Advances in Electrophoresis

Volume 1

Advances in Electrophoresis

Edited by
A. Chrambach, M. J. Dunn, B. J. Radola

Advances in Electrophoresis

Edited by
A. Chrambach, M. J. Dunn, B. J. Radola

Volume 1

Contributions from

P. Gebauer, V. Dolník, M. Deml, P. Boček, Brno
M. J. Dunn, London
J. M. Gershoni, Rehovot
R. Horuk, Glenolden
C. R. Merril, Bethesda
N. C. Stellwagen, Iowa
J. G. Sutton, Reading
K. Takeo, Ube

VCH

CHEMISTRY

Dr. Andreas Chrambach
Building 10, Room 8 C 413
National Institutes of Health
Bethesda MD 20892
USA

Dr. Michael J. Dunn
Muscle Research Centre
Royal Postgraduate
Medical School
Ducane Road
London W12 0HS
England

Professor Bertold J. Radola
Institut für Lebensmittel-
technologie und
Analytische Chemie
Technische Universität München
D-8050 Freising-Weihenstephan
Federal Republic of Germany

Editorial Director: Dr. Hans F. Ebel
Production Manager: Elke Littmann

Deutsche Bibliothek Cataloguing-in-Publication Data

Advances in electrophoresis. – Weinheim ; New York, NY :
VCH.
  Erscheint jährl. – Aufnahme nach Vol. 1 (1987)
  ISSN 0932-3031

  Vol. 1 (1987) –

British Library Cataloguing in Publication Data

Advances in electrophoresis.
  Vol. 1
  1. Electrophoresis
  541.3'7   QD79.E44

  ISSN 0932-3031

Distribution

VCH Verlagsgesellschaft, P.O. Box 1260/1280, D-6940 Weinheim (Federal Republic of Germany)

Switzerland: VCH Verlags-AG, P.O. Box, CH-4020 Basel (Switzerland)

Great Britain and Ireland: VCH Publishers (UK) Ltd., 8 Wellington Court, Wellington Street,
    Cambridge CB1 1HW (Great Britain)

USA and Canada: VCH Publishers, Suite 909, 220 East 23rd Street, New York,
    NY 10010-4606 (USA)

ISBN 3-527-26741-7 (VCH Verlagsgesellschaft)   ISBN 0-89573-669-1 (VCH Publishers)
ISSN 0932-3031

Composition: K + V Fotosatz GmbH, D-6124 Beerfelden
Printing and bookbinding: Graphischer Betrieb Konrad Triltsch, D-8700 Würzburg
Printed in the Federal Republic of Germany

Preface

Like all first births, that of *Advances in Electrophoresis* has been a difficult one. Now that the pains of parturition lie behind us and will undoubtedly soon be forgotten, it seems appropriate to reflect on the reasons behind the production of an annual review series on electrophoresis. The monthly journal *Electrophoresis* provides space for reviews and so do many other methodological journals. Moreover, the meetings of the international and some national electrophoresis societies produce proceedings also containing review articles. The purpose of *Advances in Electrophoresis* is to assemble these multiple sources into a central "review bank" that is readily available to everyone using electrophoretic methods.

A central review bank should provide a forum for the authoritative voices in each specialized field of electrophoresis, thereby helping to resolve problems created by discordant advice at different levels of expertise. It should serve to unify research areas whose results are published in a wide range of journals, for example, those of the two most challenging classes of substances – proteins and nucleic acids. Rather than summarizing all available information, the reviews in *Advances in Electrophoresis* will present the essence of each topic and demonstrate its potential. The reviews will be directed to the great many readers who already use electrophoretic techniques but do not follow their development in the original literature. Also, the reviews should become indispensible to those interested in the application of a new technique or entering a field requiring the use of electrophoresis. Ideally, the reviews should become the key references for the following years in a particular area.

Advances in Electrophoresis will contain reviews dealing either with selected techniques or important areas of application of electrophoresis. We have already alluded to the need for reviews on methodological progress. However, we consider it equally essential to provide reviews on important areas of application. Electrophoresis is not an esoteric method employed by only a small group of experts. On the contrary, its range of applications is increasing at an astonishing pace and, in many areas, it is already established as an indispensible tool. By publishing in *Advances in Electrophoresis* a balanced blend of reviews covering applications and techniques we expect a crossfertilizing effect which should stimulate further developments in the field of electrophoresis.

In order to accomplish these aims, we should like to encourage our readers to send us their comments, criticisms and suggestions for important topics to be included in forthcoming volumes. Finally, we wish to thank the authors for the sacrifice they have made in filling these pages and thereby in providing the field of electrophoresis with its first centralized retrieval bank.

November 1987

Andreas Chrambach
Michael J. Dunn
Bertold J. Radola

Contents

Contributors

Petr Boček
Institute of Analytical Chemistry
Czechoslovak Academy of Sciences
Leninova 82
CS-61142 Brno, Czechoslovakia
p. 281

Mirko Deml
Institute of Analytical Chemistry
Czechoslovak Academy of Sciences
Leninova 82
CS-61142 Brno, Czechoslovakia
p. 281

Vladislav Dolník
Institute of Analytical Chemistry
Czechoslovak Academy of Sciences
Leninova 82
CS-61142 Brno, Czechoslovakia
p. 281

Michael J. Dunn
Jerry Lewis Muscle Research Centre
Royal Postgraduate Medical School
Ducane Road
London W12 0HS, UK
p. 1

Petr Gebauer
Institute of Analytical Chemistry
Czechoslovak Academy of Sciences
Leninova 82
CS-61142 Brno, Czechoslovakia
p. 281

Jonathan M. Gershoni
Department of Biophysics
The Weizmann Institute of Science
Rehovot 76100, Israel
p. 141

Richard Horuk
Medical Products Division
E. I. Du Pont De Nemours and Co.
Glenolden, PA 19036, USA
p. 361

Carl R. Merril
Section on Biochemical Genetics
Clinical Neurogenetics Branch
National Institute of Mental Health
National Institutes of Health
Bethesda, MD 20892, USA
p. 111

Nancy C. Stellwagen
Department of Biochemistry
University of Iowa
Iowa City, IA 52242, USA
p. 177

John G. Sutton
Home Office Forensic Science
Service, Central Research
Establishment, Aldermaston
Reading, Berkshire, UK
p. 381

Kazusuke Takeo
Department of Biochemistry
Yamaguchi University School
of Medicine
Kogushi-1144
Ube 755, Japan
p. 229

TWO-DIMENSIONAL POLYACRYLAMIDE GEL ELECTROPHORESIS

Michael J. Dunn

Royal Postgraduate Medical School, London, UK

Abbreviations: Bis, N,N'-methylenebisacrylamide; **CBB**, Coomassie Brilliant Blue; **CHAPS**, 3-(cholamidopropyl)dimethylammonio-1-propanesulphonate; **CSF**, cerebrospinal fluid; **2-D**, two-dimensional; **DATD**, N,N'-diallyltartardiamide; **DTT**, dithiothreitol; **IEF**, isoelectric focusing; **IPG**, immobilized pH gradient; M_r, relative molecular mass; **NEPHGE**, non-equilibrium pH gradient electrophoresis; **NP-40**, Nonidet P-40; **PAGE**, polyacrylamide gel electrophoresis; **pI**, isoelectric point; **PMSF**, phenylmethylsulphonyl fluoride; **SB**, sulphobetaine; **SDS**, sodium dodecyl sulphate; **TACT**, N,N',N'', trilallylcitrictriamide; **TCA**, trichloroacetic acid; **Vh**, volt×hours

1   Introduction

More than 10 years have elapsed since the publication of the paper by O'Farrell [1] describing a method of high-resolution two-dimensional polyacrylamide gel electrophoresis (2-D PAGE) optimised for the separation of *Escherichia coli (E. coli)* proteins. This procedure has formed the basis for most developments in 2-D PAGE in the last 10 years, during which time it has become established as the most popular technique for the analysis and characterization of complex protein mixtures. The popularity of 2-D PAGE can be judged on the basis of the number of citations to O'Farrell's paper [1] (several thousand citations in 1985). Of course, the methodology devised by O'Farrell was based on previous developments in electrophoretic technology. In fact, the first 2-D electrophoretic separation of proteins can probably be ascribed to Smithies and Poulik [2] who separated serum proteins using a 2-D combination of paper and starch gel electrophoresis. Subsequent innovations in electrophoresis, such as the use of polyacrylamide gel as a support matrix [3] and the development of discontinuous (multiphasic) buffer systems [4, 5], were rapidly applied to 2-D procedures. For example, the ability of gels of different concentrations to resolve different components of complex mixtures was exploited in 2-D separations of serum proteins [6]. The sharpness of protein zones can be enhanced using gradient polyacrylamide gels [7, 8]. Margolis and Kenrick [9] applied this approach for 2-D separations using low concentration polyacrylamide gels in the first dimension, separating proteins predominantly by mobility, coupled with convex gradient polyacrylamide gels in the second dimension, separating proteins according to size.

The application of isoelectric focusing (IEF) techniques to 2-D separations made it possible for the first-dimension separation to be based solely on charge, and was used in combination with either single concentration [10, 11] or gradient [12, 13] polyacrylamide gels. The further advance of using polyacrylamide gels containing the anionic detergent, sodium dodecyl sulphate (SDS), which separates proteins according to their molecular weight [14, 15] for the second-dimensional separation resulted in a 2-D method capable of resolving proteins according to two independent parameters, that is charge and size [16]. IEF methods in use at that time were only applicable to soluble proteins, necessitating the development of modified procedures so that this technique of 2-D protein mapping could be applied to a wider range of samples with differing solubility properties. The most significant of these modified IEF techniques were (i) the inclusion of urea for 2-D separations of non-histone nuclear proteins [17 – 19] and EDTA-extractable erythrocyte membrane proteins [20], and (ii) the use of nonionic detergents such as Triton X-100 in combination with high urea concentrations for 2-D separations of hydrophobic membrane proteins [21, 22]. Thus, by 1975 a 2-D PAGE system had been developed which separated proteins on the basis of charge in the first, IEF dimension followed by size in the second, SDS-PAGE dimension. The resolution capacity of this method was such that it could be applied to the analysis of complex protein mixtures from whole cells or tissues [23–26]. It was on the basis of these developments that O'Farrell [1] devised the optimised 2-D separation procedure which has formed the basis for most of the subsequent developments in 2-D PAGE which will be described in this article.

2   Two-dimensional electrophoresis under native conditions

Techniques for 2-D separations of proteins under native conditions were used early in the development of 2-D PAGE [6, 9, 10]. These methods have been generally superseded by procedures based on that of O'Farrell [1] using denaturing conditions. This is due to the latter technique's increased resolution capacity and its adaptability to a wide variety of samples with differing solubility properties. 2-D electrophoresis under native conditions is limited to the analysis of soluble proteins, but it can be used to advantage for investigation of the native physicochemical properties and biological activities of proteins. The technique most commonly used today is based on the 2-D combination of first-dimensional rod-gel IEF under native conditions with second-dimension PAGE in the absence of urea or detergents developed by Latner and his coworkers [10, 13]. The resolution capacity of this technique can be improved by the use of 4 to 17% T linear gradient PAGE in Tris buffer in the second dimension [27, 28]. Manabe and his coworkers [29] have developed a microscale procedure by decreasing gel size in both dimensions (first-dimensional IEF gels 35×1.3 mm; second-dimensional 4 to 17% T linear gradient slab gels 35×38×1.0 mm). Using this procedure, 16 first- and second-dimensional gels can be run simultaneously [29] and about 100 spots can be resolved (*cf.* 250 using larger gels [27] from 2 µL samples of serum [30]). The reproducibility of this technique can be inproved using a micro-computer-controlled automatic gradient gel former for the preparation of batches of gradient slab gels [31]. A typical micro 2-D pattern of human plasma proteins obtained using this technique is shown in Fig. 1 and a reference map of those proteins which have been identified using immunoblotting

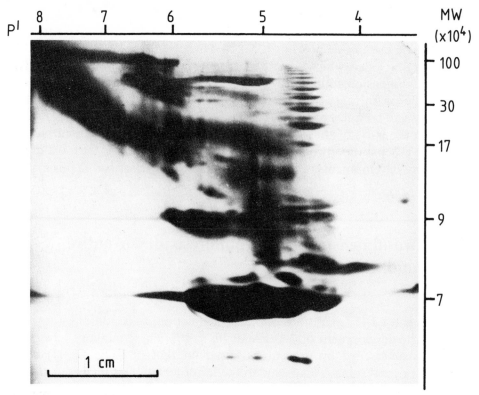

Figure 1. Micro 2-D electrophoretic pattern of human plasma proteins. Normal human plasma (2 µL), containing 40% w/v sucrose, was subjected to 2-D electrophoresis under native conditions followed by CBB staining. Reproduced with permission from [32].

and specific antisera [32] is illustrated in Fig. 2. In a recent modification of this technique [33] conventional IEF rod-gels using synthetic carrier ampholytes were replaced with flat-bed immobilised pH 4 to 6 gradient (IPG) IEF gels for the first-dimensional separation. Gels loaded with 18 samples were cast on plastic sheets (Gel-Fix, Serva) which were cut up into strips after the IEF dimension and applied to second-dimensional gels containing step layers of 8%, 5% and 12% polyacrylamide. Some examples of the use of this technique are the analysis of serum [28, 30, 32, 34], cerebrospinal fluid (CSF) [29, 35] and salivary [29, 36] proteins. As this technique is carried out in the absence of denaturing reagents, enzymes can be demonstrated directly on the gels after 2-D separation, *e.g.* α-amylase iso-enzymes [37]. Similary, protein-protein complexes and interactions can also be analysed [38]. 2-D gel patterns produced using this technique can be visualized using silver-staining procedures. However, the sensitivity of such staining techniques is low in the absence of protein denaturants [36]. The sensitivity of detection can be sig-

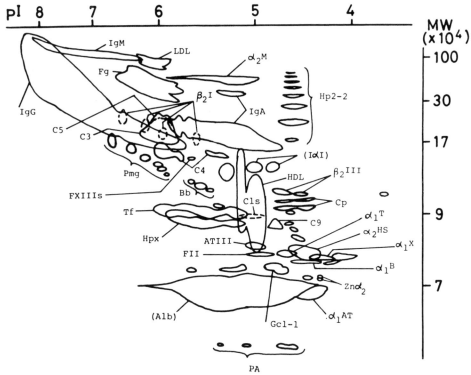

Figure 2. Reference map of human plasma proteins separated by micro 2-D electrophoresis under native conditions. Reproduced with permission from [32].

nificantly enhanced by pre-treatment of gels with Coomassie Brilliant Blue [39] of SDS [36, 40] prior to silver staining.

3　Two-dimensional polyacrylamide gel electrophoresis under denaturing conditions

It is possible to use electrophoresis under denaturing conditions in both dimensions for 2-D separations of most protein samples. However, the ability of IEF to separate proteins on the basis of their charge properties alone has resulted in the almost universal adoption of IEF for the first dimension in 2-D PAGE. Nevertheless, 2-D separations using denaturing conditions in both dimensions are still used for particular types of sample.

3.1   Ribosomal proteins

The strongly basic nature of both prokaryotic and eukaryotic ribosomal proteins makes them not amenable to analysis by IEF. Therefore, a special system was required for 2-D separation of ribosomal proteins, and this problem was initially solved for *E. coli* ribosomal proteins by Kaltschmidt and Wittmann [41, 42] using electrophoresis in polyacrylamide gels containing urea in both dimensions. The first-dimension gels, containing 8% or 4% T polyacrylamide, 6 M urea, Tris-borate-EDTA buffer, pH 8.6 or pH 9.6 were cast in glass tubes. After electrophoresis in the first-dimension, gels were removed from their tubes and equilibrated for 3 h before application to the second-dimension gels, containing 18% T polyacrylamide, 6 M urea, acetate buffer, pH 4.6. Separation was achieved both by exploiting differences in protein mobility in gels of low and high concentration and by the use of a different pH in each dimension, thereby creating conditions for separation of proteins according to charge properties in addition to their size. In the original procedure, a large pore polyacrylamide gel containing the sample was polymerised in the middle of the first-dimension resolving gel [41] so that anodically- and cathodically-migrating proteins could be resolved similtaneously. However, significant sample loss often occurred as a result of protein immobilisation within the sample gel [42]. This problem can be alleviated by substituting a 1% agarose gel (mixed 1:1 with the sample) for the polyacrylamide sample gel [43]. In a further modification of this system, an acidic pH was used in both dimensions so that all the ribosomal proteins migrated as cations [44].

The 2-D analysis of ribosomal proteins can be improved using SDS-PAGE for the second-dimensional separation, so that the ribosomal protein subunits are resolved on the basis of their molecular weight. A low percentage gel (*ca.* 4%T) containing 8 M urea, usually run at low pH (*ca.* pH 4.3), is used in the first dimension. This is followed by an SDS-PAGE second-dimensional separation in the presence [45–47] or absence [48] of urea. The inclusion of SDS in the second-dimensional buffer systems not only permits direct estimation of molecular weights of ribosomal protein subunits, but also greatly reduces the time required for the separation [49]. In a further modification of this procedure [50], the non-ionic detergent Triton X-100 was added to the buffer used for the first-dimensional separation. By varying the concentration of urea and Triton X-100 in the gels, it was found that the relative electrophoretic mobility of many ribosomal proteins could be retarded. It is claimed [50] that this binding of Triton X-100 is specific for the hydrophobic regions on the proteins and is not directly dependent on their net charge. In this way, it is possible to resolve two ribosomal subunits with similar net charge and molecular weight if Triton X-100 micelles bind selectively to one of the proteins and retard its mobility in the first-dimension. Thus, it appears that in the presence of Triton X-100 first-dimensional separation occurs on the basis of hydrophobic character (for those proteins that bind the detergent) in addition to net charge of the proteins [50].

A general nomenclature was developed for each ribosomal protein species deived from the coordinates of each spot identified by the original Kaltschmidt and Wittmann procedure [42]. This resulted in problems with the development of the improved 2-D separation procedures for ribosomal proteins described above as protein spots had to be correlated with those classified according to the original nomenclature. Such identification was made possible by coelectrophoresing each purified protein together with total ribosomal proteins and by determining its specific position on 2-D gel patterns, see for example [44, 51, 52]. To avoid the necessity for purification of individual components, Madjar and his colleagues [53] developed a pro-

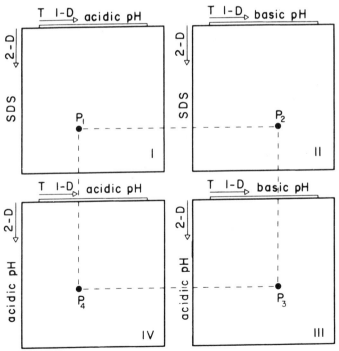

Figure 3. Schematic representation of the position of one given protein in the four different 2-D gel systems used for the method of four corners separation of ribosomal proteins. Reproduced with permission from [53].

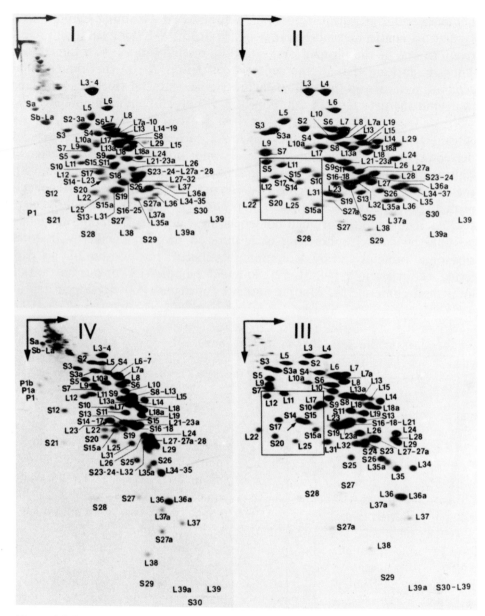

Figure 4. 2-D PAGE of Chinese hamster ovary cell ribosomal proteins using the method of four corners. Reproduced with permission from [58].

cedure for 2-D separation of ribosomal proteins in which the same protein sample is analysed using four different 2-D gel system. The first-dimensional separation is run either at acidic or at basic pH. Separation in the second dimension is carried out either at acidic pH or in the presence of SDS. The four systems used are (i) acidic-SDS, (ii) basic-SDS, (iii) basic-acidic, and (iv) acidic-acidic. This so called method of four corners permits the direct correlation of the electrophoretic mobility of proteins from one system to another (Fig. 3). This methodology has been applied to 2-D separations of ribosomal proteins from *E. coli* [53], *Bombyx mori* [54] and various mammalian cells and tissues [55–58]. It has also been used to investigate amino acid misincorporation into *E. coli* ribosomal proteins [59]. An example of the method of four corners applied to the analysis of ribosomal proteins of Chinese hamster ovary cells is shown in Fig. 4.

3.2   Histone proteins

Histones, which constitute the major protein components of chromosomes, are very difficult to separate using 2-D PAGE techniques of the O'Farrell [1] type due to their highly basic character and the similarity of their molecular weights. Histones can be readily isolated from nuclei by acid extraction (usually 0.2 M H_2SO_4). They can than be separated on the basis of their charge using an acetic acid-urea gel system [60]. In this procedure the proteins are separated on 15% T polyacrylamide gels containing 2.5 M urea and 0.9 M acetic acid (pH 2.7) and several successful 2-D separation procedures have been devised using this technique in either the first or second-dimension. The acetic acid-urea system can be used in a rod-gel system for the first-dimension coupled with a second-dimensional SDS-PAGE separation on the basis of molecular weight [61–63]. This technique has also been miniaturised [64] using special minislab apparatus for both the acid-acid urea [65] and SDS-PAGE [66] dimensions. Caution must be exercised, however, as there is evidence for anomalous behaviour of histone proteins during SDS-PAGE. A more serious problem is that lateral migration and tailing of spots in the second SDS-PAGE dimension reduces resolution of those histone species (H3, H2A and H2B) which migrate closely to each other [64]. This problem could be alleviated by a reduced sample loading, but this resulted in loss of the minor modified species of the histones from 2-D maps [64]. A better solution was found to be separation of histones on a 2-D gel system consisting of a 15% T SDS-PAGE minislab gel in the first-dimension followed by an acetic acid-urea gel in the second-dimension [64] (Fig. 5). To remove the SDS from the proteins an equilibration buffer containing 1% protamine sulphate and

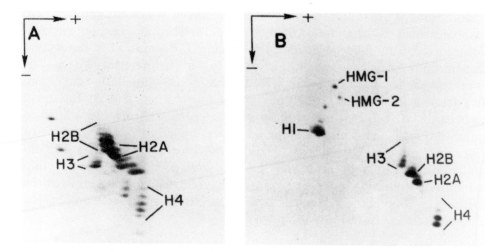

Figure 5. 2-D minislab gel separations of yeast (A) and calf thymus (B) histones. Yeast (9 µg) and calf thymus (6 µg) histones were electrophoresed on a 15% T polyacrylamide SDS minislab gel. The lanes were excised, prepared for electrophoresis and electrophoresed on an acetic acid-urea minislab gel. Reproduced with permission from [64].

6 M urea at pH 4.8 was used between the two dimensions. It was claimed that the combined action of urea and protamine resulted in the splitting of SDS-protein complexes into insoluble protamine-dodecyl sulphate complexes and free proteins [64]. Some histone modifications, such as the phosphorylation modifications of lysine residues in H1 and histidine residues in H4, are known to be extremely unstable at low pH and should therefore be separated using a gel system containing urea at neutral pH (glycylglycine buffer, pH 7.8) [67].

It is possible to include nonionic detergents such as Triton X-100, Triton DF-16 or Lubrol-WX in the acetic acid-urea gels for separation of histone proteins [68]. Several 2-D procedures for histone proteins have used this modification. In one approach, acetic acid-urea gels containing detergent are used in a 2-D combination with the same acetic acid-urea gel system in the absence of detergent [69, 70]. This produces an essentially diagonal distribution of spots but certain histone variants are retarded in their electrophoretic mobility in the detergent dimension as a consequence of interaction with the detergent. These retarded spots are not aligned on the diagonal and can, therefore, increase the resolution of certain histone species. A potential problem in this technique is that oxidation, especially of methionine residues, can result in altered mobilities on acetic acid-urea-detergent gels [71] leading to artefactual heterogeneity. Triton has a reduced affinity for oxidised histones,

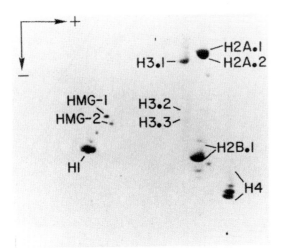

Figure 6. 2-D minislab gel separation of calf thymus histones. The first dimension was as described in Fig. 5. The second dimension was an acetic acid-urea-Triton X-100 minislab gel. Reproduced with permission from [64].

so that it is essential to maintain sample proteins in a reducing environment, for example by the addition of dithiothreitol (DDT) to the system. It might also be advantageous to use riboflavin catalysis for gel polymerisation as ammonium persulphate could oxidase histone proteins during electrophoresis [64]. It is also possible to combine acetic acid-urea gels containing nonionic detergents with SDS-PAGE [64] (Fig. 6). Recently, Pipkin *et al.* [72] have achieved good resolution of histone variants in 15% T polyacrylamide gels using 5% acetic acid, 2.5 M urea for the first-dimension followed by second-dimensional gels containing 6.5 M urea and 6 mM Triton X-100 (Fig. 7).

3.3   Non-histone nuclear proteins

Procedures of 2-D PAGE based on the O'Farrell [1] method are generally used for 2-D analysis of non-histone nuclear proteins. Nucleolar proteins have a similar overall composition to ribosomal proteins, but the solubility properties of the acid-extractable nucleolar proteins precludes their analysis by those 2-D systems optimised for ribosomal proteins (see Section 3.1). To overcome this problem a 2-D combination of acetic acid-urea and SDS-PAGE gels can be used [73] (Fig. 8). Nucleosomes can be initially separated using low percentage (5% T) polyacrylamide gels containing EDTA and triethanolamine, followed by separation of their constituent proteins by second-dimensional acetic acid-urea gels [74].

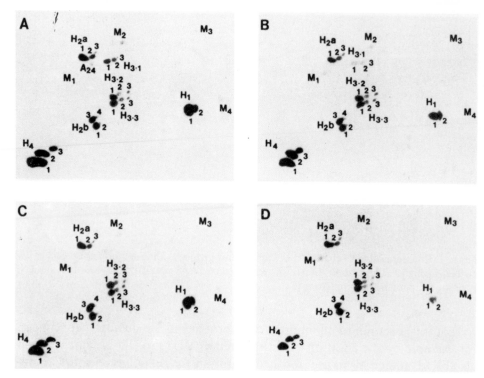

Figure 7. 2-D PAGE analysis of silver-stained histone variants from regenerating mouse liver. Sample loading was 150 µg protein. The first dimension 15% T polyacrylamide gels contained 5% w/v acetic acid and 2.5 M urea. The second dimension 15% T gels contained 6.5 M urea and 6 mM Triton X-100. Reproduced with permission from [72].

3.4   Membrane proteins

Membrane proteins can be analysed by the classical O'Farrell 2-D PAGE technique [1] using an IEF separation in the first dimension. However, the hydrophobic nature of many membrane components can result in problems of solubility under conditions compatible with IEF (see Section 6) leading to smearing of patterns, ill-defined spots and absence of proteins from 2-D maps. In attempts to overcome this problem, 2-D combinations of electro-phoretic procedures using detergents or other solubilising agents have been used. Some examples of such methods which have been employed for 2-D analysis of membrane proteins are (i) acetic acid-urea gels containing Triton X-100 in combination with SDS-PAGE [75], (ii) a combination of SDS-PAGE and SDS-Triton CF10-urea gels [76], and (iii) gels containing chloral hydrate in combination with gels containing organic-base dodecyl sulphates

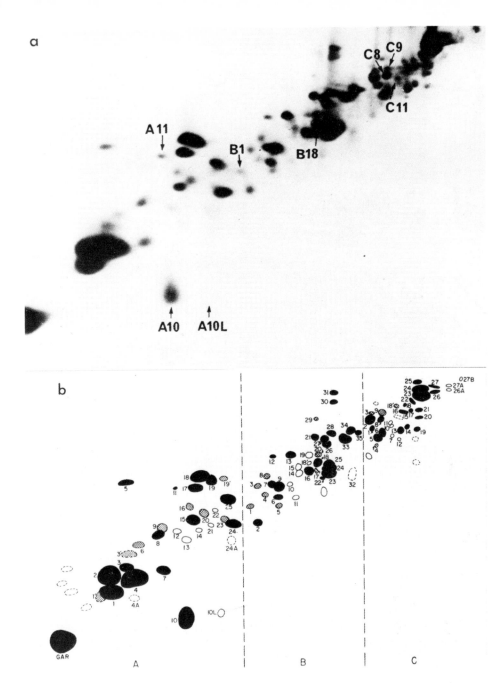

Figure 8. (a) 2-D separation of 250 μg of Novikoff hepatoma nuclear proteins. Samples were loaded on tube gels of 10% T acrylamide-6 M urea and run in the first dimension for 5 h at 120 V. For the second dimension, a 12% T acrylamide-0.1% w/v SDS slab gel was run for 14 h at 50 mA. Reproduced with permission from [73]. (b) Map of the 2-D pattern in (a). The most dense spots are black, the less-dense spots are cross-hatched, and even less-dense spots are open circles. Minor species are shown as broken circles. Reproduced with permission from [73].

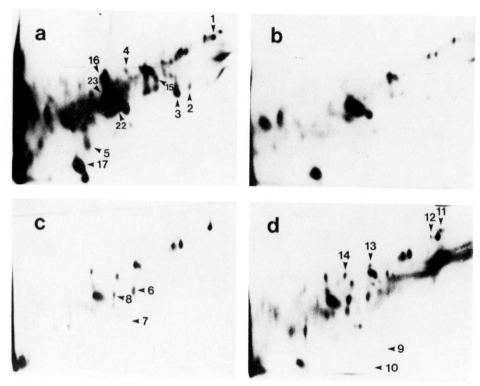

Figure 9. 2-D separation of C6 rat glioma cell plasma membrane proteins. The first-dimensional gels contained 2% T acrylamide, 0.1% w/v SDS, 0.3% w/v Triton CF10 and 9 M urea. The second dimension was conventional SDS-PAGE. (a) Total iodinatable surface proteins, (b) integral surface proteins, (c) [^{14}C]fucose-containing proteins, and (d) [^{14}C]glucosamine-containing proteins. Reproduced with permission from [78].

[77]. Unfortunately, a characteristic of these techniques is a general lack of resolution manifested by diagonal distribution of protein spots on the 2-D maps. This diagonal effect can be attributed to the fact that separation by size differences contributes to a considerable degree in both dimensions. Improved separations can be achieved if the molecular sieving effect of the polyacrylamide matrix is minimised using gels of a low concentration in the first dimension. For example, improved resolution of plasma membrane proteins from C6 rat glioma cells was obtained using 2% T polyacrylamide gels containing 0.1% SDS, 0.3% Triton CF10 and 9 M urea in the first dimension followed by conventional SDS-PAGE in the second dimension [78] (Figs. 9 and 10). This technique has also been utilised successfully in studies of cell differentiation [581], investigation of cyclic AMP effects in CHO cells [582] and fibroblasts [583], and the tentative assignment of a structural gene encoding a M_r 200000 human cell surface protein to the long arm of chro-

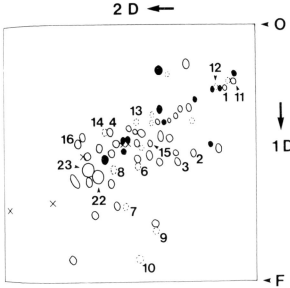

Figure 10. Diagrammatical representation of C6 glioma cell surface glycosylated and nonglycosylated proteins. Reproduced with permission from [78].

mosome 11 [584]. Such systems can also be useful for particular types of samples. For example, in studies of labile phosphate-containing proteins of *Salmonella typhimurium* and *E. coli* which would be lost in systems employing basic conditions, good resolution was obtained using a 2-D combination of acetic-acid-Triton X-100 gels and a neutral SDS gel system [79].

3.5   Disulphide-bonded and polymeric proteins

Proteins which contain disulphide bonds often exhibit different molecular weight values when analysed by SDS-PAGE in the absence and presence of reducing agents. Reductive cleavage of inter-polypeptide disulphide bonds will clearly result in a sharply-defined decrease in molecular weight. In addition, cleavage of intrapolypeptide disulphide bonds can lead to a greater unfolding of the polypeptide chain and increased binding of SDS, both of which can alter the apparent molecular weight. A comparison of mobilities by SDS-PAGE can give structural information and two-dimensional SDS-PAGE techniques have been developed using a nonreducing first dimension and a reducing second dimension [80, 81]. Recently, a similar approach has been used to analyse the subunit composition of polymeric proteins by a 2-D technique [82]. In this procedure electrophoresis is carried out on a single slab, in the absence of SDS in the first dimension and in the presence of SDS in the second dimension. The method is possible without the presence of SDS in the slabs at the start of the second-dimension as SDS from the cathodic buffer migrates into the gel during electrophoresis.

3.6   Peptide mapping

An elegant method for one-dimensional peptide mapping was developed by Cleveland *et al.* [83]. The method consists of the partial digestion of proteins by one (or more) proteolytic enzymes in an SDS-containing buffer which generates a mixture of peptides of molecular weight sufficiently large for separation by SDS-PAGE. The banding pattern is characteristic for the protein and related proteins generate a number of identical peptides. This method has been adapted to a 2-D procedure for peptide mapping analysis of heterogeneous protein samples [84–87]. The proteins of the mixture are separated in the first dimension by slab [84, 85] or rod-gel [86, 87] SDS-PAGE. All the proteins of the sample are then subjected to limited proteolysis in the gel and a second-dimension SDS electrophoresis at right angles to the first gel resolves the peptides of each individual protein as a series of spots located below the original position of the undigested protein. A similar 2-D method for diagonal peptide mapping after cyanogen bromide cleavage of proteins in SDS gels has been described [88]. In a different approach, peptide mapping can be carried out using the O'Farrell [1] system of IEF followed by SDS-PAGE [89, 90]. Zhang *et al.* [90] have described a method for electrophoretic elution of proteins out of spots cored from 2-D gels. These proteins were then subjected to partial proteolysis and the peptide products analysed by IEF followed by 9–17% T gradient SDS-PAGE. An example of peptide analysis by this procedure is shown in Fig. 11.

4   The O'Farrell system

The 2-D PAGE technique described by O'Farrell [1] included several important modifications to pre-existing procedures optimised for separation of *E. coli* proteins and has formed the basis for most subsequent developments in 2-D technology. Resolution in 2-D PAGE depends on proteins being separated in each dimension according to independent parameters so that

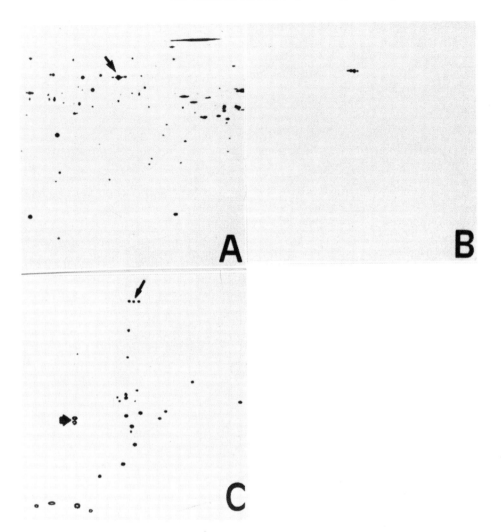

Figure 11. 2-D peptide mapping of mouse liver proteins. (A) Original 2-D pattern, arrow indicates protein extracted; (B) 2-D pattern of protein after extraction; (C) 2-D map of products of tryptic digestion of extracted protein. Reproduced with permission from [90].

proteins are distributed evenly across the 2-D gel. O'Farrell [1] chose to use a combination of IEF in cylindrical 4% T, 5% C gels containing 9 M urea and 2% w/v Nonidet P-40 (NP-40) with the discontinuous SDS polyacrylamide gradient gel slab system of Laemmli [91] on the basis of both the high resolution capacity of the methods and their ability to separate proteins according to different properties, *i.e.* charge and molecular weight. Gradients were also engineered to obtain maximum separation of *E. coli* proteins and high sensitivity of detection was achieved using autoradiography. We have

Table 1. Features and disadvantages of the O'Farrell [1] 2-D PAGE procedure compared with features required for optimal resolution (reproduced with permision from [92])

Features of the O'Farrell system	Optimal features	Disadvantages of the O'Farrell system
Separation by charge and molecular weight	Separation by two different physiochemical parameters	Hydrophobic properties not analysed
Samples solubilised using 9.5 M urea and 2% w/v NP-40	Complete solubilisation and disruption of all non-covalent interactions, complete entry of sample into both dimensions, solubilising agents should be stable and have low viscosity	Incomplete solubilisation and disaggregation, incomplete entry of sample into gels, urea is viscous and problems with carbamylation
Polyacrylamide support medium	Stable and inert support medium over a wide pH range, no sieving during charge separation, good sieving properties for molecular weight separation	Deamidation at extreme alkaline pH, sieving of high molecular weight proteins in IEF
IEF run for 30 to 59.2 Vh l^{-2}, long focusing time to get sharper spots	Stable pH gradients, true equilibrium and maximum resolution, separate systems to detect mobility variants, *i.e.* amino acid substitutions involving $pK_a = pI$	Cathodic drift, final pH gradient does not extend above pH 7, equilibrium not tested
Low field strength used	High field strengths to minimise focusing time and to sharpen bands	High field strengths cannot be used due to heating and gradient drift
Final gradient pH 4.5 to pH 7.0, Ampholine used	Optimisation of pH gradient to fit distribution of protein pI values, maximise number of ampholyte species	Gradient cannot be extended due to excess drift and loss of resolution, only one type of ampholyte used
Equilibration of first dimension gel to allow reaction of proteins with SDS	Minimisation of diffusion and protein loss with complete elution of proteins and no streaking	Diffusion and loss of proteins giving reduced resolution
Laemmli stacking gel	Rapid elution with stacking into second dimension	Slow and incomplete elution
Exponential gradient polyacrylamide SDS gels for second dimension	Good resolution of all proteins in second dimension	High molecular weight proteins poorly resolved, low molecular weight proteins form diffuse spots
	Use of large, thin gels to maximise area of gel used for separation	

Table 1. (continued)

Features of the O'Farrell system	Optimal features	Disadvantages of the O'Farrell system
Good reproducibility under standard conditions	Good reproducibility to facilitate inter-gel comparisons	Pattern matching can be difficult
	Simultaneous processing of multiple gels	Single gel procedure
High sensitivity using radiolabelled proteins	High sensitivity of detection with minimum spreading of spots, high dynamic range	Spreading of spots, limited dynamic range
	Quantitative evaluation of gels, identification and characterisation of separation polypeptides	Limited qualitative and quantitative analysis

previously compared [92] the features of the O'Farrell system with features which we considered to be desirable for optimal resolution in 2-D PAGE as shown in Table. 1. Some of these features may be difficult to achieve in practice, but a number of these problems have been overcome and some of the more recent approaches to these problems will be described in this article.

5   Sample preparation

No single method of sample preparation for 2-D PAGE can be universally applied due to the diverse nature of samples which are subjected to 2-D analysis. Soluble protein samples, typically those represented by body fluids or extracts of cells and tissues, can often be analysed by 2-D PAGE without pretreatment, but concentration will be required if the protein concentration in the sample is too low. In contrast, samples of solid tissues, circulatory cells or cells grown in tissue culture must be disrupted and solubilised prior to 2-D PAGE. It is essential to minimise the effects of chemical modification and degradation of proteins during sample preparation for 2-D PAGE. The standard 2-D PAGE technique is generally considered to resolve proteins differing by as little as 0.1 pH units in their isoelectric point (pI) and by 1000 Da in their molecular mass. The system is, therefore, exquisitely sensitive to charge changes which can result in artefactual multiple spots from a single polypeptide on 2-D maps. Thus, samples containing urea should not be heated as this can introduce considerable charge heterogeneity due to carbamylation of the proteins by isocyanate formed by decomposition of urea. Protease enzyme activity present in samples can also readily produce artefactual spots on 2-D maps, so that samples should always be subjected to the minimum of handling and kept cold at all times. Protease inhibitors, such as phenylmethane-sulphonyl fluoride (PMSF), can be added, but their use is best avoided as they can cause protein charge modifications.

5.1   Body fluids

Serum, plasma and a variety of other body fluids, including urine, CSF, semen, prostatic fluid, amniotic fluid, aqueous humour of the eye and suction blister fluid, have been successfully analysed by 2-D PAGE. Samples of these fluids can be stored at $-20\,°C$ to $-70\,°C$ prior to 2-D separation, but this can result in minor changes in the final 2-D maps [93]. Seminal plasma samples are very sensitive to proteolytic modification [94] so that they should be processed as rapidly as possible. Serum and plasma samples have a sufficiently high protein concentration that they can be directly analysed by 2-D PAGE after the addition of sample dissociation buffer (see Section 6). A particular problem with serum samples is the high relative abundance of certain proteins, particularly albumin and immunoglobulins, which can obscure some of the minor components on 2-D maps. One approach to this problem is to use a deletion technique, where serum is subjected to affinity chromatography on Affi-Gel Blue and Sepharose-bound protein A to remove albumin and immunoglobulins respectively [93]. However, these techniques are not totally specific so that there is always a possibility that other protein components can be deleted from the 2-D pattern.

In contrast to plasma and serum, most other body fluid samples have a low total protein concentration and contain high levels of salts which can interfere with the IEF dimension of 2-D PAGE. Prior to 2-D analysis these samples must, therefore, be subjected to a technique, such as dialysis, to remove salt and then concentrated, for example by lyophilisation or precipitation. The detection method used to visualize the 2-D protein maps is, of course, an important factor as sensitive methods such as silver staining can obviate excessive concentration and high sample loadings. For example, Merril *et al.* [95] obtained satisfactory 2-D maps using 15 µL loadings of CSF samples which had been concentrated four-fold by dialysis against 10% polyethylene glycol.

The analysis of urine samples by 2-D PAGE is complicated by their low protein concentration (*ca.* 100 mg/L), necessitating extensive sample concentration (500 to 1000-fold) coupled with procedures for removing salts and other non-protein components. Several methods have been devised to overcome this problem, including (i) dialysis and gel chromatography [96–98], (ii) gel chromatography and centrifugation [96], (iii) dialysis against polyethylene glycol [99], and (iv) acidified acetone extraction and gel exclusion chromatography [100]. Tracy *et al.* [101] recommend the following procedure as being in general the most practical: (i) Apply 10 mL of urine to a 1.5×60 cm column containing Fracto-Gel HW40-F equilibrated in 0.1 M ammonium formate, pH 6.5, pumped at 120 psi. (ii) Collect the protein peak, allowing the remainder to flow to waste. (iii) Lyophilise and weigh the sample. (iv) Weigh 1 mg of sample, dissolve it in 50 μLl of dissociation buffer and analyse the sample for protein. A 20 to 30 μg sample loading is recommended for 2-D gels which are to be silver stained. It should be noted that lyophilisation can result in protein modifications such as deamidation of asparagine and glutamine residues or oxidation of cysteine residues [1]. Marshall *et al.* [102] have detected over 600 polypeptides in silver-stained 2-D maps of unconcentrated, unprocessed human urine, but the resolution was not as good or reproducible as that obtained with desalted samples. Similarly, satisfactory 2-D maps of unconcentrated CSF and amniotic fluid samples have also been obtained [103].

Similar methods can be used for processing dilute samples of other body fluids prior to 2-D PAGE, except that an extensive desalting step is usually unnecessary. Salivary proteins have been processed by dialysis and concentration using a centrifugal concentrator [104]. Samples which do not require dialysis can be concentrated using apparatus such as a Minicon concentrator (Amicon Ltd) [102] or by precipitation with acetone [105]. Acids such as trichloroacetic acid (TCA) can be used for precipitation, but there is then a risk of protein modification and the precipitates can be difficult to redissolve. Specific antibodies can also be used to selectively precipitate particular proteins and the resulting immunoprecipitates analysed by 2-D PAGE. This latter approach has become less widely used since the advent of blotting techniques for the immunoanalysis of proteins separated by 2-D PAGE (see Section 13.4).

5.2   Solid tissue samples

Most procedures for processing solid tissue samples for 2-D PAGE involve disruption of the specimen in the presence of solubilisation buffer. The tissue, while frozen if possible, should be broken into small fragments by mechanical disruption. The tissue fragments can then be homogenized in solubilisation buffer using a Polytron or Ultra-Turrax homogeniser. Heating and foaming should be kept to a minimum during the homogenisation procedure and it is possible to add the solubilising detergent after homogenisation [106] or to include an antifoam reagent in the solubilisation mixture. Many tissues contain proteases that can be inhibited by protease inhibitors and/or alkaline pH [101]. Specimens of solid tissues for 2-D PAGE must be prepared very carefully to ensure homogeneity of the tissue. If possible, the tissue should be monitored by histological, histochemical and immunocytochemical analysis of frozen sections [106]. Sensitive detection methods, such as silver staining, have made it possible to perform 2-D PAGE on small amounts of tissue, even on single cryostat sections of frozen biopsy specimens routinely used for histological analysis. Cryostat sections can be collected on a cooled fine brush or probe and placed directly in solubilisation buffer or can be applied to the hydrophobic surface of GelBond squares and subsequently scraped off into solubilisation buffer [107]. The sensitivity of visualization of 2-D maps of cryostat sections can be increased by radiolabelling prior to solubilisation with [^{14}C]iodoacetamide [108, 109] or by reductive methylation with [^{3}H]sodium borohydride or [^{14}C]formaldehyde [110]. However, it should be remembered that such postsynthetic radiolabeling procedures, particularly iodination, can introduce charge heterogeneity [110, 111]. Reductive methylation has been found to be a particularly mild treatment in this respect [112]. The ability to analyse such small samples of tissue using these techniques should make a much wider range of tissues amenable to analysis by 2-D PAGE [105].

5.3   Circulating and cultured cells

Circulating cells (erythrocytes, leukocytes, platelets) and cells grown *in vitro* in suspension culture can be simply harvested by centrifugation, washed in phosphate buffered saline (PBS) or a balanced salts solution (BSS) and solubilised in sample solubilisation buffer. Cells should not be stored frozen prior to solubilisation, but after the addition of solubilisation buffer can be stored for several months at −70 °C prior to 2-D PAGE. Cells cultured *in vitro* on glass or plastic substrates also require little preparation for 2-D PAGE. The medium should be carefully aspirated and, if desired, the cell layer can be washed with PBS, BSS or an isotonic sucrose solution to reduce contamination with medium proteins. The cell layer can be scraped off with a rubber policeman, but the use of proteolytic enzymes should be avoided.

The best procedure is to lyse the cells directly in the culture plate or well by the addition of a minimum amount of solubilisation buffer. Samples can then be stored at $-70\,°C$ for several months prior to 2-D PAGE analysis. The nucleic acids present is small samples of cells will not interfere with the first-dimensional IEF separation, but larger quantities of cells should be treated with DNAase or RNAase [113, 114]. In the recommended procedure [114], cells scraped in 20 mM Tris, pH 8.8, 2 mM $CaCl_2$ and dispersed through a narrow gauge needle are treated with 0.3% w/v SDS to solubilise the proteins. A solution containing nucleases ($10\times$ nuclease solution: $1\,\mu L\,mL^{-1}$ DNAase I, $500\,\mu g\,mL^{-1}$ RNAase A, 0.5 M Tris, pH 7, 50 mM $MgCl_2$) is then added and the sample left in the cold until it is no longer viscous. Following freeze-drying the sample is resuspended in solubilisation buffer and stored at $-70\,°C$.

5.4   Plant tissues

The majority of plant tissues, such as seed [115, 116] and membrane [117] preparations, can be treated in a similar way to animal tissues. However, leaf proteins must first be extracted with acetone to remove phenolic pigments [118].

6   Sample solubilisation

The aim of solubilisation for 2-D PAGE is the disruption of all non-covalently bonded protein complexes and aggregates into a solution of individual polypeptides. When such interactions are not completely disrupted then proteins within the sample may be present both in the aggregated state and as individual polypeptides. Resultant 2-D maps will therefore be complicated by the appearance of new spots due to protein complexes, with a concomitant reduction in the intensity of those spots representing the single polypeptides [92]. For this reason, we consider solubility and disaggregation to be crucial factors in 2-D PAGE. The most popular, almost canonical, solubilisation procedure for 2-D PAGE is that described by O'Farrell [1] using a combination of 2% w/v of the non-ionic detergent NP-40 and 9.5 M urea. This procedure gives satisfactory results for the majority of samples but not all protein complexes are fully disrupted by this mixture and it is commonly found that not all sample proteins enter the first-dimensional IEF gels. These phenomena are exacerbated for more difficult samples such as histone [119], ribosomal [1], and membrane [120] proteins.

The detergent SDS disrupts the majority of non-covalent protein interactions [14, 121, 122], but its anionic nature precludes its inclusion in IEF gels. However, SDS can be used as a pre-solubilisation procedure for samples prior to 2-D PAGE [1]. This method is particularly useful for membrane or particulate proteins where SDS is used to initially solubilise the sample, followed by dilution in 9.5 M urea, 2% w/v carrier ampholytes, 5% v/v 2-mercapto-ethanol and 8% w/v NP-40 [120]. The ratios of SDS to protein (1:3) and SDS to NP-40 (1:8) should be carefully controlled to achieve effective solubilisationm while minimising the effects of high levels of SDS on the IEF dimension. The method is based on a competition effect where it is assumed that the lower critical micelle concentration (CMC) of NP-40 compared to SDS and the increased CMC due to urea leads to removal of SDS from the proteins.

In general the inclusion of SDS in the sample solubilisation procedure gives improved solubilisation and entry of proteins into 2-D gels, and we have found this to be the case in studies of human skin fibroblast proteins [123]. It is essential that the amount of SDS finally applied to the IEF gels is kept to a minimum. However, it does result in some loss of resolution in the acidic (anodic) region of 2-D maps, possibly due to the interaction of sulphate with synthetic carrier ampholytes. This method has also been found to result in streaking and loss of proteins from 2-D maps of particular types of sample [124 – 127]. It is also important to realise when using this procedure that any free SDS will form mixed micelles with NP-40 and these will then migrate to the anode during IEF [1]. Even small amounts of SDS can remove all the free detergent from the IEF gels [123], thus exposing proteins to an environment which may result in their precipitation. Another important point to consider is the temperature at which the interaction of SDS with the sample proteins should occur. Optimal solubilisation with SDS is usually achieved by heating at 100 °C for 3 to 5 min. However, heating at 70 °C for 30 min was used in the procedure of Ames and Nikaido [120], and there is some evidence that sample modification can occur at 100 °C [124, 128]. This has been attributed to an animo group reaction [124], deamidation of asparagine and glutamine [92], or even cleavage of peptide bonds [128, 129], the latter effect being due to the catalytic activity of detergents or to the presence of trace contamination with proteases [130]. Stirring in SDS for extended times at a lower temperature (*e.g.* 30 min at 40 °C) has been recommended [131], but this can also result in proteolysis [128]. Inclusion of 8 M urea in the SDS procedure can increase solubilisation efficiency without resort to elevated temperatures

[124]. Finally, the addition of an inhibitor of autoxidation, butylated hydroxytoluene, to the SDS solubilisation procedure has been recommended [132] on the basis that autoxidation of membrane lipids can be involved in crosslinking of membrane proteins and/or lipids [133].

A variety of alternative procedures for solubilisation of samples prior to 2-D PAGE analysis have been described, reviewed in [92], but most of these have not been optimised. Most of these methods were developed for 2-D analysis of specific types of sample and have not gained acceptance as general procedures for 2-D PAGE. A combination of urea and NP-40 can be used under alkaline conditions (pH 10.3) for solubilisation of membrane [125], seed [134] and leaf [118] proteins. However, this technique increases the risk of protein carbamylation and of β-elimination of O-glycosidically linked oligosaccharides and phosphoserine as a result of high pH [125]. Deoxycholate has been used to selectively solubilise those microsomal proteins not solubilised by SDS [135]. A modified lysis buffer containing 9 M urea, 6.5% w/v Triton X-100, 205 mM lysine (free base), 5 mM DTT and 15 mM sodium thioglycolate has recently been reported to result in improved resolution of erythrocyte membrane proteins [136]. Another interesting recent approach is based on the ability of the non-ionic detergent Triton X-114 to fractionate selectively integral membrane proteins by a temperature-induced phase separation [137, 138]. The latter technique has been modified and applied to 2-D PAGE analysis of leukocyte membrane proteins [139].

Zwitteronic detergents of the sulphobetaine (SB) type are effective solubilising agents [140–142]. SB12 and SB14 have been used for sample solubilisation prior to 2-D PAGE [117], but zwitterionic detergent was not used in the IEF gel. Although SB detergents are compatible with IEF as they behave as poor carrier ampholytes, they cannot be used in the presence of 8 M urea due to their precipiion in this medium [123]. However, an alternative zwitterionic detergent, CHAPS (3-[(cholamidopropyl)dimethylammonio]-1-propane sulphonate), can be used in IEF gels containing urea and has been found to be an effective solubilising agent in 2-D separations of microsomal proteins [143]. An urea/CHAPS mixture can be used instead of the urea/NP-40 mixture for routine 2-D PAGE applications [144, 145].

Little attention has been paid to the use of alternative deturants to urea for 2-D PAGE. An increased denaturing potential should disrupt more protein interactions and the absence of urea would overcome problems associated with protein charge modifications resulting from carbamylation. An extensive list of denaturants can be found in Gordon and Jencks [146]. Reagents such as tetramethylurea and dimethylethyleneurea have excellent solvent properties [147, 148] and have been used successfully for the solubilisation of myelin and oligodendroglial proteins prior to 2-D PAGE [149]. However, these reagents cannot be incorporated at a sufficiently high concentration into IEF gels as they inhibit the polymerization of polyacrylamide [148]. Guanidinium thiocyanate has been used for 2-D PAGE [120] but was found to result in protein loss and the appearance of extreme charge heterogeneity. A combination of urea and *n*-butyl urea has been used as a denaturant for the analysis of membrane proteins [150].

7   The first dimension

7.1   Order of dimensions

IEF under denaturing conditions in polyacrylamide gels containing both urea and nonionic or zwitterionic detergent has been almost universally adopted for the first-dimension of 2-D PAGE. However, some procedures have been described using SDS gels in the first dimension followed by IEF in a flat-bed gel containing 8 M urea and non-ionic detergent [151 – 155]. These systems were designed to overcome problems of protein solubility, but it is quite possible that, after solubilisation and SDS-PAGE, proteins may again become insoluble when subjected to subsequent procedures not using SDS. An additional disadvantage is that proteins must be eluted form a restrictive first-dimension gel into a non-restrictive second-dimension gel which can result in increased lateral diffusion and loss of resolution compared with the standard procedure [92]. Moreover, first-dimensional SDS gels contain a relatively high salt concentration which is potentially deleterious to the subsequent IEF separation.

7.2   Gel matrix

Polyacrylamide is used almost exclusively as the gel matrix for the first-dimensional IEF separation in 2-D PAGE. Gel concentration should be kept low (3% to 5% T) to minimise molecular sieving, but this parameter can still exert an influence on the separation particularly of high molecular weight proteins. Polyacrylamide gels prepared using high levels (50% to 60% C) of N,N'-methylenebisacrylamide (Bis) have a very large pore size but they are mechanically unstable and rather hydrophobic [156, 157]. Alternative crosslinkers, such as N,N'-diallyltartardiamide (DATD) and N,N',N''-triallylcitric-triamide (TACT) are not recommended as they can inhibit gel polymerisation resulting in the presence of agents that can react with proteins [157, 158]. Agarose is a separation medium which has considerable potential for IEF of high molecular weight proteins. Highly purified [159, 160] and charge-balanced (agarose IEF, Pharmacia) agarose preparations suitable for use in IEF are available and agarose IEF in gels containing 6 M urea has been used for the first dimension of 2-D PAGE [161]. However, there are considerable problems in the use of agarose for the IEF-dimension of 2-D PAGE associated with high urea concentrations [162], pH gradient instability [163, 164], and incompatibility with powerful denaturants which can inhibit gelation [92].

7.3   Urea and detergents

The IEF dimension of high-resolution 2-D PAGE is carried out under denaturing conditions, with both 8 M urea and nonionic (*e.g.* Triton X-100, NP-40) or zwitterionic (*e.g.* CHAPS) detergent present in the gels. In the original O'Farrell [1] procedure, nonionic detergent is used at 2% w/v, although this can be reduced to 0.5% w/v without any adverse effect on protein resolution [165, 166]. Indeed, this may have definite advantages as high NP-40 concentrations have been found to result in artefacts in SDS-PAGE [166]. The zwitterionic detergent, CHAPS, has been found to result in enhanced solubility of microsomal membrane proteins [143] and it can be routinely included at 0.5% w/v in IEF gel for 2-D PAGE [144, 145]. The use of high (8 M) urea concentrations in IEF gels necessitates extended focusing times if equilibrium is to be approached due to an increase in (i) viscosity of the system [123], (ii) gel restrictivity [158, 167] and (iii) Stokes radius of proteins after denaturation by urea [162, 167].

7.4   Synthetic carrier ampholytes

IEF first became a practical possibility when Vesterberg [168] devised a synthesis of low molecular weight carrier ampholytes by a procedure involving coupling of propanoic acid residues to polyethylene polyamines. The synthetic carrier ampholytes are the most important components of the IEF gels as they are responsible for the generation and maintenance of the pH gradient on which the quality of 2-D separations depends. Carrier ampholytes based on the Vesterberg synthetic procedure (Ampholine, LKB) have been the type most commonly used for 2-D PAGE, although useful alternative carrier ampholyte preparations are available from other manufacturers (Pharmalyte from Pharmacia, Servalyt from Serva and Resolyte from BDH). Alternative methods for the synthesis of ampholytes are reviewed in [92, 157, 169]. As these various carrier ampholytes are synthesised by different procedures, they consequently contain different species. These differences can be exploited to improve resolution in 2-D PAGE by blending the different carrier ampholyte preparations to produce a mixture containing more species with different fractional charges [165, 170]. It is also possible by blending various wide and narrow pH-range carrier ampholytes to manipulate, albeit somewhat empirically, the shape of the pH gradient generated within the IEF gel to match the distribution of protein p*I* values within the sample, thereby maximising resolution [165].

7.5   Tube-gel isoelectric focusing

Methods of 2-D PAGE based on the original O'Farrell [1] procedure usually involve the use of cylindrical first-dimension IEF gels cast in glass tubes. The tubes normally have an internal diameter of 1.2 to 3.0 mm and their length varies between 12 and 20 cm. Gels of this type are very easy to prepare. The bottom of the tubes should be sealed with several layers of Parafilm or a small plug of concentrated polyacrylamide. The gel solution can then be introduced into the tubes using a long, blunt-ended, narrow-gauge needle. The needle should initially be inserted into the bottom of the tube and slowly withdrawn to avoid trapping air bubbles. In order to ensure inter-gel reproducibility, care should be taken to fill all tubes to the same level. The gel mixture is then overlaid with water and allowed to polymerise for at least 2 h. Despite the simplicity of this methodology, inter-gel reproducibility can be difficult to control resulting in difficulties in comparison of 2-D maps. This problem can be alleviated using devices which allow the IEF gels to be prepared in batches [114, 171, 172].

Tube-gel IEF is often carried out in apparatus designed for gel electrophoresis rather than IEF. Such apparatus suffers from major disadvantages for IEF including (i) poor cooling which precludes the use of high field strengths resulting in extended focusing times, and (ii) large electrolyte volumes which result in increased pH gradient drift and protein loss [157]. In the standard procedure, the apparatus is arranged with the cathodic electrolyte (typically 20 mM NaOH) in the upper buffer reservoir and the anodic electrolyte (typically 10 mM H_3PO_4) in the lower reservoir. The gels are usually prefocused at 200 V for 15 min, 300 V for 30 min and finally 400 V for 60 min (total 600 Vh). Samples are then applied, using a suitable microsyringe or dispenser, to the top of the IEF gels and under a thin layer (*ca.* 10 µL) of buffer containing urea, detergent and ampholytes to protect the sample proteins from the basic catholyte solution. For non-radioactive samples, the exact sample loading to be applied to 2-D gels can be difficult to estimate by standard protein assay techniques due to interference by the combination of urea, detergent, and carrier ampholytes and other compounds present in the simple buffer. Recently, a method has been described based on the standard Bradford-assay with Coomassie Brilliant Blue G-250 that allows direct, accurate estimation of protein concentration in 2-D PAGE sample buffer [173]. The gels are then focused for the appropriate time (see Section 7.10). After IEF the gels are removed from the tubes by injecting water around the gels or by application of air pressure. Care must be taken not to damage, stretch or break the rather delicate gels. To overcome this problem, apparatus has been described for ejecting simultaneously 20 gels from their tubes [172] and for their automatic application directly onto the second-dimension SDS-PAGE gels [174].

The 2-D PAGE system using tube-gel IEF for the first-dimension separation is capable of producing good high-resolution 2-D protein patterns as illustrated in Figs 12 and 13. However, a major disadvantage of this technique is that the IEF dimension as a result of electroendosmotic effects suffers

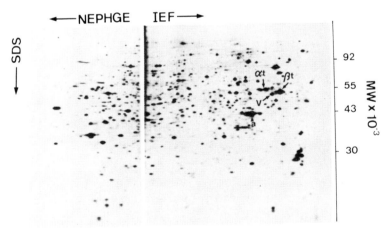

Figure 12. 2-D gel map of acidic (IEF) and basic (NEPHGE) polypeptides of asynchronous HeLa cells. In IEF the pH ranges from 7.5 (left) to 4.5 (right). In NEPHGE the pH ranges from 7.5 (right) to 9.5 (left). a, actin, αt, α-tubulin, βt, β-tubulin. Reproduced with permission from [114].

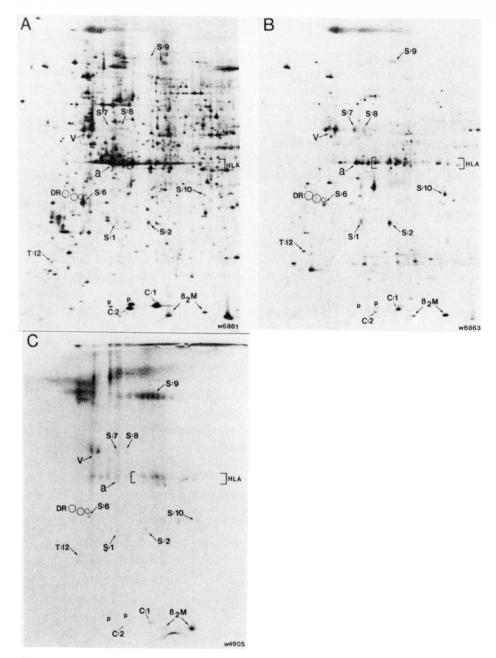

Figure 13. 2-D gel patterns of normal human leukocyte proteins labelled with [^{35}S]methionine. (A) Whole cell proteins. (B) Membrane proteins extracted with Triton X-114. (C) ^{125}I-iodinated cell surface proteins. Unidentified surface proteins and the normal human T-cell marker T:12 are indicated by number. The positions of the identified DR antigens (DR), human class I antigens (HLA), β_2-microglobulin (β_2-M), the Calgon proteins (C), and their phosphorylated versions (p) are shown. Actin (a) and vimentin (v) are identified for reference. Reproduced with permission from [139].

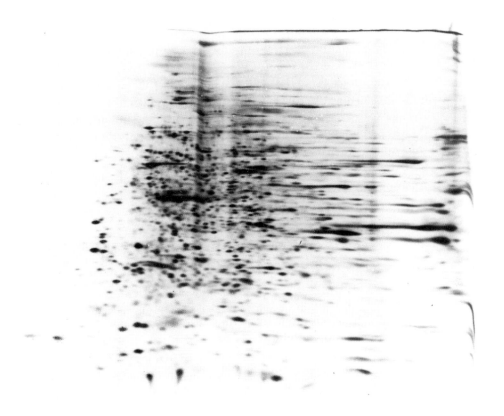

Figure 14. A 2-D gel of [^{35}S]methionine-labelled skin fibroblast proteins using tube-gel IEF in the first dimension. The glass tubes were treated with methylcellulose to reduce electroend-osmosis and the IEF gels run from 10 000 Vh. The second-dimension was 7 – 20% T linear gradient SDS-PAGE. Reproduced with permission from [165].

from serve cathodic drift, so that pH gradients rarely extend above pH 8 and basic proteins are absent from 2-D maps [175, 176]. Polyacrylamide can contain agents which can contribute to cathodic drift including acrylic acid impurities, presence of catalysts, and hydrolysis of amides above pH 10 [177]. Acrylic acid contamination can be minimised by the use of freshly prepared, deionised acrylamide solutions for IEF [178]. Dimethylaminopropylmethacrylamide and methacrylamide-propyltrimethylammonium chloride can be incorporated into polyacrylamide gels in stoichiometric amounts to balance negatively charged groups. This technique produces balanced matrices which show little cathodic drift even after focusing for 5000 Vh [177]. Another approach to increasing the stability of pH gradients is the use of alternative electrolyte solutions [179, 180] and the inclusion in IEF gels of arginine, lysine [180, 181] and alkaline carrier ampholytes [180]. Uncharged methylcellulose can be used to treat the inner walls of the glass tubes used for IEF and so reduce electroendosmosis [182]. We have used this technique in conjunction with manipulation of anolyte pH as suggested by Chrambach *et al.* [183, 184] for 2-D PAGE of [^{35}S]methionine-labelled human skin fibroblast proteins [165, 185]. The pH gradients were found to extend to pH 10 and cathodic proteins were present in the 2-D patterns, but these tended to form elongated streaks rather than discrete spots (Fig. 14) even using extended focusing times (20 000 Vh).

7.6   Non-equilibrium pH gradient electrophoresis

Another approach to the problem of resolution of basic proteins in 2-D PAGE is known as non-equilibrium pH gradient electrophoresis (NEPHGE) [175]. NEPHGE is performed in the same way as IEF except that the electrodes are reversed, the sample is applied at the acidic end rather than the basic end of the gel, and the voltage is applied for a shorter time than in equilibrium IEF, typically 5 to 21 Vh/(cm gel length)^2 [92]. Few proteins will reach their isoelectric points in this time, so that separation occurs on the basis of both charge and size in the presence of a rapidly forming pH gradient. Such transient state, non-equilibrium focusing is difficult to control reproducibly and is sensitive to experimental conditions, carrier ampholytes, focusing time, gel length and sample composition [92]. Thus, considerable care must be taken to ensure that samples are subjected to NEPHGE under identical conditions in order to obtain comparable 2-D maps. Furthermore, acidic proteins are often not well resolved by NEPHGE and small charge differences cannot be distinguished [175]. A typical NEPHGE separation is shown in Fig. 12. Some problems, in particular failure of samples to enter the gels, have been encountered with the use of NEPHGE in 2-D PAGE studies of histone proteins [100, 119, 186]. Digestion of samples with S1 nuclease [110, 186] or solubilisation using 0.5% w/v phosphatidyl choline and 8 M urea [119] can alleviate this problem. A further disadvantage of the use of NEPHGE for 2-D analysis of basic proteins is that two different types of first dimension (equilibrium IEF and NEPHGE) are necessary for the analysis of each sample. However, equilibrium and non-equilibrium methods can resolve different types of charge mutations [187]. For example, neutral amino acid substitutions which do not result in a net change in protein p*I* will be silent by conventional IEF, but might be detectable by NEPHGE on the basis of an alteration in protein mobility.

7.7   Flat-bed isoelectric focusing gels

In contrast to the system of tube-gels used for the IEF dimension of 2-D PAGE, horizontal flat-bed gels are almost always the method of choice for one-dimensional IEF separations. Purpose-designed apparatus is available for flat-bed IEF. The more efficient cooling systems of this type of equipment allow the use of high field strengths giving reduced IEF run times. Furthermore, small electrolyte volumes can be used and the electrodes can be positioned close to the ends of the gels, thus minimising pH gradient drift and protein loss from the gels [157]. Perhaps the most important advantage of this methodology is that basic proteins can be resolved into discrete components using flat-bed horizontal slab IEF gels. Thick gels were used in initial attempts to adapt this technology to the first dimension of 2-D PAGE [23, 188, 189], but recently more successful methods have been developed using thin [165] and ultrathin [115, 190] IEF gels.

We have developed a method [144, 165, 191] in which 0.5 mm thick first-dimensional IEF gel slabs are cast on a plastic support in a simple glass cassette with a U-shaped gasket. The success of this procedure depends on reliable binding of the IEF gels to the plastic supports, as handling steps are involved in equilibration and transfer to the second dimension SDS-PAGE gels. At the time we developed our original procedure [165], none of the commercially available supports were found to bind reliably polyacrylamide gels containing both 8 M urea and nonionic detergent. To overcome this problem we developed a method in which polyester sheets were treated with Dow Corning Prime Coat 1200, followed by reaction with silane A-174 [165]. However, we have found more recently that polyacrylamide gels can be bound reliably to GelBond PAG supports in the presence of 8 M urea and 0.5% w/v NP-40 or CHAPS provided that polymerisation catalyst concentration are increased two- to three-fold [144]. After polymerisation, the gel is removed from the cassette and placed on the cooling plate of the flat-bed apparatus which is cooled to 15 °C using a thermostatically-controlled circulator. Lower temperatures cannot be used as there would be a risk of crystallisation of urea within the gel. A thin film of silicon fluid (Dow Corning 200/10 cs), which has excellent thermal conductivity properties and a low viscosity, is used to ensure good contact between the gel support and the cooling plate. The gel can be focused with its upper surface exposed to the atmosphere, but in this case humidity must be maintained and a N_2 atmosphere or NaOH pellets must be used to minimise the effects of CO_2 [165]. We find it better to cover the top surface of the gel with a plastic sheet in which holes have been punched for sample application [144]. A significant advantage of flat

Figure 15. Separation of [^{35}S]methionine-labelled fibroblast proteins using a flat-bed 2-D PAGE system. The first-dimensional flat-bed IEF gel contained Pharmalyte 3–10 (0.92% w/v), Servalyt 2–11 (0.92% w/v), Ampholine 3–10 (0.92% w/v), Servalyt 4–6 (0.12% w/v), Pharmalyte 58 (0.24% w/v) and CHAPS (0.5% w/v). The gel was focused for 88 Vhl^{-2}. The second dimension was 8–20% T non-linear gradient SDS-PAGE.

bed IEF is that small electrolyte volumes can be used but they must be stronger than those used for tube gel IEF. We currently use 1 M NaOH at the cathode and 1 M oxalic acid at the anode, and four layers of glass fibre paper (Whatman GF/B) strips are used as the wicks [192]. Another important advantage of flat-bed systems is that the sample can be applied at any point along the gel, thereby avoiding the extreme acid or alkaline conditions associated with anodic or cathodic sample application as used in tube-gel IEF. After focusing (see Section 7.10 for a discussion of running conditions), the cover sheet is removed and the gel covered with Saranwrap plastic food film. Sample strips are then simply cut off with scissors using a template of lane markings made on the reverse side of the GelBond PAG sheet prior to gel casting. The single strips can be treated immediately for the second-dimension or can be stored at $-70\,^{\circ}$C for future use. For appropriately labelled radioactive samples, the wrapped gel can be placed in contact with a sheet of X-ray film and exposed overnight (or longer) at $-70\,^{\circ}$C. The film is then developed and this autoradiograph is used as a template to cut out the individual sample tracks. A typical 2-D separation of [^{35}S]methionine-labelled human skin fibroblast proteins obtained using this technique is shown in Fig. 15.

Despite the advantages described above, flat-bed IEF systems are more limited in sample loading capacity and less tolerant to the presence of salt in samples than tube-gel IEF. Overloading with protein or salt can often result in distorted protein zones in flat-bed IEF [193]. However, skewed bands can also occur in tube-gel IEF [194] as a result of physical disturbance of the gel (flat-bed gels are more mechanically stable) or due to unequal distribution of electrolyte [110, 193]. Thus, band distortion during IEF depends on the running conditions used rather than the nature of the gel system *per se*.

7.8   Rehydratable gels for isoelectric focusing

A significant problem in 2-D PAGE is pattern variability in 2-D maps resulting from variability in the physical and chemical properties of the gels used for the first and second dimensions. This considerably complicates the task of comparative analysis of 2-D gel maps from a series of samples. For the IEF dimension, this problem has been approached for tube-gel IEF using special apparatus for the preparation of large batches of gels [114, 171, 172] (see Section 7.5). However, these gels should be used for IEF as soon as possible after their preparation and cannot be stored for future use due to the risk of urea decomposition and other chemical changes. Therefore, the problem of inter-batch variability remains. A similar situation exists in the case of flat-bed gels. An advantage here is that 15 to 20 samples can be run under identical conditions on a single gel, thereby increasing reproducibility. However, it is again not possible to store gels for future use. In addition, there are other factors associated with tube- or flat-bed gels prepared in the normal manner which are potentially deleterious to IEF. These include (i) the presence within the gels of unpolymerized monomers and linear polymers [158, 195, 196], (ii) poor standardisation of polymerisation conditions in the presence of additives and/or electrolytes with undefined composition or extreme pH values [197], (iii) the presence of residual amounts of catalysts which can modify proteins and interfere with pH gradient stability, (iv) inhibition of gel polymerisation by some additives [149, 198], and (v) changes in gel composition necessitate polymerisation of different batches of gels.

An answer to these problems, at least for flat-bed, slab IEF gels can be found in the methods which have been developed recently [119, 202] for the preparation of rehydratable thin and ultrathin gels for IEF which in dry form can be stored for extended periods and which prior to use can be rehydrated with solutions of any desired composition. This methodology has several advantages including (i) the preparation of batches of gels under defined conditions which can be stored, thereby improving inter-gel reproducibility, (ii) the removal at the washing stage of unreacted catalysts, unpolymerised monomers, linear polymers and salts which can interfere with IEF, (iii) the addition at gel rehydration of additives which can interfere with gel polymerisation, and (iv) rehydratable gels appear to be the best method for preparing immobilised pH gradient (IPG) gels containing 8 M urea [203 − 205] (see Section 7.14). Thin and ultrathin rehydratable IEF gels which need to contain only acrylamide, Bis and polymerisation catalysts are cast on plastic supports (Gel-Fix, GelBond PAG) using standard procedures. After polymerisation the gels are washed extensively to remove contaminants and dried. Radola and his colleagues [199 − 201] have found that gels should be impregnated with 1 to 10% w/v of a suitable polyol (glycerol, sorbitol, dextran) or synthetic polymer (polyethylene glycol, polyvinylpyrrolidone) before drying in order to preserve gel functionality on storage. Heating at elevated temperatures should be avoided during the drying process. It appears that such gels can be stored for extended periods without detriment to their functional properties [201].

Four methods have been described for the rehydration of dried IEF gels. (i) Frey *et al.* [199] have described a rolling technique in which the dry gel is rolled onto a calculated amount of the required solution, care being taken to spread the solution uniformly over the entire gel surface. After contact for 10 − 15 s, the gel is lifted, rotated through 90° and rolled again over the residual solution. (ii) A flap technique [201, 202] in which the gel on its plastic support is placed on a glass plate and two spacers [201] or a gasket [202] of the same thickness as the original gel are placed on the gel. The solution required for rehydration is then applied in the middle of the gel and uniformly distributed by slowly lowering a glass cover plate. (iii) Righetti and his coworkers [204–207] have used solvent regain to monitor rehydration. The wet gel is weighed prior to washing and drying from which the weight of the backing and gel monomers is subtracted to calculate the solvent weight. Dried gels are rehydrated in a large volume of solution until 100% solvent regain has occurred as estimated by repeated weighing. Solvent regain in solutions containing 8 M urea must be corrected for the density increment. (iv) Probably the most reliable method is to use volume to control gel rehydration as recommended by Altland [203]. The wet gel is weighed and the thickness of the dried gel is measured, so that the dry gel volume can be calculated and the displacement of this volume accounted for when using solutions such as 8 M urea for reswelling. The dry gel is reassembled into a cassette of the same dimensions as that in which it was cast and reswollen in a controlled amount of the required solution.

Ideally, for most 2-D PAGE applications, dry IEF gels should be rehydrated in solutions containing both 8 M urea and nonionic (NP-40, Triton X-100) or zwitterionic (CHAPS) detergent to ensure maximum sample solubility. However, rehydration of polyacrylamide gels in the presence of both these reagents is very inefficient [204]. Using a controlled volume of solution containing 8 M urea and 0.5% w/v Triton X-100 in a cassette system we have found that gels never reswell fully [145, 208]. This problem can be overcome by including nonionic detergent in the gels when they are cast and in all subsequent washing solutions used prior to gel drying [208]. Note that detergent should not be included in the solution used for rehydration as it is already present within the dry gel matrix.

7.9   Sample application

Using a tube-gel IEF system, the samples must either be applied directly to the cathodic or anodic end of the IEF gels. Thus the samples are at risk of damage due to the highly acidic or alkaline environment prevailing in these regions. Therefore, the samples should be applied under a thin layer (*ca.* 10 µL) of a solution containing urea and carrier ampholytes to protect the proteins. In theory it is possible to incorporate the sample throughout the IEF gel by including it in the gel solutions before polymerisation. However, this method is not recommended due to risk of protein modification due to heat of polymerisation and the presence of urea and catalysts. Horizontal flat-bed IEF systems have much more flexibility as samples can be applied at any desired position on the IEF gel. However, sample volumes must be relatively small and should not contain high salt concentrations. Very small samples can be applied as droplets directly to the gel surface, but there is always a risk of spreading of the sample zone when detergents are present. Sample wells can be formed as indentations in the gel during polymerisation [210], but this can result in distortion of protein zones due to disturbance of the electrical field during IEF. Samples can be absorbed onto a piece of material such as filter paper, cellulose acetate, plastic sponge or desiccated polyacrylamide and these then applied to the gel surface. However, there is the danger that proteins can bind strongly to such substrates so that they are not eluted efficiently during IEF. Narrow strips of silicon rubber (1 mm thick) containing holes (for 10 μL samples) ot slits (for 20 μL samples) can be placed directly on the gel surface and we have found these to be an excellent application method in 2-D PAGE procedures. Alternatively, the IEF gel can be covered with a plastic sheet to protect it from the effects of the atmosphere desiccation and urea crystallisation during IEF [144]. In this case, slots (*ca.* 10×3 mm) can be punched in the cover sheet to allow the application of up to 25 μL of sample.

7.10   Focusing conditions

IEF is an equilibrium technique so that it is important to ascertain whether equilibrium has been attained if the positions on the gel occupied by protein zones are to reflect the p*I*s of those proteins. Little attention has been devoted to this aspect by most practitioners of 2-D PAGE. Focusing conditions are usually reported in terms of the product of voltage and time, *i.e.* volt×hours (Vh) [1, 172]. However, this parameter is virtually meaningless unless the other parameters used for IEF gels are defined. IEF gel length often varies, particularly between laboratories, and it is important to realise that the Vh product required for equilibrium to be attained varies with the square of the interelectrode gel length (l) [211]. We have, therefore, recommended [92] that Vhl^{-2} is a better parameter for the documentation of IEF running conditions. On this basis, O'Farrell [1] recommended using between 30 and 59 Vhl^{-2} and it is interesting to note that in a survey of several 2-D PAGE procedures [92] it was calculated that conditions varied from as few as 12.9 Vhl^{-2} to as many as 80 Vhl^{-2}. It should be noted that Vhl^{-2} does not compensate for changes in gel resistance, which can be achieved using watt×hours (Wh) [192] or $Whvol^{-1}$ (where vol represents gel volume) [92].

Various methods can be used to determine equilibrium such as constancy of the IEF separation pattern over long focusing times or by coincidence of protein zones when samples are migrated from the anode and cathode [194,

212]. Using the latter criterion, we have found that as many as 87 Vhl^{-2} are required for zone coincidence during IEF of human skin fibroblast proteins [123]. Therefore, IEF equilibrium conditions should be determined for the particular mixture of proteins being analysed. It should also be noted that the presence of urea in IEF gels used for 2-D PAGE extends the time required to reach equilibrium (see Section 7.3) and it may be impossible to focus fully certain high molecular weight proteins. The use of IEF under equilibrium conditions is important for inter-gel reproducibility and resolution of small charge differences between proteins, but it should be stressed that it is the quality of the final separations rather than equilibrium *per se* which is of importance in 2-D PAGE. Thus, non-equilibrium techniques (*e.g.* NEPHGE, see Section 7.6) can be used to advantage in particular circumstances, but the reproducibility of such gels can be very difficult to control.

7.11   Estimation of pH gradients

Protein p*I* values can be used in characterisation of spot positions on 2-D maps [213] but this approach requires that the pH gradient determined during IEF must be calibrated with accuracy. Often, particularly using tube-gel IEF systems, pH gradients are determined by transversely slicing the gel into thin segments, eluting them in water or 8 M urea and measuring the pH of the resulting solution. The conductivity of this solution can be increased with 10 mM KCl [120]. However, this method suffers from the disadvantage that urea is present, often at an unknown concentration, therefore complicating pH measurement as urea decreases the activity of H^+ ions [214]. Correction factors can be used [214] but the magnitude of the urea effect is pH dependent so that the correction factor increases with increasing pH [215, 216]. It is difficult, but not impossible [217], to measure pH gradients directly using IEF tube-gels. However, this can be achieved relatively easily for flat-bed IEF gels using a flat membrane electrode. This method is also complicated by urea effects and it is important that the temperature of focusing and pH measurement are identical.

Another approach to pH gradient calibration is to use a series of marker proteins of established p*I*. These can be either components of the sample itself (*e.g.* actin, tubulin, tropomyosin, vimentin and lactate dehydrogenase) [114, 218, 219] or purified proteins added to the sample being analysed [220]. Most commercial p*I* marker kits are not suitable for 2-D applications as they often contain multimeric proteins which would be dissociated under the denaturing conditions used in 2-D PAGE and their p*I* values have been established only under native conditions. An exception here is a set of acetylated cyto-chrome C markers (Calibiochem) which have the advantage that their colour facilitates the visual monitoring of the gel during IEF. Undoubtedly, the best method currently available for calibrating pH gradients in first-dimensional IEF gels is the use of carbamylated charge standards [221 – 224]. These stan-dards are generated by heating a suitable protein in the presence of urea for varying lengths of time. The sequential loss of free amino groups below pH 8.5 resulting in unit charge changes produces in 2-D maps a horizontal row or train of spots of constant mass and spaced apart by about 0.1 pH units. The length of this train depends on the amino acid composition of the prote-in, so that human haemoglobin β-chain forms 12 spots, bovine erythrocyte carbonic anhydrase produces 20 spots, and rabbit muscle creatine phospho-kinase gives 30 or more spots [157]. Commercial preparations of such stan-dards are now available as Carbamylyte (Pharmacia) derived from carbonic anhydrase (20 spots, pI 4.8 to 6.7), creatine phosphokinase (34 to 36 spots, pI 4.9 to 7.1), and glyceraldehyde-3-phosphate-dehydrogenase (34 spots, pI 4.7 to 8.3) [225]. These commercial standards have already proved useful in analysis of 2-D gels and their derivative Western blot transfer patterns [226]. It should be noted that while such standards can be useful for calibrating spot positions in NEPHGE gels, they do not indicate the true pH at the alkaline end of the gels [223].

7.12   Disadvantage of synthetic carrier ampholytes

Several problems are associated with the use of synthetic carrier ampholytes for first-dimensional IEF gels. Batch-to-batch variability of such carrier am-pholyte preparations is inevitable as a result of the synthetic procedures used. The effect of this variability on the reproducibility of 2-D separations is a topic often discussed at meetings on 2-D PAGE but, unfortunately, seems to be poorly documented in the literature. Artefacts can also be caused by in-teraction of sample proteins with synthetic carrier ampholytes, but there ap-pear to be very few documented instances of this phenomenon, reviewed in [157]. It is also difficult to engineer non-linear pH gradients using synthetic carrier ampholytes so that pH gradient shape can be optimised for resolution of particular protein mixtures. This can be achieved to a certain extent, albeit empirically, by blending of different wide and narrow pH range carrier am-pholyte preparations, but this process is unpredictable and difficult to con-trol. The most severe problem associated with the use of synthetic carrier am-pholytes for IEF in polyacrylamide gels is the inherently high electroen-dosmosis resulting in severe cathodic drift with concomitant loss of basic proteins from 2-D maps. This problem is most severe in tube-gel IEF (see Section 7.5), which resulted in the development of the NEPHGE technique (see Section 7.6), but is not completely overcome using horizontal flat-bed IEF procedures (see Section 7.7). There is, therefore, a requirement for alternative approaches for the first-dimension separation in 2-D PAGE.

7.13   Buffer isoelectric focusing

It is possible to generate pH gradients using simple, even non-amphoteric, buffers [227–229]. A mixture of 47 components, available commercially as

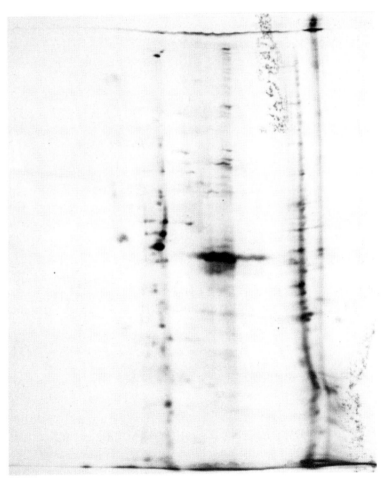

Figure 16. A 2-D separation of [^{35}S]methionine-labelled skin fibroblast which were focused in the first dimension using PolySep 47 for 100 Vhl^{-2}. The second dimension was 10% T SDS-PAGE. Reproduced with permission from [231].

PolySep 47 (Polysciences), has been used for analytical IEF [192] with claimed advantages [230] of defined chemical properties, increased reproducibility, low cost, ease of pH gradient engineering and minimal interactions with proteins. These properties appeared ideal for 2-D PAGE so that we recently assessed the suitability of buffer IEF using PolySep 47 as a first-dimensional separation procedure [145, 231]. However, 2-D separations of [^{35}S] methionine-labelled human skin fibroblasts were markedly inferior (Fig. 16) to those obtained by conventional 2-D PAGE (*cf.* Fig. 15). In the conventional procedure protein spots were distributed over the entire gel, whereas using buffer IEF the proteins were concentrated into four major zones in the IEF dimension. We believe [231] that in buffer IEF there may be insufficient or incorrect intermediate amphoteric species or separators, compared with the diversity of species of synthetic carrier ampholytes, to produce the required separation. This approach does not, therefore, appear to have much promise for the solution of the problems associated with the use of synthetic carrier ampholytes for 2-D PAGE.

7.14   Immobilised pH gradients

A recent important and exciting innovation in IEF has been the development of Immobiline reagents (LKB, Bromma, Sweden) [232] for the generation of immobilized pH gradients (IPGs). In this article there is space only for discussion of the basic essentials of this technology and of those aspects of particular relevance to 2-D PAGE. For a more detailed discussion of all aspects of IPGs the interested reader is referred to some recent reviews [157, 210, 233, 234].

The Immobilines are a series of seven acrylamide derivates with the general structure:

$$CH=CH-\underset{\underset{O}{\|}}{C}-\underset{\underset{H}{|}}{N}-R$$

where R contains either a carboxyl (acidic Immobilines) or a tertiary amino (basic Immobilines) group. IPG IEF gels are made by forming a gradient using the appropriate Immobiline solutions. Thus, during polymerisation the buffering groups forming the pH gradient are covalently attached and immobilised *via* vinyl bonds to the polyacrylamide backbone. This immobilisation of the pH gradient results in the elimination of pH gradient drift, but not electroendosmosis, making it possible to generate reproducible, stable and extremely narrow pH gradients (spanning from 0.1 to 1 pH unit). Initial efforts were, therefore, concentrated on the development of Immobiline formulations and procedures for the generation of narrow and ultra-narrow pH gradients to exploit the extremely high resolving power of such systems. Details of formulations for a series of narrow and ultra-narrow pH gradients can be found in [210, 235].

Narrow and ultra-narrow pH gradients are generally of limited use in 2-D PAGE applications as wide pH gradients are usually necessary to provide adequate resolution of complex protein mixtures. The formation of extended pH gradients, spanning greater than 1 pH unit, is complicated by the necessity to mix several buffering species. This problem was resolved by the development of computer programmes to calculate the mixtures required for this purpose [236, 237]. This approach has been used to generate recipes for the formation of pH gradients spanning 2 to 6 pH units [205, 237]. Unfortunately, very wide (pH 4−10) IPGs best suited to 2-D PAGE could only be generated using two non-buffering species, very acidic ($pK < 1$) and alkaline ($pK > 12$) Immobilines, as titrants. These reagents are not available commercially from LKB at present, but this problem has been recently overcome by the development of formulations for 4 to 6 pH unit wide IPGs using only the commercially available Immobiline buffers [238]. Gradients extending from pH 4 to 10 can now be readily constituted, but IPGs still cannot be extended down to pH 3 without resort to the use of the strongly acidic Immobiline species. It has also proved possible to generate non-linear IPGs of any desired shape [239, 240]. This technique of pH gradient engineering can be used to match the shape of the pH gradient to the distribution of protein pIs, thereby optimising protein distribution and maximizing resolution during IEF.

With the foregoing developments it became possible to exploit the advantages of IPG technology, including improved reproducibility, ease of pH gradient engineering, stability of pH gradients, for first-dimensional separations in 2-D PAGE. Immobiline gels have been used in capillary tubes for 2-D PAGE [241, 575]. However, it is simpler to use slab IPG IEF gels which should be cast on suitable plastic supports, such as GelBond PAG, using cassettes with U-shaped gaskets. Gels of any thickness can be produced in this manner but should generally be 1 mm or less in thickness. We currently use 0.5 mm thick IPG gels for 2-D PAGE [209, 242]. Whatever gel thickness is used, care should be taken to use high precision material for the gaskets as this will contribute significantly to gel reproducibility. It is possible to form sample application wells in the gel at the time of gel casting using strips of adhesive embossing tape (*e.g.* Dymo) [210]. The depressions formed can accommodate volumes of about 10–12 µL, but although this technique appears to work in practice it should be remembered that the depressions in the gel can disrupt the electric field during IEF.

Once the appropriate recipe for the desired pH gradient has been selected, the IPG gel can be formed using a simple two-chamber gradient mixing device. This procedure is described in detail in [210, 234, 235, 243]. An interesting variation on this approach has recently been published [244]. Alternatively, a computer-controlled stepmotor-driven high-precision burette apparatus can be used [245, 246]. This apparatus (Fig. 17) is commercially

Figure 17. Computer-controlled stepmotor-driven burette system for preparing IPG IEF gels. From left to right: printer (3), floppy disk unit (2), computer (1), four burettes (4), mixing chamber (5) on magnetic stirrer (6), polymerisation stand and gel cassettes (7). Reproduced with permission from [203].

available from Desaga and in general improves reproducibility, flexibility and documentation (Fig. 18) of gradients used in gels. It is especially useful in the preparation of wide-range IPG gels where pH gradient engineering, for example localized flattening of the pH gradient, can be used to selectively improve resolution.

In the standard recommended procedure [235] IPG gels are polymerised by heating at 50 °C for 1 h. This procedure has been adopted since it has been shown that the optimal polymerisation efficiency (in the range 84–88% incorporation for all seven Immobilines) was obtained at 50 °C [234, 247]. However, these conditions are potentially disastrous for wide pH gradients due to the great instability of the Immobilines of pK 8.5 and 9.3 at pH 9 and 60 °C (85% destruction of the former in less than 1 h) [248]. To minimize this problem, Righetti and his colleagues [248] recommend careful control of the

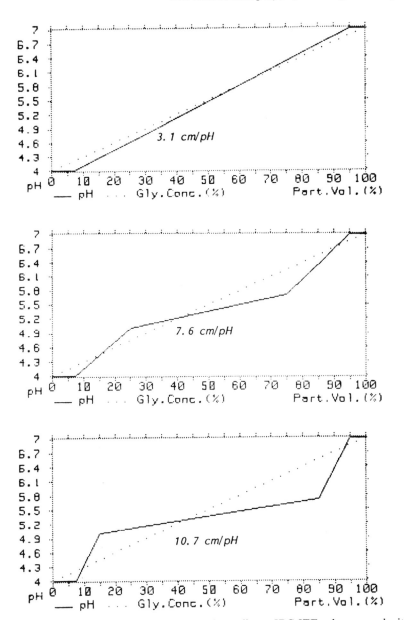

Figure 18. Documentation of linear and non-linear IPG IEF gels prepared with the apparatus shown in Fig. 17. Reproduced with permission from [240].

pH of the gel mixture, by suitable titration with acids or bases, to around pH 7.5 to 8. Altland [249] has devised a different strategy which allows polymerisation of IPG gels at ambient temperature. Stock Immobiline reagents are titrated to pH 6.8 with either 1 M Tris (acidic Immobilines) or 1 M phosphoric acid (basic Immobilines) and then diluted to 0.25 M by the addition of 0.1 M Tris-phosphate, pH 6.8. The volume required to obtain 0.25 M Immobiline solutions can be calculated using the following formula:

$$V = M \times (1/C - 1C_0 + V_0/M_0)$$

where V is the added total volume, M the amount of Immobiline in mmoles, M_0 the standard amount of Immobiline per bottle (5.11, 5.13, 5.14, 5.17, 5.19, 5.15 and 5.17 mmoles for Immobilines of pK 3.6, 4.4, 4.6, 6.2, 7.0, 8.3 and 9.3 respectively), C the concentration of Immobiline to be adjusted for, C_0 the standard concentration of 0.2 M in an Immobiline bottle after addition of the standard volume, V_0, of 25 mL [249]. The titrated and diluted Immobilines should be stored in aliquots at $-20\,°C$ to $-70\,°C$, under which conditions they are sufficiently stable to be used for up to 6 months [577]. However, the apparent hydrolysis rate of the Immobiline pK 9.3 reagent at $-20\,°C$ is 20% per year [577]. Polymerisation in neutral buffer at ambient temperature is a controlled and convenient procedure, but it should be pointed out that this advantage is gained at the expense of the necessity for removing the buffer by washing and prerunning the gels prior to sample application [249].

After polymerisation is complete the gel on its plastic support can be removed from the cassette. Unfortunately, the IPG gel cannot be used for IEF immediately, but must go through a washing procedure to remove catalysts and unpolymerised Immobilines, followed by reduction of the gel, with the aid of a fan, to its original weight [234]. This process is time-consuming and difficult to control, so that it is much preferable to use a rehydratable gel system for IPG gels [204, 206] similar to that already described for conventional IEF gels (see Section 7.8). Thus, after polymerisation, gels are washed, dried and stored for future use. This has the additional advantage that large numbers of gels can be cast in batches so minimising inter-gel variability and increasing the reproducibility of 2-D gel patterns.

Two strategies have been described for rehydration of IPG gels. The first procedure described by Righetti and his colleagues involves the use of gel weight to control the rehydration process [204, 206]. After gel polymerisation, the cassette is opened and the gel weight recorded. From this value, the combined weights of the plastic backing and of the gel monomers are subtracted. This tare-free value represents 100% solvent regain during rehydration. The gels are then washed in excess distilled water, dried with a cool fan, wrapped in Saranwrap, and stored at 4°C in a desiccator. Under these conditions it is claimed that gels can be stored for up to 6 weeks without deterioration of

IEF separation patterns [248]. When required for use, the gels are allowed to swell in a large volume of the desired solution, for example containing urea, and brought back, under weight control, to the desired % T and urea molarity by evaporation. The alternative strategy developed by Altland is to use volume rather than weight to control the rehydration [203, 249]. After polymerisation the gels are removed and washed, the final wash solution containing 1% v/v of 87% w/v glycerol. The gels are dried with a cool fan and stored, sealed in plastic bags, at $-20\,°C$. Under these conditions of storage the gels are stable for several months. When required for use, the gel is reassembled in a cassette of the same dimensions as that in which it was cast, and reswollen in a controlled amount of the required solution, for example 8 M urea. This procedure is less time consuming than that using weight control and is rather easier to perform reproducibly.

In 2-D PAGE separations it is usually desirable to perform IEF under denaturing conditions. Although it is relatively easy to incorporate 8 M urea into IPGs using the rehydratable gel system described above, it should be remembered that, due to its influence on hydrogen ion activity, urea will increase the pK of the Immobiline buffers and thereby modify the predicted pH range [206]. Suitable formulations for linear and non-linear IPGs containing 8 M urea have been developed [206, 239]. Using IPGs containing 8 M urea as the first dimension in 2-D PAGE, Righetti and his colleagues [205, 207, 239, 250] have established good 2-D maps of serum proteins. The various parameters in this procedure have been examined in detail [251]. Briefly, after IEF is complete, the IPG gel is cut up into individual sample strips. These strips are equilibrated for 15 min in 25 mM Tris-glycine buffer, pH 8.6, containing 3% w/v SDS and 2% v/v 2-mercaptoethanol. The equilibrated strip is then placed onto the scond dimensional, vertical SDS-PAGE gel and cemented in place with 1% w/v agarose in electrode buffer. An example of such a 2-D separation of serum proteins is shown in Fig. 19.

IPG gels containing 8 M urea have also beeen used by Görg and her colleagues [252−255] for the first-dimension in 2-D PAGE separations of soluble protein extracts from legume seeds. In these studies narrow and ultra-narrow IPGs were employed and for the second dimension thin, horizontal gradient SDS-PAGE was used. Successful 2-D maps of myosin light chains have also been obtained using IPGs showing additional isoforms to those found by conventional 2-D PAGE [256].

Satisfactory 2-D maps were obtained using first-dimensional IPG gels in the studies described above, but it should be pointed out that it was only soluble proteins (serum samples, seed and muscle extracts) which were being sub-

non–linear 4-10   **8 M urea**

sample pretreatment

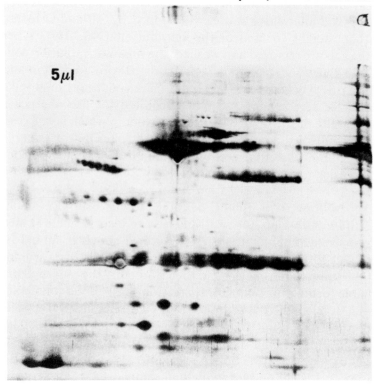

Figure 19. Silver-stained 2-D separation of normal human serum proteins using non-linear pH 4 to 10 IPG IEF in the first dimension. Reproduced with permission from [239].

jected to 2-D analysis. However, in many applications of 2-D PAGE the complex mixtures to be analysed can contain aggregated, multimeric or insoluble proteins. Such samples generally require the presence of both 8 M urea and 0.5% to 3% w/v nonionic (NP-40, Triton X-100) or zwitterionic (CHAPS) detergent to ensure adequate solubilisation for 2-D analysis [92] It has already been mentioned that the presence of 8 M urea has a marked effect on the theoretically predicted pH range of IPGs. Detergents might also be expected to modify the course of IPGs but, in fact, it has been established that the effect of 2% w/v NP-40 on Immobiline pKs is small; it is virtually negligible for the basic species (*ca.* 0.01 pH unit) and only slightly larger for the acidic compounds [206]. Unfortunately, a rather more serious problem is associated with the use of urea and nonionic detergents in rehydratable IPG systems as reswelling of polyacrylamide gels in the presence of both these reagents is very inefficient [204]. Using an open system with a large volume of solution equilibration swelling can take up to 24 h [204]. Using a cassette system with a controlled volume of solution we have found [145, 208] that gels never reswell fully in the presence of both 8 M urea and 0.5% w/v detergent (Triton X-100 or CHAPS). To overcome this problem, we recommend including 0.5% w/v Triton X-100 in the IPG gels when they are cast and in all subsequent washing solutions used prior to gel drying [209]. In this case it must be remembered that no detergent need be included in the solution used for rehydration as it is already present within the matrix of the dry gel.

Although narrow and ultra-narrow IPGs function very satisfactorily, it soon became apparent that several problems were associated with the use of wide-range IPGs of the type best suited to general 2-D PAGE applications. These problems included slow entry of sample proteins, lateral band spreading, prolonged focusing times, and increased electroendosmosis. These problems can be attributed to the inherently low conductivity of the Immobiline system and it has been found that improved separations can be obtained by the additon of low concentrations, typically 0.5% w/v, of synthetic carrier ampholytes of the appropriate range to the solution used for gel rehydration [249, 257, 258]. This technique has been termed hybrid IEF by Altland [249] or mixed carrier ampholyte-IPG IEF by Righetti [259] and has proved to be beneficial in 2-D separations [208, 209, 242, 260]. Interestingly, Righetti and his collaborators independently devised a similar technique when they attempted to analyse bacterial membrane proteins by 2-D PAGE using IPG gels. They found that addition of 4% w/v synthetic carrier ampholytes to a mixture of 2% w/v NP-40 and 8 M urea was extremely effective for solubilisation of *Streptococcus cremoris* membranes [261]. Moreover, when 4% w/v synthetic carrier ampholyte was also included in the IPG dimension, a marked improvement in the quality of 2-D protein maps was observed [259].

In our 2-D PAGE studies of [^{35}S]methionine-labelled human skin fibroblast proteins, a problem that we soon encountered was that of streaking in both the horizontal and vertical directions. This problem was apparent using both pH 4−7 [145, 208, 209, 242] and pH 4−10 [209, 242] IPGs. We concluded that the horizontal streaking was likely to be due to incomplete focusing and was significantly diminished by increasing the total Vh for the focusing run [208, 209, 242]. The vertical streaking was more serious and appears to be associated with difficulties in elution and transfer of proteins from the first-dimensional Immobiline gels to the second-dimensional SDS-PAGE gels [209, 208, 242] . Interestingly, Görg and her coworkers [253, 255] experienced

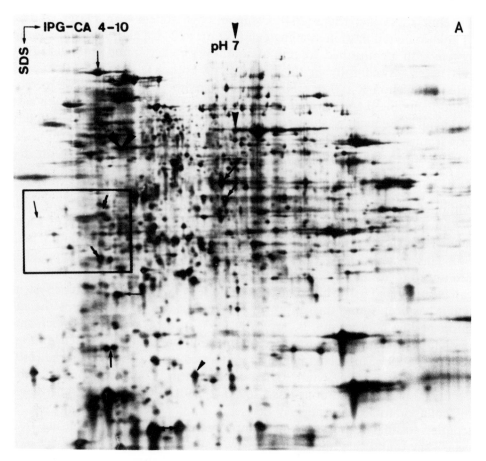

Figure 20. Horizontal 2-D PAGE of human myeloblast proteins using (A) pH 4–10 or (B) (see p. 53) pH 4–7 IPG IEF gels in the first dimension. Reproduced with permission from [265].

similar problems of streaking. They attributed this phenomenon to the presence of fixed charges on the Immobiline gel matrix, leading to increased electroendosmosis in the region of contact between the first-dimensional IPG gel and the second-dimensional SDS-PAGE gel [260, 262]. As a result there is a disturbance in migration of proteins from the first to the second dimension. Although horizontal, flat-bed SDS-PAGE gels were used in these studies, the same phenomenon probably occurs in the standard, vertical SDS-PAGE systems.

In our initial studies we had used equilibration for 30 min in a buffer containing 125 mM Tris, 2.5% w/v SDS and 100 mM DTT at pH 6.8 [145, 208]. Increasing the ionic strength of the equilibration buffer (300 mM Tris) was ineffective, whereas increasing the pH of the equilibration buffer to pH 8.6

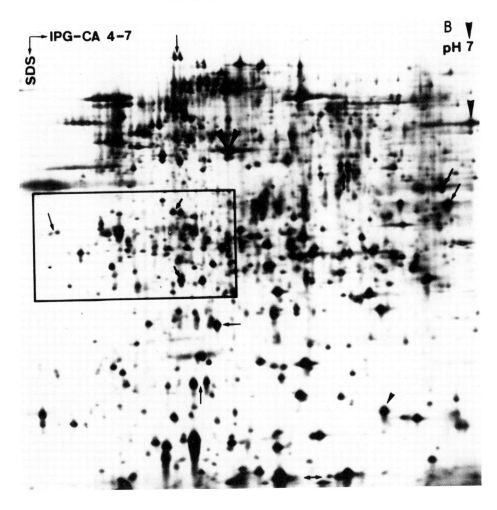

produced improved 2-D maps [209, 242] in agreement with the results of
Gianazza *et al.* [251]. Inclusion of 8 M urea in the equilibration buffer
resulted in a significant reduction in vertical streaking [209, 242], but the
overall separation was still markedly inferior to that obtained using our standard method of 2-D PAGE. In a different approach, Görg [253, 255] partly
overcame the problems of electroendosmosis and streaking by applying the
IPG IEF strip to a starting gel, adjacent to the cathodal side of the SDS-
PAGE separation gel. This starting gel contained small amounts of Immobilines (2.5 mM of each species) in order to compensate for the charges of
the IEF strip in the area of IPG gel to SDS gel contact. However, more
recently an alternative strategy has been devised [260]. In this procedure,
15% w/v glycerol was included in the solution used for rehydration of the
IPG gels and the equilibration buffer, 0.05 M Tris-HCl (pH 6.8), contained

1% w/v DTT, 2% w/v SDS plus 6 M urea and 30% w/v glycerol to minimise electroendsmosis effects. This method has been applied to the 2-D analysis of extracts of *Saccharomyces cerevisiae* using either vertical or horizontal SDS-PAGE methods in the second dimension. In the latter case an additional modification to the standard procedure [115, 190] involved the use of a laying-on procedure [263] for application of the first-dimensional IPG gel strip to the horizontal SDS gel. In this study [260] 2-D analysis of a yeast protein extract was compared using conventional synthetic carrier ampholyte IEF, IPG IEF and hybrid IEF. The latter technique using pH 4−10 IPG gels containing 0.5% w/v Ampholine (pH 3.5−9.5) was found to produce the best 2-D maps with the largest number of spots observed. This methodology has been subsequently applied to 2-D separations of pea [264] and human myeloblast (Fig. 20) [265] proteins.

When Righetti's group attempted 2-D analysis of a wider range of complex protein samples they also experienced considerable problems during elution and transfer between dimension, involving streaking, band splitting and distortion of low molecular weight spots [266, 585]. They attributed this effect to the formation of mixed micelles of SDS and non-ionic detergent. However, if this was the source of the problems encountered, it is difficult to see why these phenomena were only observed when IPG gels were used for the IEF dimension. This problem has been partially overcome [266, 267, 585] using an equilibration protocol based on that originally devised by Jäckle [268] and used by Görg *et al.* [115] for 2-D PAGE. The first-dimensional IPG gel strip is fixed for 1 h in 12% v/v acetic acid/50% v/v methanol, and then washed 2×15 min in 250 mM Tris-glycine buffer, pH 8.8, 1% w/v SDS, followed by 15 min in 25 mM Tris-glycine buffer, pH 8.8, 5% w/v SDS, 2% v/v 2-mercaptoethanol (or 15 mM DTT) prior to application to the SDS-PAGE dimension. Using this procedure samples of bacterial plasma membranes, microvilli from beef kidney cortex, rat erythrocyte plasma membranes and human heart biopsies have been analysed. This technique appears to work satisfactorily. However, a possible caveat is that it seems likely that some proteins may remain insolubilised within the IEF gel subsequent to the fixation procedure, resulting in their loss from the final 2-D maps.

In conclusion, IPG technology is of great potential value when applied to the IEF dimension of 2-D PAGE, particularly with the increased reproducibility in spot positions that can be obtained [269, 270]. Acceptable 2-D maps of a variety of complex protein mixtures are now being obtained. However, there are still problems associated with the elution and transfer of proteins between the IPG IEF and the SDS-PAGE dimensions which must be fully overcome before this technique is likely to replace conventional synthetic carrier ampholyte IEF as the first dimensional separation routinely used in 2-D PAGE.

8   Equilibration between dimensions

An equilibration step is usually used between the two dimensions of 2-D PAGE in which the IEF gels are incubated at room temperature in a Tris buffer, pH 6.8, containing SDS under reducing conditions prior to application to the SDS-PAGE gels. The function of this step is to allow the proteins within the IEF gel matrix to interact fully with SDS so that they migrate with the proper characteristics in the SDS dimension. IEF gels from tube-gel techniques are usually equilibrated for 30 to 40 min [1], while thin and ultrathin flat-bed IEF gels require only 5 to 10 min [165] and 1 to 2 min [263] respectively. The broadening of protein zones due to diffusion during this procedure can be a serious problem. O'Farrell [1] found that band width increased by 40% using a 30 min equilibration procedure. Perhaps more importantly, a considerable loss of proteins (5 to 50%) from the IEF gels can occur during this procedure [1, 114, 165, 271]. Consequently, some investigators have attempted to dispense with this procedure [127, 272], but this can result in streaking especially of high molecular weight proteins [1]. Streaking has been found to be a particular problem using IPG gels for the first dimension of 2-D PAGE, which necessitates extended (30 min) equilibration times and the use of special conditions (discussed in Section 7.14). An alternative strategy that has found some application is to fix and stain IEF gels with 50% v/v methanol/10% v/v acetic acid and Coomassie Brilliant Blue R-250 prior to equilibration to the second dimension SDS-PAGE gels [268]. This method appears to work satisfactorily for thin flat-bed slab IEF gels but results in significant amounts of sample proteins remaining in tube IEF gels after SDS-PAGE [115]. It is, therefore, probably best avoided.

9   Transfer between dimensions

First-dimensional IEF gels must be applied, after equilibration, to the top of the vertical second-dimensional SDS-PAGE gels. In order to obtain good 2-D separations, it is essential that a good contact is made at the interface between the two gels over their entire length. Fast-polymerising polyacrylamide can be used to embed the IEF gels on top of the SDS slab gels [127], but this can result in loss of proteins [273] due to their interaction with the gel during polymerisation. In most procedures using tube-gel IEF, the gels are cemented in place using buffered agarose [1] which does not cause protein retention [273]. However, many commercial agarose preparations are contaminated with amino acid-containing impurities which result in the appearance of artefacts on 2-D maps when sensitive silver staining visualization techniques are used [274]. It has been found possible [113] to apply tube IEF gels directly to the second-dimensional gels without the use of an embedding medium as, during subsequent electrophoresis, the IEF gels became bonded to the surface of the SDS gels. Care must be taken when handling tube IEF gels as they are easily stretched which can result in distortion of 2-D maps, thereby complicating inter-gel comparisons.

When flat-bed slab IEF gels are used for the first-dimensional separation, the samples to be applied to the second dimension are in the form of thin strips of gel bound to a flexible plastic support. These strips are relatively easy to handle and are not susceptible to stretching. If a vertical SDS-PAGE gel system is to be used for the second dimension, the space in the cassettes above the SDS gels should be filled with equilibration buffer. The IEF strips can then be simply slid into place, taking care to avoid the entrapment of air bubbles. It is not usually necessary, although possible, to cement the strips in place with buffered agarose [165]. Using horizontal flat-bed second-dimension SDS gels, the IEF sample strips is placed, gel layer downwards, into a trench formed in the SDS gels during casting [115]. This laying-in technique does not work well for IPG IEF gels [260] as due to electroendosmosis effects during SDS electrophoresis the IPG gel shrinks at the anode, swells at the cathode and is subject to distortion. In this case it was found preferable to use a simple laying-on procedure avoiding the use of an application trench [263].

10   The second dimension

10.1   Gradient *versus* non-gradient gels

The distribution of proteins on 2-D gels can significantly affect resolution [1]. If the protein spots from a complex mixture are restricted to one region of the gel, much of the area available for protein separation will not be utilised with a consequent loss of resolution. Unfortunately, a survey of molecular weight and pI values for a large series of proteins shows that these tend to cluster around certain mean values [1, 275]. Linear pH gradients are not likely, then, to result in optimal IEF resolution for most protein mixtures. Thus, there is a need for pH gradient engineering to generate a pH gradient shape optimised for the separation of the particular protein mixture under investigation. This is very difficult to achieve in a controlled and reproducible manner using synthetic carrier ampholytes for IEF (see Section 7.12). IPG IEF gels seem to have much more promise in this respect (see Section 7.14) but this aspect of IPG technology has not yet been exploited for 2-D PAGE.

Similarly, a gel of a single polyacrylamide concentration is unlikely to produce a uniform protein distribution in SDS-PAGE [1]. One approach to this problem, recommended by Garrels [113], is to use for each sample a series of second-dimensional SDS gels of different polyacrylamide concentrations. A series of five different polyacrylamide concentrations is suggested (7.5, 9, 12, 15 and 18% T) which results in a set of 2-D maps with good resolution in different molecular weight ranges. Bravo [114] recommends a 15% T gel for routine analysis of eukaryotic cell extracts. This approach is usually used in conjunction with a series of first-dimensional gels of different pH ranges, including NEPHGE. A rather large series of 2-D maps is generated for each sample which complicates comparative analysis between samples. The several 2-D gels of each sample must be concatenated to give a single master 2-D protein maps for that sample. This can be readily achieved using an appropriate automated computer analysis system [276] (see Section 14) but is difficult, if not impossible, to achieve visually.

The alternative approach, which was used in the original O'Farrell [1] procedure, is to exploit the ability of gradient polyacrylamide SDS gels to improve the sharpness and resolution of protein zones. Such gradient gels can separate proteins with a wide range of molecular weights. Linear gradients are unlikely to give optimal resolution due to the distribution of protein molecular weight values [275]. Generally, it is best to flatten the mid-region of the polyacrylamide gradient to maximise resolution in the region of the gradient where most proteins are usually located, while steeper gradients can be used at the extremes of high and low molecular weight where fewer proteins are found. Gianazza *et al.* [251] have recently described a method of statistical analysis of the distribution of protein molecular weight and p*I* values and using weighting factors to derive the optimal gradient shape to maximise resolution.

10.2   Gel preparation

SDS-PAGE using the discontinuous buffer system of Laemmli [91] is almost universally used for the second dimension of 2-D PAGE. Gels of a single polyacrylamide concentration can be prepared using standard procedures. It is advantageous to cast gels in batches, rather than individually, as this improves reproducibility of 2-D maps and facilities inter-gel comparisons.

Various procedures have been developed for the preparation of gradient polyacrylamide gels. The simplest approach is to use a two-chamber gradient forming apparatus of fixed shape [8, 115, 277, 278]. Equipment of this type is commercially available, reproducible and easy to use, but it lacks the flexibility required for the generation of gradients of different shapes. A greater degree of flexibility can be achieved using a two-chamber system of variable complementary shape [279, 280], but the reproducibility of this device depends on the accuracy with which the moveable baffle between the chambers can be positioned. Electromechanical gradient forming devices such as the Ultrograd (LKB) can be used to prepare gradient polyacrylamide gels [186, 280] in a reliable and reproducible manner [282]. We use this apparatus in conjunction with a casting tower of the type described by Jones *et al.* [283] for the preparation of batches of gradient polyacrylamide SDS

Gradient Control

Program: Polyacrylamide Gel Gradient

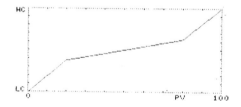

Data:

TV= 63 mL;   BV= 10 mL;   MV= 0.2 mL;   TV/BV= 6.3 ;   Speed: 65 %
LC= 8.5 Units;   HC= 22 Units;
H1= 3 % ;   L1= 7 % ;   H2= 2 % ;   L2= 10 % ;

ENDPOINTS OF LINES

EP No.	PV(%)	C(U)	EP No.	PV(%)	C(U)	EP No.	PV(%)	C(U)	EP No.	PV(%)	C(U)	EP No.	PV(%)	C(U)
0	0	8.5	1	20	13.5	2	80	17	3	100	22			

(EP=End Point; PV(%)=Partial Vol.; C(U)=Conc. in Units; TV=Total Vol.; BV=Burette Vol.; MV=Mixing Vol.; LC=Low Conc.;HC=High Conc. ;
L1,H1,L2,H2 = Proportions of catalyst solutions 1 and 2 admixed to solutions with low and high conc. of gradient constituent)

Figure 21. Documentation of gradient SDS-PAGE gel produced by the apparatus shown in Fig. 17. Reproduced with permission from [203].

gels for 2-D PAGE [105, 165]. However, this device is expensive and limited in flexibility as it will mix up to only three solutions and generates gradients as a function of time rather than volume, reflecting its design origin as a gradient former for column chromatographic applications. The micro-computer controlled stepmotor-driven burette system devised by Altland [245] (Fig. 17), already described for the generation of IPG IEF gels (see Section 7.14), is considerably more versatile and provides full documentation of the gradient produced (Fig. 21). The high precision stepmotor-driven burettes used in this system are expensive, but a commercial version of this equipment, using less expensive proportional pumps, is available from Desaga.

Polyacrylamide gels containing SDS can be bound to glass supports using silanes [284], but large batches of gels are easier to handle if they are bound to plastic supports (*e.g.* Gel-Fix, GelBond PAG). This approach should have considerable advantages for 2-D PAGE as the gels are more mechanically stable and are not prone to stretching/shrinking effects which result in distortion of 2-D maps. However, such gels cannot be exposed to TCA fixation for extended times and must be dried using special methods [92, 170]. An alternative crosslinking agent, AcryAide (an olefinic agarose derivative), can overcome this problem, as polyacrylamide gels crosslinked with AcryAide and bound to GelBond PAG are resiliant and can be dried, without vacuum, in an oven at 60 °C [285].

10.3   Stacking

In most 2-D PAGE procedures a large-pore stacking gel cast on top of the homogeneous or gradient polyacrylamide separating gel has been used in conjunction with the discontinuous (multiphasic) buffer system of Ornstein [4] and Davis [5], but with the addition of SDS [91]. This stacking gel serves to concentrate proteins from the IEF gel into narrow starting zones. Garrels [113] omitted this step on the basis that protein zones within IEF gels are concentrated already and that the non-restrictive IEF gel will itself act as a stacking gel. The nature of the stacking process is modified in the presence of SDS as SDS-coated proteins ideally (there are exceptions) have a constant charge to mass ratio. Thus, all proteins have a uniform charge, will migrate with the same mobility and will automatically stack. In addition, SDS-protein complexes are not titratable between pH 7 and 10, so that mobility is not variable within this range and unstacking will occur by the change in gel concentration alone [286].

10.4   Gel size

The resolution capacity of SDS-PAGE can be increased by a simple increase in the length of the separating gel [287] as has also found to be the case for DNA sequencing gels [288]. Nikodem *et al.* [289] demonstrated the effectiveness of this approach for 2-D PAGE using 29 cm long second-dimension SDS-PAGE gels in combination with tube IEF gels of standard (*ca.* 13 cm) size.

Resolution in the IEF dimension depends on a number of factors and can be improved by increasing gel length or by increasing the voltage gradient applied during IEF [169, 290, 291]. The latter option can only be adopted if adequate cooling is available to dissipate the increased Joule heating. For flat-bed gels, this can be readily achieved as efficient cooling systems, such as a Peltier device [169], can be used in conjunction with ultrathin gels. For example, Allen and his colleagues have used voltage gradients of 700 Vcm^{-1} in 125 µm thick IEF gels containing 4% w/v carrier ampholytes and cast on plastic supports [169, 292]. In contrast, the cooling facilities with which most tube-gel IEF apparatus is provided are non-existent or at best rudimentary. With such apparatus, voltage gradients are normally limited to about 50 Vcm^{-1}.

Resolution in 2-D PAGE can be increased using increased gel lengths in both the IEF and SDS-PAGE dimensions. This approach has been exploited by Young and his coworkers in a technique they call giant gels [211, 293] in which 32 cm IEF gels are used in combination with 41 cm SDS-PAGE gels, giving a six-fold increase in gel area compared with the O'Farrell [1] system. Using this technique, as many as 5000 proteins have been detected in rat thymus cells (Fig. 22) [294] and 10 000 species have been claimed to be observed in 2-D maps of human Hep cells [295]. This technique has also been used to investigate the *in vitro* translation products of mRNA isolated from thymus cells, where an increased resolution of 1500 species was obtained [579], and to characterise glucocorticoid-mediated induction of specific proteins in rat thymus cells [580]. Additional advantages of this technology are that (i) proteins spots are more discrete and streaked regions are resolved into multiple spots, (ii) sample loading capacity is significantly (up to 100-fold) higher [293], and (iii) effects of autoradiographic spreading are reduced allowing improved resolution of ^{125}I-iodinated proteins and [^{32}P]phosphoproteins [294].

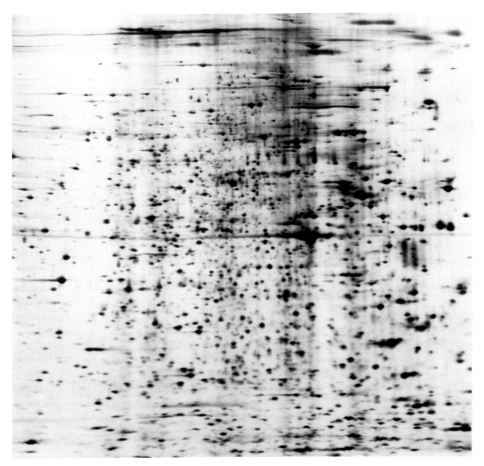

Figure 22. Giant gel 2-D PAGE separation of [^{35}S]methionine-labelled mouse embryonic fibroblast proteins. Reproduced with permission from [294].

At the other extreme, some investigators have recommended microscale systems for 2-D PAGE [273, 296, 297]. Rüchel's [296] system of IEF followed by non-detergent gradient gel electrophoresis is extremely small and has resulted in such methods being known as postage stamp gels. The gels used by Neuhoff and his coworkers [273] measure 3 cm×3.5 cm and involve a combination of IEF in 10 µL capillary tubes with homogeneous and gradient SDS-PAGE gels. This technique has proved useful in studies of urinary proteins in proteinuric disease [571] and its reproducibility for quantitative evaluation of 2-D gels has been recently assessed [298]. Such microscale procedures undoubtedly have advantages of reduced run times, shorter staining and destaining times (especially if thin gels are used), and low cost. However, these advantages are counterbalanced by a possible decrease in resolution potential as a result of the decreased distances between the separated protein components on the 2-D maps.

10.5   Molecular weight standards

In the same way that pI markers are essential for calibration of the IEF dimension of 2-D PAGE (see Section 7.11), so a series of M_r standards are required to provide a reference for the SDS-PAGE dimension. These standards are usually mixtures of purified proteins of known M_r which are electrophoresed down one side of the SDS gels. Several kits of suitable markers, both radiolabelled and non-radioactive, are available commercially. Cross-linked polymers of a single protein can be used [299], but such polymers can exhibit anomalous behaviour in SDS gels [105]. Giometti *et al.* [300] recommend the use of rat whole heart homogenate which is added to the buffered agarose medium used to cement the IEF gels in place. This generates a series of 80 references bands, ranging from M_r 300–100000, which strech horizontally across the 2-D maps. The M_r markers described so far and the pI markers discussed in Section 7.11 are used independently. A set of combined pI and M_r markers would be useful and as an approach to this problem bacteriophage T4 coat proteins [301] and fluorescent dansylated proteins [302] have been used as simultaneous markers for both pI and M_r. The various methods for standardisation of protein position in 2-D PAGE have been compared and their efficiency assessed [303].

11   Fixation

After 2-D electrophoresis has been completed, gels are usually fixed to precipitate and immobilise the separated components within the gel matrix and to remove non-protein components which can interfere with subsequent staining procedures. Aqueous and methanolic solutions of acetic acid have become very popular for fixation of 2-D gels. This method is often efficient for high M_r proteins but it should be remembered that smaller proteins, basic proteins and glycoproteins may not be adequately fixed by this procedure, especially in the presence of detergents [304]. The best general purpose fixative is TCA which is usually found to be most efficient at the 20% w/v level. Sulphosalicylic acid (10–20% w/v) or mixtures of TCA and sulphosalicylic acids (10% w/v of each) have been recommended [305], but these procedures are generally less efficient than TCA alone [306]. As an alternative to TCA, proteins can be chemically immobilized by covalently cross-linking them to the gel matrix. This can be achieved using either 5% w/v formaldehyde [307] or 2% w/v glutaraldehyde, but these reagents have also been found to give inadequate fixation in some circumstances [306]. However, as we have previously pointed out [111] the reactions have been carried out under acidic conditions, whereas optimal reaction conditions should occur under alkaline conditions. Recently Gersten *et al.* [308] have devised a method using a microwave dryer for rapid (3 min) mechanical fixation of gels crosslinked with AcryAide and cast on GelBond PAG. This technique might be useful for the development of alternative staining strategies incompatable with prior acid fixation.

12   Detection methods

In the early days of electrophoresis, methods for the detection of separated protein zones were somewhat limited and insensitive, for example (i) studies of coloured proteins [309], (ii) absorption [310], and (iii) Schlieren optical methods [311]. However, the development of organic dyes able to react with proteins soon made stains such as Bromophenol Blue [312] and Amido Black [313] popular. However, it is the Coomassie Brilliant Blue dyes, originally developed as acid wool dyes [314], which have been almost universally adopted as general protein staining reagents due to the high sensitive of detection (*ca.* 0.5 μg). The level of sensitivity of detection was further increased with the development of autoradiographic and fluorographic methods for radiolabelled proteins, and fluorescent (1 ng sensitivity) [315] and silver (0.1 ng sensitivity) [316, 317] staining techniques. Only a brief review of the most important staining and detection methods as applied to 2-D PAGE can be discussed here and for a further account the reader should consult [318].

12.1   Coomassie Brilliant Blue

The most popular general protein staining procedures are based on the use of non-polar, sulphated triphenylmethane Coomassie stains developed for the textile industry [314]. Coomassie Brilliant Blue (CBB) R-250 is most often used and requires an acidic medium for electrostatic reaction between the dye molecules and the amino groups of the proteins. Staining with CBB R-250 is usually out in 40% v/v methanol, 10% v/v acetic acid followed by removal of excess dye with the same acidic alcohol solution. An alternative strategy [319], which was used by O'Farrell [1], is to use CBB R-250 dissolved in TCA. A dimethylated form of the dye, CBB G-250, can be used to advantage here as its diminished solubility permits its use in colloidal dispersion. The colloidally dispersed dye selectively forms dye-protein complexes but does not penetrate the gel matrix, thus rapidly staining proteins without the development of background staining [320]. Alternative Coomassie dyes such as Coomassie Violet R-150 and Serva Violet 49 have also been used for staining polyacrylamide gels [284]. The general CBB staining procedures are insensitive, being capable of detecting about 0.5 µg protein cm^{-2} of gel [318]. Neuhoff and his coworkers [321] have recently reinvestigated CBB staining methods. In a test of over 600 modifications, they developed an optimal staining technique using CBB R-250 in perchloric acid in the presence of ammonium sulphate which is claimed to have a detection sensitivity as high as 0.7 ng protein cm^{-2} of gel.

12.2   Fluorescent staining methods

An increased sensitivity of detection of proteins separated in polyacrylamide gels can be achieved using fluorescent compounds. Two approaches are possible using such reagents. In the first type of procedure, pre-electrophoretic staining, proteins are covalently labelled with fluorescent molecules prior to electrophoresis. A comprehensive list of reagents which have been used in this way is given in [322]. Examples of pre-electrophoretic stains are dansyl chloride and fluorescamine which have sensitivieties as low as 10 ng [315] and 6 ng [323, 324] respectively. Of particular interest is the compound 2-methoxy-2,4-diphenyl-3(2H)-furanone which can detect as little as 1 ng of protein [325] and makes it possible to detect the labelled proteins directly in 2-D gels using a cooled charge-coupled device (CCD) imaging system [326]. However, it is important to note that such pre-electrophoretic staining procedures can cause protein charge modifications which can result in anomalous 2-D separation patterns [111]. To overcome this problem, fluorescent stains can be used as post-electrophoretic stains and 1-anilinonaphthalene-8-sulphonate (ANS) has been particularly used in this manner [327, 328]. We have recently applied this staining procedure to 2-D gels [329] but have not found it to be particularly sensitive for this application. Another disadvantage of fluorescent stains is that ultraviolet illumination is required for their visualisation which has resulted in the general lack of popularity of this group of procedures.

12.3 Silver staining

The ability of silver to develop images was discovered in the mid-17th century. This property was initially exploited in the development of photography, followed closely by its use in histological procedures. Recently, numerous silver staining methods have been developed for the detection of proteins separated by polyacrylamide gel electrophoresis, reviewed in [111, 318, 330, 331]. These techniques are claimed to be between 20 and 200 times more sensitive than CBB R-250, and can detect about 0.05 to 0.1 ng protein mm^{-2} of gel.

12.3.1 Fixation

In most published silver staining procedures, mixtures of alcohol, acetic acid and water are recommended for gel fixation, although we believe that TCA should be used due to its better fixative properties (see Section 11). TCA fixation is fully compatible with silver staining provided that the gels are washed well after fixation to remove TCA and other reagents such as glycine and detergent which can interfere with the stain [317, 332]. Glutaraldehyde has been recommended as a fixative [333], but it can result in excessive yellow background staining due to reactivity of glycine present in the electrophoresis buffer [332, 334].

12.3.2 Pretreatment of gels

In most procedures gels before silver staining are treated with formaldehyde [290, 317] or glutaraldehyde [333, 335]. Alternative pretreatments include potassium ferricyanide [336], potassium dichromate [95], and DTT [335]. Such pretreatment of the gel is not essential [334, 337, 338], but it undoubtedly enhances subsequent staining intensity. Dichromate, permanganate and ferricyanide are thought to enhance staining by converting protein hydroxyl and sulphydryl groups to aldehydes and thiosulphates, thereby altering the oxidation-reduction potential of the proteins. We have previously suggested [111] that these enhancers of silver staining can form complexes with proteins and that these complexes may act as nucleation centres for silver reduction.

12.3.3 Diamine silver stains

The first procedures for staining polyacrylamide gels with silver were based on histological silver impregnation methods used for studying degeneration in the central nervous system [316, 317]. This method was complex and time-consuming, but a simpler procedure employing fewer steps was soon developed [333]. In these methods an ammoniacal silver or diamine solution, prepared by adding silver nitrate to a sodium-ammonium hydroxide mixture was used. A high ammonia to sodium ratio was employed resulting in a very low concentration of free silver ions as most are complexed in the form $[Ag(NH_3)_2]^+$ and making the staining procedure more sensitive for glycoproteins than for proteins not conjugated with carbohydrates [339]. If this specificity is not required, it can be minimised by lowering the ammonium to sodium ratio by the addition of more NaOH [290]. Marshall and Latner [340], using 3 mm thick gels, found that improved staining was obtained by substituting methylamine for ammonia in the diamine solution. Copper is included in several diamine procedures as it increases its sensitivity and the mechanism of this may be similar to that of the Biuret reaction [316]. The silver ions in the gel complexed with proteins are developed by reduction to metallic silver, usually achieved via oxidation of formaldehyde. In the diamine stains, the ammoniacal silver must be acidified, usually with citric acid, which reduces the rate of reduction and prevents non-selective deposition of silver [339].

12.3.4 Non-diamine chemical silver stains

These stains use a simple silver nitrate solution instead of a diamine solution and are based on photographic protocols [95, 330, 335, 336, 341]. These stains depend on the reaction of silver ions with proteins under acidic conditions, followed by the selective reduction of ionic silver to metallic silver by formaldehyde made alkaline with either sodium carbonate or NaOH. Under these conditions, silver ions complexed to the proteins will be rapidly precipitated and reduced. However, care must be taken to wash out free silver nitrate from the gel before development to prevent precipitation of silver oxide leading to a high background.

12.3.5 Photodevelopment silver stains

Photodevelopment silver stains [342, 343] provide a rapide, simple and sensitive method of protein detection. These methods utilise energy from photons of light to liberate electrons so reducing ionic to metallic silver and require the use of only a single solution to achieve staining. During the fixation step the gel is impregnated with 0.2% w/v of sodium chloride. Upon transfer to a silver nitrate solution, a fine bluish-white precipitate of silver chloride is formed within the gel. Then, using either incident light or transillumination, the image is visualised as clear protein zones while the rest of the gel contains a fine bluish-white precipitate. With light of sufficient intensity, the protein zones will subsequently darken to give a black or brown image [342]. The clear protein zones are not due to exclusion of silver from these regions [342] but may rather be due to altered solute structures affecting interactions between silver and chloride ions [318, 331].

12.3.6 Colour silver staining

Silver stains are essentially monochromatic producing a dark brown or black image, but if image development is allowed to proceed further, dense spots become saturated and colour effects can be produced [336]. The colours produced depend on three variables; (i) the size of the silver particles, (ii) the refractive index of the gel, and (iii) the distribution of the silver particles within the gel [318]. Small grains (<0.2 µm) transmit reddish or yellow-red light, grains >0.3 µm give bluish colours, while larger grains produce black images. Colour development can be enhanced by modifications to staining procedures such as lowering the concentration of reducing agent in the developer, prolonging development, adding alkali, or using elevated temperatures. Some staining protocols have been developed to exploit these colour effects [338, 344, 345]. Glutaraldehyde fixation has been recently shown to enhance the sensitivity of this method [346]. The colours produced can aid in identification of certain proteins, but variations in protein concentration and conditions of image development can produce colour shifts, so confusing identification. A serious disadvantage of these colour methods is that saturation and negative staining effects often occur and these result in considerable problems if quantitative analysis is attempted.

12.3.7 Protein reactive groups

The precise mechanism involved in silver staining of proteins has not been fully established but all methods involve the reduction of ionic silver to its metallic form. It has been proposed that silver cations complex with protein amino groups [331, 347] and with cysteine and methionine sulphur residues [348]. However, more recently Gersten and his collaborators [349] have implicated 3-dimensional (3-D) protein structure and, therefore, the steric presentation of reactive moieties in 3-D space as being of most consequence and proposed that other factors such as amino acid composition are of secondary importance.

12.3.8 Silver staining and two-dimensional polyacrylamide gel electrophoresis

Silver staining procedures generally produce excellent results when used to visualise 2-D gel patterns (see Figs. 19, 23–25). However, certain problems specific to 2-D PAGE have been encountered. The presence of 2-mercaptoethanol from the equilibration buffer can result in the appearance of small, vertical streaks [93, 340]. Two or more horizontal lines which have been observed across the entire gel in the M_r 50000–68000 region have also been attributed to 2-mercaptoethanol [337, 350]. Agarose used for cementing first-dimensional IEF gels to the tops of second-dimension SDS-PAGE gels can

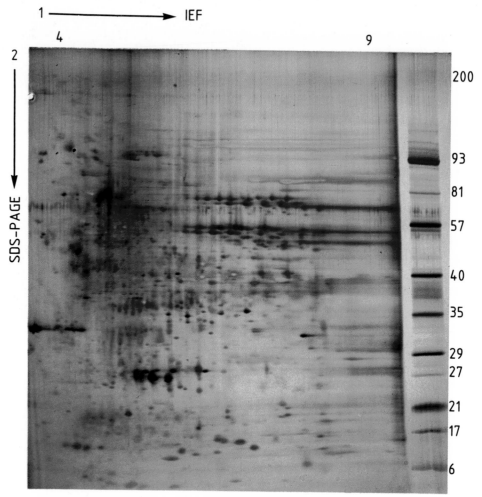

Figure 23. Colour silver stain of 2-D gel of proteins from a single wheat kernel. Reproduced with permission from [587].

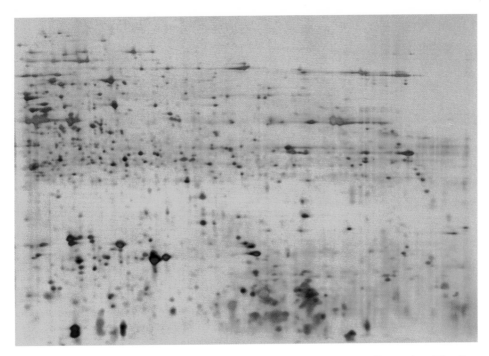

Figure 24. Colour silver-stained horizontal 2-D separation of yeast cell proteins. The first dimension was a hybrid IPG-carrier ampholyte pH 7 – 10 IEF gel containing 0.5% w/v NP-40 and 8 M urea. The second dimension was according to [265]. Illustration by courtesy of Dr. A. Görg.

have amino acid-containing contaminants which can cause increased background staining of 2-D gels [274]. Silver staining can severely quench the detection of radioactivity both by autoradiographic and fluorographic procedures and by scintillation counting [351, 352]. This effect is particularly serious for the detection of ^{3}H and for methods using dual labelling techniques. In addition, caution should be exercised in the interpretation of protein staining patterns as certain proteins, for example calmodulin [353], fail to respond to single step silver staining procedures. In such situations, increased sensitivity can sometimes be achieved through the use of a combined CBB silver stain procedure [353, 354]. Salivary proteins are similarly poorly stained by silver procedures alone, which may be due to their acidic proline-rich nature [355], particularly if they are separated using native 2-D PAGE. Silver-staining can be improved using CBB pre-staining [39] or by equilibrating non-denaturing 2-D gels in Tris buffer (pH 6.8) containing 2% w/v SDS [36, 40]. Silver staining followed by CBB R-250 has been found to enhance differentiation of sialoglycoproteins as these and lipids stained yellow with silver, while other membrane proteins were counterstained with CBB [356].

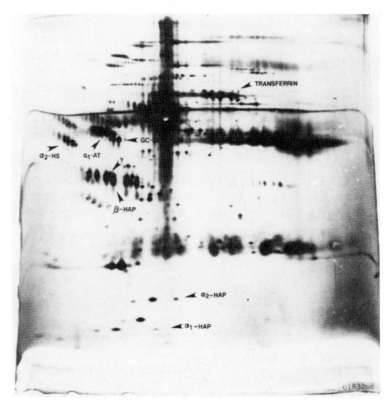

Figure 25. Silver-stained 2-D separation of normal human serum proteins. Reproduced with permission from [93].

12.3.9 Quantitation

Considerable dispute has occurred concerning the use of silver staining for quantitative analysis. Poehling and Neuhoff [334] found an S-shaped calibration curve was derived by silver staining, with the linear portion being in the range 1 to 30 ng. They concluded that silver staining was far from stoichiometric, but it is clear from this [334] and other [330, 343, 351, 586] reports that a linear relationship between silver stain density and protein concentration extends over a 40-fold range in concentration. This surely compares well with the 20-fold range (10–200 ng) of linearity found for CBB [334]! However, protein concentrations greater than $2\ \text{ng mm}^{-2}$ generally cause saturation and consequent non-linearity above that concentration. Another problem is that the slope of silver staining (stain density/ng protein) is characteristic for each protein [330, 351, 357, 586], but this is also true, although generally disregarded, for CBB staining [358] and for protein estimation by the commonly used Lowry protein assay [304, 359]. This phenomenon requires that rigorous inter-gel quantitative analysis should be limited to homologous protein spots on each gel [331]. Such quantitative inter-gel comparisons also require the presence of reference proteins for the normalisation of spot staining intensities. Although it is recommended that equivalent amounts of proteins be loaded on the gels for comparison, it has been shown that a 10-fold variation in initial protein loading can be tolerated [341]. Stastny and Fosslien [586] suggest that 2-D PAGE, staining and scanning of each sample should be performed in duplicate or triplicate to reduce the effect of possible random errors particularly caused by variation in the staining procedure.

12.4   Radioactive detection methods

12.4.1 Radiolabelling methods

Protein samples to be analysed by 2-D PAGE can be radiolabelled synthetically by the incorporation of radioactive amino acids (usually leucine or methionine) or amino acid mixtures. This method is generally used in conjunction with tissue culture techniques where the culture medium should be deficient in the amino acid(s) used for radiolabelling. It is also possible to synthetically radiolabel the proteins of small pieces of fresh tissue in this way [360]. The most frequently used radioisotopes used in conjunction with 2-D PAGE are ^{3}H, ^{14}C, ^{35}S, ^{32}P and ^{125}I. Techniques are also available for synthetic labelling of specific proteins, *e.g.* ^{32}PO$_4$ for phosphoproteins and [^{3}H]glucosamine for glycoproteins. Synthetic incorporation of radiolabel should not introduce artefacts, except perhaps by damage caused by ionising radiation although in practice this has been found not to alter 2-D protein patterns [361].

As an alternative to *in vivo* synthetic radiolabelling, proteins can be radiolabelled *in vitro* prior to separation by 2-D PAGE. Such postsynthetic radiolabelling procedures can readily result in charge modifications deleterious to 2-D PAGE, as has been found to be the case for iodination [110]. Reductive methylation with [^{3}H]borohydride has been found not to introduce charge modifications [112] and gives good results with 2-D PAGE [110]. Modified amino acids can be used to radiolabel proteins *in vitro* [362] and recently a [^{35}S]methionine derived reagent (SLR, Amersham) has been used to radiolabel proteins prior to 2-D PAGE, but this method was found to result in some charge heterogeneity [363].

The third approach is to detect the proteins separated by 2-D PAGE by staining the gels with a radiolabelled reagent. Examples of such stains are [^{59}Fe]ferrous bathophenanthroline sulphonate [364] and neutron activated Ponceau Red S and Serva Blue R [365]. Radiolabelled lectins can also be used to detect glycoproteins separated by electrophoresis [366–368] although this has been largely replaced by lectin-staining of blot transfers (see Section 13.4). Background staining can be a problem with radiolabelling procedures, for example as a result iodination of contaminants present in acrylamide [369], or arising from neutron activated components [365].

12.4.2 Autoradiography

Radiolabelled proteins separated by 2-D PAGE are usually detected by autoradiography in which the dried 2-D gels are placed in contact with an X-ray film and exposed for the appropriate time. Sequential exposures for different times are often necessary in 2-D studies of complex protein mixtures such as whole cells due to the wide range in protein abundances. Gels can be subjected to autoradiography without drying but then the film must be protected from the adverse effects of moisture by wrapping the gel in Saranwrap plastic film. Direct autoradiography of isotopes such as ^{14}C, ^{35}S, ^{32}P and ^{125}I is relatively efficient, but ^{3}H is very inefficiently detected as its low-energy β-particles do not penetrate the gel matrix and thus are severely quenched [370, 371]. Quenching, particularly of ^{3}H, is also a problem if gels are stained, for example by silver techniques [352], prior to autoradiography.

12.4.3 Fluorography

A more sensitive method of scintillation autoradiography, called fluorography, was developed for the detection of weak β-emitters such as ^{3}H in polyacrylamide gels [372], based on methods used for thin-layer chromatograms [373]. In this procedure, the fixed wet gel is impregnated with a scintillant, usually 2,5-diphenyloxazole (PPO), so that low-energy β-particles unable to penetrate through the gel can excite the fluor molecules to emit photons which can form a photographic image. Most fluors emit blue light so that blue-sensitive X-ray film should be used. Dimethyl sulphoxide (DMSO) is the solvent usually employed for impregnation of gels with PPO [372], but other safer and less expensive solvents (*e.g.* acetic acid) can be used [374]. Water-soluble fluors such as sodium salicylate can be used as an inexpensive substitute to PPO [375, 376] although they do appear to result in increased autoradiographic spreading [375]. Pre-exposure of the photographic film to a brief flash of light (*ca.* 1 ms) greatly increases (2- to 3-fold) the sensitivity of fluorography [370, 377]. This process also facilitates quantitative analysis since it corrects the non-linear relationship between radioactivity and absorbance of the film image [370, 377]. The use of low temperature during fluorography can also substantially increase detection sensivity, so that most investigators carry out fluorography exposures at $-70\,°C$ to $-80\,°C$. This results in a 12-fold increase in sensitivity for ^3H and a nine-fold increase for ^{14}C and ^{35}S. However, the mechanism for this somewhat paradoxical response to temperature is unclear and possible theories are discussed in [318]. Unfortunately, fluorographic procedures cause spreading of spots on 2-D gels compared with conventional autoradiography, resulting in a decrease in effective resolution [377, 378].

12.4.4 Intensification screens

In autoradiography of high-energy β-isotopes such as ^{32}P and γ-emitters such as ^{125}I much of the emission passes directly through the film. It is, therefore, more efficient to place the film between the dried gel and an image intensification screen (*e.g.* calcium tungstate) [371, 377]. The strong emissions which pass through the film can then excite the fluor or phosphor in the screen, thereby creating a secondary fluorographic image superimposed on the primary autoradiographic image. Two screens, arranged in the order gel, screen, film, screen, can further increase sensitivity of detection of ^{32}P (but not ^{125}I) [379] and this method is often used for visualization of DNA (Southern) and RNA (Northern) blot transfers.

12.4.5 Dual isotope methods

A major problem in 2-D PAGE is that irreproducibility between 2-D separations severely complicates comparative analysis between 2-D gels. This problem can be approached using sophisticated automated computer analysis systems (see Section 14). However, a simpler approach which gives excellent results for the comparison of pairs of samples is to use a dual radiolabelling procedure. In these techniques, the two samples to be compared are radiolabelled with different radio-analogs of the same amino acid (*e.g.* [^3H]- and [^{14}C]- or [^{35}S]labelled methionine). After radiolabelling, the samples are solubilised, mixed in the appropriate ratio, and co-electrophoresed on the same 2-D gel [378, 380–383]. The resultant 2-D gel is then processed for fluorography which will detect those proteins labelled with either isotope (*i.e.* ^3H or $^{14}C/^{35}S$) and produce a composite image of both samples. Subsequently, the gel is subjected to direct autoradiography to detect only the stronger (^{14}C or ^{35}S) emissions. The patterns derived from the proteins of each samples are then interpreted subtractively. The success of this method depends on using the appropriate input ratio of ^{3}H dpm/^{35}S (or ^{14}C) dpm in the sample mixture used for 2-D PAGE. This ratio is dependent on the isotopes used, gel thickness, the fluor used for the fluorographic step, and the X-ray films used for autoradiography and fluorography [380].

An alternative dual-labelling procedure has been described by Lecocq and his coworkers [384] using a combination of [^{35}S]methionine and [^{75}Se]selenomethionine. ^{75}Se is a γ-emitter (max. 0.4 MeV; 120 days half-life) and allows reduced exposure times compared with techniques using a combination of ^{3}H and ^{14}C/^{35}S. The 2-D gel is again subjected to a fluorographic exposure to detect both isotopes, while a second autoradiographic exposure with an exposed X-ray film interposed between the gel and the film is used to detect only the γ-emitter. This method can result in some loss of resolution due to the increased autoradiographic spreading commonly encountered with γ-emitting isotopes [385].

A considerable disadvantage of dual-labelling techniques described above is that two separate films have to be exposed as black-and-white emulsions cannot discriminate between decays of different energies. To overcome this problem, Kronenberg [386] used colour negative film which contains three photographic emulsion layers. Used in autoradiography, the first layer produces a yellow image, the second a magenta image, and the third layer a cyan image. A weak β-emitter such as ^{3}H exposes only the upper emulsion producing a yellow inage. Stronger β-emitting isotopes (^{14}C and ^{35}S) penetrate to the second layer producing a red image (yellow + magenta), while very energetic β-emitters (^{32}P) or γ-isotopes (^{75}Se, ^{125}I) will expose all three layers giving a neutral density. This method works best with films designed for tungsten illumination and is also compatible with fluorographic procedures [386].

12.4.6 Non-autoradiographic detection methods

Despite their inherent simplicity, techniques based on autoradiography suffer from the disadvantage that long exposure times are often necessary and problems of non-linearity, fogging and limited dynamic range complicate quantitative analysis. Radioactive proteins, located on a 2-D gel by staining or autoradiography, can be cut out and counted by liquid scintillation spectrometry [387]. However, this procedure is too laborious for routine use. Therefore, electronic techniques which would allow rapid and quantitative analysis would have considerable advantages in the analysis of 2-D gels.

One approach to the elimination of film in the detection of radioactive proteins separated by electrophoresis is to use gas-filled multiwire proportional counters or spark chambers. A spark chamber has been used to detect β-emissions directly on thin-layer chromatograms. However, although images were obtained in less than 1 h, the resolution of the system was poor and quantitative analysis was not possible. A single-wire proportional counter for the detection of β-emissions in one-dimensional gels has been described [388] and has been applied to 2-D gels by means of a multiwire proportional counter [389]. The apparatus is capable of analysing gels up to 20 cm × 20 cm and gave a claimed several thousand-fold increase in detection speed for ^{3}H over conventional autoradiography [389]. The method is potentially quantitative, but unfortunately the spatial resolution (2 mm) is rather poor.

Another non-autoradiographic method to record the distribution of radiolabels in 2-D gels has been developed by Burbeck [390]. This procedure employed a microchannel plate (MCP) [391] electron multiplier and a resistive anode position detector. The MCP used measured 40 mm in diameter so that only a small portion of a 2-D gel could be analysed, but a relatively high resolution (200 µm) was achieved. For ^{35}S-labelled proteins the process was rapid (5 min for strong spots, 80 min for weak spots), linear and had a good dynamic range [390]. Disadvantages of the technique are (i) that the dried 2-D gel is exposed to a vacuum in the apparatus causing problems of shrinkage, cracking and distortion, and (ii) that the MCP device is quite delicate, any scratches on the surface generating artefactual hot spots [390].

The third approach which has been employed is the use of low flux photon image intensifiers to obtain images from gels to which fluors have been previously added [392, 393]. This technique has been termed electronic autofluorography and can quantitatively analysis full size 2-D gels very rapidly and with good sensitivity (2 min to detect 6000 dpm cm^{-2} ^{3}H compared with 24 h using X-ray film).

13 Identification and characterisation of proteins

2-D PAGE has an almost unique ability to resolve the components of complex protein mixtures making it an invaluable research tool for a variety of areas of basic research and application. Components separated on a 2-D gel can be quantitated and characterised in terms of their apparent pI and M_r. However, 2-D PAGE itself does not provide directly any further information on the physicochemical nature or functional properties of the separated proteins. Some identification may be possible by comparing cell lines with known protein changes due to mutation, viral infection, or the presence of additional chromosomes. However, this is complicated if more than one spot difference is observed by 2-D PAGE [394]. Alternatively, gene expression can be altered by treatments such as drugs, hormones, heat shock and virus infection and the differences in 2-D maps of expected and control cells used to identify particular sets of proteins [394]. However, there is a general need for additional techniques for the characterisation of separated proteins to add a third dimension to 2-D PAGE.

13.1   Cell subfractionation

Sets of proteins associated with particular cellular compartments such as nuclei, mitochondria, microsomes, plasma membrane and cytoskeletal structures can be established by 2-D PAGE analysis of cellular subfractions. These proteins can then be identified in the 2-D map of the corresponding total cell proteins. However, difficulties can arise with this approach due to protein modifications which can occur during the subfractionation process and as a result of cross-contamination with proteins from other cellular compartments.

13.2   Co-electrophoresis with standard proteins

There is an extensive panel of proteins isolated from a variety of tissues and organisms which have been purified and characterised. These purified proteins can be used in co-electrophoresis experiments to identify these proteins as components of complex protein mixtures. This approach has been quite successful for the characterisation of the protein components of *E. coli* [395, 396]. This approach has also been used extensively in establishing the identity of many of the components observed in 2-D maps of human serum and plasma [93, 101, 271, 397]. A typical 2-D separation of normal human serum is shown in Fig. 25 and a map of those proteins identified (Table 2) is shown in Fig. 26. This information has been used to identify the same set of proteins and to detect sample-specific proteins in other body fluids such as urine [98, 398], CSF [399, 400] and sweat [103]. This method of protein identification

Table 2. List of spots observed in serum and plasma (reproduced with permission from [101])

	Number	Name	Comments
A	1	a_2-Macroglobulin	a, b
	3	Ceruloplasmin	a, b
	10	Ceruloplasmin	a, b
	14	Unknown plasma protein	Protein in freeze-thaw plasma
	19	C_1S	a
	22	Prothrombin	b, k
	25	a_1B-glycoprotein	a
	30	Hemopexin	a
	31	Albumin	Two genetic variants; a, b
	32	IgM heavy chain	b, c
	33	a_1-Antitrypsin dimer	a
B	1	IgG, polymers	c
	5	C_3 activator	a
	6, 7	Unknown plasma protein	Protein in serum, not plasma
	10	Transferrin	Two genetic variants; a
	15	Plasminogen	Glu form is larger, lys form smaller; a
C	1	a_1-Antichymotrypsin	a
	2	a_2HS-glycoprotein	Two genetic variants; a
	5	IgA, heavy chains	b, c
	6	Antithrombin III	a, b
	8	a_1-Antitrypsin	Three genetic variants; a
	9	GC-globulin	Two genetic variants; a
	16	Fibrinogen, γ chain	a, d
	21	Haptoglobin, β chain	Three genetic forms of halohaptoglobin; a, e
	23, 24, 26	Unknown plasma protein	Protein in freeze-thaw serum or plasma
	27	Unknown plasma protein	Unknown genetic variant; two forms seen
	30	Unknown plasma protein	Becomes a major urine protein; f
	31	J-chain	b, k
	46	Apolipoprotein E	Four forms seen; a
	47	G4-glycoprotein	a
	52	IgM, heavy chain fragments	b
D	1	Fibrinogen, a chain	a, d
	16	Fibrinogen, β chain	a, d
	17	IgG, heavy chains	a, b, c
	45–47	IgG, heavy chain fragments	g
	50	$C_4\gamma$	a
	52	κ, λ Light chains	a, b, c
	53–58, 61, 63	Nonlight chains	h
	59, 62	Nonlight chains	pH dependent; h, i
	64	Creatine phosphokinase	Present in patients with muscle damage; j
	65	Unknown plasma protein	Unknown nonlight chain present in patient with idiopathic urticaria

Table 2. (continued)

	Number	Name	Comments
E	1	Apoliopoprotein A-I	a
	3	Retinol binding protein	c
	6	Haptoglobin, a_2 chain	a, e
	7	Prealbumin	a, c
	8	Haptoglobin, a_1 chains	a, e
	9	Apolipoprotein A-II	a
	10, 11	LDL-related lipoproteins	a
	4	Hemoglobin, β chain	a
	5	β_2-Microglobulin	Only seen in cases of renal transplant rejection; b

a Comparison to map in [397].
b Co-electrophoresis with pure protein.
c Immunologic identification (precipitate/electrophoresis or electroblot).
d Comparison of 2-D PAGE analysis of serum and plasma.
e 2-D PAGE analysis of ahaptoglobinemic serum.
f Comparison of 2-D PAGE analysis of serum and urine.
g These spots were adsorbed onto protein A, but did not react with antilight chain serum.
h These spots in the light chain region were not adsorbed onto protein A.
i These spots were present when samples were prepared at pH 6.5, but absent at pH 9.5.
j Comparison to map in [129].
k Data from N.L. Anderson.

works well but is limited by the relatively small number of proteins which have been isolated and characterised compared with the large number of components detected by 2-D PAGE analysis of most complex protein mixtures.

13.3   Specific staining and affinity

Specific affinities of proteins for substances such as dyes, cofactors, vitamins, neurotransmitters, hormones and specific inhibitors can be used to identify proteins on 2-D gels [394]. Staining methods are also available for the detection of specific classes of polypeptides [322].

13.4   Immunological affinity and Western blotting

The high specificity and affinity of antibodies, and other ligands such as lectins, makes these highly sensitive reagents for identification and characterisa-

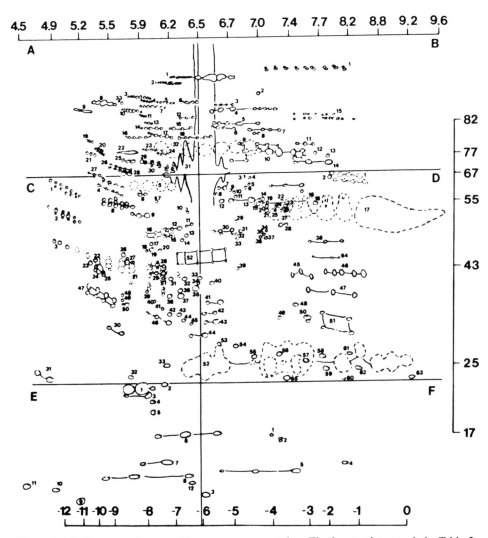

Figure 26. Reference 2-D map of human serum proteins. The key to the map is in Table 2. Reproduced with permission from [101].

tion of proteins separated by 2-D PAGE. Protein samples can be incubated with an antiserum of defined specificity to remove by immunoprecipitation a specific component(s). The resulting immunoprecipitate can then be analysed by 2-D PAGE and the protein spot(s) identified on the 2-D gel pattern of the total sample. This approach has been used extensively to establish the identity of components in 2-D maps of human serum [101, 397] and CSF [410]. Alternatively, 2-D PAGE is used to analyse samples from which a specific component has been removed by immunoprecipitation. This technique is known as immunodeletion [169, 402]. Antibodies can be used to precipitate protein components separated by electrophoresis. This technique of immunofixation [403–405] works well with cellulose acetate membranes, agarose gels and low concentration polyacrylamide gels as used for IEF. However, it is much more difficult to apply to polyacrylamide gels of high concentrations due to the slow rates of diffusion of the rather large immunoglobulin molecules into the restrictive gel matrix. Procedures have been described for immunofixation after SDS-PAGE [368, 406, 407], but these are very time-consuming as washing steps of 3 to 4 days are used between each application of antiserum with consequent loss of resolution and development of high background [368].

The problems encountered with immunofixation have been largely overcome by a technique known as blotting in which the separated proteins are transferred from the gel onto the surface of a thin matrix, such as nitrocellulose. The proteins are immobilised on the matrix and are readily accessible to interaction with antibodies and other ligands such as lectins. This technique was based on techniques developed by Southern [408] for blot transfer of DNA (Southern blotting). This technique was then applied to RNA analysis [409] and became known as Nothern blotting. Thus, when it was subsequently applied to protein analysis [410, 411] it became known as Western blotting and this name continues to be popular. Protein transfer can be achieved by capillary [410], contact diffusion [572] or vacuum [412] techniques. However, more rapid and efficient transfer is achieved if the proteins are electrophoretically removed from the gel onto the immobilising matrix by application of an electric field perpendicular to the plane of the 2-D gel. This technique was pioneered by Towbin [411] and is known as electroblotting. This technique has been reviewed elsewhere [413–417] and is the subject of the contribution to this volume by Gershon [418]. Only brief details of this technology will be outlined here and the reader is referred to those articles for a fuller account.

There are various designs of electroblotting apparatus [414, 419–421], many of which are available commercially (see Table 1 in [416]). In the standard vertical apparatus, the gel and the blotting matrix are held in intimate contact by a sandwich of filter papers and sponge pads held under pressure in a frame fixed between the electrodes. The design of the electrode assemblies for such apparatus is of paramount importance since rapid, efficient, even transfer of proteins depends on the generation of a homogeneous electrical field over the whole gel area combined with a high current. The most common electrode used is an array of platinum wire, the geometry of such arrays determining the topography of the field at the plane of the gel [422]. In vertical blotting apparatus of this type, the electrode assemblies are usually several cm apart so that the maximum voltage gradient that can be applied is limited (typically 10 V cm^{-1}), even if an efficient cooling system is available to deal with Joule heating. This problem can be overcome using flat-surface electrodes arranged in a horizontal apparatus, providing a homogeneous electrical field, with a short inter-electrode distance and using small amounts of buffers. One such horizontal. semi-dry blotting apparatus has graphite plates for both electrodes [423, 424], while another design uses a surface-conductive glass anode and a stainless steel plate cathode [425].

Several types of filters with different properties can be used for protein blotting. Nitrocellulose is the most widely used matrix for blotting as it does not require derivitisation prior to use and it is compatible with general protein stains such as Amido Black. Sensitive staining of protein patterns transferred to nitrocellulose can be obtained with India ink [426] or with colloidal gold or silver particles [427, 428], especially after alkali pretreatment [429]. Transferred proteins are not covalently bound to nitrocellulose filters, and binding has been suggested to involve hydrophobic and ionic interactions [414]. Proteins are bound covalently to diazo papers, such as diazobenzyloxymethyl cellulose and diazophenylthioether cellulose, but these matrices are not popular as they must be activated immediately prior to use. Positively charged nylon-based membranes have an extremely high binding capacity for proteins [430] but, until recently, they suffered from the disadvantage that there was no satisfactory general protein staining procedure. A general immunostaining procedure can be used [431] if the appropriate reagents are available. However, sensitive protein staining is now possible on nylon matrices either using a cationic iron cacodylate colloid followed by treatment with acidic potassium ferrocyanide [573] or by *in situ* biotinylation of the blotted proteins followed by reaction with enzyme-conjugated avidin and an appropriate substrate.

Numerous transfer systems are available for different proteins and types of filter matrix. The two most important factors are elution efficiency of proteins from the gel and the binding capacity of the matrix for proteins. Elution efficiency is determined by the polyacrylamide concentration and buffer pH and composition, while binding efficiency is dependent both on the nature of the matrix used and the buffer [416]. After the proteins have been transferred to nitrocellulose, all the unoccupied potential binding sites on the filter must be blocked before probing with a specific ligand. Bovine serum albumin (3 – 5% w/v) is the most commonly used blocking agent, although other animal sera [432, 433], ovalbumin [434] and haemoglobin [435] have also been used. Gelatin has also been recommended as a blocking agent for nitrocellulose [436]. Unfortunately, these proteins are not always non-reactive during subsequent probing leading to a high background. This problem can be overcome using a dilute solution of the nonionic detergent polyethylene sorbitan monolaurate (Tween 20) [437], but there is a risk of displacing proteins form the matrix by detergent treatment [416].

After blocking the blot is reacted with the specific antibody or ligand of interest. This primary reagent can be fluorescently labelled (*e.g.* fluorescein isothiocyanate, FITC), radiolabelled (usually with ^{125}I) or conjugated to an enzyme (*e.g.* horseradish peroxidase, alkaline phosphatase, β-galactosidase or glucose oxidase). Fluorescent methods require UV illumination and radiolabel procedures require a delaying autoradiographic step, so that the methods dependent on enzyme activity are becoming increasingly popular. Indirect sandwich techniques using second or third ligands are generally used for immunodetection due to the significant increase in sensitivity which can be achieved. In this procedure the primary antibody is unlabelled and it is the second antibody which is labelled (fluorescence, radiolabel, enzyme activity). Alternatively, in some cases the secondary antibody can be replaced by *Staphylococcus aureus* protein A, which binds specifically to the Fc region of most animal immunoglobulins.

Recently, even more sensitive methods for the detection of specific proteins transferred to nitrocellulose have been described. One approach is the use of gold-labelled antibodies [438, 439] or protein A [440]. This has the additional advantages that the stain is visible due to its red colour without further development and the sensitivity of the method can be increased by silver enhancement. Another method exploits the specificity of the interaction between the low M_r vitamin, biotin, and the protein, avidin. Biomolecules such as antibodies and proteins can be conjugated with biotin and the resulting conjugates used as the secondary reagent for probing blot transfers. A third step must then be used for visualisation using avidin conjugated with a suitable enzyme (*e.g.* peroxidase, β-galactosidase, alkaline phosphatase, glucose oxidase). Even greater sensitivity can be achieved at this stage using pre-formed complexes of a biotinylated enzyme with avidin as many enzyme molecules are present in these complexes giving rise to an enhanced signal. Egg white avidin (M_r 68 000) is often used in these procedures, but has distinct disadvantages; (i) it is highly charged at neutral pH so that it can bind to proteins non-specifically, and (ii) it is a glycoprotein which can interact with other biomolecules such as lectins *via* the carbohydrate moiety. It is, therefore, advantageous to use streptavidin (M_r 60 000) isolated from *Streptomyces avidinii* which has a p*I* close to neutrality and is not glycosylated.

A considerable problem in the application of Western blotting techniques to 2-D PAGE is that correlation between a single stained spot detected on a blot by immuno- or ligand-probing and the same spot in a 2-D pattern stained for total proteins can be difficult or impossible. Recently, Zhang *et al.* [226] have approached this problem using a train of carbamylated creatine phosphokinase charge standards to provide reference spots in both gel patterns and corresponding nitrocellulose blots to simplify recognition of individual protein spots in complex 2-D gel patterns. An elegant alternative method has

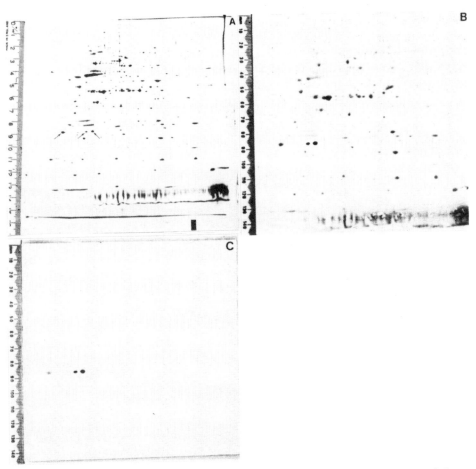

Figure 27. Rat cerebellum proteins. (A) CBB-stained 2-D gel; (B) electroblot on nitrocellulose (16 h, 5 V cm⁻¹); (C) same as (B) but photographed through a Wratten 47 B blue filter showing peroxidase stained spots. Immunodetection after blocking with bovine haemoglobin and NP-40. Polyclonal antibodies against protein gene produce 9.5 were used and sheep anti-rabbit IgG conjugated with horseradish peroxidase. Reproduced with permission from [441].

been described by Jackson [441] in which proteins were transferred onto nitrocellulose after fixing and staining 2-D gels with CBB. This allowed the spots to be transferred to the matrix as a visible pattern. Particular components were then detected using specific antisera and a second antibody coupled to horseradish peroxidase. The CBB and horseradish stains were distinguishable by a suitable filter (Wratten 47B), allowing precise correlation of spots stained by CBB with spots identified with the brown immunoperoxidase reaction product (Fig. 27).

13.5 Amino acid analysis

Computerised microdensitometry can be used to measure amino acid compositions of polypeptides resolved in 2-D gels [442, 443]. In this method, 20 parallel cultures of the cell line under investigation were radiolabelled with each of the 20 different ^{14}C- or ^{35}S-labelled amino acids and the resulting proteins analysed by 2-D PAGE. For each amino acid label the relative amount of radioactivity in an unknown protein was computed using the measured radioactivity simultaneously incorporated into the reference protein, β-, γ-actin, whose precise amino acid composition is known. This technique is based on the assumptions that (i) amino acid interconversion is minimal, and (ii) errors introduced by microdensitometry and quantitation are small and are not correlated with the amino acid used. The alternative approach which has been used is to cut out the protein spot(s) of interest from a 2-D gel and use a method of microscale amino acid analysis [28]. In this method, the excised piece of gel was extracted with a NaOH/thiodiglycol mixture, followed by hydrolysis in 6 N HCl. A piece of blank gel served to compensate for background, levels of about 0.1 µg protein being observed. The amino acids were detected by fluorimetry using o-phthaldialdehyde. Amino acid analysis of individual protein spots containing 0.6 to 1.0 µg protein was possible.

13.6 Peptide mapping

Peptide mapping analysis can be carried out on protein spots excised from 2-D gels [444]. In order to gain sufficient sensitivity it is usually necessary to resort to radiolabel procedures. Metabolically radiolabelled proteins (e.g. [^{35}S]methionine) separated by 2-D PAGE can be used [445]. Alternatively radioiodination with [^{125}I]sodium iodide using chloramine T can be carried out on proteins after elution from the gel [446] or while they are still within the gel matrix [369, 447]. This method detects only tyrosine-containing peptides. Labelling with ^{125}I of the N-terminus and more common lysyl residues can be achieved using 3-(4-hydroxyphenyl) propionic acid N-hydroxysuccinimide ester (Bolton-Hunter reagent) [448]. The radiolabelled proteins are then subjected to proteolytic digestion and the resultant peptides separated by 2-D thin-layer electrophoresis and chromatography [369, 445]. Alternatively, peptide mapping based on the method of Cleveland *et al.* [83] using partial proteolysis with *Staphylococcus aureus* V8 protease with subsequent SDS-PAGE of the peptide fragments can be used [449].

13.7   Protein sequencing

Automated Edman degradation is currently the most widely used method for protein sequencing [450]. The original method required several mg of protein, but sensitivity in the sub-nmol range is required for the direct sequencing of proteins recovered from 2-D gels. The gas-phase sequenator, which employs gas-phase reagents instead of the liquid-phase reagents used in the original method, can produce useful sequence information from as little as $10-20$ pmol of protein (0.5 to 1 µg for a M_r 50000 molecule) [451]. Hood and his collaborators have recently devised a procedure for the isolation and subsequent microsequencing of proteins from SDS-PAGE [452], IPG IEF [453], and 2-D PAGE [452] gels. The principle of this methodology is shown diagrammatically in Fig. 28. Whatman GF/C or GF/F glass fibre filter paper is activated by etching with trifluoroacetic acid and then used for electrophoretic transfer (electroblotting) of proteins from gels. The proteins are immobilised on the glass fibre sheets by ionic interactions or by covalent attachment. This technique can be applied to a variety of proteins with no apparent restriction due to size, charge or solubility properties of the proteins. The transferred proteins are detected by staining with CBB or by fluorescence with 3,3'-dipentyloxacarbocyanine iodide. The detected protein species of interest are then cut out and inserted directly into the gas phase-sequenator. The piece of glass fibre acts as a support for the protein during sequencing. Protein in the range 5 to 150 pmol can be sequenced and extended runs obtained as a result of improved stepwise yields and reduced backgrounds.

14   Computer analysis of two-dimensional gels

Techniques of 2-D PAGE are often used for the simultaneous resolution of as many components as possible from complex protein mixtures. This results in complicated 2-D maps from which only a limited amount of information

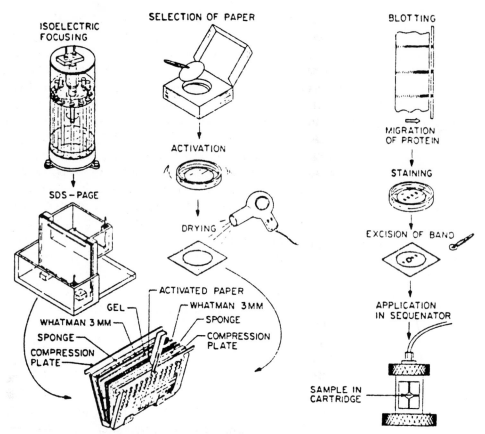

Figure 28. Method of microsequencing of proteins from 2-D gels. After electrophoresis, the 2-D gel is electroblotted using a standard apparatus onto a sheet of chemically activated glass fibre filter paper. The proteins are then visualised by staining or autoradiography, the selected spots excised and loaded directly into a gas-phase sequenator. Reproduced with permission from [452].

can be extracted by simple visual inspection. The assimilation of this mass of information requires automated computer analysis systems which can (i) extract both qualitative and quantitative information from individual gels, (ii) provide pattern matching betweeen gels, and (iii) construct databases for different types of samples. A detailed review of this topic is planned for a future volume in this series, so that only a brief outline will be given here. For further details, interested readers are referred to [111, 276, 454–465]. We have previously [111] identified the essential steps in the quantitative analysis of 2-D gel patterns as (i) data acquisition, (ii) calibration, (iii) filtering or noise reduction, (iv) spot detection, (v) spot quantitation, (vi) inter-gel pattern matching, and (vii) database construction.

Many systems have used scanning microdensitometers to digitise 2-D gels. These scanners are often of the rotating drum type which are capable of digitisting 2-D gel patterns rapidly with a resolution selectable from 12.5 µm to 200 µm over a 0 to 3 OD scale. However, this type of scanner is only suitable for digitisting autoradiographs of 2-D gels or, possibly, 2-D gels bound to flexible supports. Alternatively, flat-bed scanning densitometers [466] or laser denistometers [467, 468] can be used. Vidicon cameras have been used by some investigators to capture images of 2-D gels [457, 469–471] and are compatible with both stained and autoradiographic images using either trans- or epi-illumination. Unfortunately these devices have a limited dynamic range (ca. 0 to 1.4 OD [454]) and their resolution compares unfavourably with scanning densitometers [471]. Recently, increasing use is being made of charge coupled devices (CCD) which are essentially solid state vidicon cameras made in the form of arrays of phototransistors [464, 472–474]. These devices have a high resolution capacity combined with a good dynamic range. Most use has so far been made of linear CCD array cameras (*e.g.* Eikonix or Datacopy). Recently, a cooled 2-D CCD imaging system developed for astronomy has been applied to the digitisation of 2-D gels [326].

Most of the computer systems which have been developed for automated quantitative analysis of 2-D gels have required the use of dedicated large and expensive minicomputer systems (*e.g.* VAX 11/750 [463, 464] and VAX 11/780 [455, 473]), specialised ancillary hardware such as array processors [455, 473] and image processors [455, 463, 464, 473], or even custom-built hardware. However, recent advances in microprocessor technology combined with the availability of cheap memory and mass storage devices have made it a practical possibility to perform 2-D gel analysis on the present generation of microcomputers. Thus, it seems probable that in the near future investigators using 2-D PAGE will be able to have computer workstations capable of analysing 2-D gels in their own laboratories. The comprehensive suite of 2-D gel analysis software developed by Garrels [276] has been implemented on a Masscomp microcomputer system and is available commercially as PDQUEST (Protein Databases Inc.) [475]. An additional advantage of this system and the ELSIE III software system developed by Miller [463, 464] is that they are written in the C programming language and operate under the UNIX (AT & T Corporation) operating system. This should give these software systems considerable machine-independence, so that they should be capable of being implemented without undue difficulty on the many mini- and micro-computer systems which use the UNIX operating system.

The first generation of computer analysis systems for 2-D gels has used traditional serial or pipeline computers able to perform only a single operation at a time. This has to a large extent dictated the strategy of 2-D gel analysis resulting in a series of steps from the raw digitisted image to an abstracted, idealised model consisting of a spot list containing spatial and quantitative information on the separated components. The principle sequential processes that have been employed are: (i) Filtering (noise reduction) and background correction usually using Sobell operators [457, 476−478] or Fourier transformation [454]. Some systems also remove streaks from the 2-D images at this stage [455, 479] although this represents true sample protein. (ii) Spot detection by thresholding [461, 465, 469], chain assembly [113], central cores [457] or convolution techniques [455, 478]. (iii) Spot modelling, ususally by 2-D least-squares Gaussian fitting [276, 455, 478]. The spot list model of the 2-D gel abstracted by this series of processes is then used in the matching process used to combine and compare the results of multiple gels within an experiment or series of experiments. Most of these matching systems require operator intervention to identify a set of landmark spots on which the automatic matching is then based [113, 455, 456, 458, 461, 462, 480], although attempts have been made to develop automatic systems obviating the need for manually identified landmarks [463, 481].

Recent developments in the fields of computer vision and massively parallel computers advance the possibility of fast processing of raw 2-D gel images, without the necessity for resorting to a modelled image, within a consistent mathematical framework. A good computer architecture should significantly increase the speed and efficiency of 2-D gel analysis and provide a novel environment within which to develop second generation 2-D gel analysis algorithms [482−484]. Possible new strategies could include the application of Markov random field probabilistic theory using simulated annealing and iterated conditional node techniques [484] and artificial intelligence systems [483, 485−489].

15   Estimates of resolution

Data based on polysomal mRNA-DNA hybridisation experiments suggest that there are between 5000 and 20000 mRNA species present in mammalian cells. If 2-D PAGE is to be used for the analysis of such a complex set of gene products as represented by a particular mammalian cell type, then it is essential to have an estimate of the resolution potential of the 2-D PAGE procedure being used. O'Farrell [1] assessed the theoretical resolution capacity of his 2-D PAGE system to be 7000 components for total *E. coli* proteins, on the basis that IEF and SDS-PAGE separated 70 to 100 protein bands respectively. However, lateral diffusion of components during equilibration and transfer degraded resolution to about 500 spots in practice [1]. Other factors which can decrease the resolution potential of 2-D PAGE are spot spreading during staining, autoradiography and fluorography due to highly abundant proteins, streaking of high M_r proteins and insolubility of components in the IEF dimension. It is, therefore, not surprising that a maximum of about 1000 spots is normally observed on 2-D maps of total mammalian cell proteins. This finding prompted McConkey [490] to speculate that not more than 2000 primary gene products were actively expressed in mammalian cells. However, recent investigations using large-format 2-D gels (see Section 10.4) have shown that as many as 5000 to 10000 protein components can be resolved [294, 295, 491].

Taylor *et al.* [491] have devised a more objective mathematical test to measure the resolution capacity of 2-D gels. The test is essentially a ratio of areas and determines the number of spots of a certain size can be packed into the 2-D pattern and still be resolved. This procedure results in theoretical resolution capacities ranging from 15000 spots for 18 cm × 18 cm gels to 50000 spots for 20 cm × 25.5 cm gels. However, these theoretical estimates assume uniform distribution and size of spots on 2-D gels, a situation never encountered in practice. Taking these factors into account, it was suggested [491] that in practice the small and large format gels should resolve 2000 and 6000 components respectively. Thus, there appears to be a good correlation between these theoretical estimates of resolution [491] and resolution capacities observed in practice [294].

16   Applications

It is an impossible task to attempt to distil into just a few pages the many areas of biology, biochemistry and biomedicine in which 2-D PAGE has been applied. Rather, I will attempt to give a flavour of the power of 2-D PAGE by briefly describing a few areas where 2-D PAGE has been applied. The majority of applications have exploited the ability of 2-D PAGE to separate the components of complex protein mixtures, but the technique is also very powerful for the analysis of mixtures of a few proteins with similar charge and/or size properties and for monitoring the purity of protein preparations.

16.1   Genetic variation

The ability of 2-D PAGE to resolve simultaneously the components of complex protein mixtures, coupled with its sensitivity for the detection of the results of mutation (*ca.* 0.1 pH units into the first dimension, 1000 Da in the second dimension) make this technique an ideal tool for the study of genetic variation. Prior to the development of 2-D PAGE, such studies were carried out using electrophoretic techniques developed in the mid-1960's [492–494], usually involving the analysis of enzyme activities after one-dimensional starch or polyacrylamide gel electrophoresis. A high degree of genetic variability was found in studies of a diverse range of organisms [485] and Harris [496] has reported genetic polymorphism to occur in 24 of 104 human loci surveyed, resulting in an average heterozygosity of 6.3%.

When 2-D PAGE was applied to measurements of average heterozygosity in natural populations of *Drosophila melanogaster* [497] and mice [498, 499] low frequencies of polymorphisms were observed. In human populations, the heterozygosity rates initially reported for fibroblast cell lines [381, 383, 500], kidney [501] and brain proteins [502] using 2-D PAGE were only in the range 1 to 2%. However, more recent 2-D PAGE studies of human genetic variability have demonstrated substantially higher heterozygosity indexes for plasma proteins (6.2%) [503], red cell lysate (3.1% for Caucasoids [504], 4.0% for Japanese [578]), platelet polypeptides (3.1%) [505] and lymphocyte proteins (3%) [506–509]. The reasons for the discrepancy in these estimates of heterozygosity have not been established definitively, but it appears that the choice of spots for analysis is an important factor. Conditions which might hamper the detection of variants, such as overcrowding, streaking, edge effects and regions of overlapping spots, should be avoided [506, 510]. Hanash *et al.* [506] also believe that the availibility of parental gel data is crucial to the proper interpretation of spot variability. The differences between the heterozygosity rate measured by one-dimensional and 2-D PAGE are likely to be due to the nature of the proteins sampled by these techniques. The former technique has concentrated on less abundant enzymes, for which the percentage heterozygosity appears to be approximately 6%, while 2-D PAGE is concerned with the analysis of the most abundant cellular proteins, for which heterozygosity is closer to 3%. These findings suggest that the more abundant cellular proteins have evolved more slowly than the more commonly investigated soluble proteins [511].

16.2   Studies of body fluids

Many human diseases, both inherited and acquired, can result in alterations of the biochemical composition of body fluids. The proteins of normal human plasma and serum have been extensively characterised by 2-D PAGE [93, 101, 271, 397, 512]. A typical 2-D gel of normal human serum is shown in Fig. 25 together with a schematic map of the proteins (Fig. 26), many of which have been identified (Table 2). Many of the proteins in 2-D maps of serum can be seen to form trains of charge variants due to glycosylation. A paricular problem in 2-D analysis of serum samples is the high relative abundance of certain proteins, particularly albumin and the immunoglobulins. One solution to this problem is to use affinity chromatography on Affi-Gel Blue and Sepharose-bound protein A to delete albumin and immunoglobulins respectively [93]. However, it is important to realise that the specificity of these techniques is not absolute, so that it is possible that other components will be deleted from 2-D patterns. Another approach to this problem is the fractionation of serum proteins by size exclusion gel filtration chromatography prior to 2-D PAGE [513].

The composition of serum has been analysed by 2-D PAGE in a number of clinical conditions. Changes in 2-D maps of serum proteins have been observed in muscle trauma [101], a patient bitten by a rattlesnake [514], in myocardial infarction [515], in cases of alcohol abuse [516, 517], in Tangier disease [518], in fish-eye disease [519] and after chemical exposure [520, 521]. In the case of multiple myeloma and monoclonal gammopthies, 2-D PAGE has shown the immunoglobulin heavy and light chain to be highly restricted in terms of map location [180, 522, 523]. The analysis of urine proteins by 2-D PAGE is complicated by the low protein concentration (*ca.* 100 mg/L) necessitating extensive concentration (5000 to 1000-fold) coupled with procedures for removing salts and other non-protein components (see Section 5.1). These procedures have been used to produce detailed reference 2-D maps of urine proteins and to detect abnormal 2-D patterns associated with prostatic adenocarcinoma [398], multiple myeloma [98], muscle disease and damage [524, 525], occupational exposure to cadmium [102], rheumatoid arthritis [99] and renal disease [526]. A variety of other body fluids such as CSF [343, 401, 513, 527–530, 574], semen [94], prostatic fluid [531, 532], amniotic fluid [399, 400, 533, 534], saliva [103, 535], sweat [103, 104], aqueous humour [536], and suction blister fluid [523, 537] have been analysed by 2-D PAGE. These samples have been demonstrated to contain tissue-specific proteins in addition to expressing a common set of serum components [538].

16.3   Genetic diseases

Molecular biology techniques have had a great impact on our understanding of several human genetic disorders at the gene level. However, in very few cases has this approach given direct information on the gene products involved in these diseases. An alternative approach is to use the high resolution capacity of 2-D PAGE to search for altered gene products in protein samples of whole cells and tissues from patients with such disorders. Goldman and Merril [539] have identified four areas where they believe 2-D PAGE can contribute to human medical genetics. (i) The identification of primary mutations in genetic diseases, (ii) characterisation of patterns of secondary metabolic effects, (iii) identification of disease-associated markers, and (iv) detection of protein polymorphisms useful in linkage analysis. In human fibroblasts a mutation in the β-actin gene has been detected following neoplastic transformation [540, 541]. Disease-associated alterations in 2-D gel patterns have been described for a variety of disorders including Duchenne muscular dystrophy [542 – 544], Ataxia-Telangasctica [545], Lesch-Nyhan syndrome [341, 546], trisomy 18 [547], trisomy 21 (Down's syndrome) [548 – 551], Joseph Disease [552], Tangier disease [518] and cystic fibrosis [553]. In some cases it has not yet been established whether the changes that have been described by 2-D PAGE are the result of the primary genetic mutation or of secondary protein modulations. Such quantitative and qualitative protein modulations have also been found to occur in response to a variety of non-genetic and experimental conditions such as malignancy and neoplastic transformation [101, 106, 554 – 564], heat shock [554, 555], rheumatoid arthritis [556], hormones [289, 565, 576], drugs [566], lymphokines [567], mitogenic stimulation [568, 569], and toxic compounds [474, 570].

17   Conclusion

Procedures of 2-D PAGE based on the method of O'Farrell [1] have an almost unique capacity for resolving simultaneously the components of complex protein mixtures. Some of the limitations inherent in the standard technique of 2-D PAGE have, perhaps, limited the usefulness of this technique for certain applications. Recent developments in IPG technology have the potential to substantially improve the resolution and reproducibility of 2-D gels. The availability of affordable sophisticated automated computer analysis systems and the development of sensitive techniques such as immunoblot and microsequence analysis of the separated components have now added a third dimension to 2-D PAGE. These advances are likely to result in an increase in the use of 2-D PAGE in a wide variety of areas of biological, biochemical and biomedical research.

I would like to express my gratitude to Mrs. C. Trand for typing the manuscript and Mrs. K. Davidson for preparing the illustrations. I am grateful to Dr. Angelika Görg for allowing me access to her results prior to their publication. I am indebted to the many colleagues who have allowed me to use their work to illustrate this review. Financial support of the Muscular Dystrophy Group of Great Britain is acknowledged.

18   References

[1] O'Farrell, P. H., *J. Biol. Chem.* 1975, *250*, 4007–4021

[2] Smithies, O., Poulik, M. D., *Nature* 1956, *177*, 1033.

[3] Raymond, S., Weintraub, L., *Science* 1959, *130*, 711.

[4] Ornstein, L., *Ann. N.Y. Acad. Sci.* 1964, *121*, 321–349.

[5] Davis, B. J., *Ann. N.Y. Acad. Sci.* 1964, *121*, 404–436.

[6] Raymond, S., Nakamichi, M., *Anal. Biochem.* 1964, *7*, 225–232.

[7] Slater, G. G., *Fed. Proc.* 1965, *24*, 225.

[8] Margolis, J., Kenrick, K. G., *Nature* 1967, *214*, 1334–1336.

[9] Margolis, J., Kenrick, K. G., *Nature* 1969, *221*, 1056–1057.

[10] Dale, G., Latner, A. L., *Clin. Chim. Acta* 1969, *24*, 61–68.

[11] Macko, V., Stegemann, H., *Hoppe-Seyler's Z. Physiol Chem.* 1969, *350*, 917–919.

[12] Emes, A. V., Latner, A. L., Martin, J. A., *Clin. Chim. Acta* 1975, *64*, 69–78.

[13] Latner, A. L., Emes, A. V., in: Righetti, P. G. (Ed.), *Progress in Isoelectric Focusing and Isotachophoresis*, North-Holland, Amsterdam 1975, pp. 223–233.

[14] Shapiro, A. L., Vinuela, E., Maizel, J. V., *Biochem. Biophys. Res. Commun.* 1967, *28*, 815–820.

[15] Weber, K., Osborn, M., *J. Biol. Chem.* 1969, *244*, 4406–4412.

[16] Stegemann, H., *Angew. Chem.* 1970, *82*, 640–641.

[17] Barret, T., Gould, H. J., *Biochim. Biophys. Acta* 1973, *294*, 165–170.

[18] Suria, D., Liew, C. C., *Can. J. Biochem.* 1974, *52*, 1143–1153.

[19] MacGillivray, A. J., Rickwood, D., *Eur. J. Biochem.* 1974, *41*, 181–190.

[20] Bhakdi, S., Knüfermann, M., Wallach, D. F. H., *Biochim. Biophys. Acta* 1974, *345*, 448–457.

[21] Bhakdi, S., Knüfermann, H., Wallach, D. F. H., in: Righetti, P. G. (Ed.), *Progress in Isoelectric Focusing and Isotachophoresis*, North-Holland, Amsterdam 1975, pp. 281–291.

[22] Chignell, D. A., Wingfield, P. T., *Fed. Proc.* 1974, *33*, 1283.

[23] Iborra, G., Buhler, J. M., *Anal. Biochem.* 1976, *74*, 503–511.

[24] Klose, J., *Humangenetik* 1975, *26*, 231–243.

[25] Klose, J., in: Neubert D., Merkes, H. J., (Eds.), *New Approaches to the Evaluation of Abnormal Embryonic Development*, G. Thieme, Stuttgart 1975, pp. 375–387.

[26] Scheele, G. A., *J. Biol. Chem.* 1975, *250*, 5375–5385.

[27] Manabe, T., Tachi, K., Kojima, K., Okuyama, T., *J. Biochem.* 1979, *85*, 649–659.

[28] Manabe, T., Kojima, K., Jitzukawa, S., Hoshino, T., Okuyama, T., *Clin. Chem.* 1982, *28*, 819–823.

[29] Manabe, T., Hayama, E., Okuyama, T., *Clin. Chem.* 1982, *28*, 824–827.

[30] Manabe, T., Takahashi, Y., Okuyama, T., Maeda, Y. Y., Chihara, G., *Electrophoresis* 1983, *4*, 242–246.

[31] Manabe, T., Okuyama, T., in: Dunn, M. J. (Ed.), *Electrophoresis '86*, VCH, Weinheim 1986, pp. 613–616.

[32] Manabe, T., Takahashi, Y., Higuchi, N., Okuyama, T., *Electrophoresis* 1985, *6*, 462–467.

[33] Gahne, B., Juneja, R. K., in: Neuhoff, V. (Ed.), *Electrophoresis '84*, Verlag Chemie, Weinheim 1984, pp. 285–288.

[34] Manabe, T., Okuyama, T., *J. Chromatogr.* 1981, *225*, 65–71.

[35] Manabe, T., Takahashi, Y., Okuyama, T., in: Hirai, H. (Ed.), *Electrophoresis '83*, de Gruyter, Berlin 1984, pp. 179–187.

[36] Marshall, T., *Electrophoresis* 1984, *5*, 245–250.

[37] Kadofuku, T., Sato, T., Manabe, T., Okuyama, T., *Electrophoresis*, 1983, *4*, 427–431.

[38] Manabe, T., Takahashi, Y., Okuyama, T., *Electrophoresis* 1983, *4*, 359–362.

[39] Hallinan, F. M., *Electrophoresis* 1983, *4*, 265–269.

[40] Marshall, T., *Electrophoresis* 1984, *5*, 377–379.

[41] Kaltschmidt, E., Wittmann, H. G., *Anal. Biochem.* 1970, *36*, 401–412.

[42] Kaltschmidt, E., Wittmann, H. G., *Proc. Natl. Acad. Sci. USA* 1970, *67*, 1276–1282.

[43] Howard, G. A., Traut, R. R., *FEBS Lett.* 1973, *29*, 177–180.

[44] Knopf, U. L., Sommer, A., Kenny, J., Traut, R. R., *Molec. Biol. Rep.* 1975, *2*, 35–40.

[45] Martini, O. H. W., Gould, H. J., *J. Molec. Biol.* 1971, *62*, 403–405.

[46] Leister, D. E., Dawid, I. B., *J. Biol. Chem.* 1974, *249*, 5108–5118.

[47] Mathews, D. E., Hessler, R. A., Denslow, N. D., Edwards, J. S., O'Brien, T. W., *J. Biol. Chem.* 1982, *257*, 8788–8794.

[48] Mets, L. J., Bogorad, L., *Anal. Biochem.* 1974, *57*, 200–210.

[49] Hoffman, W. L., Ilan, J., *Prep. Biochem.* 1976, *6*, 13–26.

[50] Hoffman, W. L., Dowben, R. M., *Anal. Biochem.* 1978, *89*, 540–549.

[51] Subramanian, A. R., *Eur. J. Biochem.* 1974, *45*, 541–546.

[52] Kyriakopoulos, A., Subramanian, A. R., *Biochim. Biophys. Acta* 1977, *474*, 308–311.

[53] Madjar, J.-J., Michel, S., Cozzone, A. J., Reboud, J.-P., *Anal Biochem.* 1979, *92*, 174–182.

[54] Madjar, J.-J., Fournier, A., *Molec. Gen. Genet.* 1981, *182*, 273–278.

[55] Madjar, J.-J., Arpin, M., Buisson, M., Reboud, J.-P., *Molec. Gen. Genet.* 1979, *171*, 121–134.

[56] Madjar, J.-J., Traut, R. R., *Molec. Gen. Genet.* 1980, *179*, 89–101.

[57] Madjar, J.-J., Nielsen-Smith, K., Frahm, M., Roufa, D. J., *Proc. Natl. Acad. Sci. USA* 1982, *79*, 1003–1007.

[58] Madjar, J.-J., Frahm, M., McGill, S., Roufa, D. J., *Molec. Cell. Biol.* 1983, *3*, 190–197.

[59] Laughrea, M., Filion, A.-M., Boulet, L., *Electrophoresis* 1986, *7*, 484–485.

[60] Panyim, S., Chalkley, R., *Arch. Biochem. Biophys.* 1969, *130*, 337–346.

[61] Davie, J. R., Candido, E. P. M., *Proc. Natl. Acad. Sci. USA* 1978, *75*, 3574–3577.

[62] Davie, J. R., Saunders, C. A., Walsh, J. M., Weber, S. C., *Nucl. Acid Res.* 1981, *9*, 3205–3216.

[63] Sinclair, J., Rickwood, D., in: Hames, B. D., Rickwood, D. (Eds.), *Gel Electrophoresis of Proteins*, IRL Press, Oxford 1981, pp. 189–218.

[64] Davie, J. R., *Anal. Biochem.* 1982, *120*, 276 – 281.

[65] Spiker, S., *Anal. Biochem.* 1980, *108*, 263 – 265.

[66] Matsudaira, P. T., Burgess, D. R., *Anal. Biochem.* 1978, *87*, 386 – 396.

[67] Hoffmann, P. J., Chalkley, R., *Anal. Biochem.* 1976, *76*, 539 – 546.

[68] Franklin, S. G., Zweidler, A., *Nature* 1977, *266*, 273 – 275.

[69] Bhatnagar, Y. M., Bellvé, A. R., *Anal. Biochem.* 1978, *86*, 754 – 760.

[70] Bonner, W. M., West, M. H. P., Stedman, J. D., *Eur. J. Biochem.* 1980, *109*, 17 – 23.

[71] Zweidler, A., *Methods Cell. Biol.* 1978, *17*, 223 – 265.

[72] Pipkin, J., Anson, J. F., Hinson, W. G., Burns, E. R., Wolff, G. L., *Electrophoresis* 1985, *6*, 306 – 313.

[73] Orrick, L. R., Olson, M. O. J., Busch, H., *Proc. Natl. Acad. Sci. USA* 1973, *70*, 1316 – 1320.

[74] Goodwin, G. H., Wright, C. A., Johns, E. W., *Nucl. Acid Res.* 1981, *9*, 2761 – 2765.

[75] Fernandez, P. B., Nardi, R. V., Franklin, S. G., *Anal. Biochem.* 1978, *91*, 101 – 114.

[76] Imada, M., Hsieh, P., Sueoka, N., *Biochim. Biophys. Acta* 1978, *507*, 459 – 469.

[77] Booth, A. G., *Biochem. J.* 1977, *163*, 165 – 168.

[78] Imada, M., Sueoka, N., *Biochim. Biophys. Acta* 1980, *625*, 179 – 192.

[79] Ames, G. F.-L., Nikaido, K., *Eur. J. Biochem.* 1981, *115*, 525 – 531.

[80] Wang, K., Richards, F. M., *J. Biol. Chem.* 1979, *249*, 8005 – 8018.

[81] Allore, R. J., Barker, B. H., *Anal. Biochem.* 1984, *137*, 523 – 527.

[82] Blomendal, H., Jansen, K., *Electrophoresis* 1986, *7*, 387 – 388.

[83] Cleveland, D. W., Fischer, S. G., Kirschner, M. W., Laemmli, U. K., *J. Biol. Chem.* 1977, *252*, 1102 – 1106.

[84] Bordier, C., Crettol-Jarvinen, A., *J. Biol. Chem.* 1979, *254*, 2565 – 2567.

[85] Tijssen, P., Kurstak, E., *Anal. Biochem.* 1983, *128*, 26 – 35.

[86] Lam, K. S., Kasper, C. G., *J. Biol. Chem.* 1980, *255*, 259 – 266.

[87] Lam, K. S., Kasper, C. G., *Anal. Biochem.* 1980, *108*, 220 – 226.

[88] Lonsdale-Eccles, J. D., Lynley, A. M., Dale, B. A., *Biochem. J.* 1981, *197*, 591 – 597.

[89] Steinberg, R. A., *Anal. Biochem.* 1984, *141*, 220 – 231.

[90] Zhang, J.-S., Giometti, C. S., Tollaksen, S. L., in: Dunn, M. J. (Ed.), *Electrophoresis '86*, VCH, Weinheim 1986, pp. 621 – 625.

[91] Laemmli, U. K., *Nature* 1970, *227*, 680 – 685.

[92] Dunn, M. J., Burghes, A. H. M., *Electrophoresis* 1983, *4*, 97 – 116.

[93] Tracy, R. P., Currie, R. M., Young, D. S., *Clin. Chem.* 1982, *28*, 890 – 899.

[94] Edwards, J. J., Tollaksen, S. L., Anderson, N. G., *Clin. Chem.* 1981, *27*, 1335 – 1340.

[95] Merril, C. R., Goldman, D., Sidman, S. A., Ebert, M. H., *Science* 1981, *211*, 1437 – 1438.

[96] Anderson, N. G., Anderson, N. L., Tollaksen, S. L., Hahn, H., Giere F., Edwards, J., *Anal. Biochem.* 1979, *95*, 48 – 61.

[97] Anderson, N. G., Anderson, N. L., Tollaksen, S. L., *Clin. Chem.* 1979, *25*, 1199 – 1210.

[98] Edwards, J. J., Tollaksen, S. L., Anderson, N. G., *Clin. Chem.* 1982, *28*, 941 – 948.

[99] Clark, P. M. S., Kricka, L. J., Whitehead, T. P., *Clin. Chem.* 1980, *26*, 201 – 204.

[100] Guevara, J. G., Herbert, B. H., Martin, B. A., *Electrophoresis* 1985, *6*, 613 – 619.

[101] Tracy, R. P., Young, D. S., in: Celis, J. E., Bravo, R. (Eds.), *Two-dimensional Gel Electrophoresis of Proteins,* Academic Press, Orlando 1984, pp. 193 – 240

[102] Marshall, T., Williams, K. M., Vesterberg, O., *Electrophoresis* 1985, *6*, 47 – 52.

[103] Marshall, T., Williams, K. M., in: Dunn, M. J. (Ed.), *Electrophoresis '86*, VCH, Weinheim 1986, pp. 523 – 537.

[104] Rubin, R. W., Penneys, N. S., *Anal. Biochem.* 1983, *131*, 520 – 524.

[105] Dunn, M. J., Burghes, A. H. M., in: Dunn, M. J. (Ed.), *Gel Electrophoresis of Proteins,* Wright, Bristol 1986, pp. 203 – 261.

[106] Tracy, R. P., Wold, L. E., Currie, R. M., Young, D. S., *Clin. Chem.* 1982, *28*, 915–919.
[107] Thompson, B. J., Burghes, A. H. M., Dunn, M. J., Dubowitz, V., *Electrophoresis* 1981, *2*, 251–258.
[108] Giometti, C. S., Anderson, N. G., *Clin. Chem.* 1981, *27*, 1918–1921.
[109] Giometti, C. S, Danon, M. J., Anderson, N. G., *Neurology* 1983, *33*, 1152–1156.
[110] Kuhn, O., Wilt, F. M., *Anal. Biochem.* 1980, *105*, 274–280.
[111] Dunn, M. J., Burghes, A. H. M., *Electrophoresis* 1983, *4*, 173–189.
[112] Means, G. E., Feeney, R. E., *Biochemistry* 1968, *77*, 2192–2201.
[113] Garrels, J. I., *J. Biol. Chem.* 1979, *254*, 7961–7977.
[114] Bravo, R., in: Celis, J. E., Bravo, R. (Eds.), *Two-dimensional Gel Electrophoresis of Proteins,* Academic Press, Orlando 1984, pp. 3–36.
[115] Görg, A., Postel, W., Westermeier, R., in: Allen, R. C., Arnaud, P. (Eds.), *Electrophoresis '81,* de Gruyter, Berlin 1981, pp. 259–270.
[116] Westermeier, R., Postel, W., Görg, A., in: Allen, R. C., Arnaud, P. (Eds.), *Electrophoresis '81,* de Gruyter, Berlin 1981, pp. 281–287.
[117] Booz, M. L., Travis, R. L., *Phytochemistry* 1981, *20*, 1773–1779.
[118] Hari, V., *Anal. Biochem.* 1981, *113*, 332–335.
[119] Willard, K. E., Giometti, C. S., Anderson, N. L., O'Connor, T. E., Anderson, N. G., *Anal. Biochem.* 1979, *100*, 289–298.
[120] Ames, G. F. L., Nikaido, K., *Biochemistry* 1976, *15*, 616–623.
[121] Maizel, J. V., *Science* 1966, *151*, 988–990.
[122] Griffith, I. P., *Biochem. J.* 1972, *126*, 553–560.
[123] Burghes, A. H. M., Dunn, M. J., Statham, H. E., Dubowitz, V., *Electrophoresis* 1982, *3*, 185–196.
[124] Wilson D. L., Hall, M. E., Stone, G. C., Rubin, R. W., *Anal. Biochem.* 1977, *83*, 33–44.
[125] Horst, M. N., Mahaboob, S., Basha, M., Baumbach, G. A., Mansfield, E. H., Roberts, R. M., *Anal. Biochem.* 1980, *102*, 399–408.
[126] Archer, D. B., Rodwell, A. W., Rodwell, E. S., *Biochim. Biophys. Acta* 1978, *513*, 268–283.
[127] Klose, J., Feller, M., *Electrophoresis* 1981, *2*, 12–24.
[128] Hodges, S. C., Hirata, A. A., *Clin. Chem.* 1984, *30*, 2003–2007.
[129] Giometti, C. S., Anderson, N. G., Anderson, N. L., *Clin. Chem.* 1979, *25*, 1877–1884.
[130] Putnam, F. W., *Adv. Protein Chem.* 1948, *4*, 79–122.
[131] Novak-Hofer, I., Siegenthaler, P. A., *Biochim. Biophys. Acta* 1977, *468*, 461–471.
[132] Booz, M. L., Travis, R. L., *Plant Physiol.* 1980, *66*, 1037–1043.
[133] Minssen, M., Munkries, K. D., *Biochim. Biophys. Acta* 1973, *291*, 398–410.
[134] Basha, S. M. M., *Plant Physiol.* 1979, *63*, 301–306.
[135] Kaderbhai, M. A., Freedman, R. B., *Biochim. Biophys. Acta* 1980, *601*, 11–21.
[136] Dockham, P. A., Steinfeld, R. C., Stryker, C. J., Jones, S. W. Vidaver, G. A., *Anal. Biochem.* 1986, *153*, 102–115.
[137] Bordier, C., *J. Biol. Chem.* 1981, *256*, 1604–1607.
[138] Pryde, G. *TIBS* 1986, *11*, 160–163.
[139] Willard-Gallo, K. E., Humblet, Y., Symann, M., *Clin. Chem.* 1981, *30*, 2069–2077.
[140] Gonenne, A., Ernst, R., *Anal. Biochem.* 1978, *87*, 28–38.
[141] Hjelmeland, L. M., Nebert, D. W., Chrambach, A., *Anal. Biochem.* 1979, *95*, 201–208.
[142] Matuo, Y., Matsui, S.-I., Nishi, N., Wada, F., Sandberg, A. A., *Anal. Biochem.* 1985, *150*, 337–344.
[143] Perdew, G. H., Schaup, H. W., Selivonchick, D. P., *Anal. Biochem.* 1983, *135*, 453–455.
[144] Dunn, M. J., Burghes, A. H. M., Patel, K., Witkowski, J. A., Dubowitz, V., in: Neuhoff, V. (Ed.), *Electrophoresis '84,* Verlag Chemie, Weinheim 1984, pp. 281–284.

[145] Dunn, M. J., Burghes, A. H. M., Patel, K., *Protides Biol. Fluids* 1985, *33*, 479−482.

[146] Gordon, J. A., Jencks, W. P., *Biochemistry* 1963, *2*, 47−57.

[147] Barker, B. J., Rosenfarb, J., Caruso, J. A., *Angew. Chemie* 1979, *91*, 560−564.

[148] Righetti, P. G., Gianazza, E., Brenna, O., Galante, E., *J. Chromatogr.* 1977, *137*, 171−181.

[149] Althaus, H.-H., Klöppner, S., Poehling, H.-M., Neuhoff, V., *Electrophoresis* 1983, *4*, 347−353.

[150] Steinfeld, R. C., Vidaver, G. A., *Biophys. J.* 1981, *33*, 185.

[151] Shackelford, D. A., Mann, D. L., Van Rood, J. J., Ferrara, G. B., Strominger, J. L., *Proc. Natl. Acad. Sci. USA* 1981, *78*, 4566−4570.

[152] Tuszyncki, G. P., Buck, C. A., Warren, L., *Anal. Biochem.* 1979, *85*, 224−229.

[153] Shackelford, D. A., Strominger, J. L., *J. Exp. Med.* 1980, *151*, 141−165.

[154] Siemankowski, R. F., Giambalvo, A., Dreizen, P., *Physiol. Chem. Phys.* 1978, *10*, 415−434.

[155] Singer, B. S., Morrissett, H., Gold, L., *Anal. Biochem.* 1978, *85*, 224−229.

[156] Bianchi Bosisio, A., Lochenstein, C., Snyder, C., Snyder, R. S., Righetti, P. G., *J. Chromatogr.* 1980, *189*, 317−330.

[157] Righetti, P. G., *Isoelectric Focusing: Theory, Methodology and Application.*, Elsevier, Amsterdam 1983.

[158] Gelfi, C., Righetti, P. G., *Electrophoresis* 1981, *2*, 213−219.

[159] Saravis, C. A., Zamcheck, N. J., *J. Immunol. Methods* 1979, *29*, 91−96.

[160] Rosen, A., Ek, K., Aman, P., *J. Immunol. Methods* 1979, *28*, 1−11.

[161] Hirabayashi, T., *Anal. Biochem.* 1981, *117*, 443−451.

[162] Olsson, I., Läas, T., *J. Chromatogr.* 1981, *215*, 273−378.

[163] Serwer, P., Hayes, S. J., *Electrophoresis* 1982, *3*, 80−85.

[164] Thompson, B. J., Dunn, M. J., Burghes, A. H. M., Dubowitz, V., *Electrophoresis* 1982, *3*, 307−314.

[165] Burghes, A. H. M., Dunn, M. J., Dubowitz, V., *Electrophoresis* 1982, *3*, 354−363.

[166] Marshall, T., *Electrophoresis* 1983, *4*, 436−438.

[167] Creighton, I. E., *J. Molec. Biol.* 1979, *129*, 235−264.

[168] Vesterberg, O., *Acta Chem. Scand.* 1969, *23*, 2653−2666.

[169] Allen, R. C., Saravis, C. A., Maurer, H. R., *Gel Electrophoresis and Isoelectric Focusing of Proteins,* de Gruyter, Berlin 1984.

[170] Burghes, A. H. M., Dunn, M. J., Witkowski, J. A., Dubowitz, V., in: Stathakos, D., (Ed.), *Electrophoresis '82*, de Gruyter, Berlin 1983, pp. 371−380.

[171] Garrels, J. I., *Methods Enzymol.* 1983, *100*, 411−423.

[172] Anderson, N. L., Anderson, N. G., *Anal. Biochem.* 1978, *85*, 331−340.

[173] Ramagli, L. S., Rodriguez, L. V., *Electrophoresis* 1985, *6*, 559−563.

[174] Ramasamy, R., Spragg, S. P., Jones, M. I., Amess, R., *Electrophoresis* 1985, *6*, 43−46.

[175] O'Farrell, P. Z., Goodman, M. M., O'Farrell, P. H., *Methods Cell. Biol.* 1977, *12*, 1133−1142.

[176] O'Farrell, P. H., O'Farrell, P. Z., *Methods Cell. Biol.* 1977, *16*, 407−420.

[177] Righetti, P. G., Macelloni, G. J., *J. Biochem. Biophys. Methods* 1982, *5*, 1−15.

[178] Burghes, A. H. M., Dunn, M. J., Statham, H. E., Dubowitz, V., *Electrophoresis* 1982, *3*, 177−185.

[179] Duncan, R., Hershey, J. W. B., *Anal. Biochem.* 1984, *138*, 144−155.

[180] Tracy, R. P., Currie, R. M., Kyle, R. A., Young, D. S., *Clin. Chem.* 1982, *28*, 900−907.

[181] Breithaupt, T. B., Nystrom, I. E., Hodges, D. H., Babitch, J., *Anal. Biochem.* 1978, *84*, 579−582.

[182] Vanderhoff, J. W., Micale, F. J., Krumrine, P. H., *Sep. Pur. Methods* 1977, *6*, 61−87.

[183] Nguyen, N. Y., Chrambach, A., *Anal. Biochem.* 1977, *82*, 226–235.

[184] An der Laan, B., Chrambach, A., in: Allen, R. C., Arnaud, P., (Eds.), *Electrophoresis '81*, de Gruyter, Berlin 1981, pp. 41–48.

[185] Burghes, A. H. M., Dunn, M. J., Statham, H. E., Dubowitz, V., in: Allen, R. C., Arnaud, P. (Eds.), *Electrophoresis '81*, de Gruyter, Berlin 1981, pp. 295–308.

[186] Sanders, M. M., Groppi, V. E., Brooming, E. T., *Anal. Biochem.* 1980, *103*, 157–165.

[187] Righetti, P. G., *J. Chromatogr.* 1979, *173*, 1–5.

[188] Goldsmith, M. R., Rattner, E. C., Maay, M., Koehler, D., Balikov, S. R., Bock, G. C., *Anal. Biochem.* 1979, *99*, 33–40.

[189] Rangel-Aldao, R., Kupiec, J. W., Rosen, O. M., *J. Biol. Chem.* 1979, *254*, 2499–2508.

[190] Görg, A., Postel, W., Westermeier, R., Gianazza, E., Righetti, P. G., *J. Biochem. Biophys. Methods* 1980, *3*, 273–284.

[191] Dunn, M. J., Burghes, A. H. M., Witkowski, J. A., Dubowitz, V., *Protides Biol. Fluids* 1985, *32*, 973–976.

[192] Cuono, C. B., Chapo, G. A., *Electrophoresis* 1982, *3*, 65–75.

[193] Jonssen, M., *Electrophoresis* 1980, *1*, 141–149.

[194] Finlayson, G. R., Chrambach, A., *Anal. Biochem.* 1971, *40*, 292–311.

[195] Gelfi, C., Righetti, P. G., *Electrophoresis* 1981, *2*, 220–228.

[196] Righetti, P. G., Gelfi, C., Bianchi Bosisio, A., *Electrophoresis* 1981, *2*, 291–295.

[197] Chrambach, A., Rodbard, D., *Sep. Sci.* 1972, *7*, 663–703.

[198] Heukeshoven, J., Dernick, R., *Electrophoresis* 1981, *2*, 91–98.

[199] Frey, M. D., Atta, M. B., Radola, B. J., in: Neuhoff, V. (Ed.), *Electrophoresis '84*, Verlag Chemie, Weinheim 1984, pp. 122–125.

[200] Frey, M. D., Kinzhofer, A., Kögel, F., Radola, B. J., in: Neuhoff, V. (Ed.), *Electrophoresis '84*, Verlag Chemie, Weinheim 1984, pp. 126–127.

[201] Frey, M. D., Kinzkofer, A., Atta, M. B., Radola, B. J., *Electrophoresis* 1986, *7*, 28–40.

[202] Allen, R. C., Budowle, B., Lack. P. M., Graves, G., in: Dunn, M. J. (Ed.), *Electrophoresis '86*, VCH, Weinheim 1986, pp. 462–473.

[203] Altland, K., Banzhoff, A., Hackler, R., Rossmann, U., *Electrophoresis* 1984, *5*, 379–381.

[204] Gelfi, C., Righetti, P. G., *Electrophoresis* 1984, *5*, 257–262.

[205] Gianazza, E., Frigerio, A., Tagliabue, A., Righetti, P. G., *Electrophoresis* 1984, *5*, 209–216.

[206] Gianazza, E., Artoni, G., Righetti, P. G., *Electrophoresis* 1983, *4*, 321–326.

[207] Gianazza, E., Righetti, P. G., in: Neuhoff, V. (Ed.), *Electrophoresis '84*, Verlag Chemie, Weinheim 1984, pp. 87–90.

[208] Dunn, M. J., Patel, K., Burghes A. H. M., in: Galteau, M. M., Siest, G. (Eds.), *Progrès Récents en Electrophorèse,* Presses Universitaires, Nancy 1986, pp. 3–9.

[209] Dunn, M. J., Patel, K., *Protides Biol. Fluids* 1986, *34*, 695–699.

[210] Righetti, P. G., Gelfi, C., Gianazza E., in: Dunn, M. J. (Ed.), *Gel Electrophoresis of Proteins,* Wright, Bristol 1986, pp. 141–202.

[211] Voris, B. P., Young, D. A., *Anal. Biochem.* 1980, *104*, 478–484.

[212] Delincee, H., Radola, B. J., *Anal. Biochem.* 1978, *90*, 603–623.

[213] Fosslien, E., Prasad, R., Stastny, J., *Electrophoresis* 1984, *5*, 102–109.

[214] Ui, N., *Ann. N.Y. Acad. Sci,* 1973, *209* 198–209.

[215] Gelsema, W. J., de Ligny, C. L., van der Veen, N. G., *J. Chromatogr.* 1978, *151*, 161–174.

[216] Gelsema, W. J., de Ligny, C. L., van der Veen, N. G., *J. Chromatogr.* 1979, *171*, 171–181.

[217] Chidakel, B.-E., Nguyen, N. Y., Chrambach, A., *Anal. Biochem.* 1977, *77*, 216–225.

[218] Bravo, R., Bellatin, J., Celis, J. E., *Cell Biol. Intl. Rep.* 1981, *5*, 93–96.
[219] Bravo, R., Celis, J. E., *Clin. Chem.* 1982, *28*, 766–781.
[220] Peters, K. E., Comings, D. E., *J. Cell Biol.* 1980, *86*, 135–155.
[221] Steinberg, R. A., O'Farrell, P. H., Friedrich, U., Coffino, P., *Cell* 1977, *10*, 381–391.
[222] Anderson, N. L., Hickman, B. J., *Anal. Biochem.* 1979, *93*, 312–320.
[223] Hickman, B. J., Anderson, N. L., Willard, K. E., Anderson, N. G., in: Radola, B. J. (Ed.), *Electrophoresis '79*, de Gruyter, Berlin 1980, pp. 341–360.
[224] Tollaksen, S. L., Edwards, J. J., Anderson, N. G., *Electrophoresis* 1981, *2*, 155–160.
[225] Lizana, J., Johansson, K.-E., *Protides Biol. Fluids* 1986, *34*, 741–744.
[226] Zhang, J.-S., Tollaksen, S. L., Giometti, C. S., in: Dunn, M. J. (Ed.), *Electrophoresis '86*, VCH, Weinheim 1986, pp. 617–620.
[227] Nguyen, N. Y., Chrambach, A., *Anal. Biochem.* 1976, *74*, 145–153.
[228] Nguyen, N. Y., Chrambach, A., *Electrophoresis* 1980, *1*, 14–22.
[229] Chrambach, A., *The Practice of Quantitative Gel Electrophoresis*, VCH, Weinheim 1985.
[230] Cuono, C. B., Chapo, G. A., Chrambach, A., Hjelmeland, L. M., *Electrophoresis* 1983, *4*, 404–407.
[231] Burghes, A. H. M., Patel, K., Dunn, M. J., *Electrophoresis* 1985, *6*, 453–461.
[232] Bjellqvist, B., Ek, K., Righetti, P. G., Gianazza, E., Görg, A., Westermeier, R., Postel, W., *J. Biochem. Biophys. Methods* 1982, *6*, 317–339.
[233] Righetti, P. G., Gianazza, E., Bjellqvist, B., *J. Biochem. Biophys. Methods* 1983, *8*, 89–108.
[234] Righetti, P. G., *J. Chromatogr.* 1984, *300*, 165–223.
[235] LKB Application Note No. 324, 1984, LKB Produkter AB., Bromma, Sweden.
[236] Dossi, G., Celentano, F., Gianazza, E., Righetti, P. G., *J. Biochem. Biophys. Methods* 1983, *7*, 123–142.
[237] Gianazza, E., Dossi, G., Celentano, F., Righetti, P. G., *J. Biochem. Biophys. Methods* 1983, *8*, 109–133.
[238] Gianazza, E., Astrua-Testori, S., Righetti, P. G., *Electrophoresis* 1985, *6*, 113–117.
[239] Gianazza, E., Giacon, P., Sahlin, B., Righetti, P. G., *Electrophoresis* 1985, *6*, 53–56.
[240] Altland, K., Hackler, R., Banzhoff, A., von Eckardstein, A., *Electrophoresis* 1985, *6*, 140–142.
[241] Hochstrasser, D. F., Augsburger, V., Funk, M., Appel, R., Pellegrini, C., Muller, A. F., in: Dunn, M. J. (Ed.), *Electrophoresis '86*, VCH, Weinheim 1986, pp. 566–568.
[242] Dunn, M. J., Patel, K., in: Dunn, M. J. (Ed.), *Electrophoresis '86*, VCH, Weinheim 1986, pp. 574–578.
[243] Gianazza, E., Celentano, F., Dossi, G., Bjellqvist, B., Righetti, P. G., *Electrophoresis* 1984, *5*, 88–97.
[244] Fawcett, J. S., Chrambach, A., *Electrophoresis* 1986, *7*, 260–266.
[245] Altland, K., Altland, A., *Electrophoresis* 1984, *5*, 143–147.
[246] Altland, K., Altland, A., *Clin, Chem.* 1984, *30*, 2098–2103.
[247] Righetti, P. G., Ek, K., Bjellqvist, B., *J. Chromatogr.* 1984, *291*, 31–42.
[248] Pietta, P., Pocaterra, E., Fiorino, A., Gianazza, E., Righetti, P. G., *Electrophoresis* 1985, *6*, 162–170.
[249] Altland, K., Rossmann, U., *Electrophoresis* 1985, *6*, 314–325.
[250] Gianazza, E., Astrua-Testori, S., Giacon, P., Righetti, P. G., *Protides Biol. Fluids* 1985, *33*, 463–466.
[251] Gianazza, E., Astrua-Testori, S., Giacon, P., Righetti, P. G., *Electrophoresis* 1985, *6*, 332–339.
[252] Görg, A., Postel, W., Westermeier, R., Bjellqvist, B., Ek, K., in: Stathakos, D. (Ed.), *Electrophoresis '82*, de Gruyter, Berlin 1983, pp. 354–361.

[253] Görg, A., Postel, W., Weser, J., Westermeier, R., in: Hirai, H. (Ed.), *Electrophoresis '83*, de Gruyter, Berlin 1984, pp. 525–532.

[254] Görg, A., Postel, W., Weser, J., *Protides Biol. Fluids* 1985, *33*, 467–470.

[255] Westermeier, R., Postel, W., Weser, J., Görg, A., *J Biochem. Biophys. Methods* 1983, *8*, 321–330.

[256] Pernelle, J.-J., Chafey, P., Lognonne, J.-L., Righetti, P. G., Bosisio, A. B., Wahrmann, J. P., *Electrophoresis* 1986, *7*, 159–165.

[257] Fawcett, J. S., Chrambach, A., *Protides Biol. Fluids* 1985, *33*, 439–442.

[258] Fawcett, J. S., Chrambach, A., *Electrophoresis* 1986, *7*, 266–272.

[259] Righetti, P. G., Gianazza, E., in: Galteau, M. M., Siest, G. (Eds.), *Progrès Récents en Electrophorèse Bidimensionelle*, Presses Universitaires, Nancy 1986, pp. 11–19.

[260] Görg, A., Postel, W., Günther, S., Weser, J., *Electrophoresis* 1985, *6*, 599–604.

[261] Rimpilainen, M. A., Righetti, P. G., *Electrophoresis* 1985, *6*, 419–422.

[262] Görg, A., Postel, W., Günther, S., Weser, J., in: Dunn, M. J. (Ed.), *Electrophoresis '86*, VCH, Weinheim 1986, pp. 435–449.

[263] Görg, A., Postel, W., Westermeier, R., in: Radola, B. J. (Ed.), *Electrophoresis '79*, de Gruyter, Berlin 1980, pp. 67-78.

[264] Weser, J., Postel, W., Günther, S., Görg, A., in: Dunn, M. J. (Ed.), *Electrophoresis '86*, VCH, Weinheim 1986, pp. 607–612.

[265] Görg, A., Postel, W., Weser, J., Günther, S., Strahler, J. R., Hanash, S. M., Somerlot, L., *Electrophoresis* 1987, *8*, 45–51.

[266] Righetti, P. G., Gelfi, C., Gianazza, E., *Chimica Oggi* 1986, *March*, 55–60.

[267] Gianazza, E., Astrua-Testori, S., Caccia, P., Quaglia, L., Righetti, P. G., in: Dunn, M. J. (Ed.), *Electrophoresis '86*, VCH, Weinheim 1986, pp. 563–565.

[268] Jäckle, H., *Anal. Biochem.* 1979, *98*, 81–84.

[269] Fawcett, J. S., Chrambach, A., in: Dunn, M. J. (Ed.), *Electrophoresis '86*, VCH, Weinheim 1986, pp. 569–573.

[270] Gianazza, E., Astrua-Testori, S., Caccia, P., Giacon, P., Quaglia, L., Righetti, P. G., *Electrophoresis* 1986, *7*, 76–83.

[271] Tracy, R. P., Currie, R. M., Kyle, R. A., Young, D. S., *Clin. Chem.* 1982, *28*, 908-914.

[272] Rosenmann, E., Kreis, C., Thomson, R. G., Dobbs, M., Hamerton, J. L., Wrogemann, K., *Nature* 1982, *298*, 563–565.

[273] Poehling, H. M., Neuhoff, V., *Electrophoresis* 1980, *1*, 90–101.

[274] Amess, R., Fox, J. E., Spragg, P. S., *Electrophoresis* 1985, *6*, 186–188.

[275] Gianazza, E., Righetti, P. G., *J. Chromatogr.* 1980, *193*, 1–8.

[276] Garrels, J. I., Farrar, J. T., Burwell, C. B., in: Celis, J. E., Bravo, R. (Eds.), *Twodimensional Gel Electrophoresis of Proteins*, Academic Press, Orlando 1984, pp. 37–91.

[277] Rothe, G. M., Purkhanbaba, H., *Electrophoresis* 1982, *3*, 33–42.

[278] Rothe, G. M., Maurer, W. D., in: Dunn, M. J. (Ed.), *Gel Electrophoresis of Proteins*, Wright, Bristol 1986, pp. 37–140.

[279] Anderson, N. L., Anderson, N. G., *Anal. Biochem.* 1978, *85*, 341–354.

[280] Anderson, N. G., Anderson, N. L., *Behring Inst. Mittl.* 1979, *63*, 169–210.

[281] Groppi, V. E., Browning, E. T., *Molec. Pharmacol.* 1980, *18*, 427–437.

[282] Poduslo, J. F., *Anal. Biochem.* 1981, *114*, 131–139.

[283] Jones, M. I., Massingham, W. E., Spragg, S. P., *Anal. Biochem.* 1980, *106*, 446–449.

[284] Radola, B. J., *Electrophoresis* 1980, *1*, 43–56.

[285] Nochumson, S., Gibson, S. G., in: Stathakos, D. (Ed.), *Electrophoresis '82*, de Gruyter, Berlin 1983, pp. 177–182.

[286] Wyckoff, M., Rodbard, D., Chrambach, A., *Anal. Biochem.* 1977, *78*, 469–482.

[287] Anderson, D. W., Peterson, C., in: Allen, R. C., Arnaud, P. (Eds.), *Electrophoresis '81*, de Gruyter, Berlin 1981, pp. 41–48.

[288] Ansorge, W., Garoff, H., in: Allen, R. C., Arnaud, P. (Eds.), *Electrophoresis '81*, de Gruyter, Berlin 1981, pp. 635–646.

[289] Nikodem, V. M., Trus, B. L., Rall, J. E., *Proc. Natl. Acad. Sci. USA* 1981, *78*, 4411–4415.

[290] Allen, R. C., *Electrophoresis* 1980, *1*, 32–37.

[291] Läas, T., Olsson, I., in: Allen, R. C., Arnaud, P., *Electrophoresis '81*, de Gruyter, Berlin 1981, pp. 191–203.

[292] Allen, R. C., Arnaud, P., *Electrophoresis* 1983, *4*, 205–211.

[293] Young, D. A., Voris, B. P., Maytin, E. V., Colbert, T. A., *Methods Enzymol.* 1983, *91*, Part 1, 190–214.

[294] Young, D. A., *Clin. Chem.* 1984, *30*, 2104–2108.

[295] Klose, J., Zeindl, E., *Clin. Chem.* 1984, *30*, 2014–2020.

[296] Rüchel, R., *J. Chromatogr.* 1977, *132*, 451–468.

[297] Beltle, W., Zimmermann, S., Bobb, M., Murach, K.-F., *Electrophoresis* 1983, *4*, 143–148.

[298] Arold, N., Ehrhardt, W., Kruska, S., Neuhoff, V., in: Dunn, M. J. (Ed.), *Electrophoresis '86*, VCH, Weinheim 1986, pp. 626–629.

[299] Inouye, M., *J. Biol. Chem.* 1971, *246*, 4834–4838.

[300] Giometti, C. S., Anderson, N. G., Tollaksen, S. L., Edwards, J. J., Anderson, N. L., *Anal. Biochem.* 1980, *102*, 47–58.

[301] Kurian, P., Gersten, D. M., Suhocki, P. V., Ledley, G., *Electrophoresis* 1981, *2*, 184–187.

[302] Lubit, B. W., *Electrophoresis* 1984, *5*, 358–361.

[303] Johnston, D. A., Capetillo, S., Ramagli, L. S., Guevara, J., Gersten, D. M., Rodriguez, L. V., *Electrophoresis* 1984, *5*, 110–116.

[304] Dunn, M. J., Maddy, A. H., in: Maddy, A. H. (Ed.), *Biochemical Analysis of Membranes*, Chapman and Hall, London 1976, pp. 197–251.

[305] Vesterberg, O., in: Radola, B. J. (Ed.), *Electrophoresis '79*, de Gruyter, Berlin 1980, pp. 95–104.

[306] Frey, M. D., Radola, B. J., *Electrophoresis* 1982, *3*, 27–32.

[307] Steck, G., Leuthard, P., Burk, R. R., *Anal. Biochem.* 1980, *107*, 21–24.

[308] Gersten, D. M., Zapolski, E. J., Ledley, R. S., *Electrophoresis* 1985, *6*, 191–192.

[309] Davis, B. D., Cohn, E. J., *Ann. N.Y. Acad. Sci.* 1939, *39*, 209–212.

[310] Tiselius, A., *Nova Acta Reg. Soc. Sci. Uppsala* 1930, *IV 7*, No. 4.

[311] Tiselius, A., *Trans. Faraday Soc.* 1937, *33*, 524–531.

[312] Durrum, E. L., *J. Am. Chem. Soc.* 1950, *72*, 2943–2948.

[313] Grassman, W., Hannig, K., *Z. Physiol. Chem.* 1952, *290*, 1–27.

[314] Fazekas de St. Groth, S., Webster, R. G., Datyner, A., *Biochim. Biophys. Acta* 1963, *71*, 377–391.

[315] Talbot, D. N., Yaphantis, D. A., *Anal. Biochem.* 1971, *44*, 246–253.

[316] Merril, C. R., Switzer, R. C., Van Keuren, M. L., *Proc. Natl. Acad. Sci. USA* 1979, *76*, 435–439.

[317] Switzer, R. C., Merril, C. R., Shifrin, S., *Anal. Biochem.* 1979, *98*, 231–237.

[318] Merril, C. R., Harasewych, M. G., Harrington, M. G., in: Dunn, M. J. (Ed.), *Gel Electrophoresis of Proteins*, Wright, Bristol 1986, pp. 323–362.

[319] Chrambach, A., Reisfeld, R. A., Wyckoff, H., Zaccari, J., *Anal. Biochem.* 1967, *20*, 150–154.

[320] Diezel, W., Koppenschläger, G., Hofmann, E., *Anal. Biochem.* 1972, *48*, 617–620.

[321] Neuhoff, V., Stamm, R., Eibl, H., *Electrophoresis* 1985, *6*, 427–448.

[322] Hames, B. D., Rickwood, D., *Gel Electrophoresis of Proteins: A Practical Approach*, IRL, London 1981, pp. 249–263.

[323] Pace, J. L., Kemper, D. L., Ragland, W. L., *Biochem. Biophys. Res. Commun.* 1974, *57,* 482–488.

[324] Ragland, W. L., Pace, J. L., Kemper, D. L., *Anal. Biochem.* 1974, *59,* 24–33.

[325] Burger, B. O., White, F. C., Pace, J. L., Kemper, D. L., Ragland, W. L., *Anal. Biochem.* 1976, *70,* 327–335.

[326] Mackay, C. D., in: Dunn, M. J. (Ed.), *Electrophoresis '86,* VCH, Weinheim 1986, pp. 720–722.

[327] Hartman, B. K., Udenfriend, S., *Anal. Biochem.* 1969, *30,* 391–394.

[328] Aragay, A. M., Diaz, P., Daban, J-R., *Electrophoresis* 1985, *6,* 527–531.

[329] Patel, K., Easty, D., Dunn, M. J., in: Dunn, M. J. (Ed.), *Electrophoresis '86*, VCH, Weinheim 1986, pp. 662–667.

[330] Merril, C. R., Goldman, D., in: Celis, J. E., Bravo, R. (Eds.), *Two-dimensional Gel Electrophoresis of Proteins,* Academic Press, Orlando 1984, pp. 93–109.

[331] Merril, C. R., in: Dunn, M. J. (Ed.), *Electrophoresis '86,* VCH, Weinheim 1986, pp. 273–290.

[332] Wray, W., Boulikas, J., Wray, V. P., Hancock, R., *Anal. Biochem.* 1981, *118,* 197–203.

[333] Oakley, B. R., Kirsch, D. R., Morris, N. R., *Anal. Biochem.* 1980, *105,* 361–363.

[334] Poehling, H. M., Neuhoff, V., *Electrophoresis* 1981, *2,* 141–147.

[335] Morrissey, J. M., *Anal. Biochem.* 1981, *117,* 307–310.

[336] Merril, C. R., Dunau, M., Goldman, D., *Anal. Biochem.* 1981, *110,* 201–207.

[337] Guevara, J., Johnston, D. A., Ranageli, L. S., Martin, B. A., Capetillo, S., Rodriguez, *Electrophoresis* 1982, *3,* 197–205.

[338] Sammons, D. W., Adams, L. D., Nishizawa, E. E., *Electrophoresis* 1982, *2,* 135–141.

[339] Nauta, W. J. H, Gygax, P. A., *Stain Technology* 1951, *26,* 5–11.

[340] Marshall, T., Latner, A. L., *Electrophoresis* 1981, *2,* 228–235.

[341] Merril, C. R., Goldman, D., *Clin. Chem.* 1982, *28,* 1015–1020.

[342] Merril, C. R., Harrington, M., Alley, V., *Electrophoresis* 1984, *5,* 289–297.

[343] Merril, C. R., Harrington, M., *Clin. Chem.* 1984, *30,* 1938–1942.

[344] Nielsen, B. L., Brown, L. R., *Anal. Biochem.* 1984, *141,* 311–315.

[345] Sammons, D. W., Adams, L. D., Vidmar, T. J., Hatfield, A., Jones, D. H., Chuba, P. J., Crooks, S. W., in: Celis, J. E., Bravo, R. (Eds.), *Two-dimensional Gel Electrophoresis of Proteins,* Academic Press, Orlando 1984, pp. 112–127.

[346] Slisz, M. L., Van Frank, R. M., *Electrophoresis* 1985, *6,* 405–407.

[347] Dion, A. S., Pomenti, A. A., *Anal. Biochem.* 1983, *129,* 490–496.

[348] Heukeshoven, J., Dernick, R., *Electrophoresis* 1985, *6,* 103–112.

[349] Gersten, D. M., Wolf, P. H., Ledley, R. H., Rodriguez, L. V., Zapolski, E. J., *Electrophoresis* 1986, *7,* 327–332.

[350] Ochs, D., *Anal. Biochem.* 1983, *135,* 470–474.

[351] Merril, C. R., Goldman, D., Van Keuren, M. L., *Electrophoresis* 1982, *3,* 17–23.

[352] Van Keuren, M. L., Goldman, D., Merril, C. R., *Anal. Biochem.* 1981, *116,* 248–255.

[353] Rochette-Egly, C., Stussi-Garaud, C., *Electrophoresis* 1984, *5,* 285–288.

[354] De Moreno, M. R., Smith, J. R., Smith, R. V., *Anal. Biochem.* 1985, *151,* 466–470.

[355] Friedman, R. D., *Anal. Biochem.* 1982, *126,* 346–349.

[356] Dzandu, J. K., Deh, M. M., Barratt, D. L., Wise, G. E., *Proc. Natl. Acad. Sci. USA* 1984, *81,* 1733–1737.

[357] Yüksel, K. U., Gracy, R. W., *Electrophoresis* 1985, *6,* 361–366.

[358] Tal, M., Silberstein, A., Nusser, E., *J. Biol. Chem.* 1985, *260,* 9976–9980.

[359] Lowry, O. H., Rosenbrough, N. J., Farr, A. L., Randall, R. J., *J. Biol. Chem.* 1951, *193,* 265–275.

[360] Gold, M. A., Heydorn, W. E., Creed, G. J., Weller, J. L., Klein, D. C., Jacobowitz, D. M., *Electrophoresis* 1984, *5,* 116–121.

[361] Zeindl, E., Klose, J., *Electrophoresis* 1984, *5,* 303 – 309.
[362] Assoian, R. K., Blix, P. M., Rubenstein, A. H., Tager, H. S., *Anal. Biochem.* 1980, *103,* 70 – 76.
[363] Rabilloud, T., Therre, H., *Electrophoresis* 1986, *7,* 49 – 51.
[364] Zapolski, E. J., Gersten, D. M., Ledley, R. S., *Anal. Biochem.* 1982, *123,* 325 – 328.
[365] Zapolski, E. J., Padrasky, F., Ledley, R. S., Gersten, D. M., *Electrophoresis* 1984, *5,* 354 – 357.
[366] Robinson, P. J., Bull, F. D., Anderton, B. M., Roitt, I. M., *FEBS Lett.* 1975, *58,* 330 – 333.
[367] Tanner, M. J. A., Anstee, D. J., *Biochem. J.* 1976, *153,* 265 – 270.
[368] Burridge, K., *Methods Enzymol.* 1978, *50,* 54 – 64.
[369] Elder, J. H., Pickett, R. A., Hampton, J., Lerner, R. A., *J. Biol. Chem.* 1977, *252,* 6510 – 6515.
[370] Laskey, R. A., Mills, A. D., *Eur. J. Biochem.* 1975, *56,* 335 – 341.
[371] Laskey, R. A., Mills, A. D., *FEBS Lett.* 1977, *82,* 314 – 316.
[372] Bonner, W. M., Laskey, R. A., *Eur. J. Biochem.* 1974, *46,* 83 – 88.
[373] Randerath, K., *Anal. Biochem.* 1970, *34,* 188 – 205.
[374] Pulleybank, D. E. Booth, G. M., *Biochem. Biophys. Methods* 1981, *4,* 339 – 346.
[375] Chamberlain, J. P., *Anal. Biochem.* 1979, *98,* 132 – 135.
[376] Heegaard, N. H. H., Hebsgaard, K. P., Bjerrum, O. J., *Electrophoresis* 1984, *5,* 263 – 269.
[377] Laskey, R. A., *Methods Enzymol.* 1980, *65,* 363 – 371.
[378] McConkey, E. H., *Anal. Biochem.* 1979, *96,* 39 – 44.
[379] Swanstrom, R., Shanks, P. R., *Anal. Biochem.* 1978, *86,* 184 – 192.
[380] McConkey, E. H., Anderson, C., *Electrophoresis* 1984, *5,* 230 – 232.
[381] Choo, K. H., Cotton, G. H., Danks, D. M., *Anal. Biochem.* 1980, *103,* 33 – 38.
[382] Gruenstein, E. Z., Pollard, A. L., *Anal. Biochem.* 1976, *76,* 452 – 457.
[383] Walton, K. E., Styer, D., Gruenstein, E. Z., *J. Biol. Chem.* 1979, *254,* 7951 – 7960.
[384] Lecocq, R., Hepburn, A., Lamy, F., *Anal. Biochem.* 1982, *127,* 293 – 299.
[385] McConkey, E. H., Anderson, C., *Electrophoresis* 1984, *5,* 233 – 235.
[386] Kronenberg, L. M., *Anal. Biochem.* 1979, *93,* 189 – 195.
[387] Bravo, R., Celis, J. E., *J. Cell Biol.* 1980, *84,* 795 – 802.
[388] Goulianos, K., Smith, K. K., White, S. N., *Anal. Biochem.* 1980, *103,* 64 – 69.
[389] Scott, B. J., Bateman, J. E., Bradwell, A. R., *Anal. Biochem.* 1982, *123,* 1 – 10.
[390] Burbeck, S., *Electrophoresis* 1983, *4,* 127 – 133.
[391] Wiza, J. L., *Nucl. Instrum. Methods* 1979, *162,* 587 – 601.
[392] Davidson, J. B., Case, A. L., *Science* 1982, *215,* 1398 – 1400.
[393] Davidson, J. B., in: Neuhoff, V. (Ed.), *Electrophoresis '84,* Verlag Chemie, Weinheim 1984, pp. 235 – 251.
[394] Anderson, N. G., Anderson, N. L., *Clin. Chem.* 1982, *28,* 739 – 748.
[395] Block, P. L., Phillips, T. A., Neidhardt, F. C., *J. Bacteriol.* 1980, *141,* 1409 – 1420.
[396] Phillips, T. A., Block, P. L., Neidhardt, F. C., *J. Bacteriol.* 1980, *144,* 1024 – 1033.
[397] Anderson, N. L., Anderson, N. G., *Proc. Natl. Acad. Sci. USA* 1977, *74,* 5421 – 5425.
[398] Edwards, J. J., Anderson, N. G., Tollaksen, S. L., von Eschenbach, A. C., Guevara, J., *Clin. Chem.* 1982, *28,* 160 – 163.
[399] Jones, M. I., Spragg, S. P., Webb, T., *Biol. Neonate* 1981, *39,* 171 – 177.
[400] Jones, M. I., Spragg, S. P., *Electrophoresis* 1983, *4,* 291 – 297.
[401] Goldman, D., Merril, C. R., Ebert, M. H., *Clin. Chem.* 1980, *26,* 1317 – 1322.
[402] Allen, R. C., Arnaud, P., Spicer, S. S., in: Allen, R. C., Arnaud, P. (Eds.), *Electrophoresis '81,* de Gruyter, Berlin 1981, pp. 161 – 179.
[403] Alper, C. A., Johnson, A. M., *Vox. Sang.* 1969, *17,* 445 – 452.

[404] Johnson, A. M., in: Allen, R. C., Arnaud, P. (Eds.), *Electrophoresis '81,* de Gruyter, Berlin 1981, pp. 127–132.

[405] Ritchie, R. F., Smith, R., *Clin. Chem.* 1976, *22,* 497–499.

[406] Burridge, K., *Proc. Natl. Acad. Sci. USA* 1976, *79,* 4457–4461.

[407] Adair, W. S., Jurivich, D., Goodenough, U. W., *J. Cell Biol.* 1978, *79,* 281–285.

[408] Southern, E. M., *J. Molec. Biol.* 1975, *98,* 503–517.

[409] Alwine, J. C., Kemp, D. J., Stark, G. R., *Proc. Natl. Acad. Sci. USA* 1977, *74,* 5350–5354.

[410] Renart, J., Reiser, J., Stark, G. R., *Proc. Natl. Acad. Sci. USA* 1979, *76,* 3116–3120.

[411] Towbin, H., Staehelin, T., Gordon, J., *Proc. Natl. Acad. Sci. USA* 1979, *76,* 4350–4354.

[412] Peferoen, M., Huybrechts, R., De Loof, A., *FEBS Lett.* 1982, *145,* 369–372.

[413] Gooderham, K., in: Walker, J., Gaastra, W. (Eds.), *Techniques in Molecular Biology,* Croom Helm, London 1983, pp. 49–61.

[414] Gershoni, J. M., Palade, G. E., *Anal. Biochem.* 1983, *131,* 1–15.

[415] Symington, J., in: Celis, J. E., Bravo, R. (Eds.), *Two-dimensional Gel Electrophoresis of Proteins,* Academic Press, Orlando 1984, pp. 127–168.

[416] Beisiegel, U., *Electrophoresis* 1986, *7,* 1–18.

[417] Gershoni, J. M., in: Dunn, M. J. (Ed.), *Electrophoresis '86,* VCH, Weinheim 1986, pp. 305–313.

[418] Gershoni, J. M., *Adv. Electrophoresis* 1987, *1,* 141–175.

[419] Stott, D. I., McLearie, J., Marsden, H. S., *Anal. Biochem.* 1985, *149,* 454–460.

[420] Shuttelworth, A. D., *Electrophoresis* 1984, *5,* 178–179.

[421] Anderson, N. L., Nance, S. L., Pearson, T. W., Anderson, N. G., *Electrophoresis* 1982, *3,* 135–142.

[422] Gershoni, J. M., Davis, F. E., Palade, G. E., *Anal. Biochem.* 1985, *144,* 32–40.

[423] Khyse-Anderson, J., *J. Biochem. Biophys. Methods* 1984, *10,* 203–209.

[424] Bjerrum, O. J., Schafer-Neilsen, C., in: Dunn, M. J. (Ed.), *Electrophoresis '86,* VCH, Weinheim 1986, pp. 315–327.

[425] Svoboda, M., Meuris, S., Robyn, C., Christophe, J., *Anal. Biochem.* 1985, *151,* 16–23.

[426] Hancock, K., Tsang, V. C. W., *Anal. Biochem.* 1983, *133,* 157–162.

[427] Moeremans, M., Daneels, G., De Mey, J., *Anal. Biochem.* 1985, *145,* 315–321.

[428] Moeremans, M., Daneels, G., De Raeymaeker, M., De Mey, J., in: Dunn, M. J. (Ed.), *Electrophoresis '86,* VCH, Weinheim 1986, pp. 328–329.

[429] Wrigley, C. W., Skerritt, J. H., in: Dunn, M. J. (Ed.), *Electrophoresis '86,* VCH, Weinheim 1986, pp. 291–303.

[430] Gershoni, J. M., Palade, G. E., *Anal. Biochem.* 1982, *124,* 396–405.

[431] Kittler, J. M., Meisler, N. T., Vicepo-Madore, D., Cidlowski, J. A., Thanassi, J. W., *Anal. Biochem.* 1984, *137,* 210–216.

[432] Hawkes, R., *Anal. Biochem.* 1983, *123,* 143–146.

[433] Bhullar, B. S., Hewitt, J., Candido, E. P. M., *J. Biol. Chem.* 1981, *256,* 8801–8806.

[434] Hanff, P. A., Fehninger, T. E., Miller, J. N., Lovett, M. A., *J. Immunol.* 1982, *129,* 1287–1291.

[435] Winter, J., *Nature* 1982, *298,* 471–472.

[436] Saravis, C. A., *Electrophoresis* 1984, *5,* 54–55.

[437] Batteiger, B., Newhall, W. J., Jones, R. B., *J. Immunol. Methods* 1982, *55,* 297–307.

[438] Moeremans, M., Daneels, G., Van Dijk, A., Langanger, G., De Mey, J., *J. Immunol. Methods* 1984, *74,* 353–360.

[439] Daneels, G., Moeremans, M., De Raeymaeker, M., De Mey, J., *J. Immunol. Methods* 1986, *89,* 89–91.

[440] Perides, G., Plagens, U., Traub, P., *Anal. Biochem.* 1986, *152,* 94–99.

[441] Jackson, P., Thompson, R. J., *Electrophoresis* 1984, *5*, 35–42.

[442] Latter, G. I., Metz, E., Burbeck, S. Leavitt, J., *Electrophoresis* 1983, *4*, 122–126.

[443] Latter, G. I., Burbeck, S., Fleming, J., Leavitt, J., *Clin. Chem.* 1984, *30*, 1925–1932.

[444] Fey, S. J., Bravo, R., Larsen, P. M., Celis, J. E., in: Celis, J. E., Bravo, R. (Eds.), *Two-dimensional Gel Electrophoresis of Proteins,* Academic Press, Orlando 1984, pp. 169–189.

[445] Bravo, R., Fey, S. J., Small, J. V., Larsen, M. P., Celis, J. E., *Cell* 1981, *25*, 195–202.

[446] Bray, D., Brownlee, J. M., *Anal. Biochem.* 1973, *55*, 213–221.

[447] Christopher, A. R., Nagpal, M. L., Carroll, A. R., Brown, J. C., *Anal. Biochem.* 1978, *85*, 404–412.

[448] Bolton, A. E., Hunter, W. M., *Biochem. J.* 1973, *133*, 529–538.

[449] Fey, S. J., Bravo, R., Larsen, P. M., Bellatin, J., Celis, J. E., *Cell Biol. Int. Rep.* 1981, *5*, 491–500.

[450] Edman, P., Begg, G., *Eur. J. Biochem.* 1967, *1*, 80–91.

[451] Hewick, R. M., Hunkapiller, M. W., Hood, L. E., Dreyer, W. J., *J. Biol. Chem.* 1981, *256*, 7990–7997.

[452] Aebersold, R. H., Teplow, D. B., Hood, L. E., Kent, S. B. H., *J. Biol. Chem.* 1986, *261*, 4229–4238.

[453] Aebersold, R. H., Teplow, D. B., Hood, L. E., Kent, S. B. H., *Protides Biol. Fluids* 1986, *34*, 715–718.

[454] Spragg, S. P., Amess, R., Jones, M. I., Ramasamy, R., in: Dunn, M. J. (Ed.), *Gel Electrophoresis of Proteins,* Wright, Bristol 1986, pp. 363–394.

[455] Anderson, N. L., Taylor, J., Scandora, A. E., Coulter, B. P., Anderson, N. G., *Clin. Chem.* 1981, *27*, 1807–1820.

[456] Taylor. J., Anderson, N. L., Scandora, A. E., Willard, K. E., Anderson, N. G., *Clin. Chem.* 1982, *28*, 861–866.

[457] Lemkin, P. F., Lipkin, L. E., *Comput. Biomed. Res.* 1981, *14*, 272–297.

[458] Lemkin, P. F., Lipkin, L. E., *Comput. Biomed. Res.* 1981, *14*, 355–380.

[459] Lemkin, P. F., Lipkin, L. E., *Comput. Biomed. Res.* 1981, *14*, 407–416.

[460] Lemkin, P. F., Lipkin. L. E., *Electrophoresis* 1983, *4*, 71–81.

[461] Vo, K.-P., Miller, M. J., Geiduschek, E. P., Nielsen, C., Olson, A., Xuong, N.-H., *Anal. Biochem.* 1981, *112*, 258–271.

[462] Miller, M. J., Vo, K. P., Nielsen, C., Geiduschek, E. P., Xuong, N., *Clin. Chem.* 1982, *28*, 867–875.

[463] Miller, M. J., Olson, A. D., Thorgeirsson, S. S., *Electrophoresis* 1984, *5*, 297–303.

[464] Miller, M. J., in: Dunn, M. J. (Ed.), *Electrophoresis '86,* VCH, Weinheim 1986, pp. 539–551.

[465] Bossinger, J., Miller, M. J., Vo, K. P., Geiduschek, E. P., Xuong, N. H., *J. Biol. Chem.* 1979, *254*, 7986–7998.

[466] Kronberg, H., Zimmer, H.-G., Neuhoff, V., *Clin. Chem.* 1984, *30*, 2059–2062.

[467] Marsman, H., van Resandt, R. W., *Electrophoresis* 1985, *6*, 242–246.

[468] Tyson, J. J., Haralick, R. M., *Electrophoresis* 1986, *7*, 107–113.

[469] Aycock, B. F., Weil, D. E., Sinicropi, D. V., McIlwain, D. L., *Comput. Biomed. Res.* 1981, *14*, 314–326.

[470] Mariash, C. N., Seelig, S., Oppenheimer, J. H., *Anal. Biochem.* 1982, *121*, 388–394.

[471] Schneider, W., Klose, J., *Electrophoresis* 1983, *4*, 284–291.

[472] Toda, T., Fujita, T., Ohashi, M., *Electrophoresis* 1984, *5*, 42–47.

[473] Anderson, N. L., Nance, S. L., Tollaksen, S. L., Giere, F. A., Anderson, N. G., *Electrophoresis* 1985, *6*, 592–599.

[474] Anderson, N. L., Swanson, M., Giere, F. A., Tollaksen, S., Gemmell, A., Nance, S., Anderson, N. G., *Electrophoresis* 1986, *7*, 44–48.

[475] Blose, S. H., in: Dunn, M. J. (Ed.), *Electrophoresis '86,* VCH, Weinheim 1986, pp. 552–555.

[476] Brown, W. T., Ezer, A., *Clin. Chem.* 1982, *28,* 1041–1044.

[477] Kronberg, H., Zimmer, H. G., Neuhoff, V., *Electrophoresis* 1980, *1,* 27–32.

[478] Taylor, J., Anderson, N. L., Coulter, B. P., Scandora, A. E., Anderson, N. G., in: Radola, B. J. (Ed.), *Electrophoresis '79,* de Gruyter, Berlin 1979, pp. 329–339.

[479] Skolnick, M. M., Sternberg, S. R., Neel, J. V., *Clin. Chem.* 1982, *28,* 969–978.

[480] Taylor, J., Anderson, N. L., Anderson, N. G., in: Allen, R. C., Arnaud, P. (Eds.), *Electrophoresis '81,* de Gruyter, Berlin 1981, pp. 383–400.

[481] Skolnick, M. M., *Clin. Chem.* 1982, *28,* 979–986.

[482] Potter, D. J., *Comput. Biomed. Res.* 1985, *18,* 347–362.

[483] Potter, D. J., Skolnick, M. M., in: Dunn, M. J. (Ed.), *Electrophoresis '86,* VCH, Weinheim 1986, pp. 556–559.

[484] Smith, K. A., Dunn, M. J., in: Dunn, M. J. (Ed.), *Electrophoresis '86,* VCH, Weinheim 1986, pp. 560–562.

[485] Vincens, P., Paris, N., Pujol, J.-L., Gaboriaud, C., Rabilloud, T., Pennetier, J.-L., Matherat, P., Tarroux, P., *Electrophoresis* 1986, *7,* 347–356.

[486] Vincens, P., *Electrophoresis* 1986, *7,* 357–367.

[487] Vincens, P., Tarroux, P., *Electrophoresis* 1987, *8,* 100–107.

[488] Vincens, P., Tarroux, P., *Electrophoresis* 1987, *8,* 173–186.

[489] Tarroux, P., Vincens, P., Rabilloud, T., *Electrophoresis* 1987, *8,* 187–188.

[490] Duncan, R., McConkey, E. H., *Clin. Chem.* 1982, *28,* 749–755.

[491] Taylor, J., Anderson, N. L., Anderson, N. G., *Electrophoresis* 1983, *4,* 338–346.

[492] Harris, H., *Proc. R. Soc. Lond. (B) Biol. Sci.* 1966, *164,* 298–310.

[493] Johnson, F. M, Kanapi, C., Richardson, R. H. Wheeler, M. R., Stone, W. S., *Proc. Natl. Acad. Sci. USA* 1966, *56,* 119–125.

[494] Lewontin, R. C., Hubby, J. L., *Genetics* 1966, *54,* 595–609.

[495] Powell, J., *Evol. Biol.* 1975, *8,* 79–120.

[496] Harris, H., *The Principles of Human Biochemical Genetics, 3rd Edition,* Elsevier, Amsterdam 1980.

[497] Brown, A. J. L, Langley, C. H., *Proc. Natl. Acad. Sci. USA* 1979, *76,* 2381–2384.

[498] Aquadro, C. F., Avise, J. C., *Proc. Natl. Acad. Sci. USA* 1981, *78,* 3784–3788.

[499] Racine, R. R., Langley, C. H., *Nature* 1980, *283,* 855–857.

[500] McConkey, E. H., Taylor, B. J., Phan, D., *Proc. Natl. Acad. Sci. USA* 1979, *76,* 6500–6504.

[501] Smith, S. C., Racine, R. R., Langley, C. H., *Genetics* 1980, *96,* 967–974.

[502] Comings, D., *Clin. Chem.* 1982, *28,* 798–804.

[503] Rosenblum, B. B., Neel, J. V., Meisler, M. H., *Am. J. Hum. Genet.* 1982, *34,* 209–215.

[504] Rosenblum, B. B., Neel, J. V., Hanash, S. M., Joseph, J. L., Yew, N., *Am. J. Hum. Genet.* 1984, *36,* 601–612.

[505] Hanash, S. M., Neel, J. V., Baier, L. J., Rosenblum, B. B., Niezgoda, W., Markel, D., *Am. J. Hum. Genet.* 1986, *38,* 352–360.

[506] Hanash, S. M., Baier, L. J., Welch, D., Kuick, R., Galteau, M. M., *Am. J. Hum. Genet.* 1986, *39,* 317–328.

[507] Hamaguchi, H., Yamada, M., Shibaski, M., Mukai, R., Yabe, T., Kondo, I., *Hum. Genet.* 1982, *62,* 142–147.

[508] Goldman, D., Merril, C. R., Polinsky, R. J., Ebert, M. H., *Clin. Chem.* 1982, *28,* 1021–1025.

[509] Goldman, D., Merril, C. R., *Am. J. Hum. Genet.* 1983, *35,* 827–837.

[510] Damerval, C., de Vienne, D., Zivy, M., Thiellement, H., *Electrophoresis* 1986, *7,* 52–54.

[511] McConkey, E. H., *Proc. Natl. Acad. Sci. USA* 1982, *79*, 3236–3240.
[512] Marshall, T., Williams, K., Vesterberg, O., *Clin. Chem.* 1984, *30*, 2008–2013.
[513] Wiederkehr, F., Büeler, M., Vonderschmitt, D. J., in: Dunn, M. J. (Ed.), *Electrophoresis '86*, VCH, Weinheim 1986, pp. 635–637.
[514] Bagley, E. A., Lanberg-Holm, K., Pandya, B. V., Budzynski, A. Z., *Electrophoresis* 1983, *4*, 238–241.
[515] Gomo, Z. A. R., Clark, P. M. S, Kricka, L. J., Woods, K., Buckley, B., Whitehead, T. P., *Electrophoresis* 1983, *4*, 298–302.
[516] Marshall, T., Vesterberg, O., Williams, K. M., *Electrophoresis* 1984, *5*, 122–128.
[517] Marshall, T., Williams, K. M., Vesterberg, O., in: Neuhoff, V. (Ed.), *Electrophoresis '84*, Verlag Chemie, Weinheim 1984, pp. 258–261.
[518] Visvikis, S., Dumon, M. F., Steinmetz, J., Galteau, M. M., Clerc, M., Siest, G., in: Dunn, M. J. (Ed.), *Electrophoresis '86*, VCH, Weinheim 1986, pp. 638–641.
[519] Marshall, T., Williams, K. M., Holmquist, L., Carlson, L. A., Vesterberg, O., *Clin. Chem.* 1985, *31*, 2032–2035.
[520] Marshall, T., Vesterberg, O., *Electrophoresis* 1983, *4*, 363–366.
[521] Marshall, T., Williams, K. M., Vesterberg, O., *Electrophoresis* 1985, *6*, 392–398.
[522] Latner, A. L., Marshall, T., Gambi, M., *Electrophoresis* 1980, *1*, 82–89.
[523] Jellum, E., Thorsrud, A. K., *Clin. Chem.* 1982, *28*, 876–883.
[524] Frearson, N., Taylor, R. D., Perry, S. V., *Brit. Med. J.* 1981, *282*, 2002–2003.
[525] Frearson, N., Taylor, R. D., Perry, S. V., *Clin. Sci.* 1981, *61*, 141–149.
[526] Bauer, H., Nagel, J., Franz, H.-E., in: Dunn, M. J. (Ed.), *Electrophoresis '86*, VCH, Weinheim 1986, pp. 677–679.
[527] Harrington, M., Merril, C. R., *Clin. Chem.* 1984, *30*, 1933–1937.
[528] Harrington, M. G., Merril, C. R., Goldman, D., Xu, X.-H., McFarlin, D., *Electrophoresis* 1984, *5*, 236–245.
[529] Wiederkehr, F., Ogilivie, A., Vonderschmitt, D. J., *Clin. Chem.* 1985, *31*, 1537–1542.
[530] Bergenbraut, S., Gallo, P., Gudmunson, C., Sidén, A., *Protides Biol. Fluids* 1986, *34*, 855–858.
[531] Dermer, G. B., Silverman, L. M., Chapman, J. F., *Clin. Chem.* 1982, *28*, 759–765.
[532] Tsai, Y. C., Harrison, H. H., Lee, C., Daufeldt, J. A., Oliver, L., Grayhack, J. T., *Clin. Chem.* 1984, *30*, 2026–2030.
[533] Kronquist, K. E., Crandall, B. F., Cosico, L. G., in: Hirai, H. (Ed.), *Electrophoresis '83*, de Gruyter, Berlin 1984, pp. 229–236.
[534] Burdett, P., Lizana, J., Eneroth, P., Bremme, K., *Clin. Chem.* 1982, *28*, 935–940.
[535] Giometti, C. S., Anderson, N. G., in: Radola, B. J. (Ed.), *Electrophoresis '79*, de Gruyter, Berlin 1980, pp. 395–404.
[536] Segers, J., Rabaey, M., Van Oye, R., *Electrophoresis* 1984, *5*, 48–53.
[537] Volden, G., Thorsrud, A. K., Bjornsen, I., Jellum E., *J. Invest. Dermatol.* 1980, *75*, 421–424.
[538] Dermer, G. B., Edwards, J. J., *Electrophoresis* 1984, *4*, 212–218.
[539] Goldman, D., Merril, C. R., in: Celis, J. E., Bravo, R. (Eds.), *Two-dimensional Gel Electrophoresis of Proteins*, Academic Press, Orlando 1984, pp. 241–258.
[540] Leavitt, J., Kakunaga, T. J., *J. Biol. Chem.* 1980, *255*, 1650–1661.
[541] Leavitt, J., Goldman, D., Merril, C., Kakunaga, T., *Clin. Chem.* 1982, *28*, 850–860.
[542] Patel, K., Guest, J., Dunn, M. J., in: Dunn, M. J. (Ed.), *Electrophoresis '86*, VCH, Weinheim 1986, pp. 652–657.
[543] Guest, J., Patel, K., Dunn, M. J., in: Dunn, M. J. (Ed.), *Electrophoresis '86*, VCH, Weinheim 1986, pp. 658–661.
[544] Hughes, A. E., Graham, C. A., McLean, W. H. I., Burn, J., Nevin, N. C., in: Dunn, M. J. (Ed.), *Electrophoresis '86*, VCH, Weinheim 1986, pp. 723–726.

[545] Murnane, J. P., Painter, R. B., *Biochemistry* 1983, *22*, 1217–1222.

[546] Merril, C. R., Goldman, D., Ebert, M., *Proc. Natl. Acad. Sci. USA* 1981, *78*, 6471–6475.

[547] Willers, I., Singh, S., Goedde, H. W., Klose, J., *Clin. Genet.* 1981, *20*, 217–221.

[548] Weil, J., Epstein, C., *Am. J. Hum. Genet.* 1979, *7*, 478–488.

[549] Van Keuren, M. L., Goldman, D., Merril, C. R., in: Allen, R. C., Arnaud, P. (Eds.), *Electrophoresis '81*, de Gruyter, Berlin 1981, pp. 355–369.

[550] Van Keuren, M. L., Goldman, D., Merril, C., *Ann. N.Y. Acad. Sci.* 1982, *396*, 55–67.

[551] Klose, J., Zeindl, E., Sperling, K., *Clin. Chem.* 1982, *28*, 987–992.

[552] Rosenberg, R. N., Thomas, L., Baskin, F., Kirkpatrick, J., Bay, C., Nyhan, W. L., *Neurology* 1979, *29*, 917–926.

[553] Kirkpatrick, C., Lecocq, R., Lamy, F., Defleur, V., Dedobeleer, G., Baran, D., Rodesch, F., Dumont, J. E., *Pediat. Res.* 1985, *19*, 1341–1345.

[554] Anderson, N. L., Giometti, C. S., Gemmell, M. A., Nance, S. L., Anderson, N. G., *Clin. Chem.* 1982, *28*, 1084–1092.

[555] Miller, M. J., Xuong, N. H., Geiduschek, E. P., *Proc. Natl. Acad. Sci. USA* 1979, *76*, 5222–5225.

[556] Willard, K. E., Thorsrud, A. K., Munthe, E., Jellum, E., *Clin. Chem.* 1982, *28*, 1067–1073.

[557] Unteregger, G., Zang, K. D., Issinger, O.-G., *Electrophoresis* 1983, *4*, 303–311.

[558] Stastny, J., Prasad, R., Fosslien, E., *Clin. Chem.* 1984, *30*, 1914–1918.

[559] Motte, P., Bidart, J. M., Delarue, J. C., Comoy, E., Moingeon, P., Bohuon, C., *Clin. Chem.* 1984, *30*, 1947–1949.

[560] Wirth, P. J., Benjamin, T., Schwartz, D. M., Thorgeirsson, S. S., *Cancer Res.* 1986, *46*, 400–413.

[561] Marshall, T., Latner, A. L., *Electrophoresis* 1984, *4*, 354–358.

[562] Forchhammer, J., Macdonald-Bravo, H., in: Celis, J. E., Bravo, R. (Eds.), *Gene Expression in Normal and Transformed Cells*, Plenum Press, New York 1983, pp. 291–314.

[563] Thorsrud, A. K., Vatn, M. H., Jellum, E., *Clin. Chem.* 1982, *28*, 884–889.

[564] Celis, J. E., Bravo, R., Larsen, P. M., Fey, S. J., Bellatin, J., Celis, A., in: Celis, J. E., Bravo, R. (Eds.), *Two-dimensional Gel Electrophoresis of Proteins,* Academic Press, Orlando 1984, pp. 307–362.

[565] Garrels, J. I., *Devl. Biol.* 1979, *73*, 134–152.

[566] Floros, J., Phelps, D. S., Smith, B. T., *Electrophoresis* 1985, *6*, 238–241.

[567] Anderson, N. L., *Electrophoresis* 1985, *6*, 277–282.

[568] Braun, A., Waldinger, D., Cleve, H., *Electrophoresis* 1985, *6*, 512–516.

[569] Waldinger, D., Braun, A., Cleve, H., *Electrophoresis* 1985, *6*, 605–613.

[570] Phillips, P. G. N., Stonard, M. D., in: Dunn, M. J. (Ed.), *Electrophoresis '86*, VCH, Weinheim 1986, pp. 646–647.

[571] Weber, M. H., Cheong, K.-S., Schott, K.-J., Neuhoff, V., *Electrophoresis* 1986, *7*, 134–141.

[572] Bowen, B., Steinberg, J., Laemmli, U. K., Weintraub, H., *Nucl. Acid Res.* 1980, *8*, 1–20.

[573] Moermans, M., De Raeymaeker, M., Daneels, G., De Mey, J., *Anal. Biochem.* 1986, *153*, 18–22.

[574] Wiederkehr, F., Ogilvie, A., Vonderschmitt, D. J., *Electrophoresis* 1986, *7*, 89–95.

[575] Hochstrasser, D., Augsburger, V., Funk, M., Appel, R., Pellegrini, C., Muller, A. F., *Electrophoresis* 1986, *7*, 505–511.

[576] Guest, J. F., Elder, M. G., White, J. O., *Electrophoresis* 1986, *7*, 512–518.

[577] Astrua-Testori, S., Pernelle, J.-J., Wahrmann, J. P., Righetti, P. G., *Electrophoresis* 1986, *7*, 527–529.

[578] Takahashi, N., Neel, J. V., Nagahata-Shimoichi, Y., Asakawa, J., Tanaka, Y., Satoh, C., *Ann. Hum. Genet.* 1986, *50*, 313–325.

[579] Colbert, R. A., Young, D. A., *J. Biol. Chem.* 1986, *261*, 14733–14739.

[580] Colbert, R. A., Young, D. A., *Proc. Natl. Acad. Sci. USA* 1986, *83*, 72–76.

[581] Imada, M., Sueoka, N., *Devl. Biol.* 1980, *79*, 199–207.

[582] Imada, S., Imada, M., *J. Biol. Chem.* 1982, *257*, 9108–9113.

[583] Imada, M., Imada, S., *Biochim. Biophys. Acta* 1986, *885*, 162–169.

[584] Imada, M., Kao, F.-T., Law, M. L., Jones, C., *Som. Cell Molec. Genet.* 1986, *12*, 197–201.

[585] Gianazza, E., Caccia, P., Quaglia, L., Righetti, P. G., Rimpiläinen, M. A., Forsén, R. J., *Electrophoresis* 1986, *7*, 537–543.

[586] Stastny, J. J., Fosslien, E., *Electrophoresis* 1986, *7*, 544–555.

[587] Dunbar, B. D., Bundman, D. S., Dunbar, B. S., *Electrophoresis* 1986, *6*, 39–42.

DETECTION OF PROTEINS SEPARATED BY ELECTROPHORESIS

Carl R. Merril

National Institutes of Health, Bethesda, MD, USA

1   Historical introduction

The physicist Ferdinand Frederic Reuss initiated the development of electrophoretic separation techniques with his observations in 1807 that colloidal particles migrate in electrical fields [1]. The application of electrophoretic methods to the problems of protein and nucleic acid purification would not have been possible without the development of complementary detection methods. The earliest applications of electrophoresis relied on direct observations of objects, including cells, colloidal particles, bacteria, and the naturally colored proteins, such as myoglobin, hemogloin, ferritin, and cytochrome C [2]. However, most protein molecules could not be observed directly with visible light and their electrophoretic properties were studied by observing quartz microspheres with the proteins adsorbed to their surface [3 – 5]. Detection of non-colored proteins by the specific absorption of ultraviolet light was first demonstrated by Tiselius in the 1930s [6]. Protein detection by ultraviolet absorption requires a special light source, filters, and optical components that are transparent to ultraviolet light. Tiselius also utilized schlieren, or shadows, created by boundaries between regions with different refractive indices due to the varrying concentrations of proteins in electrophoretic sytems as a detection method [6]. This system also required complex optical systems.

Introduction of organic stains for detection of proteins eliminated many of the complications inherent in the ultraviolet and schlieren detection systems. The organic stains also provided increased sensitivities. The use of moist filter paper as an electrophoretic support medium or carrier for zonal electrophoretic separation stimulated the adaptation of a number of histochemical stains for the detection of uncolored proteins [7]. These stains were usually employed after the proteins were "fixed" or made immobile, to decrease proteins loss in the staining solutions. Early organic protein stains included Bromophenol Blue [8] and Amido Black [9]. Lipoproteins were preferentially stained by Oil Red O [10], while glycoproteins were detected by a red color that was produced upon their oxidation with periodic acid and subsequent reaction with fuchsin sulfurous acid (Schiff's reagent) [11]. Coomassie Brilliant Blue stains, with their capability of detecting as little as half a microgram of protein, are the most sensitive of these organic protein stains [12]. This increased sensitivity of the Commassie Brilliant Blue stains was originally used to detect proteins separated on cellulose acetate. It also complemented the increased protein resolution of acrylamide gel electrophoretic methods. Most of the early organic stains were employed to detect proteins after their electrophoretic separation (post-electrophoretic stains). Fluorescent protein stains, which were introduced by Talbot and Yaphantis in 1971 [13], can now detect as little as one nanogram of protein [14]. However, these fluorescent stains usually require reaction conditions that are best provided prior to electrophoresis (pre-electrophoretic stains). Moreover, the formation of covalent bonds with the protein molecules generally alters the charge of the proteins [15]. This charge alteration is not of consequence for electrophoretic techniques that separate proteins on the basis of molecular weight, such as sodium dodecyl sulfate (SDS) electrophoresis, but it can alter separations by isoelectricfocusing [15].

Radioactively labeled proteins may be visualized without staining by autoradiographic methods, which were first introduced by Becquerel and Curie in their discovery of the phenomenon of radioactivity [16], or by fluorographic techniques, which were introduced by Wilson to study tritium-labeled metabolites involved in photosynthesis [17]. Proteins radioactively labeled to a high specific activity can be detected with sensitivities equal to, and often better than, those obtained by most stains. However, the use of radioactively labeled proteins is limited, as it is difficult to achieve high specific activities in animal studies and unethical to utilize such high specific activities in research involving humans.

Silver staining was introduced as a general protein detection method for proteins separated by polyacrylamide gel electrophoresis in 1979 [18, 19]. It was demonstrated to provide more than a 100-fold increase in sensitivity over that attained by the most commonly used organic protein stain, Coomassie Brilliant Blue [18, 19]. Histological silver stains had been employed prior to their use as general proteins stains for the detection of specific proteins separated electrophoretically. Frederick in 1963 [20] first used a histological silver stain, a modified Gomori method, to study phosphorylases separated on polyacrylamide gels [21–22], and Kerenyi and Gallyas adapted another histological silver stain in 1972 to study cerebrospinal fluid proteins electrophoresed in agarose. This latter stain did not achieve widespread acceptance, perhaps because it did not work well in polyacrylamide. Hubbell et al.. in 1979 [23] utilized a histological silver stain, developed to visualize nucleoli, to detect nucleolar proteins separated on polyacrylamide.

The adaptation of silver stains for protein detection and the recognition of the large quantitative gain in sensitivity that silver staining offers over the commonly used organic stain [18, 19] have stimulated the recent widespread use of silver staining for the detection of proteins separated by polyacrylamide gel electrophoresis. The first silver stains used for the detection of proteins were adapted directly from histological stains and they were often tedious, requiring hours of manipulation and numerous solutions. In the seven years since the introduction of silver staining as a general method for the detection of proteins in polyacrylamide gel electrophoresis numerous, often simplified, staining protocols have been developed [24]. These silver stain protocols can be divided into three categories; first, the diamine or ammoniacal silver stains, second, the non-diamine stains, including stains based on photographic chemistry, and third, the stains based on the photodevelopment or photoreduction of silver ions to form a metallic silver image. Some of the newer silver stain protocols can be performed in less than fifteen minutes and many of them may be employed in quantitative analyses.

2   Post-electrophoretic organic protein stains

2.1   Coomassie Brilliant Blue stains

Coomassie Brilliant Blue stains are the most commonly used organic stains for post-electrophoretic detection of proteins separated on polyacrylamide gels. They were originally developed as acid wool dyes and were named "Coomassie dyes" to commemorate the 1896 British occupation of the Ashanti capital, Kumasi or "Coomassie", now in Ghana. In a collaborative effort to find a highly sensitive protein stain that could be used in quantitative studies, a microbiologist of the Australian National University, Fazekas de St. Groth, and textile chemists at the Universtity of New South Wales School of Textile Technology (Australia) tested numerous dyes and dyeing techniques [12]. Their studies demonstrated the intense protein staining abilities of the triphenylmethane Coomassie stains.

Coomassie Brilliant Blue R-250 (the letter "R" stands for a reddish hue while the number "250" is a dey strength indicator) was the first of the triphenylmethane stains to be introduced. It can detect as little as 0.5 µg/cm of protein and gives a linear response up to 20 µg/cm^2. However, it should be noted that the relationship between stain density and protein concentrations varied for each of the four proteins tested [12]. Fazekas de St. Groth *et al..* originally introduced this stain to detect proteins on cellulose acetate, agar or starch gels [12]. Meyer and Lamberts [25] in 1965 adapted the Coomassie Brilliant Blue R-250 stain for polyacrylamide gels [25]. They used electrophoresis to remove excess stain, but a number of proteins displayed some mobility during this destaining [25–27]. Non-electrophoretic methods of destaining have largely eliminated this problem and Chrambach *et al.*. have used R-250 without destaining [29]. Other Coomassie stains, such as Coomassie Brilliant Blue G-250 ("G" indicates that this stain has a greenish hue), have augmented the stain introduced by Fazekas de St. Groth *et al.*. [12]. Coomassie Brilliant Blue G-250 has a diminished solubility in 12% TCA. permitting its use as a colloidal dispersion. Such a colloidally dispersed dye does not penetrate gels, permitting rapid staining of proteins without an undesired background [29]. Another derived Coomassie stain, Coomassie Violet R-150, has gained some favor by virtue of its ability to rapidly stain proteins on polyacrylamide gels while not staining carrier ampholytes, and its ease of destaining [30–31]. Although Coomassie Violet R-150 is no longer produced by Imperial Chemical Industries, Ltd., a very similar dye, Serva Violet 49, is available. Serva Violet 49 differs from Coomassie Violet R-150 by the substitution of a diethylamine group for a dimethylamine group. Imperial Chemical Industries, Ltd. no longer produces Coomassie Brilliant Blue R-250 or G-250, but still holds the trademark "Coomassie", so that manufacturers who are currently producing Coomassie type dyes have had to introduce their own trademarked names [32].

2.2   Mechanism of Coomassie Brilliant Blue staining

Coomassie Brilliant Blue staining requires an acidic medium for electrostatic attraction to be exerted between the dye molecules and the amino groups of the proteins. This ionic attraction, together with van der Waals' forces, binds the dye-protein complex together. The binding, however, is fully reversible by dilution under appropriate conditions [12]. The relatively high staining intensity of Coomassie Blue stains, compared to other organic dyes, is apparently due to secondary bonds formed between dye molecules. Additional dye may be bound by dye-dye interactions to dye molecules that are ionically bound to, or are in hydrophobic association with, protein molecules [33]. Recent studies concerning the mechanisms of Coomassie dye staining of proteins have indicated the importance of the basic amino acids. Righetti and Chillemi [34] noted that polypeptides rich in lysine and arginine were aggregated by Coomassie G-250 dye molecules, suggesting that the dye interacts with the basic groups in the polypeptides [34]. Studies of proteins with known sequences, by Tal *et al.*. [35], have confirmed these observations and demonstrated a significant correlation between the intensity of Coomassie Brilliant Blue staining and the number of lysine, histidine, and arginine residues in the protein.

2.3   Metachromatic effects

Secondary dye-binding or dye-dye interactions may play a fundamental role in the metachromatic effects that have been observed with some polypeptides that are stained with Coomassie Brilliant Blue R-250 [36–37]. Some peripheral nerve proteins stain with both red and blue bands with Coomassie Brilliant Blue R-250 after separation by SDS-polyacrylamide electrophoresis. Calf skin collagen and histone-1 protein display similar red-staining bands, as do most other collagen samples [37]. Metachromatic shifts are often observed when dye molecules are stacked together [38]. Such dye stacking or close aggregation may affect the dye's electron resonance structure, resulting in an altered response to excitation by light. These metachromatic shifts are affected by a number of variables. Bands containing more than 5 µg of a protein, which normally produces a red hue, have been shown initially to stain blue in the center of the band. Only with continued destaining does the red become apparent. Red-staining proteins such as histone-1 or collagen may be converted to blue bands by placing the gels in solutions containing alcohol, sodium dodecyl sulfate on trichloroacetic acid (TCA) [37]. Metachromasy is also diminished by staining at elevated temperatures [36]. The dependence of metachromatic effects on protein specificity, concentration, temperature, solvents, and the type of spectral shift observed with Coomassie Brilliant Blue, are characteristic of metachromatic mechanism rather than staining artifacts due to dye contaminants.

2.4   Other common post-electrophoretic organic protein stains

Amido Black (Acid Black 1) and Fast Green (Food Green 3) are commonly utilized for protein detection following polyacrylamide gel electrophoresis. However, Coomassie Brilliant Blue R-250 staining exhibits three times the intensity of Fast Green and six times the intensity of Amido Black staining [32]. The staining intensities of these dyes are approximately proportional to their relative molar adsorption coefficients. Wilson [33] estimated that 1 mg of protein will bind approximately 0.17 mg of Amido Black, 0.23 mg of Fast Green, 1.2 mg of Coomassie Brilliant Blue R-250, and 1.4 mg of Coomassie Blue G-250. It is unlikely that this 7 fold variation is due to variations in molecular weight between these dyes since their weights only vary over a 1.4 fold range, between 616.5 for Amido Black and 854.0 for Coomassie Brilliant Blue G-250. Variations in binding must be due to differences in the number of dye molecules bound per protein molecule. The higher staining intensity of Coomassie Brilliant Blue G-250 may be due to this dye's higher efficiency at forming dye-dye interactions or hydrophobic interactions between the dye molecules and the proteins. Secondary binding mechanisms also occur with Amido Black and Fast Green dyes, although perhaps not at levels observed with Coomassie Brilliant Blue R-250, as these dyes display metachromatic effects with certain proteins similar to the metachromasy observed with Coomassie Brilliant Blue R-250. Amido Black produces blue-green bands with certain histones rather than its characteristic blue-black color, while Fast Green produces a difference in the ratio of blue to green hues [39].

3   Pre-electrophoretic organic protein stains

Pre-electrophoretic organic stains usually involve the covalent binding of either a fluorescent or colored residue to the protein prior to electrophoresis. Potential advantages of these stains include: the possibility of performing stoichiometric reactions with proteins without the diffusion limitations imposed by staining within a gel matrix, the feasibility of following the process of electrophoresis visually with "stained" proteins, and the absence of background problems due to dye-trapping or reaction of the dye with the gel. An often cited disadvantage of covalently bound pre-electrophoretic stains is that they usually alter the charge of proteins, unless amphoteric dyes are employed [15]. This objection is not of consequence for sodium dodecyl sulfate electrophoresis, as the protein's mobility depends solely on molecular weight, and the dye molecules are usually too small to produce an appreciable size effect. Furthermore, as long as the stains react with proteins in a stoichiometric manner, shifts in protein pattern should be highly reproducible, permitting construction of valid protein maps and protein identifications.

3.1   Non-fluorescent stains

Remazol Brilliant Blue R, was the first anionic dye used for prestaining proteins [40]. A major disadvantage was its lower limit of sensitivity (3 μg of protein). Bosshard and Datyner [15] introduced anionic dyes with sensitivities comparable to the Coomassie Blue stains, Drimarene Brilliant Blue K-BL and Uniblue A. These dyes are capable of detecting bands containing as little as 0.5 μg of protein. They react primarily with the amino groups of proteins as well as the hydroxyl groups of serine and tyrosine. A similar range and sensitivity has been achieved with a cationic dye that binds to the protein's amino groups, causing less alteration in isolectric focussing patterns than anionic dyes [41].

3.2   Fluorescent stains

Fluorescent stains are currently the most sensitive pre-electrophoretic stains in use. The first fluorescent stain used to visualize proteins in gels was anilinonaphthalene sulfonate, a post-electrophoretic stain which is thought to bind to a protein's hydrophobic sites, to form a fluorescent complex [43]. Its limit of sensitivity is about 20 µg of protein. Pre-electrophoretic fluorescent staining with dansyl chloride was first introduced by Talbot and Yaphantis [13]. This stain reacts with proteins to form fluorescent derivatives in 1−2 min at 100 °C, with a sensitivity limit of 8−10 ng. Reagents that were first designed to increase the detection limits of amino acid analyzers have resulted in a number of highly sensitive fluorescent stains [42]. The first of these, fluorescamine, is a non-fluorescent compound. However, at room temperature and at alkaline pH, it reacts with the primary amines of the basic amino acids within each protein and the N-terminal amino acids to yield a fluorescent derivative. It has proven capable of detecting as little as 6 ng of myoglobin [44−45]. A related compound, 2-methoxy-2,4-diphenyl-3(2H)-furanone (MDPF), has the same speed and simplicity of reaction as fluorescamine, and its protein derivative is 2.5 times as fluorescent-labeled protein. Furthermore it does not fade as rapidly. As little as 1 ng of protein has been detected with MDPF. It also has a linear response from 1−500 ng. As with most other protein stains, a plot of relative fluorescence versus protein concentration revealed a different slope for each of the four proteins studied [14]. Although these fluorescent stains achieve greater sensitivity than other organic stains, they require ultraviolet light for visualization, and direct quantitation requires fairly sophisticated equipment. These problems, coupled with the altered mobility of the proteins during isolectric focusing (a result of the addition of the charged fluorescent group(s) on each protein), has tended to inhibit utilization of these fluorescent stains.

4   Silver stains

Silver nitrate, the main ingredient in silver stains, was first described by the Arabian alchemist, Gâbir Dschâbir ibn Hajjam in the eighth century. The observation that this compound has the ability to blacken when in contact with organic substances, including human skin, is usually credited to Count Albert von Bollstädt in the twelfth century [46]. Although experimentation was performed with silver nitrate between the twelfth and the nineteenth centuries, it was not until the middle of the nineteenth century that this property of silver nitrate to stain organic substances was exploited by modern science. The first modern application of silver nitrate as a stain was Krause's use of it to stain fresh tissues for histological examination in 1844 [47]. By 1873, Golgi, followed by Cajal, were utilizing silver stains to revolutionize the understanding of the anatomy of the central nervous system [48–50]. The turn of this century was also a period of intense development of photographic methods, based on silver compounds which had been discovered to be light sensitive. Cajal [49] adapted many of the then newly developed photochemical methods to produce histological stains.

Silver was introduced as a general stain for proteins separated by polyacrylamide gel electrophoresis in 1979 [18–19]. This silver stain, an adaptation of a histological silver stain, was demonstrated to be 100-fold more sensitive than previous stains; it permitted the detection of as little as 0.1 ng of protein [18–19]. Other histological silver stains adapted for protein detection were limited to the detection of specific proteins, modifying subgroups, or to proteins electrophoresed in agarose. A modified histological Gomori silver stain was used to study phosphorylase [20] in 1963, while another histological silver stain, originally developed to visualize nucleoli, was used in 1979 to detect nucleolar proteins [23]. Kerenyi and Gallyas adapted a histological silver stain in 1972 to visualize cerebrospinal fluid proteins separated on agarose [21–22]. This stain did not achieve widespread acceptance, perhaps because it produced numerous staining artifacts, did not work well in polyacrylamide, or because of a report that it was quantitatively irreproducible [51]. However, recent work by Peats [52] has improved this stain's performance in agarose. In the seven years since the introduction of silver staining as a general method for the detection of proteins separated by polyacrylamide gel electrophoresis, numerous staining protocols have been developed. These protocols van be divided into three basic categories: the diamine or ammoniacal silver stains, the non-diamine chemical development silver stains, and the silver stains that depend on light for the photoreduction of the silver ions to form the metallic image.

4.1 Diamine silver stains

These stains rely on the stabilization of the silver ions by the formation of silver diamine complexes with ammonium hydroxide. Diamine silver stains were first developed for the visualization of nerve fibers [53]. Silver ion concentrations are usually very low in these stains, as most of the silver is bound in diamine complexes [54]. Diamine stains tend to become selectively sensitive for glycoproteins if their concentration of silver ions is decreased. This specificity can be minimized by maintaining a sufficient sodium to ammonium ion ratio in the diamine solution [55]. However, in some applications, an emphasis on the diamine stain's specificity has proven useful, as in the adaptation of a diamine histological silver stain to visualize neurofilament polypeptides in electrophoretic analyses of spinal cord homogenates [56]. In the diamine stains, the ammoniacal silver solution must be acidified, usually with citric acid, for image production to occur. The addition of citric acid lowers the concentration of free ammonium ions, thereby liberating silver ions to a level where their reduction by formaldehyde to metallic silver is possible. The optimal concentration of citric acid also results in a controlled rate of silver ion reduction, preventing a non-selective deposition of silver.

4.2 Non-diamine chemical development silver stains

Most of the non-diamine chemical development silver stains were developed by adapting photographic photochemical protocols [57–61]. These stains rely on the reaction of silver nitrate with protein sites under acidic conditions, followed by the selective reduction of ionic silver by formaldehyde under alkaline conditions. Sodium carbonate and/or hydroxide and other bases are used to maintain an alkaline pH during development. Formic acid, produced by the oxidation of formaldehyde, is buffered by the sodium carbonate [62].

4.3 Photo-development silver stains

Photo-development stains utilize energy from photons of light to reduce ionic to metallic silver. Scheele in 1777 recognized that the blackening of silver chloride crystals by light was due to the formation of metallic silver [62]. This ability of light to reduce ionic to metallic silver was adapted by William Fox Talbot, in 1839, as the basis of a photographic processes that dominated photography from its introduction until 1862, when photo-development was replaced by "chemical development" processes [64]. The use of photo-reduction provides for a rapid, simple, sensitive silver stain method for detecting proteins [65 – 66].

Most chemical development stains require a minimum of two solutions, in addition to the fixing solutions. This requirement for multiple solutions is a result of the use of alkaline solutions for the chemical reduction of silver. The presence of silver ions and an organic reducing agent in an alkaline solution often results in the uncontrolled reduction of silver. However, since light can reduce silver in an acidic solution, a photo-development stain may utilize a fixation solution followed by a single staining solution. Such single-solution photo-development silver stains have two major advantages over chemical-development silver stains. First, pH gradient effects are eliminated. In chemical development, one solution, containing silver ions, diffuses out of the gel, while the solution containing the reducing agent diffuses into the gel. The interactions of these solutions creates complex pH gradients within the gel. A single-solution photo-development stain reduces such diffusion effects, minimizing staining artifacts due to variations in gel thickness. Proteins on ultrathin supporting membranes, such as cellulose nitrate, stain poorly with the "chemical stains" because they retain very little silver nitrate when transferred into alkaline solution for image development. Because the photo-development stain contains the silver ions in the image-developing solution, proteins may be visualized even when bound to thin membranes.

4.4   Combinations of photo-development and chemical-development stains

By combining photo-development and chemical-development methods, a staining method has been developed which can detect proteins and nucleic acids in the nanogram range. It can be performed in less than, 15 min, with minimal background staining [67]. This stain utilizes: a silver halide, to provide a light sensitive detection medium, and to prevent the loss of silver ions from membranes of thin layer plates; photo-reduction, to initiate the formation of silver nucleation centers; and chemical-development, to provide a high degree of sensitivity by depositing additional silver on the silver nucleation centers (formed by the photo-reduction of the silver halide). This stain displays an average detection sensitivity of 1 ng of protein or 10 ng of DNA. The stain's rapidity of action, and its ablility to stain samples spotted on membranes, such as cellulose nitrate, permits the use of the method as a general quantitative protein assay. Futhermore, by spotting and staining proteins of known sequence, the method has yielded information on the specificity of the staining reaction.

The first step in this stain protocol employs copper acetate, a metal salt that is both a good fixative [68] and a silver stain enhancer. The mechanism of copper's stain enhancement, in this and other silver stains, may be similar to its action in the biuret reaction [19], in which a characteristic color shift, from violet to pink, is achieved by titrating peptides in the presence of copper ions. Copper complexes formed with the *N*-peptide atoms of the peptide bonds are primarily responsible for this reaction. There are also a number of secondary sites which may interact with copper. Any elemental copper formed may displace positive silver ions from solution as copper has a greater tendency to donate electrons than silver, as indicated by its position in the electromotive series of the elements. Following the treatment with copper acetate, the membrane is sequentially soaked in a solution containing chloride and citrate ions and then in a solution containing silver nitrate. The membrane is then irradiated with light while it is in the silver nitrate solution. The presence of the resulting silver chloride in the membrane produces a significant increase in light sensitivity over that which can be achieved with silver nitrate alone. Herman Vogel, a 19th century photochemist, suggested that, although silver chloride is more sensitive to the reducing action of light than silver nitrate, it is fixed in position by its insolubility and the potential density of its image would be limited unless the free silver ions supplied by the silver nitrate are present to diffuse into the photo-reduction centers [67]. This increase in sensitivity was further enhanced in this stain by the presence of acetate and citrate ions [66, 69 – 70]. White fluorescent light proved to be the most effective for this photo-reduction. Ultraviolet light produced a denser image, but it also produced an unacceptable background stain. Continued irradiation with white light would provide sufficient photo-reduction to produce an image of the protein pattern on the membrane. However, photo-reduction alone usually results in a dense background stain when applied to thin membranes [66]. By limiting the light irradiation to a total of four minutes, only enough to initiate the formation of a latent image, formation of a visiable image is achieved by chemical reduction. The chemical reduction of ionic to metallic silver was effected by placing the membrane in a solution containing the reducing reagents hydroquinone and formaldehyde. During image formation, ionic silver is reduced to metallic silver, formaldehyde is converted to formic acid [62], and hydroquinone to quinone. Unreacted silver chloride is removed from the membrane, to prevent a grayish cast background, and continued darkening of the membrane as the silver ions in the unreacted silver chloride are photo-reduced by exposure to light. Removal of the silver chloride is accomplished by complexing the silver chloride with sodium thiosulfate to form a series of complex argentothio-sulfate sodium salts, most of which are soluble in water [64]. The argentothiosulfate sodium salts, unreacted reagents, and silver grains formed in solution that may have precipitated onto the surface of the membrane, are washed away with water.

4.5   General silver stain mechanisms

The basic mechanism underlying all protein detection silver stains involves reduction of ionic to metallic silver. Detection of proteins in the gel or membrane requires a difference in the oxidation-reduction potential between the sites occupied by proteins and adjacent sites of the gel or membrane. If a protein site has a higher reducing potential than the surrounding gel or matrix, then the protein will be positively stained. Conversely, if the protein site has a lower reducing potential than the surrounding gel or matrix, the protein will appear to be negatively stained. These relative oxidation-reduction potentials can be altered by the chemistry of the staining procedure. Proteins separated on polyacrylamide gels have been shown to stain negatively if the gel is soaked in the dark in silver nitrate followed by image development in an alkaline reducing solution (such as Kodak D76 photographic developer). By treating the gel with potassium dichromate prior to the silver nitrate incubation, followed by development of the image in an alkaline reducing solution (utilizing formaldehyde as the reducing agent), a positive image is produced [60]. Positive images may also by obtained by substituting potassium ferricyanide [57], potassium permanganate [71], or dithiothreitol [72] for the potassium dichromate in this stain. Dichromate, permanganate and ferricyanide are thought to enhance the formation of a positive image by converting the protein's hydroxyl and sulfhydryl groups to aldehydes and thiosulfates, thereby altering the oxidation-reduction potential of the protein. Although the formation or presence of aldehydes has often been suggested as essential for silver staining in certain histological stains neither aldehyde-creating or aldehyde-blocking reagents appreciably affect silver staining [71]. Dithiothreitol, a reducing agent, also creates a positive image, perhaps by maintaining the proteins in a reduced state. However, other reducing agents, such as beta-mercaptoethanol, do not enhance positive image formation. Alternatively, all of the positive image enhancing compounds may form complexes with the proteins and these complexes may act as nucleation centers for silver reduction [24].

4.6 Reactive groups on proteins which affect silver stains

The combination photo-development, chemical-development silver stain has been utilized to study amino acid homopolymers and individual amino acids to gain information about reactive groups that may be involved in silver staining reactions [67]. The only individual amino acids which stained were cysteine and cystine (Fig. 1). Polymethionine and the hydrophilic basic amino acid polymers: polylysine, polyarginine, polyhistidine, and polyornithine also stained (Fig. 2) [67]. Staining of the basic amino acids in their homopoly-

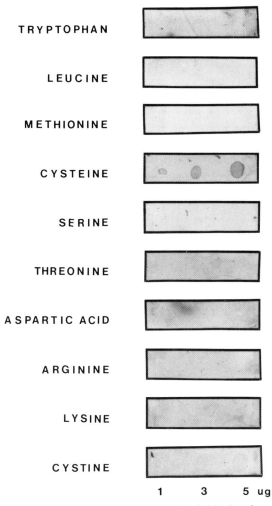

Figure 1. Silver staining response of individual amino acids [67]. Of the 20 natural amino acids tested only cysteine and cystine produced a detectable staining reaction.

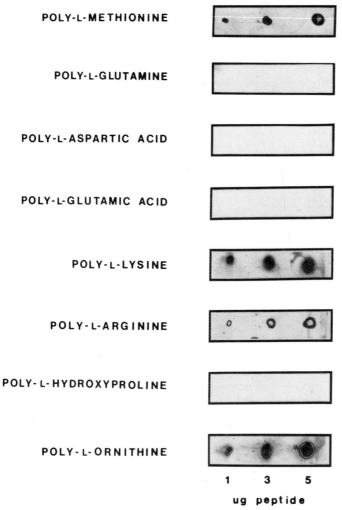

Figure 2. Silver staining response of 8 of the 14 polyamino acids tested with the silver stain protocol on nitrocellulose membranes [67]. Only the basic amino acid homopolymers, including poly-L-histidine (not illustrated) and the homopolymer poly-L-methionine stained with this protocol. These amino acids did not stain when tested in a non-polymeric form. Most of the homopolymers ranged in molecular weight from 11 000 to 44 000 (the exceptions were poly-L-tyrosine with M_r 81 000 and polyglycine with M_r 6000).

meric form, but not as individual amino acids, may be related to the shift of pKs that is normally associated with the incorporation of amino acids into peptides. This shift in pK toward the neutral range results in an increased presence of ionized amino acid side chains closer to the physiological pH. The ability of the reactive group in an amino acid side chain to from complexes with metal ions may be enhanced by such a shift. For example, a shift in the pK of an amino group would reduce the proton competition that a metal ion must overcome for the amino group's *N*-atom electron pair, Staining of the basic amino acid and methionine homopolymers, but not their individual amino acids may also indicate the need for cooperative effects of several intramolecular functional groups to form complexes with the silver or copper ions [73].

Heukeshoven and Dernick [74] also observed silver staining of the basic homopolymers of histidine, arginine, and ornithine, although they did not report staining of the basic amino acid homopolymer polylysine. Furthermore, Nielsen and Brown [75] noted that the basic amino acids; lysine, arginine, and histidine, (in both a free and homopolymeric form) produced colored complexes with silver. Heukeshoven and Dernick [74] reported silver staining of the homopolymers of glycine, serine, proline, and aspartic acid while Nielsen and Brown [75] reported the formation of colored silver complexes with: aspartate, and tyrosine. Staining of these homopolymers was not observed in the study of Merril and Pratt [67]. In this regard prior metal binding studies have failed to demonstrate metal interactions with the side-chain hydroxyl groups of serine, threonine or tyrosine [73]. These discrepancies concerning the non-basic amino acids may be due to differences in the staining procedures employed; the Heukeshoven and Dernick study stained homopolymers on a polyacrylamide gel, while Nielsen and Brown studied formation of silver-amino acid complexes in solution. Both of these studies used formaldehyde in an alkaline sodium carbonate solution for image development, while Merril and Pratt utilized acidic conditions and a combination of light, hydroquinone and formaldehyde for image formation.

The importance of the basic and the sulfur containing amino acids has been corroborated by observations with purified peptides and proteins of known amino acid sequence (Fig. 3) [67]. Leucine enkephalin, which has neither sulfur containing nor basic amino acids does not stain with silver, while neurotensin which also has no sulfur containing amino acids but does have three basic amino acid residues (one lysine and two arginines) does stain. Gastrin produced a weak staining reaction. It lacks basic amino acids but it has one sulfur containing amino acid, methionine. Oxytocin stains fairly vigorously. It also has no basic amino acids but it does have two sulfur containing cysteines. The staining reaction of angiotensin II was rather anomalous. It produced a negative stain rather than a positive silver stain despite its two basic amino acids, arginine and histidine. All the other polypeptides; insulin, somatostatin, alpha-melanocyte stimulating hormone, thyrocalcitonin, aprotinin, vasoactive intestinal peptide, and ACTH, contained both basic

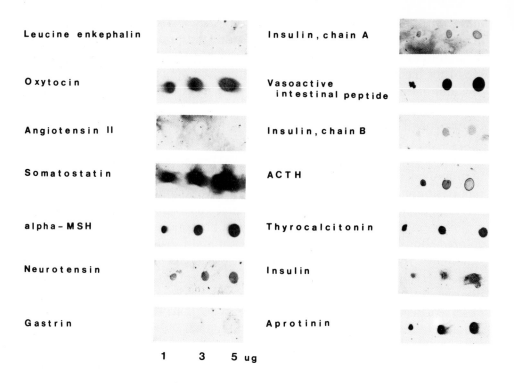

Leucine enkephalin

Oxytocin

Angiotensin II

Somatostatin

alpha – MSH

Neurotensin

Gastrin

Insulin, chain A

Vasoactive
intestinal peptide

Insulin, chain B

ACTH

Thyrocalcitonin

Insulin

Aprotinin

1   3   5 ug

SMALL MOLECULAR WEIGHT PEPTIDES

Figure 3. Silver staining response of 12 polypeptides containing known sequences [67]. The three spots represent 1.3 and 5 μg of each polypeptide. Leucine enkephalin which contains neither sulfur nor basic amino acids does not stain with the silver protocol in this study. Neurotensin contains no sulfur but it has three basic amino acids, one lysine and two arginines and it stains fairly well. Oxytocin also stains, but it contains no basic amino acids. However, it does contain two sulfur containing cysteines. Angiotensin II contains two basic amino acids but produces an anomalous negative staining reaction. All of the other polypeptides illustrated produce a positive silver stain, and they all contain basic amino acids and/or sulfur containing amino acids.

and sulfur containing amino acids and they all produce positive silver staining reactions [67].

The importance of the basic amino acids has been further substantiated by evaluations of the relationship between the amino acid mole percentages of proteins and their ability to stain with silver. The best correlations were achieved when comparisons were made between the slopes of the staining curves of the denatured proteins and the protein's mole percentages of basic amino acids, particularly of histidine and lysine [67]. A similar correlation has been observed by Dion and Pomenti [76]. Dion and Pomenti suggested that this correlation may be due to an interaction between lysine and glutaraldehyde, which was used in their stain protocol. The bound glutaraldehyde could supply aldehyde groups to facilitate the reduction of ionic silver. While this mechanism may play a role in the stain protocol employed by Dion and Pomenti, it is unlikely to be a factor in the Merril and Pratt [67] protocol, since that protocol did not employ glutaraldehyde. Dion and Pomenti also suggested that alkaline conditions may be important for the formation of silver complexes with lysine and histidine. However the Merril and Pratt protocol utilized acidic conditions. No significant correlations have been found between protein amino acid mole percentages and the proteins's ability to stain with silver in a native, or non-denatured state [67]. This lack of a significant correlation with non-denatured proteins is probably due to the inaccessibility of many of the potentially active amino acid side chains in the non-denatured protein structures. The observation of a significant correlation between silver staining intensity and the mole percent of lysine is most likely due to the reactive amino group at the terminus of lysine's side chain. The amino group has been known to have significant metal binding ability due to its strong electron-donor qualities and the ligand-field effect of its nitrogen atoms [72]. However, amino groups involved in peptide bonding and N-terminal amino groups are in themselves insufficient for visualization with silver stain. If they were capable of independently reducing silver ions, all peptides, proteins, and amino acids would stain positively. Amino groups involved in peptide bonding and N-terminal atoms may be of some importance for the intensity of the stain, as these atoms have been observed to form 13 different complexes with copper between pH 1.5 to pH 11.0 [77]. Copper may be reduced under the conditions of some stain protocols and then be displaced by silver. Alternatively, silver may also interact directly, but weakly, with these groups.

The contribution of histidine to silver staining is not surprising, since the imidazole groups in the histidine side-chains are often important for metal-binding in the metalloproteins. The effectiveness of histidine in metal binding is probably due to the fact that imidazole groups are good electron donors [73]. The enthalpy changes in the formation of metal-nitrogen (imidazole) bonds are only slightly less than those found with metal-nitrogen (amino) bonds [78]. The slightly lowered ability of the imidazole group, relative to the amino group, to donate electrons for the formation of metal complexes may be balanced by imidazole's lower pK. The lower imidazole group's pK, in contrast to the higher pK of an amino group, reduces the metal ion's competition with protons for the imidazole's nitrogen atom's electron-pair [73].

The guanidine group in arginine's side chain has proven to be less active than either the amino or the imidazole groups in the side chains of lysine and histidine respectively. Arginine's correlation coefficient was not found to be significant in studies of comparing staining densities to mole percent of arginine. This lack of activity of the guanidine group may have been, in part, responsible for the negative staining reaction of the peptide angiotensin II which contains the two basic amino acids arginine and histidine (one residue of each). However, neurotensin, which contains two arginine residues and one lysine residue, stained well. Cooperative metal binding effects between active groups may play a role in the staining process. In angiotensin II the arginine residue is separated from the histidine by three residues, while in neurotensin the two arginines are adjacent to each other and only one residue separates them from a lysine residue.

Of the nonpolar and uncharged polar amino acids, only the sulfur containing amino acids, methionine, cysteine and cystine, showed any silver staining reactivity with the Merril-Pratt [67] protocol. Cysteine and cystine were the only amino acids to stain as an individual amino acids and they may account for the silver staining properties of the peptide oxytocin. Oxytocin contains no basic amino acids and its only sulfur containing amino acids are two cysteine residues. The ability of cysteinyl side-chains to form complexes with silver ions is well known. At the low pH utilized in this protocol, the predominant species is $Ag(HCys)_2^+$ [73]. It has been suggested that the ability of reducing agents, including: thiosulfates, sulfides, borohydrides, cyanoborothydrides, mercaptoethanol, thioglycolic acid, cysteine, tributylphosphine reducing metal salts (such as $FeCl_2$, $SnCl_2$ and $TiCl_3$ and dithiothreitol, to intensify silver stains may be related to the generation of thiol groups in cysteine residues [78]. However, proteins that contain no cysteine or proteins with an alkylated cysteine(s) were also affected by these reducing agents in some stain protocols [74].

Methionine's ability to participate in the silver staining process has been demonstrated by silver staining of methionine homopolymers. Methionine may also be responsible for the staining of the peptide gastrin (Fig. 3). Gastrin contains no basic amino acids and only one methionine residue. In general the thioether sulfur atoms in the methionine residues are weaker electron donors than the sulfhydryl sulfur atoms in the cysteine residues. The only metal ions that have been observed to bind to the thioether's sulfur atoms are those with electrons in the d^8 and d^{10} configurations (Pd^{++}, Pt^{++}, Ag^+, Cu^+, and Hg^{++}). The affinity of sulfur ligands for metal ions may be explained by the highly polarized state sulfur atoms achieve during interactions with small metal ions containing high charge densities. Sulfur's electron distributions and energies enhance the enthalpies of metal ion bonding (they have high crystal field stabilization energies). There may also be electron resonance bonding in the metal-sulfur bond [73]. Insignificant staining correlations were observed between staining densities and mole percentages of the sulfur containing amino acids methionine and cysteine [67]. This observation may indicate a relatively minor silver staining role in proteins containing large numbers of basic amino acids. However, this poor staining correlation is somewhat of a paradox since poly-methionine stained with a higher silver densitiy than the basic amino acid homopolymers [67]. This paradox may ·be explained by a strong requirement for cooperative effects between sulfur atoms and silver atoms which may be disrupted in heteropolymers.

5   Properties of silver stains

5.1   Color effects

Most proteins stain with monochromatic brown or black colors. However, the ability of silver to produce colors was first noted when certain lipoproteins tended to stain blue while some glycoproteins appeared yellow, brown or red in a study of cerebrospinal fluid proteins [80]. This color effect is most likely an analogue of a photographic phenomenon first described by Herschel in 1840 [60, 81]. Herschel noted in 1840 that if he projected the spectrum of visible light obtained by passing sunlight through a prism onto a silver chloride-impregnated paper, the colors of the spectrum appeared on the paper, particularly a "full and fiery red" at the focal point of the red light [81]. Since these observations by Herschel it has been found that the color produced depends on three variables: the size of the silver particles, the refractive index of the photographic emulsion or electrophoretic gel, and the distribution of the silver particles. In general, studies with photographic emulsions have shown that smaller grains (less than 0.2 µm in diameter) transmit reddish or yellow-red light, while grains above 0.3 µm give bluish colors, and larger grains produce black images [70]. Modifications of the silver staining procedures, such as lowering the concentration of reducing agent in the image development solution, prolonging the development time, adding alkali, or elevating the temperature during staining often enhance color formation. Some silver stain protocols have been developed to produce colors that may aid in identification of certain proteins [75, 82–83]. Production of color with silver stains depends on many variables. Amino acid side groups play a major role in color formation [74]. Furthermore, variations in protein concentration and conditions of image development may also produce color shifts. Color-enhanced silver stains tend to become saturated at low protein levels and often produce negatively stained bands or spots. These factors tend to make quantitative analysis with silver stain protocols that enhance color effects more difficult.

5.2   Protein specific silver stains

Silver stains can demonstrate considerable specificity. Hubbell *et al.* [23] stained nucleolar proteins with a histological stain, while Gambetti *et al.* [56] adapted a silver stain specific for neurofilament polypeptides [56]. Many silver stain protocols detect not only proteins but also DNA [84–86], lipopolysaccharides [87], and polysaccharides [88]. In a study of erythrocyte membrane proteins, sialoglycoproteins and lipids stained yellow with a silver stain protocol, while other membrane proteins counterstained with Coomassie Brilliant Blue [89]. All silver stains do not detect proteins such as calmodulin or troponin C. However, pretreatment with gluteraldehyde often permits positive silver staining of these proteins [90]. Histones may also fail to stain with silver. Fixation with formaldehyde coupled with simultaneous prestaining with Coomassie Brilliant Blue partly alleviates this problem. However, even with this fixation procedure, sensitivity for histones is decreased 10-fold compared with detection of neutral proteins [91]. Another example of differential sensitivity was demonstrated in a study utilizing four different silver stain protocols to stain salivary proteins. Different protein bands were visualized with each of the stains [92].

5.3   Quenching of autoradiography by silver stains

Quenching of ^{14}C-labeled proteins is minimal with most of non-diamine silver stains and even the most intense diamine stained, labeled proteins can be detected by autoradiography with only a 50% decrease in image density. This loss of autoradiographic sensitivity can generally be compensated for by longer film exposures. However, detection of ^{3}H-labeled proteins is severely quenched by all silver stains. Destaining of the silver stained gel with photographic reducing agents can often permit detection of as much as half of the fluorographic density of ^{3}H-labeled proteins, providing that the initial staining was performed with a non-diamine silver stain. Many diamine stains continue to quench, even after treatment with photographic reducing agents, so that fluorographic detection of ^{3}H-labeled proteins is not feasible. This impediment to ³H-detection with diamine stains is likely to be due to a greater amount of residual silver deposited in the gels by the diamine stains, which block the weak-beta emissions from ³H. Residual silver has been demonstrated in gels that have been "cleared" by photographic reducing agents, by the reappearance of a faint silver image of the proteins, in "cleared" gels which are dried with heat. Silver has also been demonstrated in these "cleared" gels by electron beam analysis [93].

5.4   Sensitivity

Silver stains offer the most sensitive non-radioactive method for detecting proteins separated by gel electrophoresis. They are 100-fold more sensitive than the Coomassie stains for most proteins [18 – 19]. Chemical-development silver stains are, in general, more sensitive than photo-development silver stains. This loss in sensitivity may be compensated for by the ability of photo-development stain to produce an image within 10 to 15 min after gel electrophoresis [66]. Attaining high sensitivities with silver stains requires care in selecting reagents; small traces of contaminants may cause a loss of sensitivity and result in staining artifacts. Artifactual bands with molecular weights ranging from 50 000 – 68 000 have commonly been observed in silver stained gels. Evidence has been presented indicating that these contaminating bands are due to keratin skin proteins [94]. Water used to make solutions should have a conductivity of less than 1 mho/cm.

6   Quantitation with protein stains

6.1   Quantitation using organic stains

Fazekas de St. Groth *et al.* [12] demonstrated an accuracy of plus or minus 10% in measuring the concentration of a protein in the range of 0.5 – 20 µg/cm² using Coomassie Brilliant Blue R-250 [12]. He noted that, although individual proteins displayed linear relationships between absorbance and concentration, the slopes differ for each protein. This variation in Coomassie Brilliant Blue staining now appears to be related to the mole percent of the basic amino acids in the protein [35]. Therefore, a standard curve must be produced for each protein assayed and quantitative comparisons limited to equivalent protein spots on two-dimensional or equivalent protein bands on one-dimensional electrophoretograms. This is especially frue for metachromatically staining proteins, which often display an additional complication, in that their bands fade more rapidly than the non-metachromatically staining proteins. In one study with Amido Black, certain metachromatic histone bands faded by 30−50%, while other protein bands in the same gel faded by only 5−15% [38]. This fading reflected a disproportionate loss of stain, rather than a loss of histone protein, since the bands could be restained. In the case of smaller proteins, such as insulin, decreases in band densities have been demonstrated to be due to the loss of protein during staining [12]. Another problem in utilizing post-electrophoretic organic stains occurs because diffusion of the dye into the gel is slow. This results in "ring-dyeing" if staining is terminated prematurely [15]. In ring-dyeing, the stain concentration is less in the center of a band or spot than at the edge, due to the insufficient diffusion of dye molecules. Regional nonstoichiometric processes, as occur in ring-dyeing, require careful control of staining parameters to assure that they are not present in protein bands or spots that are to be quantitatively analyzed.

6.2   Quantitation using silver stains

A reproducible relationship between silver stain density and protein concentration has been found with most silver stain protocols. The linear portion of this relationship extended over a 40-fold range in concentration, beginning at $0.02 \, \text{ng/mm}^2$ for most proteins [19, 59−60, 65]. Protein concentrations greater than $2 \, \text{ng/mm}^2$ generally cause saturation of silver images, resulting in non-linearity above that concentration. Saturation can usually be recognized by bands or spots with centers which are less intensely stained than the regions near the edges. This effect is similar to the ring-dyeing noted with some of the organic stains. An often quoted report by Poehling and Neuhoff [95] states that "silver does not stoichiometrically stain proteins, unlike Coomassie Blue". However, their own silver-stain data actually are linear over a 30-fold range in protein concentration, while their Coomassie Brilliant Blue data are only linear over a 20-fold range [24, 59]. Employment of curve-fitting techniques, as described by Coakley and James [96], for the analysis of curvilinear relationships found in the Folin-Lowry [97] method of protein estimation may be utilized for quantitative analysis of silver stain curves. With careful measurement of total stain densities, estimates of relative protein concentrations have been made over a 220-fold concentration range with six purified proteins [66]. Plots of silver stain densities *versus* protein concentrations produced different staining curves for each protein studied [18–19, 59–60, 67]. Protein specific staining curves have also been observed with the organic stains, including Coomassie Brilliant Blue [12, 35], as noted above, and with most protein assays such as the commonly used Lowry protein assay [97]. The observation that each protein produces a unique density *versus* concentration curve in these studies, illustrates a dependence on specific reactive groups contained in each protein. Further-more, the occurence of protein-specific curves argues against a stain mechanism that depends on some fundamental subunit common to all pro-teins, for example the peptide bond, or a unique element in each protein, such as the terminal amino acid. A stain that depended on a subunit, such as the peptide bond, would result in similar staining curves for all proteins when the density of staining for each of the protein bands or spots was plot-ted against the mass of protein contained in each of the bands or spots. Similarly, a stain that was based on a reaction with a unique element in each protein, for example the terminal amino group, would produce similar plots for each protein when the stain's densities were plotted against the number of molecules contained in each band or spot. It is possible that these protein-specific curves may be utilized to differentiate proteins and to provide in-sights concerning the reactive groups responsible for the staining reactions. The importance of the basic amino acids, particularly lysine and histidine as discussed in Section 4.6 illustrates the use of these protein specific staining curves. It indicates the need for a careful choice of a "standard protein(s)" if a stain is used quantitatively to estimate protein concentrations. A protein containing an abnormally large number of stain reactive groups would pro-duce a curve which would tend to underestimate the concentration of pro-teins containing normal numbers of reactive groups. A similar correlation be-tween the intensity of Coomassie Brilliant Blue staining and the number of basic amino acids in proteins [34–35] caused Tal *et al.* [35] to suggest the use of egg white lysozyme rather than the more commonly used bovine serum albumin as a protein standard. This suggestion is based on their observation that the basic amino acid content of proteins ranges between 10–17 mole percent, with a modal content of 13 mole percent [35]. Egg white lysozyme has a basic amino acid mole percent of 13.2 while bovine serum albumin has a basic amino acid content of 16.5 mole percent. For similar reasons, egg white lysozyme may also prove to be an optimal standard for quantitative silver stain applications.

6.3   Quantitative inter-gel protein comparisons

The occurence of protein specific staining curves with most staining pro-tocols, and with detection of radiolabeled proteins by autoradiography and fluorography (for proteins that were labeled with specific amino acids containing radioisotopes), requires that quantitative inter-gel comparative studies limit comparisons to homologous protein bands or spots on each gel. For example, the actin spot on one gel can be compared with an actin spot on another gel, but not with a transferrin spot. Furthermore, gels to be compared must have been run under similar conditions (percentage acrylamide, stacking gel specifications, etc.), as migration distance affects band or spot compression which inturn may influence the dyeing reactions [98]. Quantitative inter-gel comparisons require the presence of reference proteins for the normalization of spot or band staining densities. One scheme for normalization utilizes "operationally constitutive proteins", a subset of proteins contained in each gel that have constant intra-gel density ratios to each other in all of the gels in a study. The sum of the densities of the "operationally constitutive proteins" in an arbitrarily designated "standard gel" are compared with the sums of the densities of the constitutive proteins in all other gels, and a specific normalization factor is determined for each gel. These gel specific normalization factors are then utilized to correct the densities of all the proteins on each of the gels to those of the standard gel. This scheme corrects for variations in staining, in image digitization, and initial protein loading; a variation of initial protein loading of up to 10-fold may be tolerated [59, 65].

7   Conclusions

The introduction and development of electrophoretic techniques has produced ever more powerful means of resolving proteins from complex mixtures. Development of these separation techniques has been paralleled by the development of protein detection methods with ever-increasing sensitivities. Techniques have progressed from direct observation of protein-coated microspheres and colored proteins, to the detection of proteins by their absorption of ultraviolet light, the observation of schlieren patterns, and, more recently, by direct staining with organic, fluorescent and, silver stains. During this technical evolution, sensitivity has increased from the milligram to the tenth of a nanogram level. This range of sensitivity coupled with high resolution separation techniques, now permits clinical studies of proteins in body fluids that were not possible even a decade ago. Similar sensitivities can be achieved with proteins labeled to high specific activities with radioactive tracers. However, radioactive labeling is often not possible in animal and human studies for economic and, in the latter case, ethical considerations.

Many of the protein staining techniques may be employed quantitatively, provided that their methodological limitations are respected. Most protein stains and autoradiographic methods exhibit protein-specific quantitative responses. Optical density/concentration relationships are usually linear over a 30- to 40-fold range in concentration and quantitation may be extended beyond this range by the use of curve fitting techniques. Protein-specific staining slopes are indicative of a dependence of these staining methods on the content of specific groups within each protein. These protein-specific staining slopes may be utilized to differentiate proteins, and emphasize the need to limit quantitative comparisons to homologous proteins. So long as inter-gel studies are confined to comparisons of homologous proteins and observations are made within the linear range of the detection procedures, valid quantitative results may be obtained.

Parts of this manuscript were adapted from the Proceedings of the 1986 Meeting of the Americas' Branch of the Electrophoresis Society.

8   References

[1] Gray, G.W., *Sci. Am.* 1951, *185*, 45−49.
[2] Davis, B.D., Cohn, E.J., *Ann. N.Y. Acad. Sci.* 1939, *39*, 209−212.
[3] Porret, R., *Annals of Philosophy,* 1816, July, 78−83.
[4] Abramson, H.A., *Electrokinetic Phenomena and Their Applications to Biology and Medicine.* The Chemical Catalog Co. Inc., New York 1934, pp. 17−104.
[5] Picton, H., Linder, S.E., *J. Chem. Soc.* 1892, *61*, 148−172.
[6] Tiselius, A., *Trans. Faraday Soc.* 1937, *33*, 524−531.
[7] Koenig, P., *Act. E. Tab. Terceiro Congr. Sud-Americano Chim; Rio de Janeira e Sao Paulo* 1937, *2*, 334−337.
[8] Durrum, E.L., *J. Am. Chem. Soc.* 1950, *72*, 2943−2948.
[9] Grassmann, W., Hannig, K., *Hoppe-Seylev's Z. Physiol. Chem.* 1952, *290*, 1−27.
[10] Durrum, E.L., Paul, M.H., Smith, E.R.B., *Science* 1952, *116*, 428−430.
[11] Koiw, E., Gronwell, A., *Scand. J. Clin. Lab. Invest.* 1952, *4*, 244−246.
[12] Fazekas de St. Groth, S., Webster, R.G., Datyner, A., *Biochim. Biophys. Acta* 1963, *71*, 377−391.
[13] Talbot, D.N., Yaphantis, D.A., *Anal. Biochem.* 1971, *44*, 246−253.
[14] Barger, B.O., White, F.C., Pace, J.L., Kemper, D.L., Ragland, W.L., *Anal. Biochem.* 1976, *70*, 327−335.
[15] Bosshard, H.F., Datyner, A., *Anal. Biochem.* 1977, *82*, 327−333.
[16] Becquerel, A.H., *Comp. Rend. Acad. Sci. (Paris)* 1896, *122*, 420−421.
[17] Wilson, A.T., *Nature* 1958, *182*, 524.
[18] Merril, C.R., Switzer, R.C., Van Keuren, M.L., *Proc. Natl. Acad. Sci. USA* 1979, *76*, 4335−4339.

[19] Switzer, R.C., Merril, C.R., Shifrin, S., *Anal. Biochem.* 1979, *98*, 231–237.
[20] Frederick, J.F., *Phytochemistry* 1963, *2*, 413–415.
[21] Kerenyi, L., Gallyas, F., *Clin, Chem. Acta* 1972, *38*, 465–467.
[22] Kerenyi, L., Gallyas, F., *Clin. Chem. Acta* 1973, *47*, 425–436.
[23] Hubbell, H.R., Rothblum, L.I., Hsu, T.C., *Cell. Biol. Int. Rep.* 1979, *3*, 615–622.
[24] Dunn, M.J., Burghes, A.H.M., *Electrophoresis* 1983, *4*, 173–189.
[25] Meyer, T.S., Lamberts, B.L., *Biochim. Biophys. Acta.* 1965, *107*, 144–145.
[26] Marshall, W.E., Porath, J., *J. Biol. Chem.* 1965, *240*, 209–217.
[27] Polter, C., *Z. Naturforsch* 1967, *22 b*, 340–347.
[28] Chrambach, A., Reisfeld, R.A., Wychkoff, M., Zaccari, J., *Anal. Biochem.* 1967, *20*, 150–154.
[29] Diezel, W., Kopperschläger, G., Hofmann, E., *Anal. Biochem.* 1972, *48*, 617–620.
[30] Frater, R., *J. Chromatogr.* 1970, *50*, 469–474.
[31] Radola, B.J., *Electrophoresis* 1980, *1*, 43–56.
[32] Wilson, C.M., *Methods Enzymol.* 1983, *91*, 236–247.
[33] Wilson, C.M., *Anal. Biochem.* 1979, *96*, 236–278.
[34] Righetti, P.G., Chillemi, F., *J. Chromatogr.* 1978, *157*, 243–251.
[35] Tal, M., Silberstein, A., Nusser, E., *J. Biol. Chem.* 1985, *260*, 9976–9980.
[36] Miko, S., Schlaepfer, W.W., *Anal. Biochem.* 1978, *88*, 566–572.
[37] Duhamel, R.C., Meezan, E., Brendel, K., *Biochim. Biophys. Acta* 1980, *626*, 432–442.
[38] Schubert, M., Hamerman, D., *J. Histochem. Cytochem.* 1956, *4*, 159–189.
[39] McMaster-Kaye, R., Kaye, J.S., *Anal. Biochem.* 1974, *61*, 120–132.
[40] Griffith, I.P., *Anal. Biochem.* 1972, *46*, 402–412.
[41] Datyner, A., Finnimore, E.D., *Anal. Biochem.* 1973, *55*, 479–491.
[42] Hartman, B.K., Udenfriend, S., *Anal. Biochem.* 1969, *30*, 391–394.
[43] Stein, S., Bohlen, P., Stone, J., Dairman, W., Udenfriend, S., *Arch. Biochem. Biophys.* 1973, *155*, 203–212.
[44] Ragland, W.L., Pace, J.L., Kemper, D.L., *Anal. Biochem.* 1974, *59*, 24–33.
[45] Pace, J.L., Kemper, D.L., Ragland, W.L., *Biochem. Biophys. Res. Commun.* 1974, *57*, 482–488.
[46] Eder, J.M., in: Eptean, E., *History of Photography*, Columbia University Press, New York 1945, pp. 22–24.
[47] Krause, C., in: Wagner, R. (Ed.), *Handwörterbuch der Physiologie,* Vieweg and Sohn, Braunschweig, Germany 1844, pp. 108–186.
[48] Golgi, C., *Gazz. Med. Ital. Lombarda* 1873, *33*, 244–246.
[49] Cajal, S.R., *Trab. Lab. Invest. Biol. Univ. Madrid,* 1903, *2*, 129–222.
[50] Gibson, W.C., in: *Creative Minds in Medicine*, Charles C. Thomas Publisher, Springfield, Illinois 1963, pp. 53–70.
[51] Verheecke, P., *J. Neurol.* 1975, *209*, 59–63.
[52] Peats, S., *Biotechniques* 1983, *1*, 154–156.
[53] Bielschowsky, M., *J. Psychol. Neurol.* 1904, *3*, 169–189.
[54] Nauta, W.J.H., Gygax, P.A., *Stain Technol.* 1951, *26*, 5–1.
[55] Allen, R.C., *Electrophoresis* 1980, *1*, 32–37.
[56] Gambetti, P., Autilio-Gambetti, L., Papasozomenos S.C.H., *Science,* 1981, *213*, 1521–1522.
[57] Merril, C.R., Dunau, M.L., Goldman, D., *Anal. Biochem.* 1981, *110*, 201–207.
[58] Merril, C.R., Goldman, D., Sedman, S.A., Ebert, M.H., *Science* 1981, *211*, 1437–1438.
[59] Merril, C.R., Goldman, D., Van Keuren, M.L., *Electrophoresis* 1982, *3*, 17–23.
[60] Merril, C.R., Goldman, D., in: Celis, J.E., Bravo, R., (Eds.), *Two-Dimensional Gel Electrophoresis of Proteins*, Academic Press, New York 1984, pp. 93–109.

[61] Morrisey, J.H., *Anal. Biochem.* 1981, *117,* 307 – 310.

[62] Ehrenfried, G., *Photogr. Sci. Tech.* 1952, *18 B,* 2 – 6.

[63] Eder, J.M., in: Eptean, E., *History of Photography,* Columbia University Press, New York 1932, pp. 96 – 99.

[64] Newhall, B., *Latent Image, the Discovery of Photography,* University of New Mexico Press, Albuquerque, New Mexico 1983, pp. 8 – 17 and 117 – 118.

[65] Merril, C.R., Harrington, M.G., *Clin. Chem.* 1984, *30,* 1938 – 1942.

[66] Merril, C.R., Harrington, M., Alley, V., *Electrophoresis* 1984, *5,* 289 – 297.

[67] Merril, C.R., Pratt, M.E., *Anal. Biochem.* 1986, *117,* 307 – 310.

[68] Sheinin, J.J., Davenport, H.A., *Stain Technol.* 1931, *6,* 131 – 148.

[69] Reilly, J.M., *The Albumin and Salted Paper Book,* Light Impressions Corporation, Rochester, New York 1980, p. 4.

[70] Mees, C.E.K., *The Theory of the Photographic Process,* 1st Edition, MacMillan, New York 1952, p. 305 and pp. 563 – 583.

[71] Ansorge, W., in: Stathakos, D. (Ed.), *Electrophoresis '82,* de Gruyter, Berlin 1983, pp. 235 – 242.

[72] Thompson, S.W., Hunt, R.D., *Selected Histochemical and Histopathological Methods* Thomas, Springfield, Illinois 1966, pp. 798 – 802.

[73] Freeman, H.C., in: Eichhorn, G.L., (Ed.), *Inorganic Biochemistry,* Vol. 1, Elsevier, Amsterdam/New York 1973, pp. 121 – 166.

[74] Heukeshoven, J., Dernick, R., *Electrophoresis,* 1985, *6,* 103 – 112.

[75] Nielsen, B.L., Brown, L.R., *Anal. Biochem.* 1984, *144,* 311 – 315.

[76] Dion, A.S., Pomenti, A.A., *Anal. Biochem.* 1983, *129,* 490 – 496.

[77] Osterberg, R., Sjoberg, B., *J. Biol. Chem.* 1968, *243,* 3038 – 3042.

[78] Meyer, J.L., Bauman, J.E., *J. Am. Chem. Soc.,* 1970, *92,* 4210 – 4215.

[79] Morrissey, J.H., *Anal. Biochem.* 1981, *117,* 307 – 310.

[80] Goldman, D., Merril, C.R., Ebert, M.H., *Clin. Chem.* 1980, *26,* 1317 – 1322.

[81] Herschel, J.F.W., *Phil. Trans. Roy. Soc.,* London, 1840, *131,* 1 – 59.

[82] Sammons, D.W., Adams, L.D., Nishizawa, E.E., *Electrophoresis* 1981, *2,* 135 – 141.

[83] Sammons, D.W., Adams, L.D., Vidmar, T.J., Hatfield, A., Jones, D.H., Chuba, P.J., Crooks, S.W., in: Celis, J.E., Bravo, R., (Eds.) *Two-Dimensional Gel Electrophoresis of Proteins,* Academic Press, New York 1984, pp. 112 – 127.

[84] Somerville, L.L., Wang, K., *Biochem. Biophys. Res. Commun.* 1981, *10,* 53 – 58.

[85] Boulikas, T., Hancock, R.J., *Biochem. Biophys. Methods* 1981, *5,* 219 – 222.

[86] Goldman, D., Merril, C.R., *Electrophoresis* 1982, *3,* 24 – 26.

[87] Tsai, C.M., Frasch, C.E. *Anal. Biochem.* 1982, *119,* 115 – 119.

[88] Dubray, G., Bezard, G. *Anal. Biochem.* 1982, *119,* 325 – 329.

[89] Dzandu, J.K., Deh, M.H., Barratt, D.L., Wise, G.E., *Proc. Natl. Acad. Sci. USA* 1984, *81,* 1733 – 1737.

[90] Schleicher, M., Watterson, D.M., *Anal. Biochem.* 1983, *131,* 312 – 317.

[91] Irie, S., Sezaki, M., *Anal. Biochem.* 1983, *134,* 471 – 478.

[92] Friedman, R.D., *Anal. Biochem.* 1982, *126,* 346 – 349.

[93] Van Keuren, M.L., Goldman, D., Merril, C.R., *Anal. Biochem.* 1981, *116,* 248 – 255.

[94] Ochs, D., *Anal. Biochem.* 1983, *135,* 470 – 474.

[95] Poehling, H.M., Neuhoff, V., *Electrophoresis* 1981, *2,* 141 – 147.

[96] Coakley, W.T., James, C.J., *Anal. Biochem.* 1978, *85,* 90 – 97.

[97] Lowry, O.H., Rosenbrough, N.J., Farr, A.L., Randall, R.J., *J. Biol. Chem.* 1951, *193,* 265 – 275.

[98] Fishbein, W.N., *Anal. Biochem.* 1972, *46,* 388 – 401.

PROTEIN BLOTTING: A TOOL FOR THE ANALYTICAL BIOCHEMIST

Jonathan M. Gershoni

The Weizmann Institute of Science, Rehovot, Israel

Abbreviations: BSA, bovine serum albumin; **NC,** nitrocellulose membrane filters; **PAGE,** polyacrylamide gel electrophoresis; **PBS,** phosphate buffered saline; **PCM,** positively-charged nylon membranes; **SDS,** sodium dodecyl sulfate

1   Introduction

Protein blotting is the process of transferring electrophoretic protein patterns from supporting gels to immobilizing matrices. The latter are then subjected to further analyses. Most commonly, proteins resolved by sodium dodecyl sulfate-polyacrylamide gel electrophoresis (SDS-PAGE) are electroblotted onto nitrocellulose (NC) membrane filters which are then probed with an antibody to reveal the corresponding antigen. Since the appearance of Towbin's article in 1979 [1] it has been quoted well over 5000 times and the subject of "immunoblotting" and blotting in general has been reviewed extensively (see for example [2−9]). Therefore, this article will give special attention to the variety of applications of protein blotting rather than to its technical aspects. As will be demonstrated, this method is far more versatile than simply being a solid phase immunoassay. It can be incorporated as part of biochemical analyses or used to characterize protein/protein interactions. Nonetheless, in the first sections of this text I provide a pragmatic description of the basic technique so that the reader with little first-hand experience should gain sufficient insight to the practical side of this methodology. Moreover, by comparing the routine immunoblot procedure with other protocols, the novelty of each becomes more apparent. For a more extensive in-depth analysis of the technical aspects of protein blotting the reader is referred to Gershoni [9].

2   Typical immunoblot protocol

The following protocol describes a basic immunoblot assay. Although each step and the reagents can be modified, this procedure serves as a good starting point. Following the "methods" section are a series of "comments" which elaborate on various steps as indicated.

2.1   Reagents and software

All the reagents used are of analytical grade, representative companies and catalogue numbers are suggested when considered particularly helpful. Deionized water is usually quite adequate for the preparation of the solutions.

Transfer buffer: 15.6 mM Tris/120 mM glycine, pH 8.3.
This solution is routinely prepared by adding 7.56 g Tris and 36 g glycine to 4 L cold (4 °C) water (a ten-fold concentrated solution is easily achieved).

Phosphate buffered saline (PBS): 10 mM sodium phosphate/150 mM NaCl, pH 7.4. This can be prepared by mixing 200 mM disodium phosphate (84 mL), 200 mM monosodium phosphate (16 mL), and 17.52 g NaCl, with 1.9 L water.

Quench solution: 2% (w/v) bovine serum albumin (BSA; *e.g.* Sigma A-8022 fraction V powder) and 0.05% w/v sodium azide in PBS (see Section 2.3.1).

Immobilizing matrix: NC (see Section 2.3.2).

First probe: *e.g.* rabbit serum containing polyclonal antibody against the antigen in question (see Section 2.3.3).

Second probe: *e.g.* radioiodinated *Staphylococcus aureus* protein A (see Section 2.3.4).

Polyacrylamide gel of choice: see Section 2.3.5.
Protein blot apparatus: see Section 2.3.6.
Compartmentalized plastic box: see Section 2.3.7.

2.2   Methods

All incubations of the blot are performed by rocking or shaking the filter in adequate volumes of solutions so that it is wet well on both surfaces (0.5 mL per cm^2 of filter is usually sufficient).

2.2.1   Preparation of gel for blotting

After electrophoresis, remove one glass plate from the gel. The gel can be blotted as one piece or individual lanes can be transferred separately (see Section 2.3.8). In all cases the stacking gel should be removed as this tends to stick to NC causing background. No further treatment of the gel is necessary; however, some protocols [10, 11] prescribe an equilibration step to remove SDS to allow possible renaturation. The gel should be maintained moist by applying transfer buffer to its surface.

2.2.2   Assembly of the cassette

The empty gel filter cassette should be placed in the electroblot apparatus (Fig. 1). Cold transfer buffer is added so as to just cover the uppermost surface of the cassette. In the mean time a piece of NC is cut to size, slightly

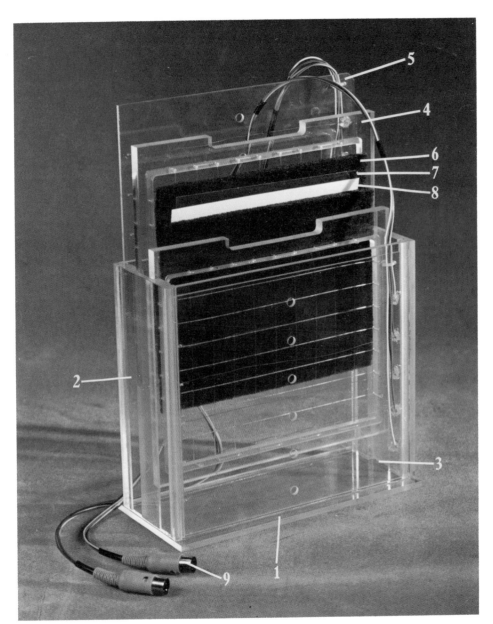

Figure 1. Electroblot apparatus. Photograph of an electroblot apparatus based on the original design developed at the Yale University School of Medicine Medical Instrument Facilities and produced at the Weizmann Institute of Science Workshop. This apparatus is basically a Plexi-glass container (3.5 L capacity) which can accommodate two electrode mounts (5) situated ad-jacent to the chamber walls (3) and a cassette (4) which is held midway between the electrodes. A blue print for this apparatus is provided in Fig. 3. Other parts: (1) chamber bottom; (2) chamber side; (6) "Scotch-brite" hand pad; (7) polyacrylamide gel; (8) NC; (9) 5-pin plug which fits the resistor box described in Fig. 4.

Figure 2. Cassette. The cassette consists of two Plexiglass frames ((4) in Figs. 1 and 3) strung with nylon fish line or surgical silk thread, between which "Scotch-brite" hand pads, the gel and the blotting matrix are secured. The loaded cassette is placed midway between the electrodes in the accommodating groove in the chamber sides ((2) in Figs. 1 and 3).

larger than the area of the gel to be transferred. Excess transfer buffer is poured into a plastic box for wetting the NC. Wetting microporous membrane filters is achieved by floating them on the surface of the buffer as opposed to dunking them (this prevents the entrapment of air in the depth of the matrix). The cassette is now removed from the apparatus and placed onto a tray (Fig. 2). The first mechanical support facing down is covered with one Scotch-brite pad (*e.g.* #7447 general purpose hand pad, Scotch-brite 3M, St. Paul, MN 55144). The moist gel is placed directly onto the pad and wet thoroughly with transfer buffer. The wet NC is applied to the gel. This is most conveniently achieved by curling the filter and making contact with the gel, center to center. Then the rest of the filter is rolled outward, over the surface of the gel making sure that air bubbles are not entrapped. The gel/filter is covered with another pad or more, followed by the second mechanical support so to insure a snug fit of the cassette in the apparatus. This assembly is placed into the blot apparatus with the filter facing towards the appropriate electrode (for SDS-complexed or other anionic proteins, the filter should face the anode).

2.2.3   Electroblotting

The blotting apparatus is connected to its power supply and run for 2 to 3 h at 40–50 V constant voltage or 200–300 mA constant current (see Section 2.3.9).

2.2.4   Quenching

After blotting, the NC is removed from the gel, rinsed briefly with PBS and incubated for 1 to 2 h in quench solution. Room temperature is commonly used yet higher temperatures (*e.g.* 35−45 °C) may improve the quality of the quench.

2.2.5   Probing

The blot is incubated in a dilute solution of primary antibody. When rabbit polyclonal antibodies are used, a reasonable starting dilution is 1:200. Culture media containing monoclonal antibodies are frequently used at 1:10 dilutions and purified IgG fractions may be used at a 10 µg/mL concentration. Obviously these figures are average values and are given only as a first approximation, to be changed based on the actual titre or quality of the reagents used. Probing blots with protein (*i.e.* IgG, lectins, *etc.*) should be performed in quench buffer. One or two hours at room temperature is often sufficient.

2.2.6   Washing

The probe solution is decanted and the blot is rocked for 10 min in an excess of PBS (no quencher is necessary). This is repeated 4 or 5 more times. If the final signal to background ratio is poor, background can be reduced by introducing to the wash regimen a 10 min cycle of 0.1% w/v Tween 20 in PBS (see Section 2.3.10).

2.2.7   Second probing

Most immunoblot assays require the use of a second probe to achieve visualization of the antigen-antibody complex. When rabbit antibodies are employed, use of *S. aureus* protein A is recommended. Radioiodinated reagent should be used at approximately $1-5 \times 10^6$ cpm per blot and 1 h incubation at room temperature should suffice (see Section 2.3.11).

2.2.8   Washing

Repeat washing step as above.

2.2.9 Autoradiography

The washed filters are mounted between two layers of plastic wrap (*e.g.* "Saran Wrap"). The blots are mounted while they are still damp. This allows the eventual re-use of the blot for additional probing (see, for example, [12]). Removal of probes from filters that have been dried is sometimes less efficient. The mounted filter is placed against an X-ray film for 12 h (store at −70 °C when using an intensifying screen). Upon development of the autoradiogram more appropriate exposure time can be determined.

2.3   Comments

2.3.1   Quenchers

The function of a quencher is to prevent nonspecific binding of the probe to the matrix. When using a probe that does not bind to the matrix (*e.g.* heparin [13]), no quench is necessary. However, in most cases some degree of quenching is required. Two approaches have evolved. The first entails blocking unoccupied areas of the matrix with a presumably inert molecule (*e.g.* BSA, hemoglobin, milk, polyvinylpyrrolidone). Table 1 lists studies in which various quenchers have been used. The other approach has been to reduce the mutual "stickiness" of the probe and matrix by including a nonionic

Table 1. Quenchers

Quencher	Concentration % w/v	Buffer	Matrix	Time	Temperature °C	Remarks	References
BSA	0.5	PBS	NC	1 h	20	Colloidal gold probes	[14]
	2.5	PBS	NC	1 h	RT	Con A overlay	[15]
	3	TBS	NC	ON	RT	Streptavidin overlay	[16, 17]
	4	PBS	NC	1 h	40	−	[18]
	5	PBS	NC	ON	40	Streptavidin-acid phosphatase complex	[19]
	5	TBS	NC	30 min	40	−	[20, 21]
	10	PBS	PCM	12 h	45	−	[22]
Hemoglobin	0.1	TBS[a]	NC	2 h	RT	Con A overlay	[23, 24]
	1	PBS	PCM	1 h	45	Toxin overlay	[25]
	3	TBS[b]	NC	6 h	RT	−	[26]
Ovalbumin	1	PBS	NC	2 h	RT	Cell overlay	[27]
	5	TBS	NC	1 h	RT	−	[28]

Table 1. (continued)

Quencher	Concen-tration % w/v	Buffer	Matrix	Time	Temper-ature °C	Remarks	References
Casein	1	PBS	NC	3 h	RT	Comparison with 10% fetal calf serum or 4% BSA	[29]
	2	TBS	NC	1 h	RT	See text for preparation	[30]
	Sat. sol.	–	NC	–	–	–	[31]
Gelatin	0.25	TBS	NC	1 h	37	Immunoblot	[32]
	3	TBS	NC	1 h	RT	Con A overlay	[33, 34]
Gelatin (liquid)	3	TBS[c]	NC	1 h	RT	–	[35]
Milk	5	PBS	NC	–	–	Comparison with BSA	[36, 37]
PVP	2	PBS	NC	30 min	RT	WGA overlay	[38]
Ethanol-amine	10	–	NC	1 – 3 h	37	After glutaraldehyde treatment followed by 3% BSA quench	[39]
	10	Tris[d]	DBM DPT	2 h	37	Standard quench for diazo papers	[40, 41, 42]
Tween 20	0.05	PBS	NC	1 h	37	Controlled comparison with TX-100, NP-40, sarkosyl, BSA and gelatin	[43]
	0.5	PBS	NC	30 min	–	Histochemical detection of alkaline phosphatase	[44]
Newborn calf serum	5	PBS[e]	NC	30 min	–	*In situ* biotinylation followed by avidin overlay	[45]
Fetal calf serum	10	TBS	NC	–	–	Con A overlay	[46]

This table gives examples of some quenchers that have been used in blotting. Combinations of the above are also commonly employed, yet it is advisable to establish optimal and simple conditions where possible. This is best achieved by testing different regimens in dot blots [9]. Abbreviations: Con A, concanavalin A; DBM, diazobenzyloxymethyl paper; DPT, diazo-phenylthioether paper; ON, overnight; PVP, polyvinylpyrrolidone; RT, room temperature; TBS, Tris buffered saline; WGA, wheat germ agglutinin.

a) Supplemented with 10 mM $CaCl_2$ and 10 mM $MnCl_2$.
b) Supplemented with 1 mM EDTA, 7.5 mM 2-mercaptoethanol, 0.5 mL toluene/mL.
c) Supplemented with 0.05% Nonidet P-40.
d) 100 mM Tris, pH 9.0, supplemented with 0.25% gelatin.
e) Supplemented with 3% BSA.

detergent in the reaction mixtures. Commonly used are Tween 20 and Triton X-100 (see also Section 2.3.10). Generally, a quencher should be selected that does not interfere with the assay. BSA, for example, contains sugar contaminants that can increase the background in lectin overlays of protein blots [47]. Hemoglobin, due to its intrinsic peroxidase activity, may be less than optimal when blots are probed with horseradish peroxidase conjugates. Polyvinylpyrrolidone has been found to be particularly well suited for wheat germ agglutinin overlays [38]. Milk [36] has undoubtedly become extremely popular as an universal quencher. Blots quenched with milk appear to have exceptionally low backgrounds; however in some cases it has been noticed that signal intensity may be reduced as well.

2.3.2   Immobilizing matrices

In all blot procedures a macromolecule is either directly applied to an immobilizing matrix ("dot blotting" [48]; see also [49−51]) or transferred from an electrophoretic gel to such a matrix. Table 2 lists examples of matrices which have been employed in protein blotting. Common to all is the requirement that the protein be bound firmly. Covalent binding has been achieved using modified cellulosic papers. Thus diazo papers [59] or CNBr-activated papers [64] have been exploited. Their main drawbacks have been: the requirement to activate them just prior to use; limited binding capacity; the requirement to use buffers (such as borate or phosphate buffers) devoid of free-amine-containing constituents (*e.g.* Tris or glycine); and poor mechanical stability of the papers, limiting extensive re-use. Nonetheless, where irreversible binding is advantageous, diazo papers, and especially diazophenylthioether (DPT) paper should be considered. A case in point is the affinity purification of monospecific antibodies *via* protein blotting [42].

Microporous membrane filters [68] are the most easily and commonly used blotting matrices. NC is by far the most popular type available. Interestingly, this negatively-charged medium can bind as much as $80-100\,\mu g$ protein/cm². Cellulose acetate, on the other hand, has little capacity for firm binding. Apparently proteins adhere to NC *via* hydrophobic interactions, a phenomenon demonstrated by the fact that nonionic detergents can remove from it substantial amounts of bound protein [22]. NC is easily quenched and also allows quick and efficient staining of transferred proteins on its surface. Improved microporous membrane filters should therefore have better binding characteristics than NC.

Positively-charged nylon membranes (PCM) were introduced as blotting matrices for this purpose [22]. PCM can bind over $500\,\mu g$ protein/cm².

Table 2. Matrices[a)]

Matrix	Capacity μg/cm²	Remarks
NC	80 – 100	(i) Majority of blotting is performed with nitrocellulose, some filters are mixed esters also containing cellulose acetate, this reduces the filter's binding capacity for protein (ii) Small pore size improves the retention of low molecular weight proteins [20] (iii) Comparison of filters manufactered by Millipore, Sartorius, Schleicher & Schuell [32]
PCM	> 500	(i) Exceptional binding capacity requires special treatment for staining and quenching [22, 52, 53] (ii) Can be silver stained or stained with colloidal iron or by haptenizing the proteins [54, 55] (iii) Can effectively be quenched with milk
Cellulose acetate	–	Very low capacity for proteins; not recommended [56]
DBM	20	Covalent linkage [57 – 60]
DPT	–	Covalent linkage, easier to prepare than DBM [41,42, 58, 61]
Modified glass	10 – 20	Used for direct amino acid sequencing [62, 63]
CNBr paper	–	Covalent linkage [64 – 66]
DEAE paper	–	Reversible electrostatic linkage [67]

a) Abbreviations, see Table 1

However, as a result of its exceptional binding capacity it demands more attention for quenching. High concentrations of BSA (10%) have been found to quench PCM quite well, and milk has proven to be an excellent quench. PCM differs from NC also in that it is difficult to stain transferred protein patterns on its surface. This is due to the fact that conventional protein dyes (*e.g.* Amido Black, Coomassie Brilliant Blue, Ponceau S) stain the PCM as well. Therefore two different approaches have developed for protein staining on PCM. The first entails nonspecific binding of iron to the bound proteins [22], which renders a very sensitive dye when colloidal iron is used [55]. The second method entails haptenizing the bound proteins to be later detected immunologically [54, 69, 70] or with avidin [45]. Moreover, silver staining of blots has recently been improved and is now compatible with both NC and PCM [71]. Therefore, PCM has gradually gained wider use as novel protocols are being developed.

Other factors which can effect blot analyses, beside the chemical composition of the blotting matrices, are the mechanical strength of the filter and its pore size. When multiple use of a blot is anticipated (either for double labeling, or sequential reprobing), NC is acceptable and PCM is optimal. When low molecular weight proteins (less than 20000) are to be blotted, then matrices with increased matrix density (smaller pore size, *i.e.* 0.2 μm *vs.* 0.45 μm) are suggested [20, 32]. Often PCM is markedly superior for the analysis of small peptides [72].

2.3.3   Probes

Protein blots can be probed with a wide variety of reagents. The term "immunoblotting" is used for the most common application of this technique, namely probing blots with antibodies. However, any binding of a protein to a ligand or to another protein may be amenable to protein blot analysis (see Section 3). Lectin overlays can provide much information on the sugar content and structure of transferred glycoproteins. Toxin or hormone overlays have been extensively used for the analyses of their corresponding receptors. Subunit/subunit interactions have also been revealed using protein blots.

2.3.4   Second probes

Often the bound primary probe must be detected with a second-probe such as radiolabeled anti-antibody. Radioactively labeled blots are then subjected to autoradiography. This approach allows considerable flexibility in evaluating one's results, as repeated exposures can be performed to optimize the signal to background ratio. Moreover, the signal can be easily quantified either by densitometric scanning of the autoradiogram [73] or by direct counting of excised bands [22, 25, 43, 73 – 75]. The obvious objections against the use of radioactive probes are the relative health hazards involved, the necessity to maintain freshly prepared reagents, and the slight loss of band resolution. Therefore, an alternative approach has been used, namely histochemical detection of enzyme conjugates (Table 3). Horseradish peroxidase or alkaline phosphatase conjugates of *S. aureus* protein A or anti-antibodies have most commonly been used (see for example [17, 77, 81, 82]). These reagents provide comparatively safer assays and often clearer, more detailed, results. Yet, these advantages are at the expense of loss of flexibility, "multiple exposures" are not possible and quantification is more difficult. The precipitated dye can be extracted from the blot and quantified spectrophotometrically (dichloromethane, for example, extracts the red precipitate formed in the alkaline phosphatase reaction and OD_{512nm} can be determined). Densito-

Table 3. Histochemical detection of enzymes

Reagent and Reaction Mixtures	References
Alkaline Phosphatase[a]	
(a) Working solution: 5 mg naphthol-AS-MX phosphate (dissolve in 200 µL dimethylformamide) + 15 mg Fast Red TR salt in 50 mL 100 mM Tris-HCl, pH 8.4	[76]
(b) Stock solutions:	[77]
(i) 10 mg Fast Blue B in 10 mL water	
(ii) 10 mg β-naphthyl phosphate + 24 mg $MgSO_4$ in 10 mL 50 mM boric acid 50 mM KCl/NaOH pH 9.2	
Working solution: mix stock solutions 1:1	
(c) Stock solutions:	[44, 78]
(i) 5-Bromo-4-chloroindoxyl phosphate (BCIP), 5 mg/mL in dimethylformamide	
(ii) Nitro Blue Tetrazolium (NBT), 1 mg/mL in veronal acetate buffer	
(iii) 2 M $MgCl_2$ in water	
Working solution: Add 0.1 mL BCIP + 1 mL NBT + 20 µL $MgCl_2$ to 9 mL veronal acetate buffer	
Glucose Oxidase	
Working solution: 0.75% D-glucose/0.01% phenazine methosulfate/0.05% *p*-Nitro-Blue Tetrazolium chloride in 100 mM phosphate buffer, pH 6.8	[79]
Horseradish Peroxidase	
(a) Working solution: 0.05% diaminobenzidine[b]/0.01% H_2O_2 in 50 mM Tris-HCl, pH 7.6	[80[c]]
(b) Working solution: 0.6 mg/ml a-chloronaphthol/0.01% H_2O_2 in PBS	[45, 46]
(c) Working solution: 200 µg/mL aminoethyl carbazole/0.01% H_2O_2 in 50 mM sodium acetate buffer, pH 5.0	[15]
Clearing Agents	
(a) Xylene	[29, 82]
(b) Decalin	[75]
(c) Paraffin oil	[83]

The above protocols have been used for the histochemical detection of various enzymes. Alkaline phosphatase is gaining popularity as its reaction products are stable and it obviates the health hazards associated with diaminobenzidine. The clearing agents have been used to make microporous membrane filters transparent to increase the efficiency in densitometric scanning of blots.

a) For use of acid phosphatase, see Brower *et al.* [19].

b) The tetrahydrochloride salt of diaminobenzidine is preferred over the free acid as it is more soluble in water.

c) See also reference [81] for signal intensification.

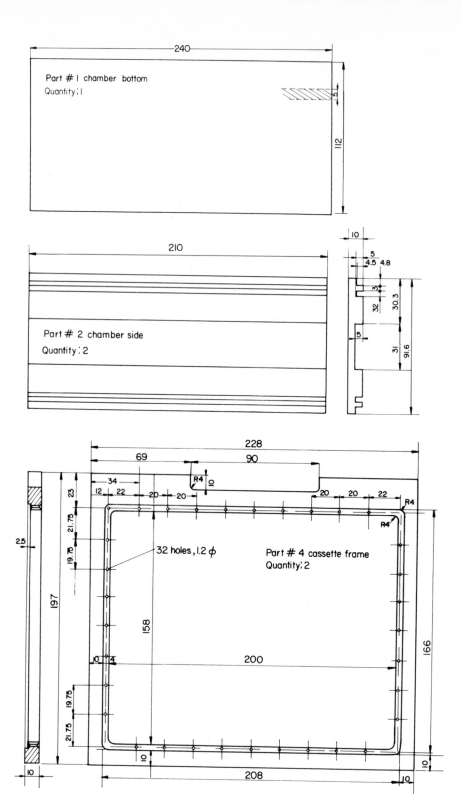

Part #1 chamber bottom
Quantity: 1

Part #2 chamber side
Quantity: 2

32 holes, 1.2 φ

Part #4 cassette frame
Quantity: 2

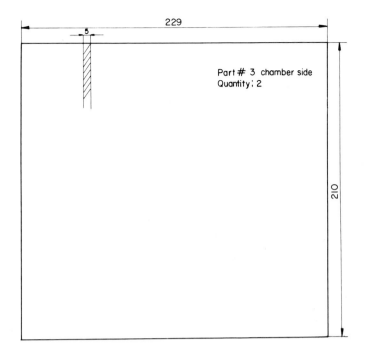

Part # 3 chamber side
Quantity : 2

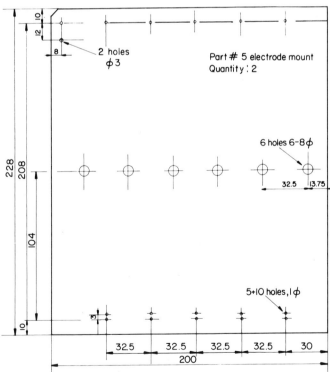

2 holes
φ3

Part # 5 electrode mount
Quantity : 2

6 holes 6-8 φ

5+10 holes, 1 φ

Figure 3. Blue print of electroblot apparatus. The parts are made of plexiglass. Parts 1, 2, and 3 make the chamber, whereas parts 4 and 5 are to be inserted into the corresponding grooves of part 2.

metric scans of histochemically processed blots can be performed either by reflectance [84] or by making the stained blot transparent [29, 82, 83]. A number of reagents have been used for this purpose (Table 3). A third approach to signal detection has been to use colloidal gold complexes [14, 85–90]. As the gold signal can be amplified by silver intensification, these techniques should gain wider use.

2.3.5 Gels

Although SDS-PAGE is usually the first step in protein blotting, many other gel systems have also been used. For the blotting of agarose gels and isoelectric focusing gels [34, 85, 91–96] diffusion blotting seems optimal. Transfer of nondenatured proteins to blots from "native" gels (*e.g.* [97, 98]) allows subsequent demonstration of enzyme activity [67, 99]. Strongly basic proteins [100], or proteins resolved in urea gels [1, 101], or agarose/acrylamide composite gels [102] can and have been used in protein blotting experiments. When two-dimensional gels are to be transferred one should refer to [4] (see also [103]).

2.3.6 Blot apparatus

The process of transferring proteins from gels to immobilizing matrices entails two steps: elution and adsorbance. The elution requires the application of some driving force to the gel. Diffusion [10, 104], convection [105], and even vacuum [106] have been used; however, electroelution is most routinely applied today. In designing an electroblot apparatus, one must consider the electrodes used. In principle, a uniform electric field is most easily obtained by using plate electrodes [107]. However, platinum wire arrays provide some technical advantages and are widely used [60]. The placement of such wires will determine the "topography" of the electric field generated which, in turn, directly affects the elution efficiency over the surface of the gel [108]. Therefore, well controlled electric fields are desired. Figs. 1 to 4 provide a detailed description of a blot apparatus that generates not only a uniform electric field but also a gradient electric field. The latter has three advantages over a completely uniform field: (i) high molecular weight proteins experience the highest field strength, thus exerting the maximal driving force where needed; (ii) the lower molecular weight proteins are subjected to mild or weak electric fields so as not to over-accelerate them, thus providing more time for them to interact with the matrix thereby reducing their loss through the filter; and (iii) the high potential differences are generated at the expense

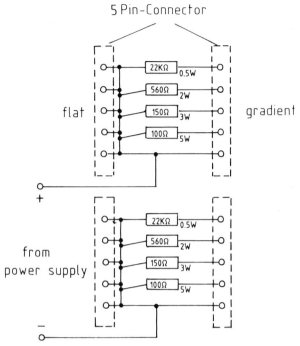

Figure 4. Resistor box. Scheme for a resistor box which accommodates the electroblot apparatus described in Figs. 1 and 3. Five platinum wires are mounted onto the electrode mount (5). Each platinum electrode is wired individually and connected to a five-pin connector. The resistor box is equipped with four 5-pin sockets. Two sockets are simply short circuited. When these are connected to the anode and the cathode, a uniform electric field is generated. The other two sockets connect the platinum wires to the power supply *via* a series of resistors as indicated. The greatest resistance should be applied to the bottom most electrode pair whereas the top electrode pair should experience only the minimal resistance of the wiring. An intermediate gradient can be produced by employing one series of resistors and one short-circuited socket.

of the lower aspects of the field, thus reducing the overall current used (see Section 2.3.9). Other concepts in electroblotting have also been developed, such as semi-dry electroblotting [109, 110].

2.3.7   Incubation chambers

Nucleic acid blot procedures often include the use of "seal-a-meal" type plastic bags. The advantages of these are that they conserve the volume of probes used and are also disposable and cheap. Regretably, this practice usually produces less satisfactory results when applied to protein blotting. This is mainly due to the development of blotched, non-uniform and relatively high background. Protein blots should be incubated in volumes approximately 0.5 to 2 mL/cm^2 of matrix (about 10 to 15 mL/blotted lane). In principle, the blot should float as it is rocked or shaken. Fluid should be constantly flushing the surface of the matrix. The most efficient mode of incubation is in plastic boxes which are rocked. Compartmentalized plastic boxes can be purchased from Althor Products (496 Danbury Rd., Wilton, CT 06897). Recently the possibility to simultaneously probe a blot with a variety of agents has been provided by the development of novel incubation chambers, "slot-blots" [111, 112].

2.3.8   Mixed dye fronts

In order to cut out lanes of a gel without endangering some of the pattern, samples should be run in every second well. Pyronin Y (Sigma P-7017, 2 to 3 µL of 0.1% w/v in 25% glycerol in water) can be applied to those wells that do not contain samples. In doing so the areas free of relevant bands will be marked with distinct, well confined, pink dye fronts. Thus, cutting along the line connecting the pink dye front and the well which initially contained Pyronin Y allows safe excision of intact protein patterns.

2.3.9   Electroblotting

As is the case for gel electrophoresis, the question of constant current *vs.* constant voltage exists for blotting. The driving force in blotting is the potential difference between the anode and the cathode, thus constant voltage is preferable. As blotting proceeds, however, three phenomena occur: (i) electrolytes are eluted out of the gel and contribute to the conductivity of the transfer buffer; (ii) some buffers break down during electrophoresis and thus increase the conductivity; (iii) Joule heating causes a drop in resistance. The mutual effect of the above is a steadily increasing rise in current. So long as the power supply can cope with this rise, and the currents do not exceed 300–400 mA, then blotting with constant voltage is permissible. If, on the other hand, currents greater that 400–500 mA develop, Joule heating becomes problematic and cooling systems must be introduced. Therefore, constant current may be advantageous in situations where the current is to be restricted. Application of gradient electric fields can cut the overall current by 50% (see Section 2.3.6). Blotting should proceed 2 to 3 h at 40–50 V (or 200–300 mA).

2.3.10 Detergents

The application of detergents as quenchers is extremely appealing. This is due to their low cost and high efficiency. However, caution should be used as nonionic detergents can remove as much as 80% of the bound protein off the blot. Interestingly, this appears to require the presence of salt, and is particularly noticable with Triton X-100 (or Nonidet P-40). Tween 20 is milder yet just as efficient as a quencher [43]. An added advantage in exclusively using detergent quenchers is that general protein staining can be performed after probing the blot.

2.3.11 Over-probing

Often, when unsure of the incubation conditions, there is a tendency to add more probe than is actually necessary or to incubate the blot longer than required. These practices sometimes lead to an effect opposite to that intended. As little probe as possible should be used and normally 10^5 cpm/mL is quite adequate. When immunoassays are performed the specific binding reaches equilibrium within an hour. Thus, excess probe and prolonged incubation will probably result in increased background rather than accentuated signals.

3   Specific applications

Besides its by now classical use as an immunoassay, protein blotting can be employed as an efficient tool for the analytical biochemist. The following sections provide examples of this. In general, four aspects of the use of protein blotting will be described: (i) the analysis of polypeptide composition; (ii) the analysis of receptors; (iii) the analysis of protein/protein interactions; and (iv) the analysis of enzymatic activities.

3.1   The analysis of polypeptide composition

Once the constituents of a protein mixture have been resolved by gel electrophoresis, the pattern of bands can be immobilized *via* protein blotting. The blot can then be subjected to a variety of procedures designed to chemically characterize individual polypeptides. Numerous approaches have been developed to stain proteins on the blot. Most commonly used are the classical stains (*e.g.* Amido Black [1] and Coomassie Brilliant Blue [20]). Recently efficient silver staining of blots has been developed [71] and the use of colloidal metals has provided exceptionally sensitive stains [14, 55, 86–90]. However, the detection of discrete amino acids or glycomoieties or haptens in the polypeptides is also possible.

General sugar staining can be achieved by use of an enzyme hydrazide [76]. By oxidizing the blot with sodium periodate, aldehydes are selectively produced in sugar-containing proteins. The aldehydes form stable Schiff bases with the enzyme hydrazides. The blot is then reacted for the appropriate enzyme and the complex is thus revealed. Differential oxidation can distinguish between sialoglycoconjugates and other glycoconjugates. Moreover, by treating cells with periodate prior to their solubilization and gel electrophoresis, subsequent detection of surface proteins by enzyme-hydrazide staining is made possible [113]. Selective sugar staining can be accomplished by probing blots with different lectins [15, 22–24, 38, 46, 47, 114, 115]. Furthermore, by treating the blot with glycosidases followed by lectin analyses, a more detailed picture of the composition and structure of the oligosaccharide moiety can be achieved [22–24, 114]. A case in point is glycophorin, for which the galactose residue becomes available for peanut agglutinin binding once the sialyl moiety is removed by treating a blotted erythrocyte pattern with sialidase [7]. A particularly interesting approach in oligosaccharide detection is the one introduced by Clegg [15]. Here mannose-containing proteins are demonstrated by their ability to bind concanavalin A. However, instead of using radioactive lectin or an enzyme-conjugated probe, the blot is probed a second time with horseradish peroxidase. This enzyme is in itself an *N*-linked glycoprotein and therefore recognized by concanavalin A as well. Thus, *via* the multivalency of the lectin, the enzyme is bound to the site of the blotted glycoprotein being studied. This approach was slightly modified by Rohringer and Holden [85] for the detection of wheat germ agglutinin *via* the glycoprotein probe avidin, followed by interaction with a biotinylated enzyme. Figs. 5 and 6 demonstrate the analysis of glycoconjugates.

Some proteins retain their hapten even after gel electrophoresis and electroblotting. For example, natural biotin-binding proteins are easily detected by probing blots with avidin or streptavidin [16]. Of particular importance are the recent advancements of Wilchek and his coworkers. Over the years, Bayer and Wilchek [116, 117] have repeatedly demonstrated the utility of the avidin-biotin complex as a diagnostic tool. This approach has been applied to protein blots as well. By designing novel biotinylated probes specific for individual amino acid residues, one can gain insight into the amino acid com-

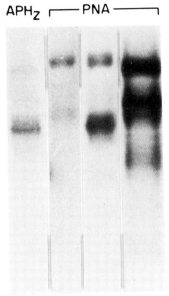

APH$_Z$ ┌———PNA———┐

Sialidase   −   −   +   +

Figure 5. Effect of desialylation before and after blotting. Mouse thymocytes were homogenated and subjected to SDS-PAGE (first three lanes) or treated with sialidase followed by homogenization and SDS-PAGE (last lane). The gel was blotted to NC. One lane was stained for sialoglycoprotein with alkaline-phosphatase-hydrazide (APHz, first lane). The remaining blots were probed with ^{125}I-labeled peanut agglutinin (PNA), a galactose specific lectin. Note that only one band is labeled with the lectin in untreated cells. Sialidase treatment of the blot prior to lectin overlay renders the sialoglycoprotein detectable by PNA (PNA⁺). The *in situ* method modifies the chemical composition of the immobilized glycoprotein without affecting its mobility. This is demonstrated by comparing lanes (3) with (4). Whereas desialylation of the protein before electrophoresis generates new PNA⁺ proteins, their electrophoretic mobilities are changed. Thus, matching of the precursor sialoglycoprotein with its desialylated product can be confusing. This problem is obviated by performing the enzymatic treatment "post-blotting" (Courtesy of Antonio De Maio, The Weizmann Institute of Science).

position of blotted polypeptides. The use of 3-(*N*-maleimido-propionyl)biocytin [118] allows the detection of reduced cysteine residues. By manipulating the reductive conditions of the assay, one can ascertain the presence or absence of disulfide bridges. This probe has been extremely useful in identifying the disulfide-linked cysteines of the α-subunit of the acetylcholine receptor [119]. Use of *p*-diazobenzoyl biocytin [120] can reveal tyrosine and histidine groups. The application of biotinyl *N*-hydroxysuccinimide ester [121] or sulfosuccinimido biotin [45] can demonstrate amino groups, *etc.* Fig. 7 demonstrates the use of some of these biotinylated probes.

Probably the most exciting achievement in the structural analysis of blotted polypeptides has been the studies of Vandekerckhove *et al.* [62] and Aeber-

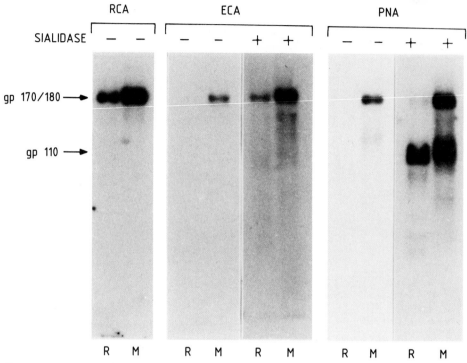

Figure 6. Detailed analysis of galacto-glycoproteins. There are many galactose specific lectins. To the novice they may be wrongly considered to be interchangable galactose detectors. In fact, they each have their preferred sugar configurations and are thus quite distinct. This is demonstrated in the above autoradiogram. Thymocytes were derived from rats (R) or mice (M) and homogenized, subjected to SDS-PAGE, blotted to NC and overlayed with *Ricinus communis* agglutinin (RCA), *Erythrina cristagalli* agglutinin (ECA) or peanut agglutinin (PNA) with or without *in situ* sialidase treatment. They were then autoradiographed. Two glycoproteins were detected, gp170/180 and gp110. Note that gp170/180 of rat is recognized only by RCA; after sialidase treatment it is detectable with ECA but not with PNA. Both the murine and rat gp110 are detectable only with PNA. (Courtesy of Antonio De Maio, The Weizmann Institute of Science).

sold *et al.* [63]. Both groups have successfully demonstrated micro N-terminal sequencing of blotted polypeptides. The pivotal innovation has been the introduction and use of modified glass fiber filters as immobilizing matrices. Vandekerckhove *et al.* have conveniently charge-modified Whatman GF/C by merely impregnating the filter with "Polybrene" (1,5-dimethyl-1,5-diazoundecamethylene; Janssen Chimica, Belgium). The filters can be stored and only require a brief rinse in water prior to their use. These filters have a reasonable binding capacity for protein (20 to 30 μg/cm^2). Blotted polypeptides can be detected by fluorescamine staining. The total amino acid composition of individual bands can be efficiently determined

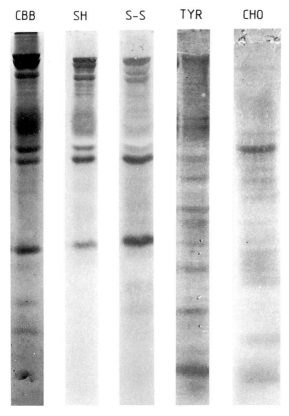

CBB   SH   S-S   TYR   CHO

Figure 7. Selective biotinylation and detection of specific amino acid residues. Comparative staining patterns for blotted proteins and glycoproteins using different group-specific biotin-containing reagents are shown. Human erythrocyte membranes were subjected to SDS-PAGE, and lanes were either stained with Coomassie Brilliant Blue R-250 (CBB) or the proteins were transferred electrophoretically to NC. One lane was treated directly for sulfhydryl groups (SH) using 3-(N-maleimido-propionyl)biocytin. For disulfides (S-S), blots were treated sequentially with N-ethylmaleimide, 2-mercaptoethanol and 3-(N-maleimido-propionyl) biocytin. For tyrosine and histidine residues (TYR), the appropriate lane was treated with diazobenzoyl biocytin. Carbohydrate groups on blotted glycoproteins (CHO) were treated successively with sodium periodate and biocytin hydrazide. This last approach is comparable with the use of the enzyme hydrazide demonstrated in Fig. 5. Lanes containing the blotted biotinylated proteins were then incubated with avidin- or strepatavidin-containing enzyme conjugates or complexes. Note the differential staining patterns of the various biotinylating procedures (Courtesy of Edward A. Bayer and Meir Wilchek, The Weizmann Institute of Science).

with the exceptions of methionine residues lost and over-abundance of glycine. More important though is the fact that only 1 to 2 µg protein is necessary for Edman degradation. As little as 80 pmol of actin proteolytic fragments could be sequenced directly in a gas-phase microsequenator (as many as 18 cycles for some of the proteins tested). The protocol of Aebersold *et al.* [63] is a bit more cumbersome, but in essence is the same. These authors have described 4 different modified glass filters. Acid-etched filters allow blotting at low pH. The other three filters are positively charge-modified or contain 1,4-phenylenediisothiocyanate, which enables covalent linkage of polypeptides to the glass support. These filters bind 7 to 10 µg protein/cm^2. In essence, protein blotting *per se* can be conducted with no significant modification except for the replacement of NC or PCM by the new matrices. Undoubtedly this approach will become widely used.

3.2   Receptor analysis

Whereas it is clear that a blot can be probed with an antibody revealing its antigen, or a lectin to demonstrate a glycoprotein, the analysis of receptors is less than obvious. The reason for this is that the binding activity must be retained in the blotted polypeptide rather than in the probe. Indeed, receptor binding sites are often associated with the maintenance of quaternary structure and tertiary configuration. By definition, the mere dissociation and resolution of a receptor into its subunits prohibits all possible quaternary interactions. Yet, there have been quite a number of systems where blotted receptor proteins continue to bind their natural ligand. Quite a few hormone receptors have been studied (*e.g.* for the epidermal growth factor [122], the human growth hormone [123], or thyroid stimulating hormones [124]). The study of viral receptors is also amenable to blot analysis [125–127]. Notable has been the analysis of the low density lipoprotein receptor [31, 128].

The most extensively studied receptor by protein blotting has been the nicotinic acetylcholine receptor. This protein is a pentameric complex ($a_2\beta\gamma\delta$) situated at the post-synaptic side of the neuromuscular junction. It binds two molecules of acetylcholine which elicit channel activity which results in membrane depolarization and eventual muscle contraction [129]. The activity of this ligand-induced channel is inhibited by the competitive antagonist, a-bungarotoxin. Whereas the acetylcholine binding site is known to be associated with the a-subunit of the receptor, the toxin binding site was less well characterized. Protein blotting of membrane preparations enriched for the acetylcholine receptor demonstrated that the a-subunit contained the toxin binding site [25, 130, 131] (Fig. 8). By quantitative blot analysis it was shown that the affinity of the toxin/subunit interaction was four orders of magnitude less than that of the intact receptor [25]. Moreover, purified a-subunit could be proteolysed to produce peptide fragments that continued to bind toxin [132]. By mapping these fragments to the amino acid sequence of

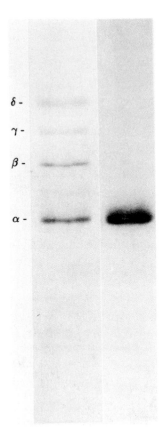

Figure 8. Ligand overlay of the nicotinic acetylcholine receptor. The nicotinic acetylcholine receptor was affinity purified from the electric organ of *Torpedo californica*. The receptor subunits were resolved on a 10% polyacrylamide gel and blotted to PCM. All four subunits of the receptor are demonstrated in the Coomassie Brilliant Blue stained gel (left lane). The blot was overlayed with ^{125}I-labeled α-bungarotoxin and autoradiographed (right lane). Overexposure of the blot emphasizes that only the α-subunit binds the ligand.

the α-subunit, it was discovered that the binding site was concealed in a sequence of some 20 amino acids [133−135]. More recently, a cDNA sequence corresponding to this area has been cloned into an *Escherichia coli* expression vector rendering transformants capable of binding neurotoxin (see Fig. 9) [136]. Clearly this achievement has been made feasible by employing quantitative blot analysis of the gene product prior to manipulating the gene itself.

3.3   Protein-protein association

The formation and maintenance of structures in cells is often established by the construction of cytoskeletons. Moreover, cell function is sometimes elicited by protein modulators such as calmodulin. Protein blotting has been employed to reveal various protein/protein interactions which can then provide a more detailed picture of cellular processes. For instance, protein

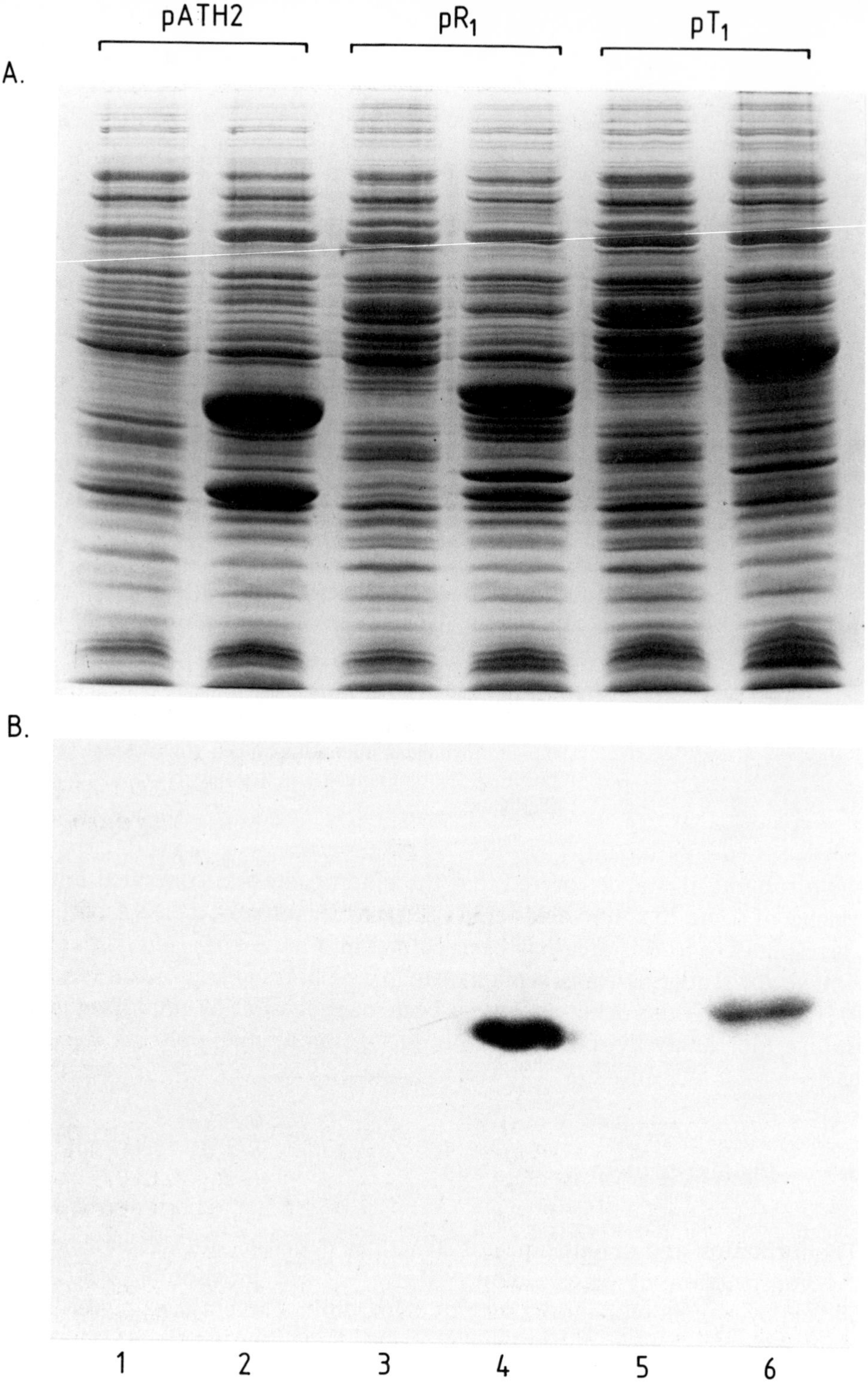
pATH2
pR1
pT1
A.
B.
1
2
3
4
5
6

phosphorylation is mediated *via* specific protein kinases. In studying the phosphorylation of pancreatic proteins, Gorelick *et al.* [137] have demonstrated by protein blotting that a 51 kDa polypeptide is a specific calmodulin-binding phosphoprotein. Other calmodulin-binding proteins have since been detected using this approach [53]. The recognition process between the acrosome of sperm and proteins of the zona pellucida is also amenable to blot analysis [21, 138, 139]. The 43 kDa protein associated with the acetylcholine receptor has been shown to bind actin on blots [80].

Protein blot analysis of vinculin-binding polypeptides has also been performed [140]. Thus it appears that cytoskeletal structures are particularly amenable to this mode of investigation. Most notable has been the work of Bennett and his coworkers. A series of extensive studies of the interaction between the elements of brain cytoskeleton has been accomplished employing protein blotting. The α chain of brain spectrin was shown to specifically associate with its β chain, and hybrid molecules could be demonstrated by binding a porcine brain α chain to an erythrocyte β chain [141]. Ankyrin could also be shown to specifically bind to spectrin β-subunit and to brain tubulin [142]. Recently synapsin I was shown to be a spectrin-binding protein [143]. A detailed analysis of tubulin binding to microtubule-associated proteins has been performed using dot blots. Littauer *et al.* [51] have applied a series of CNBr cleavage peptides of tubulin to filters and subsequently tested their capacity to bind radioactive microtubule-associated proteins. In doing so they have been able to locate those areas of the tubulin molecule which are responsible for binding.

Cell overlays of blots has allowed the detection of cell adhesion proteins. Hayman *et al.* [104] demonstrated that normal rat kidney cells bound to blotted fibronectin as well as to a 70 kDa polypeptide. Moreover, blotted trophic factors can continue to exert physiological effects [27, 144]. Cell overlays have also been used in the analysis of the binding of intact bacteria to specific dot-blotted glycoproteins. In this case, a filter containing dot-blotted

---

Figure 9. Functional expression of the toxin binding sequences in bacteria. A cDNA clone of the α-subunit of the nicotinic acetylcholine receptor from *T. californica* was cut by the restriction enzymes *Pst, Xho*II and *Eco*RV to generate DNA fragments corresponding to the amino acid sequences 166–200 (pR$_1$) and 166–315 (pT$_1$). These were cloned into the inducible expression vector pATH2. *Escherichia coli* were transformed with pATH2, pR$_1$ and pT$_1$, respectively. The bacterial transformants were grown under noninductive conditions (1), (3), (5) or inductive conditions (2), (4), (6). (A) Homogenates of the cells were resolved by SDS-PAGE and stained with Coomassie Brilliant Blue or (B) blotted to NC, overlayed with ^{125}I-labeled α-bungarotoxin and autoradiographed. Note that the fusion proteins of pR$_1$ and pT$_1$ are the only polypeptides which bind toxin.

Ovalbumin

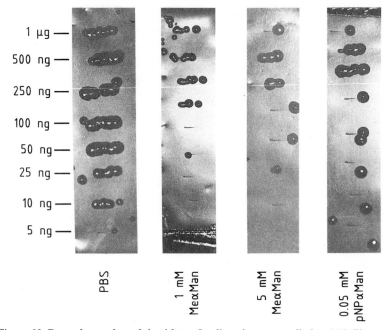

Figure 10. Bacteria overlay of dot-blots. Ovalbumin was applied to NC filters at various concentrations using a Beckman single point applicator (#324399). The filters were overlayed with *E. coli* strain 346 in the absence of competing sugars or in PBS containing methyl *a*-mannoside (Me*a*Man) or *p*-nitrophenyl-*a*-mannoside (*p*NP*a*Man) as indicated. Note that the efficacy of competition of *p*NP*a*Man is at least 100 times better than that of Me*a*Man (Courtesy of Nurit Firon and Nathan Sharon, The Weizmann Institute of Science).

proteins is incubated with a solution of live, diluted bacteria. After incubation and washing, the filters are placed on agar plates and stored at 37 °C for 12 h. Colonies of bacteria grow where even one bacteria initially associated specifically with a particular protein (Fig. 10) [145]. Clearly such an application is not only extremely sensitive but benefits from the possible recovery of functional probes, *i.e.* bound bacteria.

3.4   Enzymatic activity

The ability to ascribe enzymatic activity to a specific band is a goal of appreciable importance. Blotting of nondenaturing gels has allowed the demonstration of functional enzymes on the blot [67]. However, efficient resolution of proteins is often achieved only in the presence of SDS. Most enzymes are extremely sensitive to the denaturative effect of this detergent. Nonetheless, there has been some success in the application of protein blotting of SDS gels to the study of enzymes. For example, the activity of β-galactosidase can be demonstrated on blots by simply incubating the blot with the substrate X-Gal (5-bromo-4-chloro-3-indolyl-β-D-galactopyranoside). At the area of the ac-

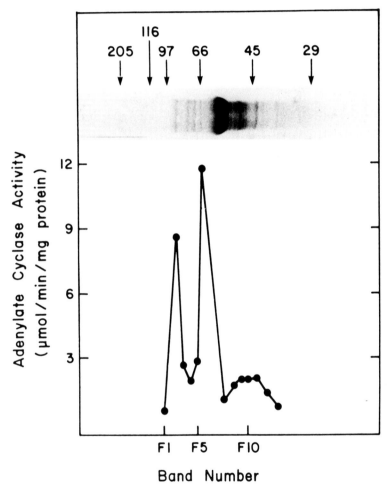

Figure 11. Blot detection of adenylate-cyclase active polypeptides. *B. pertusis* were extracted with urea, and the resultant extract was subjected to gel filtration. Three peaks of adenylate cyclase activity were detected. Peak No. 2 was collected and applied to a calmodulin affinity column. The gel shown is a Coomassie Brilliant Blue pattern of the eluted active peak. Such a gel was blotted to NC and stained with Ponceau S. Individual bands were excised out of the NC and eluted off the filter by overnight incubation in a 1% Triton X-100 buffered solution. The removed adenylate cyclase activity and protein content were determined for each band. Note that two major bands were found active and that neither correspond to the major 55 kDa polypeptide (Courtesy of Emanuel Hanski, The Weizmann Institute of Science).

tive band a blue precipitate is formed. However, such activity can only be associated with the oligomeric forms of the enzyme and complete dissociation of the tetramer abolishes enzyme activity. Attempts to reconstitute activity by incubating the blots with urea-dissociated enzyme subunits have not been successful.

Another approach toward overcoming the loss of activity upon dissociation has been that of Muilerman *et al.* [146]. Protein blots of partially purified rat liver phosphodiesterase I were incubated with an excess of antibody directed against the enzyme. Then the filter was treated with an intact and functional enzyme followed by reacting the blot with its appropriate substrate. In doing so the inactive subunit became apparent via the intact enzyme localized by the bifunctional antibody. This approach has also been employed by Van der Meer *et al.* [147].

Another approach to assaying enzymes has been to elute the active polypeptide off the blot. Hanski and Rogel (Weizmann Institute of Science) have been studying the different classes of adenylate cyclase derived from *Bordetela pertusis*. Indeed, by classical chromatography, cyclase activity can be ascribed to at least three well-separated peaks yet by no means are the fractions homogenous. Therefore, the various fractions have been subjected to protein blotting. The resolved bands are excised out of the NC which is then incubated for 12 h in a buffer containing 1% Triton X-100. Afterwards the supernatant is assayed for enzyme activity. As seen in Fig. 11, adenylate cyclase activity is easily associated with discrete polypeptides. This activity is restored only after prolonged Triton X-100 treatment. This is most probably an indication of enzyme renaturation and restoration of its activity. Valtorta *et al.* [148] have used blotting to seek specific substrates for enzymes and in particular phosphorylases. The procedure which they have developed entails incubating the blots with soluble enzymes and radioactive ATP. Efficient substrates are revealed after autoradiography of the blot.

4   Concluding remarks

The process of protein blotting is an extension of polyacrylamide gel electrophoresis. It provides the ability to identify and characterize small amounts of well-resolved polypeptides. The technique has been employed as an intermediate step in a variety of procedures. The purpose of this article has been to demonstrate that this technique has an enormous potential as an analytical tool. The examples quoted provide only a superficial glimpse of the many applications possible, only very few of which have yet been attempted.

I thank the many colleagues that have provided me with material, suggestions and criticism, all of which make this a more useful article. In particular I thank Yoav Eshel for preparing Fig. 9, Rachel Samuel for typing the text, Dvorah Ochert for her extensive help in editing and preparing the manuscript, and of course Jean-Michel Lebleautte for his insight. The work on the acetylcholine receptor was supported in part by the Israel Institute for Psychobiology and by the Leo and Julia Forscheimer Center for Molecular Genetics at the Weizmann Institute.

5   References

[1] Towbin, H., Staehelin, T., Gordon, J., *Proc. Natl. Acad. Sci. USA* 1979, *76*, 4350–4354.

[2] Gershoni, J.M., Palade, G.E., *Anal. Biochem.* 1983, *131*, 1–15.

[3] Gooderham, K., in: Walker, J.M. (Ed.), *Methods in Molecular Biology*, Humana Press, Clifton, New Jersey 1984, Vol. 1, pp. 165–178.

[4] Symington, J., in: Celis, J.E. Bravo, R. (Eds.), *Two-Dimensional Gel Electrophoresis of Proteins*, Academic Press, New York 1984, pp. 127–168.

[5] Towbin, H., Gordon, J. *J. Immunol. Methods* 1984, *72*, 313–340.

[6] Bers, G., Garfin, D., *Bio Techniques* 1985, *3*, 276–288.

[7] Gershoni, J.M., *Trends Biochem. Sci.* 1985, *10*, 103–106.

[8] Beisiegel, U., *Electrophoresis* 1986, *7*, 1–18.

[9] Gershoni, J.M., *Methods Biochem. Anal.* 1987, in press.

[10] Bowen, B., Steinberg, J., Laemmli, U.K., Weintraub, H., *Nucl. Acids Res.* 1980, *8*, 1–20.

[11] Bradbury, J.M., Thompson, R.J., *Biochem. J.* 1984, *221*, 361–368.

[12] Erickson, P.F., Minier, L.N., Lasher, R.S., *J. Immunol. Methods* 1982, *51*, 241–249.

[13] Cardin, A.D., Witt, K.R., Jackson, R.L., *Anal. Biochem.* 1984, *137*, 368–373.

[14] Brada, D., Roth, J., *Anal. Biochem.* 1984, *142*, 79–83.

[15] Clegg, J.C.S., *Anal. Biochem.* 1982, *127*, 389–394.

[16] Nikolau, B.J., Wurtele, E.S., Stumpf, P.K., *Anal. Biochem.* 1985, *149*, 448–453.

[17] O'Connor, C.G., Ashman, L.K., *J. Immunol. Methods* 1982, *54*, 267–271.

[18] Kakita, K., O'Connell, K., Permutt, M.A., *Diabetes* 1982, *31*, 648–652.

[19] Brower, M.S., Brakel, C.L., Garry, K., *Anal. Biochem.* 1985, *147*, 382–386.

[20] Burnette, W.N., *Anal. Biochem.* 1981, *112*, 195–203.

[21] O'Rand, M.G., Matthews, J.E., Welch, J.E., Fisher, S.J., *J. Exper. Zool.* 1985, *235*, 423–428.

[22] Gershoni, J.M., Palade, G.E., *Anal. Biochem.* 1982, *124*, 396–405.

[23] Kerjaschki, D., Noronha-Blob, L., Sacktor, B., Farquhar, M.G., *J. Cell Biol.* 1984, *98*, 1505–1513.

[24] Kerjaschki, D., Sharkey, D.J., Farquhar, M.G., *J. Cell. Biol.* 1984, *98*, 1591–1596.

[25] Gershoni, J.M., Hawrot, E., Lentz, T.L., *Proc. Natl. Acad. Sci. USA* 1983, *80*, 4973–4977.

172   J.M. Gershoni

[26] Jackson, P., Thompson, R.J., *Electrophoresis* 1984, *5*, 35−42.
[27] Carnow, T.B., Manthorpe, M., Davis, G.E., Varon, S., *J. Neurosci.* 1985, *5*, 1965−1971.
[28] Hanff, P.A., Fehniger, T.E., Miller, J.N., Lovett, M.A., *J. Immunol.* 1982, *129*, 1287−1288.
[29] Ramirez, P., Bonilla, J.A., Moreno, E., Leon, P., *J. Immunol. Methods* 1983, *62*, 15−22.
[30] Mandrell, R.E., Zollinger, W.D., *J. Immunol. Methods* 1984, *67*, 1−11.
[31] Dresel, H.A., Schettler, G., *Electrophoresis* 1984, *5*, 372−373.
[32] Lin, W., Kasamatsu, H., *Anal. Biochem.* 1983, *128*, 302−311.
[33] Faye, L., Chrispeels, M.J., *Anal. Biochem.* 1985, *149*, 218−224.
[34] Hoffman, W.L., Jump, A.A., *J. Immunol. Methods* 1985, *76*, 263−271.
[35] Saravis, C.A., *Electrophoresis* 1984, *5*, 54−55.
[36] Johnson, D.A., Gautsch, J.W., Sportsman, J.R., Elder, J.H., *Gene Anal. Techn.* 1984, *1*, 3−8.
[37] Miskimins, W.K., Roberts, M.P., McClelland, A., Ruddle, F.H., *Proc. Natl. Acad. Sci. USA* 1985, *82*, 6741−6744.
[38] Bartles, J.R., Hubbard, A.L., *Anal. Biochem.* 1984, *140*, 284−292.
[39] Kay, M.M.B., Goodman, S.R., Sorensen, K., Whitfield, C.F., Wong, P., Zaki, L., Rudloff, V., *Proc. Natl. Acad. Sci. USA* 1983, *80*, 1631−1635.
[40] Symington, J., Green, M., Brackmann, K., *Proc. Natl. Acad. Sci. USA* 1981, *78*, 177−181.
[41] Reiser, J., Wardale, J., *Eur. J. Biochem.* 1981, *114*, 569−575.
[42] Olmsted, J.B., *J. Biol. Chem.* 1981, *256*, 11955−11957.
[43] Batteiger, B., Newhall, W.J., Jones, R.B., *J. Immunol. Methods* 1982, *55*, 297−307.
[44] Blake, M.S., Johnston, K.H., Russell-Jones, G.J., Gotschlich, E.C., *Anal. Biochem.* 1984, *136*, 175−179.
[45] LaRochelle, W.J., Froehner, S.C., *J. Immunol. Methods* 1986, *92*, 65−71.
[46] Hawkes, R., *Anal. Biochem.* 1982, *123*, 143−146.
[47] Glass, W.F., Briggs, R.C., Hnilica, L.S., *Anal. Biochem.* 1981, *115*, 219−224.
[48] Hawkes, R., Niday, E., Gordon, J., *Anal. Biochem.* 1982, *119*, 142−147.
[49] Glenney, J.R. Jr., Glenney, P., Weber, K., *J. Mol. Biol.* 1983, *167*, 275−293.
[50] Jahn, R., Schiebler, W., Greengard, P., *Proc. Natl. Acad. Sci. USA* 1984, *81*, 1684−1687.
[51] Littauer, U.Z., Giveon, D., Thierauf, M., Ginzburg, I., Ponstingl, H., *Proc. Natl. Acad. Sci. USA* 1986, *83*, 7162−7166.
[52] Rochette-Egly, C., Daviaud, D., *Electrophoresis* 1985, *6*, 235−238.
[53] Flanagan, S.D., Yost, B., *Anal. Biochem.* 1984, *140*, 510−519.
[54] Kittler, J.M., Meisler, N.T., Viceps-Madore, D., Cidlowski, J.A., Thanassi, J.W., *Anal. Biochem.* 1984, *137*, 210−216.
[55] Moeremans, M., de Raeymaeker, M., Daneels, G., De Mey, J., *Anal. Biochem.* 1986, *153*, 18−22.
[56] Schaltman, K., Pongs, O., *Hoppe-Seyler's Z. Physiol. Chem.* 1980, *361*, 207−210.
[57] Renart, J., Reiser, J., Stark, G.R., *Proc. Natl. Acad. Sci. USA* 1979, *76*, 3116−3120.
[58] Renart, J., Sandoval, I.V., *Methods Enzymol.* 1984, *104*, 455−461.
[59] Alwine, J.C., Kemp, D.J., Parker, B.A., Reiser, J., Renart, J., Stark, G.R., Wahl, G.M., *Methods Enzymol.* 1979, *68*, 220−242.
[60] Bittner, M., Kupferer, P., Morris, C.F., *Anal. Biochem.* 1980, *102*, 459−471.
[61] Reiser, J., Stark, G.R., *Methods Enzymol.* 1983, *96*, 205−215.
[62] Vandekerckhove, J., Bauw, G., Puype, M., van Damme, J., van Montagu, M., *Eur. J. Biochem.* 1985, *152*, 9−19.
[63] Aebersold, R.H., Teplow, D.B., Hood, L.E., Kent, S.B.H., *J. Biol. Chem.* 1986, *261*, 4229−4238.

[64] Clarke, L., Hitzeman, R., Carbon, J., *Methods Enzymol.* 1979, *68*, 436–443.

[65] Newman, P.J., Kahn, R.A., Hines, A., *J. Cell Biol.* 1981, *90*, 249–253.

[66] Bhullar, B.S., Hewitt, J., Candido, E.P.M., *J. Biol. Chem.* 1981, *256*, 8801–8806.

[67] McLellan, T., Ramshawm J.A.M., *Biochem. Genet.* 1981, *19*, 647–654.

[68] Presswood, W.G., in: Dutka, B.J. (Ed.), *Membrane Filtration, Applications, Techniques and Problems*, Dekker, Basel 1981, pp. 1–17.

[69] Wojtkowiak, Z., Briggs, R.C., Hnilica, L.S., *Anal. Biochem.* 1983, *129*, 486–489.

[70] Wolff, J.M., Pfeifle, J., Hollman, M., Anderer, F.A., *Anal. Biochem.* 1985, *147*, 396–400.

[71] Merril, C.R., Pratt, M.E., *Anal. Biochem.* 1986, *156*, 96–110.

[72] Miribel, L., Peltre, G., Arnaud, P., David, B., in: Dunn, M.J. (Ed.), *Electrophoresis '86*, VCH Verlagsgesellschaft, Weinheim 1986, pp. 703–706.

[73] Lin, W., Hata, T., Kasamatsu, H., *J. Virol.* 1984, *50*, 363–371.

[74] Howe, J.G., Hershey, J.W.B., *J. Biol. Chem.* 1981, *256*, 12836–12839.

[75] Maruyama, K., Ebisawa, K., Nonomura, Y., *Anal. Biochem.* 1985, *151*, 1–6.

[76] Gershoni, J.M., Bayer, E.A., Wilchek, M., *Anal. Biochem.* 1985, *146*, 59–63.

[77] Turner, B.M., *J. Immunol. Methods* 1983, *63*, 1–6.

[78] Leary, J.J., Brigati, D.J., Ward, D.C., *Proc. Natl. Acad. Sci. USA* 1983, *80*, 4045–4049.

[79] Porter, D.D., Porter, H.G., *J. Immunol. Methods* 1984, *72*, 1–9.

[80] Walker, J.H., Boustead, C.M, Witzemann, V., *EMBO J.* 1984, *3*, 2287–2290.

[81] De Blas, A.L., Cherwinski, H.M., *Anal. Biochem.* 1983, *133*, 214–219.

[82] DuBois, D.B., Rossen, R.D., *J. Immunol. Methods* 1983, *63*, 7–24.

[83] Nakamura, K., Tanaka, T., Kuwahara, A., Takeo, K., *Anal. Biochem.* 1985, *148*, 311–319.

[84] Merrifield, P.A., Konigsberg, I.R., *Biochem. Biophys. Res. Commun.* 1986, *136*, 778–784.

[85] Rohringer, R., Holden, D.W., *Anal. Biochem.* 1985, *144*, 118–127.

[86] Moeremans, M., Daneels, G., van Dijck, A., Langanger, G., de May, J., *J. Immunol. Methods* 1984, *74*, 353–360.

[87] Moeremans, M., Daneels, G., De Mey, J., *Anal. Biochem.* 1985, *145*, 315–321.

[88] Hsu, Y.-H., *Anal. Biochem.* 1984, *142*, 221–225.

[89] Surek, B., Latzko, E., *Biochem. Biophys. Res. Commun.* 1984, *121*, 284–289.

[90] Daneels, G., Moeremans, M., de Raeymaeker, M., De Mey, J., *J. Immunol. Methods* 1986, *89*, 89–91.

[91] Wilson, J.M., Daddona, P.E., Simmonds, H.A., Acker, K.J.V., Kelley, W.N., *J. Biol. Chem.* 1982, *257*, 1508–1515.

[92] McMichael, J.C., Greisiger, L.M., Millman, I., *J. Immunol. Methods* 1981, *45*, 79–94.

[93] Reinhart, M.P., Malamud, D., *Anal. Biochem.* 1982, *123*, 229–235.

[94] Grace, A.M., Strauss, A.W., Sobel, B.E., *Anal. Biochem.* 1985, *149*, 209–217.

[95] Lum, M.A., Reed, D.E., *J. Immunol. Methods* 1983, *64*, 377–382.

[96] Handman, E., Jarvis, H.M., *J. Immunol. Methods* 1985, *83*, 113–123.

[97] Baumann, E.A., Hand, R., *J. Virol.* 1982, *44*, 78–87.

[98] Berman, J., Gershoni, J.M., Zamir, A., *J. Biol. Chem.* 1985, *260*, 5240–5243.

[99] Thorpe, R., Bird, C.R., Spitz, M., *J. Immunol. Methods* 1984, *73*, 259–265.

[100] Szewczyk, B., Kozloff, L.M., *Anal. Biochem.* 1985, *150*, 403–407.

[101] Van Dongen, W.M.A.M., Moorman, A.F.M., Destree, O.H.J., *Cell Diff.* 1983, *12*, 257–264.

[102] Elkon, K.B., Jankowski, P.W., Chu, J.-L., *Anal. Biochem.* 1984, *140*, 208–213.

[103] Anderson, N.L., Nance, S.L., Pearson, T.W., Anderson, N.G., *Electrophoresis* 1982, *3*, 135–142.

[104] Hayman, E.G., Engvall, E., A'Hearn, E., Barnes, D., Pierschbacher, M., Ruoslahti, E., *J. Cell Biol.* 1982, *95*, 20–23.

[105] Southern, E.M., *J. Mol. Biol.* 1975, *98*, 503–517.

[106] Perferoen, M., Huybrects, R., de Loof, A., *FEBS Lett.* 1982, *145*, 369–372.

[107] Gibson, W., *Anal. Biochem.* 1981, *118*, 1–3.

[108] Gershoni, J.M., Davis, F.E., Palade, G.E., *Anal. Biochem.* 1985, *144*, 32–40.

[109] Kyhse-Anderson, J., *J. Biochem. Biophys. Methods* 1984, *10*, 203–209.

[110] Bjerrum, O.J., Schafer-Nielsen, C., in: Dunn, M.J. (Ed.), *Electrophoresis '86*, VCH Verlagsgesellschaft, Weinheim 1986, pp. 315–327.

[111] Smith, E., Roberts, K., Butcher, G.W., Galfre, G., *Anal. Biochem.* 1984, *138*, 119–124.

[112] Westgeest, A.A.A., Bons, J.C., van den Brink, H.G., Aarden, L.A., Smeenk, R.J.T., *J. Immunl. Methods* 1986, *95*, 283–288.

[113] Keren, Z., Berke, G., Gershoni, J.M., *Anal. Biochem.* 1986, *155*, 182–187.

[114] De Maio, A., Lis, H., Gershoni, J.M., Sharon, N., *FEBS Lett.* 1986, *194*, 28–32.

[115] De Maio, A., Lis, H., Gershoni, J.M., Sharon, N., *Cell. Immunol.* 1986, *99*, 345–353.

[116] Bayer, E.A., Wilchek, M., *Methods Biochem. Anal.* 1980, *26*, 1–45.

[117] Wilchek, M., Bayer, E.A., *Immunol. Today*, 1984, *5*, 39–43.

[118] Bayer, E.A., Zalis, M.G., Wilchek, M., *Anal. Biochem.* 1985, *149*, 529–536.

[119] Mosckovitz, R., Gershoni, J.M., submitted for publication.

[120] Wilchek, M., Ben-Hur, H., Bayer, E.A., *Biochem. Biophys. Res. Commun.* 1986, *138*, 872–879.

[121] Roffman, E., Meromsky, L., Ben-Hur, H., Bayer, E.A., Wilchek, M., *Biochem. Biophys. Res. Commun.* 1986, *136*, 80–85.

[122] Fernandez-Pol, J.A., *FEBS Lett.* 1982, *143*, 86–92.

[123] Haeuptle, M.-T., Aubert, M.L., Djiane, J., Kraehenbuhl, J.-P., *J. Biol. Chem.* 1983, *258*, 305–314.

[124] Islam, M., Briones-Urbina, R., Bako, G., Farid, N.R., *Endocrinology* 1983, *113*, 436–438.

[125] Co, M.S., Gaulton, G.N., Fields, B.N., Greene, M.I., *Proc. Natl. Acad. Sci. USA* 1985, *82*, 1494–1498.

[126] Wolff, P., Gilz, R., Schumacher, J., Reisner, D., *Nucl. Acids Res.* 1985, *13*, 355–367.

[127] Gershoni, J.M., Lapidot, M., Zakai, N., Loyter, A., *Biochim. Biophys. Acta* 1986, *856*, 19–26.

[128] Daniel, T.O., Schneider, W.J., Goldstein, J.L., Brown, M.S., *J. Biol. Chem.* 1983, *258*, 4606–4611.

[129] Popot, J.-L., Changeux, J.-P., *Physiol. Rev.* 1984, *6*, 1162–1239.

[130] Gershoni, J.M., Palade, G.E., Hawrot, E., Klimowicz, D.W., Lentz, T.L., *J. Cell. Biol.* 1982, *95*, 422a.

[131] Oblas, B., Boyd, N.D., Singer, R.H., *Anal. Biochem.* 1983, *130*, 1–8.

[132] Wilson, P.T., Gershoni, J.M., Hawrot, E., Lentz, T.L., *Proc. Natl. Acad. Sci. USA* 1984, *81*, 2553–2557.

[133] Neumann, D., Gershoni, J.M., Fridkin, M., Fuchs, S., *Proc. Natl. Acad. Sci. USA* 1985, *82*, 3490–3493.

[134] Wilson, P.T., Lentz, T.L., Hawrot, E., *Proc. Natl. Acad. Sci. USA* 1985, *82*, 8790–8794.

[135] Neumann, D., Barchan, D., Safran, A., Gershoni, J.M., Fuchs, S., *Proc. Natl. Acad. Sci. USA* 1986, *83*, 3008–3011.

[136] Gershoni, J.M., *Proc. Natl. Acad. Sci. USA* 1987, *84*, 4318–4321.

[137] Gorelick, F.S., Cohn, J.A., Freedman, S.D., Delahunt, N.G., Gershoni, J.M., Jamieson, J.D., *J. Cell Biol.* 1983, *97*, 1294–1298.

[138] Sullivan, R., St. Jacques, S., Roberts, K.D., Chapdelaine, A., Bleau, G., *Fertil. Steril.* 1983, *40*, 283 – 284.

[139] Sullivan, R., Bleau, G., *Gamete Res.* 1985, *12*, 101 – 116.

[140] Wilkins, J.A., Chen, K.Y., Lin, S., *Biochem. Biophys. Res. Commun.* 1983, *116*, 1026 – 1032.

[141] Davis, J., Bennett, V., *J. Biol. Chem.* 1983, *258*, 7757 – 7766.

[142] Davis, J.Q., Bennett, V., *J. Biol. Chem.* 1984, *259*, 13550 – 13559.

[143] Baines, A.J., Bennett, V., *Nature* 1985, *315*, 410 – 413.

[144] Laurent, P., Beal, B., Gaspar, A., Guilloux, L., *J. Immunol. Methods* 1985, *82*, 181 – 184.

[145] Firon, N., Studies on the sugar combining site and the receptors of mannose specific bacteria. Ph. D. Thesis, Weizmann Institute of Science, Rehovot 1985.

[146] Muilerman, H.G., ter Hart, H.G.J., van Dijk, W., *Anal. Biochem.* 1982, *120*, 46 – 51.

[147] Van der Meer, J., Dorssers, L., Zabel. P., *EMBO J.* 1983, *2*, 233 – 237.

[148] Valtorta, F., Schiebler, W., Jahn, R., Ceccarelli, B., Greengard, P., *Anal. Biochem.* 1986, *158*, 130 – 137.

ELECTROPHORESIS OF DNA IN AGAROSE AND POLYACRYLAMIDE GELS

Nancy C. Stellwagen

University of Iowa, Iowa City, IA, USA

Abbreviations: Bis, N,N′-methylenebisacrylamide; **EEO,** electroendosmosis; **kbp,** kilobase pair; K_R, retardation coefficient; M_r, relative molecular mass; R_g, radius of gyration

1   Introduction

Electrophoresis is the movement of charged particles suspended in a medium under the influence of an electric field [1, 2]. In free solution, the electrophoretic mobility of DNA fragments is independent of molecular weight [3], because the DNA molecules have a constant linear charge density. However, when electrophoresis takes place in a supporting gel medium, molecular weight separation occurs. Various applications of gel electrophoresis have ranged from sequence analysis, involving the separation of DNA fragments containing a few base pairs, to the separation of whole chromosomes containing hundreds of thousands of base pairs [4]. The actual mechanism of the molecular weight separation of DNA fragments in a gel is not clear [5, 6]. Two different mechanisms have been proposed. The first, based on the Ogston model of a random meshwork of fibers [7], hypothesizes that the electrophoretic mobility of a macromolecule is proportional to the volume fraction of the pores of a gel that the macromolecule can enter [5, 8–10]. Since the average pore size decreases with increasing gel concentration [5, 8–11], electrophoretic mobility is predicted to decrease with increasing gel concentration and with increasing molecular weight. The second mechanism is based on reptation, the "worm-like" or "snake-like", end-on migration of DNA molecules through the pores of a gel [12–14]. This mechanism has been invoked to explain the inverse relationship between electrophoretic mobility and DNA molecular weight observed experimentally [15]. In this review, recent experiments involving the gel electrophoresis of DNA will be summarized. The different types of experiments for which gel electrophoresis is useful will be illustrated, rather than an exhaustive survey of the literature. Current ideas about the mechanism of DNA gel electrophoresis will also be discussed. Two types of gel matrices are commonly used: agarose and polyacrylamide. Since different types of experiments are carried out in the two media, the results will be presented separately. Some practical aspects of DNA gel electrophoresis are discussed in [16–18].

2   Agarose gel electrophoresis

2.1   Background

Agarose is a polymer consisting primarily of alternating 1,3-linked β-D-galactopyranose and 1,4-linked 3,6-anhydro-a-L-galactopyranose residues

[19, 20]. The agarose backbone may be esterified with sulfate, methoxyl, ketal pyruvate and/or carboxyl groups, with significant effects on the gelation behavior [19, 20]. However, X-ray diffraction studies of oriented films and fibers indicate that the backbone geometry is the same in all cases [21]. In native agarose some 4-linked residues occur in an unbridged open ring form, which can lead to the formation of a three-dimensional gel network by allowing each chain to participate in more than one intermolecular junction [20]. Solid agarose is dissolved by heating the suspended powder in an appropriate buffer, and undergoes gelation upon cooling. Gelation is preceded by the formation of double-stranded helices, which then aggregate to form the gel [22, 23]. The aggregates appear to contain 10–30 double helices [20, 22, 23], depending on the initial agarose [23, 24] and salt [23] concentration. The type of buffer is also important; gels formed in borate buffer instead of acetate buffer appear to have decreased interfiber spacing and increased fiber radius [25]. Static and dynamic light scattering experiments indicate that aqueous solutions of agarose undergo a sol-sol transition after a characteristic incubation period [26]. This transition may reflect the coil-to-helix transition preceding gelation [26]. The coil-to-helix transition is accompanied by sharp changes in optical activity, which can be used to monitor the transition [22, 27]. The dynamics of the sol-sol and sol-gel transitions have been studied by polarimetric stopped-flow measurements on non-gelling solutions of structurally regular chain segments of agarose sulfate [20]. An initially rapid conformational ordering is observed, which follows the dynamics expected for the process: 2 coil ⇌ helix. Subsequent slow relaxation to the equilibrium state follows second-order kinetics, consistent with the sequential aggregation of individual helices [20].

2.2   Linear DNA restriction fragments

2.2.1   Relation between mobility and molecular weight

Molecular weights of DNA fragments of unknown size are frequently inferred by interpolation from plots of the logarithm of molecular weight versus distance migrated on the gel. To try to rationalize such relationships, several investigators have studied the quantitative relationship between gel electrophoretic mobility and DNA molecular weight. The absolute mobility of DNA fragments depends on experimental parameters such as gel concentration and electric field strength [6]. However, relative mobilities are independent of electric field strength if the DNA molecular weight is less than about 1 kilobase pair (kbp) [28, 29]. Southern [15] showed that there is a linear relationship between DNA fragment length (L) and the reciprocal of mobility:

$$L = \frac{k_1}{(m-m_0)} + k_2 \tag{1}$$

where m is the mobility of the fragment and k_1, k_2 and m_0 are constants chosen to provide the best fit of the data. Since the mobility or, alternatively, the time required to pass through the gel pores is inversely dependent on macromolecular length, this equation suggests that DNA molecules migrate end-on through the gel. This concept is the basis of reptation theory, to be discussed in Section 2.5. The methods used to calculate the mobilities and empirical constants have been improved by Schaffer and Sederoff [30] and by Gough and Gough [31]. Bearden [32] proposed that the electrophoretic mobility of DNA fragments is related to DNA molecular weight, M_r, by the equation:

$$m = m_0 + k M_r^{-2/3} \tag{2}$$

where m is the observed mobility, m_0 is the "limiting mobility" of very large molecules, and k is a constant depending on the agarose concentration. The DNA molecules are assumed to be deformed into prolate ellipsoids of revolution by the electric field, leading to the fractional exponent for M_r. This relationship provides a more linear presentation of mobility data than the conventional plot of $\log M_r$ vs. mobility [32].

Stellwagen [6] found that the logarithm of the molecular weight of DNA restriction fragments is a sigmoidal function of the mobility (Fig. 1 a). In the commonly used 1.0–1.5% w/v gels, the smallest fragments (≤ 100 base pairs) approach a constant mobility, because the pore size of the gel is larger than the end-to-end lengths of the fragments in free solution ([33]; see also Section 2.4.4). Gels of higher agarose concentration cause the mobilities of the small fragments to be dependent on molecular weight (Fig. 1 b). The electrophoretic patterns obtained in agarose gels depend markedly on the applied electric field strength, as shown by double logarithmic plots in Fig. 2. These double logarithmic plots also show that the inverse mobility-molecular weight relationship proposed by Southern [15] is only observed for fragments larger than about 2 kbp in relatively weak electric fields. The deviations from linearity observed at higher electric field strengths [6, 15] are compensated by the parameter m_0 in Eq. (1). Stellwagen [29] found that the logarithm of the mobility of restriction fragments ≤ 1 kbp in size decreased as $M_r^{-0.8}$, because of the dependence of the effective "hydrodynamic surface area" of the DNA fragments on molecular weight. The hydrodynamic surface areas of various fragments were calculated from experimentally determined electric birefringence relaxation times [29]. She also found that the logarithm of the

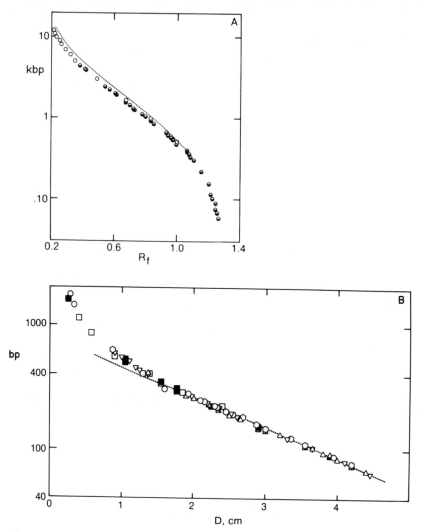

Figure 1. (A) Dependence of the logarithm of molecular weight (in kilobase pairs, kbp) on the relative mobility (R_f) of various DNA restriction fragments. 1.0% w/v SeaKem LE agarose gel, $E = 2.6$ V/cm. ○, ◑, results obtained with two different gels containing ethidium bromide. ······, observed mobility with no ethidium in the gel. Gel soaked in ethidium bromide after electrophoresis was completed. Mobility of a 506–516 bp doublet taken as 1.00. Reproduced with permission from [6]. (B) Dependence of the logarithm of molecular weight (in bp) on the distance migrated, *D*, in a 5.0% w/v SeaKem LE agarose gel. $E = 2.6$ V/cm. The different symbols represent fragments cut by different restriction enzymes. The dotted line represents a straight line connecting the low molecular weight points.

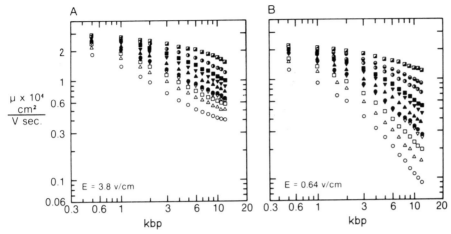

Figure 2. Dependence of the logarithm of the absolute mobility, μ, on the logarithm of molecular weight (in kbp) in agarose gels of different concentrations. (A) $E = 3.8$ V/cm; (B) $E = 0.64$ V/cm. The agarose concentrations (w/v) were: ○, 1.5%; △, 1.25%; □, 1.0%; ▽, 0.9%; ●, 0.8%; ▲, 0.7%; ▼, 0.6%; ■, 0.5%; ◑, 0.4%; ◒, 0.3%; ◪, 0.2%. Reproduced with permission from [6].

mobility of larger fragments decreased as $M_r^{-1/2}$, if the mobilities were first extrapolated to zero electric field strength [6].

Edmonson and Gray [34] studied the electrophoretic mobilities of double stranded DNA and RNA molecules in 0.4–1.8% w/v agarose gels using an electric field gradient of 1.0 V/cm. They found that the mobilities could be described by Eq. (3)

$$m = m_1'(L/L_0)^{-x} - m_2 \qquad (3)$$

where m is the mobility, L is the contour length of the fragment, m_1' and L_0 are constants, and x and m_2 depend on the agarose concentration. This equation provided a linear correlation for the mobility of DNA molecules ranging from 3.5 to 13 kbp in size, in 0.34–1.53% w/v agarose gels.

2.2.2   Determination of retardation coefficients

The negative slope of the line describing the dependence of the natural logarithm of the apparent mobility on gel concentration is called the retardation coefficient, K_R [5, 8–10]. Semi-logarithmic plots of the absolute mobility as a function of agarose gel concentration are linear for small (≤ 1 kbp) DNA restriction fragments [5, 6, 29, 32, 34, 36], except for a region

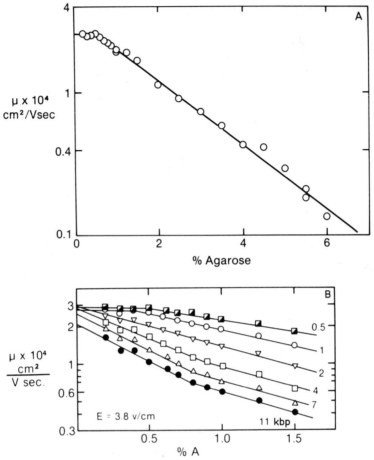

Figure 3. Ferguson-type plots of the dependence of the logarithm of the absolute mobility, μ, on the concentration of agarose, %A (w/v). The units of mobility are cm^2/Vs. (A) $E = 2.6$ V/cm, 510 bp fragment, wide range of agarose concentrations. (B) $E = 3.8$ V/cm, molecular weights (in kbp) indicated. (C) $E = 0.64$ V/cm, molecular weights indicated. (D) Mobilities extrapolated to zero electric field strength, molecular weights indicated. Reproduced with permission from [6].

of constant mobility at very low agarose concentrations (Fig. 3a). Similar plots for larger DNA fragments show concave upward curvature at high gel concentrations, with no horizontal region at low gel concentrations (Figs. 3b and 3c and [6, 29, 32, 35, 36]). The degree of curvature depends on the DNA molecular weight and applied voltage, becoming more pronounced for higher molecular weight fragments and higher electric fields [6, 36]. The curvature can be decreased by decreasing the electric field strength (Fig. 3c), and can essentially be eliminated by extrapolating the mobilities observed at each gel

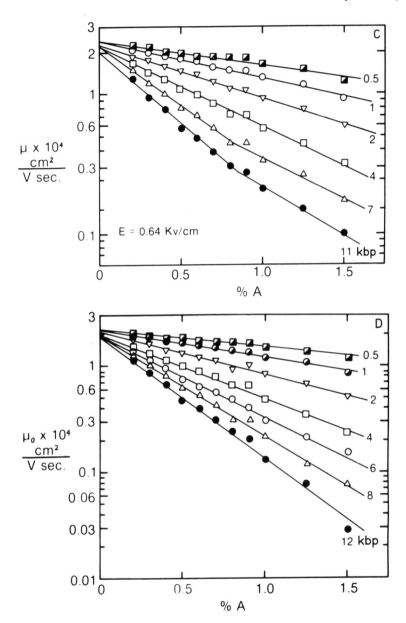

concentration to zero electric field strength [6], as shown in Fig. 3 d. Decreasing the electric field strength also changes the intercept and the slopes of the lines near the origin (compare Figs. 3 b – 3 d). Hence, retardation coefficients and apparent mobilities calculated from plots exhibiting curvature may depend on experimental conditions, such as electric field strength [6] and agarose concentration [24].

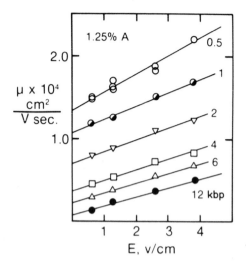

Figure 4. Dependence of the absolute mobility, μ, of DNA restriction fragments on electric field strength, E. Molecular weights (in kbp) indicated. Agarose gel concentration 1.25% w/v. Reproduced with permission from [6].

All of these electric field-dependent effects are due to the fact that the apparent mobilities of DNA restriction fragments in agarose gels increase linearly with increasing electric field strength (Fig. 4). The rate of increase decreases with increasing molecular weight [6]. It has been suggested that high electric fields may not give the particles enough time to accelerate to their free solution electrophoretic velocities before colliding with a gel fiber [37]. Alternatively, the conformation of the DNA molecules may be distorted by the electric field [14, 36]; complete stretching of the DNA molecule would lead to end-on migration through the gel [14, 38, 39]. Electric birefringence experiments also provide evidence for the stretching of DNA molecules in agarose gels [33], as will be discussed in Section 2.4.4. A third contribution to the electric field-dependent mobility might be distortion of the agarose gel matrix by the electric field, increasing the effective pore size in high electric fields (N. Stellwagen, unpublished).

According to pore size distribution theory [5, 8–10], the retardation coefficients can be related to molecular parameters by

$$K_R^{1/2} = a + b(R + r) \tag{4}$$

where a and b are empirically determined constants, R is the radius of a spherical particle moving through the gel, and r is the gel fiber radius. For highly asymmetric particles, such as DNA restriction fragments, the correct value to use for R has been a matter of debate [5]. Bearden [32] used a prolate ellipsoid of revolution with constant axial ratio to determine the surface area of an equivalent sphere. Stellwagen [29] used the hydrodynamic surface area

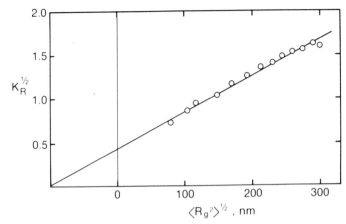

Figure 5. Dependence of the square root of the retardation coefficient, $K_R^{1/2}$, on the root-mean-square radius of gyration, $(R_g^2)^{1/2}$, of linear DNA fragments. The retardation coefficients were determined from mobilities extrapolated to zero electric field strength. The DNA molecular weights ranged from 0.5 to 12 kbp. Reproduced with permission from [6].

calculated from electric birefringence measurements for restriction fragments ≤ 1 kbp, and, for larger fragments, the root-mean-square radius of gyration, $(R_g^2)^{1/2}$, calculated from equations for the worm-like coil [6]. Serwer and Allen [36] used an effective hydrodynamic radius calculated from the radius of gyration. Edmonson and Gray [34] approximated Eq. (4) by a logarithmic function. Stellwagen [29] showed that a linear relationship exists between K_R and the effective hydrodynamic surface area for fragments ≤ 1 kbp in size and $K_R^{1/2}$ and $(R_g^2)^{1/2}$ for larger fragments [6], if the mobilities observed at each gel concentration are first extrapolated to zero electric field strength. The dependence of $K_R^{1/2}$ on $(R_g^2)^{1/2}$ is illustrated in Fig. 5. The linearity of this plot, as well as the linearity of Fig. 3d, both calculated with mobilities extrapolated to zero electric field strength, indicates that the Ogston theory of pore size distribution [5, 7–10] gives a good description of the electrophoresis of linear DNA fragments through agarose gels at zero electric field strength. This conclusion is reasonable, because the Ogston theory is based on random collisions between the macromolecules and the gel fibers. The theory breaks down in finite electric fields, where the collisions are no longer random.

2.2.3 Apparent mobility at zero gel concentration

From semi-logarithmic plots of the mobility as a function of gel concentration, such as shown in Fig. 3d, estimates can be made of the mobility of linear DNA fragments at zero gel concentration. This mobility should be close to the values observed in free solution [3, 40]. A summary of the literature values obtained for the mobility at zero gel concentration is given in Table 1.

Table 1. Mobility at zero gel concentration

Author	References	Type of DNA	$\mu \times 10^4$, cm^2/Vs
Olivera *et al.*	[3]	T2, T4 fragments	1.51 [a]
Ross and Scruggs	[40]	Calf thymus	1.85 [a]
Johnson and Grossman	[41]	PM2	1.4
Stellwagen	[6]	0.5 – 12 kbp fragments	2.0 [b]
Serwer and Allen	[36]	Linearized pBR322	3.1 [c]
Edmonson and Gray	[34]	λ-DNA restriction fragments	1.5 – 3.0

a) Free solution, 0.1 M NaCl
b) Mobilities extrapolated to zero electric field strength
c) Corrected for EEO

2.3   Spherical DNA molecules

2.3.1   Mobility as a function of topological conformation

The mobility of linear, open circle (relaxed) and closed circle (supercoiled) DNA molecules of the same molecular weight is identical at zero gel concentration [36] (Fig. 6a). Different mobilities for the different conformational isomers are observed at finite gel concentrations. Voltage gradient and molecular weight-dependent reversals of mobility can be observed under some experimental conditions [36, 42].

The dependence of the mobility on molecular weight is different for linear and for supercoiled DNA molecules [43] (Fig. 6b). In both cases, the molecular weights were known from independent measurements. Supercoiled plasmid DNAs migrate much more slowly, relative to linear standards, in gels made and electrophoresed in Tris-borate buffers than in Tris-acetate buffers [43], probably because of the decreased effective pore size of agarose gels formed in borate buffer [25]. The agarose concentration and electric field strength also affect the relative mobilities of linear and supercoiled DNAs [43]. Hence it is not possible to estimate the molecular weight of supercoiled DNA molecules from linear standards, and *vice versa*.

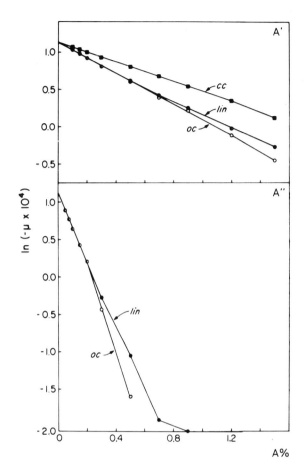

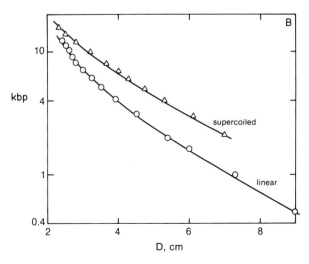

Figure 6. (A) Ferguson-type plot of the logarithm of the mobility of linear, open-circle, and supercoiled DNA molecules of the same molecular weight as a function of agarose concentration, A, in percent (w/v). (A') linear (lin), open-circle (oc) and supercoiled (cc) pBR 322, $E = 1.0$ V/cm; (A") T7 linear (lin) and λ590 open circle (oc) DNAs, $E = 0.34$ V/cm. Reproduced with permission from [36]. (B) Comparison of the mobility of linear and supercoiled DNA molecules in 0.9% w/v agarose gels, $E = 8$ V/cm. The gel was formed and run in Tris-acetate buffer. The logarithm of the molecular weight (in kbp) is plotted as a function of the distance migrated in the gel, D. Adapted and reproduced with permission from [43].

2.3.2   Determination of retardation coefficients

A semi-logarithmic plot of the mobility of spherical bacteriophage particles as a function of gel concentration was found to be concave downward at high gel concentrations [36, 44, 45], opposite to the direction of curvature observed with linear DNA molecules [35]. Typical data obtained from bacteriophage particles in HGT(P) [46] agarose are shown in Fig. 7a. The square root of the retardation coefficients calculated from the linear portion of the curves near the origin can be correlated with the radius of the bacteriophage particles (Fig. 7b).

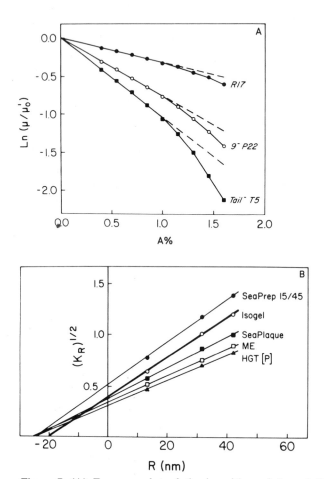

Figure 7. (A) Ferguson plot of the logarithm of the relative mobility of three spherical bacteriophage particles as a function of the agarose concentration, A, in percent (w/v); SeaPlaque agarose, $E = 0.71$ V/cm. (B) Dependence of $K_R^{1/2}$ on the radius of the bacteriophage particle, for different types of agarose. $E = 0.71$ V/cm. From [45].

In SeaPlaque [46] agarose the mobilities of bacteriophages and related spherical particles were found to be lineary dependent on gel concentration [47]; semi-logarithmic plots exhibited curvature. The intercepts of the mobilities of the linear plot with the axis of zero gel concentration were linearly related to bacteriophage radius [47], and were used to estimate the pore sizes of the gels ([47]; see also Section 2.8).

2.3.3 Temperature dependence of mobility

Serwer and Allen [36] determined the temperature dependence of the mobility of a supercoiled yeast plasmid DNA. The mobility, extrapolated to zero agarose concentration, varied inversely with the viscosity of water, between temperatures of 20 and 40 °C. Therefore the increase in mobility observed with increasing temperature can be attributed to a decrease in solvent viscosity. Similar results were obtained with linear and open circle DNAs.

2.3.4 Superhelix density

One application of agarose gel electrophoresis is the determination of the superhelix density of closed circular DNA molecules. In closed circular molecules the number of times one strand is linked through the other is called the linking number; it is a fixed integral number in the absence of strand scission. The linking number (Lk) is given by the sum of twist (Tw) and writhe (Wr):

$$Lk = Tw + Wr \tag{5}$$

where twist is the number of times one strand is wrapped about the other and writhe is the number of turns described by the helix axis in space (superhelical turns). When DNA molecules containing several thousand base pairs are first nicked and then covalently joined into circles, a distribution of topological isomers, termed topoisomers, is formed. These topoisomers can be clearly resolved on agarose gels [48, 49], as shown in Fig. 8. The slowest moving band of each sample is the nicked circular DNA. All the other bands represent closed DNA circles of distinct electrophoretic mobilities, each differing by one in linking number [48]. The intensities of the bands represent the relative population densities of the various topoisomers, which are found in an approximately Gaussian distribution due to thermal fluctuations in the conformation of the DNA helix at the moment of ring closure. Variations in the super helix density under different conditions have been used to determine the helical periodicity of DNA molecules

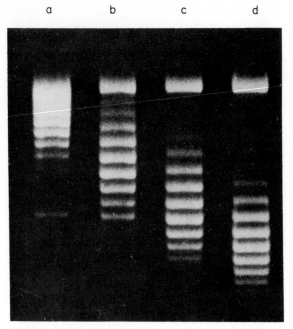

Figure 8. Electrophoresis patterns of supercoiled PM2 DNA molecules covalently closed by ligase at different temperatures. The temperatures of ligase reaction for the four samples (a)–(d) were 37, 29, 21 and 14 °C, respectively. Each band represents DNA molecules of the same molecular weight, differing by one in linking number. 0.7% Agarose gel, $E = 2.5$ V/cm. (From [48]).

in solution [50], evaluate the dependence of conformational transitions on superhelix density [51], study the $B \rightleftharpoons Z$ conformational transition [52, 53], and determine the temperature dependence of the helix rotation angle [48]. Changes in the topoisomer distribution of an *E. coli* plasmid DNA after infection of the host by bacteriophage T4 have also been studied [54]. Post infection topological changes were attributed to the relaxation of torsional stress.

A variant of the method of determining superhelix density is running the electrophoresis in each of two perpendicular directions, usually using the same electric field strength in each direction [55]. Alternatively, electrophoresis in the first direction can be carried out in a tube gel, and the tube gel placed in a wide slot in a horizontal gel before electrophoresis in the second direction [56]. Before electrophoresis in the second direction, the gel is soaked in an intercalating agent to partially unwind the helix [55]. The topoisomers are resolved into distinct spots that lie along a smooth curve [55], each spot differing by one in linking number (Fig. 9). An abrupt shift

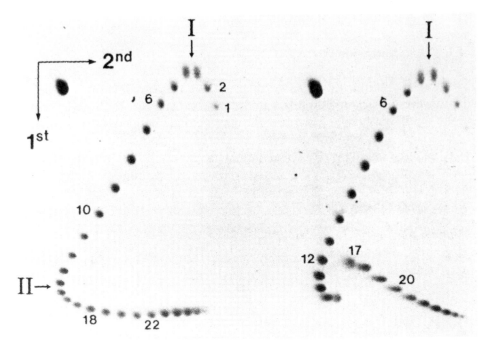

Figure 9. Two-dimensional agarose gel electrophoresis of the dependence of the right-to-left-handed conformational transition of cloned d(pCpG)·d(pCpG) on superhelicity. The electrophoretic pattern on the left represents a mixture of topoisomers of plasmid pTR161; that on the right represents the d(pCpG)-insert-containing plasmid. The discontinuity in the right panel is indicative of a conformational transition. Both samples were electrophoresed in the same 0.7% gel; within a panel the topoisomers differ only in linking number. The directions of electrophoresis are indicated. Prior to electrophoresis in the second dimension, the gel was equilibrated with buffer containing 1.3 μM chloroquine, which unwound the plasmids about 12 turns. The dark spot in the upper left-hand corner of each panel corresponds to nicked circular DNA. From [55].

in the curve, evident in the pattern on the right, is an indication of a conformational transition. Current applications of this technique include determining the helical periodicity of different conformations of DNA [55], studying the B$\rightleftharpoons$Z conformational transition [55, 57], detecting cruciform formation [58], and studying the *in vivo* occurrence of Z DNA [59]. The temperature dependence of the mobility of superhelical DNA has also been determined [56]. Two-dimensional electrophoresis in acrylamide-agarose composite gels [60] has been used to study cruciform formation in d(AT)$_n$·d(AT)$_n$ inserts in supercoiled DNA. Branched DNA molecules have been separated from linear molecules by electrophoresis in two perpendicular directions, using different agarose concentrations and electrical field strengths in each direction [61]. The branched molecules appear on the gel diagonal, in order of increasing molecular weight.

2.4   Pulsed electric field electrophoresis

2.4.1   One dimension

Instead of a continuously applied electric field, it is possible to use a pulsed square wave of varying amplitude and duration. The electrophoretic pattern can be significantly changed, even though the total energy (voltage×time) of the electric field is kept constant [62]. The amplitude, duration, and frequency of the pulse can be varied to maximize the gel resolution in any given molecular weight range [62]. A systematic study [63] of mobility as a function of pulse length and interval has shown that the apparent mobility increases and approaches the steady state (constant field) value as the pulse length increases, if the interval between pulses remains constant. If the pulse length is constant, the apparent mobility decreases as the interval between pulses becomes longer. These effects become more apparent for higher molecular weight fragments [63]. Pulse amplitudes of a few V/cm, applied for a few seconds, are generally used in these experiments.

2.4.2   Two perpendicular dimensions, non-uniform fields

Schwartz and Cantor [64] have devised an electrophoresis procedure using pulsed, alternating electric fields in perpendicular directions to separate chromosome-sized DNA molecules containing up to 2000 kbp. At least one of the perpendicular electric fields is inhomogeneous. The periods and amplitudes of the applied pulses are varied to optimize the separation in a desired molecular weight range. Electrophoresis occurs on the diagonal of the gel [64]. Alternatively, the gel can be placed at an angle of 45° to the mutually perpendicular electrodes, so that the electrophoretic pattern becomes essentially linear [65]. Typical applications of this technique include separating and identifying individual chromosomes [64, 66] and studying chromosomal rearrangements [67]. The agarose gel concentration is typically 1.0−1.5%, with electric fields ~3 V/cm and switching times of 20−50 s. Running the gels at 35 °C improves the separation of very large chromosomes [68].

2.4.3   Alternating polarity

Carle *et al.* [69] have made further improvements in the technique of large molecule electrophoresis by using alternating positive and negative electric fields of uniform voltage. Net migration in the "forward" direction is achieved when the portion of each switching cycle in the "forward" direction

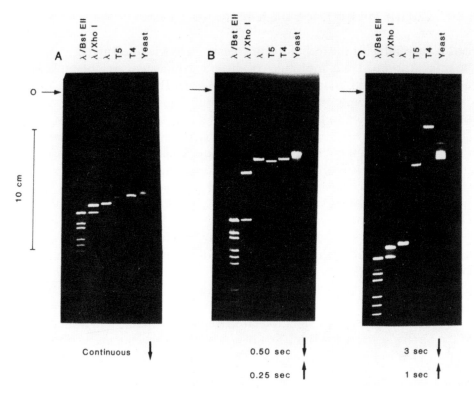

Figure 10. Field-inversion gel electrophoresis of DNA molecules in the size range 15 to 200 kbp. The DNAs used and their molecular weights are: BstE II-cleaved bacteriophage λ, ≤14.1 kbp; Xho I-cleaved λ, 15.0 and 33.5 kbp; λ, 48,5 kbp; T 5, 125 kbp; T 4, 170 kbp; yeast chromosomal DNAs, 260–700 kbp. (A) Control experiment in which forward electrophoresis was continuous for 4 h, leading to little size separation for molecules larger than 14 kbp. (B) Enhanced resolution of the two Xho fragments by periodic inversion of the electric field; the switching cycle was 0.5 s of forward migration followed by 0.25 s of reverse migration for 12 h; $E = 10.5$ V/cm; (C) Enhanced resolution of the λ, T 5 and T 4 DNAs by using a switching cycle of 3 s in the forward direction followed by 1 s in the reverse direction. All gels contained 1% agarose; the origin of electrophoresis is indicated by 0. Reproduced with permission from [69].

is about twice as long as the portion in the "reverse" direction. The switching interval can be varied to optimize the separation in any desired molecular weight range. Typical results are illustrated in Fig. 10. The mobility is found to go through a minimum as a function of molecular size [69]. The double-valued relation between mobility and size can be overcome by varying the switching interval in the forward direction during the experiment. The success of the electric field inversion technique in achieving molecular weight fractionation of large DNA molecules suggests that they have "directional" conformations during electrophoresis [69], at least under non-steady state conditions.

2.4.4   Electric birefringence, single pulses

Stellwagen [33] used the technique of transient electric birefringence to study the orientation of DNA molecules of different molecular weights imbedded in agarose gels of different concentrations. Electric birefringence uses refractive index differences to measure the orientation of macromolecules, whether imbedded in a gel or in free solution. The DNA molecules are oriented by a pulsed electric field; the applied voltage is on the order of 1 kV/cm, with durations in the millisecond range. The time constant for the loss of the orientation after removal of the electric field is characteristic of the size and shape of the macromolecule being oriented [70].

Three DNA restriction fragments, ranging in size from 622 to 2936 bp, imbedded in agarose gels ranging in concentration from 0.2% to 1.5%, were studied. The birefringence relaxation times of all three fragments were equal to the values observed in free solution, if the median pore diameter of the gel was greater than the effective hydrodynamic length of the fragment. The median pore diameter is discussed in Section 2.8. However, if the median pore diameter was smaller than the effective hydrodynamic length, the decay of the birefringence signal (*i.e.,* loss of orientation) became markedly slower, as illustrated in Fig. 11 for a 1426 bp DNA fragment. The longest time constant observed in the decay curve corresponds to that expected for the disorientation of a fully stretched 1426 bp DNA molecule. Since DNA molecules larger than one persistence length are not fully stretched in free solution (Fig. 11a and [71–74]), the 1426 bp fragment must become stretched out in the agarose gel while being oriented by the electric field.

A summary of the longest birefringence relaxation times observed for each of the three fragments in free solution and in agarose gels of various concentrations is given in Table 2. Apparent hydrodynamic lengths, calculated from the observed relaxation times using standard equations [70], are also given. To have a feeling for what these lengths represent, the percentage of the fully streched contour length (based on 0.34 nm rise/base pair) is also given. The median pore diameters of the gels were estimated from Eq. (9), below. The gel concentrations at which the three fragments became fully stretched were 1.0–1.5% for the 622 bp fragment, 0.5% for the 1426 bp fragment and 0.3% for the 2936 bp fragment, corresponding to the gel concentration at which the median pore diameter became comparable to the hydrodynamic length of the DNA fragment in free solution (Table 2). The commonly used marker dye, Bromophenol Blue, comigrates with ~500 bp DNA in 1.5% agarose, ~1300 bp DNA in 0.5% agarose and ~2400 bp DNA in 0.3% agarose. Therefore, in all three of these gels the fully stretched DNA fragments would

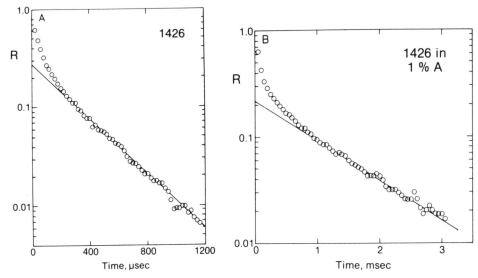

Figure 11. Comparison of the decay of the electric birefringence of a 1426 bp DNA fragment (A) in free solution and (B) imbedded in a 1% agarose gel. The logarithm of the relative bire-fringence, *R*, is plotted as a function of time after removal of the electric field. The applied electric fields were: (A) 4.3 kV/cm, applied for 100 μs; and (B) 4.6 kV/cm applied for 30 μs. The straight lines characterize the slowest decay process. The longest relaxation time is defined as the time required for this signal to decrease to 1/e of its initial value (intercept at *t* = 0). Reproduced with permission from [33].

have migrated behind the dye front; fragments ahead of the dye front (*e.g.,* the 622 bp fragment in 0.5% agarose) appear to be unstretched, with relaxation times comparable to those observed in free solution.

When DNA molecules ≥ 1 kbp are imbedded in an agarose gel matrix, the birefringence signal (*i.e.,* orientation) appears only after a significant lag period [75], as illustrated in the insert of Fig. 12. This delay of orientation decreases with increasing electric field strength, but is relatively independent of molecular weight, as shown in Fig. 12. Assuming the relationship in Fig. 12 to hold at still lower values of the applied electric field, the delay time before orientation would be ~10 ms at *E* = 10 V/cm and ~30 ms at *E* = 3 V/cm (typical electric field strengths used for electrophoresis). The delay in orientation can be attributed to the time required for one end of the DNA molecule to find a pore or "tube" oriented in the direction of the electric field [75]. The orientation of the head of the DNA molecule thus eventually determines the orientation of all the other segments, leading to elongation and reptation [14].

Table 2. Birefringence relaxation times of DNA fragments in free solution and in agarose gels of different concentrations[a]

bp	Free solution (0.2 mM Tris buffer)	Concentration of agarose gel				
		0.2%	0.3%	0.5%	1.0%	1.5%
622	$\tau = 52 \pm 3$ μs $L = 155$ nm 74% of contour length		$\tau = 59 \pm 4$ μs $L = 163$ nm 77% of contour length	$\tau = 59 \pm 3$ μs $L = 163$ nm 77% of contour length	$\tau = 74 \pm 5$ μs $L = 185$ nm 84% of contour length	$\tau = 106 \pm 10$ μs $L = 204$ nm 100% of contour length
1426	$\tau = 305 \pm 30$ μs $L = 306$ nm 64% of contour length	$\tau = 290 \pm 90$ μs $L = 300$ nm 62% of contour length	$\tau = 850 \pm 30$ μs[b] $L = 452$ nm 93% of contour length	$\tau = 1.02 \pm 0.17$ ms $L = 483$ nm 100% of contour length	$\tau = 1.12 \pm 0.11$ ms $L = 496$ nm 100% of contour length	$\tau = 1.29 \pm 0.14$ ms $L = 527$ nm 109% of contour length
2936	$\tau = 880 \pm 50$ μs $L = 578$ nm 46% of contour length	$\tau = 2.2 \pm 0.4$ ms[b] $L = 646$ nm 65% of contour length	$\tau = 5.3 \pm 0.5$ ms $L = 894$ nm 88% of contour length	$\tau = 6.6 \pm 1.1$ ms $L = 969$ nm 100% of contour length	$\tau = 6.9 \pm 1.2$ ms $L = 986$ nm 100% of contour length	$\tau = 8.8 \pm 1.1$ ms $L = 1088$ nm 109% of contour length
Estimated median pore diameter of gel	–	750 nm	520 nm	330 nm	190 nm	140 nm

a) From [33]
b) With 80 μs orienting pulse; τ increases with increasing pulse length

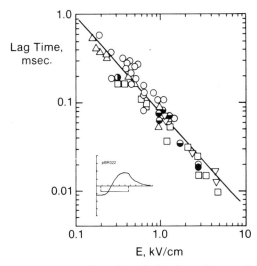

Figure 12. Log-log plot of the dependence of the lag period before orientation of DNA molecules in agarose gels, on the applied electric field strength, *E*. The various DNA samples were: ◐, 1426 bp restriction fragment; ○, 2936 bp fragment; □, linear pBR 322; ◒, supercoiled pBR 322; ▽, plasmid 82-6 B, 8600 bp; △, λ DNA. Insert: birefringence signal observed for supercoiled pBR 322 (upward-going signal), along with the applied electric field (downward-going signal). *E* = 1.2 kV/cm, pulse duration = 240 μs. The horizontal scale corresponds to 50 μs between tic marks. From [75].

The orientation of DNA molecules in agarose gels parallel to the electric field lines has also been observed by electric dichroism [76], using pulsed alternating perpendicular inhomogenous electric fields, and by polarized fluorescence [77]. In both of these cases very large DNA molecules were studied in continuous electric fields, using voltage gradients typical of electrophoresis experiments. The orientation of DNA molecules in agarose gels observed by these techniques can also be interpreted as evidence that reptation is a likely mechanism for the gel electrophoresis of high molecular weight linear DNA molecules.

2.4.5   Electric birefringence, reversing fields

If electric field pulses which are rapidly reversed in polarity are applied to DNA molecules imbedded in agarose gels, the birefringence (*i.e.*, orientation) decreases at the moment of field reversal, and then increases again, as shown in Fig. 13 a. The time interval between the moment of field reversal and the minimum in the orientation depends on pulse voltage, pulse length, and

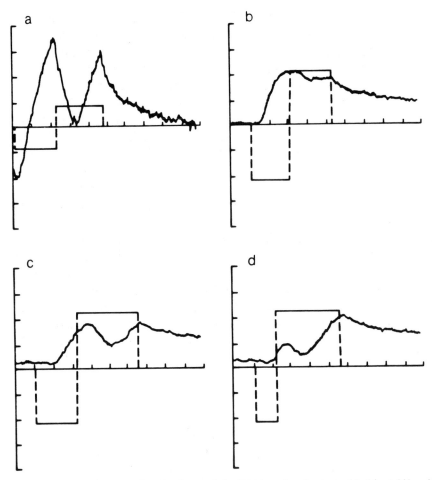

Figure 13. Birefringence signals observed for DNA molecules imbedded in 1.0% w/v agarose gels after rapidly reversing the polarity of the applied electric field. (a), λ DNA, 1.2 ms/1.2 ms orienting pulse, $E = 0.57$ kV/cm, 0.5 ms between horizontal tic marks; (b)–(d), 2936 bp restriction fragment, $E = 1.0$ kV/cm, 100 μs between horizontal tic marks, illustrating the effect of varying the initial pulse length: (b) 430 μs/430 μs orienting pulse; (c) 210 μs/430 μs orienting pulse; (d), 120 μs/430 μs orienting pulse. From [75].

DNA molecular weight [75]. Very little change in orientation (*i.e.*, essentially no decrease in the amplitude of the birefringence) is observed if the DNA molecules had reached steady state orientation (equilibrium birefringence) before field reversal occurred (Fig. 13b). Since steady state birefringence is accompanied by stretching and orientation (Section 2.4.4), the completely stretched, oriented DNA molecule can reverse its direction of migration quickly without having to find a "tube" or pore in the opposite direction.

Complicated orientation patterns are observed if the DNA orientation is far from equilibrium before field reversal occurs (Fig. 13 c). If the field "on" time is very short compared to the time required to reach the equilibrium orientation, almost no orientation occurs in the first field direction (Fig. 13 d). When the field is reversed in polarity, incompletely stretched molecules experience a delay in orientation similar to that observed when the field is first applied (Fig. 12 insert), because the unoriented (and unstretched) end of the molecule must find a "tube" or pore in the new field direction. At the same time, the DNA molecules begin to lose their original orientation (as shown in Fig. 11), so that a minimum in orientation occurs during the second half of the reversing pulse. To achieve equal orientation in the second field direction, the second pulse must be longer than the first pulse. However, most current protocols call for the second pulse to be only one-third or one-half as long as the first pulse [66, 69]. Small DNA molecules, which had reached their equilibrium orientations before field reversal, would remain relatively completely oriented in the reversed field, while larger molecules would be relatively little oriented in the new field direction. The switching times necessary for improved molecular weight separation would depend on the molecular weights of the DNA molecules in the mixture, because the characteristic orientation and disorientation times are dependent on molecular weight [75].

2.5   Reptation theory

Lumpkin *et al.* [13, 14] have developed a theory for electrophoresis based on the length-wise movement, or reptation [78, 79], of DNA molecules through "tubes" or pores in the gel. The direction of the tube is random, except for possible bias introduced by the applied electric field. When the electric field is small, the mobility is inversely dependent on length, as observed experimentally [6, 12, 15]. At higher electric fields the tubes become oriented, because the field biases the direction of the leading segment of the DNA molecule. This effect leads to an increase of mobility with increasing field strength, because the equation for mobility now contains two terms:

$$m = \frac{Q}{3\xi} \left[\frac{1}{N} + \frac{E'^2}{3} \right] \tag{6}$$

where m is the mobility, Q is the total charge of the polyion, ξ is the frictional coefficient for translational motion along the tube, N is the number of tube segments (directly related to L, the contour length of the molecule) and E' is a dimensionless reduced electric field. The first term, which varies inversely as the molecular weight, is independent of E at low field strengths; the second term, which is independent of molecular weight, goes to zero at low fields but becomes dominant at high field strengths. As a result the mobility becomes independent of molecular weight at high field strengths, as observed experimentally [28, 80].

In very high electric fields, the DNA segments would be expected to be completely oriented along the field direction, so that further increases in electric

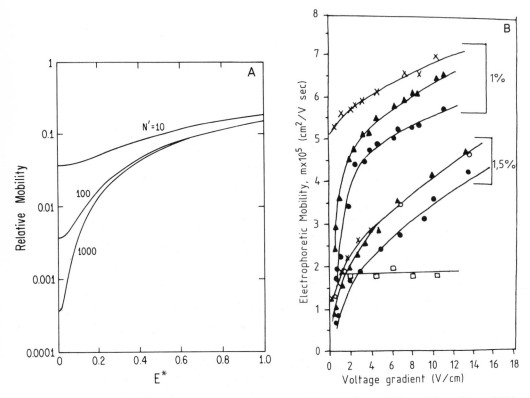

Figure 14. (A) Theoretical plot of the logarithm of the relative mobility of three linear DNA chains differing in molecular weight by factors of 10, on the reduced electric field, E. Reproduced with permission from [14]. (B) Experimental determination of the dependence of the electrophoretic mobility of several DNA molecules on the applied electric field strength. The upper three curves were measured for linear DNA molecules in 0.5% agarose-1.0% polyacrylamide gels; the middle curves were measured in 0.5% agarose-1.5% polyacrylamide gels. The various DNA samples were: ●, T2; ▲, T1; x, PPSX; ○, T2 DNA fragments; □, bacteriophage T1. Reproduced with permission from [81].

field strength would have no effect on the mobility. A theoretical calculation [14] of the dependence of the relative mobility on electric field strength is shown in (Fig. 14a) for three DNA chains differing in length by factors of 10. The mobilities of the three chains approach each other at high values of E, but differ markedly at low E. Very similar experimental results have been obtained for linear DNA molecules by Lishenskaya and Mosevitsky [81] (Fig. 14b). However, the mobility of a spherical bacteriophage particle was independent of electric field strength, as also shown in Fig. 14b.

Slater and Noolandi [82] have independently developed a reptation theory for DNA electrophoresis. They showed that the time constant for chain stretching is small compared with the duration of an electrophoresis experiment [82, 83]. This leads to a field dependent mobility only weakly dependent on chain length, in agreement with Eq. (6). Hervet and Bean [84] have used reptation theory to correlate the mobilities of DNA restriction fragments with "effective persistence lengths" determined by gel concentration. Reptation

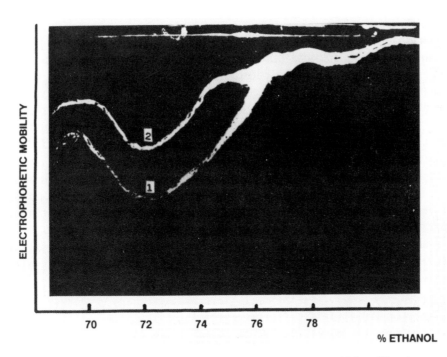

Figure 15. The mobility of linear (1) and open circular (2) plasmid pA03 in a 2% w/v agarose gel containing an ethanol gradient ranging from 70–80%. The direction of electrophoresis is from top to bottom. Reproduced with permission from [86].

theories have also been extended to mobilities in pulsed electric fields [14, 82, 85].

2.6   Structural transitions

The $B \rightleftharpoons A$ conformational transition in DNA has been studied by gel electrophoresis in an ethanol gradient [86]. DNA molecules at the mid-point of the transition, where alternating stretches of A-form and B-form DNA exist, have the highest electrophoretic mobility (Fig. 15). Therefore, B/A junction zones must be flexible and act as hinges for the rest of the molecule [86]. A pH dependent structural transition in a homopurine-homopyrimidine tract in a superhelical DNA has been studied by two-dimensional electrophoresis [87]. A new structural conformation, based on a cruciform structure, has been suggested [87].

2.7   Binding studies

An electrophoretic assay has been developed to study the cooperative binding of an *E. coli* single-strand binding protein to single-stranded nucleic acid [88]. Complexes containing a constant concentration of DNA and various concentrations of protein were electrophoresed in 0.3% w/v agarose gels. Since the dissociation rate of the complex was small, electrophoresis separated the complexes according to the amount of protein bound to each DNA molecule. Typical electrophoresis patterns obtained for two different binding modes are shown in Fig. 16. The pattern on the left indicates random binding of the protein to the DNA; at all binding ratios only a single rather diffuse band is observed, suggesting that all DNA molecules have approximately the same number of bound protein molecules. The electrophoretic pattern on the right is indicative of cooperative binding. Lanes C and D contain a bimodal distribution of DNA molecules, some containing a large number of protein molecules and others migrating close to the position of free DNA.

2.8   Pore size and fiber radius

Three estimates have been made of the pore size of agarose gels as a function of concentration. Righetti *et al.* [89] used polystyrene latex particles of

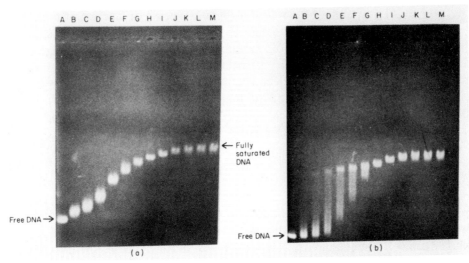

Figure 16. Electrophoresis of complexes of single-strand binding protein with M13mp7 DNA (circles) in 0.3% w/v agarose gels. Each lane contains 0.61 μg of DNA and increasing amounts of protein. (a) Complexes formed in high salt; (b) complexes formed in low salt. From [88].

known diameter to determine the limiting pore size of Isogel [46] agarose gels between 0.16% and 1.0% w/v in concentration. The limiting pore size was estimated from an extrapolation of migration distance *vs.* particle diameter; the intercept at zero particle mobility was assumed to be the limiting pore size. The relationship between pore size and gel concentration was found to be:

$$P = 140.7 \, c^{-0.7} \tag{7}$$

where P is the mean pore diameter in nm and c is the concentration in percent (w/v) of the hydrated gel powder. Serwer and Allen [47] studied the electrophoresis of spherical virus particles of known molecular radius in SeaPlaque [46] agarose. They found that the intercept of a linear plot of mobility *vs.* agarose concentration was related to particle radius (see Section 2.3.2), and proposed the following equation for agarose gels ≤0.9% (w/v) in concentration:

$$P = 117.4 \, c^{-1.71} \tag{8}$$

where P is the pore diameter in nm and c is the concentration in percent (w/v) of the hydrated gel powder.

Stellwagen [6] determined the retardation coefficients of a series of high molecular weight DNA restriction fragments in Seakem LE [46] agarose, using
the root-mean-square radius of gyration to estimate molecular size. She
assumed that when the mobility of a DNA fragment was equal to half its
mobility at zero gel concentration, the median pore size of the gel would be
equal to the average diameter of the macromolecule [8, 9]. The relationship
between pore size and gel concentration, for gels between 0.25% and 1.5%
w/v in concentration, was found to be:

$$P = 50 + 140 \, c^{-1.0} \tag{9}$$

where P is the median pore diameter in nm and c is the gel concentration in
per cent. From Eqs. (7)−(9), the median pore diameter of a 1% gel would
be 280 nm for Isogel agarose, 230 nm for SeaPlaque agarose, and 190 nm for
Seakem LE agarose. The decrease in estimated pore size is opposite in direction to the sieving order determined by Serwer et al. [45] for these three types
of agarose, probably because very different methods were used to estimate
pore size. The sieving power, S, of an agarose preparation was defined by
Serwer et al. [45] as the dependence of the retardation coefficient on molecular radius. Values of S, calculated from the data in Fig. 7b, are summarized
in Table 3. They correlate with pore diameters of 4% gels determined by electron microscopy [46], but not with the pore diameters of 1% gels estimated
from electrophoresis measurements (see above).

The gel fiber radii of various types of agarose were determined by Serwer et
al. [45] from plots of $K_R^{1/2}$ vs. the radius of spherical bacteriophage particles, using Eq. (4) and the data in Fig. 7b. The results were found to be
nearly independent of the type of agarose, as summarized in Table 3. However, a recalculation of the fiber radius of SeaPlaque agarose using the same
data fitted to non-linear Ferguson plots [24] showed that the effective fiber
radius was dependent on the agarose concentration, decreasing from 54 to
21 nm as the agarose concentration increased from 0.4 to 1.6%.

The gel fiber radius calculated from Eq. (4) may also depend on the type of
macromolecule undergoing electrophoresis. For example, the value of the gel
fiber radius calculated for Seakem LE agarose from the mobilities of linear
DNA molecules (Fig. 5) would be 100 nm, much larger than the value of
~25 nm determined for various types of agarose from the mobility of (relatively compact) bacteriophage particles [45] (see also Table 3). The gel fiber
radius of HGT(P) agarose estimated from Eq. (4) and the mobility of protein
molecules (much smaller than bacteriophage particles or linear DNA frag-

Table 3. Characteristics of various types of agarose

Agarose[a]	Sulfur[b] %	EEO[b]	Calculated pore diameter		Sieving power[e], $nm^{-1} \times 10^2$	Fiber radius[e], nm
			1% gel[c], nm	4% gel[d], nm		
Seakem HGT	≤0.15	≤0.10	–	–	1.69	25
Seakem ME	≤0.35	0.16–0.19	–	106	1.94	27
Seakem LE	≤0.35	0.10–0.15	190	–	–	–
SeaPlaque	≤0.15	<0.15	230	69	2.53	25
Isogel	≤0.10	–	280	–	3.82	20
SeaPrep	≤0.10	<0.05	–	42	4.63	24

a) All are trademark names of Marine Colloids
b) Data from the manufacturer [46]
c) Section 2.8
d) Determined by electron microscopy, data from the manufacturer [46]
e) Ref. [45]

ments) is 1–2 nm [24, 90]. Electron microscopy [23] of freeze fractured agarose gels has indicated that the fiber radius is about 3–5 nm. Tietz and Chrambach [24] have reconciled these variations by suggesting that gels have an "effective fiber structure" which is a function of both the agarose concentration and the size of the molecule passing through it.

2.9 Electroendosmosis

Electroendosmosis (EEO) refers to the flow of buffer toward the cathode during electrophoresis; it occurs because the fixed anionic groups in the agarose gel matrix are unable to migrate in the electric field, while the counterions are free to move toward the cathode. One manufacturer [46] has provided estimates of a "coefficient of electro-osmosis" for various types of agarose. These values are given in Table 3. Johnson *et al.* [91] proposed an empirical correction for EEO based on multiplying the mobility observed at a given gel concentration by $(m_r)^{-0.5}$, where m_r is the electro-osmosis coefficient. Serwer and Hayes [92] devised an empirical correction for EEO, subtracting a constant from the mobility observed at zero gel concentration. The constants were determined by comparing the mobilities of mixtures of bacteriophage particles in different types of agarose.

Stellwagen [6] found that the mobility of linear DNA fragments in Seakem LE agarose, extrapolated to zero gel concentration and zero electric field strength, was equal to the mobility observed in free solution [3, 40], and concluded that EEO was negligible under these conditions. However, EEO may be responsible for the fact that the mobilities extrapolated to zero gel concentration at finite electric field strengths are different from the free solution value (compare Figs. 3a–3c with Fig. 3d).

2.10   Experimental improvements

Serwer [39] has described an apparatus and techniques for running several agarose gels of different concentrations simultaneously. Gels as low as 0.035% w/v in concentration have been formed and run [94]. Improved procedures for controlling voltage gradient and temperature have also been described [95]. If the different lanes contain the same agarose concentration but different concentrations of ethidium bromide, superhelix density can be measured in horizontal gels instead of tube gels [96]. An apparatus in which two-dimensional electrophoresis can be performed without manipulating the gel before electrophoresis in the perpendicular direction has been described [97]. Electrophoresis in a gel almost dilute enough to be non-retarding, followed by electrophoresis in an orthogonal direction, has been developed as a procedure to determine the radius of spherical particles [98].

The effect of sample load on DNA mobility has been studied for several types of agarose [99]. As the sample load is increased, the DNA fragments move faster in the direction of migration [91, 99]. This effect was attributed to a binding reaction; as the load increases a larger fraction of the DNA binding sites are occupied and the DNA zone moves forward until reaching a region with free binding sites. As the loading increases still further, the band splits into two sharp components [99]. Overloading effects are minimized at high gel concentrations. Sharp, well-resolved zones are obtained with very low DNA loads only in high salt, high pH, high EDTA buffers, or when unlabeled "carrier" DNA is added [99]. These results suggest that electrophoresis should be viewed as a dynamic association-dissociation reaction with the gel matrix [39, 99]. The resolution of DNA fragments ranging from 30 bp to 15 kbp in a single agarose gel has been achieved by pouring a slab gel of increasing thickness from cathode to anode [100].

Methods of quantifying the fluorescence of ethidium bromide-stained horizontal gels have been developed for one-dimensional [101] and two dimensional [102] gels. Methods of making quantitative measurements of photographs of fluorescently stained DNA gels have been described [103]. A computer-automated method of evaluating one-dimensional gel electrophoretic radiograms has also been described [104]. Silver staining has been developed as a method to visualize DNA bands, with a sensitivity comparable to fluorescence techniques using ethidium bromide [105].

3 Polyacrylamide gel electrophoresis

3.1 Background

Polyacrylamide gels are formed by the polymerization of acrylamide and a cross-linking agent, such as N,N'-methylenebisacrylamide (Bis). The reaction mechanism is a free radical polymerization, using, for example, ammonium persulfate as the initiator and N,N,N',N'-tetramethylethylenediamine (TEMED) as catalyst. The rate of the reaction and its extent are governed by the concentration of initiator [18]. Control of the polymerization reaction depends on reagent purity and stoichiometry [106]. Dynamic light scattering measurements [107] have been used to measure the shear modulus of polyacrylamide gels containing $4-6\%$ w/v acrylamide and $0.005-0.015\%$ Bis. For a given concentration of initiator, the number of chains per gel is independent of monomer concentration, although the mass per chain increases with increasing monomer concentration [107, 108]. The number of chains per gel can be increased by increasing the initiator concentration [107]. Small angle x-ray, neutron, and light scattering studies [109] have indicated that 8% w/v polyacrylamide gels polymerized with $0-0.5\%$ Bis contain two phases, a homogeneous phase of constant polymer content, and an inhomogeneous phase, characterized by large concentration fluctuations. In the homogeneous phase, the fiber radius increases from 0.25 nm to 0.4 nm with increasing Bis concentration. The correlation length also increases.

3.2 Linear DNA restriction fragments

3.2.1 Relation between mobility and molecular weight

The polyacrylamide gel electrophoresis of linear DNA restriction fragments between 30 and 4000 bp in size has been studied by Stellwagen [110]. A

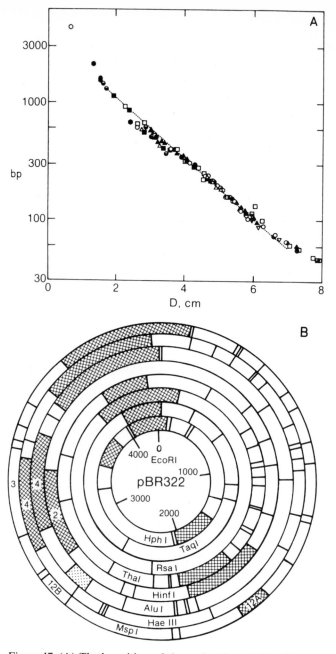

Figure 17. (A) The logarithm of the molecular weight of DNA restriction fragments (in kbp) is plotted as a function of the distance, D, migrated in a 6.9% w/v polyacrylamide gel. $E = 11.3$ V/cm. The different symbols represent fragments cut by different restriction enzymes. The dotted line represents a straight line drawn through many of the low molecular weight points. Reproduced with permission from [110]. (B) Schematic diagram of pBR322 sequence [111]. Segments migrating anomalously slowly (by at least 10%) in 6.9% w/v polyacrylamide gels are crosshatched. Reprinted with permission from [110].

typical plot of the logarithm of the molecular weight as a function of distance migrated on the gel is shown in Fig. 17a. The distribution of mobilities is similar to that observed for the same fragments in 5% agarose (Fig. 1b). However, in the polyacrylamide gel, a significant number of fragments in the 350–700 bp size range have mobilities below the straight line describing the electrophoretic behavior of the smaller fragments. The mobilities were determined in a single multiple-lane gel, so that conditions of temperature and applied voltage were the same for all fragments. These anomalous mobilities will be discussed in Section 3.3.3. The electric field dependence of the absolute or relative mobilities of fragments ≤ 4 kbp in size is small [38, 110] and virtually independent of molecular weight [38]. However, the mobilities of DNA molecules larger than about 10 kbp depend on electric field strength [38, 39, 112], approaching a constant value in high electric fields [39, 112]. The mobilities of high molecular weight samples also decrease abruptly at very low electric field strengths [81] (Fig. 14b).

3.2.2   Determination of retardation coefficients

Stellwagen [110] determined the mobility of a series of linear restriction fragments in polyacrylamide gels of three different concentrations. Typical results are illustrated in Fig. 18. The apparent absolute mobilities observed for small DNA fragments, extrapolated to zero gel concentration, ranged between 1.9 and 3.4×10^{-4} cm^2/V s. [110]. The upper range of these values is higher than the free solution mobility of DNA [3, 40], possibly because curvature would have been observed at low polyacrylamide concentrations if it had been possible to form more dilute gels (compare Fig. 3a; see also [113]). Specific interactions between the aromatic DNA molecules and the polyacrylamide gel matrix may also be important. Stellwagen [110] observed that the absolute mobility of the Bromophenol Blue marker dye decreased linearly with increasing polyacrylamide gel concentration, as shown in the insert of Fig. 18b. This effect may be due to the affinity of polyacrylamide gels for aromatic compounds [114]. The mobility of the marker dye was independent of gel concentration in agarose gels [110], and independent of electric field strength in both gel media.

The absolute mobilities of DNA fragments in polyacrylamide gels were larger than the mobilities observed in agarose gels of the same concentration, as can be seen from a comparison of Fig. 18a with Fig. 3a. It is possible that DNA molecules interact more strongly with the agarose gel matrix [99] than with polyacrylamide [39]. However, it is more likely that the different mobilities reflect the fact that the average pore radius in agarose and polyacrylamide

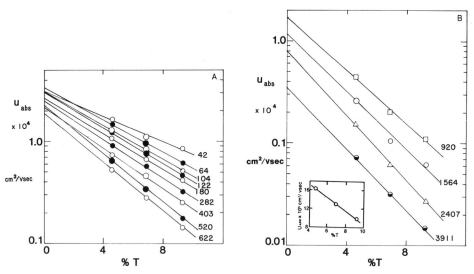

Figure 18. Ferguson-type plots of DNA restriction fragments in polyacrylamide gels. The logarithm of the absolute mobility, extrapolated to zero electric field strength, is plotted as a function of the polyacrylamide gel concentration. The number next to each curve indicates the molecular weight of the fragment. Insert: absolute mobility of the Bromophenol Blue marker dye as a function of polyacrylamide gel concentration. Adapted and reprinted with permission from [110].

gels is different, even though the nominal concentration is the same. Equal absolute mobilities were observed for a 510 bp DNA fragment in 4% polyacrylamide and 2.8% agarose gels (Fig. 3a and 18a). If Eq. (9) can be extended to higher concentrations, the pore radius of a 2.8% agarose gel can be estimated to be 5.0 nm. The pore radius of a 4% polyacrylamide gel is estimated to be 5.8 nm from Fig. 26 (see Section 3.8). These two values calculated for the pore radii are reasonably close, considering the assumptions made in estimating gel pore size. Hence, equal absolute mobilities observed for the same macromolecule in different gel media indicate that the pore sizes of the gels are approximately equal.

Retardation coefficients, K_R, were determined for the different DNA restriction fragments from the slopes of the lines in Fig. 18 [110]. The value of K_R was approximately constant for fragments larger than about 800 bp, as observed previously [38, 112]. The values of K_R observed for smaller fragments can be related to molecular dimensions by Eq. (4), if the molecular radius is chosen to be the geometric mean radius, $\bar{R}$ [110]. The geometric mean radius, $\bar{R}$, in nm, is defined as

$$\bar{R} = [3\,V/4\pi]^{1/3} = 0.755\,bp^{1/3} \tag{10}$$

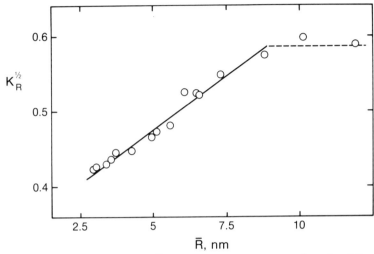

Figure 19. Dependence of $K_R^{1/2}$ on the geometric mean radius, $\bar{R}$, of linear DNA restriction fragments. Adapted and reprinted with permission from [110].

if the equivalent volume (V) of the DNA molecule is taken to be that of a right circular cylinder of radius 1.3 nm and length 0.34 nm $\times$ bp. A plot of $K_R^{1/2}$ vs. $\bar{R}$ is shown in Fig. 19. The linear correlation indicates that the retardation coefficients are dependent on the mass of the DNA molecules (raised to the 1/3 power), even though these short DNA fragments are highly asymmetric in shape. Hence molecular mass, not molecular shape, appears to be the controlling factor in the polyacrylamide gel electrophoresis of DNA restriction fragments. It is possible that the DNA molecules act as "magic bullets" and deform the polyacrylamide gel during electrophoresis. Alternatively, the DNA molecules may interact specifically with the gel matrix during electrophoresis. Both of these processes would be expected to be mass dependent. A third possibility is that curvature of the plots at lower gel concentration would lead to a different dependence of K_R on molecular radius if gels could be formed in this concentration region [113]. However, composite agarose-polyacrylamide gels exhibit no curvature at polyacrylamide concentrations as low as 1% w/v [81].

3.2.3   Anomalous migration

When a series of linear DNA restriction fragments is electrophoresed in a polyacrylamide gel, the mobility of a significant number of fragments in the 300–500 bp range is found to be lower than the smooth curve describing the mobility of the rest of the fragments (Fig. 17a) [110]. Molecular weights of these anomalously migrating fragments, if calculated from their electrophoretic mobilities, would be 10–20% larger than their sequenced molecular weights [110]. The anomalous mobilities are enhanced by increasing the polyacrylamide gel concentration [110, 115], lowering the temperature of electrophoresis [110, 116], or adding Mg^{++} to the electrophoresis buffer [116]. Decreasing the polyacrylamide gel concentration [110, 115], raising the temperature of electrophoresis [110, 116] or adding Na^+ to the electrophoresis buffer [116] has the opposite effect. Anomalous mobilities are not observed in denaturing gels [117]. The anomalously migrating fragments derived from plasmid pBR 322 were found to originate from three specific regions of the plasmid, as shown in Fig. 17 b [110]. Therefore, a conformational feature such as a kink or bend in the DNA helix may be responsible for the anomalously slow migration of these fragments. Head-to-tail dimers of an anomalously migrating fragment migrate even more anomalously [110].

The anomalously slow electrophoresis of some DNA fragments is particularly apparent for a 410 bp sequence present in a kinetoplast DNA minicircle [115, 116]. The molecular weight which would be calculated from the electrophoretic mobility of this fragment in 10–12% polyacrylamide gels is 3–4 times larger than its sequenced molecular weight [115, 116]. The anomalously slow electrophoretic migration has been attributed to stable curvature of the DNA helix axis [115, 116, 118]. Analysis of the electrophoretic mobility of subfragments of this sequence has led to the conclusion that two sequences, located at 100–170 bp and 190–250 bp (numbering from one end of the fragment), are most responsible for the anomalous gel mobility [116]. Both sequences contain short runs of adenosine residues spaced at intervals of about 10 bp. Electric birefringence [118] and electric dichroism studies [119] have been used to estimate the bending angle of the helix axis.

Wu and Crothers [120] have used gel electrophoresis to map the bending locus in the kinetoplast fragment more precisely. Dimers of the kinetoplast fragment were cloned into a plasmid and digested with different restriction enzymes, each of which cut the sequence once. A series of fragments of identical molecular weight was obtained, with the putative bend located in different positions with respect to the ends of the fragment. Fragments with the bend located near one end would be expected to have a higher gel mobility than the more C-shaped fragments with the bend located near the center. Therefore, extrapolating to the position of maximum mobility would locate the center of the bend (Fig. 20). Extrapolation of the nearly linear portions of the curve gives an estimate that the bend center is located at ~148 bp [120]. The maximum and the minimum (located at bp ~380) of the mobility

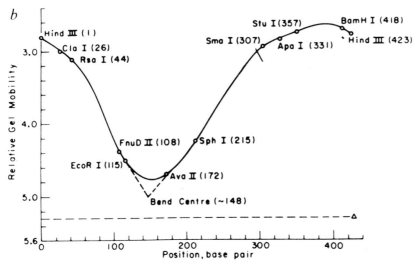

Figure 20. Dependence of the relative gel mobilities of circularly permuted DNA fragments on the position of the restriction site in the fragment. A linear extrapolation was used to estimate the position of the bend center. ○, circularly permuted K·DNA fragments; △, normal 423 bp fragment. The polyacrylamide gel concentration was 5% w/v. From [120].

curve are separated by about one half the fragment length, as expected. This technique has also been used to map the position of the bend induced when catabolite gene activating protein binds to its DNA recognition sequence [120].

Several systematic studies have been undertaken to characterize the anomalous electrophoretic behavior of certain DNA sequences. Hagerman [121] prepared a series of oligomers of the form $(G_iA_3T_3C_i)_N$, $(N>1; i = 1, 2,$ or 3). For each series the electrophoretic behavior was essentially normal for $N \leq 6$. However, the electrophoretic mobilities of higher polymers of the series constructed with a 10 bp repeat, $[G_2A_3T_3C_2]_N$, were markedly slower than predicted from their known molecular weights, while the mobilities of higher polymers constructed with an 8 bp repeat $(i = 1)$ or a 12 bp repeat $(i = 3)$ were essentially normal (Fig. 21). The abnormally slow electrophoresis of the decamer series $(i = 2)$ suggests that local distortions of the helix axis, when occurring in phase with the helix repeat, lead to macroscopic curvature of the DNA molecule. Similar results have been obtained by Koo *et al.* [122], who suggested that bending may occur at the junctions between oligo (dA) sequences and adjacent B-form DNA.

Ulanovsky *et al.* [123] synthesized a series of 21 bp oligomers with runs of adenosine residues repeating every 10.5 bp. Two-dimensional electrophoresis

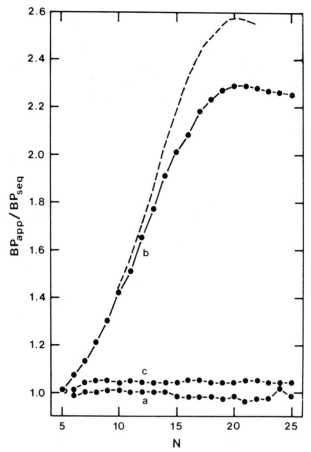

Figure 21. Plot of the relative electrophoretic behavior of four oligomer ladders as a function of the number of sequence repeats. In each case, the ratio of the apparent number of base pairs (BP_{app}) to the actual number of base pairs (BP_{seq}) is plotted as a function of the degree of oligomer polymerization, N. a), $5'$-$[GA_3T_3C]_N$; b), $5'$-$[G_2A_3T_3C_2]_N$; c), $5'$-$[G_3A_3T_3C_3]_N$; $---$, $5'$-$[GA_4T_4C]_N$. Reprinted with permission from [121].

gave two families of spots: linear oligomers containing 1 to 11 repeats of the monomer sequence, and circular molecules containing 5–8 repeats. All of the linear molecules exhibited anomalously slow migration, as if they were about three times larger than their actual size. Circular molecules containing 126 bp (6 repeats) were most abundant; circles of this size should be nearly non-constrained in terms of bending. Assuming the dinucleotide wedge hypothesis for DNA curvature, the AA-TT wedge angle was estimated to be 8.7° [123]. Anomalously slow migration in polyacrylamide gels has also been observed when pseudo-cruciform formation structures are formed by certain DNA sequences [124].

3.2.4 Electric birefringence studies

Wijmenga and Maxwell [125] studied the electric birefringence of small linear DNA fragments imbedded in polyacrylamide gels of different concentrations. The DNA fragments ranged in size from 55 bp to 250 bp. The birefringence relaxation times observed in 4% or 10% w/v polyacrylamide gels were larger than the values observed in free solution, even though molecules this small are essentially completely stretched in free solution [71–74]. The relaxation times also increased markedly with increasing gel concentration. The increase of the relaxation times with increasing molecular weight agreed with predictions from the Odijk theory [126] for the dynamics of slightly flexible rods imbedded in a network. These results are very different from the results observed for DNA fragments imbedded in agarose gels (Section 2.4.4), and suggest that specific interactions may occur between the DNA molecules and the polyacrylamide gel matrix. A "cooperative interaction" between DNA and polyacrylamide gels has also been postulated by Flint and Harrington [39] on the basis of electrophoretic studies.

3.3 Spherical DNA molecules

Shore and Baldwin [127] have developed a gel electrophoretic method to resolve small (250–500 bp) closed circular DNA molecules, using thin 5% w/v polyacrylamide gels and high voltage gradients (25–35 V/cm). The temperature of the glass plates is held at 50–60 °C. Under these conditions the migration of small DNA circles is extremely sensitive to small differences in conformation. A typical autoradiogram is shown in Fig. 22 for a series of DNA circles ranging from 237 to 254 bp in size. Only a single topoisomer is observed, indicating that the free energy of twisting half a turn is large compared to $k_B T$ (k_B is Boltzmann's constant) in this size range. The mobility goes through a minimum between 245 and 249 bp, where the position of half-integral helical twist occurs. The difference in fractional twist of two fragments differing in size by 10 bp was used to determine that the helix repeat is $10.45 \pm .02$ bp/turn. The relative concentrations of topoisomers between 245 and 1361 bp were used to analyze the importance of twist and writhe during ring closure. Horowitz and Wang [128] used 5% w/v polyacrylamide gels containing ethidium bromide to resolve topoisomers of ~200 bp DNA circles, and 4% w/v gels to resolve ~500 bp circles. By analyzing topoisomer populations the torsional rigidity of the DNA helix was calculated to be 2.9×10^{-19} erg cm and the helical repeat was found to be 10.54 bp/turn.

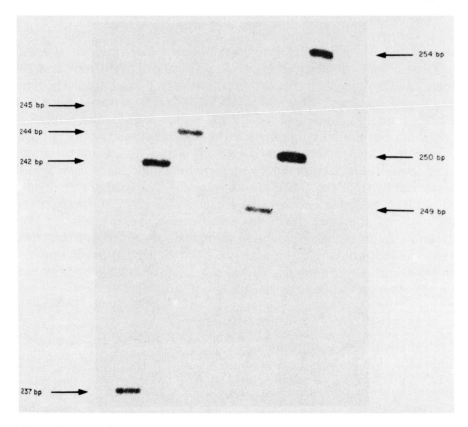

Figure 22. Autoradiogram of small closed circular DNAs separated by electrophoresis on 5% w/v polyacrylamide gels. The lanes contain DNAs with (from left to right) 237, 242, 244, 245, 249, 250 and 254 bp. $E = \sim 30$ V/cm. From [127].

3.4   Protein-DNA interactions

Quantitative gel electrophoresis binding assays have been developed for the study of protein-DNA interactions [129–132]. Significant reductions in mobility occur when the DNA fragments are complexed with protein molecules, as shown in Fig. 23. The relative mobility of each complex is determined by the number of protein molecules bound [130]. The relative amounts of free and complexed DNA can be determined by the intensity of each band. The gel binding assay has been used to obtain accurate measurements of equilibrium constants [130, 131, 133], and to study the kinetics and mechanism of the reaction of gene regulatory proteins with DNA [132]. For proteins with high affinity, the protein concentration and, hence, the DNA concentrations required are very low ($10^{-12} – 10^{-14}$ mol).

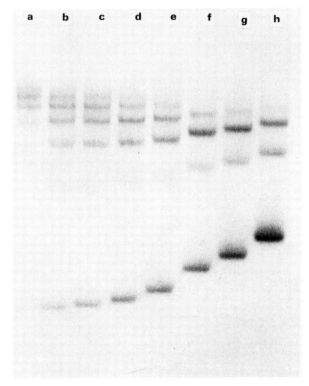

Figure 23. Effect of DNA concentration on the kinetics of *lac* repressor dissociation. Following equilibration of the *lac* repressor with the 203 bp L8-UV5 *lac* promoter fragment, dissociation was initiated by addition of more L8-UV5 DNA. Samples were withdrawn and assayed at 0, 60, 120, 240, 480, 960, 1320, and 1920 s, lanes (a) to (h) respectively. The bottom band in each lane consists of free DNA. Each band above the first contains one equivalent of repressor more than its predecessor. Equivalent gel bands differ in position because the samples were placed sequentially on a running gel. After [132].

Some question exists about whether protein-DNA complexes are stabilized by the polyacrylamide gel matrix. Complexes that would dissociate in a few seconds in binding buffer can be electrophoresed in a gel for several hours without apparent dissociation [130]. A "caging" effect was proposed to explain the apparent stabilization; the gel matrix may bind the DNA and/or the protein molecules and prevent them from diffusing away from each other during electrophoresis [130]. However, Revzin *et al.* [134] found that the dissociation rates of DNA-protein complexes in a gel were the same as the dissociation rates in free solution, if the buffer type and concentration were the same in both media. They also found that the gel matrix does not hinder the separation of DNA and protein molecules which have dissociated.

3.5   Denaturing gels

The electrophoretic mobility of a double-stranded DNA molecule decreases abruptly when a portion of the molecule is denatured or "melts" [135, 136]. Since melting is a cooperative phenomenon, the mobility transition is very sharp if electrophoresis takes place in a gel containing a gradient of denaturing solvent (Fig. 24). The onset of melting depends on base sequence, since large DNA molecules melt in domains of different A-T content [138]. Mutations affecting gradient penetration lie within the first cooperatively melting sequence. Fischer, Lerman, and coworkers have used this technique to separate DNA fragments differing by single base-pair substitutions [137,

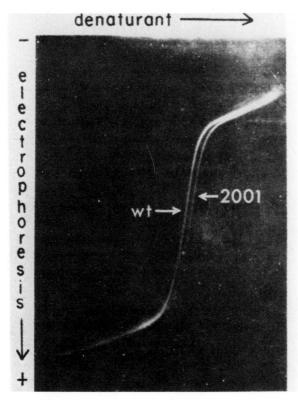

Figure 24. Comparison of the mobilities of wild-type and cy 2001 DNA fragments in a denaturing gradient perpendicular to the electric field. The denaturant concentration was constant along the path of electrophoretic movement but increased linearly in the perpendicular direction, from 2.1 M urea-12% v/v formamide to 3.5 M urea-20% v/v formamide. The sample was applied uniformly across the top from a strip of agarose gel containing the same total amount of both fragments at every point. The acrylamide gel concentration was 6.5% w/v. Both DNA samples were 586 bp in size, but the cy 2001 fragment contained a G·C base pair instead of T·A at position 136. From [137].

139]. If restriction fragments of the mutant DNA molecules are first separated in size by agarose gel electrophoresis, and then electrophoresed in the perpendicular direction in a polyacrylamide gel containing a denaturing gradient, two-dimensional separation of about one thousand fragments is possible [140]. The effects of the size of the denatured region, the position of the denatured region in the molecule, and the molecular weight of the undenatured portion of the molecule on the mobility of the partially melted DNA molecule have also been investigated [141]. A different procedure has been developed to detect single-base substitutions in DNA fragments, based on ribonuclease cleavage of single-base mismatches in RNA:DNA heteroduplexes [142]. The digestion products are analyzed by electrophoresis in denaturing polyacrylamide gels. Single base mutations have been detected in DNA obtained from persons with β-thalassemia, a genetic disorder [142].

3.6   Sequencing gels

In the chemical DNA sequencing method, the DNA is radioactively end-labeled, partially cleaved at each of the four bases in four separate reactions, and the digestion products electrophoresed in separate lanes on denaturing polyacrylamide gels [143]. From the nucleotide ladders produced, the base sequence of the DNA fragment can be read by inspection. Several hundred nucleotides can be separated in a single gel using current electrophoresis procedures. An important application of sequencing gels, besides determining unknown sequences, involves the technique of "foot-printing". In this procedure, a ligand is bound to the DNA before the cleavage reaction. A modulated cutting pattern results; the absence of bands in the sequencing ladder indicates the location of the ligand [144, 146]. Alternatively, the DNA is first chemically modified, then incubated with a ligand, and the modified sites that interfere with binding are determined from the sequencing gel [146]. A typical gel of this type is shown Fig. 25. Footprinting and affinity cleaving techniques have been used to design a synthetic, crescent shaped oligopeptide that binds nine contiguous adenine-thymine base pairs in the minor groove of double-helical DNA [148]. Other applications of these techniques include identifying the binding sites of a naturally occurring quinoxaline antitumor antibiotic [147], and measuring the helical repeat of B-conformation DNA [149]. Hydroxyl radical footprints, generated by the reduction of hydrogen peroxide by iron (II), have been used to show that bacteriophage λ repressor and Cro protein bind only to one side of the DNA helix [150].

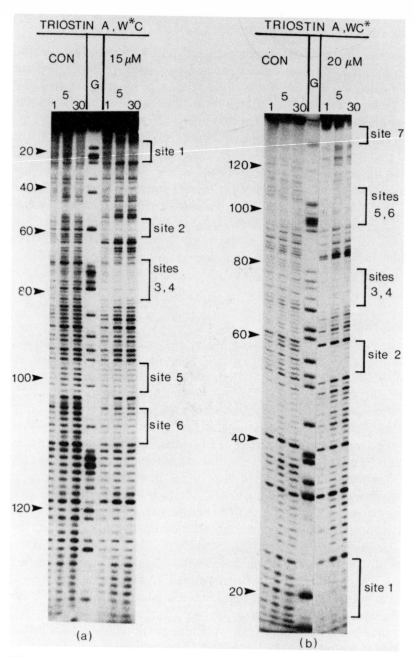

Figure 25. DNase I footprinting of triostin A on a 160 bp DNA fragment from *E. coli.* Symbols W*C and WC* indicate which of the two strands bears a radioactive 3′ end-label. The time in minutes (1, 5, 30) after the addition of enzyme is shown at the top of each gel lane. The extent of digestion was limited to 20–40% of the starting material so as to minimize the incidence of multiple cuts in any strand. Tracks labelled "G" are dimethyl sulfate-piperidine marker lanes specific for guanine. Sites of protection from DNase I digestion are identified on the right: numbers on the left refer to base pair sequence position. From [147].

3.7   Pore size

Righetti *et al.* [89] measured the pore size of polyacrylamide gels using polystyrene latex particles of known diameter. Very dilute polyacrylamide gels (2% acrylamide, 2.2% crosslinker) were gluey and did not admit the latex particles, suggesting that the maximum pore diameter was smaller than 100 nm. Highly cross-linked gels containing 3% total acrylamide were prepared using several cross-linking agents; highly porous gels were obtained only when using cross-linking agents with very short chain lengths between the two terminal double bonds. For gels polymerized with Bis, the average pore diameter increased from 100 nm to 600 nm as the Bis concentration increased from 25% to 60%. Increased gel porosity was accompanied by increased gel turbidity [89]. Stellwagen [110] estimated the median pore radius of 4−9% polyacrylamide gels from the mobility of DNA restriction fragments of known molecular weight. She assumed that when the mobility of the DNA molecule was equal to one half its mobility at zero gel concentration, the median pore radius of the gel should be equal to the average radius of the DNA molecule [8, 9]. Using the mean geometric radius as the measure of molecular size (Section 3.2.2), the median pore radius was found to be inversely dependent on $T^{1/2}$, where T is the total acrylamide concentration (Fig. 26).

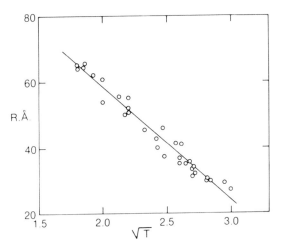

Figure 26. Dependence of average pore radius, *R*, on the square root of total polyacrylamide concentration, %T w/v. The cross-linking agent was 3% Bis (calculated from the concentration of acrylamide). All data were obtained from mobilities extrapolated to zero electric field strength. Reprinted with permission from [110].

3.8   Experimental techniques

The progressive decrease in conductivity which is often observed during polyacrylamide gel electrophoresis has been studied by Spencer [151–153]. The decrease in conductivity was attributed to the formation of a zone of altered salt concentration at the interface between the gel and the solvent, due to the change in transport numbers of the ions on the two sides of the interface [152]. The zone of lowest salt concentration migrates slowly into the gel. Changes in pH may also occur within the zone of altered salt concentration [153]. These effects were observed during the electrophoresis of tRNA in the presence of spermine, when the tRNA precipitated in a sharp zone within the gel at a slowly moving discontinuity in salt concentration. The region of the gel behind the moving boundary contained a much lower concentration of spermine than the electrophoresis buffer.

Mills and Ilan [154] prepared highly porous polyacrylamide gels by adding 0.6% linear polyacrylamide to the acrylamide solution before polymerization. The use of 0.4% diallyltartardiamide as the cross-linking agent gave clear gels at all concentrations of acrylamide and linear polyacrylamide. Silver staining has been developed as a method of visualizing DNA bands in polyacrylamide gels [105]. DNA concentrations of 1 or 2 ng can be detected, with a sensitivity comparable to that obtained with fluorescence procedures using ethidium bromide [154]. Two notched gel plates, sandwiched together by a solid U-shaped gasket, have been used to eliminate "smiling" at the edges of sequencing gels [155].

The work in the author's laboratory was supported by Grant GM-29690 from the National Institute of General Medical Sciences, which is gratefully acknowledged.

4   References

[1] Overbeek, J. Th. G., Lijklema, J., in: Bier, M. (Ed.), *Electrophoresis,* Vol. 1, Academic Press, New York 1959, pp. 1–33.
[2] Shaw, D. J., *Electrophoresis,* Academic Press, New York 1969.
[3] Olivera, B. M., Baine, P., Davidson, N., *Biopolymers* 1964, *2,* 245–257.
[4] Sealey, P. G., Southern, E. M., in: Rickwood, D., Hames, B. D. (Eds.), *Gel Electrophoresis of Nucleic Acids: A Practical Approach,* IRL Press, Oxford 1982, pp. 39–76.
[5] Rodbard, D., in: Catsimpoolas, N. (Ed.), *Methods of Protein Separation,* Vol. 2, Plenum Press, New York 1976, pp. 145–218.
[6] Stellwagen, N., *Biopolymers* 1985, *24,* 2243–2255.

[7] Ogston, A. G., *Trans. Faraday Soc.* 1958, *54,* 1754–1757.

[8] Rodbard, D., Chrambach, A., *Proc. Nat. Acad. Sci. USA* 1970, *65,* 970–977.

[9] Chrambach, A., Rodbard, D., *Science* 1971, *170,* 440–451.

[10] Rodbard, D., Chrambach, A., *Anal. Biochem.* 1971, *40,* 95–134.

[11] Laurent, T. C., Killander, J., *J. Chromatogr.* 1964, *14,* 317–330.

[12] Lerman, L. S., Frisch, H. L., *Biopolymers* 1982, *21,* 995–997.

[13] Lumpkin, O. J., Zimm, B. H., *Biopolymers* 1982, *21,* 2315–2316.

[14] Lumpkin, O. J., Dejardin, P., Zimm, B. H., *Biopolymers* 1985, *24,* 1573–1593.

[15] Southern, E., *Anal. Biochem.* 1980, *105,* 304–318.

[16] Schleif, R. F., Wensink, P. C., *Practical Methods in Molecular Biology,* Springer-Verlag, New York 1981.

[17] Gould, H., Matthews, H. C., in: Work, T. S., Work, E. (Eds.), *Laboratory Techniques in Biochemistry and Molecular Biology,* Vol. 4, American Elsevier, New York 1976, pp. 207–471.

[18] Chrambach, A., Jovin, T. A., Svendsen, P. J., Rodbard, D., in: Catsimpoolas, N. (Ed.), *Methods of Protein Separation,* Vol. 2, Plenum Press, New York 1976, pp. 27–144.

[19] Serwer, P., *Electrophoresis* 1983, *4,* 375–382.

[20] Norton, I. T., Goodall, D. M., Austen, K. R. J., Morris, E. R., Rees, D. A., *Biopolymers* 1986, *25,* 1009–1029.

[21] Arnott, S., Fulmer, A., Scott, W. E., Dea, I. C. M., Moorehouse, R., Rees, D. A., *J. Mol. Biol.* 1974, *90,* 269–284.

[22] Dea, I. C. M., McKinnon, A. A., Rees, D. A., *J. Mol. Biol.* 1972, *68,* 153–172.

[23] Waki, S., Harvey, J. D., Bellamy, A. R., *Biopolymers* 1982, *21,* 1909–1926.

[24] Tietz, D., Chrambach, A., *Electrophoresis* 1986, *7,* 241–250.

[25] Peats, S., Nochumson, S., Kirkpatrick, F. H., *Biophys. J.* 1986, *49,* 91 a.

[26] San Biagio, P. L., Madonia, F., Newman, J., Palma, M. U., *Biopolymers* 1986, *25,* 2255–2269.

[27] Morris, E. R., Stevens, E. S., Frangou, S. A., Rees, D. A., *Biopolymers* 1986, *25,* 959–973.

[28] McDonell, M. W., Simon, M. N., Studier, F. W., *J. Mol. Biol.* 1977, *110,* 119–146.

[29] Stellwagen, N., *Biochemistry* 1983, *22,* 6180–6185.

[30] Schaffer, H. E., Sederoff, R. R., *Biochemistry* 1981, *115,* 113–122.

[31] Gough, E. J., Gough, N. M., *Nucleic Acids Research* 1984, *12,* 845–853.

[32] Bearden, J. C., Jr., *Gene* 1979, *6,* 221–234.

[33] Stellwagen, N., *J. Biomol. Struct. Dyn.* 1985, *3,* 299–314.

[34] Edmondson, S. P., Gray, D. M., *Biopolymers* 1984, *23,* 2725–2742.

[35] Serwer, P., *Biochemistry* 1980, *19,* 3001–3004.

[36] Serwer, P., Allen, J. L., *Biochemistry* 1984, *23,* 922–927.

[37] Cobbs, G., *Biophys. J.,* 1981, *35,* 535–542.

[38] Fisher, M. D., Dingman, C. W., *Biochemistry* 1971, *10,* 1895–1899.

[39] Flint, D. H., Harrington, R. F., *Biochemistry* 1972, *11,* 4858–4863.

[40] Ross, P. D., Scruggs, R. L., *Biopolymers* 1964, *2,* 231–236.

[41] Johnson, P. H., Grossman, L. I., *Biochemistry* 1977, *16,* 4217–4225.

[42] Mikel, S., Arena, Jr., V., Bauer, W., *Nucleic Acids Research* 1977, *4,* 1465–1482.

[43] Longo, M. C., Hartley, J. L., *Focus,* Bethesda Research Laboratories, Gaithersburg, MD 1986, Vol. 8 (3), pp. 3–4.

[44] Serwer, P., Hayes, S. J., in: Allen, R. C., Arnaud, P. (Eds.), *Electrophoresis '81,* deGruyter, Berlin 1981, pp. 237–243.

[45] Serwer, P., Allen, J. L., Hayes, S. J., *Electrophoresis* 1983, *4,* 232–236.

[46] Trademark name of Marine Colloids. See *The Agarose Monograph,* FMC Corp., Rockland, ME 1982, pp. 16–21, and *Marine Colloids Division 1984 Bioproducts Catalog,* FMC Corp., Rockland, ME 1983, p. 5.

[47] Serwer, P., Allen, J. L., *Electrophoresis* 1983, *4,* 273–276.

[48] Depew, R. E., Wang, J. C., *Proc. Nat. Acad. Sci. USA* 1975, *72,* 4275–4279.

[49] Keller, W., *Proc. Nat. Acad. Sci. USA* 1975, *72,* 4876–4880.

[50] Wang, J. C., *Proc. Nat. Acad. Sci. USA* 1979, *76,* 200–203.

[51] Stirdivant, S. M., Klysik, J., Wells, R. D., *J. Biol. Chem.* 1982, *257,* 10159–10165.

[52] Singleton, C. K., Klysik, J., Stirdivant, S. M., Wells, R. D., *Nature* 1982, *299,* 312–316.

[53] Peck, L. J., Nordheim, A., Rich, A., Wang, J. C., *Proc. Nat. Acad. Sci. USA* 1982, *79,* 4560–4564.

[54] Albright, L. M., Geiduschek, E. P., *J. Mol. Biol.* 1986, *190,* 329–341.

[55] Peck, L. J., Wang, J. C., *Proc. Nat. Acad. Sci. USA* 1983, *80,* 6206–6210.

[56] Lee, F. S., Bauer, W. R., *Nucleic Acids Research* 1985, *13,* 1665–1682.

[57] Ellison, M. J., Feigon, J., Kelleher, R. J., III, Wang, A. H.-J., Habener, J. F., Rich, A., *Biochemistry* 1986, *25,* 3648–3655.

[58] Greares, D. R., Patient, R. K., Lilley, D. M., *J. Mol. Biol.* 1985, *185,* 461–478.

[59] Haniford, D. B., Pulleyblank, D. E., *J. Biomol. Struct. Dyn.* 1983, *1,* 593–609.

[60] Panyutin, I., Lyamichev, V., Mirkin, S., *J. Biomol. Struct. Dyn.* 1985, *2,* 1221–1234.

[61] Bell, L., Byers, B., *Anal. Biochem.* 1983, *130,* 527–535.

[62] Kalyaniwalla, N., Bean, C. P., *Biophys. J.* 1985, *47,* 337a.

[63] Jamil, T., Lerman, L. S., *J. Biomol. Struct. Dyn.* 1985, *2,* 963–966.

[64] Schwartz, D. C., Cantor, C. R., *Cell* 1984, *37,* 67–75.

[65] Carle, G. F., Olson, M. V., *Nucleic Acids Research* 1984, *12,* 5647–5664.

[66] Carle, G. F., Olson, M. V., *Proc. Nat. Acad. Sci. USA* 1985, *82,* 3756–3780.

[67] Van der Ploeg, L. H. T., Cornelissen, A. W. C. A., Michels, P. A. M., Borst, P., *Cell* 1984, *39,* 213–221.

[68] Snell, R. G., Wilkins, R. J., *Nucleic Acids Research* 1986, *14,* 4401–4406.

[69] Carle, G. F., Frank, M., Olson, M. V., *Science* 1986, *232,* 65–68.

[70] Fredericq, E., Houssier, C., *Electric Dichroism and Electric Birefringence,* Clarendon Press, Oxford 1973.

[71] Stellwagen, N. C., *Biopolymers* 1981, *20,* 399–434.

[72] Hagerman, P. J., *Biopolymers* 1981, *20,* 1503–1535.

[73] Elias, J. G., Eden, D., *Macromolecules* 1981, *14,* 410–419.

[74] Diekmann, S., Hillen, W., Morgeneyer, B., Wells, R. D., Porschke, D., *Biophys. Chem.* 1982, *15,* 263–270.

[75] Stellwagen, N., in: Sarma, R. H. (Ed.), *Fourth Conversation in Biomolecular Stereodynamics,* Institute of Biomolecular Stereodynamics, SUNY at Albany, Albany, NY 1985, p. 70.

[76] Moore, D. P., Schellman, J. P., Baase, W. A., *Biophysical J.* 1986, *49,* 130a.

[77] Hurley, I., *Biopolymers* 1986, *25,* 539–554.

[78] deGennes, P. G., *Scaling Concepts in Polymer Physics,* Cornell University Press, Ithaca, NY 1979.

[79] Doi, M., Edwards, S., *J. Chem. Soc. Faraday Transactions* 1978, *74,* 1789–1801.

[80] Fangman, W. L., *Nucleic Acids Research* 1978, *5,* 653–665.

[81] Lishenskaya, A. I., Mosevitsky, M. I., *Biochem. Biophys. Res. Comm.* 1973, *52,* 1213–1220.

[82] Slater, G. W., Noolandi, J., *Biopolymers* 1986, *25,* 431–454.

[83] Slater, G. W., Noolandi, J., *Biopolymers* 1985, *24,* 2181–2184.

[84] Hervet, H., Bear, C. P., *Biopolymers* 1987, *26,* 727–742.

[85] Fesjian, S., Frisch, H. L., Jamil, T., *Biopolymers* 1986, *25,* 1179–1184.
[86] Shlyakhtenko, L. S., *J. Biomol. Struct. Dyn.* 1984, *1,* 1511–1516.
[87] Lyamichev, V. I., Mirkin, S. M., Frank-Kamenetskii, M. D., *J. Biomol. Struct. Dyn.* 1985, *3,* 327–338, 667–669.
[88] Lohman, T. M., Overman, L. B., Datta, S., *J. Mol. Biol.* 1986, *187,* 603–615.
[89] Righetti, P., Brost, B. C. W., Snyder, R. S., *J. Biochem. Biophys. Methods* 1981, *4,* 347–363.
[90] Buzás, Z., Chrambach, A., *Electrophoresis* 1982, *3,* 130–134.
[91] Johnson, P. H., Miller, M. J., Grossman, L. I., *Anal. Biochem.* 1980, *102,* 159–162.
[92] Serwer, P., Hayes, S. J., *Electrophoresis* 1982, *3,* 80–85.
[93] Serwer, P., *Anal. Biochem.* 1980, *101,* 154–159.
[94] Serwer, P., *Anal. Biochem.* 1981, *112,* 351–356.
[95] Serwer, P., *Electrophoresis* 1983, *4,* 227–231.
[96] Maniloff, J., Poddar, S. K., *Electrophoresis* 1984, *5,* 172–173.
[97] Serwer, P., *Anal. Biochem.* 1985, *144,* 172–178.
[98] Serwer, P., Hayes, S. J., Griess, G. A., *Anal. Biochem.* 1986, *152,* 339–345.
[99] Smith, S. S., Gilroy, T. F., Ferrari, F. A., *Anal. Biochem.* 1983, *128,* 138–151.
[100] Boncinelli, E., Simeone, A., de Falco, A., Fidanza, V., La Volpe, A., *Anal. Biochem.* 1983, *134,* 40–43.
[101] Malvy, C., *Anal. Biochem.* 1984, *143,* 158–162.
[102] Sutherland, J. C., Monteleone, D. C., Trunk, J., Ciarrocchi, G., *Anal. Biochem. 1984, 139,* 390–399.
[103] Willis, C. E., Holmquist, G. P., *Electrophoresis* 1985, *6,* 259–267.
[104] Pun, T., Trus, B., Grossman, N., Leive, L., Eden, M., *Electrophoresis* 1985, *6,* 268–274.
[105] Peats, S., *Anal. Biochem.* 1984, *140,* 178–182.
[106] Chrambach, A., Rodbard, D., *Sep. Sci.* 1972, *7,* 663–703.
[107] Nossal, R., *Macromolecules* 1985, *18,* 49–54.
[108] Rüchel, R., Brager, M. D., *Anal. Biochem.* 1975, *68,* 415–428.
[109] Hecht, A.-M., Duplessix, R., Geissler, E., *Macromolecules* 1985, *18,* 2167–2173.
[110] Stellwagen, N. C., *Biochemistry* 1983, *22,* 6186–6193.
[111] Sutcliffe, J. G., *Cold Spring Harbor Symp. Quant. Biol.* 1978, *42,* 77–90.
[112] Dingman, C. W., Fisher, M. P., Kakefuda, T., *Biochemistry* 1972, *11,* 1242–1250.
[113] Tietz, D., Gottlieb, M. H., Fawcett, J. S., Chrambach, A., *Electrophoresis* 1986, *7,* 217–220.
[114] Fawcett, J. S., Morris, C. J. O. R., *Sep. Sci.* 1966, *1,* 9–28.
[115] Marini, J. C., Levene, S. D., Crothers, D. M., Englund, P. T., *Proc. Nat. Acad. Sci. USA* 1982, *79,* 7664–7668.
[116] Diekmann, S., Wang, J. C., *J. Mol. Biol.* 1985, *186,* 1–11.
[117] Maniatis, T., Jeffrey, A., van de Sande, H., *Biochemistry* 1975, *14,* 3787–3794.
[118] Hagerman, P. J., *Proc. Nat. Acad. Sci. USA* 1984, *81,* 4632–4636.
[119] Levene, S. D., Wu, H.-M., Crothers, D. M., *Biochemistry* 1986, *25,* 3988–3995.
[120] Wu, H.-M., Crothers, D. M., *Nature* 1984, *308,* 509–513.
[121] Hagerman, P. J., *Biochemistry* 1985, *24,* 7033–7037.
[122] Koo, H.-S., Wu, H.-M., Crothers, D. M., *Nature* 1986, *320,* 501–506.
[123] Ulanovsky, L., Bodner, M., Trivonov, E. N., Choder, M., *Proc. Nat. Acad. Sci. USA* 1986, *83,* 862–866.
[124] Gough, G. W., Lilley, D. M. J., *Nature* 1985, *313,* 154–156.
[125] Wijmenga, S. S., Maxwell, A., *Biopolymers* 1986, *25,* 2173–2186.
[126] Odijk, T., *Macromolecules* 1983, *16,* 1340–1344.
[127] Shore, D., Baldwin, R. L., *J. Mol. Biol.* 1983, *170,* 983–1007.

[128] Horowitz, D. S., Wang, J. S., *J. Mol. Biol.* 1984, *173,* 75−91.
[129] Hendrickson, W., Schleif, R., *J. Mol. Biol.* 1984, *178,* 611−628.
[130] Fried, M., Crothers, D. M., *Nucleic Acids Research* 1981, *9,* 6505−6525.
[131] Garner, M., Revzin, A., *Nucleic Acids Research* 1981, *9,* 3047−3170.
[132] Fried, M. G., Crothers, D. M., *J. Mol. Biol.* 1984, *172,* 263−282.
[133] Fried, M. G., Crothers, D. M., *J. Mol. Biol.* 1984, *172,* 241−262.
[134] Revzin, A., Ceglarek, J. A., Garner, M. M., *Anal. Biochem.* 1986, *153,* 172−177.
[135] Fischer, S. G., Lerman, L. S., *Cell* 1979, *16,* 191−200.
[136] Fischer, S. G., Lerman, L. S., *Proc. Nat. Acad. Sci. USA* 1980, *77,* 4420−4424.
[137] Fischer, S. G., Lerman, L. S., *Proc. Nat. Acad. Sci. USA* 1983, *80,* 1579−1583.
[138] Gotoh, O., *Adv. Biophys.* 1983, *16,* 1−52.
[139] Myers, R. M., Lumelsky, N., Lerman, L. S.,, Maniatis, T., *Nature* 1985, *313,* 495−498.
[140] Fischer, S. G., Lerman, L. S., *Methods Enzymol.* 1979, *68,* 152−176.
[141] Lyamichev, V. I., Panyutin, I. G., Lyubchenko, Yu. L., *Nucleic Acids Research* 1982, *10,* 4813−4826.
[142] Myers, R. M., Larin, Z., Maniatis, T., *Science* 1985, *230,* 1242−1246.
[143] Maxam, A. M., Gilbert, W., *Methods Enzymol.* 1980, *65,* 499−560.
[144] Galas, D., Schmitz, A., *Nucleic Acids Research* 1978, *5,* 3157−3170.
[145] Ptashne, M., Jeffrey, A., Johnson, A., Maurer, R., Meyer, B., Pabo, C., Roberts, T., Sauer, R., *Cell* 1980, *19,* 1−11.
[146] Hendrickson, W., Schleif, R., *Proc. Nat. Acad. Sci. USA* 1985, *82,* 3129−3133.
[147] Low, C. M. L., Olsen, R. K., Waring, M. J., *FEBS Lett.* 1984, *176,* 414−419.
[148] Dervan, P. B., *Science* 1986, *232,* 464−471.
[149] Tullius, T. D., Dombroski, B. A., *Science* 1985, *230,* 679−681.
[150] Tullius, T. D., Dombroski, B. A., *Proc. Nat. Acad. Sci. USA* 1986, *83,* 5469−5473.
[151] Spencer, M., Kirk, J. M., *Electrophoresis* 1983, *4,* 46−52.
[152] Spencer, M., *Electrophoresis* 1983, *4,* 36−41.
[153] Spencer, M., *Electrophoresis* 1983, *4,* 41−45.
[154] Mills, N. C., Ilan, J., *Electrophoresis* 1985, *6,* 531−534.
[155] Brown, D. J., Bos, T. J., *Electrophoresis* 1986, *7,* 54−55.

AFFINITY ELECTROPHORESIS

Kazusuke Takeo

Yamaguchi University School of Medicine, Ube, Japan

1   Introduction

Affinity electrophoresis is a newly developed technique useful for characterizing the molecular properties of biomacromolecules, such as proteins and
nucleic acids, and for analyzing their specific interactions with corresponding affinity ligands. When two substances having opposite charges are applied at appropriate positions on a supporting medium and electrophoresed,
they cross one another. When two substances have the same charge but different mobilities, the faster moving substance migrates ahead of the slower
one. In both cases, the electrophoretic pattern changes at the crossing or
passing point if the two substances have an affinity for each other. The
higher the affinity, the stronger the change in pattern. Based on this principle, Nakamura and his collaborators developed cross electrophoresis on
paper [1, 2] and explored biospecific interactions, such as between enzymes
and substrates or inhibitors ([1, 3, 4] Fig. 1), antibodies and antigens ([1, 5]
Fig. 2), concanavalin A and glycoproteins ([6, 7] Fig. 3) and other biospecific
interactions [8, 9]. Rocket immunoelectrophoresis [10] and crossed immunoelectrophoresis [11] are both based on the same principle as cross electrophoresis. Cross electrophoresis is a simple and sensitive method for detecting biospecific interactions (Figs. 1 – 3). The basic approach [1, 8] was
developed on the basis of chromatographic theories [12, 13]. However, since
an exact measurement of mobility and its change was impossible with paper
electrophoresis, the dissociation constant could not be calculated.

In 1970 Takeo [14] observed a concentration dependent decrease in rabbit
muscle glycogen phosphorylase mobility after the addition of glycogen to the
polyacrylamide gel in disc electrophoresis. The decrease in mobility resulting
from the addition of glycogen was specific for phosphorylase. Its magnitude
was proportional to the concentration of the added glycogen (Fig. 4A, and
B). Protein bands of muscle extracts did not show alterations in mobility, except for phosphorylase. Neither dextran nor inulin affected phosphorylase
mobility. The apparent dissociation constants of the interaction were
calculated [14, 15] from the induced mobility change as a function of
glycogen concentration. This quantification of the cross electrophoresis was
the first application of electrophoresis theory in which a kinetic constant was
determined. This electrophoretic method was later called "affinity electrophoresis", in analogy to affinity chromatography.

The term affinity electrophoresis was first proposed by Bøg-Hansen [16] and
used by Hořejší and Kocourek [17, 18] and Caron [19]. Every electrophoretic
process which explores biospecific interactions falls under the category of af-

A   **B**   **C**

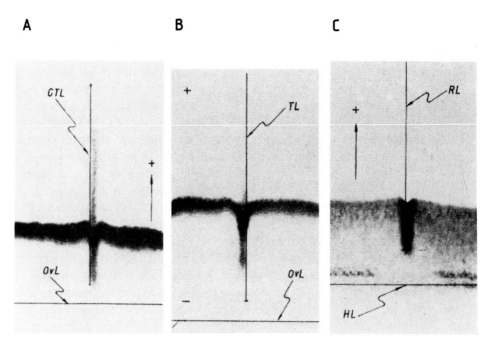

Figure 1. One-dimensional cross electrophoresis of enzyme reactions (Fig. from [1]). (A) Chymotrypsin-ovalbumin reaction. 2% Chymotrypsin solution (0.02 mL/10 cm) was applied on line CTL and 5% ovalbumin solution (0.02 mL/8 cm) on line OvL. Paper electrophoresis was carried out with phosphate buffer, pH 7.0, at 200 V, 5 mA for 150 min at 2 °C. After drying at 110 °C, the electrophoresed filter paper was stained with Bromophenol Blue. (B) Trypsin-ovalbumin reaction. 2% Trypsin solution (0.04 mL/10 cm) was applied on line TL and 5% ovalbumin solution (0.01 mL/8 cm) on line OvL. Electrophoresis and staining were the same as in (A). (C) Ribonuclease-RNA reaction. 2% Bovine pancreatic ribonuclease (0.02 mL/10 cm) was applied on line RL, and 10% yeast RNA 0.02 mL/7 cm on line HL. Electrophoresis was carried out with acetate buffer, pH 4.0, at 600 V, 3.5 mA for 20 min at 3 °C. The electrophoresed paper was stained by direct dipping into cold Victoria Blue solution without drying. When staining was performed after drying the paper, the combined RNA, observed on the line RL, disappeared completely due to enzymatic hydrolysis.

finity electrophoresis. They include: cross electrophoresis [1]; rocket affinity electrophoresis [20]; crossed affinity immunoelectrophoresis [16]; affinity electrophoresis in cellulose acetate membrane, agarose and polyacrylamide gel; countercurrent electrophoresis [21]; affinity electrophoretic titration [22]; and blotting electrophoresis [23], and some others described in Section 4. There are general reviews of affinity electrophoresis [24–29] and affinity electrophoresis of glycoproteins [30, 31]. This review describes the principles and techniques of affinity electrophoresis with its latest applications and limitations.

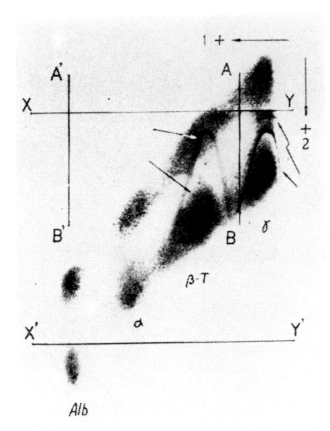

Figure 2. Two-dimensional cross electrophoresis of diphtheria antiserum-toxoid interaction (Fig. from [4]). Filter paper (30×30 cm) was used for two-dimensional cross electrophoresis. First electrophoresis: Diphtheria serum (0.06 mL/8 cm) was applied on line AB, and electrophoresis was carried out in direction 1 at 50 V, 5 mA for 12 h. Second electrophoresis: Toxoid (0.01 mL/16 cm) was applied on line XY, and electrophoresis was carried out in direction 2 at 60 V, 5 mA for 12 h. Two precipitation lines in the β-globulin fraction and two in the γ-globulin fraction were observed.

1.1   Terminology and symbols

Macromolecular affinity ligands are macromolecular substrates and antigens, such as glycogen, starch and dextran, or synthetically immobilized affinity ligands, in which low molecular affinity ligands are attached covalently to water soluble macromolecules, such as non cross-linked polyacrylamide gels or dextran.

Low molecular affinity ligands are freely mobile affinity substances of low molecular weight in the supporting medium, such as enzyme substrates, inhibitors and haptens.

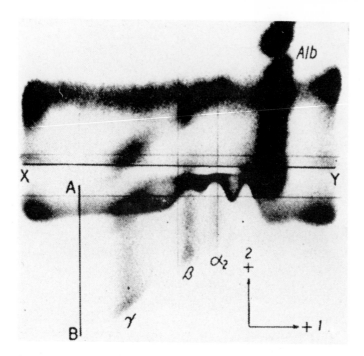

Figure 3. Two-dimensional cross electrophoresis of the concanavalin A-human serum interaction (Fig. from [7]). First electrophoresis: Human serum (0.03 mL/8 cm) was applied on line AB, and electrophoresis was carried out in direction 1 at 200 V for 7.5 h. Second electrophoresis: Jack-bean extract (0.12 mL/16 cm, 1 volume jack-bean meal − 5 volumes water) was applied on line XY, and electrophoresis was carried out at 90 V for 20 h. Three peaks corresponding to α-1, α-2 and β-globulin fractions were observed.

Relative migrating distance is the ratio of the migration distance of the protein to that of the reference substance. In electrophoresis, when the protein migrates from cathode to anode, such as in the report by Davis [32] and Ornstein [33], Bromophenol Blue (BPB) or albumin monomer can be used as the reference. When the protein migrates from anode to cathode, as in the system of Reisfeld *et al..* [34], Methylene Blue or egg white lysozyme can be used as the reference.

c,   total concentration of macromolecular affinity ligand
d,   migration distance of the sample protein
D,   migration distance of the reference substance
i,   total concentration of low molecular affinity ligand
K_a, apparent association constant, *i.e.,* the reciprocal value of the dissociation constant
K_d^{app}, apparent dissociation constant of the sample protein for macromolecular affinity ligand

K_i,   apparent dissociation constant of the sample protein for a low molecular affinity ligand

r,   relative migration distance (d/D) of protein in the presence of an affinity ligand in the electrophoresis gel

R_c,   relative migration distance of the complex between protein and affinity ligand, or that value obtained in the presence of an excess amount of affinity ligand with which all protein molecules bind the ligand

R_0,   relative migration distance of the free protein or that obtained in the absence of a macromolecular affinity ligand in electrophoresis gel.

2   Principles of affinity electrophoresis

The dissociation constant is defined here as the value for the affinity ligand concentration at which the sample protein migrates just half of the distance compared with the distance in the absence of a ligand [35]. It is thus an "apparent" value. Hořejší and Tichá [36, 37] have proposed a modified affinity equation for calculating the true dissociation constant using the term "effective ligand concentration". The equation was developed using the postulation that the sample protein migrates in polyacrylamide gel without stacking and diffusion. However, proteins are stacked at the gel surface due to a molecular sieving effect even in a continuous buffer system [38]. In the polyacrylamide gel electrophoresis system of Davis [32] and Ornstein [33], serum proteins are stacked in the stacking gel in a band thinner than 10 μm [33]. This is followed by considerable diffusion in the separating gel during electrophoresis, in spite of restricted diffusion due to molecular sieving of the polyacrylamide gel. Furthermore, in the interaction between a divalent protein (P) and its affinity ligand (L) on an immobilized matrix, the effective ligand concentration for the first step of the interaction (P + L = PL) is different from the second step of the interaction (PL + L = PL$_2$). Since the mobility of PL complex is zero, a collision of PL with L may be strongly restricted, and the effective ligand concentration for the second step becomes low. Therefore, the actual dissociation constant of multivalent protein samples cannot be determined without (i) determination of the effective ligand concentration in the gel and (ii) kinetic analysis of multistep interactions of the multivalent proteins in affinity electrophoresis. Thus, at that present time the apparent dissociation constant may be the most reliable value.

2.1   Original affinity equation

The original affinity equation [15] is valid for interactions between a protein and its neutral macromolecular affinity ligand. The equation was derived using the phosphorylase-glycogen interaction as an example.

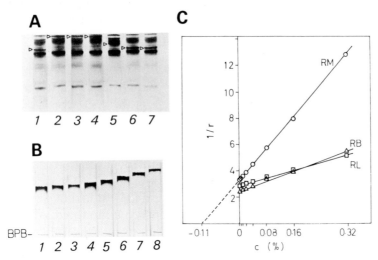

Figure 4. Affinity electrophoresis of rabbit muscle phosphorylase and polysaccharides (Figs. from [15] and [25]). (A) Polyacrylamide gel (PAG) disc electrophoresis of rabbit muscle extract in the presence of various polysaccharides. All gels (7.5% PAG) were stained with Amido Black 10 B. (1) PAG without any polysaccharide; (2) PAG containing 0.5% rabbit liver glycogen; (3) 0.5% shellfish glycogen; (4) 0.5% soluble potato starch; (5) 0.5% dextrin; (6) 0.5% dextran; (7) 0.5% inulin. ▷ indicates the phosphorylase fraction. (B) Affinity pattern of the muscle phosphorylase-glycogen interaction in 5.0% PAG. (1) PAG without glycogen; (2) PAG containing 0.005% rabbit muscle glycogen; (3) 0.010%; (4) 0.020%; (5) 0.040%; (6) 0.080%; (7) 0.16%; (8) 0.32%. Phosphorylase activity was stained with $KI\text{-}I_2$ solution after incubation of the gels in 5′-AMP containing glucose 1-phosphate solution. For (1) 1% glycogen was added to the incubation solution. BPB, Bromophenol Blue. (C) The affinity plot obtained with the original affinity equation (Eq. 6). Abscissa, glycogen concentration percentage (c), and ordinate, reciprocal value of relative migrating distance ($1/r$). RM, skeletal muscle phosphorylase; RB, brain phosphorylase; RL, liver phosphorylase.

The interaction of phosphorylase and glycogen is expressed in Eqs. (1) and (2):

$$Pl + Gn = Pl \cdot Gn \tag{1}$$

$$K_d^{app} = \frac{[Pl]\,[Gn]}{[Pl \cdot Gn]} \tag{2}$$

where Pl and Gn are free phosphorylase and glycogen, Pl·Gn is their complex; [Pl], [Gn] and [Pl·Gn] are their concentrations; and K_d^{app} is the apparent dissociation constant. When the phosphorylase sample is applied to polyacrylamide gel disc electrophoresis using a gel with a given concentration of glycogen, c, a part of phosphorylase combines reversibly with glycogen, resulting in a decrease of mobility in the phosphorylase band, as seen in Fig. 4B. The extent of the decrease in mobility is dependent on c. Since the molecular weight of glycogen is high (average molecular weight 10^6), the phosphorylase-glycogen complex cannot migrate in the polyacrylamide gel due to molecular restriction. When all phosphorylase molecules combine with glycogen, the mobility of the phosphorylase bands becomes zero. When the relative migration distance of the phosphorylase without glycogen in the gel is expressed as R_o and that obtained with glycogen at a concentration of c as r, the following equation is derived:

$$\frac{R_o}{r} = \frac{[Pl]_t}{[Pl]} \tag{3}$$

where $[Pl]_t$ is the total phosphorylase concentration. Since $[Pl]_t = [Pl] + [Pl·Gn]$, Eq. (3) can be transformed to

$$\frac{R_o}{r} = 1 + \frac{[Pl·Gn]}{[Pl]} \tag{4}$$

When Eq. (2) is substituted in Eq. (4), Eq. (5) is obtained:

$$\frac{R_o}{r} = 1 + \frac{[Gn]}{K_d^{app}} \tag{5}$$

[Gn] is the free glycogen concentration in the gel and is a variable value depending on the concentration of phosphorylase. But at a condition where the total glycogen concentration in the gel, c, is much higher than the total phosphorylase concentration ($c \gg [Pl]_t$), [Gn] is practically equal to c, and Eq. (5) can be transformed to

$$\frac{1}{r} = \frac{1}{R_o}\left(1 + \frac{c}{K_d^{app}}\right) \tag{6}$$

Therefore, when Eq. (6) is plotted, taking $1/r$ as the ordinate and c as the abscissa, a straight line is obtained. Its intercept on the abscissa gives a negative apparent dissociation constant ($-K_d^{app}$). Fig. 4C shows results obtained with rabbit glycogen phosphorylases verifying the theory. We have designated Eq. (6) the original affinity equation. Eq. (6) is applicable to interactions, such as those between α-amylase and starch, lectin and polysaccharide or glycoprotein, and antibody and macromolecular antigen or immobilized hapten. These interactions are described in Section 4.

2.2   Calculation of apparent dissociation constants of low molecular affinity ligands: inhibition affinity equation

The decrease in mobility of phosphorylase caused by glycogen is reversed by addition to the gel of a competitive substance, such as maltotriose or β-cyclodextrin. The apparent dissociation constant can be calculated from the altered mobility, as a function of the concentration of the competitive substance [39, 40]. Assuming that maltotriose and glycogen combine competitively at the binding site of phosphorylase, their equilibrium is expressed in Eqs. (7) and (8):

$$Pl + M_3 \rightleftharpoons Pl \cdot M_3 \tag{7}$$

$$K_i = \frac{[Pl][M_3]}{[Pl \cdot M_3]} \tag{8}$$

where $[M_3]$ and $[Pl \cdot M_3]$ are concentrations of the free maltotriose and the phosphorylase-maltotriose complex, respectively, and K_i is the apparent dissociation constant of phosphorylase for M_3. Assuming that the mobility of the $Pl \cdot M_3$ complex is the same as that of free phosphorylase (R_o), Eq. (9) follows:

$$\frac{R_o}{r} = \frac{[Pl]_t}{[Pl] + [Pl \cdot M_3]} \tag{9}$$

where $[Pl]_t = [Pl] + [Pl \cdot M_3] + [Pl \cdot Gn]$. When Eqs. (3) and (8) are substituted in Eq. (9), the following equation is obtained:

$$\frac{r}{R_o - r} = \frac{K_d^{app}}{[Gn]} \left(1 + \frac{[M_3]}{K_i} \right) \tag{10}$$

Under the condition where the total glycogen concentration, c, and the total maltotriose concentration, i, are much higher than those of phosphorylase ($c \gg [Pl]_t$ and $i \gg [Pl]_t$), Eq. (10) can be transformed to Eq. (11):

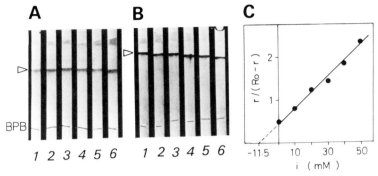

Figure 5. Affinity electrophoresis of rabbit muscle phosphorylase and maltotriose (Figs. from [25] and [40]). (A) Affinity pattern of the interaction between phosphorylase and maltotriose in the absence of glycogen. Maltotriose levels (mM): (1) 0, (2) 10, (3) 20, (4) 30, (5) 40, and (6) 50. ▷ indicates the phosphorylase fraction. (B) Affinity pattern of the interaction between phosphorylase and maltotriose in the presence of glycogen. The conditions were the same as in (A) except that all gels contained 0.2% glycogen. Other electrophoretic conditions were the same as in Fig. 4B. (C) Affinity plot obtained with the inhibition affinity equation (Eq. 11).

$$\frac{r}{R_o - r} = \frac{K_d^{app}}{c}\left(1 + \frac{i}{K_i}\right) \qquad (11)$$

Therefore, if Eq. (11) is plotted at a constant concentration of glycogen, taking $r/(R_o - r)$ as the ordinate and i as the abscissa, a straight line is obtained. The intercept of the line on the abscissa gives a negative apparent dissociation constant for maltotriose $(-K_i)$. Fig. 5A shows the affinity pattern of the interaction between rabbit muscle phosphorylase and maltotriose in the absence of glycogen. The pattern demonstrates that maltotriose has no effect on the mobility of phosphorylase, as predicted by theory. Fig. 5B shows the affinity patterns of the interaction between phosphorylase and maltotriose in the presence of 0.2% glycogen. The decreased mobility of phosphorylase by glycogen is reversed by the addition of maltotriose, and the reversal increases proportionally with the concentration of maltotriose. Fig. 5C shows the affinity plot obtained with Eq. (11), with the data in Fig. 5A and 5B. The plot results in a straight line as required by theory. We have designated Eq. (11) the inhibition affinity equation. The inhibition affinity equation is applicable to interactions between enzyme and inhibitor, lectin and oligosaccharide or antibody and hapten.

2.3   General affinity equation

The original and the inhibition affinity equations are derived from assumptions that: (i) the mobility of a protein complex with a macromolecular affinity ligand is zero and (ii) the mobility of a protein complex with a low molecular affinity ligand is identical to that of free protein. But in the case of a protein complex with a neutral substance having an intermediate molecular weight, the complex could have limited mobility because of the incomplete molecular sieving effect of polyacrylamide gel [25, 41]. Concanavalin A interacts specifically with a-$(1-4)$ and a-$(1-6)$-D-glucan [42, 43]. Fig. 6A shows the affinity patterns of concanavalin A in the presence of equal concentrations (0.5%) of dextrans of different molecular weight [41]. Concanavalin A migrates about 70% of egg white lysozyme (lane 1). When Dextran T-10 (average molecular weight 1×10^4) is added to the polyacrylamide gel (lane 2), the mobility of concanavalin A decreases to about 50% of lysozyme. When the molecular weight of the added dextran is increased, the rate of the decrease in mobility is elevated, and reaches a maximum when molecular weight of the dextran reaches 5×10^5 (lane 6, Dextran T-500) or more (2×10^6; lane 7, Dextran T-2000). While the mobility of concanavalin A decreases in the presence of dextran, that of lysozyme does not change. In addition, the kinetically determined dissociation constants for a series of maltose-type oligosaccharides were reported to have identical values regardless of the number of their glucosyl residue [44, 45]. The differences in the decrease of mobility in the presence of dextrans of different molecular weights result from molecular sieving, the complex of concanavalin A with dextran (Dn) with an intermediate molecular weight having limited mobilities. The equilibrium of the concanavalin A-dextran interaction may be expressed as follows:

$$\text{Con A} + \text{Dn} = \text{Con A} \cdot \text{Dn} \tag{12}$$

$$K_d^{app} = \frac{[\text{Con A}][\text{Dn}]}{[\text{Con A} \cdot \text{Dn}]} \tag{13}$$

When the relative migration distance of a complex of concanavalin A-dextran of intermediate molecular weight or that obtained with an excess of such dextran is expressed as R_c, the following equation is obtained:

$$\frac{R_o - R_c}{r - R_c} = \frac{[\text{Con A}]_t}{[\text{Con A}]} \tag{14}$$

Substituting Eq. (13) in Eq. (14) results in

$$\frac{R_o - R_c}{r - R_c} = 1 + \frac{[\text{Dn}]}{K_d^{app}} \tag{15}$$

When the total dextran concentration, c, is much higher than the total concanavalin A concentration, [Dn] is practically equal to c. Then, Eq. (15) is transformed to

$$\frac{1}{R_o-r} = \frac{1}{R_o-R_c}\left(1+\frac{K_d^{app}}{c}\right) \tag{16}$$

Eq. (16) is identical to the original affinity equation (Eq. (6)), when $R_c = 0$, as in the case of the phosphorylase-glycogen interaction or the concanavalin A-Dextran T-2000 interaction. When Eq. (16) is plotted taking $1/(R_o-r)$ as the ordinate and $1/r$ as the abscissa, a straight line is obtained. The intercept of the line on the abscissa gives a negative reciprocal apparent dissociation constant $(-1/K_d^{app})$, and from the intercept on the ordinate, R_c can be calculated.

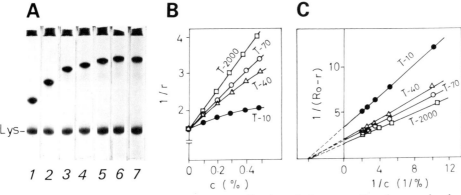

Figure 6. Affinity electrophoresis of concanavalin A and dextrans of various molecular weights (Figs. from [25] and [41]). (A) Affinity pattern of concanavalin A. Electrophoresis was carried out according to the method described by Reisfeld et al. [34] in a 5.0% polyacrylamide gel. Staining with Coomassie Brilliant Blue R-250. (1) No dextran. Gels (2) to (7) dextran added. (2) 0.5% Dextran T-10 (average molecular weight 1×10^4); (3) 0.5% Dextran T-40 (4×10^4); (4) 0.5% Dextran T-70 (7×10^4); (5) 0.5% Dextran T-150 (15×10^4); (6) 0.5% Dextran T-500 (5×10^5); (7) 0.5% Dextran T-2000 (2×10^6). Lys, egg white lysozyme band. (B) Affinity plot obtained with the original affinity equation (Eq. 6). (C) Affinity plot obtained with the general affinity equation (Eq. 16).

Fig. 6B shows the affinity plots for the interaction between concanavalin A and various dextrans obtained by Eq. (6). While plots obtained by dextrans of higher molecular weight, such as Dextran T-2000, give straight lines, those obtained by dextrans of lower molecular weight, such as Dextran T-10 or T-40, form convex curves, showing a deviation from Eq. (6). By contrast, all plots obtained with Eq. (16) result in straight lines and converge at the same point on the abscissa (Fig. 6C). Therefore, the apparent dissociation constants of concanavalin A-dextran complexes are identical regardless of the molecular weight of dextran. Eq. (16) is valid not only for interactions between proteins and substances of intermediate molecular weight, as indicated above, but also for interactions between proteins and charged ligands, where the mobility of the complex (R_c) is different from that of free protein (R_o). Bøg-Hansen and Takeo [46] have calculated the apparent dissociation constants of various human serum glycoproteins for concanavalin A with Eq. (16) in crossed affinity immunoelectrophoresis. Therefore, we have designated Eq. (16) the general affinity equation [25, 46].

3   Factors influencing the affinity pattern

3.1   Buffer systems

In general, discontinuous buffer systems are superior to continuous buffer systems for achieving a sharp electrophoretic pattern. Hauzer et al.. [49] determined the pH dependence of dissociation constants of lectin-sugar complexes in affinity electrophoresis using a series of discontinuous buffer systems. However, small charged molecules were stacked on the ion boundary or escaped into the upper electrode buffer solution during electrophoresis, making it impossible to maintain a constant concentration. A similar situation is encountered with metalloprotein. Concanavalin A contains 1 mole of Mn^{2+} ion and Ca^{2+} ion per mole of subunit. Demetalized concanavalin A showed no affinity for carbohydrates [50]. The affinity of these metal ions for concanavalin A is not particularly strong (in the order of 1 mM to 0.1 mM [51]) and during electrophoresis a sizable fraction of ions dissociates from concanavalin A, with resultant concentration on the ion boundary or loss into the upper buffer solution. In order to keep the metal composition of concanavalin A constant during electrophoresis, the metal concentration in the buffer solution should be constant. For this purpose the use of the continuous buffer system is inevitable. Clarke [38] reported a simplified disc electrophoresis system with the separating gel prepared with the same buffer as the electrode buffer (glycine-Tris mixture, pH 8.1). However, since the concentrations of the electrolyte in the separating gel (eight times dilution of the stock buffer) and the electrode buffer (10 times dilution of the stock buffer) were different and the separating gel contained a high concentration of ammonium persulfate (0.07%), the buffer was still discontinuous.

Takeo *et al..* [52, 53] have developed a continuous buffer system of pH from 3.5 to 9.3 for polyacrylamide gel disc electrophoresis. The separating gel was prepared by photopolymerization to minimize deviations from buffer continuity. The apparent dissociation constants of concanavalin A − carbohydrate obtained with this continuous buffer system were about two thirds of those obtained with a discontinuous buffer system [52, 54].

3.2   Effect of temperature

Electrophoresis is generally performed at a lower temperature to avoid the denaturation of proteins by Joule heat generated during electrophoresis.

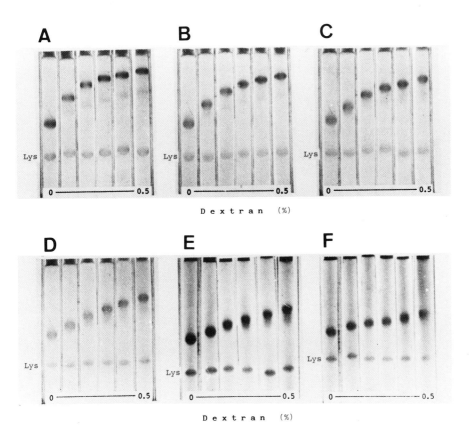

Figure 7. Affinity pattern of interactions between concanavalin A and dextran by varying temperature (Fig. from [54]). Electrophoresis was carried out in a 5% polyacrylamide gel containing 0, 0.1, 0.2, 0.3, 0.4 and 0.5% dextran. Other electrophoresis conditions were the same as in Fig. 6A. K_d^{app} determined with the original affinity equation (Eq. 6) was: (A) 0.39 mM at 11 °C, (B) 0.66 mM at 20 °C, (C) 0.95 mM at 30 °C, (D) 1.35 mM at 39 °C, (E) 2.12 mM at 50 °C, and (F) 3.83 mM at 59 °C. Lys, egg white lysozyme band.

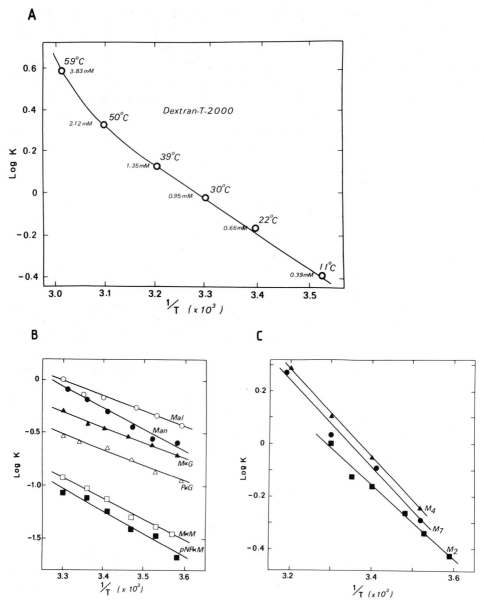

Figure 8. Van't Hoff plots for concanavalin A-carbohydrate interactions (Fig. from [54]). (A) Concanavalin A-dextran interaction. Van't Hoff plot was prepared with the results from affinity electrophoresis (Fig. 7). (B) Concanavalin A interaction with monosaccharides and their glycosides. Mal, maltose; Man, D-mannose; MaG, methyl α-D-glucoside; PaG, phenyl α-D-glucoside; MaM, methyl α-D-mannoside; pNPaM, p-nitrophenyl-α-D-mannoside. (C) Concanavain A interaction with maltose oligosaccharides. M_2, maltose; M_4, maltotetraose; and M_7, maltoheptaose.

Since affinity is a temperature-dependent interaction and patterns change with temperatures, it is important that affinity electrophoresis is performed at a constant temperature. If an efficient thermostatic electrophoresis apparatus were available, thermodynamic constants could be calculated from the apparent dissociation constants obtained at various temperatures. Fig. 7 shows the affinity patterns of concanavalin A-dextran interactions at varying temperatures using an efficient thermostatic apparatus [54]. The mobility of concanavalin A decreases in gels containing dextran. The rate of decrease was smaller when electrophoresis was carried out at higher temperature. The apparent dissociation constants are estimated to be 0.39 mM at 11 °C, 0.66 mM at 22 °C, 0.95 mM at 30 °C, 1.35 mM at 39 °C, 2.12 mM at 50 °C and 3.83 mM at 59 °C, increasing about 10-fold in this temperature range. In other words, the affinity of concanavalin A for dextran decreased by about one-tenth when the temperature was increased from 11 °C to 59 °C. Fig. 8A shows a van't Hoff plot obtained from data in Fig. 7. There was a linear relationship between 10 °C and 50 °C. From the slope, ΔH^0 was estimated to be -6.2 kcal/mol, and ΔS^0 was calculated to be -6.3 cal/mol/K. In Figs. 8B and 8C, van't Hoff plots for interactions between concanavalin A and various oligosaccharides and glycosides are presented [54]. A linear relationship was found and thermodynamic constants for the interactions could be determined [54]. The method is quite simple and the calculated values coincided closely with those obtained by substitution titration of fluorescence quenching [55]. Similar procedures were used to determine thermodynamic constants for the phosphorylase-glycogen interaction [56], for the interaction between Dnp-hapten and Dnp-specific myeloma protein [35] and for the interaction between human plasma cholinesterase and immobilized procainamide [57].

3.3   Effects of affinity ligand concentration

As mentioned in Section 2, all three affinity equations are derived under conditions where the concentration of the affinity ligand (c or i) was much higher than that of the sample protein. Since in the case of Coomassie Brilliant Blue R-250 staining, the minimal detectable concentration of protein in the polyacrylamide gel is in the order of 10^{-7} M, the added affinity ligand concentration should be higher than 10^{-6} M, preferably higher than 10^{-5} M. In high affinity interactions such as the antigen-antibody, and lectin-glycoprotein reactions, whose dissociation constants are lower than 10^{-6} M, an affinity ligand concentration in the order of 10^{-6} M could cause a complete retardation of protein mobility at the origin of the electrophoresis gel, making it impossible to estimate the exact relative migrating distance (r) and, therefore, to determine the apparent dissociation constant. For these high affinity interactions a more sensitive staining technique, such as silver staining [58 – 60], colloidal gold staining [61] or enzymo-immunochemical staining, is necessary for detecting the protein band. In silver staining, a polyacrylamide slab gel thinner than 1 mm in width and in colloidal gold and enzymo-immunochemical staining, electroblotted nitrocellulose membrane is required.

Where the affinity ligand concentration is not much higher than that of protein, plots obtained from the original affinity equation provide concave curves. A theory explaining affinity electrophoresis for these conditions has been reported [37, 62, 63]. However, when the protein and its ligand, such as antibody and antigen, lectin and polysaccharide or glycoprotein, approach equivalent concentrations, the complex tends to precipitate or aggregate, making the interaction deviate from dynamic equilibrium. Therefore, it appears safer to calculate the apparent dissociation constant under conditions where the concentration of the affinity ligand is much higher than that of the sample proteins as described in Section 2 of reference [35].

4   Applications of affinity electrophoresis

4.1   Electrophoresis

All types of electrophoresis can be adapted to affinity electrophoresis. Among reported types of affinity electrophoresis covered here are: affinity electrophoresis in polyacrylamide gel, crossed affinity immunoelectrophoresis, affinity electrophoresis in cellulose acetate membrane and agarose,

Table 1. Theoretical approach to affinity electrophoresis

Electrophoresis system	References
Protein – macromolecular affinity ligand system	[1, 8, 14, 15, 25, 46, 62, 63, 139]
Protein – macromolecular affinity ligand – low molecular affinity ligand system	[25, 37, 39, 40, 47, 48, 63, 124]
Protein – affinity ligand system	[25, 37, 41, 46, 62, 63]
Multivalent protein – macromolecular affinity ligand system	[36, 37, 143, 148]

desorption electrophoresis, affinity electrophoretic titration, affinophoresis and two-dimensional affinity electrophoresis. The theoretical approach and applications of affinity electrophoresis are summarized in Tables 1 and 2.

4.2   Plasma proteins

4.2.1   Plasma glycoproteins

A two-dimensional combination of crossed immunoelectrophoresis [11] and affinity electrophoresis was developed by Bøg-Hansen [16]. Plasma glyco-proteins with an affinity for concanavalin A were adsorbed prior to interaction with antibodies by setting an intermediate gel containing concanavalin A coupled to Sepharose between the first-dimensional gel and the reference gel containing antibodies. He identified several plasma glycoproteins which interact with concanavalin A. Later, this method was modified [64, 65]. First-dimensional electrophoresis was performed with gels containing varying concentrations of free concanavalin A instead of concanavalin A-Sepharose.

Fig. 9 shows one set of the typical affinity patterns of this crossed affinity immunoelectrophoresis [64]. Using this method, interactions between plasma

Table 2. Synopsis of affinity electrophoresis

Sample	Affinity ligand[a]	Type of electrophoresis[b]	References
1 Plasma proteins			
Plasma glycoproteins	Con A and other lectins	CAIEP	[16, 30, 46, 64 – 68]
Alpha-fetoprotein	Con A	CAIEP	[70 – 74, 79 – 82]
	Con A	AA-Blotting	[77, 78]
	LCA	CAIEP	[71, 72, 74, 79]
	LCA	AA-Blotting	[78]
Alpha-1-antitrypsin	Con A	CAIEP	[46, 66, 83, 84]
Orosomucoid	Con A	CAIEP	[46, 86, 87, 89 – 92]
Alpha-1-antichymotrypsin	Con A	CAIEP	[66, 93]
Inter-α-trypsin inhibitor	Con A	CAIEP	[94]
Ceruloplasmin	Con A	CAIEP	[66]
Transferrin	Con A	CAIEP	[97]
Haptoglobin	Con A	CAIEP	[66]
Serum ferritin	Con A	CAIEP	[99 – 102]
	Anti-ferritin	Desorption EP	[203]
Blood clotting factor VIII	Con A	CAIEP	[102]
Blood clotting factor IX	WGA	CAIEP	[103]

Table 2. (continued)

Sample	Affinity ligand[a]	Type of electrophoresis[b]	References
Serum albumin	N-alkyl-PAG	PAGDE	[111]
	Blue-dextran	PAGDE	[107]
	Cibacron Blue-agarose	AG-PAGE	[108, 109]
	Cibacron Blue-agarose	Desorption EP	[205]
	Anti-albumin	AGE	[112]
Fibronectin	Heparin	CAIEP	[113]
2 Other proteins			
Ovalbumin	Blue Dextran	PAGDE	[107]
Beta-lactoglobulin A	N-alkyl-PAG	PAGDE	[111]
Glycophorin	WGA	CAIEP	[115]
Thyroglobulin	Con A and RCA	RAIEP	[116]
Glycosylated hemoglobin	Dextransulfate	CAM-EP	[117, 118]
	Dextransulfate	AGE	[119]
Profilin, chicken	Poly-L-proline	PAGDE	[120]
I blood group substance	Lectins	Rocket lectin EP	[121]
Submaxillary mucin	Lectins	Rocket lectin EP	[121]
3 Lectins			
Con A	Dextran	PAGDE	[24, 45, 52 – 54]
	Glycogen	PAGDE	[24, 45, 53, 54]
	Starch	PAGDE	[24]
	Mannan	PAGDE	[24]
	Oligosaccharides	PAGDE	[24, 45, 54, 124, 125]
	O-mannosyl PAGs	PAGDE	[17, 125]
Succinyl con A	Dextran	PAGDE	[52, 53]
Ricinus communis agglutinin	O-galactosyl PAG	EP-Titrn	[130]
	Oligosaccharides	PAGDE	[124]
Lens culinaris agglutinin	Oligosaccharid	PAGDE	[124, 125]
	O-mannosyl PAG	PAGDE	[49, 154]
	O-mannosyl PAG	EP-Titrn	[130]
Dolichos biflorus lectin	Oligosaccharides	PAGDE	[124]
	Gal-NAc-PAG	PAGDE	[49]
	BGS (A + H)	PAGDE	[123]
Vica cracca lectin	Oligosaccharides	PAGDE	[124, 125]
	Gal-NAc-PAG	PAGDE	[49, 125]
Pisum sativum lectin	Oligosaccharides	PAGDE	[17, 125]
Glycine soja lectin	Oligosaccharides	PAGDE	[124]
	O-galactosyl-PAG	PAGDE	[49]
Marasmius oreades lectin	Oligosaccharides	PAGDE	[124]
	O-galactosyl-PAG	PAGDE	[49]

Table 2. (continued)

Sample	Affinity ligand[a]	Type of electrophoresis[b]	References
Ulex europaeus lectin	Oligosaccharides	PAGDE	[124]
Anguilla anguilla lectin	Oligosaccharides	PAGDE	[124]
Helix pomatia lectin	Oligosaccharides	PAGDE	[124]
Stinkhorn mushroom lectin	Fetuin-Sepharose 4B	PAGDE	[127]
Azrocyle aegerita lectin	Beta-lactosyl-PAG	PAGDE	[128]
Lathyrus sativus lectin	APG-dextran	PAGDE	[126]
4 Enzymes			
Alcohol dehydrogenase	Blue Dextran	PAGDE	[107]
Lactate dehydrogenase	Blue Dextran	PAGDE	[107]
	5'-AMP-PAG	PAGDE	[133]
	2'-AMP-PAG	PAGDE	[135]
	5'-AMP-PHPMA	PAGDE	[134]
Malate dehydrogenase	Blue Dextran	PAGDE	[107]
	5'-AMP-PAG	PAGDE	[135]
	2'-AMP-PAG	PAGDE	[135]
Malic enzyme	5'-AMP-PAG	PAGDE	[135]
	2'-AMP-PAG	PAGDE	[135]
Isocitrate dehydrogenase	5'-AMP-PAG	PAGDE	[135]
	2'-AMP-PAG	PAGDE	[135]
6-Phosphogluconate dehydrogenase	5'-AMP-PAG	PAGDE	[135]
	2'-AMP-PAG	PAGDE	[135]
Glucose 6-phosphate dehydrogenase	Blue Dextran	PAGDE	[107]
	5'-AMP-PAG	PAGDE	[135]
	2'-AMP-PAG	PAGDE	[135]
Glucosyltransferase	Soluble glucan	PAGDE	[173]
Glycogen phosphorylase (mammalian)	Glycogen	PAGDE	[14, 15, 24, 40, 56, 136, 140, 147, 163]
	Glycogen	EP-Titrn	[22]
	Cyclodextrin	PAGDE	[24, 40, 56]
	Oligosaccharides	PAGDE	[24, 40, 56]
	Alkylated PAG	PAGDE	[146]
	5'-AMP-PAG	PAGDE	[135]
	2'-AMP-PAG	PAGDE	[135]
Glycogen phosphorylase (potato)	Glycogen	PAGDE	[24, 40, 139, 140 – 142, 163]
	Starch	PAGDE	[24, 40, 140, 141, 163]
	Pullulan	PAGDE	[24, 40]
	Cyclodextrin	PAGDE	[24, 40]
	Oligosaccharides	PAGDE	[24, 40]
	Alkylated PAG	PAGDE	[146]
	5'-AMP-PAG	PAGDE	[135]
	2'-AMP-PAG	PAGDE	[135]

Table 2. (continued)

Sample	Affinity ligand[a]	Type of electrophoresis[b]	References
Glycogen phosphorylase (mold)	Glycogen	PAGDE	[137]
Starch phosphorylase (potato)	Starch	PAGDE	[143, 144]
Pyruvate kinase	Blue Dextran	PAGDE	[107]
Creatine kinase	Blue Dextran	PAGDE	[107]
Adenylate kinase	Blue Dextran	PAGDE	[107]
Arylesterase	Con A	CAIEP	[46]
Cholinesterase	*m*-APTMA-PAG	PAGDE	[148, 149]
	Procainamide-PAG	PAGDE	[57, 150]
Alkaline phosphatase	WGA	CAME	[152, 153, 156]
	WGA	AGE	[154, 155]
Acid phosphorylase	Con A	CAIEP	[157, 158]
	Canavalia gladiate lectin	CAIEP	[159, 160]
α-Amylase	Starch	PAGDE	[24, 161 – 164]
	Starch	AGE	[165]
	Starch	2D-PAGE	[166 – 168]
	Glycogen	PAGDE	[164]
	Beta-limit dextrin	PAGDE	[161]
	Maltotriose	PAGDE	[164]
	Maltose	SGE	[165]
α-Galactosidase	*O*-glycosyl-PAG	PAGDE	[174]
Trypsin	*p*-ABAD-PAG	PAGDE	[169]
	m-ABAD-af-finophore	AGE	[170, 171]
Chymotrypsin	Trp-affinophore	AGE	[172]
Aldolase	Blue Dextran	PAGDE	[107]
5 Immunoglobulins			
Dextran specific myeloma protein	Dextrans	PAGDE	[175, 176]
	(IM)$_n$	PAGDE	[175, 176]
Fructose specific myeloma protein	Oligofructans	PAGDE	[177]
Monoclonal anti-dextran Ig	Dextrans	PAGDE	[178 – 181]
Monoclonal anti-stearyl-(IM)$_7$	Dextrans and (IM)$_7$	PAGDE	[182]
Dnp-specific myeloma protein	Dnp-PAG	PAGDE	[35, 183]
	Tnp-PAG	PAGDE	[35, 183]
Anti-stearyl (IM)$_n$-antibodies	(IM)$_n$	PAGDE	[178]
Anti-Dnp IgG	Dnp-PAG	2D-AEP	[188 – 191]
	Tnp-PAG	2D-AEP	[189 – 191]
Human IgG subclass	Mouse monoclonal antibody	AA-Blotting	[192]
Anti-hapten antibodies	Hapten-anionic affinophore	AGE	[193]

Table 2. (continued)

Sample	Affinity ligand[a]	Type of elec- trophoresis[b]	References
6 Nucleic acids			
Polyadenosine nucleotide	Polyvinyl-uracil	PAGDE	[195]
Polyuridine nucleotide	Polyvinyl-adenine	PAGDE	[195]
Queuosine containing t-RNA	Phenylboronate- PAG	PAGDE	[199]
DNAs	DNA dye-PEG	2D-AEP	[196, 197]
7 Preparative applications			
Ferritin	Antiferritin	Desorption EP	[203]
Human serum albumin	Cibacron- Sepharose	Desorption EP	[205]
Potato glycogen phosphorylase	Glycogen- beta-cyc-Dex	Prep. PAGDE	[140]
Trypsin	*m*-ABAD- affinophore	AGE	[170]
IgG$_1$, IgG$_2$, IgG$_4$	Protein A	Desorption EP	[204]
Steroid specific antibodies	Anti-steroid	Desorption EP	[202]
Anti-Dnp IgG	Dnp-PAG	Prep. 2D-AEP	[190]

a) Abbreviations of affinity ligands: *m*-ABAD-affinophore, *m*-aminobenzamidine conjugated affinophore; *p*-ABAD-PAG, *p*-amino-benzamidine conjugated non-cross-linked polyacrylamide; alkylated dextran, water soluble alkyl dextran; N-alkyl-PAG, linear copolymer of N,N-dimethylacrylamide with *N*-alkyl-substituted acrylamides; 5'-AMP-HPMA, 5'-AMP-hydroxypropylmethacrylamide copolymer; 2'-AMP-PAG, 8-substituted 2'-AMP non-cross-linked polyacrylamide conjugate; 5'-AMP-PAG, 8-substituted 5'-AMP non-cross-linked polyacrylamide conjugate; APG-PAG, aminophenyl glycosyl conjugated non-cross-linked polyacrylamide gel; *m*-APTMA-PAG, *m*-aminophenyl trimethylammonium conjugated non-cross-linked polyacrylamide gel; BGS (A + H), blood group substance (A + H); Con A, concanavalin A; beta-cyc-Dex, beta-cyclodextrin; DNA dye-PEG, polyethylene glycol-DNA-specific dye conjugate; Dnp-PAG, 2,4-dinitrophenyl conjugated non-cross-linked polyacrylamide; Gal-NAc-PAG, N-acetyl-galactosaminyl conjugated non-cross-linked polyacrylamide gel; *O*-glycosyl PAG, *O*-glycosyl conjugated non-cross-linked polyacrylamide gel (*e.g.* *O*-mannosyl-PAG *etc.*); (IM)$_n$, isomaltose oligosaccharide; (IM)$_7$, isomaltoheptaose; LCA, *Lens curinalis* agglutinin; Phenylborate-PAG, acryloyl aminophenylborate-acrylamide copolymer; RCA, *Ricinus communis* agglutinin; Tnp-PAG, 2,4,6-trinitrophenyl conjugated non-cross-linked polyacrylamide; Trp-affinophore, tryptophan conjugated affinophore; WGA, wheat germ agglutinin
b) Abbreviations of electrophoresis: AA-blotting, antibody-affinity blotting; AGE, agarose gel electrophoresis; AG-PAGE, agarose containing polyacrylamide gel electrophoresis; CAIEP, crossed affinity immunoelectrophoresis; CAME, cellulose acetate membrane electrophoresis; 2D-AEP, two-dimensional affinity electrophoresis; Desorption EP, desorption electrophoresis; EP-Titrn, electrophoretic titration; PAGDE, polyacrylamide gel disc electrophoresis; Prep. 2D-AEP, preparative two-dimensional affinity electrophoresis; Prep. PAGDE, preparative polyacrylamide gel disc electrophoresis; RAIEP, rocket affinity immunoelectrophoresis; SGE, starch gel electrophoresis

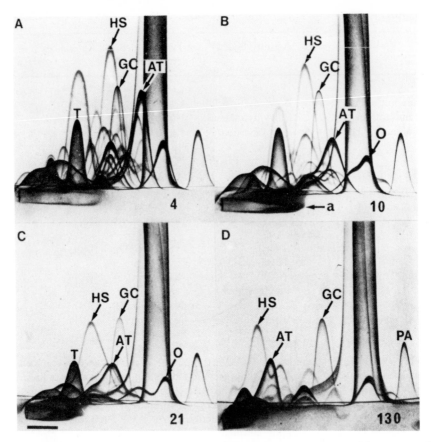

Figure 9. Crossed affinity immunoelectrophoresis of human serum with concanavalin A (Fig. from [64]). In crossed immunoelectrophoresis of 1 μL human serum the first dimensional gel contained increasing amounts of concanavalin A (Con A). (A) 4 μg; (B) 10 μg; (C) 21 μg; (D) 130 μg Con A/cm^2. The upper gel for the second electrophoresis contained anti-human serum (8 μL/cm^2). a, Affinity precipitate formed during the first electrophoresis; AT, alpha-1-antitrypsin; GC, Gc-globulin; HS, alpha-2-HS-glycoprotein; O, orosomucoid; PA, prealbumin; T, transferrin.

glycoproteins and concanavalin A were analyzed, and their apparent dissociation constants were calculated [46]. Orosomucoid was composed of three components. Component 1 did not show an affinity for concanavalin A, but components 2 and 3 showed strong affinity, with apparent dissociation constants of 1.5×10^{-5} M and 1.1×10^{-5} M, respectively. Arylesterase showed the same order of affinity (1.1×10^{-5} M) with component 3 of orosomucoid. Apparent dissociation constants for haptoglobin and transferrin were estimated to be 3.2×10^{-5} M and 3.9×10^{-5} M, respectively. Crossed affinity immunoelectrophoresis has been used as a general technique for identification and quantification of normal and pathological glycoproteins in serum and other body fluids [30].

4.2.2   Alpha-fetoprotein (AFP)

The microheterogeneity of human alpha-fetoprotein was first demonstrated by Smith and Kellerher [69]. Kerckaert *et al.* [70] first applied crossed affinity immunoelectrophoresis to characterize the molecular heterogeneity of rat, mouse and human alpha-fetoprotein. The affinity patterns of alpha-fetoprotein from different sources consisted of one to four peaks, with mobility being related to the affinity for concanavalin A. Human alpha-fetoprotein has been extensively studied by this affinity technique with lectins. Certain oncodevelopmental aspects have been verified in studies of fetal alpha-fetoprotein and of alpha-fetoprotein producing tumors [71]. Using crossed affinity immunoelectrophoresis with concanavalin A and *Lens culinaris* agglutinin, Toftager-Larsen [71] and Breborowicz and Bøg-Hansen [72] demonstrated three alpha-fetoprotein fractions: lectin non-reactive, weakly reactive and strongly reactive alpha-fetoprotein. From the affinity patterns, they calculated the apparent dissociation constants of the two lectin-reactive alpha-fetoproteins. Hay *et al.* [73] determined the proportion of concanavalin A non-reactive alpha-fetoprotein in the total concentration of alpha-fetoprotein by crossed affinity immunoelectrophoresis in amniotic fluid during pregnancies in open neural tube defect and other abnormal fetal cases. The percentage of concanavalin A non-reactive alpha-fetoprotein was significantly lower in open neural tube defects ($<3.9\%$) compared with normal pregnancy cases ($6.4-25.2\%$). These observations suggest that the total alpha-fetoprotein level may aid in the elimination of false diagnoses.

Toftager-Larsen *et al.* [74] confirmed the findings of Hay *et al.* [73]. They compared amniotic alpha-fetoprotein reactivity to *L. curinalis* agglutinin and concanavalin A in crossed affinity immunoelectrophoresis. The *L. curinalis* agglutinin most weakly reactive alpha-fetoprotein fraction correlated strongly with the concanavalin A non-reactive alpha-fetoprotein fraction. This fraction was found at significantly lower level in amniotic fluids from abnormal pregnancies (mainly neural tube defects) than in these from normal pregnancies.

Kobata and his collaborators determined the sugar chain structure of human alpha-fetoprotein from ascites fluid [75] and from a yolk sac tumor [76]. Alpha-fetoproteins isolated from the ascites fluid of patients with primary hepatocellular cancer had a series of biantennary sugar chains which had an affinity for concanavalin A. On the other hand, alpha-fetoprotein isolated from the yolk sac tumor had triantennary sugar chains which did not show affinity for concanavalin A. The structural features of the sugar chains are consistent with data reported by Toftager-Larsen *et al.* [74] and by Hay *et al.* [73] as mentioned above. Yamashita *et al.* [76] suggested that kidney brusch border cells and germ cells in yolk sac tissue contain beta-*N*-acetylglucos-aminyltransferase III which is responsible for synthesis of the triantennary sugar chain by adding bisecting *N*-acetylglucosamine to the biantennary sugar chain, while this transferase is absent in hepatocytes. The data on the structural differences of the carbohydrate sequence of alpha-fetoproteins may suggest ways to devise diagnostic procedures indicative of their tissue origin.

Taketa *et al.* [77, 78] separated the alpha-fetoprotein of different origins into eight groups by a successive affinity electrophoresis with two lectins of different carbohydrate specificity. They developed a sensitive detection technique for alpha-fetoprotein heterogeneity [78]. After affinity electrophoresis in agarose gel, alpha-fetoprotein was transferred by blotting to nitrocellulose membranes precoated with purified horse or goat polyclonal antibodies to human alpha-fetoprotein. The fixed alpha-fetoprotein was detected by successive immunofixation on the blotted nitrocellulose membrane, first with rabbit anti-alpha-fetoprotein immunoglobulin, followed by goat anti-rabbit IgG-horseradish peroxidase conjugate. They called the technique antibody-affinity blotting. Fig. 10 shows the antibody affinity blotting pattern for alpha-fetoprotein-concanavalin A interaction. Washing with an oligosaccharide inhibitor enhanced the sensitivity. Concanavalin A reactive and non-reactive alpha-fetoprotein fractions were sharply resolved.

4.2.3   Alpha-1-antitrypsin

Bayard *et al.* [83] demonstrated that human serum alpha-1-antitrypsin contains four asparagine-linked carbohydrate chains per molecule. By hydrazinolysis it released three types of carbohydrate chains: (i) biantennary (80%), (ii) biantennary with an intercalated *N*-acetylglucosamine residue (14%) and (iii) triantennary (6%). Serum alpha-1-antitrypsin itself was found to be divided into three distinct concanavalin A-reactive molecular variants, S_1, S_2, S_3, with crossed affinity immunoelectrophoresis [83, 84] or with concanavalin A-Sepharose column [83]. All four carbohydrate chains attached on each variant were composed of an identical type of carbohydrate [83]. Bayard *et al.* [83] found that S_1 had triantennary chains, S_2 biantennary chains and S_3 biantennary chains with the intercalated residue. The

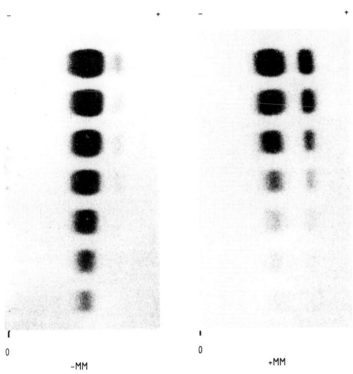

Figure 10. Antibody affinity blotting of alpha-fetoprotein (Fig. from [78]). Agarose gel plates, pH 8.6, were prepared on GelBond film with concanavalin A. The ascites fluid from a patient with hepatocellular carcinoma was serially diluted, and 5 μL were applied. Electrophoresis was carried out until Bromophenol Blue migrated 4.5 cm from the origin. After electrophoresis, the agarose plates were covered with an anti-alpha-fetoprotein (from goat or horse)-precoated nitrocellulose membrane. After 20 min of blotting, the agarose plates were removed, and the blotted nitrocellulose membrane was washed in 0.05% buffered Tween 20 solution with (+MM) or without (−MM) 0.2 M methyl-α-D-mannoside. The fixed alpha-fetoprotein was stained by a successive immunofixation, first with another anti-alpha-fetoprotein (from rabbit), followed by goat anti-rabbit IgG-horse raddish peroxidase conjugate. Color was developed with the H_2O_2-3,3'-diaminobenzidine system. The effect of the methyl-α-D-mannoside wash on band intensity was clear. Concanavalin A reactive and non-reactive alpha-fetoproteins were sharply resolved.

human leukocyte contains multiple forms of alpha-1-antitrypsin. Andersen and Noack [84] distinguished seven molecular variants on the basis of concanavalin A reactivity. Three variants were similar to variants in serum. One variant was similar to alpha-1-antitrypsin reacted with trypsin and elastase. The three remaining variants had zero or very low concanavalin A reactivity.

4.2.4   Orosomucoid (alpha-1-acid glycoprotein)

Orosomucoid has the highest carbohydrate content among human serum glycoproteins (45%). It contains heteroglycans with five different structures and has five glycosylation sites [85]. Nicollet *et al.* [86] reported that while serum orosomucoid fractionated into two fractions with concanavalin A-Sepharose chromatography (concanavalin A non-reactive and concanavalin A reactive), it was separated into three groups by crossed affinity immuno-electrophoresis with concanavalin A. When exogeneous estrogens were administered to normal subjects or to patients with prostate cancer, the level of serum orosomucoid was lowered [87]. Wells *et al.* [88] demonstrated that the strongly reactive orosomucoid fraction (type 3) disappeared after hormone administration. While neuraminidase treatment did not change the elution pattern on the concanavalin A-Sepharose column, the crossed affinity immunoelectrophoresis pattern changed strikingly. Thus, the affinity of concanavalin A weakly reactive and reactive orosomucoid was greatly enhanced. Hansen *et al.* [89] demonstrated with crossed affinity immunoelectrophoresis that orosomucoid appeared to consist of four microheterogeneity components. Type 1, an anodic component, was not retarded by concanavalin A, type 2 was a weakly retarded component of the second peak, and type 3 consisted of strongly retarded components of the third and fourth peaks. The apparent dissociation constants of type 2 and type 3 of the orosomucoid-concanavalin A complex were $1.25 - 1.68 \times 10^{-5}$ M and 1.11×10^{-5} M, respectively [89]. Using the same procedure, examinations were conducted of the microheterogeneity of serum orosomucoid from healthy individuals, patients with benign chronic inflammations and patients with various cancers in various stages before and after surgery [90, 91]. Patients with acute phase reaction of surgery differed from patients with chronic inflammation, and patients with testicular cancer differed from patients with colorectal cancer in having a greater proportion of biantennary glycan orosomucoid.

4.2.5   Alpha-1-antichymotrypsin

Bowen *et al.* [93] applied crossed affinity immunoelectrophoresis to demonstrate the microheterogeneity of human serum alpha-1-antichymotrypsin. The sera contain three protein components: (i) concanavalin A non-reactive, (ii) concanavalin A-weakly reactive and (iii) concanavalin A reactive. In normal sera the level of the concanavalin A-reactive component was low (8%). The level of alpha-1-antichymotrypsin increased in patients with acute phase reaction. While the non-reactive component was not increased significantly by the attack, the quantity of weakly reactive and reactive components increased.

4.2.6   Inter-alpha-trypsin inhibitor

Salier *et al.* [94] reported that inter-alpha-trypsin inhibitor was separated into three concanavalin A-reactive fractions by crossed affinity immunoelectrophoresis. The affinity pattern of purified inter-alpha-trypsin inhibitor was different from that obtained from normal sera. The difference in the affinity pattern was due to the presence of contaminating serum glycoprotein. Loading a sugar specific for the lectin was recommended in the second dimension gel to check for heterogeneous affinity patterns.

4.2.7   Transferrin

Human serum transferrin possesses biantennary [95] and triantennary [96] oligosaccharide chains. Kerckaert and Bayard [97] demonstrated that the oligosaccharide chains obtained from transferrin by hydrazinolysis were resolved on the concanavalin A-affinity column into unbound (15%) and bound (85%) fractions. By structural analysis [97] it was elucidated that the unbound and bound carbohydrate fractions corresponded to the triantennary and biantennary oligosaccharide chain, respectively. On the other hand, human transferrin was fractionated either by crossed affinity immunoelectrophoresis with concanavalin A or on a concanavalin A-affinity column into three fractions: (i) concanavalin A non-reactive (5%), (ii) concanavalin A weakly reactive (30%) and (iii) concanavalin A reactive (65%). From these results, Kerckaert and Bayard [97] concluded that human serum transferrin has two carbohydrate sites per molecule: the non-reactive fraction containing a pair of triantennary chains; the reactive fraction, a pair of biantennary oligosaccharide chains; and the weakly reactive fraction, one biantennary and one triantennary oligosaccharide chain.

4.2.8   Serum ferritin

While a major part of serum ferritin binds to concanavalin A-Sepharose, tissue ferritin does not interact with concanavalin A [98]. Andersen *et al.* [99] demonstrated with crossed affinity immunoelectrophoresis that the concanavalin A-binding serum ferritin was present mainly in the fast-migrating fraction of serum ferritin. Since neuraminidase treatment had no influence on serum ferritin mobility, the ferritin carbohydrate chains did not contain sialic acid [99]. Elevated serum ferritin levels have been found in various infectious, inflammatory and malignant disorders [100] and were mostly liver type isoferritins. Andersen *et al.* [99] correlated this to the relatively greater increase in the non-binding fraction compared to the concanavalin A binding fraction. Serum ferritin contains at least two different antibody reactive fractions: concanavalin A-binding, *i.e.*, carbohydrate-containing and concanavalin A-non-binding, *i.e.*, without carbohydrates. The ferritin fractions from sera of renal carcinoma patients were also analyzed by crossed affinity immunoelectrophoresis [101]. Neither the tumor ferritin concentration nor the preoperative serum ferritin concentration was correlated with the clinical tumor stage of the patients. It was concluded that ferritin was not a tumor marker.

4.2.9   Blood clotting factors

Krauss and Sheard [102] reported evidence for increased interaction of factor VIII related antigen in variant von Willebrand's disease using crossed immunoelectrophoresis and crossed affinity immunoelectrophoresis with concanavalin A. Polack and Freyssinet [103] reported that purified human blood clotting factor IX, although homogeneous by sodium dodecyl sulfate (SDS)-electrophoresis, showed two peaks in crossed affinity immunoelectrophoresis with wheat germ agglutinin. The slow migrating peak had a higher affinity for the lectin ($K_d^{app} = 5.26 \times 10^{-7}$ M) than the fast migrating peak ($K_d^{app} = 1.29 \times 10^{-5}$ M).

4.2.10   Albumin

The triazine dye Cibacron Blue 3G-A has a specific affinity for enzymes possessing a dinuceotide fold [104] and for a wide variety of proteins having hydrophobic binding regions [105, 106]. Tichá *et al.* [107] applied Blue Dextran to affinity electrophoresis for bovine serum albumin. Dean and his collaborators [108, 109] reported dissociation constants calculated by affinity electrophoresis for various serum albumins in interaction with Cibacron Blue 3G-A conjugated with agarose bead [110]. Human serum albumin ($K_d^{app} = 1.6 \times 10^{-5}$ M) had a significantly higher affinity than did albumins from other species (*e.g.*, bovine serum albumin, 1.96×10^{-4} M). The apparent dissociation constants of bovine serum albumin to the alkyl groups were reported by Chen and Morawetz [111] for polyacrylamide gel containing *N*-alkyl-substituted acrylamide-acrylamide linear copolymer. The mobilities were sharply reduced, with the effect increasing as the alkyl side chain on the copolymer extended from dodecyl to octadecyl.

4.3   Other proteins

4.3.1   Erythrocyte membrane glycoprotein

Glycophorin is one of the major components of erythrocyte membrane glycoproteins [114]. Heegaard *et al.* [115] determined the apparent dissociation constant of the glycophorin-wheat germ agglutinin interaction with crossed affinity immunoelectrophoresis. The apparent dissociation constant obtained differed from that determined in direct binding experiments using batchwise separation of glycoprotein from immobilized wheat germ agglutinin. The discrepancy seems to have arisen from differences in the assay system. Free wheat germ agglutinin is used in crossed affinity immunoelectrophoresis, while immobilized wheat germ agglutinin is used in direct binding experiments.

4.3.2   Thyroglobulin

Thyroglobulin is a glycoprotein with a molecular weight of 660000 synthesized in the thyroid gland. Hanham *et al.* [116] characterized the glycosylation of human thyroglobulin by one-dimensional affinity immunoelectrophoresis, similar to that described by Laurell [10] using various lectins. Using the affinity technique with or without neuraminidase and endoglycosidase treatment, they demonstrated that thyroglobulin contains two types of carbohydrate chains: (i) an oligomannose type, as shown by affinity for concanavalin A, and (ii) a complex oligosaccharide type, as shown by affinity for *R. communis* agglutinin.

4.3.3   Hemoglobin

Attempts to separate non-glycosylated hemoglobin, HbA, and glycosylated hemoglobin, HbA_1, with standard electrophoretic techniques have not succeeded due to minute charge differences in these two hemoglobin species. Janik *et al.* [117, 118] developed a simple method based on the facts that HbA_1 does not bind, whereas HbA binds to the sulfate group on dextransulfate, and that its mobility is retarded. They separated HbA from HbA_1 by affinity electrophoresis with dextran sulfate on cellulose acetate membrane. They called the method mobile affinity electrophoresis. Applying the same principle, Aleyassine [119] developed a simple method for quantitative determination of HbA_1 using agarose gel electrophoresis. Hemoglobin bands can be observed directly in the agarose gel, thus eliminating several preparative steps, such as the separation of red blood cells from plasma, washing the cells, staining hemoglobin after electrophoresis and rendering cellulose acetate strips translucent with liquid paraffin prior to scanning densitometry.

4.3.4   Poly(L-proline)-binding proteins

A poly(L-proline)-agarose column was used to purify two poly(L-proline)-binding proteins (PBP-1 and PBP-2) from chicken embryo [120]. PBP-1 was a profilin-actin complex (molar ratio 1 : 1) and PBP-2 was profilin itself. Affinity electrophoresis with poly(L-proline) demonstrated that PBP-2 had the stronger affinity [120]. Since actin does not have an affinity for poly(L-proline), the affinity of PBP-1 originates from the profilin moiety.

4.4   Lectins

The use of affinity electrophoresis in lectin interactions has focused on two fields: (i) characterizing lectin-carbohydrate interactions, such as dissociation constants of interactions; effects of metal ions, pH and temperature; and identifying isolating lectins and isolectins; and (ii) characterizing heterogeneous glycoproteins using the specific affinity of lectins for carbohydrate moieties of glycoproteins. Polyacrylamide gel disc electrophoresis has mainly been used for the first type of application and for the second, crossed immunoelectrophoresis, as mentioned Sections 4.2. and 4.3. The specific interaction of lectin with carbohydrates in polyacrylamide gel disc electrophoresis was first reported by Hořejší and Kocourek [17], who used cross-linked O-glycosyl polyacrylamide copolymers [122] as the macromolecular affinity ligands. Later they used water-soluble non-cross-linked O-glycosyl polyacrylamide copolymers [124] as the affinity ligands. Using the change of lectin mobility in the presence of both O-glycosyl polyacrylamide conjugate as the macromolecular affinity ligand and low molecular weight sugars as the small molecular affinity ligand, they reported dissociation constants of various lectins for glycosyl copolymer and oligosaccharides. Takeo et al. [45] reported that apparent dissociation constants of concanavalin A for the maltose type of oligosaccharides (K_i) and for glycogen (K_d^{app}) were practically equal to the dissociation constant for maltose regardless of the number of glucosyl residues. This indicates that the carbohydrate binding site of concanavalin A appears to be one glucose unit.

Hauzer et al. [49] reported the pH dependence of lectin-carbohydrate interactions using various continuous and discontinuous buffer systems in a pH range from pH 2.3 to 9.5. Lectins from seeds of *Dolichos biflorus, Glycine* (soja), *Lens esculenta* and *Vicia cracca* and from the fruiting body of *Marasmius oreades* had a maximal affinity at pH 7 to 9 [49]. Takeo *et al.* [52] developed a new continuous buffer system for polyacrylamide gel disc electrophoresis for pH 3.5 to 9.6. Using this buffer system, they demonstrated that the apparent dissociation constants of concanavalin A and succinylated concanavalin A for dextran remained unchanged at pH 3.5 to 7.5. At neutral pH, concanavalin A exists as a tetramer, while at pH values below pH 5.5 it exists predominantly as a dimer [129]. Hence it could be concluded that alterations in the quaternary structure of concanavalin A had no effect on its affinity for the carbohydrate [52]. Ek *et al.* [130] determined the apparent dissociation constants of *Ricinus communis* and *L. culinaris* agglutinins to *O*-galactosyl and *O*-mannosyl polyacrylamide conjugates [131] over a wide pH range with affinity electrophoretic titration, a combined procedure of affinity electrophoresis with electrophoretic titration [132]. For both lectins the maximum affinity was found at pH 7 − 8.

4.5   Enzymes

4.5.1   Dehydrogenases

Tichá *et al.* [107] reported on the application of affinity electrophoresis to lactate dehydrogenase (LDH) using Cibacron Blue attached dextran (Blue-Dextran). As mentioned in Section 4.2.10, Cibacron Blue may have a group specific affinity for enzymes which possess a dinucleotide fold [104]. The first report on the determination of the apparent dissociation constant by affinity electrophoresis for LDH-coenzyme analogue interaction was by Nakamura *et al.* [133], who used water-solube 8-substituted 5′-AMP-polyacrylamide conjugatè as the macromolecular affinity ligand. They demonstrated that muscle type LDH isoenzyme (LDH-5) had an approximately 35-fold stronger affinity than heart type LDH (LDH-1). Tichá *et al.* [134] reported dissociation constants independently for bovine LDH isoenzyme (LDH-1, 2, and 3) with 5′-AMP-hydroxy-propylmethacrylamide conjugate having varying lengths of spacer arms of affinity ligands. The apparent dissociation constants decreased with increasing length of spacer arm. Kinetically determined inhibition constants [134] also decreased with increasing lengths of spacer arm.

In contrast, 8-substituted 2′-AMP-polyacrylamide conjugate demonstrated specific affinity for the coenzyme binding site of various NADP⁺-depen-

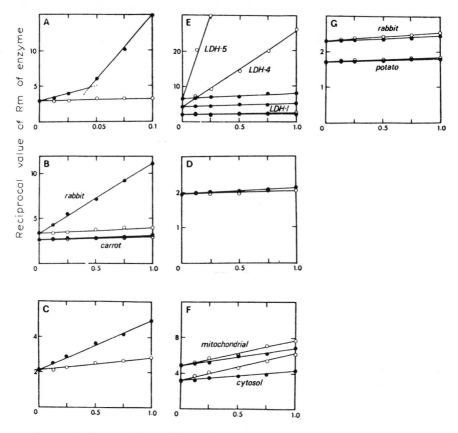

Figure 11. Affinity plots of the interactions of dehydrogenases and phosphorylases with 5'-AMP- and 2'-AMP-conjugated polyacrylamide gel (Figs. from [135]). The reciprocal values of the relative migration distance ($1/r$) of enzymes were plotted against the concentrations of 5'-AMP- or 2'-AMP immobilized on polyacrylamide gel. (A) 6-Phosphogluconate dehydrogenase (rabbit liver); (B) malic enzyme (rabbit liver and carrot); (C) glucose 6-phosphate dehydrogenase (rabbit liver); (D) isocitrate dehydrogenase (rabbit liver); (E) lactate dehydrogenase isoenzymes (rabbit brain); (F) malate dehydrogenase isoenzymes (pig heart mitochondria and cytoplasm); (G) phosphorylases (rabbit brain and potato). ● – ●, with 2'-AMP conjugated PAG, ○ – ○, with 5'-AMP conjugated PAG.

dent dehydrogenases [135]. As seen in Fig. 11 and Table 3, the apparent dissociation constants to the 2'-AMP polyacrylamide conjugate calculated by affinity electrophoresis [135] revealed that NADP$^+$-dependent dehydrogenases generally had a much stronger affinity for the 2'-AMP ligand than did NAD$^+$-dependent dehydrogenases, whereas NADP$^+$-dependent dehydrogenases had a much weaker affinity for the 5'-AMP ligand than did NAD$^+$-dependent dehydrogenases. Thus, NADP$^+$-dependent rabbit liver

Table 3. Apparent dissociation constants for 2'-AMP and 5'-AMP immobilized on polyacrylamide gel for $NADP^+$-dependent dehydrogenases, NAD^+-dependent dehydrogenases and phosphorylases [133, 135]

Enzymes	Apparent dissociation constant (M)	
	2'-AMP	5'-AMP
$NADP^+$-dependent dehydrogenase		
6-Phosphogluconate dehydrogenase (rabbit liver)	8.5×10^{-5}	1.1×10^{-2}
Malic enzyme (rabbit liver)	4.5×10^{-4}	6.1×10^{-3}
Malic enzyme (carrot)	7.3×10^{-3}	1.0×10^{-2}
Glucose 6-phosphate dehydrogenase (rabbit liver)	8.0×10^{-4}	2.6×10^{-3}
Isocitrate dehydrogenase (rabbit liver)	1.6×10^{-2}	2.2×10^{-2}
NAD^+-dependent dehydrogenase		
Lactate dehydrogenase-1 (H_4, rabbit brain)	1.6×10^{-2}	3.2×10^{-3}
Lactate dehydrogenase-2 (H_3M, rabbit brain)	1.4×10^{-2}	1.9×10^{-3}
Lactate dehydrogenase-3 (H_2M_2, rabbit brain)	9.4×10^{-3}	1.2×10^{-3}
Lactate dehydrogenase-4 (HM_3, rabbit brain)	5.6×10^{-3}	4.1×10^{-4}
Lactate dehydrogenase-5 (M_4, rabbit brain)	4.8×10^{-3}	8.6×10^{-5}
Malate dehydrogenase (rabbit brain supernatant)	2.7×10^{-3}	1.3×10^{-3}
Malate dehydrogenase (pig heart cytosol)	2.8×10^{-3}	9.6×10^{-4}
Malate dehydrogenase (pig heart mitochondrial)	2.5×10^{-4}	1.9×10^{-3}
Phosphorylase		
Phosphorylase (rabbit brain)	1.4×10^{-2}	1.0×10^{-2}
Phosphorylase (potato)	4.3×10^{-2}	1.7×10^{-2}

6-phosphogluconate dehydrogenase has a 120-fold stronger affinity and rabbit liver malic enzyme a 14-fold stronger affinity for 2'-AMP ligand than for 5'-AMP ligand, whereas the NAD^+-dependent rabbit muscle type LDH has a 50-fold stronger affinity and pig heart cytosol malate dehydrogenase has a 3-fold stronger affinity for 5'-AMP ligand than for 2'-AMP ligand.

4.5.2   Phosphorylases

Takeo and Nakamura [14, 15] classified mammalian glycogen phosphorylases into three types of isoenzymes – muscle, brain and liver types – based on their affinity differences for glycogen. The apparent dissociation constants of these three isoenzymes for rabbit liver glycogen were calculated by the original affinity equation as 0.61 mM, 1.3 mM and 2.2 mM, respectively, at pH 9.5. 5'-AMP had no effect on their affinity for glycogen. The pH-dependence of phosphorylase affinity [22] was elucidated by affinity electrophoretic titration [130]. Both rabbit muscle phosphorylase a and b had a maximal affinity at pH 8.0 [22]. In human urines from various urogenital diseases, phosphorylase activity was demonstrated in high numbers (51 of 127 cases tested) [136]. The apparent dissociation constants of urine phosphorylase from uterine carcinoma were estimated to be $2.1-2.7$ mM and that from vesicular carcinoma, 1.4 mM.

Glycogen phosphorylase of the mold, *Physarum polycephalum* has an affinity for glycogen. The apparent dissociation constant for oyster glycogen was calculated to be 0.5 mg/mL by affinity electrophoresis [137]. The dissociation constant determined by kinetic measurement was 10-fold higher. This discrepancy was probably due to differences in pH and the buffer system. Potato tubers contain one major and several minor phosphorylase fractions [14, 138−140]. Gerbrandy *et al.* [139, 141, 142] demonstrated that one of the minor fractions had a strong affinity for glycogen, and they called it potato glycogen phosphorylase. The apparent dissociation constants of the major fractions of potato phosphorylase for starch were reported by Shimomura and Fukui [143]. They [144] assumed that the potato glycogen phosphorylase contains glycogen storage sites in the molecule as mammalian glycogen phosphorylase. D-Glucose showed a very weak affinity for rabbit and potato glycogen phosphorylases, while the maltose type of oligosaccharides and beta-cyclodextrin showed strong affinity [40, 56]. The apparent dissociation constants were estimated by the inhibition affinity equation. In contrast to concanavalin A [45] (see Section 4.4), the affinity of rabbit and potato glycogen phosphorylases for these oligosaccharides progressively increased when the number of glucosyl residues was increased. The increasing rate of affinity per glucosyl unit was estimated to be about 5-fold for rabbit muscle phosphorylase and 15-fold for potato glycogen phosphorylase [40].

Dissociation constants depend on temperature. The apparent dissociation constant of potato glycogen phosphorylase for glycogen at 5 °C was about one quarter of that at 18 °C [142], and the apparent dissociation constant of rabbit muscle phosphorylase for glycogen at 5 °C was about one five-hundredth of that at 42.5 °C [56]. Thermodynamic constants calculated from the van't Hoff plots indicated that the interaction between rabbit muscle phosphorylase and glycogen was exothermic ($\Delta H^0 = -29$ kcal/mol) and that the enzyme adopted a more ordered configuration on complex formation ($\Delta S^0 = -77$ cal/mol/K) [56] and similarly on concanavalin A-dextran interaction [54]. There was no difference in carbohydrate binding specificity between rabbit muscle phosphorylase a and b. These results indicated that the carbohydrates bind to phosphorylase at the glycogen storage site.

Muscle phosphorylase has an affinity for aliphatic hydrocarbons. Thus, Shaltiel and his collaborators [145] purified muscle phosphorylase by hydrophobic chromatography. Nakamura *et al.* [146] determined the affinity of rabbit muscle glycogen phosphorylase for a series of aliphatic hydrocarbon conjugated dextrans by affinity electrophoresis. As the length of the alkyl group hydrocarbon side-chains increased, the affinity of the alkyl groups for phosphorylase increased. The introduction of a hydroxyl or an amino group at the terminal position of the hydrocarbon side-chains diminished the affinity.

4.5.3 Cholinesterases

Masson and Vallin [148] first applied affinity electrophoresis to study the multiple molecular forms of human plasma cholinesterase using *m*-aminophenyltrimethyl ammoninum – non cross-linked linear polyacrylamide copolymer as a macromolecular affinity ligand. Three forms of phenotypes (usual enzyme U, atypical A and intermediate UA) were identified. The apparent dissociation constants obtained showed that phenotype U had a twice stronger affinity to the affinity ligand than phenotype A. They suggested that the anionic site in phenotype A is altered resulting in lower affinity. Phenotype U was further separated into three molecular forms: monomer (C_1), dimer (C_3) and tetramer (C_4). Their apparent dissociation constants were calculated to be 1.70×10^{-4} M, 0.80×10^{-4} M, and 0.4×10^{-4} M, respectively [149]. Thermodynamic analysis of the tetrameric form of cholinesterase (C_4) was performed using affinity electrophoresis with immobilized procainamide as the affinity ligand [57]. Native and dealkylated cholinesterase obtained by aging of Soman (1,2,2'-trimethylpropylmethyl fluorophosphate)-alkylated cholinesterase resulted in parallel straight lines on the van't Hoff plot. Masson *et al.* [57] suggested that while affinity was altered by alkylation and dealkylation, a detectable structural change did not seem to be induced by dealkylation.

4.5.4 Alkaline phosphatases

Alkaline phosphatases are grouped into tissue specific isoenzymes of the liver, bone, intestine and placenta. In normal human sera, alkaline phosphatase activity originated mainly from the bone and liver, with a minor contribution from the intestine [151]. Placental alkaline phosphatase enters the plasma as pregnancy progressed. The resolution of such tissue-specific alkaline phosphatase isoenzymes was principally performed with electrophoresis. However, bone and liver alkaline phosphatases were insufficiently resolved. Rosalki and Ying Foo [152] separated them with affinity electrophoresis on cellulose acetate membrane with wheat germ agglutinin. Bone alkaline phosphatase was retarded and clearly separated from liver alkaline phosphatase. Neuraminidase treatment of plasma reduced the resolution of liver and bone alkaline phosphatase [153]. Peaston and Cooper [154] and Onica *et al.* [155] modified the lectin affinity electrophoresis. Wheat germ agglutinin was incorporated into the pre-cast agarose gel with and without Triton X-100. This modification enhanced the resolution of the liver and bone alkaline phosphatase isoenzymes. Komoda *et al.* [156] applied this wheat germ agglutinin-affinity electrophoresis to urine samples of various patients. They suggested that urinary alkaline phosphatases were principally derived from plasma.

4.5.5   Acid phosphatases

Lorenc-Kubis [157, 158] applied crossed affinity immunoelectrophoresis to acid phosphatase interactions. The acid phosphatase activity in the crude extract of grass seeds was separated into two groups: One exhibited a high affinity to concanavalin A and the other did not bind with concanavalin A. However, the non-binding acid phosphatase developed a binding capacity after purification. This indicated that the enzyme may exist as an aggregate complex with other proteins without exposed mannose or glucose units. In the same way, Iwasa *et al.* [159, 160] analyzed seminal acid phosphatase affinity with various lectins. Among lectins extracted from seeds, only *Canavalia gladiate* DC lectin [159] had a binding activity to seminal acid phosphatase. The enzyme was separated into two fractions, a binding and a nonbinding fraction.

4.5.6   α-Amylases

α-Amylases of various origins show affinity to α-(1 − 4) D-glucans such as starch and glycogen. Affinity electrophoresis of α-amylase can be performed by the same procedure as the phosphorylase affinity electrophoresis mentioned in Sections 2.1 and 2.2. However, α-amylase digested these glucans during electrophoresis, and the mobility decrease due to glucan interaction disappeared when a large amount of the enzyme was employed [161]. On reducing the enzyme level, the rate of mobility decrease was enhanced, and at a concentration lower than the limiting amount of enzyme, the rate of the mobility decrease reached a maximum. When the amount of enzyme was reduced further, the mobility became constant, independent of the amount of enzyme applied. Under this condition, the concentration of glucan embedded in the polyacrylamide gel remained practically constant during electrophoresis, so permitting calculation of the apparent dissociation constant. The critical amounts of enzyme were 5 μg for Taka-amylase, 0.1 μg for native, and 0.5 μg for the EDTA-treated human salivary amylases [162, 163]. At enzyme levels lower than the critical amount, the respective apparent dissociation constants for soluble potato starch were determined to be 2.5×10^{-2}, 2.6×10^{-6}, and 1.9×10^{-4} g/mL. Thus, removal of Ca^{2+} ions from salivary amylase diminished its affinity to one eightieth, whereas its enzyme activity was one two-hundredth of native amylase. In contrast, EDTA has neither an effect on affinity, nor on enzyme activity of Taka-amylase A.

Sudo and Kanno [164] detected abnormal lung α-amylase in serum from a patient with lung carcinoma. This amylase had a three-fold stronger affinity for starch than pancreatic or salivary amylase, while it had no affinity for maltotriose. The polymorphism of bovine serum amylase was demonstrated by affinity electrophoresis [165]. The addition of maltose to the starch gels or the use of a supporting medium without starch resulted in no polymorphism. The amylases share a common isoelectric point of pH 3.5.

When polyacrylamide slab gel with a concentration gradient of soluble starch was used and the amylase sample was applied in a line perpendicular to the concentration gradient, the affinity pattern of amylase resulted in a curve or curves. Dissociation constants of amylase to starch could be determined from the affinity curve(s) on one slab gel. Applying this principle, Inoue [166–168] reported the apparent dissociation constants of α-amylases from various mollusc families. While the method gave identical apparent dissociation constants for starch as those obtained with polyacrylamide gel disc electrophoresis [167], the calculation of dissociation constants (K_i) for the maltose types of oligosaccharides was impossible, due to rapid diffusion during electrophoresis.

4.5.7 Trypsins and chymotrypsin

Čeřovský *et al.* [169] reported the interaction of trypsin with immobilized *p*-aminobenzamidine on dextran by affinity electrophoresis. The apparent dissociation constants decreased with increasing lengths of spacer arm. Shimura and Kasai [170, 171] reported aminobenzamidine conjugated cationic and anionic affinity ligands (affinophores) for trypsins of various origins. In affinity electrophoresis with the cationic affinophore, soluble dextran coupled with diethyl aminoethyl bromide and *m*-aminobenzamidine. The tested trypsin samples (bovine pancreas, *Streptomyces erythreus* and *Streptomyces griseus*) migrated towards the cathode. Leupeptin, a specific inhibitor of trypsins, completely suppressed the mobility effect of the affinophore. In contrast, in affinity electrophoresis with an anionic affinophore, polyacrylyl-beta-alanyl-beta-alanine coupled with *m*-aminobenzamidine and aminomethanesulfonic acid. The mobility of *S. griseus* trypsin and bovine pancreatic trypsin shifted towards the anode, whereas the affinophore was not effective for *S. erythreus* trypsin. An anionic property of the *S. erythreus* trypsin seems to cause ionic repulsion to anionic affinophores with no effect on mobility. By the same procedure, anhydrochymotrypsin was separated from other chymotrypsin derivatives [172] by affinity electrophoresis with a tryptophan-incorporated anionic affinophore. Affinity electrophoresis with an affinophore is useful for preparative purposes, as described in Section 4.8.

4.5.8   Glycosidases and glycosyltransferases

While *a*-amylases show strong affinity to a-$(1-4)$-D-glucan, there has been no report on the interaction between *β*-amylase and glucan. Also, no interaction was found for the branching enzyme. A primer a-$(1-4)$-D-glucan is required for its activity. However, this enzyme has no activity to bind glycogen or starch in affinity electrophoresis. On the other hand, three types of glucosyltransferases were isolated from *Streptococcus* mutant 6715-13 Mutant 27 [173], one was primer independent and two primer dependent. All three glucosyltransferases bound dextran and water-soluble glucans from various streptococcal mutants in affinity electrophoresis [173]. Malý *et al.* [174] isolated two *a*-galactosidases from *Vicia faba* seeds. The enzymes interacted with D-galactose, glycogen and *O*-galactosyl polyacrylamide copolymer, but no interaction was observed with D-mannose and *O*-mannosyl-polyacrylamide copolymers.

4.6   Immunoglobulins

Takeo and Kabat [175] first applied affinity electrophoresis to immunoreactions. They calculated the apparent dissociation constants for interactions between dextran specific BALB/c mouse IgA myelomas W 3129 and QUPC 52 with dextrans and isomaltose oligosaccharides. With W 3129 myeloma protein, the dissociation constants (K_i) for methyl-a-glucoside and isomaltose were nearly equal. As the number of a-$(1-6)$-linked glucosyl residues increased, the K_i value decreased. With further increases in glucosyl residues however, the K_i value decreased, isomaltopentaose having the smallest value. The K_i of isomaltoheptaose was about three times higher than that of isomaltopentaose. With QUPC 52 myeloma protein, isomaltose oligosaccharides generally had larger K_i values than with W 3129. As the number of a-(1−6)-linked glucosyl residues increased, the K_i values decreased, reaching a minimal value with isomaltohexaose or isomaltoheptaose. The results suggested that the binding sites of these two myeloma proteins were different. W 3129 myeloma protein probably had a cavity-type binding site, whereas QUPC 52, a groove-type binding site. In the same manner, Sugii *et al.* [176] calculated apparent dissociation constants for dextran specific NZB mouse IgA myeloma PC 3858 and PC 3936. Both myeloma proteins have groove-type combining sites and showed specificity for internal a-(1−6)-linked glucoses, similarly to QUPC myeloma protein.

Using the same procedure, Sugii and Kabat [177] calculated apparent association constants of BALB/c and NZB-D-fructan specific myeloma protein with high molecular weight levans and with lower molecular weight compounds, such as rye-grass levan, inulin, sucrose and D-fructose oligosaccharides with β-(2−1)- and β-(2−6)-D-fructofuranosyl linkages. They demonstrated that there were two different groups of D-fructan specific myeloma proteins: one had a dual specificity for β-(2−1)- and β-(2−6)-D-fructofuranosyl linkages (W 3082, UPC 61), and the other had a specificity for β-(2-6)-D-fructofuranosyl linkages (PC 3660, Y 5476, and UPC 10). The combining sites of W 3082 and UPC 61 were complementary to tetrasaccharide.

Wood and Kabat [178] reported affinity electrophoresis of the rabbit anti-stearyl isomaltose oligosaccharide antibodies. In general, the specific antibodies were heterogeneous in isoelectric focusing. But anti-stearyl isomaltoheptaose-antibodies R-862 showed a restricted isoelectric focusing pattern and one band in polyacrylamide gel disc electrophoresis. Its apparent binding constants for dextran B-512 and for isomaltose oligosaccharides were determined. These data were comparable to dextran specific myeloma protein W 3129.

Sharon *et al.* [179] determined apparent association constants of dextran specific mouse IgM and IgA hybridoma antibodies for dextran B 512 and for isomaltoheptaose. The affinity of these IgA hybridoma antibodies is in the same order as that of dextran-specific W 3129 IgA myeloma protein. The apparent association constants for isomaltoheptaose ranged from $1.45 \times 10^4 \, M^{-1}$ to $7.01 \times 10^4 \, M^{-1}$, while the constant of W 3129 was $2.29 \times 10^4 \, M^{-1}$ [175]. A faint minor band was observed for IgA hybridoma in addition to the major retarded band in the affinity gel. Sodium dodecyl sulfate (SDS)-electrophoresis showed that the minor bands of IgA hybridoma antibody had two L-chains with different migrations and that the major band had a single L-chain band. Sharon *et al.* [179] suggested that the major IgA band contained a monomer composed of two specific H chains, each associated with a specific L chain, and the minor bands contained a monomer composed of two specific H chains, one of which was associated with a specific L chain and the other with a non-specific L chain. These IgA monomers containing both specific and nonspecific L-chains were shown to have association constants with dextran six-fold to 30-fold lower than monomers containing two specific light chains. Using the same procedures together with quantitative precipitin assay, Newman *et al.* [180, 181] determined the specificities in the combining site of a set of monoclonal antibodies to dextran B 512 [180] and to dextran B 1355 S [181].

Lai and Kabat [182] characterized 12 C57BL/6J hybridoma antibodies for stearyl-isomaltose oligosaccharides. Seven produced IgA and five IgM by affinity electrophoresis. The apparent association constants of monomers of these antibodies determined by affinity electrophoresis ranged from 1.4×10^3 to 4.6×10^5 mL/g for dextran B 512 and from 1.2×10^3 to 3.5×10^4 M^{-1} for isomaltoheptaose. They reported that the specificity and nature of the binding sites of these hybridoma antibodies were comparable to those of rabbit antisera to stearyl-isomaltosyl oligosaccharides [178].

Tanaka *et al.* [35] applied affinity electrophoresis to determine the apparent dissociation constants and the thermodynamic parameters for the affinity of Dnp-specific mouse myeloma MOPC 315. The myeloma protein consists of monomeric, dimeric and trimeric forms of IgA. The dimer had a higher affinity to the Dnp-hapten ($K_d^{app} = 0.83$ mM at 20 °C) than the monomer ($K_d^{app} = 2.8$ mM), and the monomer had a higher affinity than its Fab' fragment ($K_d^{app} = 4.6$ mM). All of these myeloma proteins had a higher affinity to Tnp-hapten (K_d^{app}; monomer $= 0.11$ mM) than to Dnp-hapten. The affinity increased when the temperature increased. Thus, the van't Hoff plots for these interactions produced linear relationships at 7 °C to 40 °C. At 50 °C the van't Hoff plot deviated from a straight line, and a new protein band with a very low affinity appeared. The authors stated that it appeared to be a light chain dimer. Its affinity to Tnp was found to be about one-fourteenth that of Fab' fragment. The fact that ΔH^0 and ΔS^0 were both positive, in contrast to phosphorylase and concanavalin A, suggested the MOPC-315 interactions were endothermic and hydrophobic.

Antibodies to a single antigenic determinant or hapten are heterogeneous. In spite of the high resolving power of isoelectric focusing [178, 184, 185] or standard two-dimensional electrophoresis [186, 187], a satisfactory resolu-

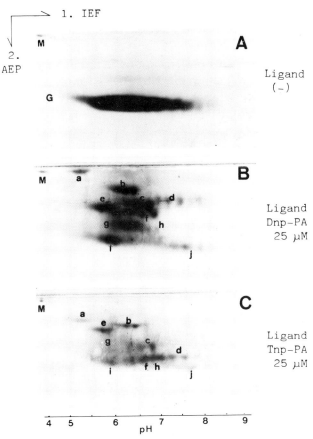

Figure 12. Two-dimensional affinity electrophoresis patterns of rabbit anti-Dnp antibody (Figs. from [189]). In the first electrophoresis, isoelectric focusing was carried out in a 5% polyacrylamide gel containing 6 M urea, 10% sucrose and eight-fold diluted Pharmalyte carrier ampholytes of an equal volume mixture of stock solution with a pH range 4.0−6.5 and 6.5−9.0. The purified rabbit anti-Dnp antibody (470 µg) was applied. In the second electrophoresis, affinity electrophoresis was carried out by using the acidic buffer system of Reisfeld et al. [34] with 5% polyacrylamide gel containing (A) no affinity ligand, (B) 25 µM Dnp-conjugated PAG, and (C) 25 µM Tnp-conjugated PAG. Silver staining of proteins.

tion of immunoglobulins has still not been attained. Takeo *et al.* [188, 189] developed a new type of two-dimensional affinity electrophoresis in which both isoelectric focusing and affinity electrophoresis were employed. Fig. 12 shows an example of two-dimensional affinity electrophoresis. Rabbit anti-Dnp antibodies were separated into a large number of IgG spots with Dnp- (Fig. 12 B) or Tnp-polyacrylamide conjugate (Fig. 12 C) as the affinity ligand. Calculations from affinity patterns indicated that the apparent dissociation constant of the individual IgG spots ranged from 2.0×10^{-6} M to

1.1×10^{-4} M for the Dnp-hapten and from 1.4×10^{-5} M to 1.3×10^{-4} M for the Tnp-hapten. On the basis of affinity electrophoresis patterns and affinity for haptens at different pH values [190], these IgG spots can be grouped into several families of monoclonal IgGs [189, 190]. One of the families of anti-Dnp IgG (family e in Fig. 12 B or 12 C) showed a 1.6 times stronger affinity for Tnp-hapten than Dnp-hapten. By the same principle, preparative affinity electrophoresis was reported for amounts of a few milligrams [190].

4.7   Nucleic acids

There have been only a few reports on affinity electrophoresis of nucleic acids. Takeo demonstrated with cross electrophoresis [2] that yeast ribonucleic acid interacts strongly with protamines [194]. Pitha [195] reported the specific interactions of polyadenoside and polyuridine nucleotide with synthesized polyvinyl uracil and polyvinyl adenine. Caffeine completely prevented a cross-reaction between polyvinyl adenine − polyadenosine nucleotide. However, quantitative evaluations of the interactions are limited, since the native histone − DNA interactions were so strong that an equilibrium could not be attained. Müller *et al.* [196, 197] reported DNA-DNA-dye interactions in electrophoresis. Various base pair specific DNA-dyes comprising phenyl phenazinium dye, triphenylmethane dye and Hoechst 33258 were covalently bound to polyethylene glycol [196]. Polyethylene glycol derivatives were used for base specific DNA separation in agarose and polyacrylamide gel electrophoresis. The resolution allows separation of DNA fragments differing as little as 0.5% in base composition [197]. Recently Igloi and Kössel [198] developed a new affinity technique for t-RNA separation. The hypermodified nucleoside Q (queuosine) in t-RNAs has an unusual cyclopentaenediol side chain [199]. Based on the observation that borate has a specific affinity to cis 1,2-diol [200, 201], an affinity gel for the queuosine side chain was prepared by copolymerization of acryloylaminophenylboric acid. By this procedure, t-RNA species containing the Q base may be specifically resolved from Q-lacking t-RNAs.

4.8   Preparative affinity electrophoresis

For preparative purposes, affinity chromatography is generally superior to affinity electrophoresis. But there have been several reports on selective preparations of proteins by affinity electrophoresis. High affinity substances cannot be eluted from the affinity column by affinity chromatography. Dean and his collaborators [202, 203] developed desorption electrophoresis to elute such high affinity proteins from the affinity column. Steroid specific antibodies adsorbed on immunoadsorbents were placed on the top of the electrophoresis gel, and antibodies were desorbed by electrophoresis [202]. The recovery was quantitative. In the same manner human IgG_1, IgG_2 and IgG_4 were desorbed from immobilized protein A [204], and ferritin from immobilized anti-ferritin [203]. Similarly, human serum albumin [205] was desorbed from the Cibacron-Sepharose 4 B gel by desorption electrophoresis with 83% recovery.

Potato tubers contain a minor phosphorylase fraction (potato glycogen phosphorylase) which has a high affinity for glycogen, as mentioned in Section 4.5.2. This phosphorylase was purified to homogeneity by combining affinity chromatography and affinity electrophoresis [140]. The eluate from potato starch granules with beta-cyclodextrin was used directly in preparative polyacrylamide gel disc electrophoresis [206, 207], the separating gel containing glycogen. After electrophoresis, the phosphorylase fraction was extracted from the gel and was reapplied in the same type of preparative electrophoresis using a separating gel without glycogen. The phosphorylase fraction was extracted, and the contaminated soluble polyacrylamide component was removed by electrophoresis with a sucrose gradient from 15 to 45% in the stacking buffer system without the supporting polyacrylamide gel [207]. The overall recovery of potato glycogen phosphorylase was 45%.

Shimura and Kasai [170] devised a separation technique which is based on the specific affinity of a protein for a macromolecular affinity ligand with either a positive or negative charge, as mentioned in Section 4.5.7. When a mixture of proteins is electrophoresed in the presence of a charged ligand, the protein having an affinity for the ligand will form a complex and its mobility will change. Using *m*-aminobenzamidine-soluble dextran conjugate as the charged affinity ligand, they separated *S. griseus* trypsin. They called the charged affinity ligand an "affinophore", and the electrophoresis process "affinophoresis".

5   References

[1] Nakamura, S., Takeo, K., Tanaka, K., Ueta, T., *Hoppe-Seyler's Z. Physiol. Chem.* 1960, *318*, 115–128.
[2] Nakamura, S., *Cross Electrophoresis,* Igaku Shoin, Tokyo and Elsevier, Amsterdam 1966.

[3] Nakamura, S., Takeo, K., Sasaki, I., Murata, M., *Nature* (London) 1959, *184*, 638–639.
[4] Nakamura, S., Takeo, K., Sasaki, I., *Hoppe-Seyler's Z. Physiol. Chem.* 1962, *328*, 139–144.
[5] Nakamura, S., Takeo K., Katuno, A., Tominaga, S., *Clin. Chim. Acta* 1959, *4*, 893–900.
[6] Nakamura, S., Suzuno, R., *Arch. Biochem. Biophys.* 1965, *111*, 499–505.
[7] Nakamura, S., Tominaga, S., Katsuno, A., Murakawa, S., *Comp. Biochem. Physiol.* 1965, *15*, 435–444.
[8] Nakamura, S., Wakeyama, T., *J. Biochem.* 1961, *49*, 733–741.
[9] Nakamura, S., Ogata, H., Suzuno, R., *Comp. Biochem. Physiol.* 1972, *41B*, 201–215.
[10] Laurell, C.-B., *Anal. Biochem.* 1966, *15*, 45–52.
[11] Svendsen, P. J., Axelsen, N. H., *J. Immunol. Methods* 1972, *1*, 169–176.
[12] De Vault, D., *J. Am. Chem. Soc.* 1943, *65*, 532–540.
[13] Weiss, J., *J. Chem. Soc.* 1943, 297–303.
[14] Takeo, K., *Annu. Rep. Soc. Protein Chem. Yamaguchi Univ. School Med.* 1970, *4*, 41–48.
[15] Takeo, K., Nakamura, S., *Arch. Biochem. Biophys.* 1972, *153*, 1–7.
[16] Bøg-Hansen, T.C., *Anal. Biochem.* 1973, *56*, 480–488.
[17] Hořejší, V., Kocourek, J., *Biochim. Biophys. Acta* 1974, *336*, 338–343.
[18] Hořejší, V., *Methods Enzymol.* 1984, *104*, 275–281.
[19] Caron, M., Faure, A., Cornillot, P., *J. Chromatogr.* 1975, *103*, 160–165.
[20] Owen, P., Salton M. R. J., *Anal. Biochem.* 1977, *73*, 20–26.
[21] Kohn, J., Raymond, J., Voller, A., Turp, P., *Lectins* 1983, *3*, 405–414.
[22] Ek, K., Righetti, P. G., *Electrophoresis* 1980, *1*, 137–140.
[23] Towbin, H., Staehelin, T., Gordon, J., *Proc. Natl. Acad. Sci. USA* 1979, *76*, 4350–4354.
[24] Takeo, K., Fujimoto, M., Suzuno, R., Kuwahara, A., *Seibutsu Butsuri Kagaku* 1978, *22*, 139–144.
[25] Takeo, K., *Electrophoresis* 1984, *5*, 187–195.
[26] Hořejší, V., Tichá, M., Kocourek, J., *Trends Biochem. Sci.* 1979, *4*, N6–N7.
[27] Hořejší, V., *Anal. Biochem.* 1981, *112*, 1–8.
[28] Hořejší, V., Tichá, M., Tichý, P., Holý, A., *Anal. Biochem.* 1982, *125*, 358–369.
[29] Hořejší, V., Tichá, M., *J. Chromatogr.* 1986, *376*, 49–67.
[30] Bøg-Hansen, T. C., in: Scouten, W. H. (Ed.), *Solid Phase Biochemistry. Analytical and Synthetic Aspects*, J. Wiley and Sons, New York 1983, pp. 223–251.
[31] Bøg-Hansen, T. C., Hau, J., *Acta Histochem.* 1982, *71*, 47–56.
[32] Davis, B. J., *Ann. N. Y. Acad. Sci.* 1964, *121*, 404–427.
[33] Ornstein, L., *Ann. N. Y. Acad. Sci.* 1964, *121*, 321–349.
[34] Reisfeld, R. A., Lewis, U. J., Williams, D. E., *Nature* (London) 1962, *195*, 281–283.
[35] Tanaka, T., Suzuno, R., Nakamura, K., Kuwahara, A., Takeo, K., *Electrophoresis* 1986, *7*, 204–209.
[36] Hořejší, V., Tichá, M., *J. Chromatogr.* 1981, *216*, 43–62.
[37] Hořejší, V., Tichá, M., in: Neuhoff, V. (Ed.), *Electrophoresis '84*, Verlag Chemie, Weinheim 1984, pp. 141–143.
[38] Clarke, J. T., *Ann. N. Y. Acad. Sci.* 1964, *121*, 428–436.
[39] Takeo, K., Suzuno, R., Nakayama, H., Kuwahara, A., Ogata, H., Nakamura, S., *Seikagaku* 1976, *48*, 638.
[40] Takeo, K., Nakamura, S., in: Hoffmann-Ostenhof, O., Breitenbach, M., Koller, F., Kraft, D., Scheiner O. (Eds.), *Affinity Chromatography*, Pergamon, Oxford and New York, 1978, pp. 67–70.
[41] Takeo K., *Yamaguchi-Igaku* 1982, *31*, 417–430.
[42] Poretz, R. D., Goldstein, I. J., *Biochemistry* 1970, *9*, 2890–2896.

[43] So, L. L., Goldstein, I. J., *J. Immunol.* 1967, *99*, 158–163.

[44] Goldstein, I. J., Reichert, C. M., Misaki, A., *Ann. N. Y. Acad. Sci.* 1974, *234*, 283–296.

[45] Takeo, K., Fujimoto, M., Kuwahara, A., Suzuno, R., Nakamura, K. in: Allen R. C., Arnaud, P. (Eds.) *Electrophoresis '81*, Walter de Gruyter, Berlin 1981, pp. 33–40.

[46] Bøg-Hansen, T. C., Takeo K., *Electrophoresis* 1980, *1*, 67–71.

[47] Hořejší, V., Matoušek, V., *Mol. Immunol.* 1985, *22*, 125–133.

[48] Mackiewicz, A., Mackiewicz, S., *Anal. Biochem.* 1986, *156*, 481–488.

[49] Hauzer, K., Tichá, M., Hořejší, V., Kocourek, J., *Biochim. Biophys. Acta* 1979, *583*, 103–109.

[50] Kuwahara, A., Fujimoto, M., Suzuno, R., Takeo, K., in: Hirai, H. (Ed.), *Electrophoresis '83*, Walter de Gruyter, Berlin 1984, pp. 643–646.

[51] Christie, D. J., Munske, G. R., Magnuson, J. A., *Biochemistry* 1979, *18*, 4638–4644.

[52] Takeo, K., Fujimoto, M., Kuwahara, A., *Lectins* 1983, *3*, 397–404.

[53] Takeo, K., Fujimoto, M., Suzuno R., Tanaka, T., Nakamura, K., Kuwahara, A., *Lectins* 1985, *4*, 213–220.

[54] Takeo, K., *Lectins* 1982, *2*, 583–594.

[55] Van Landschoot, A., Loostiens, F. G., de Bruyne, C. K., *Eur. J. Biochem.* 1980, *103*, 307–312.

[56] Suzuki, I., *Yamaguchi Igaku* 1985, *34*, 319–330.

[57] Masson, P., Marnot, B., Lombard, J.-Y., Morelis, P., *Biochimie* 1984, *66*, 235–249.

[58] Switzer, R. C., III, Merril, C. R., Shifrin, S., *Anal. Biochem.* 1979, *98*, 231–237.

[59] Oakley, B. R., Kirsch, D. R., Morris, N. R., *Anal. Biochem.* 1980, *105*, 361–363.

[60] Heukeshoven, J., Dernick, R., *Electrophoresis* 1985, *6*, 103–112.

[61] Segers, J., Rabaey, M., *Protides Biol. Fluids* 1985, *33*, 589–591.

[62] Hořejší, V., *J. Chromatogr.* 1979, *178*, 1–13.

[63] Matoušek, V., Hořejší, V., *J. Chromatogr.* 1982, *245*, 271–290.

[64] Bøg-Hansen, T. C., Bjerrum, O. J., Ramlau, J., *Scand. J. Immunol.* 1975, *4*, Suppl. 2, 141–147.

[65] Bøg-Hansen, T. C., Bjerrum, O. J., Brogren, C.-H., *Anal. Biochem.* 1977, *81*, 78–87.

[66] Raynes, J., *Biomedicine* 1982, *36*, 77–86.

[67] Bøg-Hansen, T. C., Brogren, C.-H., *Scand. J. Immunol.* 1975, *4*, Suppl. 2, 135–139.

[68] Hau, J., Larsen, P., Bøg-Hansen, T. C., Teisner, B., Nilsson, M., in: Stathakos, D. (Ed.) *Electrophoresis '82*, Walter de Gruyter, Berlin 1983, pp. 261–269.

[69] Smith, C. J., Kelleher, P. C., *Biochim. Biophys. Acta* 1973, *317*, 231–235.

[70] Kerckaert, J.-P., Bayard, B., Biserte, G., *Biochim. Biophys. Acta* 1979, *576*, 99–108.

[71] Toftager-Larsen, K., *Lectins* 1982, *2*, 433–444.

[72] Breborowicz, J., Bøg-Hansen, T. C., *Lectins* 1982, *2*, 445–456.

[73] Hay, D. L., Teisner, B., Davey, M. W., Horacek, I., Hart, A., Grudzinskas, J. G., *Aust. N. Z. J. Obstet. Gynaecol.* 1981, *21*, 170–173.

[74] Toftager-Larsen, K., Kjaersgaard, E., Nørgaard-Pedersen, B., *Clin. Chem.* 1983, *29*, 21–24.

[75] Yoshima, H., Mizuochi, T., Ishii, M., Kobata, A., *Cancer Res.* 1980, *40*, 4276–4281.

[76] Yamashita, K., Hitoi, A., Tsuchida, Y., Nishi, S., Kobata, A., *Cancer Res.* 1983, *43*, 4691–4695.

[77] Taketa, K., Ichikawa, E., Izumi, M., Taga, H., Hirai, H., in: Neuhoff, V. (Ed.), *Electrophoresis '84*, Verlag Chemie, Weinheim 1984, pp. 137–140.

[78] Taketa, K., Ichikawa, E., Taga, H., Hirai, H., *Electrophoresis* 1985, *6*, 492–497.

[79] Takeda, K., Toguchi, E., Izumi, M., Takeo, K., in: Stathakos, D. (Ed.), *Electrophoresis '82*, Walter de Gruyter, Berlin 1983, pp. 577–585.

[80] Hau, J., Teisner, B., Bøg-Hansen, T. C., *Lectins* 1982, *2*, 467–474.

[81] Hau, J., Westergaard, J. G., Ipsen, L., Teisner, B., Bøg-Hansen, T. C., Søndergaard, K., *Lectins* 1982, *2*, 457–466.

[82] Toftager-Larsen, K., Kjaersgaard, E., Jacobsen, J. C., Nørgaard-Pedersen, B., *Clin. Chem.* 1980, *26*, 1656–1659.

[83] Bayard, B., Kerckaert, J.-P., Laine, A., Hayem, A., *Eur. J. Biochem.* 1982, *124*, 371–376.

[84] Andersen, M. M., Noack, S., *Lectins* 1983, *3*, 361–370.

[85] Schmid, K., in: Putnam, F. W. (Ed.) *The Plasma Proteins,* Vol. 1, Academic Press, New York 1975, pp. 183–228.

[86] Nicollet, I., Lebreton, J.-P., Fontaine, M., Hiron, M., *Lectins* 1982, *2*, 413–421.

[87] Trautner, K., Cooper, E. H., Haworth, S., Ward, M. A., *Scand. J. Urol. Nephrol.* 1980, *14*, 143–149.

[88] Wells, C., Bøg-Hansen, T. C., Cooper, E. H., Glass, M. R., *Clin. Chim. Acta* 1981, *109*, 59–67.

[89] Hansen, J.-E. S., Lihme, A., Bøg-Hansen, T. C., *Electrophoresis* 1984, *5*, 196–201.

[90] Hansen, J.-E. S., Larsen, V. A., Bøg-Hansen, T. C., *Clin. Chim. Acta* 1984, *138*, 41–47.

[91] Hansen, J.-E. S, Jensen, S. P., Nørgaard-Pedersen, B., Bøg-Hansen, T. C., *Electrophoresis* 1986, *7*, 180–183.

[92] Kint, J. A., Leroy, J. G., *Lectins* 1985, *4*, 221–227.

[93] Bowen, M., Raynes, J. G., Cooper, E. H., *Lectins* 1982, *2*, 403–411.

[94] Salier, J.-P., Faye, L., Vergaine, D., Martin, J.-P., *Electrophoresis* 1980, *1*, 193–197.

[95] Spik, G., Bayard, B., Fournet, B., Strecker, G., Bouquelet, S., Montreuil, J., *FEBS Lett.* 1975, *50*, 296–299.

[96] Montreuil, J., Spik, G., in: Crighton, R. R. (Ed.), *Proteins of Iron Storage and Transport in Biochemistry and Medicine,* North-Holland Publishing, Amsterdam 1975, pp. 27–38.

[97] Kerckaert, J.-P., Bayard, B., *Biochem. Biophys. Res. Commun.* 1982, *105*, 1023–1030.

[98] Worwood, M., Cragg, S. J., Wagstaff, M., Jacobs, A., *Clin. Sci.* 1979, *56*, 83–87.

[99] Andersen, M. M., Lihme, A., Bøg-Hansen, T. C., *Lectins* 1982, *2*, 475–485.

[100] Andersen, M. M., Lihme, A., Bøg-Hansen, T. C., *Lectins* 1982, *2*, 487–496.

[101] Andersen, M. M., Lihme, A., Noack, S., Bøg-Hansen, T. C., *Lectins* 1985, *4*, 229–240.

[102] Kraus, J. S., Sheard, M. M., *Lectins* 1982, *2*, 423–431.

[103] Polack, B., Freyssinet, J.-M., *Electrophoresis* 1986, *7*, 413–416.

[104] Thompson, S. T., Cass, K. H., Stellwagen, E., *Proc. Natl. Acad. Sci. USA* 1975, *72*, 669–672.

[105] Edwards, R. A., Woody, R. W., *Biochemistry* 1979, *18*, 5197–5204.

[106] Dean, P. D. G., Watson, D. H., *J. Chromatogr.* 1979, *165*, 301–319.

[107] Tichá, M., Hořejší, V., Barthová, J., *Biochim. Biophys. Acta* 1978, *534,* 58–63.

[108] Johnson, S. J., Metcalf, E. C., Dean, P. D. G., *Anal. Biochem.* 1980, *109*, 63–66.

[109] Metcalf, E. C., Crow, B., Dean, P. D. G., *Biochem. J.* 1981, *199*, 465–472.

[110] Heyns, W., de Moor, P., *Biochim. Biophys. Acta* 1974, *358*, 1–13.

[111] Chen, J.-L., Morawetz, H., *J. Biol. Chem.* 1981, *256*, 9221–9223.

[112] Caron, M., Faure, A., Cornillot, P., *Anal. Biochem.* 1976, *70*, 295–301.

[113] Caron, M., Joubert, R., Bøg-Hansen, T. C., *Lectins* 1986, *5*, 631–635.

[114] Marchesi, V. T., Andrews, F. P., *Science* 1971, *174*, 1247–1248.

[115] Heegaard, N. H. H., Christensen, U., Bjerrum, O. J., *Lectins* 1983, *3*, 387–396.

[116] Hanham, C. A., Chapman, A. J., Sheppard, M. C., Black, E. G., Ramsden, D. B., *Biochim. Biophys. Acta* 1986, *884*, 158–165.

[117] Ambler, J., Janik, B., Walker, G., *Clin. Chem.* 1983, *29*, 340–343.

[118] Janik, B., Ambler, J., in: Hirai, H. (Ed.), *Electrophoresis '83*, Walter de Gruyter, Berlin 1984, pp. 631–634.

[119] Aleyassine, H., *Clin. Chim. Acta* 1984, *142*, 123–130.

[120] Tanaka, M., Shibata, H., *Eur. J. Biochem.* 1985, *151*, 291–297.

[121] Owen, P., Oppenheim, J. D., Nachbar, M. S., Kessler, R. E., *Anal. Biochem.* 1977, *80*, 446–457.

[122] Hořejší, V., Kocourek, J., *Biochim. Biophys. Acta* 1973, *297*, 346–351.

[123] Borrebaeck, C., Etzer, M. E., *FEBS Lett.* 1980, *117*, 237–240.

[124] Hořejší, V., Tichá, M., Kocourek, J., *Biochim. Biophys. Acta* 1977, *499*, 290–300.

[125] Hořejší, V., Tichá, M., Kocourek, J., *Biochim. Biophys. Acta* 1977, *499*, 301–308.

[126] Čeřovský, V., Tichá, M., Hořejší, V., Kocourek, J., *J. Biochem. Biophys. Methods* 1980, *3*, 163–172.

[127] Entlicher, G., Jesenská, K., Jarošová-Dejlová, L., Jarník, M., Kocourek, J., *Lectins* 1985, *4*, 491–503.

[128] Tichá, M., Dudová, V., Kocourek, J., *Lectins* 1985, *4*, 505–514.

[129] Kalb, A. J., Lustig, A., *Biochim. Biophys. Acta* 1968, *168*, 366–367.

[130] Ek, K., Gianazza, E., Righetti, P. G., *Biochim. Biophys. Acta* 1980, *626*, 356–365.

[131] Hořejší, V., Smolek, P, Kocourek, J., *Biochim. Biophys. Acta* 1978, *538*, 293–298.

[132] Righetti, P. G., Krishnamoorthy, R., Gianazza, E., Labie, D., *J. Chromatogr.* 1978, *166*, 455–460.

[133] Nakamura, K., Kuwahara, A., Ogata, H., Takeo, K., *J. Chromatogr.* 1980, *192*, 351–362.

[134] Tichá, M., Barthová, J., Labský, J., Semanský, M., *J. Chromatogr.* 1980, *194*, 183–189.

[135] Nakamura, K., Kuwahara, A., Takeo, K., *J. Chromatogr.* 1980, *196*, 85–99.

[136] Takeo, K., Nitta, K., Nakamura, S., *Clin. Chim. Acta.* 1974, *57*, 45–54.

[137] Nader, W., Becker, J.-U., *Eur. J. Biochem.* 1979, *102*, 345–355.

[138] Siepmann, R., Stegemann, H., *Z. Naturforsch.* 1967, *22b*, 949–955.

[139] Gerbrandy, S. J., Doorgeest, A., *Phytochemistry* 1972, *11*, 2403–2407.

[140] Takeo, K., Suzuno, R., Fujimoto, M., Kuwahara, A., *Bull. Yamaguchi Med. Sch.* 1980, *27*, 85–98.

[141] Gerbrandy, S. J., Verleur, J. D., *Phytochemistry* 1971, *10*, 261–266.

[142] Gerbrandy, S. J., *Biochim. Biophys. Acta* 1974, *370*, 410–418.

[143] Shimomura, S., Fukui, T., *Biochemistry* 1980, *19*, 2287–2294.

[144] Fukui, T., Shimomura, S., Nakano, K., *Mol. Cell Biochem.* 1982, *42*, 129–144.

[145] Er-el, Z., Zaidenzaig, Y., Shaltiel, S., *Biochem. Biophys. Res. Commun.* 1972, *49*, 383–390.

[146] Nakamura, K., Kuwahara, A., Takeo, K., *J. Chromatogr.* 1979, *171*, 89–99.

[147] Sato, T, Sato, K., *Biochim. Biophys. Acta* 1980, *612*, 344–351.

[148] Masson, P., Vallin, P., *J. Chromatogr.* 1983, *273*, 289–299.

[149] Masson, P., de Garilhe, A. P., Burnat, P., *Biochim. Biophys. Acta* 1982, *701*, 269–284.

[150] Masson, P., Marnot, B., *J. Chromatogr.* 1985, *328*, 135–144.

[151] Moss, D. W., *Clin. Chem.* 1982, *28*, 2007–2016.

[152] Rosalki, S. B., Ying Foo, A., *Clin. Chem.* 1984, *30*, 1182–1186.

[153] Rosalki, S. B., Ying Foo, A., *Clin. Chem.* 1985, *31*, 1198–1200.

[154] Peaston, R. T., Cooper, J., *Clin. Chem.* 1986, *32*, 235–236.

[155] Onica, D., Sundblad, L., Waldenlind, L., *Clin. Chim. Acta* 1986, *155*, 285–294.

[156] Komoda, T., Koyama, I., Okano, K., Miura, M., Sakagishi, K., *Seibutsu Butsuri Kagaku* 1986, *30*, 273–281.

[157] Lorenc-Kubis, I., *Lectins* 1983, *3*, 379–386.

[158] Lorenc-Kubis, I., Morawiecka, M., Bøg-Hansen, T. C., *Lectins* 1982, *2*, 509–515.

[159] Iwasa, M., Sagisaka, K., *Lectins* 1983, *3*, 371–377.

[160] Iwasa, M., Yokoi, T., Sagisaka, K., *Tohoku J. expl. Med.* 1983, *140*, 435–441.

[161] MacGregor, A. W., *Anal. Biochem.* 1977, *79*, 605–609.
[162] Takeo, K., Ogata, H., Nakayama, H., Nakamura, S., *Proc. Symp. Chem. Physiol. Pathol.* 1973, *13*, 85–88.
[163] Takeo, K., Kuwahara, A., Nakayama, H., Nakamura, S., *Protides Biol. Fluids Proc. Colloq.* 1976, *23*, 645–649.
[164] Sudo, K., Kanno, T., *Clin. Chim. Acta* 1976, *73*, 1–12.
[165] Archibald, A. L., *Anim. Blood Groups Biochem. Genet.* 1981, *12*, 249–264.
[166] Inoue, T., *Seibutsu Butsuri Kagaku* 1978, *22*, 135–138.
[167] Inoue, T., *Seibutsu Butsuri Kagaku* 1980, *24*, 1–10.
[168] Inoue, T., *Seibutsu Butsuri Kagaku* 1984, *28*, 361–368.
[169] Čeřovský, V., Tichá, M., Turková, J., Labský, J., *J. Chromatogr.* 1980, *194*, 175–181.
[170] Shimura, K., Kasai, K., *J. Biochem.* 1982, *92*, 1615–1622.
[171] Shimura, K., Kasai, K., *Biochem. Biophys. Acta* 1984, *802*, 135–140.
[172] Shimura, K., Kasai, K., *J. Chromatogr.* 1986, *376*, 323–329.
[173] McCabe, M. M., *Infect. Immun.* 1985, *50*, 771–777.
[174] Malý, P., Tichá, M., Kocourek, J., *J. Chromatogr.* 1985, *347*, 343–350.
[175] Takeo, K., Kabat, E. A., *J. Immunol.* 1978, *121*, 2305–2310.
[176] Sugii, S., Takeo, K., Kabat, E. A., *J. Immunol.* 1979, *123*, 1162–1168.
[177] Sugii, S., Kabat, E. A., *Carbohydr. Res.* 1980, *82*, 113–124.
[178] Wood, C., Kabat, E. A., *Arch. Biochem. Biophys.* 1981, *212*, 262–276.
[179] Sharon, J., Kabat, E. A., Morrison, S. L., *Mol. Immunol.* 1982, *19*, 389–397.
[180] Newman, B. A., Kabat, E. A., *J. Immunol.* 1985, *135*, 1220–1231.
[181] Newman, B. A., Liao, J., Gruezo, F., Sugii, S., Kabat, E. A., Torii, M., Clevinger, B. L., Davie, J. M., Schilling, J., Bond, M., Hood, L., *Mol. Immunol.* 1986, *23*, 413–424.
[182] Lai, E., Kabat, E. A., *Mol. Immunol.* 1985, *22*, 1021–1037.
[183] Takeo, K., Tanaka, T., Suzuno, R., Nakamura, K., Kuwahara, A., Fujimoto, M., in: Neuhoff, V. (Ed.) *Electrophoresis '84*, Verlag Chemie, Weinheim 1984, pp. 144–147.
[184] Cisar, J., Kabat, E. A., Dorner, M. M., Liao, J., *J. Exp. Med.* 1975, *142*, 435–459.
[185] Congy, N., Mihaesco, C., *Immunology* 1978, *35*, 307–315.
[186] Anderson, N. L., Nance, S. L., Pearson, T. W., Anderson, N. G., *Electrophoresis* 1982, *3*, 135–142.
[187] Manabe, T., Takahashi, Y., Higuchi, N., Okuyama, T., *Electrophoresis* 1985, *6*, 462–467.
[188] Takeo, K., Suzuno, R., Fujimoto, M., Tanaka, T., Kuwahara, A., in: Stathakos, D. (Ed.), *Electrophoresis '82*, Walter de Gruyter, Berlin 1983, pp. 277–283.
[189] Takeo, K., Suzuno, R., Tanaka, T., Fujimoto, M., Kuwahara, A., Nakamura, K., *Protides Biol. Fluids* 1984, *32*, 969–972.
[190] Takeo, K., Suzuno, R., Tanaka, T., Nakamura, K., Kuwahara, A., in: Dunn, M. J. (Ed.), *Electrophoresis '86*, Verlag Chemie, Weinheim 1986, pp. 233–240.
[191] Takeo, K., Suzuno, R., Tanaka, T., Fujimoto, M., Kuwahara, A., Nakamura, K., in: Hirai, H. (Ed.), *Electrophoresis '83*, Walter de Gruyter, Berlin 1984, pp. 627–630.
[192] Hamilton, R. G., Roebber, M., Reimer, C. B., Rodkey, L. S., *Electrophoresis* 1987, *8*, 127–134.
[193] Shimura, K., Kasai, K., *Electrophoresis* 1987, *8*, 135–139.
[194] Takeo, K., *Seibutsu Butsuri Kagaku* 1958, *5*, 138–139.
[195] Pitha, J., *Anal. Biochem.* 1975, *65*, 422–426.
[196] Müller, W., Hattesohl, I., Schuetz, H.-J., Meyer, G., *Nucleic Acid Res.* 1981, *9*, 95–119.
[197] Müller, W., Bünemann, H., Schuetz, H.-J., Eigel, A., in: Gribnau, T. C. J., Visser, J., Nivard, R. J. F. (Eds.), *Affinity Chromatography and Related Techniques*, Elsevier, Amsterdam 1982, pp. 437–444.

[198] Igloi, G. L., Kössel, H., *Nucleic Acid Res.* 1985, *19*, 6881–6898.

[199] Yokoyama, S., Miyazawa, T., Iitaka, Y., Yamaizumi, Z., Kasai, H., Nishimura, S., *Nature* (London) 1979, *282*, 107–109.

[200] Khym, J. X., *Methods Enzymol.* 1967, *12*, 93–101.

[201] Weith, H. L., Wiebers, J. L., Gilham, P. T., *Biochemistry* 1970, *9*, 4396–4401.

[202] Morgan, M. R. A., Kerr, E. J., Dean, P. D. G., *J. Steroid Chem.* 1978, *9*, 767–770.

[203] Morgan, M. R. A., Brown, P. J., Leyland, M. J., Dean, P. D. G., *FEBS Lett.* 1978, *87*, 239–243.

[204] Morgan, M. R. A., Johnson, P. M., Dean, P. D. G., *J. Immunol. Methods* 1978, *23*, 381–387.

[205] Morgan, M. R. A., Slater, N. A., Dean, P. D. G., *Anal. Biochem.* 1979, *92*, 144–146.

[206] Nakamura, S., Ogata, H., Takeo, K., Kuwahara, A., Suzuno, R., *Hoppe-Seyler's Z. Physiol. Chem. 1975, 356*, 677–692.

[207] Takeo, K., Suzuno, R., Fujimoto, M., Kuwahara, A., Ogata, H., Nakamura, S., *Bull. Yamaguchi Med. Sch.* 1976, *23*, 165–183.

RECENT TRENDS IN CAPILLARY ISOTACHOPHORESIS

Petr Gebauer, Vladislav Dolník, Mirko Deml and Petr Boček

Institute of Analytical Chemistry, Czechoslovak Academy of Sciences, Brno, Czechoslovakia

Abbreviations and symbols: ADP, adenosine 5'-diphosphate; **AMMEDIOL**, 2-amino-2-methyl-1,3-propanediol; **AMP**, adenosine 5'-monophosphate; **ATP**, adenosine 5'-triphosphate; c_i, concentration of i-th subspecies; $\bar{c}_j$, concentration of j-th substance; C_p, specific heat; $\bar{c}_{X,Y}$, concentration of substance X in zone Y; **cAMP**, adenosine 3',5'-cyclic monophosphate; d, electric-current density; D_i, diffusion coefficient of i-th subspecies; E, electric-field strength (electric-potential gradient); **EACA**, ε-aminocaproic acid; **EDTA**, ethylenediaminetetraacetic acid; **F**, Faraday constant; **GABA**, γ-aminobutyric acid; **GMP**, guanosine 5'-monophosphate; h, step height (magnitude of the detection signal); **HEPES**, N-2-hydroxyethylpiperazine-N'-2-ethane sulfonate; i, ionic subspecies; I, electric current; **IMP**, inosine 5'-monophosphate; j, substance; $\bar{J}_i$, flux of i-th subspecies; $\bar{J}_j$, flux of j-th substance; k, number of subspecies of a substance; k_j, integration constant relating to j-th substance; K_X, calibration constant for substance X; **L**, leading substance; Δl_C, boundary width at thermal convection; Δl_D, boundary width at diffusion; **MES**, 2-(N-morpholino)ethanesulfonic acid; n, number of substances in a system; N_X, amount of substance X; N_{min}, minimum detectable amount; **NAD$^+$**, nicotinamide adenine dinucleotide – oxidized form; **NADH**, nicotinamide adenine dinucleotide – reduced form; **NTA**, nitrilotriacetic acid; p, selectivity; **PTFE**, polytetrafluoroethylene; Q, electric charge; Q_L, column hold-up; Q_X, passage charge of zone X; **R**, counterionic substance; **R**, gas constant; R_i, generation rate of i-th subspecies; t, time; t_X, passage time of zone X; **T**, terminating substance; T, absolute temperature; **Tris**, tris(hydroxymethyl)aminomethane; u_i, ionic mobility of i-th subspecies; $\bar{u}_j$, effective mobility of j-th substance; $\bar{u}_{X,Y}$, effective mobility of substance X in zone Y; v, velocity; x, longitudinal coordinate; X, time-dependent longitudinal coordinate; **X**, **Y**, substances; z_i, valence of i-th subspecies; ρ, density

1 Introduction

Analytical isotachophoresis has recently become a well-established technique. Its popularity and utilization in analytical practice are growing, and the number of producers of commercial instruments has also increased. Simultaneously, a large number of published papers has been appearing, as continuous proof of the amount of basic and applied research being carried out in the field. This article describes the contemporary state of the art of analytical capillary isotachophoresis, with emphasis on recent leading trends in theory, instrumentation, methodology and applications. The objective is to provide a critical review of the method rather than a summary of all available information, since basic information on the method [1, 2] as well as a complete survey of literature [3, 4] may be found elsewhere.

2 Theory

The fundamental theory underlying isotachophoresis is based on the pioneering work of Kohlrausch in 1897 [5], and so may be considered well-founded. However, recent theoretical work, stimulated by the development of the method as a routine analytical technique, has made a significant contribution. Theoretical models have been used to obtain answers to some important questions asked in analytical practice. Progress in theory has been concentrated in three directions, aiming at (i) a better understanding of the dynamics of isotachophoretic separation, as well as the properties of an isotachophoretic system after the steady state has been reached, (ii) utilization of theoretical results in analytical practice in order to optimize the actual procedures, and (iii) determination of the possible limits of isotachophoresis as an analytical method.

2.1   Towards a better understanding of isotachophoresis

Although contemporary analytical capillary isotachophoresis is a theoretically and instrumentally advanced technique, it often happens that we obtain an isotachophoregram with distorted steps, inversions of the step heights, *etc.,* and do not know how to interpret it correctly. One reason for these difficulties lies in the fact that commercial instruments with on-line detection do not offer sufficiently complete and unambiquous information on the qualitative as well as quantitative composition of the migrating system. Moreover, the information obtained is related to a single point of the migration path. It is therefore not surprising that at the present time much consideration is being given to a technique which – indirectly – offers the illusive possiblity of looking into the separation tube and observing the whole course of the electrophoretic process in all its details. This technique is based upon the computer-simulation of the dynamic behavior of the problematic electrophoretic system.

A full mathematical description of the electrophoretic system can be presented simply, *e.g.,* in the manner of Bier *et al.* [6]. For each point of an one-dimensional separation space having the coordinate *x*, for each time *t*, and for each ionic (or neutral) subspecies of the system, the equation of continuity holds in the following form

$$\frac{\partial c_i}{\partial t} = -\frac{\partial}{\partial x}\left[Ec_iu_i - D_i\frac{\partial c_i}{\partial x}\right] + R_i \tag{1}$$

where the term in brackets expresses the flux of the *i*-th subspecies, J_i, and where c_i is the actual concentration of subspecies *i*, u_i is the ionic mobility of subspecies *i* (for anions, $u_i < 0$; for uncharged species, $u_i = 0$), D_i is the diffusion coefficient of subspecies *i*, E is the electric-field strength, and R_i is the rate of generation of the *i*-th subspecies by chemical reactions.

If we consider, *e.g.*, an electrophoretic system formed by the aqueous solution of n substances, each of which provides k subspecies, the total number of different particles found in the solution is equal to $(n \cdot k + 2)$ (including H^+ and OH^- ions). This is also the number of equations of type (1) which is valid for the system. Since the generation rate of j-th substance is zero, the last term in Eq. (1) disappears after summing up the respective k equations for the j-th substance and we obtain n equations of the type:

$$\frac{\partial \bar{c}_j}{\partial t} = -\frac{\partial}{\partial x} \bar{J}_j \tag{2}$$

where $\bar{c}_j$ is the total (analytical) concentration of substance j, and $\bar{J}_j$ is the total flux of substance j, $\bar{J}_j = \sum_i J_i$. For any system, the electroneutrality condition holds in the form

$$\sum_1^{n \cdot k + 2} z_i c_i = 0 \tag{3}$$

where z_i is the valence of the i-th subspecies. When working at constant electric current, the conservation of electric charge can be expressed by

$$\frac{\partial}{\partial x} \sum_1^{n \cdot k + 2} z_i J_i = 0 \tag{4}$$

The system in question represents $(n \cdot k + 3)$ dependent variables: $(n \cdot k + 2)$ concentrations of the individual subspecies, c_i, and the electric-field strength E. The number of equations necessary for the complete mathematical description of the system is determined by the number of dependent variables. In our case, we have to consider: n equations of type (2), Eqs. (3) and (4), and $[n \cdot (k-1) + 1]$ equations describing the protolytic equilibria for water and each substance. In the above model, the influence of both temperature and ionic strength, as well as the effect of electroosmosis and other accompanying phenomena are neglected. The set of equations quoted above is nonlinear, and a solution is to be obtained by numerical methods only. The model may be applied to any electrophoretic system; the type of electrophoresis is predetermined by the initial distribution of the working electrolytes along the separation column.

An illustration of how computer simulations can contribute to the understanding of the properties of an isotachophoretic system can be found in Fig. 1, which shows the evolution of the boundary between sodium for-

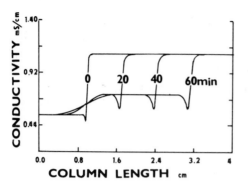

Figure 1. Computer-simulated evolution of a boundary between 10 mM sodium formate (leader) and formic acid (terminator): conductivity profiles after 0, 20, 40 and 60 min of current flow (1.2 mA/cm²). From [7], with permission.

mate (Na^+ as the leader) and formic acid (H^+ as the terminator) during cationic isotachophoresis [7]. From the resulting conductivity profiles we can distinctly see a stable drop on the rear side of the boundary. This effect, which is often observed in acidic cationic systems with H^+ as the terminator, had earlier been ascribed to either migrating impurities on the boundary or to disturbing phenomena on the detection electrodes. Computer simulation has shown that it is a natural phenomenon stemming from the properties of the given isotachophoretic system.

The mathematical model described above provides valuable results even in a simplified form for the case of strong electrolytes in which diffusion is neglected. This is exemplified in Fig. 2 [8], which shows the dynamics of the

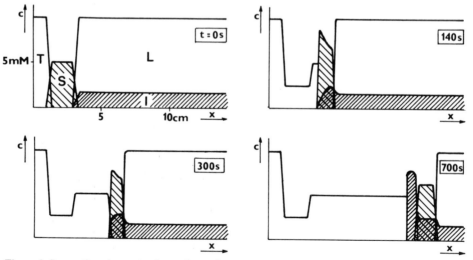

Figure 2. Separation dynamics for an impurity (I) present in the leading electrolyte: concentration profiles after 0, 140, 300 and 700 s of current flow. From [8], with permission.

separation of a sample whose migration is disturbed by the presence of an impurity in the leading electrolyte; this impurity forms its isotachophoretic zone behind the zone of the sample substance. We can see that the impurity first penetrates into the zone of the sample and deforms the concentration (and conductivity) profile of the zone. Then the impurity starts to form its own zone. However, a constant amount of impurity is permanently present in the sample zone and causes a change in both its qualitative and quantitative characteristics. In such a case, the computer simulation provides a natural explanation of the deformed plateaus of the steps in the record, as well as hinting at a possible cause for irreproducibilities.

The mathematical model can be simplified substantially if we are not interested in the dynamics of the isotachophoretic process, but only in the resulting steady state. Under these conditions, the steady-state concentration profiles of all substances are simulated along the separation column. These profiles move with velocity v in the direction of the leading electrode. Substituting $(X = x - v \cdot t)$, we can easily integrate Eq. (2) and obtain [9]

$$\bar{J}_j = E \bar{c}_j \bar{u}_j - \sum_i^k D_i \frac{\partial c_i}{\partial x} = v \bar{c}_j + k_j \tag{5}$$

where k_j is the integration constant; $\bar{u}_j$ is the effective mobility of substance j, defined by the relationship

$$\bar{c}_j \bar{u}_j = \sum_i^k c_i u_i \tag{6}$$

This quantity characterizes the migration of substance j (consisting of k subspecies of type i) as one constituent.

One important aspect of the steady state is the boundary between two neighboring zones. From the analytical point of view, we are interested especially in the factors affecting the width of the diffusion part of the boundary which is given as the result of the counteraction of diffusion broadening and electromigration sharpening. A set of equations of type (5) can serve as the starting point of the solution: This set can either be numerically integrated [9] to obtain the concentration profiles of the substances along the separation column, or we can solve the set of equations analytically [10], for simplified cases neighboring zones of strong or weak monovalent electrolytes. Both approaches arrive at the same result [9, 10], that the boundary width decreases (the boundary sharpness increases) with increasing driving electric current, with decreasing concentration of the leading electrolyte and with increasing differences in mobilities and in the pK_a values of the separated substances. Another aspect of interest in the steady state is the description of zone properties. To obtain this description, we may ignore the concentration profiles across the boundary by neglecting the diffusion term in Eq. (5). Thus, the fundamental isotachophoretic equation has the form:

$$v = E_j \bar{u}_j \tag{7}$$

(for isotachophoretically migrating substances, k_j is zero). The electric-field strength E_j stands for the value in the isotachophoretic zone of substance j.

The complete mathematical description is now given by a system of $(3\,n \cdot k + 3)$ equations, but instead of having n partial differential equations of type (2), we have the same number of algebraic equations. Among these n equations, $(n-1)$ equations are of type (7), for $(n-1)$ substances forming isotachophoretic zones, and one equation is of type (5), for the substance of the counterion R. The constant k_R can be determined, *e. g.* from Eq. (5) written for substance R in leading zone L. Eq. (5). The balance for the counterionic substance R in any zone j is thus

$$E_j \bar{c}_{R,j} \bar{u}_{R,j} - v\bar{c}_{R,j} = E_L \bar{c}_{R,L} \bar{u}_{R,L} - v\bar{c}_{R,L} \tag{8}$$

where $\bar{c}_{R,j}$ and $\bar{u}_{R,j}$ are the total concentration and the effective mobility of substance R in zone j, respectively. The solution of the equations for the isotachophoretic steady state is based on an iterative procedure described by Beckers [11] for systems containing weak protolytes. As a rule, the pH-values in a certain zone are varied until the solution of the system is obtained. Then the values of the steady-state concentration and of the effective mobility of a substance in the given zone can be calculated (see Section 2.2).

Effective mobility is the fundamental quantity characterizing a substance migrating in an isotachophoretic zone in a given electrolyte system: it is quite easy to obtain this quantity from the record provided by a universal detector. One of the recent advances is an understanding of effective mobility as a quantity related to a given isotachophoretic zone. Two kinds of data thus emerge:
- type $\bar{u}_{X,X}$ (effective mobility of substance X in its zone X),
- type $\bar{u}_{X,Y}$ (effective mobility of substance X in some other zone of substance Y).

Recently, the significance of parameters $\bar{u}_{X,Y}$ for the description and under-standing of the isotachophoretic separation process and the steady state has been established [12–14]. When describing the steady state, one of the pro-blems solvable by means of parameters of type $\bar{u}_{X,Y}$, is the question of the migration order of the zones. The starting point here is the determination of the presence or absence of a sharp boundary between two zones of a chosen sequence, based on the effective mobilities of each of the two substances in both the first and the second zone. Three fundamental possibilities arise for two given substances X and Y [12]:

$$|\bar{u}_{X,Y}| > |\bar{u}_{Y,Y}| \quad \text{and} \quad |\bar{u}_{X,X}| > |\bar{u}_{Y,X}| \tag{9}$$

i.e., the zone of substance X migrates in front of the zone of substance Y;

$$|\bar{u}_{X,Y}| < |\bar{u}_{Y,Y}| \quad \text{and} \quad |\bar{u}_{X,X}| < |\bar{u}_{Y,X}| \tag{10}$$

i.e., the zone of substance Y migrates in front of the zone of substance X;

$$|\bar{u}_{X,Y}| < |\bar{u}_{Y,Y}| \quad \text{and} \quad |\bar{u}_{X,X}| > |\bar{u}_{Y,X}| \tag{11}$$

i.e., the migration order cannot be established and the substances form a stable mixed zone.

It has already been shown that the determination of the migration order is not unimportant. In addition to its significance for qualitative analysis, it is also of great importance for the verification of separability [13]. Substances are separable if we can unambiguously establish the migration order of their individual zones, *i.e.*, either condition (9) or condition (10) holds. Substances are not separable if they form a stable mixed zone, *i.e.*, condition (11) holds (see also Section 4.2.1). In the same way, we can say that the isotachophoretic zone of a sample migrates correctly provided that the respective conditions (9) or (10) hold for neighboring zones: terminator → sample and sample → leader. Otherwise the migration of the sample zone is incorrect; this is often observed in cases when H^+ is the terminator (cationic systems).

In each isotachophoretic system, there are components present which penetrate the whole system, for example, the substance forming the counter-ion and the H^+ and OH^- ions. The influence of the solvent ions can fre-quently be neglected; however, in the acidic or alkaline region, it is necessary to take their effects into account. An exact description of the influence of these ions in terms of effective mobility has recently been given. In acidic ca-tionic systems, for example, H^+ migrates in the direction from the terminating to the leading electrode and penetrates the whole system. By using the ion of a weak acid as the counterion, the migration of the H^+ front is retarded, owing to the formation of the nondissociated weak acid, and H^+ can be directly used as the terminator [14]. The specialty of this terminator lies in the fact that, in a certain concentration, it is also present in the other zones; Eq. (5) holds in the form

$$E_H c_{H,H} u_H = v\bar{c}_{H,H} - k_j; \quad k_j = -v\bar{c}_{H,L} + E_L c_{H,L} u_H \qquad (12)$$

By combining (12) with Eq. (7), we get an expression for the effective mobility of H^+ which describes the properties of the isotachophoretic zone of H^+:

$$\bar{u}_{H,H} = c_{H,H} \bar{u}_H / (\bar{c}_{H,H} - \bar{c}_{H,L} + c_{H,L} u_H / u_L) \qquad (13)$$

Comparison with Eq. (6) shows that this relationship differs from the classical definition of the effective mobility, owing to the presence of H^+ in the leading electrolyte; when the concentration of H^+ in the leading zone can be neglected, Eq. (13) reduces to the well known form.

By analogy with the concept of effective mobility of H^+, the concept of effective mobility of OH^- in anionic isotachophoresis has also been established [13], in particular with respect to the terminating zone of OH^-. Both these concepts have contributed to an improved understanding of the effective mobility as a quantity characterizing not only a given substance in its isotachophoretic zone, but also the properties of that zone or the migration of the front boundary of the isotachophoretic zone of a given substance.

The effective mobilities of type $\bar{u}_{X,Y}$ have also proved to be useful for the description of the separation process prior to the steady state. The values for the separated substances in the transient-state mixed zones were found to be of key importance. For the separation of binary mixtures, the concept of selectivity was introduced [16] as the relative difference of effective mobilities in the transient-state mixed zone:

$$p = \frac{\bar{u}_{X,mix}}{\bar{u}_{Y,mix}} - 1 \qquad (14)$$

This parameter is experimentally easily accessible: it enables us to describe the separation power in a quantitative way, and thus it facilitates the optimization of the separation process.

2.2 Theory applied in analytical practice

Nowadays, calculations of steady-state properties of the zones can be evaluated in a new light thanks to a series of investigations which have demonstrated that such calculations can be a valuable aid to isotachophoresis in practice. The usefulness of computer simulations of the steady state has been demonstrated in detail by Hirokawa *et al.,* who utilized them both for the evaluation of physico-chemical constants (mobilities and pK_a's) from isotachophoretic measurements [17–19] and for the determination of optimum separation conditions [20, 21]. The latter is important in analytical practice. The procedure developed by the above authors makes it possible to simulate experimental isotachophoregrams for a given group of substances (with known values of mobilities, pK_a and constants of other chemical equilibria) and a given electrolyte system. Laborious experimental work to find a suitable electrolyte system is no longer necessary. Computer simulations of isotachophoregrams for various electrolyte systems are far more convenient. Later, the theoretically predicted separation can be verified by experiment.

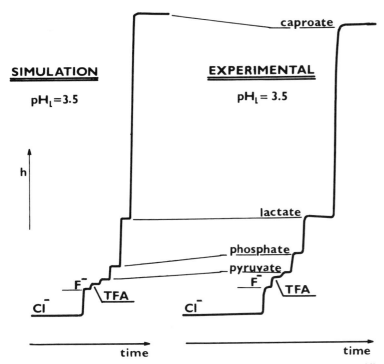

Figure 3. Simulated and experimental isotachophoregrams for F⁻, trifluoroacetate (TFA), pyruvate, phosphate and lactate. Leading electrolyte: 10 mM Cl⁻, β-alanine, pH_L 3.5. From [21], with permission.

Fig. 3 shows, as an example, the comparison of a simulated and an experimental recording for the optimum conditions of separation determined for trifluoroacetate in the presence of some other anions [21].

In many laboratories, however, the programs for the simulations are not yet readily available. It is therefore important to have representative data, which can facilitate finding of the best separation conditions, at hand. Hirokawa *et al.* [22] have published comprehensive tables containing information on the behavior of 287 anions in 31 different electrolyte systems, within the range of pH_L 3 – 10. For each anion and each electrolyte system, the following steady-state characteristics of the zones are listed: effective mobilities, effective charges, pH of the zones and slopes of the calibration graph. For a given electrolyte system, the tables also make it possible to estimate roughly

Table 1. Isotachophoretic indices of acetic acid. $RE = u_{Cl}/\bar{u}_{Ac, Ac}$, Ac = acetate, t = time-based zone length (s), $-Z$ = effective charge (from [22], with permission)

Acetic acid ($C_2H_4O_2$, 60.05), $z_{Ac} = -1$, $u_{Ac} = -42.4$, $pK_{Ac} = 4.756$

pH_L	3.00	3.25	3.50	3.75	4.00	4.00
RE	8.876	7.444	6.370	5.428	4.576	3.848
t	21.01	20.13	19.51	19.02	18.64	16.48
Z	0.206	0.247	0.289	0.340	0.404	0.485
pH_{Ac}	4.151	4.249	4.342	4.443	4.561	4.700

4.25	4.50	4.75	4.75	5.00	5.25	5.50
3.485	3.111	2.763	2.650	2.427	2.244	2.087
16.37	16.26	16.18	18.16	18.12	18.09	16.23
0.537	0.603	0.681	0.711	0.778	0.843	0.912
4.789	4.904	5.050	5.112	5.264	5.449	5.733

5.75	6.00	6.25	6.50	6.75	7.00	7.25
2.027	1.980	1.949	1.925	1.915	1.909	1.904
16.22	16.22	16.21	21.62	21.61	21.61	21.61
0.940	0.962	0.978	0.988	0.993	0.996	0.998
5.910	6.122	6.355	6.651	6.887	7.132	7.380

7.50	7.75	8.00	8.25	8.50	8.75	9.00
1.912	1.910	1.909	1.908	1.909	1.908	1.907
16.18	16.18	16.19	16.20	16.20	16.23	16.27
0.999	0.999	1.000	1.000	1.000	1.000	1.000
7.593	7.841	8.091	8.340	8.591	8.842	9.092

9.25	9.50	9.75	10.00
1.906	1.902	1.901	1.899
16.34	20.09	20.36	20.85
1.000	1.000	1.000	1.000
9.343	9.626	9.878	10.133

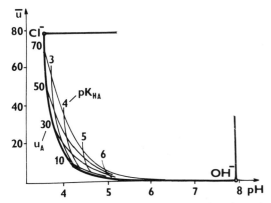

Figure 4. The zone existence diagram for the anionic system with the leading electrolyte: 10 mM Cl$^-$, 20 mM β-alanine, pH$_L$ 3.5. On the vertical axis, the absolute values of mobilities (in 10^{-9} m^2 V^{-1} s^{-1}) are plotted. From [13], with permission.

the mutual separability of substances. Table 1 shows a column taken from the table which presents the data for one of the tabulated substances.

The published tables are, incontestably, useful in practice, but their applicability is, of course, limited to the substances listed. For every other substance, we have to find the effective mobility and pH of the zone in a given electrolyte system by calculation. Such calculations can be avoided by a procedure utilizing a graphical representation of isotachophoretic zones known as the zone existence diagrams [12, 13]. For a given electrolyte system, the steady-state characteristics of the zones are simulated, whereas the constants of the substances (mobility, pK_a) are parametrically selected. A graphical representation of the results, as the dependence $(\bar{u}, \text{pH}) = f(u, pK_a)$, gives a planar network. Fig. 4 shows an example of a zone existence diagram for one of the currently used anionic electrolyte systems, using 10 mM HCl/20 mM β-alanine as the leading electrolyte. The network enables one to read off the effective mobility and zone pH for the zone of each substance, the ionic mobility and pK_a of which are known. Moreover, the diagram facilitates the determination of whether a substance in the given system provides an isotachophoretic zone: points in the area outside the existence contours do not correspond to correct isotachophoretic zones.

2.3 Limitations of the method

One question, which has lately come a matter of great interest concerns the quantitative and qualitative limits of isotachophoresis as an analytical method. The problem of limitations of the method for quantitative analysis is especially important in the area of trace analysis [23]. The minimum detectable amount is roughly given as

$$N_{min} = V_{det} \cdot \bar{c} \tag{15}$$

where V_{det} is the volume of the detection cell and $\bar{c}$ is the concentration of the analyzed substance in the isotachophoretic zone. Obviously, the amount detectable can be lowered either by diminishing the size of the detection cell or by decreasing the concentration of the leading electrolyte. However, both these parameters have their limitations, which depend on the apparatus used and physico-chemical laws, respectively (see also Section 4.3.3).

The width of the isotachophoretic boundary itself is an important factor which must be considered when evaluating very short zones. The three fundamental dispersion effects causing broadening of the boundary are electroosmosis, diffusion and axial temperature profiles. Whereas, in principle, electroosmosis can be sufficiently suppressed, the other two phenomena will always be present and cannot be neglected. The boundary width caused by diffusion can be approximated by the relationship [23]

$$\Delta l_D = 4 \frac{u}{\Delta u} \frac{RT}{FE} \tag{16}$$

where $\Delta u/u$ is the selectivity for the two separands in question, R is the gas constant, T is the absolute temperature, F is the Faraday constant and E is the average electric-field strength. From Eq. (16) we can see that the diffusional boundary width increases with decreasing selectivity and with decreasing electric-field strength. For the boundary width caused by convection generated by axial temperature profiles, the following dependence was deduced [23]

$$\Delta l_C = \rho C_p |u| \Delta T/d \tag{17}$$

where ρ is the density, C_p is the specific heat of the liquid, ΔT is the temperature difference and d the current density. As ΔT is proportional to d^2, it follows from relationship (17) that in this case the boundary width increases with increasing current density. A comparison of relationships (16) and (17) then shows that, in both cases, the key quantity is the driving current used; an increase in current density elevates the value of Δl_C and lowers the value of Δl_D. It has been shown that the optimum value of the current density is found by taking both effects into account, resulting in a value of Δl in the order of 10^{-4} m.

In qualitative analysis, a substantial problem is the question of the maximum number of components separable by a given instrument. As has been shown by Kenndler [24], according to Eq. (14), a minimum selectivity of 0.01 can be derived for two substances which are still separable (the column being 200 mm long and the zone length required being 1 mm). In practice, the required selectivity is generally estimated as ca. 2–4%. Kenndler has also provided an estimate of the information content of isotachophoretic analysis: in the limiting case of separation of a maximum number of separable components, with a selectivity of 2–3% and a mobility ratio of leader to terminator of 15:1, an information content of 6.5–7 bit is obtained. A more realistic estimation, based on the evaluation of tabulated data [22], gives an information content for isotachophoresis of 3.5–5.7 bit for a single system, which is comparable to the value for packed-column gas chromatography.

3   Instrumentation

Recently, instrumentation has been developed which takes theoretical and, in particular, practical requirements into account. These requirements are: (i) to increase the concentration ratio of major to minor substances which can be analyzed simultaneously, (ii) to shorten the analysis time, (iii) to facilitate identification of the substances contained in the zones, (iv) to enable one to perform the isotachophoretic separation combined with another analytical technique, (v) to be able to follow the separation process.

New developments in instrumentation generally appeared in response to these demands. The column system of isotachophoregraphs and detectors were developed as a result of demands for an increase in separation capacity and a decrease in analysis time. An instrument with multichannel detection made it possible to scan the course of the separation and to shorten the analysis time to a period needed for the separation of the given sample. The still difficult identification of substances has been made easier by new detection principles and by a combination of detectors. Micropreparative procedures made it possible to take out the zone from the isotachophoretic column and to identify the substance contained in it by another analytical procedure. A broader application of isotachophoresis as an analytical method was made possible by the production of advanced commercial instruments. Considerable progress has been made in preparative isotachophoresis where, by utilizing the free-flow technique, we can get amounts of prepared solutions in hundreds of mL per hour.

3.1   Enhancing the sensitivity of the method

One of the main goals of recent research work has been to increase detection sensitivity and/or separation capacity for the purposes of trace analysis. The possibilities of increasing detection sensitivity by decreasing the volume of the detection cell or by using a lower concentration of the leading electrolyte have their practical limits [25]. Currently, the limit is given by detection cells with diameters of 0.1 mm (0.3 mm for commercial instruments) and detectable zone lengths of ca. 0.1 mm. Another method of determining low concentrations consists in using conventional detection sensitivities together with an increased amount of sample. Lately, there has been an outspoken trend to use this latter method.

A larger amount of injected sample requires an increase in the hold-up of the column or the separation capacity of the column. One possible method is to use an exchangeable separation capillary. A new capillary of the same I.D. and of the required length is connected to the fixed detection cell and an injection port by means of screw joints (this system has been used, *e.g.*, in LKB-Tachophor, see Section 3.5.1). When employing so-called volume-coupling [26], which has also been introduced for the above purpose, the exchangeable capillary has a greater diameter than the detection cell (Fig. 5b). This leads to

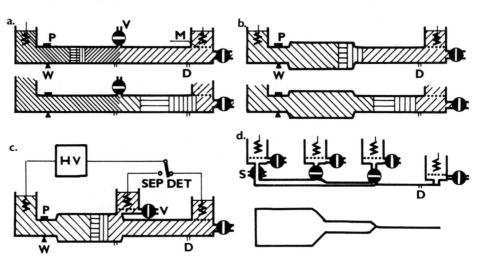

Figure 5. Column arrangements in isotachophoresis. (a) Concentration cascade; upper part – separation, lower part – detection. (b) Volume-coupling: upper-part – separation, lower part – detection. (c) Column-coupling. (d) Multicolumn isotachophoresis: lower part – shape of the channel. P, septum; M, membrane; W, drain; V, valve; D, detector; S, sampling valve; HV, high-voltage power supply.

a lower stabilization of the zones by the wall effect in the capillary and possible deterioration of the sharp boundaries during passage of the zone through the joint piece. The advantage of volume-coupling is that it is possible to work with a higher driving electric current in the period before the leading zone leaves the separation capillary without causing overheating of the analytical (detection) capillary. Compared with analysis in a simple capillary, the time of analysis is thus shortened.

Another technique is use of the concentration cascade [27], which only requires an additional inlet valve for introduction of the electrolyte with a higher concentration into the preseparation part of the capillary (Fig. 5a). During its migration, the sample follows the concentration profile of the leading electrolyte and thus, the separation capacity is increased while the detection sensitivity remains unchanged. An abrupt prolongation of the zones occurs at the point of the auxiliary inlet. Substantial progress has resulted from use of column-coupling (column-switching) [28], which employs a preseparation and an analytical capillary (Fig. 5c). It facilitates the work by using a substantially increased electric current during the total preseparation time, thus leading to a substantial reduction of the time required for analysis. Moreover, the column-switching system offers the possibility of removing the components of the sample which are not of interest to the auxiliary electrode after the separation has been attained, so that their time-consuming passage through the analytical capillary is not necessary at all.

A laboratory-made multicolumn instrument described recently [29] makes it possible to inject directly up to 1 mL of sample. The cross-section of a flat separation channel is gradually reduced from 20×1 mm down to an I.D. of 0.2 mm, corresponding to the circular capillary equipped with the detection cell (Fig. 5d). The parts of the flat channel which have a large cross-section are filled with a granulated hydrophilic gel as a stabilizing medium. The large surface of the flat channel facilitates intense cooling and the use of a high electric-current density. The connecting auxiliary electrodes between particular sections of the channel make it possible to work with an almost constant electric-current density throughout the analysis time and during removal of the sample components which are not of interest, and thus to attain a short analysis time.

3.2   Identification of substances in their zones by means of on-line detection

In order for the analytical potential of isotachophoresis to be realized, an improvement in the level of the qualitative information obtained by the method must be achieved (see Section 4.3.1). Such improvements have been observed in the sphere of detection. When using universal detectors, a qualitative evaluation of the record is limited to a comparison between the step heights of the sample and model standards. The use of selective and specific detectors offers far greater possibilities and, thus, the development of new detection principles and the improvement of existing ones have recently been the target of research interest. The already classical universal detectors used up till now measure the electric properties of the zones. The conductivity detector was introduced by Everaerts [1]. The detection cell is usually formed by a part of the separation capillary into which two platinum electrodes protrude, and the electric conductance of the electrolyte in between the electrodes is measured by a.c. current and then recorded. The principle of the electric-potential gradient detector [2] is the measurement of the electric voltage across two electrodes protruding into the capillary wall and being displaced from each other in the direction of zone migration. The design of both these detectors has been perfected and today they are widely employed for qualitative evaluations. Progress in universal detection has been marked by substantial improvements achieved in the properties of the contactless conductivity detector [30]. Its principal advantage is that the sensing electrodes in the detection cell are not in contact with the electrolytes, and thus the phenomena on the phase interface (electrolyte/electrode) are eliminated.

The UV absorption detector is the most widely used selective detector [1]. It is normally equipped with interference filters especially for 206, 254 and 280 nm wave-lengths. Combination of an UV detector with an universal detector is quite common, for it increases the identification power of the analysis. The detection cells of both detectors are usually positioned close to each other, in one block. The dual-wavelength UV absorption detector [31] measures the zone absorption at two wave-lengths simultaneously. A technique of scanning the whole UV absorption spectrum of a zone has also been demonstrated [32]: the isotachophoregraph is combined with a commercial UV spectrometer whose measuring cell has been substituted by a part of the isotachophoretic separation capillary. Top level instrumentation in this field is described by Goto *et al.* [33], who used a multichannel spectrophotometer with a photodiode array as detector. The system detects, on-line, the whole

UV and visible absorption spectrum of the zone in the detection cell, thus substantially facilitating the identification of the substance.

The fluorescence and radiometric detectors are further examples of advanced selective detectors. At the former detector [34], UV light passes through the detection cell, and any fluorescing substances present emit visible light which is (in the direction perpendicular to that of the UV light) detected by a photodiode. The latter detector [35] makes it possible to detect on-line β-emission of atoms. The electrochemical detector [36] can also be classified as selective. The separated substances are continuously eluted, via a short tube, into the electrochemical detection cell, which contains two solid electrodes. The current is measured and registered in the form of an isotachophoregram at a fixed d.c. potential applied to these electrodes.

3.3   Micropreparative procedures and combination of techniques

The aim of getting further independent information for the identification of substances in the zone led to the construction of a device for taking zones out of the separation capillary – the so-called micropreparative system. Some micropreparative devices are shown in Fig. 6 a, b, for example, devices in which the zone is taken out by an injection syringe [37] and a micropreparative valve [38], respectively. During this procedure, the driving electric current through the column is interrupted. The identification of substances in the zones is subsequently performed by one of the various other methods available. An off-line combination with mass spectroscopy should also be mentioned here [39]: the zone is extracted by a 3 µL valve, placed in a crucible, evaporated, and brought into the mass-spectrometer via a solid sample inlet. This method is very important since the analytical power of mass-spectroscopy is very high. Continuous elution (Fig. 6 c) [40] has found universal application. It even makes the on-line detection of eluted zones possible (see the electrochemical detector mentioned in Section 3.2). Another preparative principle has been described by Öfverstedt and Eriksson [41]; after having migrated to the leading electrode, the zone is forced out of the column by the hydrodynamic flow of the terminator (Fig. 6 d).

Combination of isotachophoresis with other analytical techniques should be considered in cases where another technique makes it possible to identify substances contained in the isotachophoretic zones or where isotachophoresis is unable to provide a complete separation. From the viewpoint of instrumentation, combination of isotachophoresis with other analytical tech-

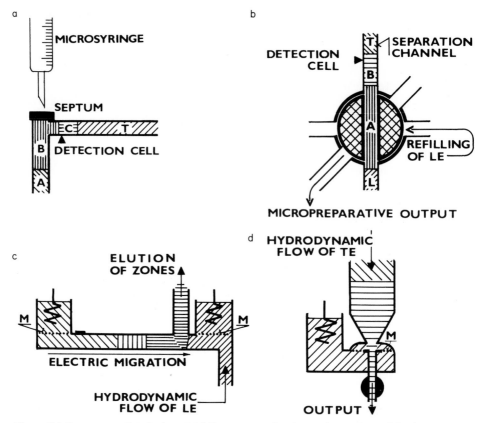

Figure 6. Micropreparative devices. (a) Micropreparation by a microsyringe; (b) micropreparative valve; (c) continuous elution; (d) discontinuous elution by hydrodynamic flow; M, membrane.

niques is accompanied by the problem of how to transfer the sample to the inlet of the isotachophoretic column if isotachophoresis is the final analytical procedure, or, alternatively, how to take the isotachophoretic zone out of the isotachophoregraph and transfer it to the inlet of the next technique (in cases when the analytical procedure starts with isotachophoresis). Combination of isotachophoresis with HPLC should be mentioned here [41] (Fig. 7). After preconcentration in the isotachophoretic column the sample is transferred to the input of the HPLC column by the procedure shown in Fig. 6d and then analyzed. This technique has been utilized for the concentration of samples containing proteins. The chromatogram of a concentrated sample of 1.2 mL (containing 28 µg of transferrin) may be compared with the chromatogram of 50 µL of a sample containing 33 µg of transferrin. The combination of HPLC with isotachophoresis as preseparation technique, using a commercial

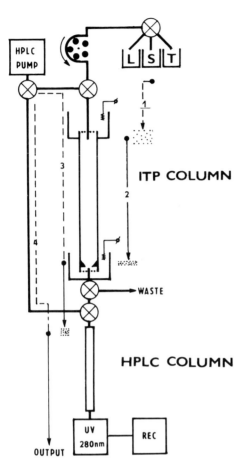

Figure 7. Combination of isotachophoresis and HPLC. (1) Sampling of the low-concentration sample by a peristaltic pump into the isotachophoretic column. (2) Preconcentration of the sample during the isotachophoretic run. (3) Transfer of the sample from the output of the isotachophoretic column to the input of the HPLC column by the HPLC pump. (4) HPLC run − separation and detection of the sample components. From [41], with permission.

device with a separation capillary made of PTFE, has been described [42]. After isotachophoretic preseparation, the capillary is removed and the sample fractions (obtained by cutting after the tracking dyes) are injected into the liquid chromatograph.

The principle of desorption isotachophoresis [43] combines two techniques − selective sorption and isotachophoresis. The analyzed sample substance is first selectively sorbed on an absorption element placed in the isotachophoretic column and then desorbed by the electric field during a normal isotachophoretic run. The substance forms an isotachophoretic zone and may thus be quantitated. Fig. 8 shows the apparatus used. In the first step (Fig. 8a) the sample is pumped by a peristaltic pump through the beginning of the isotachophoretic column equipped with the adsorption element. The bulk of the sample, which is not of interest, is not absorbed and leaves the column *via*

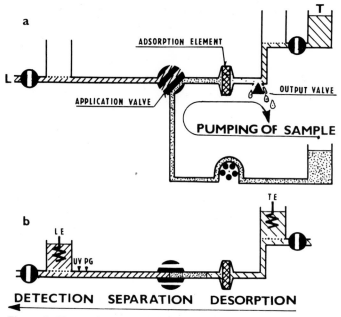

Figure 8. Desorption isotachophoresis. (a) Sorption of the sample. (b) Isotachophoretic desorption and detection by UV-absorption (UV) and potential-gradient (PG) detector. From [43], with permission.

the output valve. In the second step, the application valve is filled with the leading electrolyte from the syringe and turned to the position in Fig. 8b. Then, the isotachophoretic run is started.

3.4   Analysis automation and data treatment

Considerable attention has recently been paid to a simplification of the operation of isotachophoretic analyzers, namely, to automation of the operation and of data processing. With volume-coupling, we can work with a higher electric current during the time when only the leading electrolyte is in the analytical capillary, thus shortening the analysis time. For this technique, a time programmer which changes the value of the driving electric current, switches on the chart drive of the recorder, and switches off the power supply together with the chart drive after finishing the analysis is produced by the firm Shimadzu [44]. A control unit for column coupling [45] consists of a time programmer which switches over the power supply either to the auxiliary electrode (during passage of the leading zone or of a major sample component which is not of interest) or to the leading electrode during passage of such zones which are to be detected). For details, see Section 3.5.3.

To quantitate the analyses, various methods have been developed, to simplify the evaluation of recorded step lengths. Coulometric records [46] are based on the unambiguous relationship between mass transfer by the electric current and electric charge passed through the column (see Section 4.3.2). The record obtained is similar to the usual time record except that measurements are registered as a function of electric charge instead of time. Measurements are independent of the separation instrument used as well as of the magnitude of the electric current. A high degree of precision and the uniformity of the output information, suitable for automation, are the advantages of this method. Another way in which to process the data [47] is based on the electronic off-line evaluation of step lengths by an adapted chromatographic integrator or an on-line connected computer. The analysis is recorded as the time dependence of dt/dR (where t is the time and R the magnitude of the conductivity-detector signal); such conversion offers an isotachophoregram similar to a chromatogram.

To interpret an analysis, each zone is described by two measurable parameters: the electric charge corresponding to its passage through the detection cell and the magnitude of the detection signal. Based on these facts, a device has been developed [48] which, for each zone characterized by the level of the detection signal, measures the time of its passage and determines the relative level of the detection singal (related to suitable standard substances, *e.g.*, the leader and/or terminator). In accordance with the relative step

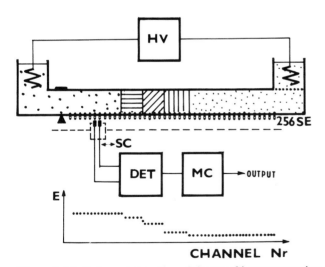

Figure 9. Multichannel detection. Scheme of instrumentation and record of a scan. SE, sensing electrodes; HV, high-voltage power supply; SC, moving contacts; DET, potential-gradient detector; MC, microcomputer. From [49], with permission.

heights, the processor recognizes the zones and uses the corresponding calibration dependences to determine and print the concentrations of the analyzed substances (see also Section 3.5.2).

A sophisticated system of automation is represented by the multichannel detector [49] which follows the course of sample separation into individual zones, as well as the electric field strength in these zones. An array of 256 thin sensing electrodes are located along the whole separation path (Fig. 9). The scanning time is sufficiently short, and each scan is stored in the memory of a computer which recognizes when the separation is complete and prints the results of the analysis. The analysis time is thus reduced to the time necessary for the separation of the sample.

3.5   Commercial instrumentation

Good commercial apparatus is now available with which to perform isotachophoretic analysis routinely. Two simultaneous trends have been observed in recent years in an increase in the number of producers of commercial instruments, and a marked endeavor to make the existing instruments yet more perfect and efficient. A description of the characteristics of various commercial instruments is presented in the following sections.

3.5.1   Isotachophoretic instrument LKB 2127 Tachophor [50]

This instrument is produced by the firm LKB Produkter AB, Bromma, Sweden. It is designed for cationic and anionic analyses in aqueous and non-aqueous media. The separation capillary is of PTFE and its length is selectable. It is enclosed in an air thermostat with efficient, enforced, air circulation; the temperature is adjustable within the range $3-29\,^\circ$C. The sample is injected by a microsyringe. The instrument is equipped with a dual detection system involving a universal conductivity detector and a UV absorption detector with wavelength selection provided by interference filters of 206, 254, 280, 340 and 365 nm. The conductivity detector has both a direct and a differential output to the recorder. The power supply provides a stabilized driving electric current, with a fine continuous setting up to 500 µA, and 30 kV as the maximum voltage. It is equipped with an adjustable trip. The protection circuits ensure the safety of the operator against an accidental electric shock, as well as the protection of the device against damage caused by incorrect operation. The column is adapted for its connection with an optional micropreparative device called Tachofrac [51]. This device permits continuous elution of the separated sample fractions out of the separation capillary and their collection on a moving cellulose acetate strip.

3.5.2   Isotachophoretic analyzer Shimadzu IP-2A [44]

The apparatus is designed for isotachophoretic analyses in aqueous and non-aqueous media. The instrument is equipped with a volume-coupling capillary system; the first capillary, of large inner diameter, is easily exchangeable, thus permitting its length to be selected in the range 40–200 mm. Furthermore, the apparatus is equipped with a device for the use of hydrodynamic counter-flow. The injection device, the separation capillary and the detection cells (of the potential-gradient detector and the UV absorption detector) are enclosed in a common thermostated bath, the temperature of which can be selected within the range 10–37 °C. Sample injection is made by a microsyringe. The maximum volume of the sample injection is 100 µL. The driving electric current can be selected in steps up to 500 µA. The trip can be adjusted up to 25 kV. The apparatus is equipped with a simple and useful programmer controlling the adjustable driving current during the analysis (see Section 3.4). For specific detection, a double-beam UV absorption detector UVD-10 A is delivered as an option.

A data processor, Isotachopac I-E 1 B, has been produced for signal processing from the potential-gradient detector [48]. It prints the month, day, hour and minute of the injection of the sample, the calibration data, the analysis number and the quantitating method used (selectable from four possible ones). Then it prints the list of sequentially numbered zones and their step lengths (in the corrresponding time scale). For each zone, it evaluates its relative step height related either to one reference substance – the leading ion, or to two reference substances – the leading ion and the terminator. The data processor also evaluates the calibration curves and prints the concentrations of all components contained in the sample. The Manual Preparative Attachment IPP-2A permits one to take out the zone, by a microliter syringe, when its length is at least 10 mm in a capillary of I. D. 0.5 mm. The detection of the respective zone prior to its preparative isolation is by potential gradient, but combination with the UVD-10A is possible.

The operation of the whole apparatus is simple and safe. It is remarkable that the whole instrument requires only a small space on the laboratory bench; a width of 275 mm is enough (when the recorder is not included). Recently, production of a new type of analyzer, IP-3A, has been started.

3.5.3   CS Isotachophoretic Analyzer [45]

This instrument is produced by the Institute of Radioecology and Applied Nuclear Techniques, Spišská Nová Ves, Czechoslovakia; it is designed for analytical and micropreparative isotachophoresis. The apparatus is designed for the analysis of anions and cations in aqueous media, but some mixed solvents can also be used, *e.g.*, up to 40% methanol or 60% ethanol. The instrument has a column-coupling system with an auxiliary third electrode and an appropriate electrolyte inlet. The driving electric current is adjustable by steps. Different current values can be chosen for the preseparation and analytical capillaries. The maximum current possible is 500 µA. The supply is equipped with a trip, adjustable within the range 6–16 kV.

For samples which require a small separation charge, the instrument can be set up as an one-column system, *e.g.*, without the preseparation capillary and the bifurcation block. The detector is of the conductivity type, with a signal output for direct and differential recordings. The control unit makes it possible to program the timing of the whole analysis. In six pre-set time intervals the unit directs control instructions to:

(i) start recording the detector signal from the preseparation capillary; (ii) switch over the current supply from preseparation to analytical capillary and, at the same time, reduce the current value to the second pre-set value; (iii) drive off a certain part of the sample, which is not to be analyzed further (this instruction may be pre-programmed twice); (iv) switch on the chart drive, to start recording of the detection signal from the analytical capillary; (v) switch off the recorder and the high-voltage power supply. The instrument has recently also been provided with an optional UV detector (254 and 405 nm).

3.5.4   Electrophoretic preparative instrument Elphor VaP 21 [52]

This apparatus for continuous free-flow electrophoresis is produced by the firm Bender and Hobein, Munich, F.R.G. The apparatus allows separations in aqueous solutions by the method of isoelectric focusing, zone electrophoresis, field-step focusing and isotachophoresis, both for preparative as well as analytical purposes. The minimum sample volume for the analytical use of the apparatus is 10 µL. For a separation by isotachophoresis the useful sampling flow-rate is 10 mL/h. The separation chambers are produced in three sizes: 200×250 mm, 100×250 mm and 50×250 mm. The range of the thermostating temperatures of the chamber is 4–25 °C. The electric high-voltage power supply provides a power of 1 kW (3 kV/0.33 A, 1.5 kV/0.66 A, 0.75 kV/1.33 A).

On-line detection is carried out by one of three modes: light absorption, fluorescence or light scattering. The signal is then evaluated by a minicomputer and the result is printed or shown on the display. Hydrodynamic flow carries the separated sample into the outlets of the electrophoretic chamber (90 holes; the distance between the holes is 1.1 mm). Each fraction may be collected in a special container.

3.5.5   Tachophor Delta [53]

Production of an instrument for capillary isotachophoretic analysis has recently been begun by the firm Itaba, Järfälla, Sweden. The instrument, named Tachophor Delta, is suitable for biochemical laboratories specializing in medicine, food chemistry, environmental monitoring *etc.* The basic version of Tachophor Delta has a single column system equipped with both conductivity and UV absorption detectors, the latter with an unusually wide range of selectable wavelengths from 206 to 530 nm. The working electrolytes are stored in glass bottles and transported to the electrolyte unit by pressurized gas. Before each run the system is automatically rinsed. The separation capillary is not thermostated but a stream of pressure gas can be used for cooling. The automatic sample loader takes 60 samples. After their introduction, the instrument works fully automatically until the output of the results is obtained. The evaluation of the results of the analysis is automatic by a computing integrator. As an option, a device for column-coupling and another one for preparation will be produced in the future.

3.5.6   Agrofor [54]

An apparatus under this name is produced by JZD Odra, Krmelín, Czechoslovakia. Agrofor is an instrument whose operation is simple. It is suitable for utilization in agriculture and food production, but may also be used for pharmaceutical analyses. The apparatus is equipped with a simple, easily exchangeable capillary, whose length can be selected as 18, 26 or 32 cm. A sample volume of ca. 20 µL is introduced by a valve; the sample consumption for one analysis is ca. 1 mL. The stabilized electric current may be varied from 60, 90, 120 to 150 µA. The power supply has a trip, fixed on the value of 16 kV. The conductometric detector also has a differential output; the detection sensitivity can be attenuated within the range 1 to 11. Agrofor is designed for aqueous media, however, water-alcoholic media containing up to 50% methanol or 25% ethanol may also be employed.

4   Methodology

In contemporary analytical isotachophoresis great importance is attached to the development of methodology, *i.e.*, the formulation of general procedures by which to solve separation problems. A significant result in this field has been the development of analytical procedures based on a deeper under-standing of zone stability and substance separability.

4.1   Zone stability − an essential feature

A method is suitable for a particular analysis only if an electrolyte system has been found in which all the substances in the sample give isotacho-phoretic zones. The classical rule of isotachophoresis, which stated that the effective mobility of a given substance had to lie between the effective mobilities of a suitable leading and terminating species, was corrected recent-ly. A new and more exact rule has been derived from the concept of stability of isotachophoretic zones. It has two separate aspects, which are described by the terms "correct migration" and "analytical stability".

4.1.1   Correct migration

The concept of correct migration stems from the simple reflection [14] that the existence of a stable isotachophoretic state is dependent on the self-sharpening of all the zone boundaries in the isotachophoretic system. This condition can easily be described in terms of parameters of the type $\bar{u}_{X,Y}$ (see Section 2.1). In order for the migration of the zones to be correct, the electrolyte system itself must have been chosen correctly, *i.e.*, the mobilities of the leading and the terminating zones must be such that [12]:

$$|\bar{u}_{T,T}| < |\bar{u}_{L,T}| \tag{18}$$

which, implicitly, includes the validity of

$$|\bar{u}_{T,L}| < |\bar{u}_{L,L}| \tag{19}$$

Then, for the correct migration of a zone, it must hold that:

$$|\bar{u}_{X,X}| < |\bar{u}_{L,X}| \tag{20}$$

$$|\bar{u}_{T,T}| < |\bar{u}_{X,T}| \tag{21}$$

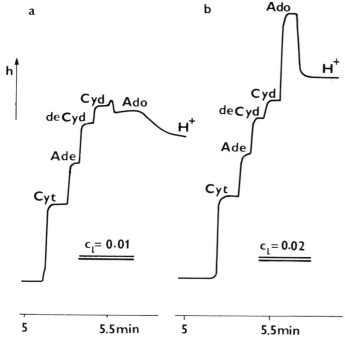

Figure 10. Cationic separation of cytosine (Cyt), adenine (Ade), deoxycytidine (deCyd), cytidine (Cyd) and adenosine (Ado). Leading electrolyte: (a) 10 mM, (b) 20 mM ammonium acetate/acetic acid (1:1); terminator: acetic acid. 0.5 µL (a) and 1 µL (b), resp., of an 5 mM equimolar solution of the substances were sampled. From [55], with permission.

The relationships quoted above state that the leading substance L must possess a higher mobility than substance X in the zone of X, and that substance X has to possess a higher mobility than the terminator in the zone of the terminator.

An important role is always played by the solvent ions, *e.g.*, H^+ and OH^- in water. These ions can penetrate the whole electrolyte system and thus, have a substantial effect on migration. The authors have given a detailed description [14, 15] of the migration behavior of H^+ in acidic cationic systems and have defined the conditions for the choice of the composition of the leading electrolyte (counterion of a certain pK, total concentration of the leading electrolyte and its pH). The fulfilment of these conditions ensures the correct migration of the system, with H^+ as terminator. Fig. 10 illustrates the influence of concentration of the leading electrolyte on the migration behavior of a mixture of bases [55]; we can see that an increase in concentration of the leading electrolyte extends the useful range of mobilities and makes the correct migration of all substances present possible. The role of OH⁻ in anionic systems has also been described (see Section 2.1) [13]. Reflections on the correct migration of substances should also include the concept of effective mobility, discussed in Section 2.1, and the zone existence diagram, described in Section 2.2.

4.1.2   Analytical stability

A zone is a stable one (from the viewpoint just mentioned) if it contains, independently of time, a constant amount of the substance being analyzed. The sample does not disappear from its zone as the result of migration of the sample into the leading or the terminating electrolyte. The analytical stability of zones is a natural stability, given by the reversibility of chemical reactions and by the arrangement of the electrolyte system. These two factors determine whether the ionic species belonging to one substance present migrate together (as one constituent) and thus cannot be mutually separated, or whether the ionic species migrate independently of each other, and are thus separable. These two factors also decide the question of whether the zones of the substances are, or are not, analytically stable (*cf.*, [2]).

Recently it has been shown that the analytical stability of the zones is not an indispensable condition for their analytical utilization, *i.e.*, there are certain conditions under which even unstable zones may be analytically utilizable. Unstable zones can be tolerated in the following two cases: either the instability can be controlled and unstable zones may be quantitated, or the instability of zones is used to increase the selectivity of the system (some components of the sample form stable zones and can be analyzed, and other components of the sample form very unstable zones and are eliminated from the system).

The isotachophoretic separation of condensed phosphates can serve as an example of the analytical utilization of unstable zones. In solution, these phosphates are subject to hydrolysis. As has been shown [56], we can separate and quantitate a mixture of mono-, di-, tri- and tetraphosphates (with a leading electrolyte of pH 4.0), although the decomposition rate of tetraphosphate cannot be neglected (the system is in a quasi-stedy state). As the authors have shown, we can compensate the effect of hydrolysis on the shortening of the zone of tetraphosphate and on the prolongation of the zones of mono- and triphosphate by using the calibration curve method. Another example is the case of anionic analysis of M-NTA complexes in acidic systems [57], where the instability of a zone is caused by the partial

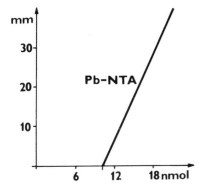

Figure 11. Calibration curve of the Pb-NTA complex. Leading electrolyte: 8 mM Cl$^-$ (HCl+KCl), pH$_L$ 3.0; terminator: benzoate. From [57], with permission.

dissociation of the complex and an escape of the free metal cation M$^+$ from the zone (bleeding zone technique). Fig. 11 shows the calibration curve obtained for the Pb-NTA complex; although it does not pass through the origin of coordinates, it provides, at a sufficient injection of the sample, the opportunity for a reproducible quantitative analysis.

It has been shown already that the stability or instability of the zones is a result of superimposing effects, which are dependent on the arrangement of the electrolyte system, reaction kinetics and thermodynamic stability. From the viewpoint of methodology we have to estimate the possible types of instabilities correctly (several types can coexist). As an example, the zone types in a simple complex-forming system M$^+$-Y$^-$-MY$_2^-$, see Fig. 12, are given below [2]: (i) Stable simple zones in which no reactions take place (non-com-

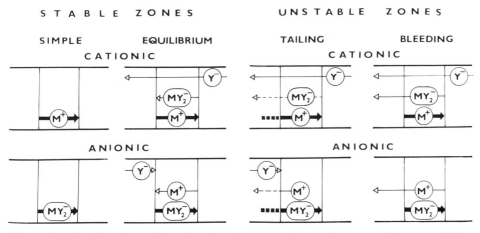

Figure 12. Classification of isotachophoretic zones of complexes according to stability. M$^+$-metal cation, Y$^-$-ligand anion.

plexed metal cations, non-complexing anions, kinetically inert complexes). (ii) Stable equilibrium zones characterized by the presence of fast complex-forming equilibria. The separand behaves as an ion constituent; the complexed ion and the kinetically labile complex are its components. The stability of this type of zone is based on the fact that the components of the separand are chemically unstable outside its zone owing to a suitable arrangement of the electrolyte system. The components undergo fast chemical reactions on the zone boundaries, where the zone is continuously restored.

As depicted in Fig. 12, in the cationic system migration of a zone of cation M^+, which forms the kinetically labile complex MY_2^- with the counterion Y^-, takes place. By a fast reaction, the cation M^+ forms the complex MY_2^- on the front zone boundary, and simultaneously this complex undergoes a fast decomposition on the rear zone boundary, owing to the tendency to re-establish the complex-forming equilibrium. (iii) Unstable tailing zones in which migration is similar to the equilibrium zones, but the reaction proceeding at the rear boundary is slow. This reaction does not reach its equilibrium at the zone boundary, and the reaction region penetrates into the following (terminating) zone. The zone is followed by a migrating "tail" of the separand. The existence of the "tailing" zone has been experimentally demonstrated in the case of cationic migration of La^{3+} with cyclohex-anediaminetetraacetic acid as the counterion [58]. (iv) Unstable bleeding zones, characterized by the fact that a subspecies of the separand leaves the zone via its rear boundary and is chemically stable in the following zone. In the anionic system (*cf.*, Fig. 12), the zone is left by the free cation M^+; in cationic systems, the complex MY_2^- leaves the zone, its decomposition rate being negligible in comparison with the migration speed. As described above (*cf.*, Fig. 12), an experimental demonstration of this type of unstable zone has been performed with anionic NTA (and EDTA) metal complexes [57].

4.2   New aspects of separation

The separation of a sample containing two substances requires that these substances are, in principle, separable (a qualitative problem of separation) and, further, that a sufficient separation capacity is available (a quantitative problem of separation).

4.2.1   Qualitative problems of separation

The classical concept of separability presupposes that one of the following theses is valid: (i) substances which have different effective mobilities are separable in pure, individual zones; (ii) substances having the same effective mobilities are not separable and form a stable mixed zone. Hence, the question of the separability of substances X and Y leads to the question of whether two given substances form, or do not form, a stable mixed zone, *i.e.*, whether the given substances show the same effective mobilities, $\bar{u}_{X,X} = \bar{u}_{Y,Y}$.

It has been shown recently [12] that the formation of stable mixed zones is a more complex phenomenon than was previously realized and that the classical description requires modification. Apart from the already mentioned ("classical") stable mixed zones, there exists another type of mixed zone (the so-called "enforced" type). These zones may be formed even when the substances show different effective mobilities in their individual zones (and the pH of these zones is different, too). This special type of mixed zone is formed in cases when the condition for a sharp boundary between two individual zones is not fulfiled; *cf.*, conditions (9)–(10) in Section 2.1. It goes without saying that in the mixed zone itself both substances have the same effective mobilities, $\bar{u}_{X,mix} = \bar{u}_{Y,mix}$ and also certain fixed ("prescribed") values of concentration. Depending on the sampling ratio of both substances, the substance in excess forms its individual zone in front of the mixed zone.

The situation just mentioned is exemplified in Fig. 13 for the case of picrate and formate. It also explains how to experimentally establish the presence of a stable mixed zone.

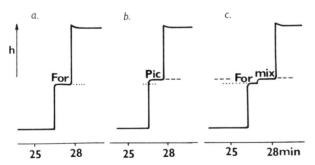

Figure 13. Example of an enforced stable mixed zone in an anionic system. Leading electrolyte: 10 mM Cl⁻/20 mM β-alanine, pH$_L$ 3.5; terminator: acetic acid. Sample: (a) 20o nmol of formate (For); (b) 20 nmol of picrate (Pic); (c) 20 nmol of formate and picrate; mix, mixed zone. From [13], with permission.

The contemporary conception of separability [13] has its roots in the determination of the migration order of zones, *i.e.*, in the testing of conditions (9)–(10). The value of $\bar{u}_{X,X}$ required can be taken directly from the tables (*cf.*, Section 2.2), and the value of $\bar{u}_{X,Y}$ can be calculated from the tabulated values of u_X and pH_Y. Another method utilizes the zone existence diagrams (*cf.*, Section 2.2) onto which one can plot the so-called sequence contours [12] and thus evaluate the group of substances X separable from a certain substance Y.

4.2.2   Quantitative problems of separation

The procedure described in the previous section considers the qualitative aspects of the separation, *i.e.*, separability. Separation also involves quantitative aspects, such as the completeness of a separation and the conditions for separation in a given electrolyte system and with given instrumentation. Here, two approaches are of interest: (i) conditions are sought under which the required amount of sample can be completely separated; (ii) the maximum amount of sample is determined which, under given conditions, can just be separated.

The first approach, (i) is related to trace analysis. The amount of sample to be analyzed is important since even the minor component of the sample must form a zone sufficiently large in comparison with the dimensions of the detection cell. Then separation conditions are sought which will enable a full separation.

It has been shown that the universal parameter for separation is the electric charge passed through the column [2]. This parameter is independent of the concentration of the leading electrolyte, the geometry of the separation column and the driving electric current used.

The following quantities (expressed in terms of the electric charge) have been defined as useful for the description of the separation process [59]: (i) The column hold-up, Q_L, defined as the electric charge passing through the column from the start of the analysis until the passage of the rear boundary of the leading zone through the detection cell. This quantity is proportional to the amount N_L of leading ion contained in the column (note that u_R and u_L have opposite signs):

$$Q_L = N_L \cdot F \left(1 - \frac{u_R}{u_L} \right) \tag{22}$$

where the subscript R refers to the counterion R. If the leading electrolyte has the same composition throughout the column, then the column hold-up is directly proportional to the volume of the column and to the concentration of the leading electrolyte. It is a quantity which is easy to measure experimentally; at constant driving electric current, one measures the time taken for the leading zone to pass through the detection cell: $Q_L = I \cdot t_L$. (ii) The passage charge of a zone X, defined as the charge which passes through the column during the passage of the zone X through a certain cross-section of the column, e.g., through the detection cell. At constant driving current it again holds that: $Q_X = I \cdot \Delta t_X$. (iii) The separation charge, Q_S, defined as the electric charge which must pass through the column so that a full separation of the dosed amount of sample may just be reached. In particular, the separation charge (for a sample containing two components A and B) depends on the injected amounts of both substances and on their effective mobilities. It is equal to the column hold-up increased by the passage charge of the first zone: $Q_S = Q_L + Q_A$. With the help of the quantities described above, we can solve the separation problem. The column hold-up can be expressed as

$$Q_L = (Q_{A,\max} + Q_{B,\max})/p \tag{23}$$

where $Q_{A,\max}$ and $Q_{B,\max}$ are the passage charges of the zones given by the maximum amounts of substances A and B which, under the given conditions, can still be separated.

The theoretical procedure is based on a rough knowledge of the composition of the sample and on an estimation of the amount of it needed for a reproducible analysis. For that amount we then calculate the required column hold-up by using relationship (23), where the corresponding charges are expressed explicitly; e.g., for a weak monovalent protolyte, it holds that:

$$Q_L = F \left[N_A \left(1 - \frac{u_R}{u_A} \right) + N_B \left(1 - \frac{u_R}{u_B} \right) \right]/p \tag{24}$$

where N_A and N_B are the sampled amounts of substances A and B. The experimental procedure is generally applied in cases where the column of a given hold-up Q_L did not provide complete separation of the required amount of sample and where a mixed zone of the unresolved remainder of the sample is detected. The column hold-up needed for the complete resolution of the given sample amount, $Q_{L,req}$, can be calculated from the following equation [2]:

$$Q_{L,req} = Q_L \frac{(Q_A + Q_B + Q_{AB}) \cdot (Q_L + Q_A + Q_{AB})}{(Q_L + Q_A) \cdot (Q_A + Q_B) + Q_{AB} \cdot Q_A} \tag{25}$$

where the subscripts A, B and AB designate the pure zones of substances A and B and the mixed zone AB, respectively. When working with a constant driving electric current, the respective step lengths can be used in place of the respective charges.

The second approach, (ii), is advantageous for the analysis of relatively concentrated samples containing a small number of components. This approach uses the concept of separation capacity [60]. The separation capacity has been defined as the maximum amount of an equimolar mixture of two substances which, under the given conditions, can be completely separated. For the separation capacity N_S of an equimolar mixture of monovalent components A and B ($N_A = N_B = N_S$), with $|\bar{u}_A| > |\bar{u}_B|$, it holds that [59]

$$N_S = p \cdot \frac{Q_L}{F} \cdot \left(2 - \frac{u_R}{u_A} - \frac{u_R}{u_B}\right)^{-1} \tag{26}$$

In practice, the concept of separation capacity is also useful when considering multicomponent samples, where the separation capacity determined for two of the worst separable substances is employed. Further, in a simplified approach, separation capacity is used as an illustrative quantity. It is determined experimentally by analyzing increasing amounts of the sample in question. The separation capacity is then expressed as the maximum amount (volume) of the sample which is still separable. When the sampled amount is increased further, a new step corresponding to the mixed zone appears in the isotachophoregram.

4.2.3 Separation control

The goal is to control separation in order to obtain full resolution of the sample. In principle, the simplest procedure would be to decrease the amount of sample, but another problem emerges here — the problem of how to evaluate small zones. Here, the relation of the passage charge of the zone to the hold-up of the detection cell is of decisive importance. The hold-up of the detection cell can only be reduced within certain limits: a further decrease in its volume (now ca. 3 nL) is complicated by technological problems and the presence of mechanical impurities in working solutions of electrolytes; decreasing the concentration of operational electrolytes (below 10^{-2} to 10^{-3} M) leads to broadening of the boundary between the zones [60] and requires the presence of a very high voltage.

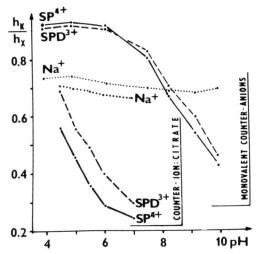

Figure 14. Dependence of the relative effective mobilities of Na, spermine (SP) and spermidine (SPD) on pH_L for a monovalent and polyvalent (citrate) counterion. From [62], with permission.

Therefore, the basic ways in which we can influence separation are by varying the separability or the separation capacity, or both. Separability can be controlled by altering the effective mobilities, and thus the selectivity, by changing the electrolyte system. The procedures most commonly adopted are based on pH-changes, utilization of the formation of complexes and associates, or use of mixed or nonaqueous solvents. It is possible to attain a high selectivity by using complex-forming equilibria. Nukatsuka *et al.* demonstrated a complete separation of 14 lanthanides with α-hydroxyisobutyric acid as the complexing counterion [61]. The quantity directly affecting the selectivity is the concentration of free ligand in the zones. Utilization of ionic associates is exemplified in Fig. 14, by the case of the polyamines spermine and spermidine [62]. The figure also demonstrates how the effective mobilities of the substances decrease with increasing charge of the substance as well as with increasing charge of the counterion, owing to the interactions between polyvalent ions.

The use of mixed and non-aqueous solvents is advantageous, since such solvents can cause a substantial alteration in the ionic mobilities (separations of alkali metals, halogenides, *etc.* [13]) and help analyze substances which are practically insoluble in water (such as fatty acids [63]) or are unstable in water. Fig. 15 shows an analysis of conjugated bile acids in 95% methanol [64]. Instrumental control of the separation capacity, while keeping the same electrolyte system, is a way of gradually increasing the hold-up of the col-

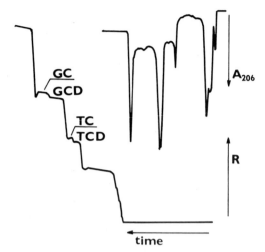

Figure 15. Analysis of taurochendeoxy-cholic (TCD), taurocholic (TC), glyco-chendeoxycholic (GCD) and glycocholic (GC) acids in human bile. Leading electrolyte: $10\,\text{mM}$ Cl^-/hydroxylamine, pH_L 5.84, 95% v/v methanol/water; terminator: *ca.* $5\,\text{mM}$ HEPES. Conductivity (R) and UV-absorption (A_{206}) detection records are depicted. From [64], with permission.

umn. Here, the best approach seems to be the use of the concentration cascade [27] with column-coupling instrumentation [28]. A promising technique is so-called multicolumn isotachophoresis [29] (see Section 3.1), which facilitates analyses of samples with volumes of 1 mL and more.

4.3   Analytical potential

4.3.1   Qualitative aspects

The identification of unknown substances in a sample by isotachophoresis is limited, above all, by the detection system used. The qualitative analysis is based on the interpretation of the detection signal, and the reliability of this signal depends on whether a universal, selective or specific detector is used and whether adequate standards are available. The separated substances form zones which are in immediate contact with one another, and it is the job of the detector to distinguish between these zones. The separation of substances into well resolved zones and the detection of these zones are related only vaguely; *e.g.*, we can detect a certain substance present in the mixed zone by a suitable selective detector but, on the other hand, two well-resolved neighboring zones may happen to be indistinguishable by a certain detector. Therefore, sometimes it is of advantage to use an isotachophoretic instrument equipped with several detectors; a description is to be found in Section 3.3.

It is often necessary to use a spacer [65], which is a substance having an appropriate intermediate mobility. When this substance is added to the sample before analysis, it creates its own zone in between two badly distinguishable zones. In this way, the two zones are separated and may then be distinguished and identified more easily. Spacers are mainly employed together with UV detectors, since the spacer may enable one to distinguish two neighboring UV-absorbing zones [66, 67]. In practice, spacers of two kinds have been used, namely, discrete spacers, and spacers with a broad mobility pattern.

Discrete spacers are composed of a defined mixture of known standard substances, most often amino acids and Good's buffers (a catalogue of 49 discrete spacers for separations at higher pH is available [68]). In cases where the sample contains a complicated mixture of unidentified substances, these discrete spacers make it possible to resolve the mixture into fractions and to characterize individual fractions (*e.g.,* fraction migrating in between valine and glycine [69]). Spacers with a broad mobility pattern are mixtures of a large number of ionogenic substances which form a large number of zones during isotachophoretic migration. The effective mobility decreases continuously and steadily from the leading to the terminating ion. Thus, a migrating gradient of mobilities (the so-called "spacing mobility gradient") and, of course, a pH-gradient are created in the zone system. Such spacers are used predominantly in protein analysis [69], where carrier ampholytes known from isoelectric focusing (Ampholine, Servalyt, Pharmalyte, Bio-Lyte) serve as spacers.

Two different procedures can be employed in order to identify the steps recorded by the detector, *i.e.*, to relate steps to zones of individual separated substances. These utilize either the sequence of the steps or the step heights in the recording. However, in order to apply these methods successfully, all the components of the sample must be available as standard substances which can be injected separately or, if necessary, in combination with another standard substance. The identification of the steps may be complicated by the fact that, in addition to individual zones of pure substances, mixed zones appear in the system. These zones are either transient, present here owing to the incomplete separation of two particular substances, or of a stable enforced type, formed by inseparable pairs of substances. The problem of zone separation can be adequately solved by calibration procedures, *cf., e.g.,* Section 4.2 and ref. [2].

For direct identification of a zone, *i.e.*, a qualitative specification of the substances which form the zone, a universal detector may be used in combination with a selective and/or specific detector. Alternatively, isotachophoresis may be combined with another identification method. In the latter case, a zone has to be withdrawn from the isotachophoretic column. For treatment of this problem in greater detail, see Section 3.3.

4.3.2   Quantitative aspects

Quantitative analysis includes a pretreatment of the sample, injection, separation and detection, evaluation of the quantitative parameters of the isotachophoregram and interpretation of the data. Each of these operations is a potential source of various difficulties and errors, which should be borne in mind when choosing the working technique. In principle, all working techniques known in column chromatography [70] may be utilized in quantitative analysis by isotachophoresis. Calibration constants are measured experimentally and are then used to determine the relationship between the amounts of analyzed substances and the experimentally found quantitative parameters [2].

The external standard technique is the most frequently used technique, especially, in combination with the calibration curve. Its advantage consists in the possibility of eliminating the systematic error involved in measuring the injected volumes, as well as further errors caused by the fact that the zone boundaries are not ideally straight and thin, the detection cell has a certain non-zero effective length in the direction of migration, *etc.* The main advantages of the internal standard technique are that the entire analyses can be carried out by a single injection and that it is not necessary to know the injected volume. The technique is especially advantageous in cases where the injected volume is difficult to define, *e.g.,* the analysis involves a pretreatment of the sample, whereby the sample is diluted or some other components are added. However, the addition of an internal standard can also cause problems, as the standard must not be present in the original sample and has to provide a zone which is well developed and completely separated from all sample components. The standard addition technique is relatively laborious, its advantage being that the influence of the sample matrix is included in the calibration. This fact can be very important, especially in analysis of biological samples. The technique of internal normalization presents results in the form of relative quantities (molar fractions); its advantage is the fact that we need not know the size of the sample analyzed.

Some of the working techniques mentioned above have already been used widely in isotachophoresis, others have been used only rarely. In practice, the pros and cons of each technique are carefully considered before selecting the most suitable technique for a particular analysis.

By definition, quantitative analysis involves the measurement of quantitative parameters. As already mentioned (*cf.,* Section 4.2.2), the passage charge of a zone is a general quantitative parameter. The amount of a substance is directly proportional to the parameter Q_X.

$$N_X = K_X \cdot Q_X \qquad (27)$$

where K_X is the calibration constant for a given substance and electrolyte system. The value of Q_X is best determined by coulometric measurements, in which the driving electric current is integrated. When the driving electric current is stabilized, the passage charge may be calculated from the passage time interval. The step lengths in the isotachophoregram may be directly used as quantitative parameters, provided all analyses are performed under identical conditions (the driving electric current and concentration of the leading electrolyte remain constant, and the same isotachophoregraph is employed).

One problem which remains to be solved is the exact measurement of the step lengths; in a real isotachophoregram the steps are not rectangular. During evaluation, real steps are substituted by idealized ones whose boundaries are derived from the inflection points of real steps, *i.e.*, the step length is obtained from the differential record by measuring the distance between two recorded peaks. For sufficiently long steps, the error involved can be neglected; for short steps, it must be eliminated by using the calibration curve technique.

When using a selective (*e.g.*, UV absorption) detector, the analyzed amount is determined from the step length, as described above. Problems are sometimes encountered when the UV absorbance steps are not sufficiently rectangular to give accurate step lengths. In such cases, it is better to use the step areas for quantitation [71]. In cases where a very short UV-absorbing zone migrates between two non-UV-absorbing zones, a peak corresponding to this zone appears in the UV detector record.

It is a great advantage of isotachophoresis that its theoretical model is well developed, since this makes it possible to simulate all the required steady-state characteristics of the zones rather easily (*cf.*, Section 2.2). Calibration procedures necessary for quantitation can thus be substituted either partially or fully by calculation. Hence, the experimental calibration may be carried out for only one reference substance, while for the other substances the steady-state concentrations in the isotachophoretic zones as well as the relative correction factors and calibration constants are calculated. Moreover, when all the required data on ionic mobilities and pK's are available, a computer simulation of the steady state may provide all the calibration constants required (see *e.g.*, Table 1).

4.3.3   Trace analysis

The problems associated with trace analysis by isotachophoresis have attracted much interest. The limits of trace analysis are given both by the method itself (*cf.*, Section 2.3) and by existing instrumentation (*cf.*, Section 3). The minimum amount of a substance whose isotachophoretic zone can still be detected depends on the concentration of the leading electrolyte and on the effective size of the detection cell. For the currently used concentrations of the leading ion, which range from 10^{-2} to 10^{-3} M, and for a volume of the detection cell of ca. 10 nL (capillary of 0.3 mm I. D., length of the detection cell being 0.15 mm), this minimum amount lies within the range $10^{-10} - 10^{-11}$ mol. The minimum concentration of a substance in the sample also depends on the volume of the sample injected: if 5 μL of the sample are injected, we can detect concentrations of $0.05 - 0.5$ mM.

When very dilute samples are to be analyzed, the concentrating effect of isotachophoresis can be an advantage. Large volumes may be sampled either by using special large-volume sampling valves [29] or by the continuous-sampling technique [73]. In either case, one problem cannot be overlooked, *viz.*, the presence of areas in the column with a very low electric conductivity and, therefore, the danger of overheating. In practice, the most frequent problems of trace analysis are associated with the determination of low concentrations of substances in samples containing a great excess of ionogenic components. For example, the determination of various metabolic substances in blood plasma at concentrations of $\leq 10^{-5}$ M may be hampered by the presence of 10^{-1} M NaCl. In order to solve such problems, large sampling volumes must be employed together with highly sensitive detectors. Further, the separation capacity must be sufficient to ensure separation of the bulk substance. One way in which to solve such problems is the use of multi-stage separations and the method of heart cutting, *i.e.*, an effective preseparation and elimination of a bulk component followed by analytical separation of a certain part of the sample (see also Section 4.2.3).

4.4   Strategy of analytical procedures

By the strategy of the isotachophoretic analysis [2], we mean a series of operations, either leading to a successful analysis or providing a reliable analytical procedure for routine purposes (see Fig. 16). Generally, the strategy is not a straightforward series of operations, but involves a repetition of certain stages under altered working conditions.

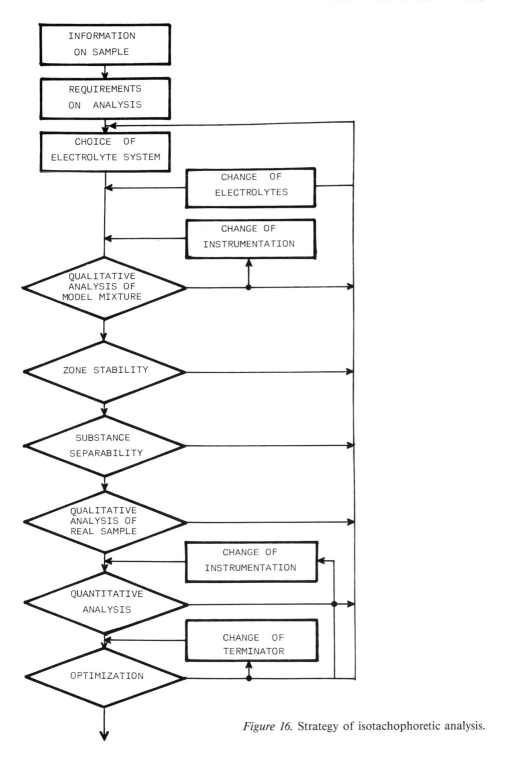

Figure 16. Strategy of isotachophoretic analysis.

4.4.1 Basic approach

In an ideal case, the primary information on the sample should include:

- the predicted qualitative composition of the sample;
- the expected concentrations of the sample components;
- the physico-chemical properties of the sample components, especially the mobilities of the ionic species and the constants of chemical equilibria.

A practical procedure starts with the choice of one of the recommended electrolyte systems based on knowledge about the sample. The next stage is the identification of the steps by analysis of a model mixture simulating the given sample. At the same time, a qualitative analysis of the sample is carried out in order to establish whether the number of steps and their character agree with the expected composition of the sample. A test follows, to ascertain whether all the substances analyzed form stable zones: (i) in the sense of a correct migration, which mainly depends on the choice of the leading and terminating electrolytes; and (ii) in the sense of a natural (chemical) stability, which is especially important in the isotachophoresis of complexes.

A universal method of verifying stability is calibration (in which we analyze each substance independently). If the calibration straight line passes through the origin of coordinates, then the substance zone is stable in the given system. Next, the separability of the substances is tested. The sequence of pure zones of the individual substances should be obtained. One also has to determine whether such an amount of the sample is separable which is required to produce sufficiently long zones for the analysis to be reproducible. In other words, the separation capacity of the system for this amount of sample has to be tested. The following stage consists of a qualitative analysis of the real sample, *i.e.*, if possible, the identification of all the steps. A quantitative evaluation is usually the final stage. When the aim is to develop a routine analytical procedure, optimization of the procedure will generally follow.

4.4.2 Modification of the system

In practice, it is often the case that at some stage a test fails. We then have to change either the electrolyte system or to modify the instrumentation. As shown in Fig. 16, unstable zones or inseparable groups of substances can only be removed by changing the electrolyte system. The amount of sample to be separated can be increased or the time of analysis decreased either by changing the electrolytes or by changing the working parameters of the instrument. As a rule, it is necessary to change the electrolyte system if some substances do not show correct migration or if the instability of the zones is caused by other effects (*e.g.*, instability of complexes). Once it has been verified that a certain pair of substances is not separable, *i.e.*, the substances form a stable mixed zone, we can follow an approximate rule which states that by increasing the difference in the effective mobilities of these substances, we can avoid the formation of a stable mixed zone. With this end in view, the leading electrolyte is changed (*e.g.*, its pH) and the test repeated. If full separation has not been attained using the amount of sample which is to be injected for the analysis, one possible remedy is to change the electrolytes. Then, the change in selectivity of the pair of substances which is difficult to separate is determined. The higher the selectivity, the higher is the separation power of the system. A general rule holds that a change of pH which causes a decrease in the degree of ionization also brings about a better separation.

When optimizing the analysis, an important question is how to change the electrolyte system so as to shorten the analysis time. One possible solution is the use of a less concentrated leading electrolyte. The use of a diluted electrolyte enables us to work with a higher electric-field strength and thus with a higher velocity of migration without increasing the Joule heat production (*i.e.*, without causing overheating). Another possibility to speed up the analysis lies in the choice of the terminator. A suitable terminator is a substance with the highest possible effective mobility which is still able to provide a reliable termination of the sample zones. In this way, the requirements concerning the voltage and the cooling of the column are minimized, and we can work at a higher voltage and obtain a faster analysis. Occasionally (*cf.*, Fig. 16), a change in the working parameters of the instrument is considered. This involves, *e.g.*, changes in the driving current, the length of the separation capillary or the application of special techniques.

One method which increases the amount of sample which can be separated is based upon an increase in the column hold-up. However, a simultaneous decrease in the sensitivity of detection must be avoided. The problem may be solved, *e.g.*, by employing the volume coupling or cascade technique. The simple use of a longer separation capillary may also have a positive effect. The instrumental procedures which can be used to decrease the analysis time depend on the actual working conditions and instrument available. The simplest solution is to work at a higher driving electric current (whether this is practicable depends on the parameters of the HV supply and the cooling of the separation capillary). On the other hand, if the actual separation capacity of the system is far greater than that required, the simplest solution is to use a shorter separation capillary, provided, of course, that the capillaries are interchangeable.

4.5   Facing accompanying phenomena

Electrophoresis has always been accompanied by the production of Joule heat, electroosmosis and diffusion. The isotachophoretic zones differ in their physico-chemical parameters and, therefore, disturbing effects manifest themselves in different ways. There are two possible methods by which to cope with these effects. The first approach aims at evaluating these effects in a defined quantitative way and at correcting the experimentally recorded parameters of the zones by a recalculation to defined standard conditions. This approach has been successfully used for the Joule heat effects [74]. Recently, another approach has been preferred, namely, to attempt to eliminate the disturbing effects by an appropriate choice of the working conditions.

Electroosmosis, which causes a spreading of the zone boundaries, may be suppressed by the following procedures [75]: (i) the increase in viscosity of the solution upon adding $0.05-0.4\%$ of (hydroxypropyl-, hydroxyethyl-, hydroxypropylmethyl-) cellulose derivative, linear polyacrylamide *etc.* into the leading electrolyte; (ii) the lowering of the electrokinetic potential by adding $0.05-0.2\%$ of nonionogenic detergents (polyvinylalcohol, Triton X-100, polyethyleneglycol *etc.*) into the leading electrolyte; (iii) the sign inversion of the electrokinetic potential upon adding a cationic detergent (1 mM cetyltrimethylammonium bromide) into the leading electrolyte.

Joule heating of the zones has a negative effect both on the boundary width [*cf.*, Eq. (17)] and on the qualitative steady-state characteristics of the zones. From a quantitative viewpoint, we can minimize the influence of heat on the boundary width by finding the optimum working electric current in the sense of the commentary to Eq. (17) in Section 2.3. From a qualitative viewpoint, we can recommend working at an electric current which is sufficiently low to ensure that the qualitative characteristics of the zones are not distorted by temperature effects; this procedure has been used by the authors [17] in the evaluation of the mobilities and of the pK_a's from isotachophoretic measurements.

5   Utilization of capillary isotachophoresis in analytical practice

5.1   Capillary isotachophoresis as an analytical tool

The advancement of an analytical method is strongly dependent on the rapid and efficient development of its theory, instrumentation and applications. Moreover, the popularity of a method depends first and foremost on its practical applications. The first papers dedicated to the practical use of capillary isotachophoresis were published at the end of the seventies. Since that time, several hundred papers covering the applications have appeared, and capillary isotachophoresis has ceased to be an esoteric proposition. Although it is not yet used as widely as the chromatographic methods, it has already found its place in many fields of applications. In practice, isotachophoresis is a method suitable, above all, for the quantitative analysis of samples of known composition. It is not very suitable for the identification of unknown components of a sample. In a qualitative analysis, it can be helpful by eliminating some of the substances suspected of being present in the sample. In many cases, it is necessary to check the individuality of the analyzed zone and to employ isotachophoresis in combination with another procedure. As an example may serve an analysis of urate in blood in which two aliquots of a sample were analyzed [76]. The first aliquot was analyzed directly; prior to analysis, the second one was incubated with the enzyme uricase, for which urate is the specific substrate. In the second aliquot the disappearance of the urate step confirmed the identity of the step with the analyzed substance and the individuality of its zone, *i.e.*, the absence of interfering substances in the zone in question.

With the help of contemporary instrumentation, capillary isotachophoresis with on-line detection can simultaneously analyze either cations or anions and quantitate several substances of one sample in one run. The actual isotachophoretic analysis is rather fast. Its time ranges from ca. 4 to 40 minutes, depending on the content of the major components. Therefore, isotachophoresis is especially suitable for urgent analyses *e.g.*, blood of critically ill patients. Data characteristic for currently performed isotachophoretic analyses with direct sample injection are summed up in Table 2. Liquid samples with sufficient conductivity can be analyzed directly. If the conductivity of the sample is low, the solution is easily overheated at the place of injection; then it is necessary to add the leading or the terminating electrolyte to the sample or to analyze a smaller volume of the sample. Solid

Table 2. Characteristic data for direct isotachophoretic analysis

Sample volume	$0.1 - 10\,\mu L$
Analysis time	$4 - 40\,min$
Analyzed concentrations	$0.1 - 100\,\mu M$
Reproducibility	$1 - 3\%$
Recovery	$98 - 102\%$
Major-minor component ratio	$100:1 - 1000:1$

and gaseous samples have also been analyzed by isotachophoresis. Before starting the analysis, the substances to be analyzed have to be dissolved in a suitable solvent.

5.2   Analysis of biological material

Body fluids are an exceptionally complex analytical material. They contain many groups of chemically very similar substances which, in current analytical procedures, react in a similar, or even the same, way. In order to analyze them, essentially only separation methods and extremely specific methods (*i.e.*, immunological and enzymatic methods) are suitable. When analyzing body fluids by isotachophoresis, attention has generally been concentrated on the analysis of blood plasma (or blood serum) and urine, less often have tissue homogenates and the cerebrospinal fluid been considered, and only very rarely saliva, semen, bile, aqueous humor and urinary calculi. Detailed technical information concerning the most important analyses of different types of substances are summarized in Addendum 1 (see page 336).

5.2.1   Carboxylic acids

Carboxylic acids, involved in the metabolism of amino acids and sugars, are important components of body fluids. In blood, they play a significant part in the acid-base balance and in its failures: In numerous pathological states the concentration of organic acids in blood increases enormously, and the resulting acidosis can lead to acidotic coma and even to death. Carboxylic acids are generally analyzed by enzymatic tests. Due to its speed and the possibility of analyzing several components in one run, isotachophoresis has a good chance of becoming a method of key importance for monitoring the clinical state of critically ill patients (Fig. 17). An increased level of some non-physiological acids appears in the blood and urine of patients suffering

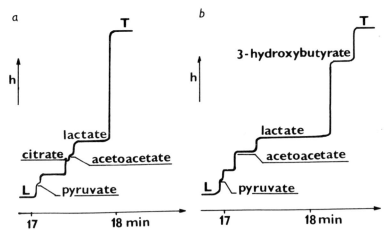

Figure 17. Analysis of carboxylic acids in human serum. (a) A healthy subject; (b) a patient with diabetes mellitus. From [78], with permission.

from an inborn error of metabolism of amino acids and sugars. In such cases, isotachophoresis can be used to obtain quantitative analyses of selected acids, *e.g.*, in load tests. Several exogenous substances are eliminated from the body in the form of carboxylic acids. A number of drugs used in human medicine contain a carboxylic acid as the main active component. Isotachophoresis enables one to follow the accumulation and the excretion of these acids from the body.

5.2.2   Amino acids and peptides

Amino acids belong to the group of substances in biological material which are analyzed very often. Owing to the wide use of well-established commercial analyzers of amino acids, isotachophoresis is not yet frequently used in this field. Moreover, the use of isotachophoresis is rather difficult owing to the relatively low concentrations of amino acids in blood and in urine and, from the viewpoint of the correct isotachophoretic migration, owing to the unfavourable pH region required for their ionization. By cationic analysis, we can, in practice, analyze only the basic amino acids. By anionic analysis, we can analyze the majority of amino acids, provided that sufficiently alkaline electrolytes are used. However, here the analyses are hampered by carbonate originating from the absorption of CO_2 from the air. Isotachophoresis cannot yet be used to analyze all amino acids occurring in proteins, as is necessary, for example, in protein sequencing.

The analysis of peptides in body fluids for clinical practice is promising but difficult, and still awaits some fundamental work. There are serious problems in the analysis of peptides, stemming from the low concentrations of the peptides and their chemical similarity. Therefore, the identification of individual peptides presents a very difficult problem. Isotachophoresis alone does not seem to be a sufficient means for their identification and analysis. It seems to be suitable only as one of the separation steps or, as a tool for a partial characterization of unidentified peptides. Therefore, the sample (serum, urine, ultrafiltrate) is first concentrated by ultrafiltration and fractionated by gel chromatography, *etc.* The individual fractions are then analyzed and characterized by isotachophoresis. Some of the steps of the isotachophoregram may be found characterisitic for the pathological state studied. The peptidic character of the zones can be checked by the amino acid analysis of its hydrolysate.

5.2.3   Purines, pyrimidines and organic bases

Among this group of substances, uric acid is most often analyzed in body fluids. This type of substances is also analyzed in order to detect and identify inborn disorders (Fig. 18).

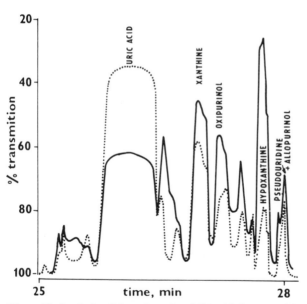

Figure 18. Analysis of the urine of a child with hypoxanthine guanine phosphoribosyltransferase deficiency during allopurinol therapy. (———) 254 nm, (······) 280 nm. From [112], with permission.

Among the exogenous substances, weak bases administered medicinally are the most often analyzed in body fluids.

5.2.4 Nucleotides and nucleosides

Owing to their large charge, nucleotides do not pass the cell membrane, and this is the reason why they are found exclusively inside the cells. Therefore, not body fluids but tissue extracts, from the liver and from the bone and heart muscles, are analyzed. The substances most often analyzed are ATP, ADP, AMP, cAMP, NADH, NAD^+, and IMP, together with phosphocreatine, glucoso-6-phosphate, phosphate, lactate, and pyruvate, by using UV detection and, sometimes, non-UV-absorbing spacers.

5.2.5 Proteins

The electromigration separation methods are widely used for the analysis of proteins. The separations are generally carried out in polyacrylamide gel or in agarose, and the zones of proteins are detected with the help of a suitable staining procedure. Capillary isotachophoresis offers on-line detection of proteins in cases where the UV detector alone is used (Fig. 19). In order to

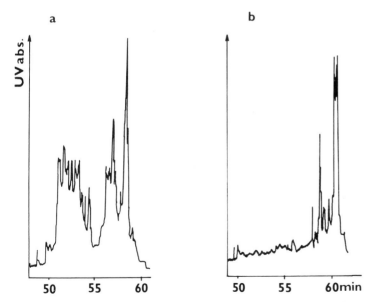

Figure 19. Cationic isotachophoresis of cerebrospinal fluid. (a) Patient with multiple sclerosis; (b) a healthy man. From [127], with permission.

distinguish the zones of proteins, it was necessary to add spacers to the sample before analysis (see Section 4.3.1). The area of the UV-absorbing peak is directly proportional to the content of protein, as has already been shown for albumin by comparing the results of isotachophoresis with those obtained by radial diffusion and with the declared content in standard human plasma [69]. In the isotachophoregrams of proteins we may often find small sharp peaks, the occurrence of which is badly reproducible [77]. These peaks are thought to belong to the proteins denatured during the course of the isotachophoretic separation.

5.2.6   Inorganic ions

In body fluids the anions of sulfate and phosphate and the cations of sodium, calcium, aluminum, iron, zinc, copper and lead are the inorganic ions most frequently analyzed.

5.3   Isotachophoresis in production control and product testing

When analyzing industrial samples and their intermediates by isotachophoresis, one usually finds that the sample contains only a small number of components, whose concentrations are generally sufficient for a direct isotachophoretic analysis. Both the quality of final products and crude pro-

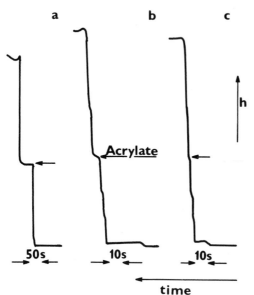

Figure 20. Analysis of acrylic acid in acrylamide. (a) Acrylic acid; (b) 2× recrystallized acrylamide; (c) LKB UltroGrade acrylamide. From [138], with permission.

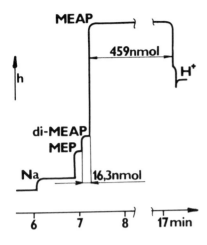

Figure 21. Cationic analysis of the artificial sweetener Aspartam (methylester of aspartylphenylalanine). MEAP, Aspartam; di-MEAP, dimethylester of aspartyl-phenylalanine; MEP, methylester of phenylalanine. From [141], with permission.

ducts, together with intermediates, can be controlled and tested (Figs. 20 and 21). In pharmacy, drugs and their intermediate products may be analyzed, especially vitamins, antibiotics, peptide drugs, alkaloids *etc*. In food production, isotachophoresis is especially useful for the analysis of additives, preservatives and natural substances (most frequently organic acids) *etc.*, including toxic substances. In agriculture, silage and feedstuffs are analyzed to test their quality. Detailed information on the analysis of particular samples is shown in Addendum 2 (see page 346).

5.4   Isotachophoresis in environmental analysis

In environmental analysis, isotachophoresis is used for the analysis of air (Fig. 22), water, and soil. In the majority of cases, the substances in question must be concentrated before the analysis is made. For information on the details of individual analyses, see Addendum 3 (page 351).

5.5   Isotachophoresis in research

Isotachophoresis can also be used as a unique analytical tool in experiments and studies of purely scientific significance and research character. In enzymology, isotachophoresis can be used to measure enzyme activity, by quantitating the concentrations of ionogenic substrates or products. It has been

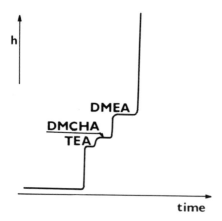

Figure 22. Analysis of a sample taken at polymerization of polyurethane foam. TEA, triethylamine; DMCHA, dimethylcyclohexylamine; DMEA, 2-dimethylaminoethanol. From [194], with permission.

used to measure the activity of prolidase and prolinase in the serum of patients with iminopeptiduria [197], and to determine the activity of hexokinase and 6-phosphofructokinase [198], adenylate kinase [199] and urokinase [200]. Further, it has been used to study the enzymatic transfer of sulfate [201], glucuronidation [202, 203], metabolism of ascorbic acid [204] and methionine [205], and the enzymatic reactions depending on nucleotides [206]. Isotachophoresis has also been employed to study reactions of glutathione-S-reductase [207] and to follow the inactivation of formate dehydrogenase [208].

In protein chemistry, isotachophoresis has been used to distinguish and characterize the subclasses of IgG [209], to demonstrate the immunocomplex of bovine serum albumin and its antibodies [210], to analyze sialic acid in glycoproteins [211], to follow the substitution of dog albumin [212], to study the bonds of dodecyl sulfate (Fig. 23) and indomethacine [213, 214], bilirubin and biliverdin [215], rifamycine [216], and 8-anilinonaphthalene sulfonic acids [217] on serum albumin. Further, isotachophoresis has been employed to study the influence of lyophilization on the composition of proteins in control sera [218], and to analyze the virus-membrane glycoproteins [219] and the conjugates of enzyme-immunoglobulin used in the enzyme immunoassays [220]. In peptide chemistry, isotachophoresis has been used to analyze the low-molecular substances in commercial peptides [221], the oxidized and reduced forms of glutathione [222], lysylalanine [223], the C-terminal pentapeptide of bombinine [224, 225], kinine, angiotensine [226], insulin [227], and to follow the deiodination of iodotyrosine and diiodotyrosine during peptide hydrolysis [228].

In nucleotide chemistry, isotachophoresis has been used for the analysis of nucleotides released by microorganisms after a high-voltage pulse and ultra-

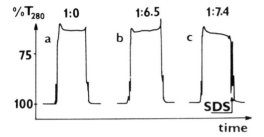

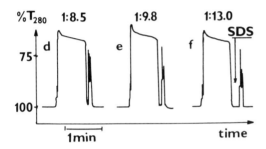

Figure 23. Analysis of mixtures containing various molar ratios of bovine serum albumin and sodium dodecylsulfate (SDS). From [214], with permission.

sonic treatment [229] and for the analysis of adenine nucleotides [230], as well as to control the synthesis of nucleotides [231]. Isotachophoresis has also been used for the analysis of venom from spiders and snakes [232] and stinging insects [233], of plant alkaloids [234–236], pollen allergens [237], and royal jelly [238], and for the analysis of the polar lobe of the first cleavage of *Nassarius reticulatus* embryos [239].

Addendum 1. Technical data of isotachophoretic analyses of biological material

Substance	Sample	Pretreatment	Leading electrolyte[a] (Sign of leading ion)	Terminating electrolyte	Comments	References
Organic acids						
Lactate, pyruvate, acetoacetate, 3-hydroxy-butyrate	Serum	None	10 mM HCl, β-alanine, pH 3.3, (−)	10 mM propionic acid	Monitoring of metabolic acidoses	[78]
Lactate, phosphate, acetate, hippurate	Uremic serum before and after hemodialysis	None	10 mM HCl, β-alanine, pH 3.5, (−)	Caproate		[79]
Lactate	Plasma of healthy men	Blood taken into EDTA + KF solution	10 mM HCl, 20 mM EACA, pH 4.4, (−)	5 mM caproic acid	Good correlation with the enzymatic test with lactate dehydrogenase	[80]
Oxalate	Urine	+ HCl, + Ca++, centrifugation and dissolution of the precipitate	10 mM HCl, β-alanine, pH 3.7, (−)	10 mM caproic acid	Any contact of the sample with iron (plunger and needle of microsyringe) should be avoided	[81]
Oxalate, citrate	Urine	Addition of ZnCl₂ up to 10 mM concentration	5 mM HCl, 1 mM NaCl, pH 2.2, (−)	20 mM acetic acid	Specificity of the analysis confirmed by the disappearance of the step of oxalate and citrate after treatment with citrate lyase and oxalate decarboxylase; good correlation of citrate determination	[82, 83]

Analyte	Sample	Sample preparation	Leading electrolyte	Terminating electrolyte	Remarks	Ref.
Oxalate, phosphate	Urinary stones	Dissolution of pulverized calculus in 1 M HCl	10 mM HCl, β-alanine, pH 3.7, (−)	10 mM caproic acid		[84]
Ascorbate	Urine, leukocytes	Ultrasonification or lyophilization of cells	10 mM HCl, β-alanine, pH 3.7 (−)	10 mM caproic acid	Purity of the ascorbate zone and its identity in the UV-isotachophoregram verified by the disappearance of its step after ascorbate oxidase treatment	[85]
Citrate, lactate, pyruvate, malate, succinate, ascorbate	Human seminal plasma	None	7 mM HCl, glycylglycine, pH 2.9, (−)	5 mM caproic acid	For lactate and citrate determination good correlation with enzymatic test and HPLC	[86]
Perhydro-1,4-thiazepine-3,5-dicarboxylic acid	Urine of a patient with cystathioninuria	None	10 mM HCl, β-alanine, pH 3.1, (−)	10 mM caproic acid	Not detected in urine of healthy subjects	[87]
Methylmalonic acid	Urine of a patient with methylmalonic aciduria	None	10 mM HCl, β-alanine, pH 3.2, (−)	10 mM glutamic acid	Not detectable in samples from healthy subjects	[88]
Lactate, acetate, formate, phosphate	Saliva, dental plaque	None	2.5 mM HCl, GABA, pH 3.9, (−)	2.5 mM caproic acid, Tris, pH 5.5		[89]
Taurochendeoxycholate, taurocholate, glycocholate, glycochendeoxycholate	Human bile	None	10 mM HCl, 20 mM hydroxylamine in 95% methanol, (−)	5 mM HEPES in 95% methanol		[64]

Addendum 1. (continued)

Substance	Sample	Pretreatment	Leading electrolyte[a] (Sign of leading ion)	Terminating electrolyte	Comments	References
Lactate, phosphate, diphosphoglycerate, ATP	Erythrocytes from blood conserves	Sedimentation, rinsing, lysis with distilled water	10 mM HCl, β-alanine, pH 4.2, (−)	10 mM caproic acid	Aging test of blood conserves	[90]
Valproate	Serum	None	5 mM HCl, EACA, pH 5.0, (−)	5 mM MES	Drug for the primary epilepsy treatment; good correlation of the results with GC	[91]
Trifluoroacetate	Serum, urine	None	10 mM HCl, β-alanine, pH 3.6−3.9, (−)	10 mM caproic acid	Metabolite of the inhalation anesthetic halothane	[92]
Acetate	Plasma of persons on hemodialysis	None	5 mM HCl, β-alanine, pH 3.2, (−)	Caproic acid	Good correlation of the results with the enzymatic test	[93]
Formate	Plasma	None	5 mM HCl, (−)	10 mM acetic acid	In subjects intoxicated with methanol, plasma levels up to 17 mM	[94]
Glycolate	Plasma	None	5 mM HCl, (−)	10 mM acetic acid	On glycol intoxications plasma levels up to 29 mM	[95]
Thiodiacetate	Urine	None	10 mM HCl, β-alanine, pH in separation capillary 3.4; in analytical	10 mM acetic acid	Found in urine of persons exposed to vapors of cancerogenous vinyl chloride	[96]

Mandelate, phenylglyoxalate, methylhippurate, hippurate	Urine	Acidification, saturation with NaCl, extraction with ethyl acetate or diethyl ether	5 mM HCl, β-alanine, pH 3.75, (−)	5 mM caproic acid	Found in urine of persons exposed to vapors of styrene, toluene, xylene	[97]
Amino acids and peptides						
γ-Aminobutyrate	Rat brain homogenate	Ionex chromatography	10 mM potassium acetate, acetic acid, pH 4.5, (+)	10 mM carnitine-HCl	Results comparable with those from an amino acid analyzer but systematically higher	[98]
Carnitine	Human serum	Incubation in alkaline medium, ionex chromatography	10 mM potassium acetate, acetic acid, pH 5.0, (+)	20 mM HCl	Determination of free carnitine and carnitine with short acyl; physiological range in healthy men: 42–62 μM	[99]
Cystathionine	Urine of patients with cystathioninuria	Acid hydrolysis, ionex chromatography	10 mM HCl, AMMEDIOL, pH 8.9, (−)	10 mM GABA, Ba(OH)$_2$, pH 10.9	Results comparable with those from an amino acid analyzer but systematically higher	[100]
Phenylalanine	Phenylketonuric serum	Deproteinization	5 mM HCl, 160 mM Tris, pH 9.7, (−)	5 mM phenol, Ba(OH)$_2$, pH 10	In healthy subjects the concentration is below detection limit	[101]

Addendum 1. (continued)

Substance	Sample	Pretreatment	Leading electrolyte[a] (Sign of leading ion)	Terminating electrolyte	Comments	References
Isovalerylglycine	Urine	None	10 mM HCl, 1 mM $CuCl_2$, β-alanine, pH 3.1, (−)	10 mM caproic acid	Pathological metabolite in isovaleric acidemia, not found in healthy subjects	[102]
Taurine	Homogenates from various rat tissues	Ionex chromatography	10 mM HCl, AMMEDIOL, pH 6.5, (−)	10 mM GABA, $Ba(OH)_2$, pH 10.9	Results comparable with those from an amino acid analyzer but systematically higher	[103]
S-Carboxymethyl-cysteine, S-2-methyl-2-carboxy-methyl-cysteine, S-1,2-dicarboxy-cysteine	Human urine	Ionex chromatography	10 mM HCl, β-alanine, pH 3.1, (−)	10 mM caproic acid		[104]
Glutathione, glutathione disulfide	Homogenates from various rat tissues	Ionex chromatography	10 mM HCl, β-alanine, pH 3.1 – 4.0, (−)	10 mM caproic acid	Purity of zones checked by analysis after treatment with N-ethylmaleimide and dithiothreitol or glutathione reductase	[105]
Iminopeptides	Urine	Alkalization, double ionex chromatography	10 mM HCl, AMMEDIOL, pH 7.5, (−)	10 mM GABA, $Ba(OH)_2$, pH 10.9	Found in the cases of prolidase deficiency; five isotachophoretic zones containing twelve dipeptides with C-terminal proline	[106]
Unidentified peptides	Serum, urine, ultrafiltrate from hemodialysis	Concentration, gel chromatography	10 mM HCl, β-alanine, pH 3.1 – 4.0, (−)	10 mM caproic acid	Steps found in the isotachophoregram, characteristic for hemolytic uremic syndrom, uremia, rheumatoid arthritis	[107 – 110]

	Sample	Sample preparation	Leading electrolyte	Terminating electrolyte	Remarks	Reference
Methotrexate	Plasma	Precipitation with Ag$^+$, dissolution of precipitate	8 mM HCl, Tris, pH 8.4, (−)	8 mM histidine, Tris, pH 9.5	Cystostatic drug	[111]
Purines, pyrimidines and organic bases						
Uric acid	Serum	None	10 mM HCl, EACA, pH 5.0, (−)	5 mM MES, Tris, pH 6.5	Good correlation of the results with the enzymatic test; purity of the urate zone checked by analysis after the uricase treatment	[76]
Uric acid, xanthine and cysteine	Urinary calculi	Dissolution of pulverized calculus in 1 M NaOH	5 mM HCl, Tris, pH 7.7, (−)	10 mM phenol, Ba(OH)$_2$, pH 9.4		[84]
Uric acid, orotic acid, hippuric acid, xanthine, hypoxanthine, allopurinol, oxypurinol, guanosine, adenine, orotidine, pseudoxanthine	Urine, serum	None	5 mM HCl, AMMEDIOL, pH 8.6, (−) or 2.5 mM HCl, Tris, pH 7.9, (−)	20 mM β-alanine, Ba(OH)$_2$, pH 10.5	In inborn deficiencies of adenine phosphoribosyltransferase, hypoxanthine guanine phosphoribosyltransferase, xanthine oxidase, purine nucleoside phosphorylase, adenosine deaminase, orotate phosphoribosyltransferase, orotidinphosphate decarboxylase; purity check of zones of hypoxanthine, xanthine, allopurinol, uric acid by the analysis of the sample after its treatment with an appropriate enzyme	[66, 112]
Hypoxanthine	Serum	Deproteinization, ionex chromatography	5 mM HCl, Tris, pH 8.4, (−)	40 mM glycine, Ba(OH)$_2$, pH 9.7	Marker of tissue hypoxia; average value in healthy subjects: 0.91 μM, in umbilical blood of newborns 3 – 75 μM; 5-fluorouracil used as internal standard	[113]

Addendum 1. (continued)

Substance	Sample	Pretreatment	Leading electrolyte[a] (Sign of leading ion)	Terminating electrolyte	Comments	References
Adriamycine, adriamycinol	Plasma	Extraction with butanol	10 mM sodium acetate, acetic acid, 60% methanol, pH 6.0, (+)	10 mM β-alanine in 60% methanol	Cystostatic drug and its main metabolite	[114]
Trimecaine	Plasma	Deproteinization, alkalization, extraction with CHCl$_3$	10 mM potassium acetate, acetic acid, pH 4.75, (+)	50 mM β-alanine	Local anesthetic; results more precise than by GC	[115]
Quinine	Urine	Extraction with isopropyl-alcohol – CH$_2$Cl$_2$	10 mM KOH, MES, pH 6.0, (+)	5 mM creatinine, MES, pH 5.5		[116]
Theophylline	Serum	Ultrafiltration	7.5 mM MES, AMMEDIOL, pH 8.9 or 5 mM HCl Tris, pH 8.4, (–)	5 mM α-alanine or 10 mM glycine, Ba(OH)$_2$, pH 9.0	Quantitation by UV-absorbance of the peak between the spacers serine and bicine; results comparable with those obtained by HPLC	[117, 118]

Choline	Semen	Deproteinization, ionex chromatography	10 mM potassium acetate, acetic acid, pH 4.0, (+)	10 mM carnitine-HCl	Results comparable with the enzymatic test, but systematically higher	[119]
Nucleotides and nucleosides						
ATP, ADP, AMP, cAMP, NAD$^+$, phosphocreatine, phosphate	Frog muscle, liver	EDTA-methanol extraction, freeze-drying	5 mM HCl, 18 mM β-alanine, (−)	5 mM caproic acid	Results comparable with the enzymatic test (ATP) and classical procedure (phosphocreatine)	[71, 120]
ATP, ADP, AMP, cAMP, IMP, NADH, NAD$^+$, phosphocreatine, pyruvate, glucoso-6-phosphate	Bone muscle and heart muscle from pig, frog, dog, hamster	EDTA-methanol extraction	7 mM HCl, 13 mM β-alanine, pH 3.9, (−)	5 mM caproic acid	Results comparable with the data from literature	[121]
ATP, ADP, AMP	Human bone muscle	EDTA-methanol extraction	5 mM HCl, β-alanine, pH 3.9, (−)	5 mM sodium caproate	Decreased level in Duchenne muscular dystrophy	[122]
ATP, ADP, AMP, NADH, NAD$^+$, glucoso-6-phosphate, phosphocreatine, phosphate, lactate	Human bone muscle	Ethanol extraction	10 mM HCl, 20 mM β-alanine, pH 3.75, (−)	10 mM caproic acid	Results of ATP, lactate and phosphocreatine determination comparable with the enzymatic tests	[123]

Addendum 1. (continued)

Substance	Sample	Pretreatment	Leading electrolyte[a] (Sign of leading ion)	Terminating electrolyte	Comments	References
ATP, ADP	Various rat tissues	Perchloric acid extraction	5 mM HCl, β-alanine, pH 3.9, (−)	5 mM caproic acid	UV detection and non-UV-absorbing spacers used	[124]
IMP, phosphocreatine, lactate	Pig muscle	EDTA-methanol extraction	5 mM HCl, β-alanine, pH 3.9, (−)	5 mM caproic acid, Tris, pH 5.0	Diagnostic test for malignant hyperthermia susceptibility	[125]
5-Fluorouracil, 5-fluorouridine	Plasma, serum	Deproteinization, ionex chromatography	5 mM HCl, Tris, pH 8.4, (−)	40 mM glycine, Ba(OH)$_2$, pH 9.4	Cytostatic drug and its metabolite	[67]
Proteins						
Serum proteins, CSF proteins	Serum, cerebrospinal fluid	Recommended microdialysis prior to isotachophoresis, to remove the excess of salts	5 mM MES, AMME-DIOL, pH 8.4–9.1, (−)	5 mM EACA, Ba(OH)$_2$, pH 10.8	UV detection und non-UV-absorbing spacers used; characteristic changes in multiple sclerosis, subarachnoid hemorrhage, neurinoma, meningitis, meningoencephalitis, acute leucemia	[69, 77, 126–133]
Serum lipoproteins	Serum	Prestaining with Sudan Black B	5 mM HCl, histidine, pH 6.5, (−)	10 mM β-alanine, 10 mM histidine, Ba(OH)$_2$, pH 9	Photometric detection at 570 nm	[134]

Inorganic ions

	Sample	Pretreatment	Leading electrolyte	Terminating electrolyte	Remarks	Ref.
Sulfate	Plasma, urine	Acidification of urine; deproteinization of plasma	5 mM HCl, 1 mM NaCl, pH 2.2, (−)	5 mM propionic acid		[135]
Pb, Cu, Zn, Fe, Al, Ca	Serum	Deproteinization, ionex chromatography	20 mM KOH, α-hydroxy-isobutyric acid, acetic acid, pH 4.1, (+)	5 mM acetic acid		[136]
Na	Serum	None	10 mM potassium citrate, pH 5.5, (+)	10 mM creatinine-HCl pH 7.0	The procedure proposed as a candidate reference method	[137]
Miscellaneous						
Unidentified compounds	Uremic serum	None	10 mM HCl, histidine, pH 6.0, (−)	HEPES	"HL-ratio" (the ratio of the sums of the step lengths of high- and low-molecular compounds) used for the evaluation of the clinical state	[79]

a) For additives added to leading electrolytes, see Section 4.5.

Addendum 2. Technical data of isotachophoretic analyses of technological products and intermediates

Substance	Sample	Leading electrolyte[a] (Sign of leading ion)	Terminating electrolyte	References
Organic acids				
Ascorbic acid	Vitamin preparations	5 mM HCl, β-alanine, pH 3.8, (−)	5 mM caproic acid	[139]
Nicotinic acid, riboflavin-5-phosphate	Vitamin preparations	10 mM HCl, AMME-DIOL, pH 8.95, (−)	20 mM β-alanine, Ba(OH)$_2$, pH 10.0	[139]
Arabonic acid	Solutions after alkaline oxidation of glucose; intermediate in riboflavine production	10 mM HCl, β-alanine, pH 3.3, (−)	10 mM propionic acid	[140]
Phosphonoacetate	Antiherpetic drug	10 mM HCl, 19 mM urotropin, 3 mM CaCl$_2$, (−)	15 mM glutamic acid	[141]
Valproate	Antiepileptic drug	2.5 mM HCl, histidine, pH 5.5, (−)	2.5 mM MES, Tris, pH 7.2	[142]
Sorbic, propionic, benzoic acid, esters of *p*-benzoic acid	Various foodstuffs	10 mM HCl, AMME-DIOL, pH 9.6, (−)	20 mM β-alanine, Ba(OH)$_2$, pH 10.0	[143, 144]
Sweeteners cyclamate, saccharine	Beverages, tinned foodstuffs	7 mM HCl, glycyl-glycine, pH 2.9, (−)	5 mM caproic acid	[145]
Additives citrate, ascorbate, glucono-δ-lactone, with glutamate, mono-, di- and triphosphate	Meat products	7 mM HCl, glycylglycin, pH 2.9, (−)	5 mM caproic acid	[146]
Ascorbic acid	Citrus concentrates	5 mM HCl, β-alanine, pH 3.8, (−)	5 mM caproic acid	[147]
Lactic, citric, acetic, phosphoric acid	Sauerkraut brine	7 mM HCl, 8 mM glycylglycine, pH 2.9, (−)	5 mM benzoic acid	[148]

Analytes	Sample	Leading electrolyte	Terminating electrolyte	Ref.
Quinic, formic, citric, phosphoric, malic, glycolic, lactic, acetic acid	Coffee	5 mM HCl, β-alanine, pH 3.8, (−)	5 mM caproic acid	[149]
Acetic, succinic, gluconic, lactic, malic, malonic, phosphoric, sulfuric acid	Wine	10 mM HCl, β-alanine, pH 2.9, (−)	5 mM sodium propionate	[150]
Tartaric, citric, malic, gluconic, lactic, succinic, phosphoric acid	Various foodstuffs	7 mM HCl, glycylglycine, pH 2.9, (−)	5 mM caproic acid	[151]
2-Pyrrolidone-5-carboxylic acid	Tomatoes	10 mM HCl, 20 mM histidine, pH 5.7, (−)	10 mM glutamic acid	[152]
Lactic, citric acid	Lactic acid beverages	10 mM HCl, 20 mM histidine, pH 6.2, (−)	10 mM caproic acid	[153]
Ascorbic, formic, citric, isocitric, lactic acid, sweetener cyclamate	Orange juice	5 mM HCl, β-alanine, pH 4.0, (−)	5 mM caproic acid	[154]
Succinic acid	Fish extracts	10 mM HCl, β-alanine, pH 3.0, (−)	10 mM ascorbic acid	[155]
EDTA	Mayonnaise, margarine	10 mM HCl, β-alanine, pH 3.3, (−)	10 mM caproic acid	[156]
Sinalbin, sinigrin	Mustard seeds	7 mM HCl, glycylglycine, pH 2.9, (−)	5 mM caproic acid	[157]
Lactate, acetate, butyrate	Silage extracts	12 mM HCl, 20 mM urotropine, pH 4.9, (−)	10 mM sodium hydrogen carbonate	[158]
Citric acid	Fermented n-alkanes	10 mM HCl, 2 mM Ca^{2+}, histidine, pH 6.0, (−)	10 mM MES	[159]

Addendum 2. (continued)

Substance	Sample	Leading electrolyte[a] (Sign of leading ion)	Terminating electrolyte	References
Chlorocarboxylic acids	Chlorinated phenol	10 mM HCl, 20 mM histidine, pH 6.1, (−)	10 mM glutamic acid	[160]
Dibutylphosphate, monobutyl-phosphate, phosphate	Aqueous extract from tributyl phosphate	10 mM HCl, histidine, pH 6.0, (−)	10 mM MES	[161]
Amino acids, peptides				
7-Aminodesacetoxycephalosporanic acid, cephalosporin G, phenylacetic acid	Control of the enzymatic cleavage of cephalosporin G	10 (100) mM HCl, 20 (200) mM 2,6-lutidine, pH 6.85, in concentration cascade, (−)	100 mM sodium 5,5′-diethylbar-biturate	[162]
Saralasine	Drug	6 mM KOH, cacodylic acid, pH 6.2, (+)	10 mM creatinine, HCl, pH 5.9	[163]
Gonadoreline	Drug	6 mM KOH, MES, pH 6.2, (+)	10 mM EACA	[163]
Protireline	Drug	6 mM KOH, acetic acid, pH 5.0, (+)	10 mM β-alanine	[163]
S-Carboxymethylcysteine, cysteinesulfonic acid	Mucolytic drug	10 mM HCl, β-alanine, pH 3.3, (−)	10 mM caproic acid	[164]
Glutamate, GMP, IMP	Various foodstuffs	10 mM HCl, histidine, pH 6.0, (−)	10 mM MES, Tris, pH 6.0	[165]
Aspartate, glutamate, theanin	Green tea	10 mM HCl, β-alanine, pH 3.9, (−)	10 mM caproic acid	[166]
Hydroxyproline	Sweet pepper fruit	10 mM HCl, 20 mM AMMEDIOL, pH 9.0, (−)	10 mM β-alanine, Ba(OH)$_2$, pH 10.0	[167]

Lysine	Fermentation broth	10 mM NaOH, 1 mM EDTA, MES, pH 6.2, (+)	5 mM tetrabutylammonium perchlorate	[168]
Aspartylphenylalanine methyl-ester	Artificial sweetener	50 mM ammonium acetate, 50 mM acetic acid, (+)	50 mM acetic acid	[141]
Organic bases				
Thiamine, pyridoxol, pyridoxal, pyridoxamine	Vitamin preparations	20 mM potassium acetate, acetic acid, pH 4.95, (+)	20 mM GABA, acetic acid, pH 4.7	[139]
Nicotinamide	Vitamin preparations	20 mM potassium acetate, acetic acid, pH 4.95, (+)	10 mM β-alanine, HCl, pH 1.8	[139]
Tobramycine, spectinomycine, clindamycine, lincomycine	Antibiotics	20 mM potassium acetate, acetic acid, pH 4.95, (+)	20 mM GABA or β-alanine or glycyl-glycine, acetic acid, pH 4.7	[169]
Ephedrine, norephedrine, norpseudoephedrine, phenylephrine, carbinoxamine, methoxymethylmorphine, yohimbine	Drugs	20 mM potassium acetate, acetic acid, pH 4.95, (+)	20 mM GABA, acetic acid, pH 4.7	[170]
Ephedrine, procaine	Drugs	2.8 mM ammonium acetate, acetic acid, pH 4.9, (+)	5 mM acetic acid	[171]
Quinine	Drugs, beverages	10 mM KOH, MES, pH 6.0, (+)	5 mM creatinine, MES, pH 5.5	[116]
Codeine, phenyltoloxamine	Drugs	10 mM potassium acetate, pH 5.5 in 70% ethanol, (+)	10 mM β-alanine, acetic acid, pH 4.95, 70% ethanol	[172]

Addendum 2. (continued)

Substance	Sample	Leading electrolyte[a] (Sign of leading ion)	Terminating electrolyte	References
Procaine, lidocaine, tetracaine	Local anesthetics	20 mM potassium acetate, acetic acid, pH 4.95, (+)	20 mM GABA, acetic acid, pH 4.7	[173]
Preservative thiabendazol	Peel of citrus fruits	20 mM potassium acetate, acetic acid, pH 4.9, (+)	20 mM β-alanine, HCl, pH 1.8	[174]
Histamine	Stored fish	5 mM Ba(OH)$_2$, 15 mM valine, pH 9.9, (+)	20 mM Tris, 5 mM HCl, pH 8.3	[175]
Tetrodotoxin	Puffer fish	5 mM potassium acetate, acetic acid, pH 6.0 in 50% dioxane, (+)	10 mM β-alanine, acetic acid, pH 4.95	[176]
Amprolium	Poultry feedstuff	5 mM KOH, butyric acid, pH 4.85, (+)	5 mM acetic acid	[177]
Inorganic ions				
Antioxidans sulfite, resulting sulfate	Drugs	10 mM HCl, 10 mM histidine, pH 4.0, (−)	10 mM caproic acid	[178]
Cyanide	Fruit, apricot kernel	10 mM HCl, AMME-DIOL, pH 7.5, (−)	10 mM β-alanine, Ba(OH)$_2$, pH 10.5	[179]
Nickel hypophosphite, nitrate	Chemical nickel plating bath	10 mM HCl, β-alanine, pH 4.0, (−)	10 mM glutamic acid	[180]
Chloride, sulfate	Ball-point pen ink	5 mM Cd(NO$_3$)$_2$ in 20% ethanol or acetone, (−)	5 mM caproic acid	[181]
Phosphate, sulfate, fluoride	Crude phosphoric acid	10 mM HCl, histidine, pH 5.7, (−)	10 mM MES	[182]

Substance	Sample	Pretreatment	Leading electrolyte (Sign of leading ion)	Terminating electrolyte	References
Sulfur oxo acids	Sodium sulfite		5 mM HCl, 10 mM histidine in 50% acetone, (−)	10 mM sodium acetate	[183]
PO_4^{3-}, $P_2O_7^{4-}$	Artificial fertilizers		5 mM HCl, 10 mM histidine, pH 6.0, (−)	10 mM glutamic acid	[189]
NO_3^-, PO_4^{3-}, SO_4^{2-}	Artificial fertilizers		5 mM HCl, glycine, pH 2.8, 5 mM $CaCl_2$, (−)	Tartaric acid	[190]

a) For the additives added to the leading electrolytes see Section 4.5.

Addendum 3. Technical data of isotachophoretic environmental analysis

Substance	Sample	Pretreatment	Leading electrolyte[a) (Sign of leading ion)	Terminating electrolyte	References
Herbicide asulam	Soil	Extraction, concentration	10 mM HCl, β-alanine, pH 3.6, (−)	Caproic acid	[191]
Herbicide diquat	Soil	Boiling with H_2SO_4, extraction	10 mM KOH, citric acid, pH 6.0, (+)	5 mM Tris, acetic acid, pH 5.8	[192]
Herbicide paraquat	Soil	Boiling with H_2SO_4, extraction	10 mM KOH, diiodotyrosine, pH 7.4, (+)	5 mM Tris, acetic acid, pH 7.0	[192]
Phenol	Industrial waste water	None	10 mM HCl, AMMEDIOL, pH 8.8, (−)	10 mM EACA, Ba(OH)₂, pH 10.9	[193]
Triethylamine, 2-dimethylethanol	Air from polyurethane foam production	Trapped by bubbling of a sample through 20 mM HCl	5 mM Ba(OH)₂, β-alanine, pH 9.6, (+)	20 mM Tris	[194]
Butylamine	Air	Trapped by bubbling of a sample through 20 mM HCl	10 mM KOH, valine, pH 8.8, (+)	20 mM Tris, 5 mM HCl, pH 8.4	[195]

Addendum 3. (continued)

Substance	Sample	Pretreatment	Leading electrolyte[a] (Sign of leading ion)	Terminating electrolyte	References
Cl^-, F^-, SO_4^{2-}, PO_4^{3-}, NO_3^-, NO_2^-	Surface water	None	1 mM HCl, (−)	1 mM citric acid	[196]
Cl^-, SO_4^{2-}, NO_3^-	Well and surface water	None	5 mM Ca(OH)$_2$, (−)	5 mM formic acid	[184]
Na^+, K^+, Ca^{2+}, Mg^{2+}	Well and surface water	None	2 mM N-oxide of nitrilotrismethylene phosphonionic acid, pH 2.4, (+)	4 mM creatinine	[184]
Fe, Cu, Ni, Cd, Co, Zn, Pb	River water	Ionex chromatography	20 mM KOH, α-hydroxyisobutyric acid, acetic acid pH 4.1, (+)	5 mM acetic acid	[137]
PO_4^{3-}	Sea water	Coprecipitation by Mg(OH)$_2$, ionex chromatography	10 mM HCl, histidine, pH 4.0, (−)	10 mM caproic acid	[185]
F^-	Sea water	Coprecipitation by Mg(OH)$_2$, ionex chromatography	10 mM histidine-HCl, (−)	10 mM caproic acid	[186]
Mg^{2+}, Ca^{2+}, as EDTA complexes	Sea water	Ionex chromatography, elution with EDTA	10 mM HCl, Tris, pH 8.5, (−)	10 mM caproic acid	[187]
Cl^-, SO_4^{2-}	Spring water	None	6 mM Cd(NO$_3$)$_2$, (−)	10 mM citric or tartaric acid	[188]

a) For additives added to the leading electrolytes see Section 4.5.

6 References

[1] Everaerts, F. M., Beckers, J. L., Verheggen, Th. P. E. M., *Isotachophoresis, Theory, Instrumentation and Applications*, Elsevier, Amsterdam, Oxford and New York 1976.

[2] Boček, P., Deml, M., Gebauer, P., Dolník, V., *Analytical Capillary Isotachophoresis*, VCH Verlagsgesellschaft, Weinheim 1987.

[3] *Acta Isotachophoretica, Literature Reference List 1967–1980*, LKB, Bromma 1981.

[4] Boček, P., Gebauer, P., Dolník, V., Foret, F., *J. Chromatogr.* 1985, *334*, 157–195.

[5] Kohlrausch, F., *Ann. Phys. Chem., N. F.* 1897, *62*, 209–239.

[6] Bier, M., Palusinski, O. A., Mosher, R. A., Saville, D. A., *Science* 1983, *219*, 1281–1287.

[7] Mosher, R. A., Thormann, W., Bier, M., *J. Chromatogr.* 1985, *320*, 23–32.

[8] Fidler, Z., Fidler, V., Vacík, J., *J. Chromatogr.* 1985, *320*, 175–183.

[9] Shimao, K., *Electrophoresis* 1986, *7*, 121–128.

[10] Thormann, W., Mosher, R. A., *Trans. SCS* 1984, *1*, 83–96.

[11] Beckers, J. L., Everaerts, F. M., *J. Chromatogr.* 1972, *68*, 207–230.

[12] Gebauer, P., Boček, P., *J. Chromatogr.* 1983, *267*, 49–65.

[13] Boček, P., Gebauer, P., *Electrophoresis* 1984, *5*, 338–342.

[14] Boček, P., Gebauer, P., Deml, M., *J. Chromatogr.* 1981, *217*, 209–224.

[15] Boček, P., Gebauer, P., Deml, M., *J. Chromatogr.* 1981, *219*, 21–28.

[16] Gebauer, P., Boček, P., *J. Chromatogr.* 1985, *320*, 49–65.

[17] Hirokawa, T., Kiso, Y., *J. Chromatogr.* 1982, *252*, 33–48.

[18] Hirokawa, T., Nishino, M., Kiso, Y., *J. Chromatogr.* 1982, *252*, 49–65.

[19] Hirokawa, T., Kobayashi, S., Kiso, Y., *J. Chromatogr.* 1985, *318*, 195–210.

[20] Hirokawa, T., Kiso, Y., *J. Chromatogr.* 1983, *257*, 197–210.

[21] Hirokawa, T., Takemi, H., Kiso, Y., Takiyama, R., Morio, M., Fujii, K., Kikuchi, H., *J. Chromatogr.* 1984, *305*, 429–437.

[22] Hirokawa, T., Nishino, M., Aoki, N., Kiso, Y., Sawamoto, Y., Yagi, T., Akiyama, J., *J. Chromatogr.* 1983, *271*, D 1–D 106.

[23] Reijenga, J. C., Verheggen, Th. P. E. M., Everaerts, F. M., *J. Chromatogr.* 1985, *328*, 353–356.

[24] Kenndler, E., *Anal. Chim. Acta* 1985, *173*, 239–251.

[25] Akiyama, J., Mizuno, T., *J. Chromatogr.* 1976, *119*, 605–608.

[26] Verheggen, Th. P. E. M., Everaerts, F. M., *J. Chromatogr.* 1982, *249*, 221–230.

[27] Boček, P., Deml, M., Janák, J., *J. Chromatogr.* 1978, *156*, 323–326.

[28] Everaerts, F. M., Verheggen, Th. P. E. M., Mikkers, F. E. P., *J. Chromatogr.* 1979, *169*, 21–38.

[29] Dolník, V., Deml, M., Boček, P., *J. Chromatogr.* 1985, *320*, 89–97.

[30] Vacík, J., Zuska, J., Muselasová, I., *J. Chromatogr.* 1985, *320*, 233–240.

[31] Reijenga, J. C., Verheggen, Th. P. E. M., Everaerts, F. M., *J. Chromatogr.* 1983, *267*, 75–84.

[32] Tamchyna, J., Zuska, J., Vacík, J., *J. Chromatogr.* 1985, *320*, 241–244.

[33] Goto, M., Irino, K., Ishii, D., *J. Chromatogr.* 1985, *346*, 167–176.

[34] Reijenga, J. C., Verheggen, Th. P. E. M., Everaerts, F. M., *J. Chromatogr.* 1984, *283*, 99–111.

[35] Kaniansky, D., Rajec, P., Švec, A., Havaši, P., Macášek, F., *J. Chromatogr.* 1983, *258*, 238–243.

[36] Kaniansky, D., Havaši, P., Marák, J., Sokolík, R., *J. Chromatogr.* 1986, *366*, 153–160.

[37] Kaniansky, D., Zelenská, V., Zelenský, I., *J. Chromatogr.* 1983, *256*, 126–134.

354   *P. Gebauer et al.*

[38] Kenndler, E., Kaniansky, D., *J. Chromatogr.* 1981, *209*, 306–309.
[39] Kobayashi, S., Shiogai, Y., Akiyama, J., *Anal. Chem. Symp. Ser.* 1981, *6*, 47–53.
[40] Arlinger, L., in: Deyl, Z. (Ed.), *Electrophoresis, A Survey of Techniques and Applications. Part A: Techniques.* Elsevier, Amsterdam, Oxford and New York, 1979, pp. 363–377.
[41] Öfverstedt, L. G., Eriksson, K. O., *Anal. Biochem.* 1984, *137*, 318–323.
[42] Schoots, A. C., Everaerts, F. M., *J. Chromatogr.* 1983, *277*, 328–332.
[43] Kašička, V., Prusík, Z., *J. Chromatogr.* 1983, *273*, 117–128.
[44] *Shimadzu Capillary-Type Isotachophoretic Analyzer IP-2A,* Shimadzu, Kyoto, Japan.
[45] *CS Isotachophoretic Analyser,* Institute of Radioecology and Applied Nuclear Techniques, Spišská Nová Ves, Czechoslovakia.
[46] Reijenga, J. C., Lemmens, A. A. G., Verheggen, Th. P. E. M., Everaerts, F. M., *J. Chromatogr.* 1985, *320*, 67–73.
[47] Reijenga, J. C., Van Iersel, W., Aben, G. V. A., Verheggen, Th. P. E. M., Everaerts, F. M., *J. Chromatogr.* 1984, *292*, 217–226.
[48] *Isotachopac I-E 1B,* Shimadzu, Kyoto, Japan.
[49] Schumacher, E., Thormann, W., Arn, D., *Anal. Chem. Symp. Ser.* 1981, *6*, 33–39.
[50] *LKB 2127 Tachophor,* LKB, Bromma, Sweden.
[51] *Tachofrac,* LKB, Bromma, Sweden.
[52] *Elphor VaP 21,* Bender and Hobein, München, FRG.
[53] *Tachophor Delta,* ITABA, Järfälla, Sweden.
[54] *Agrofor,* JZD Odra, Krmelín, Czechoslovakia.
[55] Boček, P., in: Holloway, C. J. (Ed.), *Analytical and Preparative Isotachophoresis,* Walter de Gruyter, Berlin and New York 1984, pp. 31–46.
[56] Lúčanský, D., Bátora, V., Polonský, J., Garaj, J., *Anal. Chem. Symp. Ser.* 1981, *6*, 147–158.
[57] Gebauer, P., Boček, P., Deml, M., Janák, J., *J. Chromatogr.* 1980, *199*, 81–94.
[58] Gebauer, P., Boček, P., *J. Chromatogr.* 1984, *299*, 321–330.
[59] Boček, P., Deml, M., Kaplanová, B., Janák, J., *J. Chromatogr.* 1978, *160*, 1–9.
[60] Arlinger, L., *J. Chromatogr.* 1974, *91*, 785–794.
[61] Nukatsuka, I., Taga, M., Yoshida, H., *J. Chromatogr.* 1981, *205*, 95–102.
[62] Dolník, V., Deml, M., Boček, P., in: Holloway, C. J. (Ed.), *Analytical and Preparative Isotachophoresis,* Walter de Gruyter, Berlin and New York 1984, pp. 55–62.
[63] Koval', M., Kaniansky, D., Hutta, M., Lacko, R., *J. Chromatogr.* 1985, *325*, 151–160.
[64] Reijenga, J. C., Slaats, H. J. L. A., Everaerts, F. M., *J. Chromatogr.* 1983, *267*, 85–89.
[65] Vestermark, A., Wiedemann, B., *Nucl. Instr. Methods* 1967, *56*, 151–159.
[66] Oerlemans, F., De Bruyn, C., Mikkers, F., Verheggen, Th., Everaerts, F., *Anal. Chem. Symp. Ser.* 1981, *6*, 189–194.
[67] Gustavsson, B., Almersjö, O., Berne, M., Waldenström, J., *J. Chromatogr.* 1983, *276*, 395–401.
[68] Husmann-Holloway, S., Boriss, E., *Fresenius' Z. Anal. Chem.* 1982, *311*, 465–466.
[69] Delmotte, P., *Sci. Tools* 1977, *24*, 33–41.
[70] Novák, J., *Quanitative Analysis by Gas Chromatography,* Marcel Dekker, New York 1975.
[71] Gower, D. C., Woledge, R. C., *Sci. Tools* 1977, *24*, 17–21.
[72] Svoboda, M., Vacík, J., *J. Chromatogr.* 1976, *119*, 539–547.
[73] Ryšlavý, Z., Boček, P., Deml, M., Janák, J., *J. Chromatogr.* 1978, *147*, 369–373.
[74] Boček, P., Ryšlavý, Z., Deml, M., Janák, J., *J. Chromatogr.* 1980, *191*, 271–277.
[75] Reijenga, J. C., Aben, G. V. A., Verheggen, Th. P. E. M., Everaerts, F. M., *J. Chromatogr.* 1983, *260*, 241–254.

[76] Verheggen, Th., Mikkers, F., Everaerts, F., Oerlemans, F., De Bruyn, C., *J. Chromatogr.* 1980, *182*, 317–324.
[77] Kojima, K., Manabe, T., Okuyama, T., in: Hirai, H. (Ed.), *Electrophoresis '83*, Walter de Gruyter, Berlin and New York 1984, pp. 511–517.
[78] Dolník, V., Boček, P., *J. Chromatogr.* 1981, *225*, 455–458.
[79] Mikkers, F., Ringoir, S., De Smet, R., *J. Chromatogr.* 1979, *162*, 341–350.
[80] Walterová, D., Stránský, Z., Bartek, J., Seidlová, V., *Biochem. Clin. Bohemoslov.* 1983, *12*, 147–153.
[81] Schmidt, K., Hagmaier, V., Bruchelt, G., *Anal. Chem. Symp. Ser.* 1980, *5*, 109–115.
[82] Tschöpe, W., Ritz, E., *Anal. Chem. Symp. Ser.* 1981, *6*, 63–68.
[83] Tschöpe, W., Brenner, R., Ritz, E., *J. Chromatogr.* 1981, *222*, 41–52.
[84] Bruchelt, G., Oberritter, H., Schmidt, K. H., in: Holloway, C. J. (Ed.), *Analytical and Preparative Isotachophoresis*, Walter de Gruyter, Berlin and New York 1984, pp. 229–236.
[85] Oberritter, H., Bruchelt, G., Schmidt, K. H., in: Holloway, C. J. (Ed.), *Analytical and Preparative Isotachophoresis*, Walter de Gruyter, Berlin and New York 1984, pp. 237–243.
[86] Oefner, P. J., Bonn, G., Bartsch, G., *Fresenius' Z. Anal. Chem.* 1985, *320*, 175–178.
[87] Kodama, H., Sasaki, K., Mikasa, H., Cavallini, D., Ricci, G., *J. Chromatogr.* 1984, *311*, 183–188.
[88] Mikasa, H., Sasaki, K., Kodama, H., *J. Chromatogr.* 1980, *190*, 501–503.
[89] Van der Hoeven, J. S., Franken, H. C. M., *Anal. Chem. Symp. Ser.* 1980, *5*, 69–79.
[90] Talbot, A., *Acta Med. Okayama* 1982, *36*, 431–439.
[91] Mikkers, F., Verheggen, Th., Everaerts, F., *J. Chromatogr.* 1980, *182*, 496–500.
[92] Morio, M., Fujii, K., Takiyama, R., Chikasue, F., Kikuchi, H., Ribarić, L., *Anesthesiology* 1980, *53*, 56–59.
[93] Moch, S., Schonn, D., Jahn, H., in: Holloway, C. J. (Ed.), *Analytical and Preparative Isotachophoresis*, Walter de Gruyter, Berlin and New York 1984, pp. 217–227.
[94] Øvrebø, S., Jacobsen, D., Sejersted, O. M., in: Holloway, C. J. (Ed.), *Analytical and Preparative Isotachophoresis*, Walter de Gruyter, Berlin and New York 1984, pp. 261–268.
[95] Øvrebø, S., Jacobsen, D., Sejersted, O. M., *ITP-84*, 4th International Symposium on Isotachophoresis. Hradec Králové, 2–6 September 1984, Institute of Analytical Chemistry, Czechoslovak Academy of Sciences, Brno 1984, p. 32.
[96] Křivánková, L., Samcová, E., Boček, P., *Electrophoresis* 1984, *5*, 226–230.
[97] Sollenberg, J., Baldesten, A., *J. Chromatogr.* 1977, *132*, 469–476.
[98] Ageta, T., Mikasa, H., Kojima, K., Kodama, H., *J. Chromatogr.* 1982, *233*, 361–364.
[99] Dragsholt, C., Yderstraede, K. B., in: Holloway, C. J. (Ed.), *Analytical and Preparative Isotachophoresis*, Walter de Gruyter, Berlin and New York 1984, pp. 253–260.
[100] Kodama, H., Mizoguchi, N., Sasaki, K., Mikasa, H., *Anal. Biochem.* 1983, *133*, 100–103.
[101] Kopwillem, A., Lundin, H., Righetti, A. B. B., Righetti, P. G., *Protides Biol. Fluids* 1975, *22*, 737–742.
[102] Kodama, H., Uasa, S., *J. Chromatogr.* 1979, *163*, 300–303.
[103] Mikasa, H., Ageta, T., Mizoguchi, N., Kodama, H., *J. Chromatogr.* 1980, *202*, 504–506.
[104] Kodama, H., Yamamoto, M., Sasaki, K., *J. Chromatogr.* 1980, *183*, 226–228.
[105] Mikasa, H., Ageta, T., Mizoguchi, N., Kodama, H., *Anal. Biochem.* 1982, *126*, 52–57.
[106] Mikasa, H., Sasaki, K., Kodama, H., *J. Chromatogr.* 1984, *305*, 204–209.
[107] Thimm, K., Altrogge, H., Bläker, F., *Klin. Wochenschr.* 1979, *57*, 855–856.
[108] Clark, P. M. S., Kricka, L. J., Whitehead, T. P., *J. Chromatogr.* 1980, *181*, 347–354.

[109] Zimmerman, L., Baldesten, A., Bergström, J., Fürst, P., *Clin. Nephrol.* 1980, *13*, 183–188.

[110] Gróf, J., Menyhárt, J., *Anal. Chem. Symp. Ser.* 1981, *6*, 99–107.

[111] Driesen, O., Beuckers, H., Belfroid, L., Emonds, A., *J. Chromatogr.* 1980, *181*, 441–448.

[112] Sahota, A., Simmonds, H. A., Payne, R. H., *J. Pharm. Meth.* 1979, *2*, 263–278.

[113] Gustavsson, B., Olsson, R.-M., Waldenström, J., *Anal. Biochem.* 1982, *122*, 1–5.

[114] Akedo, H., Shinkai, K., *J. Chromatogr.* 1982, *227*, 262–265.

[115] Stránský, Z., Chmela, Z., Peč, P., Šafařík, L., *J. Chromatogr.* 1985, *342*, 167–174.

[116] Reijenga, J. C., Aben, G. V. A., Lemmens, A. A. G., Verheggen, Th. P. E. M., De Bruijn, C. H. M. M., Everaerts, F. M., *J. Chromatogr.* 1985, *320*, 245–252.

[117] Reijenga, J. C., Gaykema, A., Mikkers, F. E. P., *J. Chromatogr.* 1984, *287*, 365–370.

[118] Moberg, U., Hjalmarsson, S.-G., Mellstrand, T., *J. Chromatogr.* 1980, *181*, 147–152.

[119] Ageta, T., Tsutsumi, A., Ishizu, H., Mizoguchi, N., Kodama, H., *J. Chromatogr.* 1985, *343*, 186–189.

[120] Woledge, R. C., Reilly, P., *Anal. Chem. Symp. Ser.* 1980, *5*, 103–108.

[121] Aomine, M., Arita, M., Imanishi, S., Kiyosue, T., *Jap. J. Physiol.* 1982, *32*, 741–760.

[122] Oerlemans, F., Van Bennekom, C., De Bruyn, C., Kulakowski, S., *J. Inher. Metab. Dis.* 1981, *4*, 109–110.

[123] Sjödin, B., Kopwillem, A., Karlsson, J., *Protides Biol. Fluids* 1975, *22*, 733–736.

[124] Pérez, J. A., Mateo, F., Meléndez-Hevia, E., *Electrophoresis* 1982, *3*, 102–106.

[125] Van Bennekom, C. A., Oerlemans, F. T., Verburg, M., De Bruyn, C., in: Holloway, C. J. (Ed.), *Analytical and Preparative Isotachophoresis*, Walter de Gruyter, Berlin and New York 1984, pp. 165–170.

[126] Kjellin, K. G., Hallander, L., *Anal. Chem. Symp. Ser.* 1980, *5*, 239–243.

[127] Kjellin, K. G., Hallander, L., *J. Neurol.* 1979, *221*, 235–244.

[128] Delmotte, P., in: Radola, B. J., Graesslin, D. (Eds.), *Electrofocusing and Isotachophoresis*, Walter de Gruyter, Berlin and New York 1977, pp. 559–564.

[129] Hallander, L., Kjellin, K. G., *Anal. Chem. Symp. Ser.* 1981, *6*, 129–135.

[130] Holloway, C. J., Heil, W., Henkel, E., in: Allen, R. C., Arnaud, P., (Eds.), *Electrophoresis '81*, Walter de Gruyter, Berlin and New York 1982, pp. 753–766.

[131] Smuts, H. E. M., Russell, B. W., Moodie, J. W., *J. Neurol. Sci.* 1982, *56*, 283–292.

[132] Kjellin, K. G., Moberg, U., Hallander, L., *Sci. Tools* 1975, *22*, 3–7.

[133] Del Principe, D., Colistra, C., Menichelli, A., Biancini, G., D'Arcangelo, C., Multari, G., Werner, B., Lemmo, M., Digilio, G., *J. Chromatogr.* 1985, *342*, 285–292.

[134] Schmitz, G., Borgmann, U., Assmann, G., *J. Chromatogr.* 1985, *320*, 253–262.

[135] Tschöpe, W., Brenner, R., Ritz, E., in: Holloway, C. J. (Ed.), *Analytical and Preparative Isotachophoresis*, Walter de Gruyter, Berlin and New York 1984, pp. 207–216.

[136] Everaerts, F. M., Verheggen, Th. P. E. M., Reijenga, J. C., Aben, G. V. A., Gebauer, P., Boček, P., *J. Chromatogr.* 1985, *320*, 263–268.

[137] Lemmens, A. A. G., Reijenga, J. C., Everaerts, F. M., Janssen, R. T. P., Hulsman, J. A. R. J., Meijers, C. A. M., *J. Chromatogr.* 1985, *320*, 193–197.

[138] *LKB Quality Chemicals,* LKB, Produkter AB, Bromma, p. 13.

[139] Röben, R., Rubach, K., in: Holloway, C. J. (Ed.), *Analytical and Preparative Isotachophoresis*, Walter de Gruyter, Berlin and New York 1984, pp. 109–116.

[140] Dolník, V., Boček, P., Šístková, L., Körbl, J., *J. Chromatogr.* 1982, *246*, 343–345.

[141] Boček, P., *Anal. Chem. Symp. Ser.* 1981, *6*, 203–205.

[142] Tatsuhara, T., Muro, H., Ozoe, F., *Yakugaku Zasshi* 1982, *102*, 988–991.

[143] Rubach, K., Breyer, Ch., *Getreide, Mehl, Brot* 1981, *35*, 91–93.

[144] Eichler, D., Rubach, K., in: Holloway, C. J. (Ed.), *Analytical and Preparative Isotachophoresis,* Walter de Gruyter, Berlin and New York 1984, pp. 117–124.

[145] Rubach, K., Offizorz, P., *Dtsch. Lebensm.-Rundsch.* 1983, *79,* 88–90.

[146] Klein, H., *Fleischwirtschaft* 1981, *61,* 1–5.

[147] Rubach, K., Breyer, Ch., *Dtsch. Lebensm.-Rundsch.* 1980, *76,* 228–231.

[148] Klein, H., *Ind. Obst- Gemüseverwert.* 1982, *67,* 31–36.

[149] Engelhardt, U., Maier, H. G., *Fresenius' Z. Anal. Chem.* 1985, *320,* 169–174.

[150] Reijenga, J. C., Verheggen, Th. P. E. M., Everaerts, F. M., *J. Chromatogr.* 1982, *245,* 120–125.

[151] Kaiser, K.-P., Hupf, H., *Dtsch. Lebensm.-Rundschr.* 1979, *75,* 346–349.

[152] Goto, E., Maekawa, A., Suzuki, T., *Eiyo To Shokuryo* 1980, *33,* 225–229.

[153] Yagi, T., Shiogai, Y., Akiyama, J., *Shimadzu Rev.* 1977, *34,* 37–40.

[154] Baldesten, A., Hjalmarsson, S.-G., Neumann, G., *Fresenius' Z. Anal. Chem.* 1978, *290,* 148–149.

[155] Fukuba, H., Tsuda, T., *Eiyo To Shokuryo* 1980, *33,* 247–251.

[156] Ito, Y., Toyoda, M., Suzuki, H., Iwaida, M., *J. Assoc. Off. Anal. Chem.* 1980, *63,* 1219–1223.

[157] Klein, H., *Z. Acker- Pflanzenbau* 1981, *150,* 349–355.

[158] Boček, P., Pavelka, S., Grígel'ová, K., Deml, M., Janák, J., *J. Chromatogr.* 1978, *154,* 356–359.

[159] Madajová, V., Kaniansky, D., Radej, Z., Eszéniova, A., *J. Chromatogr.* 1981, *216,* 313–320.

[160] Onodera, S., Udagawa, T., Tabata, M., Ishikura, S., Suzuki, S., *J. Chromatogr.* 1984, *287,* 176–182.

[161] Boček, P., Dolník, V., Deml, M., Janák, J., *J. Chromatogr.* 1980, *195,* 303–305.

[162] Dolník, V., Boček, P., Šistková, L., Körbl, J., *J. Chromatogr.* 1982, *246,* 340–342.

[163] Jannasch, R., *Pharmazie* 1983, *38,* 379–387.

[164] Lang, J., Büchele, B., *Acta Pharm. Technol.* 1980, *26,* 237–239.

[165] Kenndler, E., Huber, J. F. K., *Z. Lebensm.-Unters. Forsch.* 1980, *171,* 292–296.

[166] Shiogai, Y., Yagi, T., Akiyama, J., *Bunseki Kagaku* 1977, *26,* 701–705.

[167] Yamaguchi, T., Fukuda, M., *Shokumotsu-hen* 1979, *27,* 15–19.

[168] Madajová, V., Kaniansky, D., Čižmárová, E., Hudec, M., *J. Chromatogr.* 1985, *320,* 131–138.

[169] Klein, H., Teichmann, R., *J. Chromatogr.* 1982, *250,* 152–156.

[170] Klein, H., Teichmann, R., *Pharm. Zeit.* 1982, *127,* 447–451.

[171] Fanali, S., Foret, F., Boček, P., *J. Chromatogr.* 1985, *330,* 436–438.

[172] Lang, J., Büchele, B., *Anal. Chem. Symp. Ser.* 1981, *6,* 75–79.

[173] Klein, H., *Drug Res.* 1982, *32,* 795–798.

[174] Weiss, C., Rubach, K., in: Holloway, C. J. (Ed.), *Analytical and Preparative Isotachophoresis,* Walter de Gruyter, Berlin and New York 1984, pp. 125–131.

[175] Rubach, K., Offizorz, P., Breyer, Ch., *Z. Lebensm.-Unters. Forsch.* 1981, *172,* 351–354.

[176] Shimada, K., Ohtusuru, M., Yamaguchi, T., Nigota, K., *J. Food Sci.* 1983, *48,* 665–667, 680.

[177] Křivánková, L., Boček, P., *Electrophoresis* 1985, *6,* 143–144.

[178] Tatsuhara, T., Tabuchi, F., Nishimura, I., Muro, H., Ozoe, F., *Chem. Pharm. Bull.* 1982, *30,* 1347–1351.

[179] Kojima, K., Yagi, T., Okuda, T., *Shoyakugaku Zasshi* 1982, *36,* 196–201.

[180] Boček, P., Pavelka, S., Deml, M., Janák, J., *J. Chromatogr.* 1978, *151,* 436–438.

[181] Murai, S., Ozawa, T., Maki, Y., *Bunseki Kagaku* 1984, *33,* 229–233.

[182] Zelenský, I., Šimuničová, E., Zelenská, V., Kaniansky, D., Havaši, P., Chaláni, P., *J. Chromatogr.* 1985, *325*, 161–178.

[183] Yagi, T., Kojima, K., Haruki, T., *J. Chromatogr.* 1984, *292*, 273–280.

[184] Vacík, J., Muselasová, I., *J. Chromatogr.* 1985, *320*, 199–203.

[185] Fukushi, K., Hiiro, K., *Bunseki Kagaku* 1985, *34*, 21–25.

[186] Fukushi, K., Hiiro, K., *Bunseki Kagaku* 1985, *34*, 205–208.

[187] Fukushi, K., Hiiro, K., *Fresenius' Z. Anal. Chem.* 1986, *323*, 44–46.

[188] Boček, P., Miedziak, I., Deml, M., Janák, J., *J. Chromatogr.* 1977, *137*, 83–91.

[189] Boček, P., Kaplanová, B., Deml, M., Janák, J., *J. Chromatogr.* 1978, *153*, 287–288.

[190] Boček, P., Kaplanová, B., Deml, M., Janák, J., *Collect. Czech. Chem. Commun.* 1978, *43*, 2707–2710.

[191] Kaniansky, D., Madajová, V., Hutta, M., Žilková, I., *J. Chromatogr.* 1984, *286*, 395–406.

[192] Stránský, Z., *J. Chromatogr.* 1985, *320*, 219–231.

[193] Pfeifer, P. A., Bonn, G. K., Bobleter, O., *Fresenius' Z. Anal. Chem.* 1983, *315*, 205–207.

[194] Hansén, L., Kristiansson, B., Sollenberg, J., in: Holloway, C. J. (Ed.), *Analytical and Preparative Isotachophoresis,* Walter de Gruyter, Berlin and New York 1984, pp. 81–87.

[195] Hansén, L., Sollenberg, J., Wiberg, K., *J. Chromatogr.* 1984, *312*, 489–491.

[196] Zelenský, I., Zelenská, V., Kaniansky, D., Havaši, P., Lednárová, V., *J. Chromatogr.* 1984, *294*, 317–327.

[197] Mikasa, H., Sasaki, K., Arata, J., Yamamoto, Y., Ohno, T., Kodama, H., *J. Chromatogr.* 1985, *343*, 179–185.

[198] Everaerts, F. M., Verheggen, Th. P. E. M., *J. Chromatogr.* 1974, *91*, 837–851.

[199] Lüstorff, J., Holloway, C. J., *Anal. Chem. Symp. Ser.* 1981, *6*, 179–188.

[200] Katoh, K., Miyazaki, H., *J. Chromatogr.* 1980, *188*, 383–390.

[201] Anhalt, E., Holloway, C. J., in: Holloway, C. J. (Ed.), *Analytical and Preparative Isotachophoresis,* Walter de Gruyter, Berlin and New York 1984, pp. 197–203.

[202] Holloway, C. J., *Anal. Chem. Symp. Ser.* 1980, *5*, 153–175.

[203] Holloway, C. J., Husmann-Holloway, S., Brunner, G., *Anal. Chem. Symp. Ser.* 1981, *6*, 25–32.

[204] Bruchelt, G., Schmidt, K., *Anal. Chem. Symp. Ser.* 1981, *6*, 137–142.

[205] Tegtmeier, F., Holloway, C. J., in: Holloway, C. J. (Ed.), *Analytical and Preparative Isotachophoresis,* Walter de Gruyter, Berlin and New York 1984, pp. 175–185.

[206] Holloway, C. J., *Fresenius' Z. Anal. Chem.* 1980, *301*, 136–137.

[207] Battersby, R. V., Holloway, C. J., *Fresenius' Z. Anal. Chem.* 1984, *317*, 748–749.

[208] Yegorov, A. M., Osipov, A. P., Dikov, M. M., Karulin, A. Y., *Anal. Chem. Symp. Ser.* 1981, *6*, 167–172.

[209] Hedlung, K. W., Wistar, R. Jr., Nichelson, D., *J. Immunol. Methods* 1979, *25*, 43–48.

[210] Hedlung, K. W., Nichelson, D. E., *J. Chromatogr.* 1979, *162*, 76–80.

[211] Weiland, E., Thorn, W., Bläker, F., *J. Chromatogr.* 1981, *214*, 156–160.

[212] Einarsson, R., Karlsson, R., Åkerblom, E., *J. Chromatogr.* 1984, *284*, 143–147.

[213] Hjalmarsson, S.-G., Sjödahl, J., *Anal. Chem. Symp. Ser.* 1980, *5*, 267–278.

[214] Hjalmarsson, S.-G., *Biochim. Biophys. Acta* 1979, *581*, 210–216.

[215] Oefner, P., Csordas, A., Bartsch, G., Grunicke, H., in: Radola, B. J. (Ed.), *Elektrophorese Forum '85,* Technische Universität München, Freising-Weihenstephan 1985, pp. 300–305.

[216] Csordas, A., Oefner, P. J., Bartsch, G., Grunicke, H., in: Radola, B. J. (Ed.), *Elektrophorese Forum '85,* Technische Universität München, Freising-Weihenstephan 1985, pp. 294–299.

[217] Holloway, C. J., Bulge, G., *J. Chromatogr.* 1982, *234*, 454–458.

[218] Clark, P. M. S., Whitehead, T. P., Kricka, L. J., *Anal. Chem. Symp. Ser.* 1981, *6*, 109–114.

[219] Lövgren, K., Jung-Fang, L., Baldesten, A., Morein, B., in: Holloway, C. J. (Ed.), *Analytical and Preparative Isotachophoresis,* Walter de Gruyter, Berlin and New York 1984, pp. 291–296.

[220] Linpisarn, S., Clark, P. M. S., Kricka, L. J., Whitehead, T. P., in: Allen, R. C., Arnaud, P. (Eds.), *Electrophoresis '81,* Walter de Gruyter, Berlin and New York 1982, pp. 767–780.

[221] Janssen, P. S. L., Van Nispen, J. W., *J. Chromatogr.* 1984, *287*, 166–175.

[222] Holloway, C. J., Battersby, R. V., in: Holloway, C. J. (Ed.), *Analytical and Preparative Isotachophoresis,* Walter de Gruyter, Berlin and New York 1984, pp. 193–196.

[223] Fukuba, H., Tsuda, Y., *Nippon Eiyo Shokuryo Gakkaishi* 1983, *36*, 373–377.

[224] Holloway, C. J., Friedel, K., in: Allen, R. C., Arnaud, P. (Eds.), *Electrophoresis '81,* Walter de Gruyter, Berlin and New York 1982, pp. 821–826.

[225] Friedel, K., Holloway, C. J., *Electrophoresis* 1981, *2*, 116–122.

[226] Miyazaki, H., Katoh, K., *J. Chromatogr. 1976, 119*, 369–383.

[227] Baldesten, A., in: Brandenburg, D., Wollmer, A. (Eds.) *Insulin, Chemistry, Structure and Function of Insulin and Related Hormones,* Walter de Gruyter, Berlin and New York 1980, pp. 207–213.

[228] Holloway, C. J., Büssenschütt, B., Pingoud, V., in: Holloway, C. J. (Ed.), *Analytical and Preparative Isotachophoresis,* Walter de Gruyter, Berlin and New York 1984, pp. 187–192.

[229] Hülsheger, H., Husmann-Holloway, S., Borriss, E., Potel, J., in: Holloway, C. J. (Ed.), *Analytical and Preparative Isotachophoresis,* Walter de Gruyter, Berlin and New York 1984, pp. 157–164.

[230] Anhalt, E., Holloway, C. J., *Anal. Chem. Symp. Ser.* 1981, *6*, 159–166.

[231] Gavrilova, E. M., Dikov, M. M., Osipov, A. P., Kiseleva, N. I., Mitrochina, T. G., Yegorov, A. M., *Anal. Chem. Symp. Ser.* 1981, *6*, 173–177

[232] Kent, C. G., Tu, A. T., Geren, C. R., *Comp. Biochem. Physiol. B* 1984, *77*, 303–311.

[233] Einarsson, R., Moberg, U., *J. Chromatogr.* 1981, *209*, 121–124.

[234] Walterová, D., Stránský, Z., Preininger, V., Šimánek, V., *Electrophoresis* 1985, *6*, 128–132.

[235] Walterová, D., Preininger, V., Šimánek, V., *Planta Med.* 1984, *50*, 149–151.

[236] Kasahara, Y., Hikino, H., Hine, T., *J. Chromatogr.* 1985, *324*, 503–507.

[237] Einarsson, R., Karlsson, R., *Int. Arch. Allergy Appl. Immunol.* 1982, *68*, 222–225.

[238] Goto, H., Muto, Y., *Yakugaku Zasshi* 1981, *101*, 185–189.

[239] Van Dongen, C. A. M., Mikkers, F. E. P., De Bruyn, Ch., Verheggen, Th. P. E. M., *Anal. Chem. Symp. Ser.* 1981, *6*, 207–216.

PREPARATIVE POLYACRYLAMIDE GEL ELECTROPHORESIS OF PROTEINS

Richard Horuk

E.I. Du Pont De Nemours and Co., Glenolden, PA, USA

Abbreviations: IGF, insulin-like growth factor; **MBE**, multiphasic buffer electrophoresis; **PAGE**, polyacrylamide gel electrophoresis; R_f, relative electrophoretic mobility; **SDS**, sodium dodecyl sulfate; **ZEE**, zone-excision-extraction.

1   Introduction

1.1   Meaning and quantitative limits of preparativeness

Every analytical protein separation on polyacrylamide gel electrophoresis (PAGE) is necessarily preparative as well. That means that whenever zones can be separated they can also be recovered after separation. This axiomatic statement underlying the further discussion of preparative techniques contrasts with the widely held prejudice that PAGE is an analytical, but not an effective preparative tool. In fact, however, the main reason for separating proteins is to recover homogeneous species for further analysis, so that one can consider preparativeness the goal of PAGE in general.

It appears useful to define preparativeness according to the amount of protein applied to the gel and recovered. Accordingly, we will distinguish between microgram, milligram and gram-preparative methods [1], where the three indicated levels refer to the protein of interest, not to its contaminants. The inclusion of contaminants into load capacity estimates as practiced by most instrument manufacturers is highly misleading. For most purposes, the goal of separations in biochemistry is still the milligram-level of isolated proteins, since most analytical procedures one may wish to apply to the isolated product require that amount. However, the advent of gas phase sequenators [2] and recombinant DNA technology [3] promises to increasingly raise the importance of microgram and gram-preparative methods. The choice of the degree of preparativeness depends on the availability of the starting material and the purpose of the isolation. When the protein of interest represents only a small fraction of total protein, a milligram-preparative technique is required although the levels of contaminant may be in the hundreds of milligrams. In such a case, the load capacity of the gel for contaminant rather than the protein of interest becomes the determining factor in the selection of the appropriate preparative condition. This is particularly so, when the contaminants abound in the vicinity of the protein zone of interest. Thus, to obtain the desired milligram-yield of protein in such cases, pre-fractionations by chromatography or other ancillary methods may be required which enrich the zone of interest as compared to the abundance of contaminants in its vicinity. In rare lucky circumstances when contaminans exhibit mobilities strikingly different from the material of interest this may not be required. A few examples will illustrate these considerations in the choice of the conditions of preparative gel electrophoresis.

Polypeptide hormone receptors constitute less than 0.01% of total membrane protein and obviously have to be treated differently from a protein of higher abundance such as the red blood cell glucose transporter which constitutes greater than 5% of total membrane protein. The former would have to be concentrated by prepurification prior to sodium dodecyl sulfate (SDS)-PAGE, whereas the latter could be applied directly to SDS-PAGE since it would readily be detected even in sample loads as low as 1 mg. For proteins of low relative abundance, such as polypeptide hormone receptors, loads in excess of 100 mg may have to be applied in order to detect them. Increasing the relative abundance of such proteins by ancillary techniques is required; purification by isoelectric focussing (IEF) using granular gels allows sample loads in excess of 500 mg to be separated. The protein of interest can be readily recovered from the gel matrix and applied in a concentrated form to SDS-PAGE. Such an approach has been used for several proteins including (a) the rat adipose cell glucose transporter [4], (b) the insulin-like growth factor IGF 2 receptor [5] and (c) human growth hormone [6]. The IGF 2 receptor can be separated from other contaminants by treating the proteins with the reducing agent dithiothreitol (DTT) [5]. This simple procedure, which results in the reduction of disulfide bonds, generates a large number of lower molecular weight species which can be well separated from the IGF 2 receptor (which is a single chain 270 kDa polypeptide and thus does not reduce with DTT) by SDS-PAGE. Human growth hormone has been separated from bacterial proteins in a protein synthetic system utilizing recombinant DNA technology [6]. In this problem, the load could be vastly increased due to a generic difference in mobility of these two classes of protein which is most likely due to a difference in the relative abundance of glyco-moieties.

1.2   Preparative techniques in the absence of information concerning band width

The aim of any separation technique is resolution, defined as the non-overlap of adjacent zone distributions. A knowledge of resolution therefore depends on the measurement of the width of zone distributions. At this time, this knowledge, and generally available techniques to obtain it, are practically universally unobtainable, although suitable electrophoretic methods have been developed [7, 8]. Consequently, all present methods of separation between "bands" in gel electrophoresis, *i.e.* the maxima of the distribution profiles, irrespective of distribution overlap, are blind to true resolution (compare Figs. 1 and 4 of [9]). Most importantly, this is due to the methods of zone excision and extraction (ZEE) (see below). Ironically, the popularity of present-day preparative gel electrophoresis is almost entirely due to the illusion that proteins are separated to the degree indicated by the bands, while in fact the bands at the distribution maxima derive their detectability solely from the relative insensitivity of the detection methods applied. The same misinterpretation concerning the true significance of zones in gel electrophoresis has been largely reponsible for the downfall of preparative elution-PAGE in recent years (see below).

1.3   Load capacity of various electrophoretic methods

The load capacity of preparative gel electrophoresis refers mainly to a single component of interest, although it also depends on the degree of closeness and the concentration of the contaminants surrounding the band of interest. Furthermore it depends (a) on the type of electrophoretic separation and (b) on the cross-sectional area of the gel. Among the gel electrophoretic methods, the load capacity of PAGE is of the order of 0.1 mg/cm^2 of protein, for IEF it is of the order of 1.0 mg/cm^2 and for multiphasic buffer electrophoresis (MBE) 10 mg/cm^2 [10]. Load capacity is also proportional to gel surface area. A limit to gel surface area is set by the need to achieve the separation in a reasonable time period and the Joule heat dissipation efficiency of the apparatus, as well as by the limitations inherent in the design of preparative PAGE apparatus (see Sections 1.5 and 2.2). The efficient dissipation of Joule heating produced during the electrophoretic run restricts the maximum thickness of the gel to 18 mm if one is to conduct the preparative electrophoresis within a single workday [10]. The Joule heat produced in thicker gels cannot be dissipated in presently available waterjacketed apparatus unless the voltage is reduced, with consequent increase in the duration of electrophoresis and decrease in the resolution [11]. Failure to effectively dissipate the Joule heat frequently leads to protein denaturation, aggregation and precipitation. The maximum gel diameter of about 18 mm equally applies to gel slabs, gel annuli (which are slabs folded head-to-tail) and gel cylinders.

1.4   Special problems in preparative gel electrophoresis of
  membrane proteins

Membrane and other water-insoluble proteins differ from others by requiring detergent for their solubilization. Moreover, a requirement for their solubilization may be either the micellar or the monomeric state of the detergent; the concentration range of the detergent is thereby narrowly circumscribed. In addition, solubilization of native membrane proteins depends on high protein concentrations and on particular protein/detergent ratios. The delicate sensitivity of detergent states on temperature requires an exacting control of gel temperature and an efficient dissipation of Joule heating. Although all of these properties of membrane proteins affect analytical as well as preparative electrophoresis, they are accentuated in the latter, since wider gel diameters aggravate the problems of Joule heat dissipation. Ionic detergents which may be required for solubilization pose further problems: the high field strength in a sample containing SDS, for instance, will suppress the migration of the protein until such a time that the detergent is electrophoretically moved out of the sample zone. The migration of detergent of high mobility also causes an increased current density and consequent production of Joule heat which must be dissipated. The detergent load therefore rather than the protein load may therefore be the limiting factor in loading the gel.

1.5   Elution-polyacrylamide gel electrophoresis and zone-excision-extraction

It is useful at this point to distinguish between two different approaches to preparative gel electrophoresis. The first involves the migration of the zone of interest to the bottom of the gel and, from there, into a shallow buffer chamber from which it can be eluted continuously or discontinuously into a stream of buffer. This method is referred to here as "elution-PAGE". Many arrangements of elution chambers with upward, downward or sideways buffer elution and of apparatus ranging in gel surface area from less than 1 to over 20 cm^2 have been described (Table 1 of [1]). While elution-PAGE still lingers on at the present time in application to nucleic acids [12, 13], it has definitely fallen out of favor with most biochemists in other areas, due mainly to the following real or imaginary disadvantages: (i) Elution patterns consist of overlapping distributions. Since these give the appearance of inferior resolution compared to the band patterns in analytical PAGE, the widespread (erroneous, see above) conclusion is that resolution is lost in the process of zone elution. (ii) Eluate dilution at an adequate elution rate of one elution chamber volume per minute is enormous, making detection difficult and requiring a subsequent concentration step. Dilution may be reduced by measures such as a progressive lowering of elution rate with time of electrophoresis or by tying elution to the appearance of protein in the elution chamber, but such measures greatly complicate the apparatus design. (iii) The complete kit of instrumentation for elution-PAGE together with sufficient procedural detail for its operation is not yet commercially available. A detailed description of these problems and of their remedies has been reported [1, 10, 11].

The most widely used method of preparative gel electrophoresis, referred to here as ZEE, consists of zone-excision, protein elution and concentration, and is followed in some applications by purification of the concentrate. Its appeal rests on a low risk of losing the sample compared to elution-PAGE. Furthermore, several protein zones can be simultaneously excised and extracted from the same gel irrespective of their mobilities, while in elution-PAGE slowly migrating proteins are excessively diluted, making recovery difficult. Finally, ZEE provides the illusory benefit that a visible or visualizable narrow band of interest can be excised which is apparently completely resolved from its adjacent bands. That this is due to the myopia of the detection method, and not to improved resolution, has been pointed out above.

An important consideration in large-scale preparative gel electrophoresis, as exemplified by protein isolations in the recombinant DNA industry [6], concerns the degree to which elution-PAGE and ZEE can be scaled up. In elution-PAGE, the gel slab or annulus of maximally practical diameter of 18 mm (see above) can be elongated to any desired degree but only at the price of a rapidly increasing volume of the elution chamber of gel annuli (with ever increasing dead space at the center) and length of elution path along the bottom of linear slabs which prevents the simultaneous pick-up of particles independently of their position along the gel length. In view of these limitations, the presently commercially available elution-PAGE apparatus of 20 to 50 cm^2 of gel surface area are maximal in size. A convoluted gel slab, consisting of a number of concentric gel annuli, has been proposed to exceed these limitations but remains an untried design [6]. The scale-up of ZEE appears more hopeful in view of the ease with which very large blocks of gel − e.g. a longitudinal slice of 0.5−1.0 m in length − can be extracted into a small volume of buffer, using an MBE buffer system [14]. Such an extraction would require impracticably long durations of electrophoresis with present apparatus. But increasing the speed of electrophoretic extraction by increasing the field strength is merely dependent on designing apparatus with improved heat dissipation characteristics. Also needed will be slicing devices for gel slabs of great length which would allow one to obtain narrow longitudinal slices of 18 mm thickness at any position corresponding to the desired relative electrophoretic mobility (R_f). But these instrumental developments are feasible and relatively trivial. The corresponding scale-up of electrophoretic extraction apparatus using a single buffer to large volumes of gel would require enormous buffer volumes, present unsurmountable obstacles of Joule heat dissipation and dilute the extract intolerably.

2   Zone-excision-extraction

2.1   Extraction by diffusion *versus* electrophoresis

Diffusion of proteins from gels is slow and inefficient. Depending on the gel concentration and the size of the protein the rate of diffusion may vary from a few hours to several days, even when $1-2$ mm slices are used. This approach has been widely rejected by the majority of investigators. In contrast, near-unaminity exists that protein extraction needs to be electrophoretic. Differences in the approaches to ZEE exist merely with respect to the choice of buffer and of apparatus (Sections 2.2 and 2.3).

2.2   Buffers

The investigator in possession of one or many gel slices containing the protein of interest has two choices: (i) To extract the slices by electrophoresis in a single buffer, with or without subsequent concentration of the extract [15]. (ii) Or, to extract the slices electrophoretically in a MBE buffer system, *i.e.* onto a stacking gel, in which the extract is concentrated into a single zone (the stack) which may be visualized by a tracking dye; the stack is allowed to migrate into a buffer chamber of small volume [16] or a gel filtration column [17]. The latter approach may preclude the need for a separate purification step after extraction.

Extraction by electrophoresis in a single buffer is probably the most widely used preparative PAGE procedure, particularly in application to such extraction from SDS-PAGE, followed by sequence analysis [15]. This choice of extraction obviously excels in the applicability of any buffer within constraints discussed under procedure (Section 2.5), although for subsequent sequencing volatile buffers are preferred. Buffer volumes can be small or large, depending on the choice of apparatus (see below). The proponents of this approach will maintain that no advantage is gained by selection of a stacking system (see below).

ZEE coupled to a discontinuous MBE buffer system has the obvious disadvantage that one must locate such a system of convenient pH and ionic strength from the literature [11, 18, 19]. It has the following advantages: (i) The zone of extracted protein is visualized by a tracking dye and its migration into the collection chamber can be visually followed. (ii) In view of the high concentration of the protein zone, the collecting chamber may be of small volume (see Section 2.3). (iii) In view of the relatively low mobility of the buffers which make up MBE systems the ionic strength of the stacking gel is low (usually 15 mM), and thus relatively high voltages can be applied without exceeding the Joule heat dissipation capacity of the apparatus. (iv) Any number of volume of gel slices can be extracted simultaneously. The limit to the load of gel slices is solely that it may not exceed the volume of the stacking gel. Evidently, the latter may be increased nearly indefinitely within the constraints of the gel diameter discussed above. (v) No special apparatus other than a collection chamber to be attached to conventional gel tubes (Figs. 3, 4) is required [14].

2.3   Apparatus and procedures

Although several types of electrophoretic extraction devices have been reported [1, 20] or are commercially available (CBS Scientific, Isco, Shandon) only two representative apparatus types will be described and critically evaluated here, one pertaining to the use of a single extraction buffer [15], the other to the application of an MBE system [14].

2.3.1   Elution using a single buffer

A representative ZEE approach, using a single buffer, is that of Hunkapiller *et al.* [15]. The apparatus, which is now commercially available (CBS Scientific # ECU-040, CBS Scientific Co. P.O. Box 856, Del Mar, CA 92014) consists of an electrophoresis tank with two electrode chambers and a mixing chamber (Fig. 1), one or more H-shaped elution blocks (Fig. 2), which sit on a ledge in the electrophoresis tank that separates the anodic from the cathodic chamber, a three channel peristaltic pump and a low voltage power supply (0 – 500 V). The floor of the Plexiglas electrophoresis tank has a highly mirrored surface that allows the observer to see the bottom of the elution cells. The electrode chambers are separated by a barrier with a ledge on which the elution blocks sit. Up to five elution blocks can be accommodated in the chamber. Each of the two buffer chambers has a spigot through which excess buffer can flow into the common mixing chamber. The mixing chamber has a spigot connected to tubing through which the buffer can be recirculated into the electrode chambers via a peristaltic pump. Each buffer chamber has electrodes made of platinum wire which run along the bottom of the electrode chambers at opposite ends of the tank. Each of the wires is connected to a terminal lug that extends upward from a corner of the

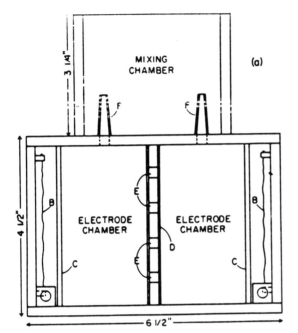

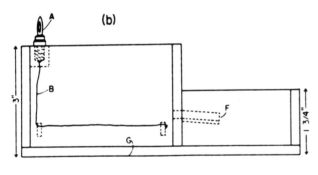

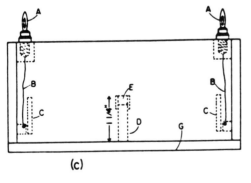

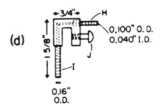

Figure 1. Electrophoretic elution tank. (a) Top view; (b) side view; (c) end view; (d) connector for pump tubing. A, terminal lug; B, platinum wire electrode; C, baffle plate; D, separation plate for electrode chambers; E, slot for elution cell; F, drain trough; H, connector to pump tubing; I, connector to tank chamber; J, set screw. Reproduced with permission from [15].

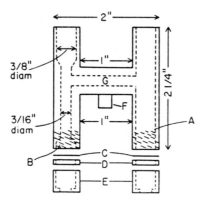

Figure 2. Electrophoretic elution cell. A, gel loading well; B, sample collection well; C, dialysis membrane; D, silicon rubber washer; E, screw cap with open top; F, peg for holding slot in elution tank; G, cross passage. Reproduced with permission from [15].

chamber. The elution blocks are machined from a single rectangular piece of plexiglas, the bottoms of which are threaded to accommodate an open-top screw cap with a teflon/silicone washer. To assemble the block for electrophoresis, the open-top screw caps are unscrewed and the washers removed. Small squares of dialysis membrane are cut slightly larger than the diameter of the screw caps and placed against the bottom of the block. The membrane is secured into place by the compression of the washers inside the open-top caps as the caps are tightened on the threaded lower end of the elution blocks. The assembled blocks are tested for leakage by filling them with buffer and letting them stand on a paper towel for 10 min before gel slices are added.

Gel slices are cut into small pieces, 1–2 mm, and placed into the large volume chamber of the elution block. The gel pieces are then carefully overlaid with soaking buffer (2% SDS in electrode buffer) sufficient to cover them and left for 1 h. The soaking buffer is overlaid with elution buffer which contains 0.1% SDS and the elution block is filled with this solution. Any large air bubbles in the elution block are carefully removed by gently tilting the cell. The loaded blocks are inserted into the electrophoresis chamber which is filled with electrophoresis buffer to a level sufficient to overflow into the mixing chamber. Air trapped beneath the open-top caps is then flushed away with the aid of a Pasteur pipette with a bent tip, care has to be taken to avoid contact with the dialysis membrane which can be easily punctured. The pump is set up so that a constant flow of buffer (3 mL/min) is moved from the mixing chamber to each of the two electrode chambers.

The electrode terminals are then connected and electrophoresis is carried out at 50–100 V constant voltage setting for around 15–20 h. Proteins from the gel pieces migrate to the anode (SDS-derivatized proteins) and collect in the small volume sample collection chamber on the left side of the block. The block is then carefully removed from the chamber and all of the buffer in the large volume chamber is removed and discarded. The eluted proteins in the sample collection chamber (150–200 µL) are then carefully removed with a Hamilton syringe and drawn up and down several times to wash off any adhered proteins from the dialysis membrane. Finally, the dialysis membrane is removed and washed in about 100 µL of buffer which is then added to the eluted protein solution.

Hunkapillar *et al.* [15] suggest using a 0.05 M NH_4HCO_3 buffer pH 7.4 at room temperature; at low temperatures (4 °C) they recommend a 0.05 M Tris/acetate buffer to avoid precipitation of SDS during the elution. They also suggest replacing the buffer after the initial electrophoresis with one of a lower molarity and then continuing the electrophoresis as a dialyzing step. We have found that 50 mM Tris-HCl, pH 7.4, is a better buffer for that purpose than either of the buffers suggested by Hunkapillar *et al.* [15], in addition we have not found it advantageous to change buffers after the initial electrophoresis since the elution buffer is compatible with standard Laemmli buffers [21], and can be applied directly to another SDS-PAGE gel if necessary. One note of caution: It is extremely important, that the electrode buffer is efficiently replenished during the course of the electrophoresis otherwise a pH discontinuity occurs between the left and right hand electrode chambers, and this will affect the recovery of proteins.

Although this apparatus has mainly been used analytically to purify proteins for amino acid sequencing [15], it can be used on a preparative scale. The elution blocks are available in two sizes, the larger of which can handle gel pieces of $1.5 \times 1.5 \times 0.3$ cm, and it is relatively simple to scale up the amount of protein handled since the electrode chambers can easily accommodate up to five elution blocks.

2.3.2 Multiphasic buffer electrophoresis-elution

Another approach to the elution of proteins from gel pieces is to exploit MBE for electrophoretic extraction since proteins concentrated into a moving boundary can be visualized as a sharply defined zone [11]. MBE automatically provides a highly concentrated (20–100 mg/mL) zone independently of the sample number or number of slices [11]. Recently, a new and improved apparatus for the application of MBE to the elution of proteins from gel slices has been described [14]. The apparatus consists of a cup shaped glass tube (Fig. 3a) having an enlarged mouth which acts as a reser-

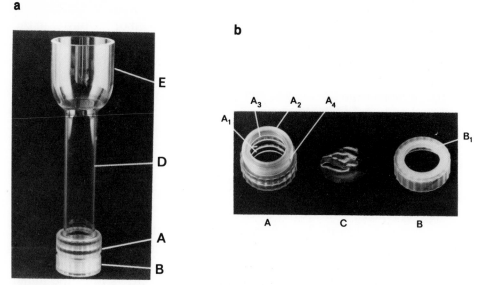

Figure 3. Collection cup attached to gel tubes. Panel (a) A, B, C collection cup; D, gel tube; E, reservoir for loading gel slices. Panel (b) collection cup: a threaded assembly of male part A and female part B. Part A features double O-ring (A1), a surface to support the dialysis membrane (A2), inner ledge (A3 faces the O-ring and is therefore not visible in this photograph) and air release groove (A4). Part B contains the freely rotating Teflon washer (B1, shown in place, visible through the polycarbonate as a white ring). A dialysis membrane disc (PartC) fits onto surface A2. Reproduced with permission from [14].

voir to hold the gel slices, and a small-volume collection cup (Fig. 3b) connected to the bottom of the gel tube. The tube fits into the upper buffer reservoir of the general purpose gel tube apparatus (Fig. 4) as indicated by the arrow in Fig. 4 section D. The exchangeable reservoirs of this apparatus (Fig. 4, parts B1 and B2) allow one to use gel tubes of 6, 8 or 18 mm inner diameter. The choice of tube diameter is dictated by the need to keep the length of the stack as short as possible and to minimize electrophoresis times. The length of the gel tube is sufficient to accommodate a gel of at least 4–5 times the sample volume which is more than sufficient to concentrate proteins into a sharp moving boundary. The collection cup (Fig. 3b) consists of a threaded assembly, and a freely rotating Teflon washer which holds a dialysis membrane in place without leaking or wrinkling. A small groove is cut across the threads to allow air to escape during the assembly of the two threaded parts. A double O-ring ensures that the gel tube is held firmly against the inner ledge of the cup and thus, that the gel tube and cup remain aligned during the elution process.

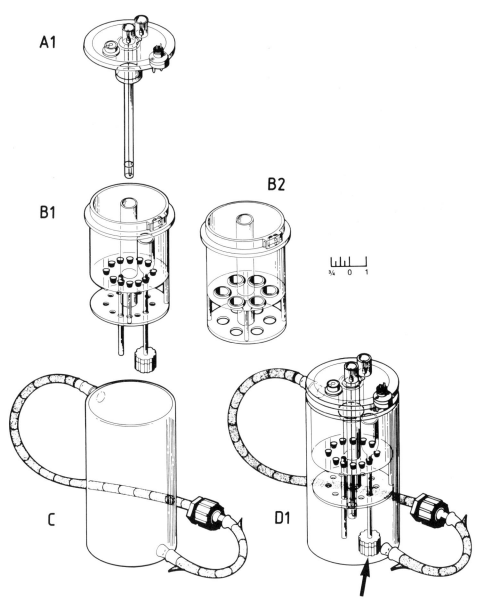

Figure 4. Gel electrophoresis tube apparatus. Apparatus materials are Pyrex unless indicated otherwise. (A1) Electrode top. Male banana plugs, male safety interlock component and spirit level are mounted on a polycarbonate plate. (B1) Upper buffer reservoir for 6 mm tubes, with or without collection cup. Tubes are seated in rubber grommets and aligned vertically by the bottom alignment plate. The sleeve is made of polycarbonate. (B2) Same for 18 mm tubes. (C) Jacketed lower buffer reservoir. (D1) Assembly. Glass-glass interfaces are bonded by Pyrex fusion; glass-plastic interfaces by RTV (General Electric). Construction details and commercial source are given in [11]. The arrow in (D1) indicates the assembled collection cup (described under Fig. 3) attached to the gel tube. Reproduced with permission from [11].

To extract and concentrate proteins from gel slices by MBE, the gel slices containing the protein to be eluted are applied onto the surface of a stacking gel (5% T. 2.5% C_{Bis}) in the apparatus described above. The gel slices are overlayered with catholyte in 10% sucrose, containing Bromphenol Blue to mark the stack. The catholyte chamber is filled with catholyte, taking care not to disturb the sucrose interface. Electrophoresis is continued until the stack has migrated to within 1 cm of the bottom of the gel. The emptied catholyte reservoir holding the gel tube is inverted on the bench surface. The male part of the collection cup is pushed onto the bottom of the gel tube to the level of the ledge in which it is held in place by the double O-ring. The male half of the cup is filled with anolyte, and a wetted dialysis membrane disc is placed smoothly onto the surface taking care to exclude air. The female half of the collection cup is carefully threaded onto its male counterpart. The reservoir is inverted, positioned in the anolyte reservoir and refilled with catholyte. Electrophoresis is resumed, and continued until at least 3 h after the tracking dye has entered the collection cup. Shorter or longer times may be needed depending on the width of the extended stack. The catholyte reservoir is then drained, inverted, placed on the bench surface and the female half of the collection cup is carefully unscrewed so as not to disturb the fluid in the collection chamber. The dialysis membrane is removed and the protein concentrate is withdrawn with a Pasteur pipet. The membrane is washed with water, and the wash combined with the extracted and concentrated protein. The apparatus and method described above has been used, in tandem with isoelectric focusing, to preparatively purify the glucagon receptor from rat liver plasma membrane protein [22]. 370 mg of rat liver plasma membrane protein was distributed over six 18 mm tube gels. The gel slice corresponding to the R_f of the glucagon receptor (previously determined) was excised from each gel, together with the slices preceding and following it.

The 18 pooled slices containing glucagon receptor were subjected to extraction and concentration on a stacking gel as described above. The recovery of the radiolabeled receptor using these procedures was 68% of the total amount of radioactivity loaded onto the gel. Although, the yields of recovered protein using this procedure are good, the multiple cylindrical gels required for loads in the range of hundreds of milligrams, as in the example cited above, is cumbersome, and the large number of gel pieces generated requires several concentration gels to extract and concentrate the protein from them. Preparative slab gels could be used instead of cylinders; these would also have the further advantage that their large surface to mass ratios, as compared to gel cylinders, would make heat dissipation more efficient. Another disadvantage that we noted with this technique was that despite its inherent simplicity it was still prone to leakage during the extraction of the protein into the collection chamber. The prime source of leakage was due to using wrinkled dialysis membranes which allowed leakage of buffer from the collection chamber, incorrect positioning of the dialysis membrane also caused some problems. However, as long as the operator takes care, high protein recoveries could be achieved with this method.

2.4   Purification after extraction

Polyacrylamide gels placed in buffer elute non-proteinaceous, soluble, non-dialyzable material, apparently structurally related to polyacrylamide, into the medium. Additonal such material is removed from the gel upon electrophoresis. Although the eluted amount decreases with time of diffusion and electrophoresis, its release has no end point [10, 11]. Therefore, protein preparations derived from gel slice extraction either by diffusion or by electrophoresis contain large amounts of non-proteinaceous impurities. When 1 or 2 mg of protein are involved, the amount of this impurity may represent up to 90% of the weight of the product, as estimated by the ratio of protein/weight [10, 11]. In some applications, such as protein sequencing or antibody production, the presence of non-proteinaceous contaminant may be innocuous. In other applications, such as spectral analysis, it is detrimental. In the latter cases, however, it is possible to purify the protein from the contaminant by gel filtration [9, 16]. Conditions of gel filtration suitable for that purpose are: 0.02 M ammonium bicarbonate buffer, pH 8.0, Sephadex G-50. The buffer needs to be prepared from ammonium hydroxide and carbon dioxide gas; the Sephadex needs to be freed from soluble dextrans, preferably on a Soxhlet extractor over boiling water. After one to three uses, the columns should be discarded since they serve as mechanical sieves rather than as gel filtration media. After purification of protein extracts in that fashion, and elution of the protein into the hold-up volume (V_0) of the column, the eluate is lyophilized.

2.5   Homogeneity, yield and purity of the product in representative applications

Homogeneity of the product depends on the effectiveness of the resolution of the protein of interest from its neighboring contaminants in the gel pattern. It is therefore an analytical as well as a preparative problem. Nevertheless it will be discussed here since product homogeneity is the primary aim of all preparative work. In gel electrophoresis the effectiveness of resolution depends on gel concentration and pH. Both can be objectively optimized: pH by systematic pH variation of stacking gels, gel concentration by calculation based on the point of intersection of two Ferguson plots [11]. Strictly, however, this optimization of gel concentration applies only at the analytical scale or its scaled up equivalent, used preparatively by the ZEE methods. In elution-PAGE, where zones to be isolated have to migrate to the end of the gel, the optimally resolving gel concentration has been approximated by that which gives rise to the maximal separation of peaks [11]. To correctly predict resolution on elution-PAGE, a knowledge of band width is needed (see below).

Homogeneity of product can also be estimated by the extent to which sequence analysis on the product has been feasible. Representative sequencing results demonstrating homogeneity in that fashion are shown in Table 1.

Yield data for proteins have been reported in a sufficient number of cases to allow for a generalization only in the case of ZEE. These cases demonstrate with surprising unanimity that independently of the isolation problem and

Table 1. Proteins recovered from PAGE using electrophoretic elution in a single buffer[a]

Protein	Molecular weight M_r	Amount recovered µg	Recovery %	Amino acids identified by N-terminal sequencing
Human cytochrome oxidase subunit I	60000	1.5	–	20
Human serum albumin	68000	8	80	–
Sperm whale myoglobin	17500	9	90	–
Mouse I_A antigen A_e^k	25000	0.5	50	21
α Receptor	50000	2	–	–
Mouse T-cell suppressor factor	70000	30	–	–
Torpedo acetylcholine receptor subunit	65000	4	71	–
V8-protease-derived fragments of *Torpedo* acetylcholine receptor subunit	9000	20	–	73
	2500	4	–	21
Eel acetylcholine receptor subunit	40000	20	–	68
Calf acetylcholine receptor subunit	42000	2	–	35
Human fibroblast interferon	18000	0.5	85	35
Diol dehydratase subunit	29000	100	80	55
Rat liver gap junction	28000	20	60	52

a) Reproduced with permission from [15].

Table 2. Protein recovery from gel slices using ZEE

Protein	Recovery (%)	Reference
[125]I-Labeled vitelline envelope proteins	60 – 85	[23]
Double stranded DNA	71 – 101	[13]
[14]C-Labeled cellular proteins, L1210 cells	72 – 96	[24]
[32]P-Labeled DNA	high	[25]
Ferritin and myoglobin	75 – 93	[26]
[14]C-Labeled sea urchin sperm histones		
(μg)	39 – 75	[27]
[125]I-Labeled human growth hormone	70	[28]
[125]I-Labeled rat FSH	70 – 80	[29]

its conditions a yield of about 70% has been nearly universally achieved (Table 2). The purity, defined as protein/weight, has been similarly uniform at better than 90% in all cases in which the purification procedure by gel filtration detailed above has been applied.

3   Impact of band width measurement on preparative polyacrylamide gel electrophoresis

All preparative gel electrophoretic separations to date, whether by elution-PAGE or by a ZEE method, have been carried out without a knowledge of the actual distribution overlap. One can only surmise that little distribution overlap occurred in those cases in which protein sequencing of the product to up to 73 residues was feasible (Table 1). But it is not known, whether this was possible only in the rare cases where the zone of interest migrates at a large distance from its closest contaminants. In other words, there exists no table correlating R_f difference between the proteins with the number of residues which can be sequenced. Nor is there a corresponding correlation between isolated stained and apparently homogeneous zones and the relative distance of the protein zone of interest from its neighbors. It appears likely, however, that in all demanding separations, where the protein of interest and its contaminants migrate closely together, substantial distribution overlap exists. This is evidenced by the overlapping elution patterns in elution-PAGE even in those cases where the flushing of the elution chamber is rapid enough to prevent the mixing of consecutively eluting protein zones. It is also evidenced by re-runs of proteins isolated by a ZEE method (*e.g.* Fig. 5 of

[30]). It is quite likely, therefore, that the extracted protein needs to be re-fractionated once or even several times before a homogeneous product is obtained; this, of course, necessarily leads to yields rapidly approaching zero with increasing degree of homogeneity of the "product". These considerations make it obvious, how undesirable the present state of preparative electrophoresis in the absence of band width information is.

We have already pointed out, that instrumentation for band width determination during electrophoresis exists [7]. However, it is still too costly to construct, difficult to operate, too insensitive and commercially unavailable. It is important to realize, nevertheless, that armed with band width measurement, one can predict the numbers of necessary consecutive separations to achieve homogeneity. Moreover, a computer program of D. Rodbard exists (Fig. 38 of [11]) which allows one to predict the time in elution-PAGE between two components of known Ferguson plot and band width needed for their complete resolution. It is also quite likely that with a facility to determine band width the apparent advantage of zone excision methods based on apparent band separation over elution-PAGE will disappear. At that time, the myriad of apparatus previously developed in that field (Table 1 of [1]) can be expected to gain renewed relevance in preparative biochemistry.

4   References

[1] Chrambach, A., Nguyen, N. Y., in: Righetti, P. J., van Oss, C. J., Vanderhoff, J. W. (Eds.), *Electrokinetic Separation Methods*, Elsevier/North Holland, Amsterdam 1978, pp. 337–367.
[2] Hewick, R. M., Hunkapiller, M. W., Hood, L. E., Dreyer, W. J., *J. Biol. Chem.* 1981, *256*, 7990–7997.
[3] Houghton, M., Eaton, M. A. W., Stewart, A. G., Smith, J. C., Doel, S. M., Catlin, G. H., Lewis, H. M., Patel, J. P., Emtage, J. S., Carey, N. H., Porter, A. G., *Nucleic Acid Res.* 1980, *8*, 2885–2890.
[4] Horuk, R., Rodbell, M., Cushman, S. W., Simpson, I. A., *FEBS Lett.* 1983, *164*, 261–266.
[5] Massague, J., Czech, M. P., *J. Biol. Chem.* 1982, *257*, 5038–5045.
[6] Kapadia, G., Jones, A. J. S., Chrambach, A., *Prep. Biochem.* 1985, *15*, 61–94.
[7] Catsimpoolas, N., *Methods of Protein Separation*, Plenum Press, New York 1975, Vol. 1, pp. 27–68.
[8] Chen, B., Chrambach, A., Rodbard, D., *Anal. Biochem.* 1979, *97*, 120–130.
[9] Yadley, R. A., Rodbard, D., Chrambach, A., *Endocrinology* 1973, *93*, 866–873.
[10] Chrambach, A., Jovin, T. M., Svendsen, P. J., Rodbard, D. in: Catsimpoolas, N. (Ed.), *Methods of Protein Separation*, Plenum Press, New York 1976, Vol. 2, pp. 27–144.

[11] Chrambach, A., *The Practice of Quantitative Gel Electrophoresis*, VCH Publications, Weinheim and Deerfield Beach, FL 1985
[12] Otto, M., Snejdarkova, M., *Anal. Biochem.* 1981, *111*, 111–114.
[13] Zassenhaus, H. P., Butow, R. A., Hannon, Y. P., *Anal. Biochem.* 1983, *125*, 125–130.
[14] An der Lan, B., Horuk, R., Sullivan, J. V., Chrambach, A., *Electrophoresis* 1983, *4*, 335–337.
[15] Hunkapiller, M. W., Lujan, E., Ostrander, F., Hood, L. E., *Methods Enzymol.* 1983, *91*, 227–235.
[16] Nguyen, N. Y., Chrambach, A., *J. Biochem. Biophys. Methods* 1979, *1*, 171–187.
[17] Öfverstedt, L. G., Johansson, G., Froman, G., Hjertén, S., *Electrophoresis* 1981, *2*, 168–173.
[18] Jovin, T. M., Dante, M. L., Chrambach, A., *Multiphasic Buffer Systems Output*, PB Numbers 259309 to 259312, 196090 National Technical Information Service, Springfield, VA 1970.
[19] Chrambach, A., Jovin, T. M., *Electrophoresis* 1983, *4*, 190–204.
[20] Guellaen, G., Goodhardt, M., Hanoune J. in: Venter, J. C., Harrison, L. C., (Eds.), *Receptor Purification Procedures*, Alan Liss, New York 1984, Vol. 2, pp. 109–124.
[21] Laemmli, U. K., *Nature* 1970, *227*, 680–685.
[22] Horuk, R., Beckner, S., Lin, M. C., Wright, D. E., Chrambach, A., *Prep. Biochem.* 1984, *14*, 99–121.
[23] Gerton, G. L., Wardrip, N. J., Hedrick, J. L., *Anal. Biochem.* 1982, *126*, 116–121.
[24] Wu, R. S., Stedman, J. D., West, M. H. P., Pantazis, P., Bonner, W. M., *Anal. Biochem.* 1982, *124*, 264–271.
[25] Clad, A., Geri, H., *Anal. Biochem.* 1982, *124*, 299–302.
[26] Bodhe, A. M., Deshpande, V. V., Lakshmikantham, B. C., Vartak, H. G., *Anal. Biochem.* 1982, *123*, 133–142.
[27] Green, G. R., Poccia, D., Herlands, L., *Anal. Biochem.* 1982, *123*, 66–73.
[28] Nguyen, N. Y., DiFonzo, J., Chrambach, A., *Anal. Biochem.* 1980, *106*, 78–91.
[29] Wachslicht, H., Chrambach, A., *Anal. Biochem.* 1978, *84*, 533–538.
[30] Nguyen, N. Y., Baumann, G., Arbegast, D. E., Grindeland, R. E., Chrambach, A., *Prep. Biochem.* 1980, *11*, 139–157.

RED CELL ENZYME MARKERS IN FORENSIC SCIENCE: METHODS OF SEPARATION AND SOME IMPORTANT APPLICATIONS

John G. Sutton

Home Office Forensic Science Service, Aldermaston, Reading, Berkshire, UK

Abbreviations: ACES, N-(2-acetamido)-2-aminoethanesulphonic acid; **AC-PI,** erythrocyte acid phosphatase; **ADA,** adenosine deaminase; **AK,** adenylic kinase; **AP,** acid phosphatase; **DP,** discriminating power; **EPPS,** N-(2-hydroxyethyl)-piperazine-N'-3-propane sulphonic acid; **ESD,** esterase D; **G-1,6-diP,** glucose-1,6-diphosphate; **G-1-P,** glucose-1-phosphate; **G-6-PD,** glucose-6-phosphate dehydrogenase; **GLO-I,** glyoxalase I; **HEPES,** N-(2-hydroxyethyl)-piperazine-N'-2-ethane-sulphonic acid; **IEF,** isoelectric focusing; **MES,** 2-(N-morpholino)-ethanesulphonic acid; **MOPS,** 3-(N-morpholino)-propanesulphonic acid; **MPFSL,** Metropolitan Police Forensic Science Laboratory; **MTT,** (3-[4,5-dimethylthiazolyl-2]-2,5-diphenyltetrazolium bromide; **PEPA,** peptidase A; **6-PGD,** 6-phosphogluconate dehydrogenase; **PGM** phosphoglucomutase; **PHI,** phosphohexose isomerase; **p*I*,** Isoelectric point; **PMS,** phenazine methosulphate; **SOD,** superoxide dismutase.

1   Introduction

Fingerprints were shown by Faulds [1] to be unique to the individual and have been used as a means of identification in criminal cases since the beginning of the century [2]. Over the same period there have also been considerable advances made using various genetically controlled polymorphisms, in the ability to individualise blood. The best known of these polymorphisms are the ABO, MN and Rh systems which can be detected in blood stains, frequently after many years. In addition to the red cell antigens there are a number of polymorphic red cell enzymes which can be separated using a number of advanced electrophoretic techniques with high resolving power. Despite this sophistication these techniques still rely on the basic principles established by Tiselius [3], who found that proteins in solution at pH values above and below their p*I*s migrate in an electric field towards the pole of opposite charge. Protein molecules of the same kind move at the same rate and form sharp boundaries.

Separations of this type can be conducted in a buffer solution, for example the Tiselius cell, or by zone electrophoresis in which a narrow band of protein is supported on a solid medium such as a starch or polyacrylamide gel or on a membrane such as cellulose acetate. The function of the support medium is to act as an anticonvective matrix for the buffer solution which is in direct contact with the electrolytes in the electrode vessels. The type of buffer and the ionic strength employed will be governed by the proteins to be separated. The current ultimately obtained from a buffer will depend upon its ionic strength $\mu = 0.5 \sum cz^2$, where c = the molarity of the buffer and z = the valency of each ion present. Therefore, buffers which are prepared from weak acids and bases and which produce ions of low valency will have a low ionic strength and will only carry a small current.

The various electrophoretic methods which have been most extensively used in forensic science are those based on the various zone techniques employing starch or polyacrylamide gels. Enzyme visualisation is achieved by preparing the appropriate overlay in 2% agarose containing all the relevant co-factors and substrate necessary for that particular enzyme. The actual position of each isoenzyme is found by linking the enzyme reaction to a suitable electron acceptor which changes colour as it becomes reduced. The most commonly used acceptors are 3-[4,5-dimethylthiazolyl-2]-2,5-diphenyltetrazolium bromide (MTT) and Meladona's Blue. Reduction of these electron acceptors results in the formation of dark purple insoluble formazan, the formation of which is catalysed by phenazine methosuphate (PMS).

1.1   Discriminating power

The value of any polymorphic system in discriminating between different individuals is most conveniently expressed in terms of its discriminating power (DP) [4]. DP has been defined as the probability that two individuals taken at random will be discriminated by a given test. If, for example, two blood samples were grouped for AB0, phosphoglucomutase (PGM) and glyoxylase I (GLO-I), then the probability of the two samples having the same phenotypes can be calculated from the known frequencies in the population [5, 6]. For example, PGM exists as three common variants observed by starch gel electrophoresis [7] whose distribution in the population are: $PGM_1 1 = 0.592$, $PGM_1 2\text{-}1 = 0.352$ and $PGM_1 2 = 0.056$. The probability of the two samples matching according to this particular system is given by:

$$P_1 = \sum_{i=1}^{3} pi^2 \text{ where } P_1 \text{ is the grouping system,}$$

which is this case is PGM, and pi is the frequency of the particular PGM variant in the population. $P_1 = 0.592^2 + 0.352^2 + 0.056^2 = 0.476$. Similarly for the AB0 system, $P = 0.3949$, and for glyoxylase I (GLO-I) system $P = 0.373$.

The probability that these two blood samples match in all three systems can be determined according to the equation:

$$P = \prod_{j=1}^{3} Pj \text{ where '}j\text{' is the number of tests}$$

$P = 0.476 \times 0.395 \times 0.373 = 0.0701$. The probability of being able to discriminate between the two blood samples using the 3 tests will be $1 - 0.0701 = 0.929$. There is, therefore, a probability of 0.929 or 92.9% of being able to discriminate between two blood samples on the basis of the three systems. Table 1 shows some examples of the polymorphic enzyme systems and their DP values used routinely in the UK Forensic Science Laboratories.

Table 1. Observed frequencies of some human red cell enzymes from the Caucasian population of South East England [5][a]

Enzymes[b]	Phenotype			DP
	1	2-1	2	
Phosphoglucomutase (PGM)	59.2	35.2	5.6	0.524
Adenosine deaminase (ADA)	90.1	9.7	0.2	0.179
Adenylate kinase (AK)	92.4	7.5	0.1	0.140
Esterase D (EsD)	79.2	19.5	1.3	0.335
Glyoxalase I (GLO I)	21.4	49.8	28.8	0.623

	A	BA	B	CA	CB	C	
Erythrocyte acid phosphatase (ACPI)	11.9	41.4	37.4	3.3	5.8	0.2	0.670

a) Frequency of occurrence of various human blood groups in the UK and regional variations are detailed by Rothwell [6].
b) Other enzymes separated by starch gel electrophoresis include: 6-phosphogluconate dehydrogenase (PGD); glucose-6-phosphate dehydrogenase (GPD); carbonic anhydrase II (CA) and peptidase A (Pep A).

1.2   Isoelectric focusing

With the advent of isoelectric focusing (IEF) the discriminating power of several red cell enzyme systems has been dramatically increased. This technique utilised the fact that proteins possess both positive and negative charges. In the presence of an electric field and a pH gradient they migrate electrophoretically until they focus at a position which corresponds to their isoelectric point, *i.e.* the point at which they have no net charge. IEF, therefore, differs from conventional electrophoresis in that the pH is not kept constant throughout the whole system; instead, the sample components migrate electrophoretically in a 'stationary' pH gradient. A steady state will eventually be reached at which all the sample components are concentrated or focused as sharp bands at their respective p*I*s. Optimal resolution by conventional electrophoresis requires that the sample is applied as a narrow zone. IEF, however, sample application is not so critical because of its concentrating property; this is reflected by a much lower detection limit than in conventional electrophoresis. Further, proteins whose p*I*s differ by a few hundredths of a pH unit can be resolved.

The charged field in the electrofocusing gel can be created by a number of commercially available compounds called carrier ampholytes; these include Ampholines (LKB, Bromma, Sweden), Servalyts (Serva Feinbiochemica, Heidelberg, FRG) and Pharmalytes (Pharmacia, Uppsala, Sweden). Like proteins, these substances possess net charges that vary with the pH and have sharply defined p*I* values. If such a mixture is subjected to an electric field, the carrier ampholytes will become arranged in order of their p*I* values so that those with the lowest p*I* will be nearest the anode and those with the highest nearest to the cathode. When the pH gradient is fully established, the net charge of the carrier ampholytes will be zero and the gradient becomes stationary.

IEF can be conducted in solution in vertical glass columns or in conjunction with a stabilising medium when used in gels. Polyacrylamide has proved to be the best stabilising medium for analytical IEF, having a high stabilising capacity and being chemically very stable. In addition, the endosmotic properties of polyacrylamide are very weak, due to an almost total lack of bound charged groups, although these endosmotic effects can only be kept to a minimum if the reagents used are of the highest purity. The introduction of IEF in polyacrylamide gels has a number of important advantages over the various column techniques. Sample application is simple and can be done at different points on the pH gradient, this is particularly important when it is feared that binding of the protein by carrier ampholyte may occur. Secondly it is possible to separate more than one enzyme system on the same gradient. These are only two advantages, but equally important are: (i) low costs (1 g of carrier ampholytes per run in the 110 mL columns), (ii) low samples loadings (10–20 mg in the columns), (iii) short focusing time (24–48 h in columns), (iv) simple component visualisation, *e.g.* by protein staining or zymogram techniques.

2   pH Gradient engineering

Early electrofocusing work was conducted on 1 mm thick polyacrylamide gels [8, 9], although with the introduction of ultrathin gels, the technique became more sensitive and economical [10, 11, 12]. Recently, the resolving power has been increased, still further, by the introduction of narrow range carrier ampholytes. Equally, narrow ranges can be produced by flattening conventional carrier ampholyte gradients with various chemical separators and also by physical means. Indeed, there are many ways in which gradient manipulations of this type can be achieved: (a) cathodal drift [13], (b) varying the anolyte pH [14, 15], (c) the addition of amino acids to the cathodal and anodal wicks [16], (d) surface application of different carrier ampholyte species in gel strips [17], (e) the incorporation of separator molecules [18−22], (f) non-equilibrium focusing [23−25] or (g) the use of a thickness modified gradient (TMG) [26, 27]. The last three methods have been used successfully in improving the resolution of a number of polymorphic enzyme systems of forensic importance including PGM_1 and esterase D (EsD).

2.1   Application of separators

One of the most effective methods of flattening a pH gradient involves the use of various zwitterionic buffers. These are buffers with different pK values whose basic or acidic nature will displace carrier ampholytes to a position either side of their pI point. However, a number of compounds including amino acids, peptides, proteins and non-amphoteric buffers (*e.g.* amines) have even been used as separators [22]. Separator gradients, based on various zwitterionic-buffers, have been applied in the separation of a number of red cell markers including the common and rare variants of EsD [27], PGM_1 [28] and the simultaneous separation of both EsD and erythrocyte acid phosphatase (EAP) [29].

In a recent paper by Gill [30] the properties of 10 zwitterionic-buffers or separators were evaluated and their effects on a number of Ampholine gradients within the pH range 4−6 reported. In addition, these buffers were studied with regard to their stability and reproducibility under different temperature conditions. Some of the best separators proved to be N-(2-hydroxyethyl)-piperazine-N′-3-propanesulphonic acid (EPPS) (pK_a 8.0 at 25 °C), N-(2-hydroxyethyl)-piperazine-N′-2-ethanesulphonic acid (HEPES) (pK_a 7.5 at 25 °C) and N-(2-acetamido)-2-aminoethanesulphonic acid (ACES) (pK_a 6.8 at 25 °C), each of which produced gradients less than 1 pH unit wide within

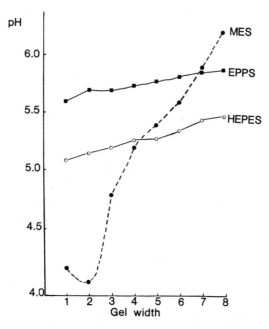

Figure 1. The effect of 3 different separators on a pH 5−7 gradient using histidine-threonine as electrolytes [28].

this pH range. This effect of EPPS and HEPES on a pH 5−7 gradient also produced gradients of less than 1 pH unit wide whereas 2-(N-morpholino)-ethanesulphonic acid (MES) (pK_a 6.1 at 25 °C) proved to be an acidic buffer displacing the gradient from pH 4.05 to pH 5.2 [28] (Fig. 1). Gradients of this type were found to be stable for up to 4 h, after which degeneration due to progressive acidification from the cathodic end took place. Although gradient stability is imperative, the practical application of these gradients is still acceptable since meaningful and reproducible patterns can be obtained within this time scale.

Different electrolytes appear to have little effect on the pH profile of the gradients, although those produced with an EPPS-pH 5 to 7 Ampholine gradient were the least effected. There was, however, some evidence that very strong anolytes such as 1 M orthophosphoric acid produced more acidic gradients with HEPES and ACES mixtures. The apparent ineffectiveness of different anolytes on the form of the pH gradient contrasts with the findings of Lan and Chrambach [15], who observed significant changes. An explanation for these contrasting observations is not obvious, although it may be related to the large volumes of electrolyte used in their vertical electrofocusing apparatus in contrast to the small volumes, limited by wick size, applied to the flat-bed gels in these studies. The effect of glycerol was to produce a more acidic gradient with both EPPS and HEPES gels, although no effect was detected with either a pH 4−6 or a pH 5−7 conventional Ampholine based gels (absence of these separators) [30].

2.1.1   Effect of temperature on separator-carrier ampholyte gradients

The temperature at which electrofocusing is undertaken in a carrier am-pholyte-separator gradient has a profound effect on the speed of migration of a protein. This is most graphically illustrated with the separation of the PGM-IEF system on a pH 5−7 (Ampholine)-EPPS gradient, when the migration rate was found to be far greater in gels run at 10 °C compared to those run at 5 °C [28]. An explanation for this phenomenon is not obvious as there was no apparent change in the pH profile of the gradient at either temperature, although the effect of changing viscosity and therefore the migration rate cannot be discounted. This fact does, however, underline the importance of controlling the temperature precisely if reproducible results are to be obtained. The application of separator-IEF systems has important and exciting implications and although it is not possible to predict exactly what effect a particular separator will have on a carrier ampholyte gradient computer program have now been developed which will determine the char-acteristics of these gradients more precisely [16].

2.2   Non-equilibrium focusing

This technique, developed by Divall [23−25], has been used successfully to increase resolution of both PGM_1, erythrocyte acid phosphatase (ACPI) and EsD systems. Essentially, the technique is one of electrophoresis in an electrofocusing gel, where a protein or isoenzyme is not allowed to reach its focusing point (Fig. 2). Separations were achieved more quickly and revealed

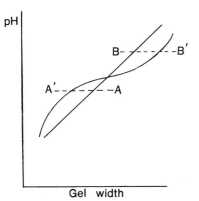

Figure 2. pH Gradient profile of an unfocused and fully focused carrier ampholyte gel. Separation be-tween proteins A^1 and B^1 is greatest in the unfocused gel (non-equilibrium focusing).

differences which would remain undetected or not completely resolved by either electrophoresis or IEF.

2.3   Application of thickness modified gradients to gradient flattening

Once a pH gradient has been created the different ampholyte species focus at their respective p*I* points, each species occupying a given volume. If the gel is made thinner over a particular area fewer ampholyte species can focus within that area with the result that the gradient will be flattened or expanded. This technique has been used to improve the resolution of the common EsD alleles [27] which will be reviewed later (Sect. 5).

2.4   Isoelectric focusing in immobilized pH gradients

Unfortunately, any carrier ampholyte (or carrier ampholyte/separator) gradient does have certain drawbacks: namely the instability of the pH gradient, uneven conductivity and buffering capacity and a limited loading capacity with regard to protein and salt concentrations. In an attempt to overcome some of these difficulties and to increase the resolving power above that achieved with a carrier ampholyte based system the technique of IEF in immobilized pH gradients have been developed [31]. Unlike the carrier ampholyte based system the various buffering groups or Immobilines (LKB trade name) are substituted onto the amide group of the acrylamide molecule. They are, therefore, bifunctional molecules having a buffering group at one end of the molecule and a double bond at the other. It is the latter group which is involved in the polymerisation process and which incorporates these derivatives into the polyacrylamide matrix. As Immobilines are co-polymerized within the matrix, their buffering groups cannot migrate in an electric field: this means that the pH gradient is indefinitely stable and must therefore be formed before polymerization takes place and can only be destroyed if and when the polyacrylamide gel is hydrolyzed.

Table 2 lists the seven Immobilines currently available. The first three are weak acids (carboxyl group) with p*K*s 3.6, 4.4 and 4.6; the other four are bases, with p*K*s 6.2, 7.0, 8.5 and 9.3. They are all crystalline powders, except for the last two bases (p*K* 8.5 and 9.3) which are liquids. All are supplied in 25 mL injection vials, the contents of which have to be dissolved in exactly 25 mL of distilled water; this is most accurately done by weight. Two addi-

Table 2. Immobiline species[a]

Immobiline	pK 3.6
Immobiline	pK 4.4
Immobiline	pK 4.6
Immobiline	pK 6.2
Immobiline	pK 7.0
Immobiline	pK 8.5
Immobiline	pK 9.3

a) Available from LKB Products (Bromma, Sweden).

tional Immobilines pK_a 2.6 and pK_b 12.0 have now been developed although these are not commercially available.

2.4.1 Principles of gradient formation

In order to cast a narrow Immobiline gradient, only a single Immobiline or buffering component is used, which is titrated around its pK with another, fully dissociated, or non-buffering Immobiline. Fig. 3 shows the titration of

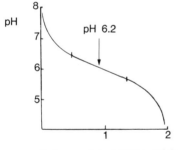

Volume of Immobiline pK 3.6

Figure 3. Titration curve of Immobiline pK 6.2, at a constant concentration, against 0.2 M Immobiline pK 3.6 [31].

Immobiline pK 6.2, at constant concentration in solution, against 0.2 M Immobiline, pK 3.6. This titration can be regarded as analogous to the titration of Tris buffer (buffering Immobiline) against HCl (non-buffering component). The free base, in solution, will give an alkaline pH upon the addition of the first few drops of Immobiline pK 3.6, the pH decreases exponentially and then approximates to linearity in the pH interval (pK+0.5 pH units to pK−0.5 pH units). By selecting the appropriate volumes of Immobilines at any two positions on the linear portion of the curve a linear pH gradient can be generated when these are incorporated into a polyacrylamide gel.

The basic equation governing the creation of an Immobiline gradient is the classical Henderson-Hasselbalch equation. This links the prevailing pH in solution to the pK of the buffering species and to the log of the ratio between the molarity of the dissociated form [A] and the molarity of the un-dissociated species [HA] or pH = pK+log [A]/[HA]. This equation will be modified depending on which species of acid or base is being used as a buffering group. If the buffer is an acidic Immobiline, the equation will have the form:

$$pH = pK_A + \log \frac{C_B}{C_A - C_B}$$

while, in the case of a basic Immobiline, the equivalent equation is:

$$pH = pK_B + \log \frac{C_B - C_A}{C_A}$$

where C_A is the molarity of an acidic Immobiline and C_B is the molarity of a basic Immobiline.

2.4.2   Creation of one unit pH gradients

In order to decide the most appropriate pH gradient, the pIs of the various proteins/isoenzymes to be separated must initially be determined. This information can most readily be obtained from a broad spectrum Ampholine gradient by measuring their pI values with a surface electrode [32, 33]. Suppose, for example, a pH 4.2 to 5.2 gradient had to be created. Initially. a buffering Immobiline must be chosen whose pK falls within the middle of the pH range, that is about pK 4.7; of the acid Immobilines available, pK 4.6 is the most suitable (Table 3). Since this Immobiline can be regarded as a fairly strong acid, an equally strong base or non-buffering Immobiline must be used; for this purpose pK 9.3 would be the most suitable. The actual volumes of Immobilines required to form this gradient can be derived from the Henderson-Hasselbalch equation although for convenience a series of tables are available in the LKB Application Note 324. The principle governing the choice of buffering and non-buffering Immobilines applies throughout the pH range 3.8 to 10 except within the pH intervals 4.6 to 6.1 and 7.2 to 8.4 where suitable buffering Immobilines are not available. Although gradients can be prepared within these particular pH ranges using single buffering and non-buffering Immobilines the volumes required to form some gradients would be excessive, consequently the cost and the destaining times of gels would be unacceptable.

Table 3. Buffering and non-buffering Immobilines required to form some 1 pH unit gradients

pH Gradient in gel 10 °C	Immobiline	
	Buffering	Non-buffering
3.8 – 4.8	pK 4.4	pK 9.3
4.0 – 5.0	pK 4.6	pK 9.3
4.9 – 5.9	pK 4.6 ⎫ pK 6.2 ⎭	pK 3.6 (acid) and pK 9.3 (basic)
5.7 – 6.7	pK 6.2	pK 3.6
6.6 – 7.6	pK 7.0	pK 3.6
7.3 – 8.3	pK 7.0 ⎫ pK 8.5 ⎭	pK 3.6 for both
8.0 – 9.0	pK 8.5	pK 3.6
9.0 – 10.0	pK 9.3	pK 3.6

2.4.3 Electrical characteristics of Immobiline- and carrier ampholyte-based gels

The current/voltage profiles of Ampholine and Immobiline-based gels are different (Fig. 4). The current associated with a carrier ampholyte-based gel will drop depending on the carrier ampholytes used to within a range of between 5 to 10 mA. The voltage will reach a plateau of approximately 2.5 kV whilst the maximum power achieved will range from 12.5 to 25 W depending on the carrier ampholytes species used. With an Immobiline gel, the current will drop to a few µA within the initial 5 to 10 min, whilst the voltage will increase rapidly to whatever voltage the power pack can provide. The power generated within the gel initially rarely exceeds 1 W so there is practically no temperature gradient within the gel. By utilizing the moveable electrodes on the 2217 LKB Ultrophor it is possible to achieve a voltage gradient of up to 2.0 kV/cm although under these conditions it is essential that both the gel and the surface of the cooling plate are free of water to avoid a direct short circuit.

2.4.4 Computer controlled systems for generating immobilized pH gradients [34]

Computerised systems for generating immobilized pH gradients have now been developed in which the basic and acid Immobilines and the catalysts are dispensed from microprocessor operated burettes. The end points of the gra-

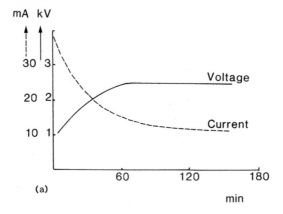

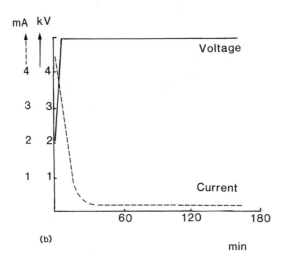

Figure 4. Variation in current and voltage in (a) carrier ampholyte and (b) in an immobilized pH gradient.

dient, or stepped gradient, are initially entered *via* a key-board and the final form of the gradient is displayed by high resolution graphics. The production of a series of stepped gradients could provide the ultimate system for multiple enzyme typing in which different polymorphic systems are separated simultaneously on gradients specific to their p*I* interval. Automation offers a number of important advantages including reproducibility, greater economy of expensive reagents, greater adaptability in preparing gels of different volumes and less demand on the practical skills of the operator.

3   Phosphoglucomutase

PGM (EC.2.7.5.1) is ubiquitous in nature; it has been found in extracts of mammalian muscle, brain, heart, liver and kidney [35], in human semen [36], vaginal secretions [37], and saliva [38, 39]. It also occurs in the plant kingdom. Cori *et al.* [40] found the enzyme in yeast while other workers have reported its presence in *Neurospora* [41] and in the potato [42]. The enzyme catalyses the reversible transfer of phosphate between the first terminal carbon of a number of a-D-sugar phosphates. In addition to glucose it can utilise phosphates of glucosamine [43] N-acetylglucosamine [44] galactose [45] and ribose [46]. PGM is activated by Mg^{2+} ions and G-1,6-diP. Considerable data on the effects of various activators and inhibitors have been described in the literature some of which is contradictory and difficult to understand. The enzyme is strongly inhibited by Zn ions [47] but it does show enhanced activity in the presence of both Mg ions and imidazole [48]. The precise function of imidazole is not fully understood, although early work considered that it acted as a chelating agent [49] while more recent studies have suggested that it played a vital role at the active site by forming a complex with G-1-P and Mg^{2+} ions [50, 51]. The mechanism of action has been reviewed by Ray and Peck [52].

3.1   Polymorphism and nomenclature

The discovery by Spencer *et al.* [7] in 1964 that human red cells show three distinct electrophoretic patterns by starch gel electrophoresis has important implications for the forensic biologist (Fig. 5). Seven bands of activity were observed designated 'a' to 'g'. Variation between individuals was found only between the 'a' to 'd' bands; the simplest explanation was that two alleles designated PGM_1^1 and PGM_1^2 were responsible each determined by the same locus (PGM_1). Subsequent studies by Hopkinson and Harris [53 – 55]

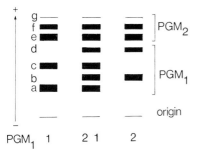

Figure 5. Diagram of the three common PGM_1 phenotypes from the human red cell as observed by starch gel electrophoresis using a 0.1 M Tris/0.1 M maleic acid/0.01 M $MgCl_2$/0.01 M EDTA buffer, pH 7.4 [7].

revealed that three separate loci, PGM$_1$, PGM$_2$ and PGM$_3$, existed each of which determined a specific group of isoenzymes. A number of variants have been recorded at the PGM$_1$ locus by starch gel electrophoresis [53–58] whilst Brinkman *et al.* [59] have reported the existence of an extremely weak PGM$_1$ allele in two generations of one family. Silent alleles have also been described by Fiedler and Pettenkofer [60] and by Ueno *et al.* [61]; these are extremely rare but when encountered could lead to errors in disputed paternity cases.

Until 1976, PGM$_1$ typing in the UK operational laboratories was conducted by starch gel electrophoresis using the basic technique described by Spencer *et al.* [7]. During that year, Bark *et al.* [9] reported the existence of 10 phenotypes determined by the PGM$_1$ locus on a pH 5–7 Ampholine (LKB) gradient which increased the DP of this system from 0.53 (starch) to 0.77. The ten phenotypes could be accounted for on the basis of a 4 allele system at the PGM$_1$ locus and not two as originally proposed [7, 62] in which the 'a' and 'b' bands were resolved into either one or two components (Fig. 6). Bark

pH5

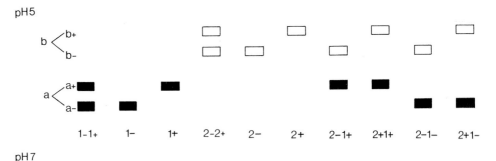

pH7

Figure 6. Diagram showing the 10 PGM$_1$ patterns ('a' and 'b' bands) separated on a pH 5–7 ampholine gradient. The proposed relationship of the new PGM$_1$ alleles to those initially described by Spencer *et al.* [7] by starch gel electrophoresis is given.

used the same nomenclature as Spencer *et al.* [7] except that he described the most cathodically focusing 'a' and 'b' bands as a- and b- and the more anodal as the a+ and b+. A PGM$_1{}^1$ phenotype observed by starch gel electrophoresis may therefore be one of three possible phenotypes by IEF designated PGM$_1$ 1–(a–), PGM$_1$ 1+(a+), PGM$_1$ 1–1+(a–a+). Similarly, a PGM$_1$ 2 could be either a PGM$_1$ 2–(b–), PGM$_1$ 2+(b+) or PGM$_1$ 2–2+(b–b+). The PGM$_1$ 2-1 heterozygote could, therefore, be one of 4 possible phenotypes 2+1+, 2–1+, 2–1– or 2+1–. These initial observations and conclusions were subsequently confirmed by other population and family studies [63].

Table 4. Comparison of the different nomenclatures describing the ten common PGM₁ phenotypes observed by IEF

Bark *et al.* [9]	Kühnl *et al.* [64]	Bissbort *et al.* [65]
1 −	a 3	1 F
1 +	a 1	1 S
2 −	a 4	2 F
2 +	a 2	2 S

Table 5. Observed frequencies of the common PGM₁ (IEF) phenotypes observed in the (a) Caucasian [5] and (b) immigrant population of South East England [6]

PGM₁ (IEF) phenotype	Frequency	
	(a)	(b)
1 −	1.6	1.7
1 +	40.4	40.3
1 − 1 +	16.9	16.8
2 −	0.3	0.4
2 +	3.2	3.4
2 − 2 +	2.1	2.0
2 − 1 −	1.4	1.3
2 − 1 +	7.3	7.0
2 + 1 +	22.1	22.3
2 + 1 −	4.7	4.8

Gene frequencies (a) PGM_11- 0.131, PGM_11+ 0.635, PGM_12- 0.057 and PGM_12+ 0.176.

In 1977 Kühnl *et al.* [64] described identical results except that IEF was conducted in commercially prepared Ampholine-polyacrylamide gels in a pH range of 3.5–9.5. They also reported that agarose gel electrophoresis could be used to detect the new polymorphic forms which they detected in leucocytes and red cell lysates and spermatozoa. Their results, like those of Bark *et al.* [9], could be explained on a 4 allele system which were numbered PGM_1a1, a2, a3 and a4; these were equivalent to 1+, 2+, 1− and 2−, respectively [9]. Finally, in 1978 Bissbort *et al.* [65] demonstrated the same polymorphism by electrophoresis in 18% acid starch gels in which the different phenotypes were classified on the basis of their electrophoretic mobility as: PGM_1F, PGM_1S, PGM_12F and PGM_12S (S, slow; F, fast). Comparison between all three systems is shown in Table 4; as yet, an universal nomenclature has not been adopted. Current data regarding the frequencies of these phenotypes in both the Caucasian and immigrant populations of the South East of England are shown in Table 5. All of the rare variants determined by the PGM_1 locus and initially described by Hopkinson and Harris have now been identified by IEF [66–68].

3.2   Characterisation of the common PGM_1 isozymes

In an attempt to locate the position of each of the isoenzymes determined by the PGM_1 and PGM_2 loci characterisation studies were conducted in this

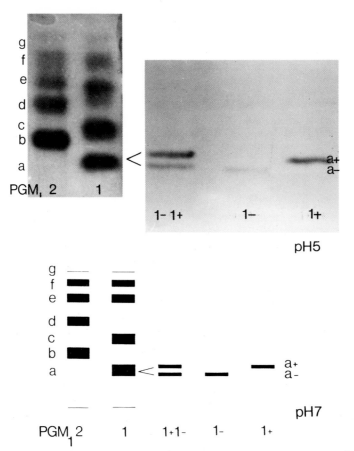

Figure 7. Characterisation of the 'a' band by IEF on a pH 5–7 gradient from three different PGM_1I lysates after their initial separation by polyacrylamide gel electrophoresis in a 0.1 M Tris/0.01 M maleic acid/0.01 M $MgCl_2$/0.01 M EDTA buffer, pH 7.4 [69].

laboratory [69] to ascertain the position of the respective 'a', to 'g' isoenzymes initially separated by polyacrylamide gel electrophoresis. The position of each band was initially located by staining the edge of the polyacrylamide gel; the unstained area associated with each band was then transferred to the IEF gel and run against control red cell lysates of known PGM_1 phenotype (Fig. 7). In a succession of experiments the position of each isoenzyme was located (Fig. 8). Comparison between the position of the various 'a' and 'c'

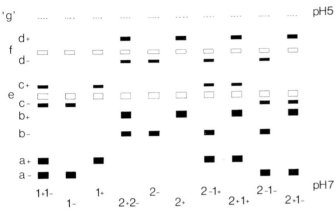

Figure 8. Proposed relationship between the first and second locus isoenzymes of PGM from human red cell lysates observed by IEF in a pH 5−7 gradient [69].

isoenzymes observed by IEF (Fig. 8) revealed that they appeared to move as isoenzyme pairs. The a+ is always paired with the less intense c+ and not the c-band. Similarly, the a− is always paired with the less intense c− band and not the c+. An identical relationship is observed with b+, d+ and the b− and d−isoenzymes. An additional feature of this separation is that the isoenzymes determined by the PGM$_1$ locus overlap those determined by the PGM$_2$ locus in the c+/− positions. Attempts at characterising the 'g' band failed primarily because the activity of the enzyme recovered after electrophoresis was too low. It was assumed that the 'g' band focused more anodally to the d+ since a common band was found in this position with all 10 phenotypes.

Theoretically it should be possible to identify the different PGM$_1$ phenotypes from the position of the c−/+ and d−/+ bands. In practice, however, it was found that the c−/c+ isoenzymes focused so close to the 'e' band (PGM$_2$), that invariably they only appeared as very weak bands or could not be recognised. The d− and d+ bands were frequently accompanied by isoenzymes (possibly secondary) which appeared predominantly between the

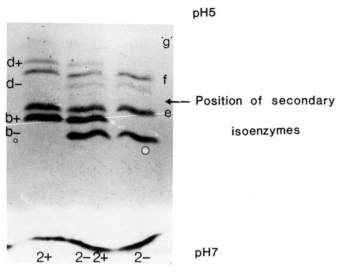

Figure 9. Separation of the b±, d± isoenzymes (PGM₁) and the'e' and 'f' isoenzymes (PGM₂ on a pH 5–7 gradient [69].

d– and 'e' positions (Fig. 9). No heterogeneity at the PGM_2 locus was observed although with prolonged electrofocusing the 'e' band was found to split into two equal components (personal observation). It is not known whether this represents further polymorphism, although the observation made by Brinkman and Koops [70] that the same band from human spermatozoa also appears as a doublet, when separated by polyacrylamide electrophoresis, suggests that this observation may represent further polymorphism at this locus.

3.3 PGM_1 typing of body fluids

An identical polymorphism was observed in human semen [71] (Fig. 10). In a survey of 100 semen stains the observed frequencies of 9 of the 10 phenotypes showed close agreement between the observed and expected gene frequencies on the basis of a 4 allele system. Enhanced activity was recorded when the semen stains were extracted in 0.1% mercaptoethanol prepared in distilled water, although in an earlier study it was shown that for maximum activity both imidazole and EDTA were also required in the overlay mixture (unpublished data). At no time was any second locus activity in stain extracts observed although this has been reported in concentrated extracts of spermatozoa [72].

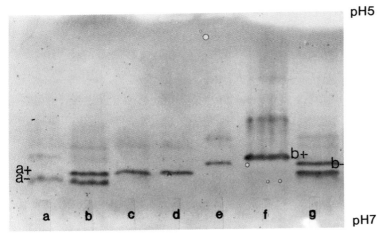

Figure 10. IEF band pattern focusing of six of the ten PGM₁ phenotypes from human seminal plasma (a) 1−, (b) 1−1+, (c) 1+, (d) 1+, (e) 2−, (f) 2+ and (g) 2−1+. (an example of a 2−2+ phenotype was not available at the time of this survey [71]).

Both PGM₁ and PGM₂ locus activity has been recorded in the buccal cells associated with whole saliva [38]. No activity was detected in the liquid phase although Divall *et al.* [39] found that the enzyme could be demonstrated if activated by an extract of a red cell lysate (free of red cell ghosts). The lysates could be derived from a number of animal species, including man, and should be mixed with the liquid saliva prior to its application on the electrofocusing gel. It was concluded that a certain co-factor(s), as yet unknown, was missing from the liquid saliva which was restored by the addition of the red cell extract.

3.4 Problem areas with PGM₁ typing

The major problems related to PGM₁ typing involve (a) the misinterpretation of certain phenotypes, (b) gradient distortion either through high salt or protein concentrations and (c) anomalous patterns observed when typing post-mortem blood samples.

3.4.1 Mistyping

The PGM₁ typing of bloodstains is routinely conducted on a conventional pH 5−7 Ampholine gradient prepared either on 1 mm or 0.15 mm gels. Instances have been reported where misinterpretation of certain phenotypes has occurred, particularly the mistyping of a PGM_11- or a PGM_11+ pheno-type as a PGM_12+1- or PGM_12+1+, respectively. This could be due to insufficient resolution in the area in which the $c+/c-$ and $b+$ band focus or poor interpretation of the relative intensities of the $a-/c-$ and $a+/c+$ bands. The apparent coincidental focusing of the $c+/c-/b+$ isoenzymes does not appear to occur in every batch of Ampholine; in those instances when it did occur it was concluded that conductivity gaps existed in the nor-mal $5-7$ pH gradient which prevented adequate separation of this group of isoenzymes with similar pI values [32, 33].

Improved resolution can be achieved in three ways, (a) by incorporating some pH $6-8$ Ampholine into a normal pH $5-7$ gradient; this will increase the number of pH intervals [33], (b) by using a non-equilibrium focusing method [23] or (c) by the construction of a pH gradient specifically designed for the resolution of the $a-/a+$ and $b-/b+$ bands. The preparation of specific gra-dients of the later type can be generated by incorporating a separator into a pH $5-7$ gradient [28] or by the construction of a specific immobilized pH gradient [73].

3.4.2   Carrier ampholyte-separator gradient

The incorporation of the separator EPPS into a conventional $5-7$ Am-pholine gradient will flatten the gradient over a pH range of approximately $5.5-5.9$ producing a dramatic increase in the separation of the $a\pm$ and $b\pm$ bands [28] (Fig. 11). This gradient is also suitable for the resolution of some of the rare variants particularly the a8 (pI 5.9) and the a9 (pI 5.89) (Dykes notation) from the common $1+$ or a1 variant and the a7 (pI 5.67) from the common $2+$ or a2 variants. Gels run at $5\,°C$ produced a much slower migra-tion rate and were therefore more suitable for the separation of other rare alleles which focus in a more cathodal position [68] (Fig. 12). Bloodstains up to 3 months old have been successfully typed using this system. However, even with the increased resolution afforded by the separator method, the $c-$ band focuses perilously close to the $b-/b+$ bands and great care must therefore be taken in interpretation. A careful note of the relative intensities of the $a-/a+$ and the bands in the c/b position should always be made.

3.4.3   Immobilized pH gradients

PGM_1 typing in an immobilized pH gradient (pH $5.8-6.8$) produces a separation as great as that obtained with an Ampholine separator system (Fig. 13) but a considerable drop in sensitivity was recorded [73] . At present,

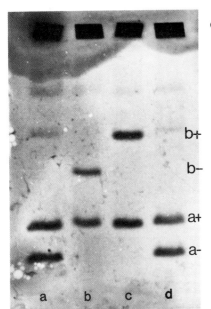

+

origin

b+

b−

a+

a−

a b c d

Figure 11. Separation of some PGM₁ phenotypes from bloodstains on an ultra-thin pH 5−7 Ampholine gradient containing 0.1 M EPPS run at 10 °C. Position (a) 1−1+, (b) 2−1+, (c) 2+1+ and (d) 1−1+ [28].

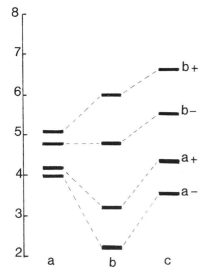

b +

b −

a +

a −

a b c

Figure 12. Separation of PGM₁ on ultrathin gels (a) using a conventional pH 5−7 gradient at 10 °C, (b) a gel containing 0.1 M EPPS run at 10 °C and (c) a gel containing 0.1 M EPPS and run at 5 °C [28].

an explanation cannot be provided for this observation although it could arise either through poor sample penetration into the gel or a loss in activity of the isoenzymes once they have reached their p*I* point in such a narrow but stable gradient in conditions of low conductivity. The effects of improving the conductivity of a pH 4−10 immobilized pH gradient have been demon-

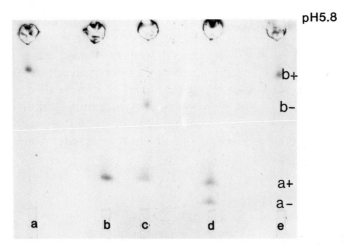

Figure 13. Separation of some PGM₁ phenotypes ('a' and 'b') bands only from week-old bloodstains on a pH 5.8–6.8 immobilized gradient. Samples (a) and (e) are PGM₁ 2+, (b) 1+, (c) 2−1+ and (d) 1−1+ [73].

strated by Fawcett and Chrambach [74], although Altland and Rossmann [75] have developed the technique of hybrid isoelectric focusing in which immobilized pH gradient gels are rehydrated in different carrier ampholytes prior to electrofocusing so combining the merits of both techniques.

3.4.4   Typing in the presence of high salt or protein concentrations

A disadvantage of electrofocusing in ultrathin carrier ampholyte gels is the instability of the pH gradient to extracts containing high concentrations of salts or protein. These deleterious effects can to a large extent be eliminated by IEF in wedge shaped polyacrylamide gels whose thickness varies from 50 μm (cathode) to 300 μm (anode). Samples are applied anodally, where the gel is thickest and the capacity is therefore the highest; thus, the effect of salts and high protein concentrations on the gradient are reduced. This technique has recently been applied successfully by Pflug [76] for PGM₁ typing of semen stains and vaginal swabs.

3.4.5   Typing of postmortem blood samples

Higaki and Newall [77] reported that certain discrepancies arose whilst typing postmortem blood samples by IEF. A number of patterns were observed which could not be related to their PGM₁ phenotype as determined by the starch gel electrophoresis. It was considered that lactic acid, the levels of which are known to rise dramatically after death [78] could possibly be contributing to these anomalous patterns. To evaluate this hypothesis a fresh postmortem blood sample (PGM$_1$+) which showed no deterioration was incubated with 20 mg/L of lactic acid. Within the initial 24 h a band appeared in the 2+ position which gradually increased in intensity over a 10 day period, although it still typed as a PGM$_1$I by starch. Extreme caution must, therefore, be exercised when typing postmortem blood samples by this method, and whenever possible it is strongly recommended that all results should be corroborated by starch gel electrophoresis.

4 Erythrocyte acid phosphatase

ACP (EAP, E.C.3.1.3.2) is systematically known as orthophosphoric mono-ester phosphohydrolase. It catalyses the transfer of phosphate from phosphate ester substrates to various alcohol acceptors such as methanol and glycerol. Its action is enhanced in the presence of these acceptors [79]; this fact has been employed to increase the sensitivity of the enzyme after electrophoresis. The enzyme has been detected in a number of tissues including the red cell [80] and human hair sheath cells [81].

4.1 Polymorphism

In 1963 Hopkinson *et al.* [80] reported genetic variants of ACPI in human red cells. Five phenotypes were observed by starch gel electrophoresis using gels made in a tris-succinate, pH 6 buffer with a citric acid-sodium hydroxide (pH 6) bridge buffer. Family studies indicated that polymorphism was based on three allelic genes called Pa, Pb and Pc each of which determined two isoenzymes and ultimately 5 phenotypes called A, BA, CA, CB and C. Gene frequencies in a British population have been quoted [80] as 0.35 Pa, 0.6 Pb, and 0.05 Pc with a DP of 0.67. Activity can be detected with phenolphthalein diphosphate or 4-methylumbelliferyl phosphate prepared in a citrate buffer, pH 5. The former substrate has proved inadequate for typing bloodstains since a long incubation time was required [82]. Successful typing of bloodstains up to 5 weeks old was possible with the latter substrate whilst Randall *et al.* [12], using an ultrathin gel IEF technique, were able to type bloodstains up to a year old.

A number of rare variants have been described. In 1965 Giblett and Scott [83] reported a new phenotype (RA) in a black person in Seattle; this proved to be a heterozygous combination of the Pa and the new allele Pr. Another variant called the BD phenotype was described by Karp and Sutton [84], whilst Giblett and Scott [83] reported further examples of the RA phenotype as well as several RB and RCs. The Pe allele was found in a Danish man [85] whilst the Pr gene appears to be restricted to both black and Chinese populations [86]. In 1970 Herbich *et al.* [87] reported a silent allele in a Viennese family, whilst Turowska *et al.* [88] reported a silent allele in a Polish family. In summary, therefore, the ACPI system is governed by three relatively common alleles Pa, Pb and Pc and three rarer alleles Pr, Pd and Pe and the occasional silent allele.

The genetic basis of the isoenzyme doublet is not known, although it has been proposed that the two isoenzymes are conformational isomers. The respective isozymes differ in their enzymatic properties and these differences are reflected in their different intensities after starch gel electrophoresis. The relative intensities of each isoenzyme can be altered by varying (a) the concentration of the substrate in the stain, (b) the pH of the staining mixture and (c) the phosphate buffer concentration in the typing gel [89]. More recent studies undertaken by Golden and Sensabaugh [90] have shown that ACPI activity is not only enhanced by various alcohol acceptors but that the acceptor activity increases with chain length to a maximum of 5 carbons, *e.g.* ribitol. In addition, they reported that the enzyme exhibits stereospecificity in which the most anodal isoenzyme (starch) determined by each allele has a significantly greater phosphotransferase activity. However, in the presence of an alcohol acceptor, such a 2 M glycerol, the degree of enhancement is dependent on the phenotype in the order B>A>C.

4.2   Thermostability studies

Thermostability studies conducted by Luffmann and Harris [91] on red cell lysates showed that the common alleles had different temperature stability profiles: the order was A>B>C. In 1976 Wraxall and Emes [92] confirmed these observations with red cell lysates, when they observed that within 30 min at 37 °C the BA type lost 'a' band activity so that it was indistinguishable from an ACPI B, while an ACPI B phenotype could lose some of its "b" band intensity giving a pattern indistinguishable from a CB type. Similar changes were reported by McWright [93]. Although temperature can influence the stability of the various isozymes, the nature of the surface on which the blood is deposited is also critical. Recent studies undertaken at the Home Office Forensic Science Laboratory, Aldermaston, UK have shown that certain strongly electropositive metals can alter the apparent phenotypic pattern. Typical changes observed were BA to CB, B to C or B to CB. An explanation for these transitions has not been established, although they could be electrochemical in nature.

4.3   Isoelectric focusing in carrier ampholyte gels and immobilized pH gradient gels

ACP1 typing of bloodstains is routinely undertaken by IEF. Initially, this was performed on 1 mm polyacrylamide gels but for reasons of economy and improved sensitivity 0.15 mm ultrathin gels have also been used. Typing of the common ACPI phenotypes can be achieved on a pH 5–8 gradient (Ampholine) prepared on 12.5 cm wide gels, although poor resolution of the rarer Pe, Pd and Pr alleles was recorded. If IEF is conducted in a pH 4–8 gradient prepared on 15 cm wide gels, using the non-equilibrium focusing method [24], a clear separation of the common and rare alleles can be achieved. This technique has the additional, but important, advantage that a clear separation between the haemoglobin and the ACPI a_1 a_2 bands, which are frequently quenched by haemoglobin, is obtained.

Separation of the common ACPI phenotypes can also be achieved on a pH 5.5–7.6 immobilized pH gradient [94]. Fig. 14 shows the IEF patterns obtained from 3 of the common phenotypes separated after 3 h at a maximum

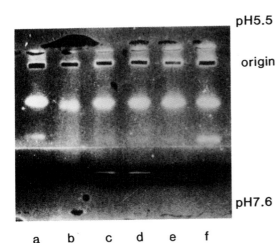

pH5.5

origin

pH7.6

a   b   c   d   e   f

Figure 14. Separation of 3 of the common ACPI phenotypes from 1 week old bloodstains by IEF using an immobilized pH 5.5–7.6 gradient. Sample (a) CB, (b) B, (c) BA, (d) BA, (e) B and (f) CB [94].

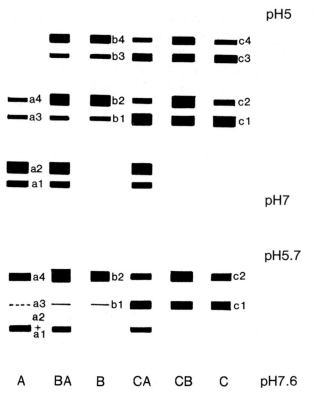

Figure 15. Diagrammatical representation of the IEF patterns of the common ACPI phenotypes separated on (a) a pH 5.7 Ampholine gradient and (b) on a pH 5.5–7.6 immobilized pH gradient [94].

voltage of 1500 V. Successful typing of 7 week old bloodstains was possible, although as the stains aged longer extraction with freshly prepared 1% w/v dithiothreitol was required. A notable feature of the IEF patterns on Immobiline gels was the straightness of the zymogen patterns across the whole width of the gel which is not always observed on a conventional IEF plate. The band patterns of the common ACPI phenotypes separated on an immobilized pH gradient and conventional carrier ampholyte gradient are shown and compared in Fig. 15.

Both systems gave similar relative positions for the ACPI isoenzymes, but a greater separation was achieved on the immobilized pH gradient. A number of differences in the profiles of the A isoenzymes was observed. It is not certain whether the most cathodal band was actually a combination of a1 + a2 or just a2 (a1 not focusing in this gradient) or whether a4 described by Divall [24] is the same as 'a4' seen in this study. The 'a4' band has a more basic p*I* value than the a4, b2 and c2 bands, which could arise either through the interaction of the ACPI isoenzymes with Immobilines or through the increased resolving power of the immobilized gradient. The application of an immobilized gradient may not always assist in the identification of certain ACPI phenotypes especially when the activity is low. Differentiation of the B and CB phenotypes may be difficult when c1+b1 activity is low especially with the CB. In other instances it might be possible to prove the existence of an A phenotype in bloodstains with weak ACPI activity by looking for activity in the 'a4' region. A further disadvantage is the identification of the rare variants 'r' and 'e' which have p*I* values less than 5 [24] and therefore cannot be resolved on this gradient.

5   Esterase D

EsD (E.C.3.1.1.1) is described as a non-specific esterase since its physiological and exact metabolic role are not known. It can be demonstrated in most tissues including the red cell [95], hair sheath cells [96] and even in spermatozoa [72]. Both the fluorogenic substrates methylumbelliferyl acetate or butyrate can be used for its detection after starch gel electrophoresis of IEF.

5.1   Polymorphism

EsD was initially reported by Hopkinson *et al.* [95] as being genetically polymorphic, showing two codominant alleles EsD 1 and EsD 2 in the human red cell. Rare alleles have been reported using different electrophoretic techniques; EsD 3 [97], EsD 4 [98], EsD 5 [99], EsD 6 [100], EsD D [101], and a null allele EsD 0 [102]. The discriminating power of the system is low when

Table 6. EsD population data (after [27]) [a]

Phenotype	1	2-1	5-1	5-2	2	5	Total
No. observed	101	16	6	2	1	0	126
No. expected	97.3	19.04	7.75	0.963	0.93	0.154	

$\chi^2 = 1.633$ with 2 degrees of freedom (P = ns)
L (phenotypes 2 and 5 were combined for the analysis)
EsD allele frequencies: EsD 1: 0.879; EsD 2: 0.086; EsD 5: 0.035
a) Samples were kindly donated by the Oxford blood transfusion centre.

based on the EsD 1 and 2 alleles (DP 0.22), although this can be increased if the EsD 5 allele is included (Table 6). Stability in bloodstains has been variously quoted as being from 3 to 4 weeks when typed by starch gel electrophoresis [103].

5.2   Isoelectric focusing studies

IEF has been used by a number of workers to improve the resolution [104, 105], particularly between the products of the EsD 2 and EsD 5 alleles, which focus within a pH range of pI 4.9 to 5.2 [25, 27]. The IEF patterns of the enzyme are complex and a thorough understanding of its subunit structure must be appreciated before the different phenotypes can be recognised. The enzyme has a dimeric structure in which each isoenzyme is composed of two subunits, each of which is determined by a separate allele. A homozygous individual will have identical subunits which are known as homodimers. In the heterozygous state some of the dimers will be formed from subunits composed of different allele products; these are called heterodimers. Since subunits combine together in a random fashion, the heterozygote will produce 3 different kinds of isoenzymes: the EsD 2-1 heterozygote will therefore produce the 1-1 and 2-2 homodimers and the 2-1 heterodimers (Fig. 16).

Olaisen *et al.* [106] resolved all the common EsD phenotypes using 200×200×1 mm thick polyacrylamine gels containing 3% carrier am-

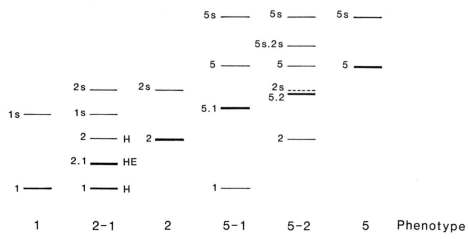

Figure 16. Diagram showing the IEF patterns of the common EsD variants separated on a pH 4.5–5.4 Pharmalyte gradient in conjunction with the separator HEPES and a thickness modifier (TMG). The position of homodimer (H) and heterodimer (HE) units associated with the 2-1 phenotype are shown [27].

pholytes. The technique was successful but it was costly and required a 6 h IEF time. However, it did show that there were relatively large p*I* differences between the principal bands of EsD 5 (p*I* 5.0) and EsD 2 (p*I* 5.1) and that separation of the EsD 2 and 1 bands was more difficult since they had a p*I* difference of approximately 0.02 units. Improved resolution for forensic application can be achieved in one of four ways (a) by IEF with selected carrier ampholytes [107]; (b) using a non-equilibrium IEF technique [23] or (c) separation in a carrier ampholyte/separator system [25] or (d) through the inclusion of a thickness modifier (TMG) in such a gradient [25].

5.2.1   pH 4.5−5.5 Servalyt gradient

Budowle [107] separated the products of all three alleles on a pH 4.5−5.5 Servalyt gradient 9.5 cm wide within 85 min using the LKB Ultrophore unit and a maximum of 3000 V. Successful typing of bloodstains up to 4 weeks old was reported with this system.

5.2.2   Ampholine gradient 'non-equilibrium method' [25]

Separation of the 6 phenotypes determined by the EsD 1,2 and 5 alleles can be achieved within 2 h at 4 °C on a pH 4−6 Ampholine gradient prepared in a 20 cm wide ultrathin gel using a field strength of 100 V/cm.

5.2.3   pH 4.5−5.5 Pharmalyte separator or thickness modified gradients [27]

Addition of HEPES to a narrow range pH 4.5−5.5 Pharmalyte gradient prepared in an ultrathin gel will flatten the gradient within a pH range of 4.85−5.35. Separation in this gradient will resolve the respective homodimers associated with the EsD 1, 2 and 5 homozygotes but not between the hetero- or homodimers associated with the 2-1 or 5-2 heterozygotes. Increased flattening, and improved resolution of these heterozygotes, can be obtained by incorporating a TMG into the gel; this produces a gradient with an overall pH range of pH 4.9−5.35 flattened over a distance of 3 cm in a region of pH 5.05−5.1. Separation can be achieved after 3 h at a maximum power setting of 1 W for the initial 30 min and 4 W for the remaining 2 $^1/_2$ h at a maximum voltage set at 1500 V.

6   Glyoxalase

GLO 1 (E.C.4.4.1.5) catalyzes the reversible conversion of reduced glutathione and methylglyoxal to S-lactoylglutathione through a thiohemiacetal intermediate; whilst glyoxalase 2 (E.C.3.1.2.6) (GLO 2) converts S-lactoylglutathione into lactate and reduced glutathione.

6.1   Distribution in human tissues

Human erythrocytes contain substantial amounts of GLO 1 but no GLO 2 [108, 109]. GLO 1 has been demonstrated in semen [110] and in hair sheath cells by Burgess and Twibell [111] and by Sutton *et al.* [112]. Blake and Sensabaugh [113] reported that there is about four times as much GLO 1 per cell in sperm cells compared to red cells and that the same phenotypic expression was observed in both. Its physiological function has been postulated as a stimulator of cell division since methylglyoxal has been reported as an inhibitor of cell division.

6.2   Polymorphism

GLO 1 exhibits polymorphism; initially, this was demonstrated by starch gel electrophoresis by Kömpf *et al.* [114] in Germany and by Bagster and Paar [115] in England. The polymorphism could be explained on the basis of two common alleles GLO_1^1 and GLO_1^2 with frequencies of 0.42 and 0.43 and a DP of 0.62. A rare allele GLO_1^3 was described by Brinkman and Püschel [116] and by Ranzani *et al.* [117], while a silent allele GLO_1^0 was described by Olaisen *et al.* [118]. The electrophoretic patterns of the GLO 1 isoenzymes display banding patterns and activity ratios which suggest a dimeric enzyme structure.

6.3   Separation by isoelectric focusing

Although starch has been the principal method of separation, Uotila and Koirvusalo [119] described a method of separation based on either a broad or narrow range carrier ampholyte gradient. Separation on a broad pH 3.5 – 10 gradient produced 2 bands from the haemolysates of all individuals examined, and although slight p*I* differences were observed between the GLO

1 and GLO 2 phenotypes, the resolution of the GLO 2-1 was poor. In a pH 3−5 gradient the three phenotypes could be more readily distinguished, although four bands were now observed from each homozygote with a p*I* range of 4.40−5.05. IEF does not increase the discriminating power of this system. The technique in its present form also suffers from the limitations caused by the interaction of methylglyoxal with Ampholine at approximately pH 5. This reaction produces a series of very dark continuous bands extending across the width of the gel masking the position of the bands. Similar observations have been made in this laboratory, although it was observed that the banding described extended further into the gradient (personal observations). Since the p*I* values of this enzyme extend over approximately 1 pH unit their separation on an immobilized pH gradient may prove to be a more effective method of separation. As yet we are not aware if an interaction between methylglyoxal and the immobilized pH gradient is likely to take place.

7   Multiple enzyme typing on isoelectric focusing gels

Various modifications have been employed to improve the resolution and to develop techniques for multi-enzyme typing of bloodstains on the same IEF gel. Randall *et al.* [12] initially described an ultrathin gel technique, using 15 mm wide glass plates, in which both the ACPI and ADA phenotypes could be separated simultaneously on a pH 4−8 gradient. In 1983 Dorrill and Sutton [120] assessed the feasibility of conducting simultaneous IEF of both PGM₁ and ACPI using different halves of the same gel, or sequential typing of both systems from the same bloodstain extract on a pH 5−8 gradient prepared on 12.5 cm plates (LKB). In practical terms sequential typing proved to be a success with only fresh or strong bloodstains. The PGM₁ typing of weak bloodstains was only partially successful because the citric acid buffer (pH 5), used in the development stage of the ACPI phenotypes, reduced the activity of the PGM₁ isozymes to be detected in the second stage. The split-plate method worked satisfactorily, although it meant that only half the number of bloodstain extracts could be typed at any one time, which is uneconomical for most forensic science laboratories with a large number of bloodstains to analyse.

The application of 15 cm wide plates has been used very effectively by Finney *et al.* [29] for the simultaneous separation of both ACPI and the six common EsD phenotypes on a pH 4−8 gradient flattened with the chemical spacer,

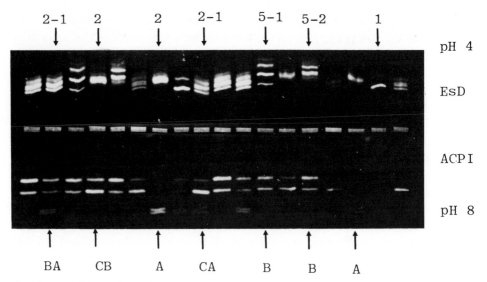

Figure 17. Photograph showing the simultaneous separation of both ACPI and EsD phenotypes from a number of bloodstains separated on a MOPS-pH 4−8 Ampholine gradient [29].

MOPS 3-(N-morpholino)-propanesulphonic acid (Fig. 17). Application was
made centrally with 'onserts' made of Whatman 1 M paper. It was found
that the ACPI isoenzymes moved cathodally whilst the EsD isozymes moved
anodally. In order to achieve the optimal conditions for separation for each
system, particular attention had to be paid to a number of parameters. Firstly, gels some 0.26 mm and not 0.15 mm thick had to be used, as they were
found to be less likely to produce band distortion. Secondly, the distance between the electrodes had to be set to 12 cm for optimal resolution of each
system, while the temperature had to be carefully regulated to 6 °C. The technique has been now fully evaluated with casework bloodstains and is in use
in a number of the UK operational laboratories.

8   Application of enzyme polymorphism to the typing of human hair

The initial attempts at typing hair were based on the AB0 system. Saki [121]
macerated hair by chemical treatment in an attempt to expose the antigenic
sites. In a later study described by Yada *et al.* [122] hairs were physically
crushed, then typed by the normal absorption-elution technique [123]. Using

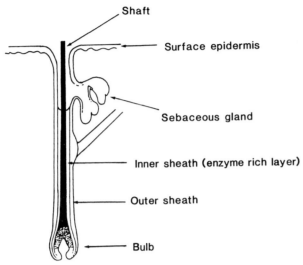

Figure 18. Diagrammatic representation of the root of a human hair showing the position of the enzyme rich sheath cell layer.

this procedure they claimed to be able to attain a good correlation with the known blood groups of the individuals from whom the hair samples were initially obtained. The experience of other workers [124] has shown that although hairs show antigenic activity, the results are not conclusive enough for routine typing and court production.

Alternative grouping methods based on the various polymorphic enzymes associated with the sheath cells (Fig. 18) of plucked head hairs were initially investigated by Twibell and Whitehead [96]. They reported the presence of PGM$_1$, adenosine deaminase (ADA), adenylic kinase (AK), EsD and PGM$_1$, although of these only PGM$_1$ was reported as being in sufficient quantity to be typed by starch gel electrophoresis (Fig. 19). Parallel studies conducted by Yoshida *et al.* [125] and Oya *et al.* [126] demonstrated the presence of PGM$_1$, PGM$_3$, EsD and 6PGD in the Japanese population; in all instances the phenotypic patterns obtained matched those obtained from the corresponding blood samples. Later studies reported the presence of 6-phosphogluconate dehydrogenase (G-6PD), phosphohexoisomerase (PHI), acid phosphatase (AP) [112], PGM$_3$ [127] (Fig. 20) and the ten PGM$_1$ phenotypes by IEF [128]. Although AP activity could be readily detected by starch gel electrophoresis, the pattern did not correlate with the ACPI patterns normally associated with blood. In a subsequent report by Kimes *et al.* [81] it was demonstrated that AP activity in sheath cells is a mixture of lysosomal AP and ACPI. Lysosomal AP activity is inhibited by tartrate, so when this is incor-

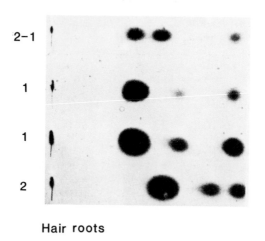

Hair roots

Figure 19. Starch gel electrophoretic pattern of the common PGM₁ phenotypes observed by starch gel electrophoresis [7] associated with the whole root of a human head hair [96].

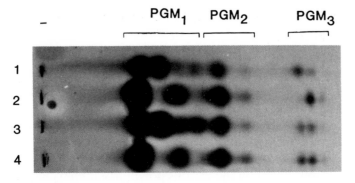

Hair roots

Figure 20. The starch gel electrophoretic patterns determined by the PGM₁ and PGM₃ hair from the sheath cells associated with a number of different human head hairs (1) PGM₁ 2-1, PGM₃ 2; (2) PGM₁ I, PGM₃ I; (3) PGM₁ 2-1, PGM₃ 2-1 and (4) PGM₁ 1, PGM₃ 2-1 [127].

porated into the developing mixture the band patterns normally associated with the ACPI complex can be revealed.

Stability studies [112] have shown that all the enzymes detected in fresh sheath cells could, with the exception of AK, be demonstrated after 3 weeks exposure to air (Table 7). Essentially the same results were obtained after 7 weeks, except that EsD activity had decreased to a point where reliable typing could not be undertaken. Probably one of the most significant features of this study was the discovery that both GLOI (DP 0.63) and PGM₁-starch (DP 0.53), which have the highest discriminating power, could be successfully typed after a 7 week period.

Table 7. Detection of hair sheath cell enzymes after a 3 and 7 week interval exposure to air [112] [a)]

System	Fresh	3 Weeks	7 Weeks	DP
Adenylic kinase (AK)	+	–	–	0.140
Esterase D (EsD)	+	+	–	0.335
Glyoxalase I (GLOI)	+	+	+	0.623
Glucose-6-phosphate dehydrogenase (G6PD)	+	+	+	Ethnic differentiation
Phosphohexose isomerase (PHI)	+	+	+	0.02
Phosphoglucomutase (PGM$_1$)	+	+	+	0.524
6-Phosphogluconate dehydrogenase (6PGD)	+	+	faint	0.081

a) Frequency data obtained from [5]. –, not detectable; +, typeable.

8.1 Multiple enzyme typing of the sheath cells associated with the root of a single hair

Studies so far described require a separate hair for each enzyme system. This is clearly a serious disadvantage, since it is not possible at present to positively identify two hairs microscopically as coming from the same individual. One approach to this problem was adopted by Yoshida *et al.* [125], who performed starch gel electrophoresis in thick starch gels which were subsequently sliced horizontally and stained for different polymorphic systems. Using this technique they were able to identify both PGM$_1$ and EsD in a single operation. Although this method has the advantage of requiring only a single electrophoretic system, it may not be applicable with other enzyme combinations unless they have the same optimal conditions for separation *i.e.* pH, ionic strength, current and voltage. A second approach [129] involves the typing of cut hair sections derived from a single root for different polymorphic systems. Probably the most important systems are the PGM$_1$ system observed by IEF (DP 0.77) and GLOI (DP 0.63). Alternatively, either EsD (DP 0.33) or AK with a DP of 0.14 could be included.

8.2 Stability studies

In a series of experiments the stability of these enzymes was examined from cut sections of single hairs which had either been retained in air or in the commonly used microscopical mountant XAM (Hopkin Williams, Romford,

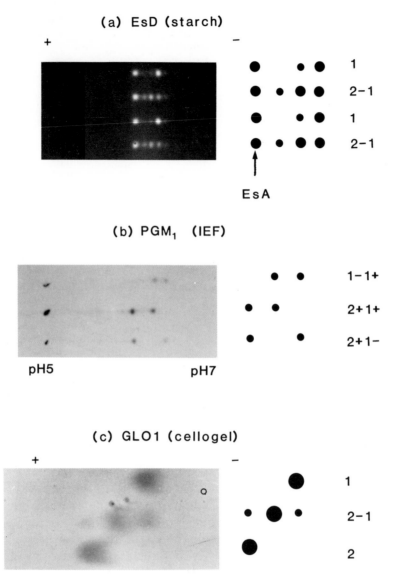

Figure 21. Multiple enzyme typing of single hair root sections (a) starch gel electrophoretic patterns of the EsD 1 and 2 phenotypes (b) IEF patterns of PGM_1 $1-1+$, $2+1+$ and $2+1-$ separated on a pH $5-7$ Ampholine gradient and (c) GLOI patterns separated on Cellogel membranes [129].

Essex) [129]. A number of solvents were capable of dissolving this mountant, although a 60/100 petroleum ether was finally adopted because of its relatively low vapour pressure and because it did not have the harmful inhalation effects experienced with solvents such as pyridine or tetrahydrofuran. Fig. 21

Table 8. Enzyme detection in hair sections after 4 and 8 weeks storage in air or XAM [129][a]

System	4 Weeks		8 Weeks	
	Air	XAM	Air	XAM
Phosphoglucomutase (PGM$_1$) Polyacrylamide Agarose	+	+	faint	+
Glyoxalase (GLO I)	+	+	faint	faint
Adenylate kinase (AK)	+	+	+	−
Esterase D (EsD)	faint	−	−	−

a) +, Typeable; −, not detectable.

shows some examples of the enzymes from hair sections taken from single head hairs, whilst Table 8 summarizes the results of the ageing studies on hairs retained in air or XAM.

The demonstration of enzyme polymorphism in human head hair sheath cells has important implications for the forensic scientist. Firstly, head hairs left at a scene of a murder or serious assault can be typed and correlated with a control blood sample taken from both defendant and accused. Secondly, head hairs can be used for reference purposes when a blood sample is not available after an extensive blood transfusion or where a pretransfused blood sample has not been obtained or is inadequate. It must be stressed that sheath cells are only found on hairs which have been forcibly removed from the scalp; it is extremely unlikely that hairs which have fallen naturally will carry any sheath cell material. Typing of other body hairs including chest and pubic hairs is possible, although in our experience overall enzyme activity is much lower and only PGM$_1$ (IEF) typing is possible.

9 Differentiation of some animal bloods on the basis of the isoenzymes of superoxide dismutase

Before any blood group analysis can be undertaken it is essential that the blood is established as being of human origin. Although very specific human anti-sera are available, this is not true of a number of animal sera produced commercially. All too frequently an anti-serum raised to detect one particular species will invariably cross-react with another, so making positive identification impossible. Of the anti-sera which are used in the forensic service are those directed against trout, deer and some farm and domestic animals. By using a red cell enzyme of very low DP [4], in conjunction with an immunological test, it is possible to discriminate between a number of the species. Of the enzyme systems examined, superoxide dismutase (SOD) was chosen because it is stable in bloodstains and is readily detected by IEF.

9.1   Polymorphism in humans

The isoenzymes of SOD are controlled by two separate gene loci SOD_A and SOD_B. SOD_B is located in the mitochrondrial fractions of most tissues, although it is absent in red cells [130]; SOD_A is found in all tissues except polymorphonuclear lymphocytes [130]. SOD exhibits polymorphism, and three electrophoretic variants have been recognised, SOD_A 1, 2-1, and 2. The SOD_A 1 variant is extremely common, the 2-1 and 2 phenotypes are very rare, but they do occur with higher frequencies in isolated communities [131, 132]. Examination of the SOD polymorphism in the red cell of a number of animal species in this and the Birmingham Forensic Science Laboratory, UK, revealed that all species examined showed enzyme activity with no apparent polymorphism within a particular species. The identification of animal bloods is routinely undertaken, particularly of trout, salmon and deer, in the investigation of poaching cases. Numerous trout and latterly salmon farms have become established in recent years, and a demand has now arisen for a definitive test for the identification of these species.

9.2   Immunological differentiation of *Salmonidae*

Anti-*Salmonidae* serum was raised in common carp (*Cyprinus carpio*), by infusing 0.25 mL of trout serum in Freund's complete adjuvant into the peritoneal cavity [133]. The fish were bled twice over a two week period, and after one month the titre of each antisera was determined using the cross-over technique of Culliford [134]. Aliquots of 0.25 mL of serum were freeze dried and stored at 4 °C before use. This antiserum was evaluated extensively against a whole range of coarse fish in addition to those members of the *Salmonidae* family [133]. All the *Salmonidae* species examined gave a positive reaction with this antiserum down to 1 : 400 dilution of serum. No coarse fish showed any cross-reaction except the grayling (family − *Thymalidae*), which is of the same order as the *Salmonidae*.

9.3 SOD polymorphism in *Salmonidae*

All the species examined showed SOD activity in their red cells which could be separated by IEF in a pH 2.5 – 8 gradient. This is shown diagrammatically in Fig. 22. Differentiation was possible with the exception of the sea trout and brown trout (p*I* 4.76), which are considered to be of common ancestry [135]. No SOD polymorphism was observed within any of the different species examined. For example, the IEF pattern obtained from sea trout caught in North Wales was identical to that obtained from fish caught in Cornwall. Similarly, brown trout caught in Cumbria had an identical pattern to brown trout held at any of the fish farms covered in this study. Although grayling could not be differentiated on an immunological basis, it could be separated from the various *Salmonidae* species by the p*I* values of its SOD isoenzymes observed in the same pH gradient.

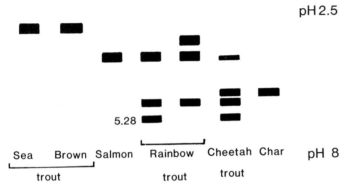

Figure 22. Diagrammatic representation of the SOD-IEF pattern from the blood of various members of the *Salmonidae* family separated on a pH 2.5 – 8 Ampholine gradient [133].

The six known varieties of rainbow trout, namely: Carabou, Washington, Shaster, White Brook, Winthrope and Grampian, could be classified into two distinct groups on the basis of the p*I* values of their SOD isoenzymes. The Carabou, Washington, Shaster, and White Brook strains all showed 3 isoenzymes whose p*I* values were 4.80, 4.90, and 5.07, respectively. Although the intensity of the isoenzymes from the Carabou, Washington and Shaster strains appeared identical, the 2 most anodic isoenzymes from the White Brook strains were of a much higher intensity. The remaining strains, that is, the Winthrope and Grampian, also possessed 3 isoenzymes, 2 of which had identical p*I* values to the most cathodic isoenzymes observed in the Carabou, Shaster, Washington, or White Brook strains. The third isoenzymes in this complex has a p*I* value of 5.28, which was the most cathodic isoenzyme recorded from any member of the *Salmonidae* family studied. The Cheetah trout was the only hybrid species examined. It was produced from a cross between rainbow trout and the American brook trout (char) and is used primarily as a game fish. The electrofocusing patterns that we observed appeared to be a mixture composed of the triple banded pattern associated with a Grampian or Winthrope strain and the single component found in the brook trout. This pattern was the most complex observed in any member of the *Salmonidae* family so far examined.

The results from this study suggest that it is possible to differentiate various members of the *Salmonidae* family on the basis of the isoenzymes of SOD from the red cell. In addition, we obtained some evidence that an identical polymorphism could be found in various tissues of the rainbow trout, although the appearance of additional but fainter bands of activity might be regarded as further evidence for an additional locus as suggested by Taggart *et al.* [136]. Although some 28 species of fish (excluding rainbow trout variants) from 8 different orders were examined, they have been few in number with the possible exception of the brown and sea trout. In forensic work, it would therefore be advisable to use control samples from the crime area in case rare variants, hitherto unreported, are present.

9.4   Identification of deer blood (*Cervidae*) on the basis of their haemoglobin and SOD patterns

As with Salmonidae identification, the forensic scientist often has very little material to work with in cases of deer poaching. Often he is presented with a car whose boot contains only a few hairs and/or bloodstains. Although deer hairs can be readily differentiated microscopically from the hairs of other animals, little can be stated about the species of deer involved. Similarly, although there are a number of commercially available anti-deer sera, these will cross-react with other animals such as sheep and goat. Initial experiments conducted in this laboratory showed that, like the Salmonidae, deer showed considerable SOD activity and that species differentiation could be undertaken on the basis of both their haemoglobin patterns and subsequently by their SOD patterns on the same IEF plate. Of a total of 40 species of deer, six species are resident in the UK. Of these six species, Red and Roe are indigenous to Britain, while Fallow, Sika, Muntjac and Chinese Water Deer have been introduced into this country in the past and are now feral [137] (Table 9). With the exception of managed herds of Reindeer in the Cairngorms, other species found in Britain are contained only in zoos.

Table 9. The six species of Deer found in Britain and their general location [137, 140]

Common name	Generic name	Areas of distribution
Red	*Cervus elaphus*	Scotland, North-West England. Few feral breeds in parks scattered throughout Midlands and Southern England.
Roe	*Capreolus capreolus*	Scotland, North, South and South-West England.
Fallow	*Dama dama*	South and South-East England. To a lesser degree Midlands and Wales.
Sika	*Cervus nippon*	Scattered in small areas throughout Britain.
Muntjac	*Muntiacus reevesi*	South and South-East England particularly Bedfordshire.
Chinese Water Deer	*Hydropotes inermis*	Bedfordshire and East Anglia.

The haemoglobin patterns in members of the Cervidae have previously been studied by IEF on a pH 6−7 gradient when marked heterogeneity in the haemoglobin patterns within this family was reported [138, 139]. Whilst providing a good basis, haemoglobin patterns alone provided insuffient data for separating all the species although further differentiation could be made on the basis of their SOD patterns [140]. Fig. 23 shows the haemoglobin and SOD patterns obtained from six British species separated on the same pH 5−8 gradient. Of the six common deer species found in the UK only Red and Sika had similar haemoglobin patterns. The subsequent development of the SOD patterns enabled all six species to be distinguished since no species showed the same combination of SOD and haemoglobin patterns.

Stability studies conducted on bloodstains showed that although methaemoglobin bands appeared these focused nearer the cathodic end of the gel than did the non-oxidised bands. Bloodstains up to two weeks old had identical haemoglobin patterns to those of the fresh lysates whilst SOD retained activity for at least a 2 month period. Bloodstains up to two weeks old had identical haemoglobin patterns to the lysates; no dimunition in SOD activity was observed during this period.

9.5 Differentiation of some farm and domestic animals

Species identification of some farm and domestic animals on the basis of their red cell SOD and haemoglobin patterns can be undertaken using a pH 5−9 gradient (unpublished data).

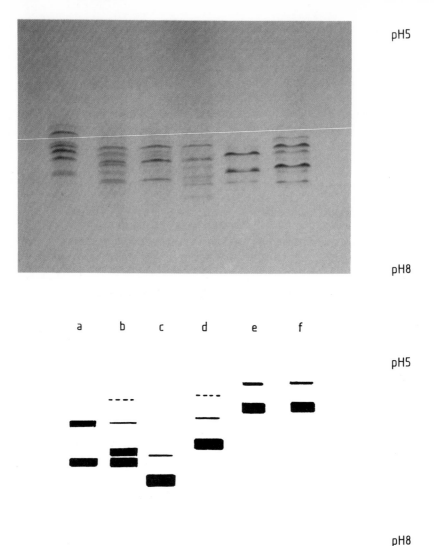

Figure 23. IEF patterns of haemoglobin and SOD patterns from the six species of British deer separated on a pH 5–8 Ampholine gradient. Position (a) Fallow, (b) Red, (c) Sika, (d) Reeves Muntjac, (e) Roe and (f) Chinese Water deer [140].

9.5.1   Cattle

No apparent differences were observed in the SOD patterns of the following breeds: Limousin, Hereford, Angus, Canadian Holstein, Charolais, Jersey or Ayrshire separated on this gradient. In addition, all these breeds had similar haemoglobin patterns with the exception of the Limousin, which had one band focusing in a more anodal position.

9.5.2 Sheep and goat

It was possible to distinguish between sheep and goat blood on the basis of their SOD patterns, but it was not possible to differentiate between varieties or strains within each species. No difference was observed between the haemoglobin patterns from a number of goat varieties examined, although the different sheep varieties did show diversity in their haemoglobin bands.

9.5.3 Dog and fox

A number of dog breeds were examined, including Lurcher, Lakeland Terrier, Red Setter, Golden Labrador, Poodle, Bassatt Hound and German shepherd dogs. No difference was observed in either the haemoglobin or the SOD patterns of any breeds, with the exception of the German shepherd dog. Fox blood showed similar haemoglobin patterns, although the SOD patterns focused in a more cathodic position and could be differentiated from the dog breeds examined.

10   Future developments

The application of DNA analysis for forensic investigation has exciting possibilities. DNA is highly polymorphic and could be applied in the differentiation of blood (white cells and platelets), semen, vaginal secretions and even sexing by utilising various restriction endonucleases and specific probes [141]. The technology is well established, although the electrophoretic techniques, particularly Southern blotting, are not used routinely in the forensic science laboratory. Future developments in the field of protein and enzyme analysis will almost certainly be directed towards improved resolution, shorter separation times, and improved sensitivities using gold-silver probes.

11   References

[1] Faulds, H., *Nature (London)* 1880, *22*, 605.
[2] Simpson, K., in: Taylor's *Principles and Practice Of Medical Jurisprudence*, 12th ed. Churchill, London 1965, p. 149.

[3] Tiselius, A., *Trans Faraday. Soc.* 1937, *33*, 524–531.
[4] Jones, D. A., *J. For. Sci. Soc.* 1972, *12*, 355–359.
[5] Stedman, R., *J. For. Sci. Soc.* 1985, *25*, 95–134.
[6] Rothwell, T. J., *J. For. Sci. Soc.* 1985, *25*, 135–144.
[7] Spencer, N., Hopkinson, D. A., Harris, H., *Nature (London)* 1964, *204*, 742–745.
[8] Burdett, P. E., Whitehead, P. H., *Anal. Biochem.* 1977, *77*, 419–428.
[9] Bark, J. E., Harris, M. J., Firth, M., *J. For. Sci. Soc.* 1976, *16*, 115–120.
[10] Görg, A., Postel, W., Westermeier, R., *Anal. Biochem.* 1979, *89*, 60–70.
[11] Radola, B. J., in: Radola, B. J. (Ed) *Electrophoresis '79*, de Gruyter, Berlin 1979, *pp.* 79–94.
[12] Randall, T., Harland, W. A., Thorpe, J. W., *Med. Sci. Law* 1980, *20*, 43–47.
[13] Viau, M., Constans, J., Boussou, C., *Sci. Tools* 1977, *24*, 25–26.
[14] Nguyen, N. Y., Chrambach, A., *Electrophoresis* 1980, *1*, 14–22.
[15] Lan, B. A., Chrambach, A., *Electrophoresis* 1980, *1*, 23–27.
[16] Arosio, P., Gianazza, E., Righetti, P. G., *J. Chromatogr.* 1978, *166*, 55–64.
[17] Altland, K., Kaempfer, M., *Electrophoresis* 1980, *1*, 57–62.
[18] Hjelmeland, L. M., Chrambach, A., *Electrophoresis* 1983, *4*, 20–26.
[19] Buzás, Z., Hjelmeland, L. M., Chrambach, A., *Electrophoresis* 1983, *4*, 27–35.
[20] Frants, R. R., Erikson, A. W., *Hum. Heredity* 1978, *28*, 201–209.
[21] Baxter, M., White, I., *J. For. Sci. Soc.* 1984, *24*, 483–488.
[22] Chrambach, A., *Mol. Cell. Biochem.* 1980, *29*, 23–46.
[23] Divall, G. B., Ismail, M., *For. Sci. Int.* 1983, *22*, 253–263.
[24] Divall, G. B., *For. Sci. Int.* 1981, *18*, 67–68.
[25] Divall, G. B., *Proceedings of the 10th International Congress of the Society of Forensic Haemogenetics,* München, 11–15 October 1983, pp. 501–505.
[26] *Isoelectric Focusing (Principles and methods)*, Pharmacia Fine Chemicals, Uppsala 1982, pp. 114–115.
[27] Gill, P., *Electrophoresis* 1985, *6*, 552–555.
[28] Gill, P., Sutton, J. G., *Electrophoresis* 1985, *6*, 23–26.
[29] Finney, S. T., Renshaw, N. A., Werrett, D. J., *For. Sci. Int.* 1985, *27*, 237–245.
[30] Gill, P., *Electrophoresis* 1985, *6*, 282–286.
[31] Righetti, P. G., *J. Chromatogr.* 1984, *300*, 165–223.
[32] Sutton, J. G., *J. For. Sci. Soc.* 1984, *24*, 111–119.
[33] Gill, P., Sutton, J. G., *Electrophoresis* 1984, *5*, 274–279.
[34] Altland, K., Altland, A., *Electrophoresis* 1984, *4*, 143–147.
[35] Cori, C. F., Cori, G. T., *Proc. Soc. Exptl. Biol. Med.* 1936, *34*, 702–705.
[36] Culliford, B. J., *Int. J. Legal Med.* 1969, *4*, 17–18.
[37] Price, C. J., Davies, A., Wraxall, B. G. D., Martin, P. D., Parkin, B. H., Emes, E. G., Culliford, B. J., *J. For. Sci. Soc.* 1976, *16*, 29–42.
[38] Sutton, J. G., *Proceedings of the 8th International Meeting of the Society for Forensic Haemogenetics,* London 23–27 September 1979, p. 265.
[39] Divall, G. B., *Proceedings of the 12th International Congress of the Society of Forsenic Haemogenetics,* Copenhagen 7–10 August 1985, p. 46.
[40] Cori, G. T., Colowick, S. P., Cori, C. F., *J. Biol. Chem.* 1938, *123*, 375–380.
[41] Reissig, J. L., *J. Biol. Chem.* 1956, *219*, 753–767.
[42] Boser, H., *Hoppe Seyler's Z. Physiol. Chem.* 1957, *307*, 240–246.
[43] Brown, D. H., *J. Biol. Chem.* 1953, *204*, 877–889.
[44] Leloir, L. F., Cardini, C. E., *Biochim. Biophys. Acta.* 1953, *12*, 15–22.
[45] Posternak, T., Rosselet, J. P., *Helv. Chim. Acta.* 1954, *37*, 246–250.
[46] Klenow, H., *Arch. Biochem. Biophys.* 1953, *46*, 186–200.

[47] Ray, W. J., Jr., *J. Biol. Chem.* 1969, *244*, 3740–3747.
[48] Harshman, S., Robinson, J. P., Bocchini, V., Najjar, V. A., *Biochemistry* 1965, *4*, 396–400.
[49] Sutherland, E. W., *J. Biol. Chem.* 1949, *180*, 1279–1284.
[50] Robinson, J. P., Najjar, V. A., *Biochem. Biophys. Res. Commun.* 1960, *3*, 62–66.
[51] Robinson, J. P., Harshman, S., Najjar, V. A., *Biochemistry* 1965, *4*, 401–405.
[52] Ray, W. J., Peck, E. J., in: Boyer, P. D. (Ed.) *The Enzymes*, 3rd ed, Academic Press, New York and London 1972, Vol. 6, pp. 407–477.
[53] Hopkinson, D. A., Harris, H., *Nature (London)* 1965, *208*, 410–412.
[54] Hopkinson, D. A., Harris, H., *Ann. Hum. Genet.* 1966, *30*, 167–178.
[55] Hopkinson, D. A., Harris, H., *Ann. Hum. Genet.* 1968, *31*, 359–367.
[56] Omoto, K., Harada, S., *Jpn. J. Hum. Genet.* 1970, *14*, 298–305.
[57] Blake, E. T., Omoto, K., *Ann. Hum. Genet.* 1975, *38*, 251–273.
[58] Turowska, B., Gawrzewski, W., *For. Sci. Int.* 1979, *13*, 129–131.
[59] Brinkmann, B., Koops, E., Klopp, O., Heindl, K., Rudiger. H. W., *Ann. Hum. Genet., London* 1972, *35*, 363–366.
[60] Fiedler, H., Pettenkofer, H., *Blut* 1969, *18*, 33–34.
[61] Ueno, S., Yoshida, H., Kiribayashi, K., Omoto, K., *Forens. Sci.* 1976, *7*, 239.
[62] Harris, H., Hopkinson, D. A., Luffman, J. E., Rapley, S., in: Beutler, E. (Ed.), *Hereditary Disorders of Erythrocyte Metabolism,* Green and Stratton, New York 1968, pp. 7–13.
[63] Sutton, J. G., Burgess, R., *Vox. Sang.* 1978, *34*, 97–103.
[64] Kühnl, P., Schmidtmann, U., Spielmann, W., *Hum. Genet.* 1977, *35*, 219–223.
[65] Bissbort, S., Ritter, E., Kömpf, J., *Hum. Genet.* 1978, *45*, 175–177.
[66] Dykes, D. D., Polesky, H. F., *Electrophoresis* 1981, *2*, 323–326.
[67] Dubosz, T., Koziol, P., *Hum. Genet.* 1981, *59*, 81–83.
[68] Dykes, D. D., Copouls, B. A., Polesky, H. F., *Electrophoresis* 1982, *3*, 165–168.
[69] Sutton, J. G., *Hum. Genet.* 1979, *47*, 279–290.
[70] Brinkmann, B., Koops, E., *Humangenetik* 1971, *14*, 78–80.
[71] Sutton, J. G., *J. For. Sci.* 1979, *24*, 189–192.
[72] Blake, E. T., Sensabaugh, G. F., *J. For. Sci.* 1976, *21*, 784–796.
[73] Sutton, J. G., Westwood, S. A., *Electrophoresis* 1984, *5*, 252–253.
[74] Fawcett, J. S., Chrambach, A., *Protides Biol. Fluids* 1984, *33*, 439–442.
[75] Altland, K., Rossmann, U., *Electrophoresis* 1985, *6*, 314–325.
[76] Pflug, W., *Electrophoresis* 1985, *6*, 19–22.
[77] Higaki, R. S., Newall, P. J., *Can. Soc. For. Sci. J.* 1979, *12*, 181–190.
[78] Jetter, W. W., *J. For. Sci.* 1959, *4*, 330–341.
[79] Tsuboi, K. K., Hudson, P. B., *Arch. Biochem. Biophys.* 1954, *53*, 341–347.
[80] Hopkinson, Ð. A., Spencer, N., Harris, H., *Nature (London)* 1963, *199*, 969–971.
[81] Kimes, D. R., Mohammad, A., Tahir, M. S., Stolorow, M. D., *J. For. Sci.* 1984, *29*, 64–66.
[82] Wraxall, B. G. D., Emes, E. G., *J. For. Sci. Soc.* 1976, *16*, 127–132.
[83] Giblett, E. R., Scott, N. M., *Ann. J. Hum. Genet.* 1965, *17*, 425–432.
[84] Karp, G. W., Sutton, H. E., *Ann. J. Hum. Genet.* 1967, *19*, 54–62.
[85] Sörensen, S. A., *Am. J. Hum. Genet.* 1975, *27*, 100–109.
[86] Shiki, L-Y., Hsia, D. Y-Y., *Hum. Hered.* 1969, *19*, 227–233.
[87] Herbick, J., Fisher, R. A., Hopkinson, D. A., *Ann. Hum. Genet.* 1970, *34*, 145–151.
[88] Turowska, B., Bugusz, M., Stojek, T., *Forensic Sci.* 1977, *10*, 109–116.
[89] Sensabaugh, G. F., *International Symposium on the Forensic Applications of Electrophoresis,* FBI Academy Quantico, 26–28 June 1984, p. 181.
[90] Golden, V. L., Sensabaugh, G. F., *Proceedings of the 11th International Congress of the Society of Forensic Haemogenetics,* Copenhagen, 7–10 August 1985, p. 45.

[91] Luffman, J. E., Harris, H., *Ann. Hum. Genet.* 1967, *30*, 387–401.

[92] Wraxall, B. G. D., Emes, E. G., *J. For. Sci. Soc.* 1976, *16*, 127–132.

[93] McWright, C. G., Kearney, S. J., Mudd, J. L., *For. Sci. A. C. S. Symposium Series No. 13*, 1975, 151–153.

[94] Westwood, S. A., Sutton, J. G., *Electrophoresis* 1984, *5*, 162–164.

[95] Hopkinson, D., Mestriner, M., Cortner, J., Harris, H., *Ann. Hum. Genet.* 1973, *37*, 119–137.

[96] Twibell, J. M., Whitehead, P. H., *J. For. Sci.* 1978, *23*, 356–360.

[97] Bender, K., Frank, R., *Hum. Genet.* 1973, *23*, 315–318.

[98] Berg, K., Schwarzfischer, F., Wischerath, H., *Hum. Genet.* 1976, *32*, 81–83.

[99] Martin, W., *Ärztl. Laboratorium* 1979, *25*, 65–67.

[100] Radam, G., Strauch, H., Martin, W., *Blut* 1980, *40*, 337–341.

[101] Henke, J., Basler, M., *Rechtsmedizin* 1984, *92*, 35–37.

[102] Marks, M. P., Jenkins, T., Nurse, G. T., *Hum. Genet.* 1977, *37*, 49–54.

[103] Jay, B. W. H., Philip, W. M. S., *J. For. Sci.* 1979, *24*, 193–199.

[104] Horscroft, G., Sutton, J. G., *J. For. Sci. Soc.* 1983, *23*, 139–143.

[105] Scherz, R., Rohner, R., Pflugshaupt, R., Butler, R., *Proceedings of the 10th International Congress of the Society for Forensic Haemogenetics*, München, 11–15 October 1983, pp. 507–510.

[106] Olaisen, B., Siverts, A., Jonassen, R., Mevag, B., Gedde-Dahl, T., *Hum. Genet.* 1981, *57*, 351–353.

[107] Budowle, B., *Electrophoresis* 1984, *4*, 314–316.

[108] Cohen, P. P., Soben, E. K., *Cancer Res.* 1945, *5*, 631–632.

[109] Paar, C. W., Bagster, I. A., Welch, S. G., *Biochem. Genet.* 1977, *15*, 109–113.

[110] Parkin, B. H., *Proceedings of the 7th International Congress of Forensic Haemogenetics*, Hamburg, 25–29 September 1977, 389–392.

[111] Burgess, R. M., Twibell, J. M., *J. For. Sci. Soc.* 1979, *19*, 283–286.

[112] Sutton, J. G., Bosley, C. M., Whitehead, P. H., *J. For. Sci. Soc.* 1982, *22*, 199–202.

[113] Blake, E. T., Sensabaugh, G. F., *J. For. Sci.* 1978, *23*, 717–729.

[114] Kömpf, J., Bissbort, S., Gassmann, S., Ritter, H., *Humangenetik* 1975, *27*, 141–143.

[115] Bagster, I. A., Paar, C. W., *J. Physiol.* 1975, *256*, 56–57.

[116] Brinkman, B., Püschel, K., *Z. Rechtsmed.* 1978, *81*, 181–190.

[117] Ranzani, G., Anotonini, G., Santachiara-Benerecetti, A. S., *Hum. Hered.* 1979, *29*, 261–264.

[118] Olaisen, B., Gedde-Dahl, T., Thorsby, E., *Hum. Genet.* 1976, *32*, 301–304.

[119] Uotila, L., Koivusalo, M., *Acta Chim. Scand.* 1980, *B34*, 63–68.

[120] Dorrill, M. J., Sutton, J. G., *J. For. Sci. Soc.* 1983, *23*, 131–134.

[121] Saki, T., *Jap. J. Leg. Med.* 1951, *5*, 19–41.

[122] Yada, S., Okane, M., Sano, Y., *Acta Criminol. Med. Leg. Japon.* 1966, *32*, 7–8.

[123] Howard, D. H., Martin, P. D., *J. For. Sci. Soc.* 1969, *9*, 28–30.

[124] Lincoln, P. J., Dodds, B. F., *Med. Sci. Law.* 1968, *8*, 38–40.

[125] Yoshida, J., Abet, T., Nakamurs, K., *Medico-Legal Soc.* 1978, *21*, 7–8.

[126] Oya, M., Ito, H., Kido, A., Suzaki, O., Katsumata, Y., Yada, S., *J. For. Sci.* 1978, *11*, 135–138.

[127] Burgess, R. M., Sutton, J. G., *Hum. Genet.* 1981, *56*, 391–393.

[128] Burgess, R. M., Sutton, J. G., Whitehead, P. H., *J. For. Sci.* 1979, *19*, 392–395.

[129] Lawton, M. E., Sutton, J. G., *J. For. Sci. Soc.* 1982, *22*, 203–209.

[130] Beckman, G., Lundgren, E., Tarnvik, A., *Hum. Hered.* 1973, *23*, 338–345.

[131] Beckman, G., Pakarinen, A., *Hum. Hered.* 1973, *23*, 346–351.

[132] Welch, S. G., Mears, G. W., *Hum. Hered.* 1972, *22*, 38–42.

[133] Sutton, J. G., Goodwin, J., Horscroft, G., Stockdale, R. E., Frake, A., *J. Assoc. Off. Anal. Chem.* 1983, *66*, 1164–1174.

[134] Culliford, B. J., National Institute of Law Enforcement and Criminal Justice, US Department of Justice NIJ Pub 71-1, 1971.

[135] Bagenal, T. B., Mackereth, F. J. H., Heron, J., *J. Fish Biol.* 1973, *5*, 555–557.

[136] Taggert, J., Ferguson, A., Mason, F. M., *Comp. Biochem. Phys.* 1981, *39B*, 393–411.

[137] Corbett, G. B., Southern, H. N., *The Handbook of British Mammals,* Blackwell Scientific Pub, Oxford 1977, pp. 410–461.

[138] Butcher, P. D., Hawkey, C. M., *Comp. Biochem. Physiol.* 1977, *57*, 391–398.

[139] Meadows, R. W., *Proceedings of Forensic Science Symposium Calgary,* Alberta, April 1977, pp. 39–44.

[140] Lawton, M. E., Sutton, J. G., *J. For. Soc.* 1982, *22*, 361–366.

[141] Gill, P., Jeffrey, A. J., Werrett, D. J., *Nature* 1985, *318*, 577–579.

Index

STABILISIERTE NETZGERÄTE

| Große Leistung |
| Geringer Platzbedarf |
| 19 × 35 cm/ca. DIN A 4 · 21 cm Höhe |
| Langzeitstabilität < 0,1 % |
| Kurzschlußfest |

Spannungs- und stromstabil
200 V/1000 mA
500 V/ 400 mA
1200 V/ 150 mA
3000 V/ 60 mA
6000 V/ 30 mA

Spannungs-, strom- und leistungsstabil
600 V/1000 mA/100 W
1200 V/ 500 mA/100 W
3000 V/ 200 mA/100 W

Die idealen Netzgeräte für Ihr Labor

ELEKTRO-BLOTTER

| Elektrophoretischer Transfer von |
| Proteinen aus Polyacrylamidgelen |
| auf Nitrozellulose-Membranen |

bestehend aus:
Pufferwanne mit Schutzabdeckung
2 Graphitplatten mit Halterungen
Druckeinrichtung mit Schnellver-
schluß

Arbeitsfläche: 160 × 240 cm